CRITICAL STUDIES
IN THE
MAHABHARATA

CRITICAL STUDIES
IN THE
MAHABHARATA

V.S. SUKTHANKAR, P. K. GODE

IN TWO VOLUMES

VOL. I

GYAN

Published by

Gyan Publishing House
5, Ansari Road
Daryaganj, New Delhi-110002
Phone: 011-47034999, 9811692060
E-mail: books@gyanbooks.com

Distribution Network
gyanbooks.com
India, USA, Canada, UK, Australia

ISBN: 978-93-7225-091-6 (Set)
978-93-7225-185-2 (HB)
First Published, 1944

2nd Impression 2025

Printed at: Gyan Press, Delhi.

CRITICAL STUDIES IN THE MAHABHARATA (VOL. I)
Author: V.S. SUKTHANKAR, P. K. GODE

V. S. SUKTHANKAR

V. S. SUKTHANKAR MEMORIAL EDITION

Edited
on behalf of the Committee
by
P. K. GODE, M.A.,
CURATOR, BHANDARKAR ORIENTAL RESEARCH INSTITUTE, POONA.

VOLUME I

CRITICAL STUDIES IN THE MAHĀBHĀRATA

Published for the
V. S. SUKTHANKAR
MEMORIAL EDITION COMMITTEE
by
KARNATAK PUBLISHING HOUSE
CHIRA BAZAR, BOMBAY 2 (INDIA).

CRITICAL STUDIES
IN THE
MAHĀBHĀRATA

BY

THE LATE

V. S. SUKTHANKAR, M.A. (Cantab.), Ph.D. (Berlin),

General Editor, Critical Edition of the Mahābhārata, Editor-in-Chief, Journal of the Bombay Branch of the Royal Asiatic Society, Honorary Member, American Oriental Society, etc.

21st January 1944

V. S. SUKTHANKAR MEMORIAL EDITION COMMITTEE
POONA 4 (India)

PREFACE

The Bhandarkar Oriental Research Institute was founded in 1915. The first verse of the Mahābhārata was written by Sir R. G. BHANDARKAR on 1st April 1919 while inaugurating the work of the Institute on the Critical Edition of the Mahābhārata. On 4th August 1925 Dr. V. S. SUKTHANKAR took charge of this work as its General Editor and reorganized it on a sound basis. For the subsequent 17 years he worked on it with an eagle eye and mature scholarship bringing international honour to himself and to the Institute. In 1940, the British Academy, London, put its seal of approval on Dr. SUKTHANKAR's work on this edition. On the 4th January 1943, the Institute conferred on Dr. SUKTHANKAR a Distinguished Services Medal in recognition of his unique services to the Institute as the helmsman of its work on the Mahābhārata on the occasion of its Silver Jubilee celebrations. On 5th January 1943, Dr. SUKTHANKAR read his statement on the Critical Edition of the Mahābhārata before the delegates for the Silver Jubilee celebrations and other audience in the Tata Hall of the Institute. This statement has proved to be his last testament more valuable than Aristotle's will as it is a national testament. I quote from it a few sentences which contain Dr. SUKTHANKAR's message about the Mahābhārata :—

"The part of the Epic critically dealt with so far is, I imagine, in bulk about four times as great as the Greek Epics, Iliad and Odyssey put together and one and a half times as our Rāmāyaṇa."

"All good work costs money now-a-days! Good manuscripts cost money. Good printing costs money. Good editors cost money."

"Amid the deepest strands that are woven in the thread of our civilization there is more than one that is drawn originally from Bhāratavarṣa and from Sanskrit literature and well in the centre of this vast mass of literature, there stands this deathless traditional book of divine inspiration, unapproachable and far removed from possibilities of human constitution."

"We must therefore grasp this great book with both hands and face it squarely. Then we shall recognise that it is our past which has prolonged itself into the present. We are it : I mean the real WE! Shall we be guilty of strangling our own soul? NEVER!"

These stirring words were read out by Dr. SUKTHANKAR on the evening of the 5th of January and within a fortnight he passed away after a brief illness on the evening of 21st January 1943! Truth is stranger than fiction!!

Such in brief is the outline of Dr. SUKTHANKAR's association with the Institute's Critical Edition of the Great Epic, which he aptly styled as "the Content of our Collective Unconscious" and in which he finally merged his being after spending every moment of his conscious life in revising his type-script of the last of his lectures on the Mahābhārata he was to deliver before the University of Bombay on the following day !

In striking him down within sight of his chosen goal, Death pierced the base of consciousness, cutting at the very joint of body and mind. No preparation for the end, no inspiring last words, were possible. Yet, those of us who knew SUKTHANKAR intimately cannot doubt that the sentiments of Valiant would also have been his own had he received the summons of an approaching end to life's journey. "Though with great difficulty I am got hither, yet now I do not repent me of all the trouble. My sword I give to him that shall succeed me in the pilgrimage, and my courage and skill to him that can get it. My marks and scars I carry with me, to be a witness for me, that I have fought His battles Who will be my Rewarder." This memorial volume represents the sword, the keen splendid-tempered image of his intellect, that he bequeathed to him that has the courage and skill to wield it. If there be such a person, undaunted by the forces of darkness, let him grasp firm the hilt and smite on.

Side by side with his text-critical work on the Mahābhārata Dr. SUKTHANKAR kept on studying its content and inner meaning and for that purpose studied many books on Philosophy and Religion. While I was editing the *Review of Philosophy and Religion* between 1930 and 1937, I received numerous books on these subjects for review. Dr. SUKTHANKAR seemed very much interested in many of them and he actually ordered some of them for his own library. I was first under the impression that Dr. SUKTHANKAR perused these books with a view to get a little diversion to his mind after his fatiguing work on the text of the Mahābhārata day after day for years without rest. I was however thoroughly surprised when he disclosed to me his scheme of lectures on the Mahābhārata which he finally prepared for being delivered before the University of Bombay and before completing which he took our final leave with a "Forget-me-not" emphasis ! The mystical vein noticed by the audience in those lectures was mainly due to the psychological changes gradually brought about in the mind of the great Savant during the ten years prior to these lectures.

The idea of bringing out a Memorial Edition of Dr. SUKTHANKAR's published writings was first discussed by myself and my learned friends Dr. S. M. KATRE and Prof. D. D. KOSAMBI with Dr. Mrs. Malinibai B. SUKTHANKAR, M.B.B.S. and the sons of Dr. SUKTHANKAR immediately after Dr. SUKTHANKAR's demise. With the substantial support promised by the Sukthankar family a Memorial Edition

Committee was formed with Shrimant Balasaheb PANT Pratinidhi, B.A. the Raja Saheb of Aundh as its Chairman and Diwan-Bahadur K. M. JHAVERI, M.A., LL.B., J.P. as its Vice-Chairman. With the assured support of these two great friends of Dr. SUKTHANKAR and with the guaranteed voluntary co-operation of my esteemed friends Dr. KATRE and Prof. KOSAMBI, it was easy for me to secure the support of the innumerable friends of Dr. SUKTHANKAR all over India and outside for the work of the Memorial Edition as will be seen from the Personnel of the Memorial Edition Committee which accompanies this Preface. A printed Appeal was subsequently issued by me on behalf of the Committee and circulated among scholars and institutions interested in the Memorial Edition. The response to this appeal from the numerous friends and admirers of Dr. SUKTHANKAR was extremely encouraging and the First Volume of the Memorial Edition that is being presented to the public today is a visible embodiment of this spontaneous response and a permanent Souvenir of the good will left behind by an Indian scholar who sacrificed himself on the altar of the Mahābhārata.

The valuable and scholarly contents of the present volume speak for themselves and will continue to speak with greater resonance as years pass by. As observed by Prof. EDGERTON they are the product of Dr. SUKTHANKAR's knowledge and experience (*Jñānam Savijñānam*) and his native ability which made reputation in three Continents. Dr. SUKTHANKAR's literary life was a life of planned action, in which every detail was scrupulously worked out and revised many times before it saw the light of the day. Every page of the Critical Edition of the Mahābhārata and the Critical Epic Studies that are being presented to the scholars to-day under one cover bear the stamp of his scholarship and fully illustrate the common adage :—"If a thing is worth doing, it is worth doing well". His Prolegomena to the Ādiparvan of the Mahābhārata, the bed-rock of the Mahābhārata Textual Criticism, was much in demand since its publication. It is being published separately for the first time in the present volume along with the other Epic Studies of Dr. SUKTHANKAR and thus brought within the means of individual research scholars through the favour of the authorities of the B. O. R. Institute. I feel confident that this First Volume of Dr. SUKTHANKAR Memorial Edition will stimulate the study of the Indian Textual Criticism on which the attention of Indian scholars has been now focussed by Dr. KATRE's able *Introduction to Indian Textual Criticism* (1940), which owes much to Dr. SUKTHANKAR's inspiration and guidance.

It now remains for me to record my feelings of gratitude for the unstinted co-operation I have received from several friends and learned bodies in bringing out this First Volume of the V. S. Sukthankar Memorial Edition. My cordial thanks are due to the authorities of the Bhandarkar Oriental Research Institute, many of whom are members of the Memorial Edition Committee, for their kind permission to include in the present volume the *Prolegomena* and other *Introductions* to the *Critical Edition of the Mahābhārata* as also Dr. SUKTHANKAR's *Epic Studies* published in the *Annals* of the Institute. Special thanks are due to Principal J. R. GHARPURE, B.A., LL.B., the Chairman of the Executive Board and Dr. R. N. DANDEKAR, M.A., PH.D., the Secretary of the Institute who is also the Editor of the *Annals*, for their uniform courtesy and kindness in securing the above permission. To Dr. S. K. BELVALKAR, M.A., PH.D., the present General Editor of the Mahābhārata, I am particularly thankful for keeping at my disposal a copy of *Epic Studies No. VI* which he found in Dr. SUKTHANKAR's office papers at the Institute. *This copy duly revised by Dr.* SUKTHANKAR *in his own hand has been incorporated in the present volume.* Evidently Dr. SUKTHANKAR had an intention to revise all his *Epic Studies* in course of time and then publish them in their final form after the completion of his work on the Great Epic. Providence, however, decreed otherwise ! As regards the other contributions of Dr. SUKTHANKAR included in the present volume I tender my most grateful thanks—

(1) To the authorities of the K. R. Cama Oriental Institute, Bombay, and the Editorial Board of *Sir J. J. Modi Volume* for permission to include Dr. SUKTHANKAR's paper on "Arjunamiśra" in this Edition.

(2) To Mr. B. T. ANKLESARIA, M.A. the Hon. Secretary of the K. R. Cama Institute for drawing my attention to the two papers of Dr. SUKTHANKAR viz. (i) Arjunamiśra and (ii) An Excursion on the Periphery of Indological Research and in securing the necessary permission of the authorities of his Institute for their inclusion in the present Edition. Mr. ANKLESARIA had collaborated with Dr. SUKTHANKAR for a number of years in connection with his work for the Cama Institute and his hearty co-operation in this work by the free supply of the press-copies of the two papers of Dr. SUKTHANKAR mentioned above deserves my best thanks.

(3) To the Editors of the *Festchrift Prof. P. V. Kane* and Dr. R. N. SARDESAI, L.C.P.S., Proprietor, Oriental Book Agency, Poona, its publisher, for permission to include Dr. SUKTHANKAR'S paper on "Rāmopākhyāna" in this Volume.

(4) To the authorities of the Deccan College Post-graduate and Research Institute, Poona and in particular Dr. S. M. KATRE, M.A.,

PH.D. its present Director and Editor of their *Bulletin* for their permission to include Dr. SUKTHANKAR's paper on "Epic Question I—Did Indra assume the form of a Swan?" in this Volume.

(5) To the Editors of *Feschrift Dr. F. W. Thomas* and its publisher Mr. M. N. KULKARNI, the Manager of the Karnatak Publishing House, Bombay for their permission to publish Dr. SUKTHANKAR's paper on "Rāmāyaṇa and Nalopākhyāna" in this Volume.

(6) To the authorities, Bombay Branch of the Royal Asiatic Society for permission to include Epic Studies I: 'Some Text-Critical Notes' in this Volume.

Every scholar who came into personal contact with Dr. SUKTHANKAR knows quite well how he loved not only the substantial contents of any scholarly publication but also its scientific and dignified presentation. He believed in the identity of Truth, Beauty and Dignity in the publication of all scholarly work worth the name. The volumes of the Critical Edition of the Mahābhārata are a visible embodiment of Dr. SUKTHANKAR's ideal in this respect. A *good edition* according to Dr. SUKTHANKAR must be good both within and without, and we have tried to make the present Memorial Edition as good as possible within the means at our disposal. But *good Editions cost money*, said Dr. SUKTHANKAR in his last public statement and the credit of achieving any goodness in the present Memorial Edition must go to those donors, subscribers and contributors who have contributed their mite towards this Edition out of sheer love and appreciation for the national work of the departed scholar as will be seen from the list of these contributors (vide Appendix). Space forbids me to thank all these contributors individually. I shall however, be failing in my duty if I do not indicate here the generosity of the following contributors but for whose spontaneous response it would have been impossible for the Memorial Edition Committee to proceed with the work of the Edition:—

Rs. 650—Dr. Mrs. Malinibai B. Sukthankar, M.B.B.S. and other members of the Sukthankar family, Bombay.

Rs. 150—University of Bombay.

Rs. 100—Shrimant Balasaheb Pant Pratinidhi, B.A., Raja Saheb of Aundh, Aundh.

Rs. 100—Right Hon'ble Dr. M. R. Jayakar, Bombay.

Rs. 100—B. J. Wadia, M.A., LL.B., Vice-Chancellor, University of Bombay, Bombay.

Rs. 100—Sir Chunilal B. Mehta, KT., J.P. and Lady Tapibai C. Mehta, Bombay.

On the completion of the Memorial Edition it is proposed to

publish a full report of the work of the Committee where all contributions and donations will be specified in detail.

I started my work in connection with the Sukthankar Memorial Edition with the assured initial support of Dr. Mrs. Malinibai B. SUKTHANKAR and other members of the Sukthankar family. This support was further strengthened by the formation of a representative Memorial Edition Committee consisting of numerous friends and admirers of Dr. SUKTHANKAR in different parts of India and outside. This support, encouraging as it was for an inexperienced man like myself, made me confident enough about the success of this enterprise but I became absolutely fearless in my work when the two great friends of Dr. SUKTHANKAR, I mean Shrimant Raja Saheb of Aundh and Dewan Bahadur K. M. JHAVERI agreed to guide me in this work as the Chairman and Vice-Chairman of the Memorial Edition Committee respectively. Their high regard for our National Epic and its Epic Editor Dr. SUKTHANKAR has been responsible in no small way for the publication of the Epic Studies of Dr. SUKTHANKAR appearing today in the form of the First Volume of the Sukthankar Memorial Edition. On 5th January 1943, Dr. SUKTHANKAR referred to the Rajasaheb of Aundh in the following glowing terms :—

> " If you want me to point out just one man who is responsible for originating and furthering the project (of the Mahābhārata) he is sitting in front of you, I mean Shrimant Balasaheb Pant Pratinidhi, the Raja of Aundh."

We are fortunate in having in our midst today, the first anniversary of Dr. SUKTHANKAR's demise, this very enlightened Rajasaheb, now in the 76th year to guide all our literary projects with undaunted zeal and optimism. I cannot adequately thank the Rajasaheb and other friends for their spontaneous and active co-operation in the work of this Edition.

I began my work in connection with the Memorial Edition with the guaranteed collaboration of my personal friends Dr. S. M. KATRE, M.A., PH.D. and Prof. D. D. KOSAMBI, M.A. These friends have fulfilled their guarantee to the very letter as they have been responsible for the entire editing of the First Volume and all credit for the careful and accurate editing of the Volume goes to them. During their personal contact with Dr. SUKTHANKAR they knew perfectly well what good *editing* meant according to Dr. SUKTHANKAR's highly critical standards and consequently the good editing of the present Volume owes everything to them as they have carried out at great inconvenience to themselves all the arduous work of seeing the Volume through the press. Though these friends have done all this labour of love out of their high sense of appreciation and respect for the work of Dr. SUKTHANKAR and though they are the members of the Memorial Committee, I take this opportunity of thanking them most cordially for their disinterested service to Indology in helping the Memorial Edition Committee to bring out the present Volume in the best possible form and get up.

Dr. SUKTHANKAR was connected with the University of Bombay in several capacities for more than two decades. His cordial relations with all the authorities of the University are evident not only from the grant sanctioned by the Syndicate towards the costs of this Edition but by the personal generosity of the Vice-Chancellor, the Registrar, the Deputy Registrar, the Librarian and many other office-bearers of the University. I am deeply touched by their prompt and spontaneous response to my appeal regarding this Edition and I convey to all these friends of Dr. SUKTHANKAR at the premier academic body of the province the grateful thanks of the Memorial Committee for their sincere appreciation of the work of the Committee.

In concluding this preface I must record the valuable services rendered to the Memorial Edition by Mr. M. N. KULKARNI, the enterprising Manager of the Karntak Publishing House, Bombay, but for whose high regard for Dr. SUKTHANKAR and spontaneous co-operation on the very day this scheme was discussed we would not have dreamt of undertaking this Edition at a time when the extraordinary high cost of printing and the scarcity of paper had chilled all academic enterprises in this country. Like my esteemed friends Dr. KATRE and PROF. KOSAMBI, Mr. KULKARNI has fulfilled his guarantee also to the letter by publishing this First Volume of the Memorial Edition most promptly and efficiently and thus kept up the high traditions of his Publishing House for excellent printing and typography, which are absolutely essential for *good editing* according to the standards of Dr. SUKTHANKAR.

In presenting this first volume of the Sukthankar Memorial Edition to-day, the first anniversary of Dr. SUKTHANKAR's lamented demise, the Memorial Committee has completed half of its promised work. Though I am thankful to all my colleagues on the Memorial Committee for their continuous co-operation so far, I must reserve my final thanks to them to a future date when the Second Volume of this Edition is completed and presented to the public.

P. K. GODE
Hon. Secretary and Managing Editor
Dr. V. S. Sukthankar Memorial Edition Committee.

Poona 4
21st January, 1944.

MEMORIAL EDITION COMMITTEE

CONTENTS

FOREWORD[1]

An elaborate introduction containing a comprehensive account of the manuscript material as also a detailed discussion of the principles of Mahābhārata textual criticism will be published with the last fascicule of the Ādiparvan. The following cursory remarks are intended merely to guide the reader meanwhile through the labyrinth of a very complicated *apparatus criticus.*

GENERAL OBSERVATIONS

In the Mahābhārata manuscript tradition, perhaps as much as in any literary tradition, the textual critic is faced with a bewildering profusion of versions as well as an amazing mixture of versions. Divers elements have been working from the earliest times in favour of the development of different types, on the one hand : on the other hand, there were not wanting elements that operated against the evolution of sharply differentiated types. To understand the phenomenon of this luxuriant growth and indiscriminate fusion of versions, one must appreciate clearly certain details of historical moment, certain special factors in the transmission of the Mahābhārata—traits which distinguish our work from every other known text except the Rāmāyaṇa and possibly the Homeric epopees. Notwithstanding the fact that we know so little that is certain and definite about the early history of the text, we may, it seems to me, with confidence assume that after its composition the great epic was for centuries handed down (in differing forms and sizes) from bard to bard merely by word of mouth. It is moreover extremely probable that even after the text had been written down, large portions of it, especially such portions as were popular, continued to be committed to memory, by itinerant *raconteurs* for purposes of recitation. It is further easy to believe that no great care was lavished on the text by these custodians of the tradition to guard it against partial corruption and elaboration or against arbitrary emendation and normalization : to reproduce the received text with any great precision would be neither attempted by these bards nor required of them. It was then inevitable that the protean oral tradition should in one form or another react on the written tradition and *vice versa.* One important and necessary consequence of such antecedents as these is the impossibility of retracing all extant versions to any fixed and authentic archetype ; since some of the modern editions could not but be descendants of fluctuating oral versions reduced to writing in some distant past, independently of each other, at different epochs and in different circumstances. In

---

1 [*Ādiparvan,* Fascicule I, 1927.]

other words, even in its early phases the Mahābhārata text tradition must have been not uniform and singular, but multiple and polygenous. To complicate matters [2] further there appears to have followed a period in which there was a free comparison of manuscripts and extensive mutual borrowings, operations which in the course of indiscriminate crossing and re-crossing have completely confused the *differentiæ* and produced a perfect wilderness of hybrid types. These are, at least in part, still mere surmises. But the assumption of some such complicated derangements, beyond the normal vicissitudes of transmission, is necessary, to account for the strange vagaries of the Mahābhārata manuscript tradition : to explain why in the best manuscripts one comes across at every step readings that are manifestly inferior and additional lines that are incontestably spurious : to elucidate how textual alterations, especially interpolations, starting from the most inconspicuous source of diaskeuasis, could extend over large areas with comparative ease and rapidity.

This state of things, if true, would make it impossible to apply to the Mahābhārata the special canons of textual criticism which are derived from a study of classical (Greek and Latin) texts and which depend ultimately upon there being a more or less complete concatenation of copies and exemplars reaching finally back to a single authentic (written) archetype. The conflation of codices may, moreover, have been carried to such an extreme that we may even have to renounce all pretensions to disentangle completely, by means of purely objective criteria, their intricate mutual relationships. It would, therefore, be well not to ignore entirely the possibility that a wholly satisfactory restoration of the text to its pristine form—even the late so-called Śatasāhasrī saṁhitā form—may be a task now beyond the powers of criticism.

Even though the problem be insoluble on the ideal plane, yet a partial solution of it is by no means impracticable and may with considerable gain be attempted. This fascicule will, I hope, demonstrate that a considerable portion of the inherited text can be incontestably proved to be authentic and unimpeachable : and that on the other hand certain portions of the " vulgate " can, equally indisputably, be shewn to be spurious. In other words, we seem entitled to assert that notwithstanding the existence of what may be termed " original doublets " (fluctuations inherited from a period of purely oral transmission), as well as a vast number of secondary variants (brought in through corruption and emendation during the period of mainly written transmission), —that despite the vagaries which surround a small part of the poem with a haze of uncertainty, the unification of the tradition could, in regard to the major part of the epic be carried to a degree of approximation which may be deemed sufficient for all intents and purposes.

Ordinarily in text reconstruction a safe expedient is to take as basis the oldest of the " best family " of manuscripts and to authenticate it in the critical edition. This expedient, though unquestionably safe and in most cases indubitably effective, fails totally in the present instance, assuming what has been said above about the fusion of types to be true : because by following any manuscript, even the oldest and the best, we shall be authenticating just that arbitrary mixture of versions which it should be the aim of criticism to avoid. The peculiar conditions of the transmission of the epic force upon us an eclectic but cautious utilization of all manuscript classes. Since all categories of manuscripts have their strong points and their weak points, each variant has to be judged on its own merits. When the criteria at our disposal fail to give a positive result, we have to content [3] ourselves with a stop-gap that will give the required sense or at least complete the metrical line. A text prepared, with due circumspection, on eclectic principles will, I am fully persuaded, present a more faithful picture of the elusive "original" than any single extant codex could do. That in these circumstances the editor will occasionally make mistakes—at times perhaps gross mistakes—is as certain as inevitable; for it is to be feared that there is no royal road to success in this incomparably difficult field. The method of Mahābhārata textual criticism can be evolved only from a special study of the Mahābhārata manuscripts and of the Mahābhārata manuscript tradition. More than one attempt will probably have to be made before the ideal is attained. It will, therefore, be prudent not to expect too much from the *first* critical edition, nor to claim too much for it.

MANUSCRIPT MATERIAL

The manuscripts utilized for this edition of the first two adhyāyas of the Ādiparvan are as follows :

I. N(ORTHERN) RECENSION

Kāśmīrī (or North-western) Version in Devanāgarī transcript (K).

K_0 = Poona, Govt. MSS. Collection, MS. No. 229 of 1895-1902.
K_1 = London, India Office Library, MS. No. 2137.
K_2 = Poona, Govt. MSS. Collection, MS. No. 182 of 1891-95. Dated V. Saṁ. 1694 (ca. 1637 A.D.).
K_3 = Baroda, Central Library, MS. No. 632. Dated V. Saṁ. 1575 (ca. 1518 A.D.).
K_4 = Poona, Govt. MSS. Collection, MS. No. 565 of 1882-83.
K_5 = Lahore, Dayanand Anglo-Vedic College, MS. No. 1.
K_6 = Poona, Govt. MSS. Collection, MS. No. 209 of 1887-91.

Maithilī Version (V).

V_1 = Nepal, Darbar Library, MS. No. 1364. Dated La. Saṁ. 411 (ca. 1530 A.D).

Bangālī Version (B).

B_1 = Bolpur, Viśvabhāratī Library, MS. No. 1.
B_2 = Bolpur, Viśvabhāratī Library, MS. No. 258.
B_3 = Bolpur, Viśvabhāratī Library, MS. No. 264.
B_4 = Bolpur, Viśvabhāratī Library, MS. No. 415.

Devanāgarī Versions (D).

Devanāgarī Version of Arjunamiśra (Da).

Da_1 = Poona, Govt. MSS. Collection, MS. No. 30 of A 1879-80.
Da_2 = Poona, Govt. MSS. Collection, Viśrāmbāg Coll. I, MS. No. 468.

Devanāgarī Version of Nīlakaṇṭha (Dn.).

Dn_1 = MS. belonging to Sardar Kibe of Indore.
Dn_2 = Mysore, Oriental Library, MS. No. 1064.
Dn_3 = Poona, Govt. MSS. Collection, MS. No. 234 of 1892-1902.

Devanāgarī Version of Ratnagarbha (Dr).

Dr_1 = Tanjore, Palace Library, MS. No. 1264.
Dr_2 = Tanjore, Palace Library, MS. No. 1199.
Dr_3 = Tanjore, Palace Library, MS. No. 1313.
Dr_4 = Tanjore, Palace Library, MS. No. 1339.

Devanāgarī Mixed Versions.

D_1 = Poona, Govt. MSS. Collection, MS. No. 29 of A 1879-80.
D_2 = Tanjore, Palace Library, MS. No. 1152.
D_3 = Tanjore, Palace Library, MS. No. 1360.
D_4 = Tanjore Palace Library, MS. No. 1126.
[4] D_5 = Lahore, Dayanand Anglo-Vedic College, MS. No. 4.
D_6 = Tanjore, Palace Library, MS. No. 1223.
D_7 = Tanjore, Palace Library, MS. No. 1269.
D_8 = Tanjore, Palace Library, MS. No. 1329.
D_9 = Tanjore, Palace Library, MS. No. 1176.
D_{10} = Tanjore, Palace Library, MS. No. 1293.
D_{11} = Tanjore, Palace Library, MS. No. 1340.
D_{12} = Tanjore, Palace Library, MS. No. 1373.
D_{13} = Poona, Govt. MSS. Collection, Viśrāmbāg Coll. II, MS. No. 191.
D_{14} = Poona, Govt. MSS. Collection, Viśrāmbāg Coll. II, MS. No. 266.

II. S(OUTHERN) RECENSION.

Telugu Version (T).

T_1 = Yadu Maṭh Collection MS. (without No.)
T_2 = Tanjore, Palace Library, MS. No. 11865.

Grantha Version (G).

G_1 = Yadu Maṭh Collection MS. (without No.)
G_2 = Yadu Maṭh Collection MS. (without No.)
G_3 = Tanjore, Palace Library, MS. No. 11823.
G_4 = Tanjore, Palace Library, MS. No. 11838.
G_5 = Tanjore, Palace Library, MS. No. 11851.
G_6 = Tanjore, Palace Library, MS. No. 11860.
G_7 = Yadu Maṭh Collection MS. (without No.)

Malayālam Version (M).

M_1 = MS. belonging to Chief of Idapillai, Cochin.
M_2 = Cochin, State Library, MS. No. 5.
M_3 = Cochin, State Library, MS. No. 1.
M_4 = MS. belonging to Kallenkara Pisharam of Cochin.

In addition to the above, two Baroda Library MSS. of the commentary by Devabodha (*without* the epic text) were collated ; the important readings found in this commentary have been cited with the symbol Cd.

GENERAL CHARACTERISTICS OF THE MANUSCRIPTS AND THEIR MUTUAL RELATIONSHIP

An important advance made in the classification of the manuscripts is the separation of archetype K (which represents Devanāgarī transcripts of the Kāśmīrī or North-western version) from other so-called Devanāgarī versions. The affinity of K is documented by the following agreements :

1\. 1. 2^b : K (except K_1) महर्षीन् ; D_{14} महर्षि ; the rest (inclusive of K_1) ब्रह्मर्षीन्.

1\. 1. 8 : K लोमहर्षणिरुवाच ; V_1 लोमहर्षण उ°; the rest सौतिरु°; सूत उ° or सूतः.

1\. 1. 49^b : K V_1 B_1 m संक्षेपतोऽब्रवीत् ; the rest संक्षेपमब्र° or संक्षिप्य चाब्र°.

1\. 1. 51^b : K विचक्षणाः; V_1 विशेषतः; the rest मनीषिणः.

1\. 1. 192^c : K (except K_6) धुतपाप्मानः; the rest (incl. K_6) शुभकर्माणः.

1\. 2. 23^b : K (except $K_{1\text{-}6}$) यथावदिह संख्यया; the rest (incl. $K_{1\text{-}6}$) संख्यातत्त्वविदो जनः.

1\. 2. 76^d : K (K_5 missing) यक्षाणामथ रक्षसां; N_2 दैत्यानामथ र°; the rest यक्षाणां च महौजसां.

Only $K_{0.1}$ represent archetype K in a *comparatively* pure form. Next to these in purity stands K_2 ; while $K_{3\text{-}6}$ are nothing but misch-codices, K_3 being conflated with the "vulgate" and $K_{4\text{-}6}$ with some Southern version (cf. 1. 1. 26 and 22*, 25*). $K_{0.1}$ contains a text which is shorter and more archaic than either the Bangālī or the [5] "vulgate." It is worthy of note that while these two manuscripts ($K_{0.1}$) have more readings in common with manuscripts of the Southern recension than either of the two latter groups, yet they contain not a single "additional" line which could be considered as a characteristic Southern interpolation.—V_1 stands, as is to be expected, nearest to the Bangālī version, but it is noteworthy that in a few cases V_1 and K agree in opposition to all other manuscripts, where it is impossible to consider the agreement as purely accidental (cf. 1. 1. 8, 49^d).—The Bangālī version is slightly superior to the "vulgate," in so far that it is not interpolated quite so heavily as the latter. Bangālī omits (like K) not only the Brahmā-Gaṇeśa episode in the first adhyāya, but (unlike K) also the short dialogue between Paraśurāma and his ancestors in the second, both unquestionably spurious and both found in the "vulgate." Occasionally Bangālī manuscripts agree with Southern manuscripts in opposition to K and the "vulgate" (cf. 1. 1. 22^b, 42^d). In these cases I have adopted as authentic the concordant readings of the Bangālī and Southern manuscripts in preference to those of K. Bangālī alone has in a few cases preserved the correct reading as compared with all the other manuscripts (cf. 1. 1. 62^c).—Closely connected with the Bangālī is the version of Arjunamiśra. It not only agrees with the Bangālī in the omission of the Brahmā-Gaṇeśa episode and of the dialogue mentioned above, but it shares with the Bangālī quite a number of isolated readings against all other manuscripts. The (epic) text in the Arjunamiśra codices is frequently contaminated from the "vulgate" and has to be corrected with the help of Arjunamiśra's commentary (cf. 1. 1. 17[b], 22[b]).—Ratnagarbha's text is eclectic, standing palpably under the influence of the Southern recension (cf. 24*, 25*, 27*).—Nīlakaṇṭha's version (which may conveniently be styled the "vulgate") presents a smooth text, with an inconsiderable amount of Southern element. It may be noted that in rare cases the Bombay edition (of Gaṇpat Kṛṣṇājī) contains readings which have no manuscript support at all or have at best very weak manuscript support.—Next we have the mixed Devanāgarī group represented by D_{1-14}, misch-codices of small trustworthiness and of no special value for critical purposes. $D_{2 \cdot 14}$ contain a very large number of old readings in common with manuscripts of the K group, but D_{14} shows at the same time some Southern readings and some unique readings not found elsewhere (cf. 1. 1. 50[c], 63[cd]; 2. 101[b]). D_{9-12} are palpably under the influence of the Southern tradition.—Telugu manuscripts have been placed in the Southern recension, but they belong in a sense to both recensions; they are eclectic on no recognizable principles.—It is difficult to define precisely the relationship between the Grantha and the Malayālam versions, which are very closely allied; each of them exhibits nevertheless certain features not found in the other (cf. 1. 1. 184[d]). On the whole the Grantha version produces the impression of being less interpolated and more archaic than the other. This version has two sub-groups, G_{1-3} and G_{4-6}; numerous cross-agreements between the two sub-groups show that our manuscripts are conflated. G_7 does not belong to either of these groups; in point of fact, it is a misch-codex contaminated from the Northern tradition and closely allied to T_1 (cf. 1. 1. 63, 64).—M_1 often stands in antagonism to M_{2-4}, sometimes agreeing with manuscripts of the Northern recension (cf. 1. 1. 32[cd], 41[cd], 71[a], 128[a]). The Southern recension, as already remarked, agrees with archetype K more closely than with any other Northern version.

[6] The Southern version of the first two adhyāyas is on the whole shorter than the "vulgate"; but the shortest version of these two adhyāyas is that preserved by $K_{0.1}$, Ko being probably even shorter than K_1. The naïve Brahmā-Gaṇeśa episode, the longest as well as the most obvious interpolation in the text of the "vulgate", has been relegated to the Appendix (cf. 1. 1. 26, 53, 60, 62, 64). Its spuriousness has now been placed beyond the domain of sane criticism through its absence in $K_{0.3}$ V_1 B Da D_1 M_1. In the Southern manuscripts (and in some conflated Devanāgarī manuscripts) Brahmā alone is introduced; in these there is no talk of Gaṇeśa, who is unquestionably a late Northern intruder. The *yadāśrauṣam* section is also evidently an interpolation, but a considerably older one. Being merely a string of stanzas summarizing some of the most important incidents and episodes of the epic, it lent itself easily to being further interpolated by revisers who wanted to

supply the omissions and thus make the summary as complete as possible. To present the oldest form of this section now recoverable, I have deemed it sufficient to accept as genuine only such stanzas as are found verbatim in both the recensions. Here again $K_{0.1}$ have the fewest interpolations. The "table of contents" in the second adhyāya is preserved in two versions, a longer and a shorter. $K_{0.1}$ S (except G_7) have the shorter version, which has been adopted in the constituted text as the authentic one.

Since I have not been able to discover any traces of "secondary interrelationship" between archetypes K and S, I consider the agreement between these two archetypes as "primitive", that is depending upon their primitive connection through the Ur-Mahābhārata. This concord is a factor of supreme importance for the reconstruction of the text. The originality of the agreement is established, in my opinion, by the following considerations. The concordant readings of K and S represent as often as not a *lectio difficilior* (cf. 1. 1. 19[a], 94[d], 158[d]). Frequently such a reading best explains the other variants (cf. 1. 1. 1. 2[a], 14[b]). Furthermore the "additional" stanzas which are found in the "vulgate" but are missing in K and S have all the appearance of being interpolations, lengthening and weakening the text (cf. 19*, 29*, 35*-38) ; the same remark applies to the additional stanzas that are found in the Southern recension but are missing in K and the "vulgate" (cf. 21*, 22*, 27*). The high position of K seems confirmed by its being the shortest of the known versions.

THE CONSTITUTED TEXT

In preparing the constituted text of the first two adhyāyas, I have endeavoured to balance the eclecticism advocated in certain matters with a rigid conservatism insisted on in others. I have been most averse to reject or correct the readings of good manuscripts. Interpretation has throughout been given precedence over emendation ; in the first two adhyāyas, no emendation seemed absolutely necessary, nor any absolutely certain. Solecisms, when shewn to be original by a clear agreement on this point between (what appeared to be) independent versions, have been allowed to stand uncorrected (cf. 1. 1. 5.[a], 170[d]). As a general rule, preference is given to a reading which best suggests how other readings might have arisen. When such a reading was not available the choice fell upon one which is common to (what *prima facie* appeared to be) more or less independent versions and which is supported by intrinsic probability ; the presumption of originality in such cases is frequently confirmed by a lack of definite agreement between the dis-[7]-cordant versions. Occasionally one comes across variants where the matter is identical but the wording of a large part or of the whole of the line is different ; one and the same primitive reading cannot in these cases account for the divergence. In the presence of such alternatives, neither of which can have come from the other and which have equal extrinsic support and equal intrinsic merit, the criteria mentioned above fail to give a positive result. A particular instance of the variation contemplated here is that of a puzzling form of a cross-agreement between the Northern and Southern versions; when, for instance, some Kāśmīrī and Malayālam manuscripts agree in opposition to say, Bangālī and Grantha (cf. 1. 1. 60[c]). In such cases, I have, owing to the much greater correctness of the K version, mostly adopted, as stopgaps, the readings of $K_{0,1}$, the manuscripts which present the archetype K in a relatively pure form.

I have given in the constituted text whatever in each case appeared to be supported by the balance of probabilities, indicating all the important elements—lines, phrases, significant words and word-parts—of the text that are less than certain by a wavy line printed below them. Insignificant differences of spelling (*e.g.* Naimiṣa-Naimiśa) are ignored for this purpose.

Doubt which cannot be resolved by a consideration of the documentary or intrinsic probability, entailing the use of the wavy line, arises in the following cases: (a) when the transmitted readings appear to be corrupt and no satisfactory emendation can be suggested; (b) when there are several readings of equal merit; in particular where the Northern and the Southern recensions offer two different readings of equal value; lastly (c) when the evidence *pro et contra* of documentary and intrinsic probability is equally balanced.

As regards interpolations, the additional lines are so ingeniously fashioned and cunningly fitted in, that in any given case the intrinsic evidence is generally inconclusive. In other words, if we leave out of account the documentary evidence, no convincing proof can in general be brought forward to establish either the originality or the spuriousness of the added lines. We cannot, however, entirely ignore the evidence of tradition. Everything points to the fact that what the epic has suffered from is inflation and elaboration, and not depletion or curtailment. On principle, therefore, lines that are peculiar to one recension, *having nothing whatsoever corresponding to them, at the same point, in the other recension*, are to be viewed with grave suspicion. Unless there is overwhelming evidence to prove their originality, they should be treated as spurious; because, the probability of error is far greater in admitting as authentic such one-recension lines on insufficient evidence of originality (both recensions being placed on an equal footing and treated with impartiality) than in rejecting them on insufficient evidence of spuriousness. It may be added that the presumption of unauthenticity is frequently confirmed by the fact that in the recension in which such lines do occur, they are found inserted in different manuscripts (or different versions) at different points of the text.

I am greatly indebted to Shrimant Balasaheb Pant Pratinidhi, Chief of Aundh, for uniform kindness and courtesy; but still more for the absolute confidence he is pleased to repose in me. I must also record my thanks, for help of various kinds, to my colleagues on the Mahābhārata [8] Editorial Board : Prof. Vaijnath K. RAJVADE, M.A.; Mr. Vishwanath P. VAIDYA, BAR-AT-LAW ; Prof. Dr. R. ZIMMERMANN, S.J., PH.D.; Prof. Dr. V. G. PARANJPE, M.A., D.LITT. ; and Mr. N. B. UTGIKAR, M.A. But I desire to make a special mention of my indebtedness to Mr. VAIDYA and to Rev. Fr. ZIMMERMANN, whose advice and ready help have accompanied my labours from the time I first accepted the responsibilities of the work. Nothing has encouraged me more in this arduous and fascinating task than the unwavering interest with which they have followed it. In connection with the help the Editorial Board has received from collaborators outside the Institute, I have to record the indebtedness of the Board to : Pandit Vidhushekhar BHATTACHARYA, M.A., Principal of the Viśvabhāratī, Bolpur ; Rajaguru Pandit HEMRAJ, Director of Public Instruction, Nepal ; M. R. Ry. Sambamurti Row, Honorary Secretary, Palace Library, Tanjore ; and Prof. K. Rama PISHAROTI, M.A., Principal of the Sanskrit College, Trippunittura, Cochin. These gentlemen have been good enough to supply the Institute with carefully prepared collations of manuscripts which are in their charge or which were kindly procured for the purpose by them. The Nirnaya Sagar Press has rendered ungrudgingly every assistance in carrying out the typographical arrangements which appeared to me best suited for the purposes of the work. The illustration accompanying this fascicule is prepared from a water-colour painting kindly supplied by the Chief of Aundh.

In conclusion, I may be permitted to remark that the renown of the Bhāratavarṣa, of its Princes and its People, is for all time inseparably linked with the Mahābhārata, which is, in more senses than one the greatest epic the world has produced. It must be manifest to anyone who bestows a thought on the subject that the monumental work of preparing the first critical edition of this colossal encyclopædia of ancient India could be carried on and completed by the young Institute by which it has been undertaken only if it can count upon substantial aid from other sources and upon co-operation on a much wider scale. If the Princes and the People of India were to associate themselves with this imposing enterprise, they would indeed be supporting a *national* work. On behalf of the Institute which I represent, I appeal to all true Indians to ally themselves with the Institute in supporting the publication of a work which is in a unique manner bound up with the history of the Indian people and the prestige of Indian scholarship.

V. S. SUKTHANKAR.

January 1927.

POSTCRIPT

Since the manuscript of this fascicule was sent to the press, I was able to make arrangements for securing collations of Śāradā and Nepāli manuscripts of the Ādiparvan. These collations will be published later. Here it may just be remarked that the collations so far received wholly support the constituted text, especially as regards the interpolated stanzas, proving the correctness of the method adopted in setting the text.

V. S. S.

May 1927.

PROLEGOMENA *

The need of a critical or as it was sometimes called a "correct" edition of the Mahābhārata has been felt (at first, of course, rather vaguely) by Sanskritists for over half a century.[1] It was voiced, however, in a clear and emphatic manner, for the first time, by Professor M. WINTERNITZ, at the XIth International Congress of Orientalists, held at Paris, in 1897, when he read a paper drawing attention to the South Indian manuscripts of the Great Epic and ending with the remark that a critical edition of the Mahābhārata was "wanted as the only sound basis for all Mahābhārata studies, nay, for all studies connected with the epic literature of India".[2] The idea received a concrete shape in his proposal for the foundation of a Sanskrit Epic Text Society, which he laid before the very next session of the Oriental Congress (XIIth), held in Rome (1899). Again, three years later, at the following session of the Congress (XIIIth), held in Hamburg (1902), Professor WINTERNITZ reiterated his requisition and endeavoured to impress again upon the assembled savants that a "critical edition of the Mahābhārata was a *sine quâ non* for all historical and critical research regarding the Great Epic of India".

The reception accorded to the various proposals made by Professor WINTERNITZ in connection with his favourite project was not as cordial as might have been expected from an enlightened, international assemblage of Sanskritists. "At first", writes Professor WINTERNITZ himself,[3] "the idea of a critical edition of the Mahābhārata met with great scepticism. Most scholars were of opinion that it was impossible to restore a critical text of the Great Epic, and that we should have to be satisfied with editing the South Indian text, while the North Indian text was represented well enough by the Calcutta and Bombay editions. Only few scholars were in full agreement with the plan of *one* critical edition".

Notwithstanding this general apathy, a committee was appointed by the Indian Section of the International Congress of Orientalists in Rome (1899) to consider the proposal of Professor WINTERNITZ for the foundation of a Sanskrit Epic Text Society, already mentioned. This committee was not in favour of the said proposal. It recommended instead that the work of preparing the critical edition should be undertaken by the International Association of Academies. The London session of this Association, held in

---

* [To the Ādiparvan.]

[1] See below.

[2] Cf. WINTERNITZ, *Indol. Prag.* 1 (1929). 58 ff

[3] ibid. p. 58.

1904, adopted the above suggestion and resolved "to make the critical edition of the Mahābhārata one of the tasks to be undertaken under its auspices and with the help of funds to be raised by the Academies." In pursuance of this decision, the Academies of Berlin and Vienna sanctioned certain funds earmarked for the Mahābhārata work, with whose help the preliminary work for the critical edition was actually begun.

[2] In furtherance of this project, then, Professor H. LÜDERS prepared a "Specimen" of a critical edition of the Mahābhārata (*Druckprobe einer kritischen Ausgabe des Mahābhārata*, Leipzig 1908) with the funds provided for the purpose by the Königliche Gesellschaft der Wissenschaften in Göttingen.[1] The Specimen, which was meant only for private circulation,[2] consisted of 18 pages, comprising the constituted text (pp. 1-11) of the first 67 stanzas of the Ādiparvan with their various readings (printed as footnotes), an Appendix (pp. 12-17), on a similar plan, containing the text of the Brahmā-Gaṇeśa interpolation (with *its* variants), and finally a list (p. 18) of the 29 manuscripts, selected exclusively from European libraries, which formed the specimen *apparatus criticus*.[3] This little brochure, which must rank in the annals of Mahābhārata studies as the first tentative critical edition of the Mahābhārata, was laid before the Indian Section of the XVth International Congress of Orientalists, held in Copenhagen (1908). The tender seedling, planted with infinite care, did not, however, thrive in the uncongenial European soil. Twenty years later, in 1928, at the XVIIth International Congress of Orientalists, held at Oxford, Professor WINTERNITZ reported that, under the scheme of the International Association of Academies, "except this specimen (*Druckprobe*) nothing has been printed".[4]

However, in the interval some preliminary work, such as the classifying and collating of manuscripts had been done by Professor LÜDERS and some of his pupils (among them my fellow-student and friend Dr. Johannes NOBEL, now Professor in the University of Marburg), by Professor WINTERNITZ and his pupil Dr. Otto STEIN, and by Dr. Bernhard GEIGER (Vienna). The last great World War gave its quietus to this ambitious project, sponsored by the Associated Academies of Europe and America, and finally diverted the attention of European scholars from the Mahābhārata Problem.

---

1 It was printed by the firm of W. Drugulin.

2 Professor WINTERNITZ had sent me, in 1926, his copy, on loan, for perusal, which I returned to him almost immediately afterwards.

3 The brochure did not contain any preface, or explanatory notes.

4 See also the remarks of Professor A. A. MACDONELL printed in the "Report of the Joint Session of the Royal Asiatic Society, Société Asiatique, American Oriental Society, and Scuola Orientale, Reale Universita di Roma, September 3-6, 1919 in *JRAS*. 1920. 149. Cf. also *ABI*. 4. 145 ff.

After the war, the Bhandarkar Oriental Research Institute, then in its early infancy, enthusiastically undertook the work, making a fresh start, fortunately without realizing fully the enormousness of the project or the complicacies of the problem. At a meeting of the General Body of the Institute, held on July 6, 1918, Shrimant Balasaheb Pant Pratinidhi, Chief (now Ruler) of Aundh—the liberal and enthusiastic patron of diverse projects calculated to stimulate research, advance knowledge, and enhance Indian prestige—the president elect on the occasion, easily persuaded by a band of young and hopeful Sanskritists who had returned to India after completing their philological training abroad, with their heads full of new ideas, urged upon the audience the need of preparing a Critical and Illustrated Edition of the Mahābhārata, offering to contribute, personally, a lakh of rupees, by annual grants, towards the expenses of producing the edition.[1] The donor was warmly thanked for this princely [3] gift and the offer was gratefully accepted by the spokesmen of the Institute, who in their turn undertook to prepare an edition that would meet with the high requirements of modern critical scholarship. In accordance with this decision of the General Body of the Institute, the late lamented Sir Ramkrishna Gopal BHANDARKAR, the doyen of the Sanskritists of Western India and the inspirer of the critical and rigorous scholarship of the present day, inaugurated, in April 1919, this monumental work by formally beginning the collation of the opening *mantra* of the works of the ancient Bhāgavata sect, which is found also at the beginning of some manuscripts of the Mahābhārata :[2]

नारायणं नमस्कृत्य नरं चैव नरोत्तमम् ।
देवीं सरस्वतीं चैव ततो जयमुदीरयेत् ॥

Then, on the basis of the promise of the donation of a lakh of rupees by the Ruler of Aundh, the Institute appealed for the very large financial support needed to Indian governments, princes, and men of wealth. Not as many favourable responses were received as might have been expected ; but very generous aid was and is being given by some, whose names are recorded elsewhere.

The reasons which have induced Sanskritists both here and abroad to undertake this gigantic enterprise are easy to understand. The pre-eminent importance of the epic is universally acknowledged. Next to the Vedas, it is the most valuable product of the entire literature of ancient India, so rich in notable works. Venerable for its very antiquity, it is one

---

[1] Cf. Bhavanrao Pandit Pratinidhi, *ABI*. 3 (1921-22). 1 f. Also *A Prospectus of a New and Critical Edition of the Mahābhārata* (Poona 1919), published by the Institute, p. v.

[2] For instance, the stanza is foreign to the entire Southern recension of the epic. Cf. also BÜHLER-KIRSTE, *Ind Stud*. No. 2, p. 4, 2 ; and Sylvain LÉVI, *R. G. Bhandarkar Commemoration Volume*, p. 99.

of the most inspiring monuments of the world, and an inexhaustible mine for the investigation of the religion, mythology, legend, philosophy, law, custom, and political and social institutions of ancient India.

As a result of researches that have been carried on during the last thirty-five years or so, there is now no doubt whatsoever that the text of the Mahābhārata has undergone numerous changes.[1] The texts of the Northern and Southern manuscripts—to mention only two of the manuscript classes—are widely divergent, and much uncertainty prevails regarding the correctness and originality of the texts preserved by them. The existing editions—which either merely reproduce the version of a particular type of manuscripts, like the Bombay edition,[2] or else are eclectic on no recognizable principles, like the Kumbhakonam edition—fail to remove the uncertainty of the text.

The present edition of the epic is intended chiefly to remedy this unsatisfactory state of things. What the promoters of this scheme desire to produce and supply is briefly this : a critical edition of the Mahābhārata in the preparation of which all important versions of the Great Epic shall have been taken into consideration, and all important manuscripts collated, estimated and turned to account. Since all divergent readings of any importance will be given in the critical notes, printed at the foot of the page, this [4] edition will, for the first time, render it possible for the reader to have before him the entire significant evidence for each individual passage. The value of this method for scientific investigation of the epic is obvious. Another feature of the new edition will be this. Since not even the seemingly most irrelevant line or stanza, actually found in a Mahābhārata manuscript collated for the edition, is on any account omitted, this edition of the Mahābhārata will be, in a sense, more complete than any previous edition.[3] It will be a veritable thesaurus of the Mahābhārata tradition.

Under the scheme outlined above, a tentative edition of the Virāṭaparvan was prepared by the late Mr. Narayan Bapuji UTGIKAR, M.A., and published by the Institute in 1923. Copies of this edition were distributed gratis among leading Sanskritists—Indian, European and American—with a view to eliciting from them a frank expression of their opinion on the method worked out by the then editor-in-chief. The opinions received were very favourable and highly encouraging. The valuable suggestions made

---

1 The earliest systematic study of the subject seems to have been made by BURNELL in his *Aindra Grammarians* ; cf. also his *Classified Index to the Sanskrit MSS. in the Palace at Tanjore* (London 1879), p. 180.

2 Representing the Nilakantha tradition.

3 The Institute intends to publish, as a supplement to this edition, a Pratika Index of the Mahābhārata, which will be an alphabetical index of every single pāda of the text of the epic.

by many eminent authorities have been to a great extent followed in the subsequent work.

COLLATION OF MANUSCRIPTS

Collation of the manuscripts is being done, regularly, not merely at the Institute, but also at the Visvabharati of Rabindranath TAGORE in Bengal under the supervision of Pandit Vidhushekhara BHATTACHARYA, and at the Saraswati Mahal in Tanjore under the supervision of M. R. Ry. Rao Saheb T. Sambamurthi RAO Avl., B.A., B.L. These outside centres were at first intended chiefly for the collation of the Bengali and the Telugu-Grantha manuscripts respectively. But provision has now been made at the Institute itself for the collation of manuscripts written in any of the seven scripts (Śāradā, Nepālī, Maithilī, Bengali, Telugu, Grantha and Malayālam), besides Devanāgarī, which are ordinarily required for our Mahābhārata work.

The *entire* Mahābhārata stands now collated from a *minimum* of ten manuscripts; many parvans have been completely collated from twenty manuscripts; some from thirty; a few from as many as forty; while the first two adhyāyas of the Ādi, which have special importance for the critical constitution of the text of the entire epic, were collated from no less than sixty manuscripts.

The collation is done by a permanent staff of specially trained Shastris (Northern as well as Southern) and University graduates. For the purposes of collation, each Mahābhārata stanza (according to the Bombay edition of Ganpat KRISHNAJI, Śaka 1799) is first written out, in bold characters, on the top line of a standard, horizontally and vertically ruled foolscap sheet. The variant readings are entered by the collator horizontally along a line allotted to the manuscript collated, akṣara by akṣara, in the appropriate column, vertically below the corresponding portion of the original reading of the "Vulgate". On the right of each of these collation sheets, there is a column four inches wide reserved for remarks (regarding corrections, marginal additions etc.), and for "additional" stanzas found in the manuscripts collated, either immediately before or after [5] the stanza in question. Very long "additions" are written out on separate "śodhapatras" and attached to the collation sheets. The collations are regularly checked by a batch of collators different from the one which did the collation in the first instance, before they are handed over to the editor for the constitution of the text.

THE CRITICAL APPARATUS

GENERAL ACCOUNT OF THE MANUSCRIPTS

It is by no means easy to answer the question how many manuscripts of the Mahābhārata there are in existence; firstly, because, no complete list of these manuscripts has ever been compiled; and, secondly, because the expression "Mahābhārata manuscript", as ordinarily used, is ambiguous in the extreme; it may apply to a small manuscript of the Bhagavadgītā alone, as well as to a complete manuscript of the Mahābhārata, in several volumes, containing all the eighteen parvans. Moreover, the parvans are mostly handed down separately, or in groups of few parvans at a time, at least in the oldest manuscripts now preserved. Therefore, in taking stock of Mahābhārata manuscripts, it is best to take as unit of measurement a manuscript of a *single* parvan.

As a very approximate computation, I may state that there are known to be about 235 manuscripts of the Ādi, counting only such as have come within my knowledge from catalogues of private and public libraries accessible to me, as also those manuscripts whose owners have sent them to the Institute for collation or inspection. But this is probably by a long way not the total number of extant manuscripts of this parvan, because there must be quite a large number of manuscripts in private hands, of which we know next to nothing. It has been the experience of most manuscript collectors in India that when one takes the trouble to look for the manuscripts, they turn up in quite astonishing numbers, though they are as a rule late and of questionable worth. Of these 235 manuscripts of the Ādi, a little less than half (107) are in the Devanāgarī script alone. The other scripts are represented in this collection as follows: Bengali 32, Grantha 31, Telugu 28, Malayālam 26, Nepālī 5, Śāradā 3,[1] Maithili 1, Kannada 1, and Nandināgarī 1.

Of these manuscripts of the Ādi about 70 (i.e. a little more than 29 per cent of the total) were fully or partly examined and collated for this edition. And of these again about 60 were actually utilized in preparing the text. The critical apparatus of the first two adhyāyas gives the collations of 50 manuscripts. Many of these were, however, discarded in the sequel as misch-codices of small trustworthiness and of no special value for critical purposes. At the same time a few other manuscripts (such as the Śāradā and Nepālī codices), which were not available in the beginning, were added to the critical apparatus subsequently. A table given below supplies all the necessary details of the critical apparatus as to where the collations of the different manuscripts begin, where they end, and so on and so forth.

[6] The choice of the critical apparatus is not easy matter, owing to the astonishing bulk and the amazing variety of the material. The number of exact duplicates among these is decidedly small and almost negligible. An exception to this rule is formed only by manuscripts of commentators' versions, which show *inter se* little difference. So that what has been said by KOSEGARTEN with respect to the manuscripts of the Pañcatantra, applies, generally speaking, equally well to the Mahābhārata manuscripts: *quot codices, tot textus*. Notwithstanding these difficulties, the choice of our critical apparatus has not been entirely arbitrary. Efforts were made to secure manuscripts written in as many different Indian scripts as possible, which is the same as saying, manuscripts belonging to as many different Indian

---

1 Of these three, our $Ś_1$ is one, while the other two are paper manuscripts, written in modern Śāradā characters, with Nīlakaṇṭha's commentary, in the Raghunatha Temple Library; cf. STEIN'S CATALOGUE (1894), p. 196, Nos. 3712-32, 3951-79. They represent probably the Nīlakaṇṭha version.

provinces as possible. Old manuscripts, even though fragmentary and partly illegible, were selected in preference to modern-looking manuscripts, though complete, neatly written and well preserved. Within the version, discrepant types were chosen in preference to similar types.[1] Of the Nīlakaṇṭha version, only three were selected, though it is by far the most numerous group; because, firstly, it is one of the latest versions; and, secondly it has been edited several times already, though not as well as it should be; and, thirdly, there is little difference between the individual manuscripts of the group. The only important scripts unrepresented in our critical apparatus are: Kannaḍa, Uriyā and Nandināgarī.

Besides the manuscripts collated specially for this edition, I have made occasional use of the collations of manuscripts preserved in European libraries made by Theodor GOLDSTÜCKER, photographic copies of which were presented to the Institute, for use in connection with this project by the University of Strassburg, through the kind offices of the late Professor Émile SENART, as also of the collations intended for the edition planned by the International Association of Academies and made by the pupils of Geheimrat Professor Dr. Heinrich LÜDERS, which have been placed at the disposal of the Institute in pursuance of a resolution on the subject passed by the Indian Section of the XVIIth International Congress of Orientalists, held at Oxford, in 1928.[2]

Sixteen of the manuscripts collated bear dates, ranging from the 16th to the 19th century. The oldest dated manuscript of our critical apparatus is a Nepālī manuscript ($\tilde{N}_3$) which bears a date corresponding to A.D. 1511.* The other dates are: A.D. 1519 (K_3), 1528 (V_1), 1598 (D_2), 1620 (Da_2), 1638 (K_2), 1694 (K_4), 1701 (Dr_3), 1739 (K_0), 1740 (B_1), 1759 (B_3), 1786 (B_5), 1802 (D_6), 1808 (Dn_2), 1838 (M_3), and 1842 (M_8). The Nīlakaṇṭha manuscripts are not all dated, but they can scarcely be much anterior to the beginning of the eighteenth century, since Nīlakaṇṭha himself [7] belongs to the last quarter of the seventeenth. Many of the Grantha

1 Consequently, our critical apparatus tends to reflect greater diversity in the material than what actually exists, but that was unavoidable.

2 The Resolutions were worded as follows:

No. 2. That in view of the eminently satisfactory manner in which the work is being done by the Institute, this Congress is of opinion that the MSS. collations made, and the funds collected, for the critical edition of the epic planned by the Association of Academies, be now utilized for the purposes of the critical edition being prepared in India, without prejudice to the original project of the Association of Academies.

No. 3. That this Congress therefore recommends that: (a) such collations of the Mahābhārata text as have already been prepared by the Association of Academies be placed, on loan, at the disposal of the Bhandarkar Oriental Research Institute.......

[* See now Epic Studies VII, *infra*.]

manuscripts do bear dates, but since they refer to a cyclic era, it is difficult to calculate their equivalents.

CLASSIFICATION OF MANUSCRIPTS

The manuscript material is divided naturally into recensions by the scripts in which they are written. Corresponding to the two main types of Indian scripts, Northern and Southern, we get two main recensions of the epic. Each of these recensions is again divided into a number of sub-recensions, which I have called "versions", corresponding to the different provincial scripts in which these texts are written. This *principium divisionis* is not as arbitrary as it might at first sight appear. The superficial difference of scripts corresponds, as a matter of fact, to deep underlying textual differences. It is common experience in India that when we have a work handed down in different versions, the script is invariably characteristic of the version.[1] The reason for this concomitance between script and version appears to be that the scribes, being as a rule not conversant with any script but that of their own particular province, could copy only manuscripts written in their special provincial scripts, exception being made only in favour of Devanāgarī, which was a sort of a "vulgar" script, widely used and understood in India.

While the principle mentioned above is not entirely mechanical or arbitrary, it is also not ideal or perfect. It is often contravened in practice, mainly through the agency of the Devanāgarī, which is the chief medium of contamination between the different recensions and versions. Thus we come across Devanāgarī copies of the commentary or version of Arjunamiśra, who was an Easterner; similar copies of the commentary or version of Ratnagarbha, who was a Southerner. There are again Devanāgarī copies of the Grantha and the Śāradā[2] versions. On the other hand, a popular version like that of Nīlakaṇṭha may be copied in any script. I have come across manuscripts of the Nīlakaṇṭha (Devanāgarī) version written in Śāradā,[3] Bengali,[4] Telugu and Grantha scripts. Another cause of disturbance was this. Along the boundaries of provinces speaking different languages or using different scripts, there are invariably bi-lingual and bi-scriptal zones. In these zones there was an ever operating impulse, tending to introduce innovations, obliterating the *differentiae* and normalizing the text. Nevertheless, though nothing is impossible, it would be passing strange if we were to find a copy of the pure Śāradā version written, say, in the Malayālam script, or of the Grantha version in the Nepālī script.

---

1 Cf. LÜDERS, *Deutsche Literaturztg*, 1929, 1140.

2 Like our K_1 (India Office, No. 2137).

3 There are two such MSS. in the Raghunatha Temple Library, Jammu, Nos. 3712-32, 3958-79.

4 Some of them were collated for the Institute at the Viśvabharati.

[8] LIST OF MANUSCRIPTS FORMING THE CRITICAL APPARATUS

The manuscripts utilized for this edition of the Ādi are as follows :

I. (Northern) Recension.

(*a*) *North-western Group* (*ν*).

Śāradā (or Kaśmīrī) Version (Ś).

Ś$_1$ = Poona, Bombay Govt. Collection (deposited at the BORI), No. 159 of 1875-76.

Devanāgarī Group allied to the (Śāradā or) Kaśmīrī Version (K).

K$_0$ = Poona, Bombay Govt. Collection (deposited at the BORI), No. 229 of 1895-1902. Dated V. Saṁ 1795 (ca. A.D. 1739).

K$_1$ = London, India Office Library, No. 3226 (2137).

K$_2$ = Poona, Bombay Govt. Collection (deposited at the BORI), No. 182 of 1891-95. Dated V. Saṁ. 1694 (ca. A.D. 1638).

K$_3$ = Baroda, Oriental Institute Library, No. 632. Dated V. Saṁ. 1575 (ca. A.D. 1519).

K$_4$ = Poona, Bombay Govt. Collection (deposited at the BORI), No. 565 of 1882-83. Dated Śaka 1616 (ca. A.D. 1694).

K$_5$ = Lahore, Dayanand Anglo-Vedic College, No. 1.

K$_6$ = Poona, Bombay Govt. Collection (deposited at the BORI), No. 209 of 1887-91.

(*b*) *Central Group* (*γ*).

Nepālī Version (Ñ).

Ñ$_1$ = Nepal, in private possession.

Ñ$_2$ = Nepal, in private possession.

Ñ$_3$ = Nepal, in private possession. Dated Nepālī Saṁ. 632 (ca. A.D. 1511).

Maithili Version (V).

V$_1$ = Nepal Durbar Library, No. 1364, Dated La Saṁ. 411 (ca. A.D. 1528).

Bengali Version (B).

B$_1$ = Santiniketan, Visvabharati Library, No. 1. Dated Śaka 1662 (ca. A.D. 1740)

B$_2$ = Santiniketan, Visvabharati Library, No. 258.

B$_3$ = Santiniketan, Visvabharati Library, No. 782. Dated Saka 1681 (ca. A.D. 1759).

B$_4$ = Santiniketan, Visvabharati Library, No. 413.

B$_5$ = Dacca, University Library, No. 485. Dated Śaka 1708 (ca. A.D. 1786).

B$_6$ = Dacca, University Library, No. 735.

Devanāgarī Versions *other than K* (D).

Devanāgarī Version of Arjunamiśra (Da).

Da$_1$ = Poona, Bombay Govt. Collection (deposited at the BORI), No. 30 of A 1879-80.

Da$_2$ = Poona, Bombay Govt. Collection (deposited at the BORI, Viśrāmbāg I, No. 468. Dated V. Saṁ. 1676 (ca. A.D. 1620).

Devanāgarī Version of Nīlakaṇṭha (Dn), the "Vulgate".

Dn$_1$ = MS. belonging to Sardar M. V. Kibe of Indore.

Dn$_2$ = Mysore, Oriental Library, No. 1064. Dated V. Saṁ. 1864 (ca. A.D. 1808).

[9] Dn_3 = Poona Bombay Govt. Collection (deposited at the BORI), No. 234 of 1895-1902.

Devanāgarī Version of Ratnagarbha (Dr.)

Dr_1 = Tanjore, Saraswathi Mahal Library, No. 1246.
Dr_2 = Tanjore, Saraswathi Mahal Library, No. 1199.
Dr_3 = Tanjore, Saraswathi Mahal Library, No. 1313. Dated Śaka 1623 (ca. A.D. 1701).
Dr_4 = Tanjore, Saraswathi Mahal Library, No. 1339.

Devanāgarī Composite Version.

D_1 = Poona, Bombay Govt. Collection (deposited at the BORI), No. 29 of A 1879-80.
D_2 = Tanjore, Saraswathi Mahal Library, No. 1152. Dated V. Saṁ. 1654 (ca. A.D. 1598).
D_3 = Tanjore, Saraswathi Mahal Library, No. 1360.
D_4 = Tanjore, Saraswathi Mahal Library, No. 1126.
D_5 = Lahore, Dayanand Anglo-Vedic College, No. 4. Dated V. Saṁ 1858 (ca. A.D. 1802).
D_6 = Tanjore, Saraswathi Mahal Library, No. 1223.
D_7 = Tanjore, Saraswathi Mahal Library, No. 1269.
D_8 = Tanjore, Saraswathi Mahal Library, No. 1329.
D_9 = Tanjore, Saraswathi Mahal Library, No. 1176.
D_{10} = Tanjore, Saraswathi Mahal Library, No. 1293.
D_{11} = Tanjore, Saraswathi Mahal Library, No. 1340.
D_{12} = Tanjore, Saraswathi Mahal Library, No. 1373.
D_{13} = Poona, Bombay Govt. Collection (deposited at the BORI), Viśrāmbāg II, No. 191.
D_{14} = Poona, Bombay Govt. Collection (deposited at the BORI) Viśrāmbāg II, No. 266.

II. S(outhern) Recension.

Telugu Version (T).

T_1 = Melcote, Yadugiri Yatiraj Math Library MS. (without number).
T_2 = Tanjore, Saraswathi Mahal Library, No. 11865.
T_3 = Tanjore, Saraswathi Mahal Library, No. 11809.

Grantha Version (G).

G_1 = Melkote, Yadugiri Yatiraj Math Library MS. (without number).
G_2 = Melkote, Yadugiri Yatiraj Math Library MS. (without number).
G_3 = Tanjore, Saraswathi Mahal Library, No. 11823.
G_4 = Tanjore, Saraswathi Mahal Library, No. 11838.
G_5 = Tanjore, Saraswathi Mahal Library, No. 11851.
G_6 = Tanjore, Saraswathi Mahal Library, No. 11860.
G_7 = Melkote, Yadugiri Yatiraj Math Library MS. (without number).

Malayālam Version (M).

M_1 = MS. belonging to Chief of Idappalli, Cochin.
M_2 = Cochin, State Library, No. 5.
M_3 = Cochin, State Library, No. 1. Dated Kollam 1013 (ca. A.D. 1838).
M_4 = MS. belonging to Kallenkara Pisharam of Cochin.
M_5 = Cochin (Jayantamangalam); property of the Paliyam family.
M_6 = Malabar (Nareri Mana); in private possession.
M_7 = Cochin (Avaṇapparambu Mana); in private possession.
M_8 = Malabar Poomulli Mana Library, No. 297. Dated Kollam 1017 (ca. A.D. 1842).

[10] DETAILED ACCOUNT OF THE MANUSCRIPTS

Ś$_1$

Poona, Bombay Government Collection (deposited at the BORI), No. 159 of 1875-76. Total number of folios 114 (some fragmentary), with about 24 lines to a page; size 12″ × 9½″. Clear Śāradā characters (of perhaps the 16th or 17th century), Birchbark (bhūrjapatra).

This unique and valuable MS. was purchased for the Government of Bombay, by BÜHLER, in Kaśmīr. It is listed on p. xi, and cursorily described at p. 64, of his *Detailed Report of a Tour in Search of Sanskrit MSS. made in Kaśmīr, Rajputana and Central India*, a report printed as Extra Number of the *Journal of the Bombay Branch of the Royal Asiatic Society* for 1877. The lines of writing of the MS. run parallel to the narrow side of the leaf. There are, on an average, 24 lines on a page, and 36 akṣaras (i.e. a little over a śloka) in a line. A page, therefore, contains, on an average, 26 (anuṣṭubh) stanzas. Each folio bears, on its reverse, in the left-hand margin, near the bottom, a cipher representing the serial number of the folio and a signature indicating the title of the work, as well as the name of the parvan.—The MS., which is unfortunately incomplete and fragmentary, must have originally contained at least the first three parvans (Ādi, Sabhā and Araṇya), written, as far as one can judge, by the same hand. The extant portion contains the Sabhā in its entirety, but only fragments of the other two parvans, the beginning of Ādi and the end of Araṇya being lost. The Ādi, which appears to have extended from the beginning of the volume up to fol. 154, is particularly fragmentary; a continuous text begins only from fol. 63 (our adhy. 82). Of the first 62 folios, the extant portion contains only the *lower* segments (with 10 to 15 lines of writing on each page) of fol. 24-25, 36-37, 39, 47-48, 53-57 and 61-62; the initial 23 folios as also 15 other intermediate folios (viz. 38, 40-46, 49-52, 58-60) are entirely missing; while only 10 of these folios are complete. Folio number 96 is repeated. The Ādi ends at fol. 154a. The colophon repeats the stanzas of the Parvasaṁgraha giving the number of adhyāyas (230) in this parvan, as also its extent in "ślokas", i.e. granthas (7984). The writing is neat and careful; erasures and corrections are few and far between. Occasionally one comes across variant readings (cf. fol. 115b), entered (probably by the same hand) in yet smaller letters between the lines; on fol. 116a, there is a stanza written in the upper margin, which is meant to be added after 1. 162. 15, and which is found, otherwise, only in K$_1$, in other words is an interpolation peculiar to Ś$_1$ K$_1$. Many of the *marginal* additions are glosses, which are rather numerous in the first 15 (extant) folios, evidently notes made from some commentary by a student who intended making a careful study of the text. In a few places—perhaps about half a dozen—corrections have been made with yellow pigment. Some of the adhyāyas bear (serial) numbers, written probably by a different hand; the first (legible) figure that we come across is 43, corresponding to adhy. 32 of our edition, involving a difference of 11 in our enumerations of adhyāyas ! The last adhyāya number noted in this parvan is 100, corresponding to our adhy. 87 : the difference between our enumerations thus rises to 13 in 55 adhyāyas. The Purāṇic *raconteur* is here called, throughout, Sūta, *not* Sauti. Moreover, the prose formula of reference generally omits उवाच [11] (resp. ऊचुः), and gives, as in S MSS., merely the name or designation of the speaker, such as वैशंपायनः. However, from the fact that towards the middle and end of the parvan, the full forms containing उवाच (resp. ऊचुः) do occur sporadically, e.g. 1. 94. 64 (fol. 73a); 98. 1 (fol. 75b); 99. 36 (fol. 77a) etc. : it follows that the usual वैशंपायनः etc. are only *abbreviations*. The names of the sub-parvans are generally added, in the colophons, agreeing mostly with the corresponding divisions of our edition. The extant fragment begins (fol. 24a) with the words कश्यपः । विदित्वा चास्य सङ्कल्पमिमं (cf. v. l. 1. 26. 10).—A facsimile of the folio (154) containing the end of the Ādi and the beginning of the Sabhā is given, facing p. 880.

K_0

Poona, Bombay Government Collection (deposited at the BORI), No. 229 of 1895-1902. Folios 181, with about 15 lines to a page ; size 14·7″ × 6·7″. Devanāgarī characters ; dated V. Saṁvat 1795 (ca. A.D. 1739). Old Indian paper.

The MS. contains the first three parvans written in the same hand, ***the date coming at the end of the Araṇya.*** The writing is clear and fairly correct ; a few corrections of scribe's errors are noted in the margin, probably by the same hand ; otherwise the margins are clean. The colophons give adhyāya numbers sporadically, and names of adhyāyas, sub-parvans or upākhyānas generally. On the last folio (181) of the Ādi is given, ***in different hand,*** a list of major parvans with the corresponding number of their adhyāyas and stanzas, in a tabular form.

K_1

London, India Office Library, No. 3226 (2137). Folios 169, with about 33 lines to a page : size 16¼″ × 9″. Devanāgarī characters ; dated (possibly) 1783 A.D. Indian Paper.

A moderately trustworthy, though somewhat modern and very incorrect transcript of a Śāradā exemplar. Even the outward form and get-up of this MS. are suggestive of Kaśmīrī origin. The lines of writing, as in Śāradā (bhūrjapatra) MSS. run parallel to the narrow side of the folio. The signatures in the margin are like those found in Kaśmīrī books. The numerous clerical errors, which disfigure every page, betray the writer to be a professional scribe, not thoroughly familiar with the awkward Śāradā script, and still less so with the language of the text, easily misled by the deceptive similarity between certain letters of the Śāradā and Devanāgarī alphabets. He frequently writes म for स (e. g. मंकुले for संकुले); उं for त and ष for थ (e. g. उषा for तथा); द for ऋ (e. g. दध्या for ऋध्या); श for म (e. g. प्रकाशं for प्रकामं) or for च (e. g. पांशाली for पांचाली); medial उ for subscript व (e. g. सुर्णं for स्वर्णं),

ब्य for ह्व; तु for र्तै, त्त, त्र (e. g. आतुस्वरं, मतुमः, वैच्चितुवीर्ये for आर्तैस्वरं, सत्तमः and विचित्रवीर्ये); श्य for च्य; श्व for च्च; medial उ for subscript त; भ for त (e. g. मभिः for मतिः); ष्ट for ष्य (e. g. शिष्टा for शिष्या). Margins are clean; very occasional corrections, in the body of the text, by yellow pigment. The pages from 42 to 45 are left blank, while 41b and 46a contain only a few lines of writing. Besides Ādi, the codex contains also Virāṭa, Bhīṣma and a portion of Anuśāsana (Dānadharma), breaking off at the first half of stanza 39 of adhy. 83 of the Bombay ed. According to statements at the end of the Bhīṣma and the beginning of the Anuśāsana, the MS. was written in V. Saṁvat 1839 (ca. A.D. 1783), by a Brāhmaṇa named Gopāla, residing in Lakṣmīmaṭha; but the writing of the volume is not quite uniform. It is, therefore, uncertain, in my opinion, whether the Ādi was written by this same Gopāla, in the said year; *contra* EGGELING, *Catalogue of the Skt.* MSS. [12] *in the Library of the India Office,* Part VI (1899), p. 1158, who regards the entire volume as written by the same scribe. The colophons, which are short, sporadically give the adhyāya numbers. This is the only MS. of the Ādi belonging to a European Library that was available for collation at the Institute and used for this edition!—The reference लो ह णिह before stanza 8 of adhy. 1 indicates the intention of the scribe to "illuminate" the MS. by writing the alternate letters (म, र्ष, वाच) which are missing, in red ink.

K_2

Poona, Bombay Government Collection (deposited at the BORI), No. 182 of 1891-96. Folios 296 (of which 220, 226-30, 232-33, 239-40 appear to be written by a different hand), with about 11 lines to a page; size 10·8" × 4·8". Devanāgarī characters (with sporadic pṛṣṭhamātrās); dated V. Saṁ 1694 (ca. A.D. 1638). Indian paper.

Marginal corrections, as also other corrections in the body of the text, are made by using yellow pigment; the colophons give names of sub-parvans, adhyāya names, and adhyāya numbers sporadically. In the marginal notes one occasionally comes across variants and glosses, and additional passages from MSS. of the central sub-recension (γ). The first folio and a part of the second (the latter stuck on to the original torn) are written in a different hand. On fol. 186b, three lines are left blank by the scribe. After the four stanzas of "phalaśruti" mentioned on p. 879, there follow two stanzas of the parva-saṁgraha, giving the number of adhyāyas (218) and ślokas (8984) and, finally, the date: संवत १६९४ वर्षे माघशुदि १० रवौ लिखितमिदं

K_3

Baroda, Oriental Institute Library, No. 632. Folios 407. Devanāgarī characters; dated V. Saṁvat 1575 (ca. A.D. 1519). Old Indian paper.

This MS. is from Gujarat. At the end of the MS. is given the date: Saṁvat 1575, śrāvaṇa, dark half, 5th day, Abhinandana. MS. written by Nāñjika, son of the Nagar Pandit Kālidāsa of village Kāndalāja, under Saṁkhetakapura (modern Sankheda, in Baroda State). For further details, see the colophon given on p. 879.

K_4

Poona, Bombay Government Collection (deposited at the BORI), No. 565 of 1882-83. Folios 237 (not counting the suppl. folios), with about 15-16 lines to a page; size 14·9" × 6". Devanāgarī characters; dated Śaka 1616 (ca. A.D. 1694), at the end of one of the subsequent parvans. Old Indian paper.

A carelessly written complete MS., with ळ for ल, throughout, which is a Southern trait; written by one hand, but preserved in the Collection in two bundles numbered 565 and 566. Supplementary folios at 2, 114, 150, 151, 205 include certain long passages (some from Southern sources), copied by the same hand; notable among them being the Brahmā-Gaṇeśa interpolation, whose point of insertion is indicated by a small mark made in the body of the text, and the marginal remark अत्र शोधपत्रमेकं (cf. v. l. 1. 1. 53). There are some excerpts in margins, intended as glosses. Marginal additions of lines and stanzas are frequent only in the first 35 folios, afterwards few and far between. Corrections are made with yellow pigment. Colophons frequently contain adhyāya names, sub-parvan names, but no adhyāya number. The copyist was Gaṇeśa, son of Trimbaka.

[13] K_5

Lahore, Dayanand Anglo-Vedic College Library, No. 1. Folios 28 (numbered 1-7 and 9-29), with about 11-13 lines to a page; size 12" × 6". Devanāgarī characters, (said to be) about 350 years old. Paper.

This MS. is incomplete, ending with 1. 3. 152. It was *collated at the Visvabharati*, up to 1. 2. 40, and was then reported to be missing.

K_6

Poona, Bombay Government Collection (deposited at the BORI), No. 209 of 1887-91. Folios 386, with about 8-10 lines to a page; size 12·2" × 5·8". Devanāgarī characters. Partly old Indian paper and partly modern European paper.

Folios 359 to end are of different paper (modern European, with watermarks) and are written by a different hand. In the margin, corrections of scribe's errors, additional lines and stanzas (some of them probably omitted while copying), and various readings, which are decidedly more numerous in the beginning. On some folios (after fol. 105) yellow pigment has been used for correction. Here and there, lacunæ mark the syllables which the scribe could not decipher, or which were missing in the exemplar. The colophons generally give the adhyāya or sub-parvan names; the adhyāya numbers were added afterwards, perhaps by a different hand, and are often crowded out or squeezed in with difficulty.—Collated up to the end of adhy. 2 only.

$Ñ_1$

MS. in Nepālī characters from Nepal, in private possession. No specifications of the MS. (such as measurements, number of folios etc.) are available.

It begins with a short eulogy (praśasti) of king (śrīmān bhūmahendra) Jayasiṁharāma, at whose bidding the MS. was copied. For a king of that name we have the date (Nepālī) Saṁ. 516 (ca. A.D. 1395). In the praśasti, he is stated to have built (?) a temple of Paśupati in Nepal. Collations of the MS. were kindly supplied by Rajaguru Pandit HEMARAJ, C.I.E., D.P.I., Nepal, who had it collated, for the Institute, by *local Pandits*.—The *Praśasti* reads :

ॐ नमो भगवते वासुदेवाय । ॐ नमः प्रजापतिभ्यः । ॐ नमः कृष्णद्वैपायनाय ।

नारायणं नमस्कृत्य नरं चैव नरोत्तमम् ।
देवीं सरस्वतीं चैव ततो जयमुदीरयेत् ॥

वर्णप्रचाराय * * श्वमेध * * * * * * * * * * * ।
[सत्त्वार्थ] चिन्तामणिकल्पवृक्षो विराजते श्रीजयसिंहरामः ॥

मत्वा तत्क्षणभङ्गुरं जगदिदं विद्युल्लताचञ्चलं
आत्मानं विनिवेश्य धर्मसरणौ दानादिसत्कर्मसु ।
येनाभ्यस्तममत्सरेण मनसा नित्यं हरिं ध्यायता
* * * * * * * * * * * * [? श्री]भारतं लेखितम् ॥

कायेन वाचा मनसा च यद्यत्पापं कृतं तस्य विनाशनाय ।
सुश्रद्धया श्रीजयसिंहरामो व्यलीलिखद्भारतमुत्तमं तत् ॥

प्रेते विष्णुसमागमाय नरकद्वारोपरोधाय च
क्रुद्धक्रूरयमास्यदर्शनप * * * * * * * * ।
एतल्लेखयति स्म पुण्यनिलयं श्रीभारताख्यं महत्
पारः श्रीजयसिंहरामसुकृती सत्त्वार्थचिन्तामणिः ॥

{14} कायवाङ्मानसैर्वित्तैर्विष्णौ भक्तिं करोति यः ।
स एव भगवान्विष्णुस्तस्मै नित्यं नमो नमः ॥

दानेनादित्यसूनुं त्रिदशपति[गुरुं]प्रज्ञया यो विजित्य
सौन्दर्येणाप्यनङ्गं रजनिकरमपि ह्रेपयन्नात्मदीप्त्या ।
दोर्दर्पेणापि भीमं दिवसकरमपि स्पर्धमानः प्रतापैः
स श्रीमान्भूमहेन्द्रो जयति पशुपतिस्थापनेनामरेन्द्रम् ॥

Collations begin at adhy. 3. *Collated in Nepal.*

$\tilde{N}_2$

MS. in Nepālī characters from Nepal ; in private possession. No further details of the MS. are available.

Collations of the MS. were kindly supplied by Rajaguru Pandit HEMARAJ (Nepal), who had it collated for the Institute by *local Pandits*.—Collations begin at adhy. 3.

Ñ$_3$

From a private library in Nepal. Nepālī characters, written in ink on palm-leaf.

Besides the Ādi, the MS. contains also Sauptika-Aiṣīka and Viśoka-Strī. The last folio of this bundle bears the date (Nepālī) Saṁ. 632 (ca. A.D. 1511). Sent to the Institute for collation, through the kind offices of Rajaguru Pandit HEMARAJ (Nepal). The MS. was returned to the owner after a hurried collation, and further details of the MS. are unfortunately not available.—Collations begin at adhy. 14.

V$_1$

Nepal, Darbar Library, No. 1364. Maithilī characters; dated La. Saṁ. 411 (ca. A.D. 1528). Palm-leaf.

No further details of the MS. are available. The MS. has two lengthy lacunæ: 1. 68. 74 to 92. 13, and 96. 37 to 127. 21.—Collations of the MS. were kindly supplied by Rajaguru Pandit HEMARAJ (Nepal), who had it collated, for the Institute by *local Pandits.*

B$_1$

Santiniketan, Visvabharati Library, No. 1. Folios 207; size 28·2″ × 2″. Bengali characters; dated Śaka 1662 (ca. A.D. 1740). Palm-leaf.

The name of the scribe, as given in a stanza following the last colophon, is Kṛṣṇarāmadvija.—*Collated at the Visvabharati.*

B$_2$

Santiniketan, Visvabharati Library, No. 258. Folios 82, with about 5-6 lines to a page; size 25½″ × 2½″. Bengali characters. Palm-leaf.

This fragmentary MS. breaks off at 1. 43. 13, in the middle of the Āstika. —*Collated at the Visvabharati.*

B$_3$

Santiniketan, Visvabharati Library, No. 782. Folios 199; size 19½″ × 4½″. Bengali characters; dated Śaka 1681 (ca. A.D. 1759). Paper.

Name of the copyist, as given at the end of the MS., is Khelārāma Vipra. —*Collated at the Visvabharati.*

[15] B$_4$

Santiniketan, Visvabharati Library, No. 413. Folios 164, with about 7-9 lines to a page; size 20″ × 5·2″. Bengali characters. Paper.

This fragmentary MS. breaks off at 1. 90. 88, in the middle of Saṁbhavaparvan.—*Collated at the Visvabharati.*

B$_5$

Dacca, University Library, No. 485. Folios 366, with about 7 lines to a page; size 17″ × 3¾″. Bengali characters; dated Śaka 1708 (ca. A.D. 1786). Much faded old Indian yellow paper.

The MS., which is well preserved and neatly written, containing a few corrections noted in the margins, was obtained from Malatinagar, Bogra District, Bengal. Collations begin at adhy. 3.—*Collated at the Visvabharati.*

B_6

Dacca, University Library, No. 735. Folios 346, with about 7 lines to a page; size 19″ × 4½″. Bengali characters. Old Indian yellow paper.

Appearance, as well as the script of this MS. (which was obtained from Ula Bisnagar, Nadia District, Bengal), is somewhat more modern than that of B_5; belongs apparently to the beginning of the 19th century. Neatly written and fairly correct; contains occasional brief glosses on margin, apparently by the same hand as that of the copyist.—Collations begin at adhy. 54. *Collated at the Visvabharati.*

Da_1

Poona, Bombay Government Collection (deposited at the BORI), No. 30 of A 1879-80. Folios 416, with about 7-10 lines to a page; size 15½″ × 6¾″. Devanāgarī characters. Old Indian glossy paper.

Text with commentary of Arjunamiśra; written neatly but extremely corrupt and unintelligible in places, on account of the scribe's inability to read the exemplar correctly. The MS. has many short and long blanks in the text, which support the latter surmise. It has very few glosses and corrections, but a large number of variants noted in the margin. The text is written in three strips: the upper and lower ones comprise the commentary, while the central band, which has generally a still wider margin, is the (epic) text. The references to speaker (such as वैशंपायन उवाच) and colophons are written in red ink. The colophons give generally adhyāya and sub-parvan names. Ślokas are generally numbered; adhyāyas are almost regularly numbered from adhy. 45 to 109. The MS. is almost consistent in writing जन्मेजय (for जनमे°) उवाच. Punctuation is most imperfect. In the numbering of the folios, number 2 is repeated.

Da_2

Poona, Bombay Government Collection (deposited at the BORI), Viśrāmbāg I, No. 468. Folios 415, with about 10 lines to a page; size 15·7″ × 6·6″. Devanāgarī characters; dated V. Saṁ. 1676 (ca. A.D. 1620). Indian paper.

Text with commentary of Arjunamiśra. The MS. is from Dambal, a Jagir in the Kanarese District of the Deccan, and the last folio contains several stanzas in praise of a certain Gopālabhaṭṭa, a learned Pandit of great fame, who got the MS. written:

[16] भावाकाङ्क्षितमर्थिनामुपनयन्निर्धार्य योग्यं फलं
साधुप्रत्ययनिर्मलप्रकृतिभागाख्यातसत्कर्मणि ।
स्फूर्जन्सत्त्वनिसर्गतोऽव्ययमते गोपालविद्वद्गुरो
यस्त्वां पश्यति तेन जीवनमिदं लोकान्तरं कल्पितम् ॥

सूक्त्या पीयूषवर्षी निरतिशयवयो दूरदर्शी वशीया–
नन्तर्वाणिप्रवीणैः परमगुरुतया वन्दनीयो वदान्यः ।
कुर्वाणः कीर्तिकान्त्या हरममृतकरं पारदं शारदं यः
श्रीमान्गोपालशर्मा जगति विजयते पुण्यकर्माग्रगण्यः ॥

निर्देशात्तस्य नानाविधविबुधगुणग्राहिणः शिक्षितानां
संतोषोत्कर्षबीजात्सरसमुनिकलाकल्पकल्याणसंवत् ।
मित्रे भीमाङ्कलग्ने प्रतिपदि सहसः सुद्यहं सौधमोदः
पर्वाद्यं चारुटीकासुघटितमखिलं ले[ख]यित्रे शुभं स्तात् ॥

प्रणेता शास्त्राणां निखिलनिगमानां प्रतिनिधि-
र्धुरीणः स्वे धर्मे गुरुभृगुभरद्वाजसदृशः ।
कृती शाब्दे शास्त्रे धरणिपतिपूजितमति-
र्वशी गोपालोऽयं जयति किल भट्टः पृथुयशाः ॥

The date of the MS. is given as a chronogram corresponding to V. Saṁvat 1676 (ca. A.D. 1620). Double daṇḍas in red ink are inserted indiscriminately in the middle of the text. The writing, which is full of mistakes, is uniform but not neat. No corrections are, however, to be seen, the MS. being, perhaps, not much used. Notwithstanding the fact that this MS. agrees, page for page, with Da_1, there are many small differences between them ; neither can be a direct copy of the other ; they must go back to a more remote common source. It appears to be older, and is less corrupt, than Da_1. In the numbering of the folios, figure 1 is repeated. The colophons contain the names of adhyāyas and sub-parvans generally ; but śloka numbers or adhyāya numbers only sporadically. The MS. has a few blanks in the text and commentary.

Dn_1

Ms. belonging to Sardar M. V. Kibe of Indore. Folios 446, with about 8-10 lines to a page ; size 18·2" × 7·3". Devanāgarī characters. Thick Indian paper.

Text with commentary of Nīlakaṇṭha. Folios 439, 442, 444-5 are written by a different hand. The commentary, and even the text, is sometimes continued on the margin. Sporadically one comes across corrections or readings noted in the margin ; occasionally also corrections in the body are made by scoring out the portion to be deleted or by writing over, or with yellow pigment. The MS. is, on the whole, correct and very clearly written. Daṇḍas are marked in red ink. What would have been blanks in the space left for the text or commentary are often filled up by the addition of pious invocations such as श्रीराम जयराम । श्रीसांबसदाशिवाय नमः । etc. Adhyāyas are sporadically numbered and ślokas are regularly numbered in both the text and the commentary. The colophons give, in general, the adhyāya name or sub-parvan name. The last colophon contains the date : Īśvara saṁvatsara, mārgaśīrṣa śuddha 13, which cannot be identified.

[17] Dn_2

Mysore, Oriental Library, No. 1064. Folios 448, with about 22 lines to a page; size 15¼" × 6¼". Devanāgarī characters; dated V. Saṁvat 1864 (ca. A.D. 1808). Paper.

Text with commentary of Nīlakaṇṭha.

Dn_3

Poona, Bombay Government Collection (deposited at the BORI), No. 234 of 1895-1902. Folios 683, with about 9 lines to a page; size 15·2" × 7·2". Devanāgarī characters. Thick Indian paper.

Text with commentary of Nīlakaṇṭha. Bold and clear letters; generally correct; margins are almost clean. Ślokas and adhyāyas are throughout numbered. As in Dn_1, blanks were filled with invocations and names of various gods. The *lemmata* do not always fit the (epic) text. Colophons and the references to the speakers (and for some initial folios even daṇḍas) are in red ink, but only up to fol. 470.

Dr_1

Tanjore, Saraswathi Mahal Library, No. 1246. Folios 448, with about 11 lines to a page; size 15" × 6½". Devanāgarī characters. Paper.

Text with the commentary of Ratnagarbha.—Collations end at adhy. 2. *Collated at Tanjore.*

Dr_2

Tanjore, Saraswathi Mahal Library, No. 1199. Folios 306, with about 10-13 lines to a page; size 16" × 6½". Devanāgarī characters. Paper.

Text with the commentary of Ratnagarbha.—Collations end at adhy. 2, *Collated at Tanjore.*

Dr_3

Tanjore, Saraswathi Mahal Library, No. 1313. Folios 366, with about 11-13 lines to a page; size 16" × 6½". Devanāgarī characters; dated Śaka 1623 (ca. A.D. 1701). Paper.

Text with the commentary of Ratnagarbha. MS. dated, in the Śaka year 1623 (current) corresponding to Vṛṣa, Sunday the 13th (of the bright half) of the month of Āṣāḍha.—Collations end at adhy. 2. *Collated at Tanjore.*

Dr_4

Tanjore, Saraswathi Mahal Library, No. 1339. Folios 108, with about 11-22 lines to a page; size 16" × 6½". Devanāgarī characters. Paper.

Text with the commentary of Ratnagarbha. This fragment contains only about 90 adhyāyas of this edition. The number of lines of each folio fluctuates with the amount of commentary which each folio contains, and which of course, varies considerably.—Collations end at adhy. 2. *Collated at Tanjore.*

[18] D_1

Poona, Bombay Government Collection (deposited at the BORI), No. 29 of 1879-80. Folios 230, with about 16-17 lines to a page ; size 12″ × 7·15″. Devanāgarī characters. Fine cream-coloured paper.

For the first 140 folios or so, colophons and part references to speakers (such as वैशंपायन उ°) are generally in red ink ; then occasionally. Colophons sporadically give adhyāya or sub-parvan name and number of adhyāyas (especially towards the end of the parvan) ; stanzas are *not* numbered. The MS. is generally correct ; margins are clean.—*This is a complete MS. of Mbh.*, copied apparently from different exemplars ; some parvans have the commentary of Nīlakaṇṭha, while others contain some old text tradition (e.g. "M" of the Tentative Edition of the Virāṭaparvan). The MS. is of modern date, being written on paper with water-marks. Some of the parvans bear dates at the end, but these seem to be copied from the originals ; thus, Śānti (Mokṣadharma) has Śaka 1680, while Dānadharma has Śaka 1675. The last parvan bears the date : १६७७ युवानामसंवत्सरे.

D_2

Tanjore, Saraswathi Mahal Library, No. 1152. Folios 340, with about 10 lines to a page ; size 13″ × 5½″. Devanāgarī characters ; dated V. Saṁ. 1664 (ca. A.D. 1598). Paper.

The MS. was written on Friday the 13th of Āṣāḍha śuddha of V. Saṁ. 1654, at Benares by a Brāhmaṇa called Govinda, and belonged to Vāsudevabhaṭṭa.—*Collated at Tanjore.*

D_3

Tanjore, Saraswathi Mahal Library, No. 1360. Folios 120, with about 10 lines to a page ; size 14″ × 6¼″. Devanāgarī characters. Paper.

Incomplete, breaking off at the end of adhy. 76 (of our edition), in the middle of the Yayāti episode which, in this MS. (as in S MSS.), precedes the Śakuntalā episode.—*Collated at Tanjore.*

D_4

Tanjore, Saraswathi Mahal Library, No. 1126. Folios 235, with about 11 lines to a page ; size 16″ × 6¾″. Devanāgarī characters. Paper.

Many corrections and additions, the MS. being compared with another of the Southern recension, extracts from which have been written out on the margin, and on supplementary folios.—*Collated at Tanjore.*

D_5

Lahore, Dayanand Anglo-Vedic College Library, No. 4. Folios 246, with about 12-14 lines to a page ; size 12″ × 5″. Devanāgarī characters ; dated V. Saṁ. 1858 (ca A.D. 1802). Paper.—*Collated at the Visvabharati.*

[19] D_6

Tanjore, Saraswathi Mahal Library, No. 1223. Folios 293, with about 12 lines to a page; size 14″ × 6½″. Devanāgarī characters. Paper.

An old MS., but with clear and legible writing; well preserved.—Collations end at adhy. 53. *Collated at Tanjore.*

D_7

Tanjore, Saraswathi Mahal Library, No. 1269. Folios 262, with about 11 lines to a page; size 14″ × 5⅞″. Devanāgarī characters. Paper.

Clear and legible writing; well preserved.—Collations end at adhy. 53. *Collated at Tanjore.*

D_8

Tanjore, Saraswathi Mahal Library, No. 1329. Folios 196, with about 16-18 lines to a page; size 15¼″ × 7″. Devanāgarī characters. Paper.

A comparatively modern MS.—Collations end at adhy. 2. *Collated at Tanjore.*

D_9

Tanjore, Saraswathi Mahal Library, No. 1176. Folios 279, with about 11 lines to a page; size 15½″ × 5¾″. Devanāgarī characters. Paper.

Fol. 1-2 are badly damaged.—Collations end at adhy. 2. *Collated at Tanjore.*

D_{10}

Tanjore, Saraswathi Mahal Library, No. 1293. Folios 352, with about 10 lines to a page; size 13½″ × 5¼″. Devanāgarī characters. Paper.

Last leaf torn; well-preserved; clear and legible writing.—Collations end at adhy. 2. *Collated at Tanjore.*

D_{11}

Tanjore, Saraswathi Mahal Library, No. 1340. Folios 290, with about 11-18 lines to a page; size 14″ × 5½″. Devanāgarī characters. Paper.

Written, perhaps, by four different scribes.—Collations end at adhy. 2. *Collated at Tanjore.*

D_{12}

Tanjore, Saraswathi Mahal Library, No. 1373. Folios 21, with about 12 lines to a page; size 14½″ × 6″. Devanāgarī characters. Paper.

Incomplete, containing only the first two adhyāyas.—*Collated at Tanjore*

[20] D_{13}

Poona, Bombay Government Collection (deposited at the BORI), Viśrāmbāg II, No. 191. Folios 221, with about 13 lines to a page; size 14·25″ × 6·05″. Devanāgarī characters. Old Indian glossy paper.

Fragmentary, folios 1-7 wanting ; begins with भ्रूणहत्याकृतं पापं (1. 1. 205). Text very similar to Arjunamiśra's ; neatly written and generally correct ; marginal corrections are few and far between. Adhyāya names or sub-parvan names are given, but the ślokas or adhyāyas are not numbered. The reference to narrators is, at first, given at random as सौतिरुवाच and सूत उ°, but then the scribe settles down to सूत उ°. The collations are given, as a matter of fact, only from 1.1.205 to the end of adhy. 2.

D_{14}

Poona, Bombay Government Collection (deposited at the BORI), Viśrāmbāg II, No. 266. Folios 1-121 (fol. 122-189 of this MS. are found under Viśrāmbāg II, No. 86), with about 15 lines to a page ; size 18″ × 6½″. Devanāgarī characters. Old Indian unglazed paper.

MS. No. 267 of the same Collection is of Sabhā with commentary and written by the same hand.—Folio 79 is wanting. Carefully written, has very few corrections, which are made by use of yellow pigment, and a few marginal additions ; gives, as a rule, numbers to ślokas and adhyāyas ; also mentions generally sub-parvan and adhyāya names,—Collated up to the end of adhy. 2 only.

T_1

Melkote, Yadugiri Yatiraj Math MS. (without number). Folios 195, with about 11 lines to a page ; size 16·1″ × 2·3″. Telugu characters. Palm-leaf.

MS. kindly lent by His Holiness the Yatiraj Swami. Contains Ādi and Sabhā, written probably by the same hand ; writing clear and correct ; adhyāya ends are shown by a small floral (or spiral) design engraved in the right and left margins of the MS. ; adhyāyas are regularly numbered, but *not* the ślokas. It is one of the few Southern MSS. which contain the (Northern) salutatory stanza नारायणं नमस्कृत्य etc.

T_2

Tanjore, Saraswathi Mahal Library, No. 11865. Folios 400, with about 6 lines to a page ; size 21″ × 1¾″. Telugu characters. Palm-leaf.

Fragmentary ; breaking off at the end of our adhy. 181 (corresponding to its adhy. 140) ; from adhy. 182, it is replaced in our critical apparatus by the next MS. T_3.—*Collated ot Tanjore.*

T_3

Tanjore, Saraswathi Mahal Library, No. 11809. Folios 164, with about 12 lines to a page ; size 29¼ × 2¼″. Telugu characters. Palm-leaf.

An old MS., containing the first five parvans ; script small, but clear.—Collations begins at adhy. 182 ; used only to supplement the portion missing in T_2. *Collated at Tanjore.*

[21] G_1

Melkote, Yadugiri Yatiraj Math MS. (without number). Folios 110, with about 16-21 lines to a page; size 18·7″ × 1·8″. Grantha characters. Palm-leaf.

Leaves are very brittle, and worm-eaten in places; large pieces have broken off, leaving many lacunæ. The holes for the string have enlarged. perhaps from constant use, destroying some parts of the text written round them.

G_2

Melkote, Yadugiri Yatiraj Math MS. (without number). Folios 202, with about 15-17 lines to a page; size 14·5″ × 2·1″. Grantha characters. Palm-leaf.

The MS. contains the first 4 parvans: Ādi, Sabhā, Araṇya and Virāṭa, written probably by the same hand. Slightly worm-eaten; but on the whole, a well preserved old MS. with clear and legible writing.

G_3

Tanjore, Saraswathi Mahal Library, No. 11823. Folios 316, with about 10 lines to a page; size 16¾″ × 1¾″. Grantha characters. Palm-leaf.—*Collated at Tanjore.*

G_4

Tanjore, Saraswathi Mahal Library, No. 11838. Folios 477, with about 6 lines to a page; size 19″ × 1⅞″. Grantha characters. Palm-leaf.

An old and well-preserved MS., with clear and legible writing, but many corrections.—*Collated at Tanjore.*

G_5

Tanjore, Saraswathi Mahal Library, No. 11851. Folios 320, with about 8 lines to a page; size 19″ × 1½″. Grantha characters. Palm-leaf.

The MS. contains the Sabhā also, probably written by the same hand. A well-preserved old MS., with clear and legible writing.—*Collated at Tanjore.*

G_6

Tanjore, Saraswathi Mahal Library, No. 11860. Folios 324, with about 8 lines to a page; size 18¼″ × 1⅜″. Grantha characters. Palm-leaf.

MS. written by Kāśīpati, on the 22nd of the month of Kumbha, in the year Krodhi.—*Collated at Tanjore.*

G_7

Melkote, Yadugiri Yatiraj Math MS. (without number). Folios 217, with about 12-14 lines to a page; size 19·2″ × 2″. Grantha characters. Palm-leaf.

[22] Clear and legible writing; worm-eaten in places. Being a conflated MS., it was discontinued after adhy. 2. It is one of the few Southern MSS. which begins with the (Northern) salutatory stanza, नारायणं नमस्कृत्य etc. added later in the narrow upper margin of the first folio, in very fine writing. Its place of insertion is indicated by a "haṁsapāda", inserted immediately after its first maṅgala stanza (9*).—Collated up to the end of adhy. 2 only.

M_1

MS. from the private library of the Chief of Idappalli, Cochin. Folios 79. Malayālam characters. Palm-leaf.

Secured on loan and got collated kindly by Prof K. Rama PISHAROTI. No further details of the MS. are available. Incomplete MS., ending with adhy. 53, the final adhyāya of the Āstīkaparvan.—*Collated at Sanskrit College, Tripunittura, Cochin.*

M_2

Cochin, State Library, No. 5. Folios 122. Malayālam characters. Palm-leaf.

The MS. was returned to the Cochin State Library after collation. No further details of the MS. are available. Incomplete MS., ending with adhy. 53, the final adhyāya of the Āstīkaparvan.

M_3

Cochin, State Library, No. 1. Folios 166, with about 12-13 lines to a page; size 19·9" × 1·6". Malayālam characters; dated Kollam 1013 (ca. A.D. 1838). Palm-leaf.

A modern MS., perhaps less than 100 years old; adhyāya numbers and śloka numbers are given. The adhyāya ends are shown by a floral design, inscribed in the margins.

M_4

MS. from the private library of Kallenkara Pisharam, Cochin. Folios 57. Malayālam characters. Palm-leaf.

The MS. was returned to the owner immediately after collation. No further details of the MS. are available. Incomplete, ending with adhy. 53, the final adhy. of the Āstīkaparvan.

M_5

MS. from the Paliyam MSS. Library, Cochin. Folios 245. Malayālam characters. Palm-leaf.

Secured for collation by courtesy of Mr. P. ANUJAN ACHAN, now Superintendent, Archæological Department, Cochin State.

M_6

MS. from the private library of Nareri Mana, Malabar. Folios 163, with about 10 lines to a page; size 18" × 1·6". Malayālam characters. Palm-leaf.

[23] Incomplete MS., adhy. 1-53 wanting (i.e. begins with the Ādivaṁśavataraṇa sub-parvan) writing clear and legible; generally correct; margins are clean—Collations begin from adhy. 54.

M_7

MS. from the private library of Avaṇapparambu Mana, Cochin. Folios 170, with about 10 lines to a page; size 20·5" × 1·8". Malayālam characters. Palm-leaf.

Clear and legible writing ; leaves are in perfect preservation, not a single leaf being worm-eaten ; probably not very old. Scribe has left many blanks in the writing space, whenever the surface of the leaf was uneven or rugged. —Collated from adhy. 54.

M_8

Malabar, Poomulli Mana Library, No. 297. Folios 183, with about 10 lines to a page. Malayālam characters ; dated Kollam 1017 (ca. A.D. 1842). Palm-leaf.

Collated from adhy. 54.

In view of the great unevenness of the critical apparatus, and of the consequent difficulty likely to be experienced by readers using the critical notes (printed at the foot of the page) in ascertaining what manuscripts have been added, discontinued, or discarded at different points of the text, I append, on the following page, a table which shows at a glance just what manuscripts have been actually collated for different portions of the text. Even the larger lacunae of the manuscripts, which cannot be easily ascertained, have been exhibited in this table. Only such (small) omissions have been, as a rule, ignored as are *specifically* mentioned in the footnote itself pertaining to the particular stanza, and which are therefore brought to the notice of the reader as soon as he reads the footnote.

TABLE SHOWING THE MSS. COLLATED FOR DIFFERENT PORTIONS OF THE TEXT[1]

Adhyāya & Śloka.	Northern Recension MSS.									South. Rec. MSS.		
1. 1–204		K_{0-6}		V_1	B_{1-4}	Da	Dn	Dr	$D_{1-12.14}$	$T_{1.2}$	G_{1-7}	M_{1-4}
1. 205–2. 39		K_{0-6}		V_1	B_{1-4}	Da	Dn	Dr	D_{1-14}	$T_{1.2}$	G_{1-7}	M_{1-4}
2. 40–191		$K_{0-4.6}$		V_1	B_{1-4}	Da	Dn	Dr	D_{1-14}	$T_{1.2}$	G_{1-7}	M_{1-4}
2. 192–243		$K_{0-4.6}$		V_1	B_{1-4}	Da	Dn	Dr	D_{1-14}	$T_{1.2}$	G_{2-7}	M_{1-4}
3. 1–44		K_{0-4}	$Ñ_{1.2}$	V_1	B_{1-5}	Da	Dn		D_{1-7}	$T_{1.2}$	G_{2-6}	M_{1-5}
3. 45–13. 45		K_{0-4}	$Ñ_{1.2}$	V_1	B_{1-5}	Da	Dn		D_{1-7}	$T_{1.2}$	G_{1-6}	M_{1-5}
14. 1–26. 9		K_{0-4}	$Ñ_{1-3}$	V_1	B_{1-5}	Da	Dn		D_{1-7}	$T_{1.2}$	G_{1-6}	M_{1-5}
26. 10–43. 13	$Ś_1$	K_{0-4}	$Ñ_{1-3}$	V_1	B_{1-5}	Da	Dn		D_{1-7}	$T_{1.2}$	G_{1-6}	M_{1-5}
43. 14–47. 19	$Ś_1$	K_{0-4}	$Ñ_{1-3}$	V_1	$B_{1.3-5}$	Da	Dn		D_{1-7}	$T_{1.2}$	G_{1-6}	M_{1-5}
47. 20–53. 36	$Ś_1$	$K_{0.2-4}$	$Ñ_{1-3}$	V_1	$B_{1.3-5}$	Da	Dn		D_{1-7}	$T_{1.2}$	G_{1-6}	M_{1-5}
54. 1–4	$Ś_1$	$K_{0.2-4}$	$Ñ_{1-3}$	V_1	$B_{1.3-6}$	Da	Dn		D_{1-5}	$T_{1.2}$	G_{1-6}	$M_{3.5-8}$
54. 5–55. 3[a]	$Ś_1$	K_{0-4}	$Ñ_{1-3}$	V_1	$B_{1.3-6}$	Da	Dn		D_{1-5}	$T_{1.2}$	G_{1-6}	$M_{3.5-8}$
55. 3[b]–60. 61[b]		K_{0-4}	$Ñ_{1-3}$	V_1	$B_{1.3-6}$	Da	Dn		D_{1-5}	$T_{1.2}$	G_{1-6}	$M_{3.5-8}$
60. 61[c]–61. 84[a]	$Ś_1$	K_{0-4}	$Ñ_{1-3}$	V_1	$B_{1.3-6}$	Da	Dn		D_{1-5}	$T_{1.2}$	G_{1-6}	$M_{3.5-8}$
61. 84[b]–62. 2		K_{0-4}	$Ñ_{1-3}$	V_1	$B_{1.3-6}$	Da	Dn		D_{1-5}	$T_{1.2}$	G_{1-6}	$M_{3.5-8}$
62. 3–68. 19		K_{0-4}	$Ñ_{1-3}$	V_1	$B_{1.3-6}$	Da	Dn		$D_{1.2.4.5}$	$T_{1.2}$	G_{1-6}	$M_{3.5-8}$
68. 20–74[a]	$Ś_1$	K_{0-4}	$Ñ_{1-3}$	V_1	$B_{1.3-6}$	Da	Dn		$D_{1.2.4.5}$	$T_{1.2}$	G_{1-6}	$M_{3.5-8}$
68. 74[b]–69. 41[c]	$Ś_1$	K_{0-4}	$Ñ_{1-3}$		$B_{1.3-6}$	Da	Dn		$D_{1.2.4.5}$	$T_{1.2}$	G_{1-6}	$M_{3.5-8}$
69. 41[d]–51	$Ś_1$	$K_{0-2.4}$	$Ñ_{1-3}$		$B_{1.3-6}$	Da	Dn		$D_{1.2.4.5}$	$T_{1.2}$	G_{1-6}	$M_{3.5-8}$
70. 1–71. 17[c]	$Ś_1$	$K_{0-2.4}$	$Ñ_{1-3}$		$B_{1.3-6}$	Da	Dn		D_{1-5}	$T_{1.2}$	G_{1-6}	$M_{3.5-8}$
71. 17[d]–72. 8[b]	$Ś_1$	K_{0-4}	$Ñ_{1-3}$		$B_{1.3-6}$	Da	Dn		D_{1-5}	$T_{1.2}$	G_{1-6}	$M_{3.5-8}$
72. 8[c]–22	$Ś_1$	$K_{0-2.4}$	$Ñ_{1-3}$		$B_{1.3-6}$	Da	Dn		D_{1-5}	$T_{1.2}$	G_{1-6}	$M_{3.5-8}$
72. 23–74. 4		$K_{0-2.4}$	$Ñ_{1-3}$		$B_{1.3-6}$	Da	Dn		D_{1-5}	$T_{1.2}$	G_{1-6}	$M_{3.5-8}$
74. 5–76. 35		K_{0-4}	$Ñ_{1-3}$		$B_{1.3-6}$	Da	Dn		D_{1-5}	$T_{1.2}$	G_{1-6}	$M_{3.5-8}$
77. 1–78. 20[b]		K_{0-4}	$Ñ_{1-3}$		$B_{1.3-6}$	Da	Dn		$D_{1.2.4.5}$	$T_{1.2}$	G_{1-6}	$M_{3.5-8}$
78. 20[c]–90. 88	$Ś_1$	K_{0-4}	$Ñ_{1-3}$		$B_{1.3-6}$	Da	Dn		$D_{1.2.4.5}$	$T_{1.2}$	G_{1-6}	$M_{3.5-8}$
90. 89–92. 13[d]	$Ś_1$	K_{0-4}	$Ñ_{1-3}$		$B_{1.3.5.6}$	Da	Dn		$D_{1.2.4.5}$	$T_{1.2}$	G_{1-6}	$M_{3.5-8}$
92. 13[e]–96. 37[b]	$Ś_1$	K_{0-4}	$Ñ_{1-3}$	V_1	$B_{1.3.5.6}$	Da	Dn		$D_{1.2.4.5}$	$T_{1.2}$	G_{1-6}	$M_{3.5-8}$
96. 37[c]–127. 21[a]	$Ś_1$	K_{0-4}	$Ñ_{1-3}$		$B_{1.3.5.6}$	Da	Dn		$D_{1.2.4.5}$	$T_{1.2}$	G_{1-6}	$M_{3.5-8}$
127. 21[b]–181. 40	$Ś_1$	K_{0-4}	$Ñ_{1-3}$	V_1	$B_{1.3.5.6}$	Da	Dn		$D_{1.2.4.5}$	$T_{1.2}$	G_{1-6}	$M_{3.5-8}$
182. 1–225. 19	$Ś_1$	K_{0-4}	$Ñ_{1-3}$	V_1	$B_{1.3.5.6}$	Da	Dn		$D_{1.2.4.5}$	$T_{1.3}$	G_{1-6}	$M_{3.5-8}$

1 D_{13} added at 1. 205.—K_5 discontinued from 2. 40.—G_1 has lacuna from 2. 192 to 3, 44.—K_6 Dr. D_{8-14} G_7 discontinued, and $Ñ_{1.2}$ B_5 M_5 added, from 3.1.—$Ñ_3$ added at 14. 1.—$Ś_1$ added at 26. 10.—B_2 ends at 43. 13.—K_1 has lacuna from 47. 20 to 54. 4.—$D_{6.7}$ $M_{1.2.4}$ discontinued, and B_6 M_{6-8} added, from 54.1.—$Ś_1$ has lacuna from 13.—K_1 has lacuna from 47. 20 to 54. 4.—$Ś_1$ has lacuna from 55, 3[b] to 60. 61[b], and from 61. 84[b] to 68. 19.—D_3 (which transp. the Śakuntalā and Yayāti episodes) has lacuna from 62. 3 to 69. 51.—V_1 has lacuna from 68. 74[b] to 92. 13.—K_3 has lacuna from 69, 41[d] to 71. 17[c], and from 72. 8[c] to 74. 4—$Ś_1$ has lacuna from 72. 23 to 78. 20[b].—D_3 ends at 76. 35.—B_4 ends at 90. 88.—V_1 has lacuna from 96. 37[c] to 127. 21[a].—T_2 ends at 181. 40.—T_3 begins from 182. 1.

[25] TESTIMONIA

As testimonia, or aids of a partial or subsidiary character, there are available, besides the numerous commentaries, the following three important epitomes of the eleventh century: (i) the Javanese adaptation *Bhāratam* (ca. A.D. 1000), (ii) the Telugu adaptation *Āndhra Bhāratamu* by the Telugu poet Nannaya Bhaṭṭa (ca. A.D. 1025), and (iii) the Sanskrit adaptation *Bhāratamañjarī* by the Kaśmīrī poet Kṣemendra (ca. A.D. 1050); as also an important Persian rendering made some centuries later (ca. A.D. 1580) at the instance of that enlightened and sagacious Emperor of India with catholic sympathies, the great Akbar.

The commentaries collated for this edition are dealt with below, under the Devanāgarī versions. Here it will suffice to observe that, even when accompanied by the (epic) text, the commentaries are, for reasons which will be explained later on, evidence only for the actual *lemmata* and the pāṭhāntaras cited. The absence of commentary on a stanza or a group of stanzas or even on an adhyāya is, in general, no proof that that particular passage was lacking in the text used by the commentator. For, clearly, his text may have contained the passage in question, but he may not have deemed it necessary to comment upon any portion of it. Nevertheless when the commentary ignores a lengthy and difficult passage, then there is a strong presumption that the text of the commentator did not contain the passage. A case in point is the Kaṇikanīti, a passage of 186 lines, which is entirely ignored in Devabodha's commentary (but has evoked lengthy comments from both Arjunamiśra and Nīlakaṇṭha), and which is missing in the Kaśmīrī version.

As regards the old Javanese adaptation, from the reports of Dutch scholars[1] who have studied the original Javanese text, it appears that only eight out of the eighteen parvans of the Mahābhārata have been traced so far; namely, Ādi, Virāṭa, Udyoga, Bhīṣma, Āśramavāsa, Mausala, Mahāprasthāna and Svargārohaṇa. Three of these (Āśramavāsa, Mausala, Mahāprasthāna) were the subject of a doctor dissertation, submitted to the Leyden University by Dr. H. H. JUYNBOLL, as early as 1893. The Javanese original was edited by the doctor in Roman characters and rendered into Dutch. Thirteen years later (1906), the same scholar published the text of the Ādi (with different readings) in Roman transcript.[2] Of the old Javanese Ādiparvan, only a few episodes have been as yet translated, to wit: the Parvasaṁgraha, the Pauṣya, the Amṛtamanthana, the story of Parikṣit and

---

[1] Cf. D. van Hinloopen LABBERTON, "The Mahābhārata in Mediaeval Javanese," *JRAS*. 1913. 1 ff., and the literature cited there; also Kurt WULFF, *Den old javanske Wirataparva* (Copenhagen 1917). On the Mbh. in the island of Bali, cf. R. FRIEDERICH. *JRAS*. 1876. 176 f., 179 ff.

[2] *Adiparwa, Oudjavaansch Prozageschrift*, uitgegeven door Dr. H. H. JUYNBOLL. S'Gravenhage 1906.

the Sauparṇa. Unfortunately these translations are not available in India; at least they were not available to me.

The chief value of the Javanese adaptation for us lies in the fact that throughout the old Javanese text are scattered Sanskrit quotations, which appear to have "served as landmarks for writers and hearers or readers." The text prepared by Dr. JUYNBOLL, which is based upon eight manuscripts, is reputed to be very accurate. But it is admitted that the Sanskrit excerpts in the extant Javanese manuscripts are extremely corrupt, and it is a [26] question how far the conjectural restorations by the editor correctly represent the original readings. It seems to me likely that in his reconstructions Dr. JUYNBOLL was to a certain extent influenced by the wording of the Vulgate, which is certainly not always original. To give only one instance. On p. 70, the Javanese manuscripts read (in the Śakuntalā episode):

paripatyādayaḥ sunu, hāraṇireṇuguṇḍitaḥ |,

which is corrupt; it conveys no sense. In the text the editor gives:

pratipadya padā sūnur, dharaṇīreṇu gunthitaḥ |,

which is nearly the reading of the Calcutta edition (3040). Though the Javanese manuscripts are palpably corrupt, yet they have preserved the correct *paripatya* (for *pratipadya* of the Vulgate), which is the reading of the Śāradā and K manuscripts of our edition. We have here to thank the Vulgate for the *pratipadya* of Dr. JUYNBOLL's text!

Notwithstanding, that the period from which this adaptation dates is comparatively speaking recent, it yet precedes the known date of the manuscripts by several centuries and is hence of considerable importance for critical purposes, as a witness[1] independent of and uninfluenced by the main line of our extant Indian witnesses. Most of the Sanskrit quotations of the Javanese text can be traced both in the Northern and the Southern recensions, as may be seen from our Appendix II, at the end of this volume, which contains a concordance of the Javanese extracts with the Critical Edition, the Calcutta Edition, and SASTRI's Southern Recension. A few of the quotations are to be traced to the "additional" passages in the Northern manuscripts, but none to the specific Southern "additions." The conclusion is inevitable that the text of the Sanskrit Ādiparvan used by the Javanese writers must have belonged to the Northern recension, a conclusion already suggested by the sequence of the Śakuntalā and Yayāti episodes, which is the Northern sequence. This does not necessarily mean that the entire Javanese Bhāratam represents the Northern recension. It is quite likely that some of the parvans utilized by the Javanese adapters belonged to the Southern recension. The late Mr. UTGIKAR[2] was inclined to think that the Javanese Virāṭaparvan

---

1 Particularly valuable, as the Indian MSS. are mostly conflated.

2 The Virāṭaparvan (Poona 1923), Introduction, p. XIII, and *ABI.* 2. 167 f.

was of the Southern type. The point will have to be re-examined in the light of further evidence.* The books were preserved and handed down separately; consequently the genesis of each parvan must be investigated separately.

The Telugu adaptation, the *Āndhra Bhāratamu*,[1] is a metrical epitome of the Mahābhārata, commenced by Nannaya Bhaṭṭa, a court poet of the Eastern Cālukya king Viṣṇuvardhana, who had his capital at Rajahmundry, on the East Coast of India, and who appears to have ruled between 1022 and 1066.[2] The torso of the Telugu rendering left behind by Nannaya, consisting of a version of the first two parvans and of a part of the third, was completed many years later by two others poets. Nannaya's version is valuable for the light it throws on the condition of the Southern recension—or, strictly speaking, of the Telugu version—in the eleventh century of the Christian era, especially in view of [27] the fact that Nannaya has included in his poem an accurate rendering of the Parvasaṁgraha, giving the number of ślokas in each of the parvans of *his* Mahābhārata.[3] The figure for the stanzas of the Ādi is 9984, which shows that the text used by Nannaya must have been substantially of the same size as that preserved in the extant Southern manuscripts. The poet is reported to have followed the original fairly closely. Notable is consequently his omission of Brahmā's visit to Vyāsa.[4]

Curiously enough, the third old important epitome of the Mahābhārata which we possess, the *Bhāratamañjarī* by Kṣemendra,[5] belongs to the same century as the two epitomes mentioned above, since this Kaśmīri poet must also be assigned to the middle of the eleventh century.[6] BÜHLER and KIRSTE have given in their *Indian Studies*, No. 2 (pp. 30 ff.), the results of a careful comparison of Kṣemendra's abstract with the Bombay text of the Mahābhārata. They show that Kṣemendra's text contains both additions and omissions as compared with the latter.[7] Of the omissions they note: adhy. 4, 24, 45-48, 66, 94, 139, and parts of adhy. 141 and 197 of the Vulgate. Of these, adhy. 4 is, as pointed out by BÜHLER and KIRSTE, a short introductory chapter, a variant of adhy. 1; adhy. 45-48 are a repetition (with variations) of adhy. 13-15; adhy. 66 is a variant of the preceding adhyāya; adhy. 94 is a variant of adhy. 95 (prose), which is selected by Kṣemendra

* [In this connection see the Introduction to Dr. Raghu VIRA's Critical Edition of the Virāṭaparvan, pp. xi-xv.]

1 V. Ramasvami & Sons, Madras 1924-29.

2 Cf. Venkatachellam IYER, *Notes of a Study of the Preliminary Chapters of the Mahābhārata* (Madras 1922), pp. 97-100.

3 The figures of Nannaya's *Āndhra Bhāratamu* are now given by Professor P. P. S. SASTRI in his edition of the Mahābhārata, Southern Recension, Vol. II, Introduction, p. xxx (Scheme of Slokas). They were first published by Venkatachellam IYER, op.cit. p. 311.

4 Cf. Venkatachellam IYER, op. cit. p. 99. 5 Ed. Kāvyamālā, No 64 (1898).

6 KEITH, *A History of Sanskrit Literature*, p. 136. 7 Op. cit. p. 30.

for his purpose ;[1] finally, stanzas 44 to end of adhy. 197 are a repetition of a part of adhy. 169. The reason for the omission of *these* adhyāyas is thus clear : they are mere repetitions. The remaining adhyāyas, which are missing and whose omission BÜHLER-KIRSTE could not account for, namely, adhy. 24, 139, and 141 (stanzas 1-19) are also missing in many of our Mahābhārata manuscripts and have accordingly been omitted in the constituted text as well. To these must be added the important omission of adhy. 140 of the Vulgate, the Kaṇikanīti, which is likewise omitted by Kṣemendra, an omission which appears to have been overlooked by BÜHLER and KIRSTE.

The collaborating authors felt justified in concluding that the omissions and additions "are just such liberties as any Kāvya poet would take in making a similar abridgement." They were also of opinion that the original cannot have differed very essentially from our current texts, that is, the Vulgate. This is correct up to a certain point. A comparison with the different versions shows that Kṣemendra's version agrees, as was to be expected, most closely with the Śāradā. On comparing the divisions of the *Mañjarī* with those given in Bombay or Calcutta editions of the Mahābhārata, BÜHLER and KIRSTE were struck by the fact that the *Mañjarī* divisions agreed better with the course of the narrative ; and they give examples to show that the arrangement of the *Mañjarī* is more logical. That is quite natural, because the old Northern manuscripts, which this edition [28] follows, fully support the arrangement of the *Mañjarī*, whereas the divisions adopted in the Vulgate are secondary and quite corrupt.

The Persian translation[2] of the Mahābhārata, made in the reign of Emperor Akbar, being still unedited, could not be consulted. A very full account of this rendering has, however, been given by the late Dr. Sir Jivanji Jamshedji MODI in a paper read before the First Oriental Conference at Poona in November 1919 and published in the *Annals* of this Institute.[3] Of all the Sanskrit works Akbar got translated, the Mahābhārata, it appears, had his most earnest attention.

Several eminent poets and scholars had a hand in translating the Great Epic of India into Persian. The *Ā'in-e-Akbarī* gives the following names : Naqīb Khān, Maulānā 'Abdu'l-Qādir Badāyūnī, and Shaikh Sulṭān of Thanesar, to which the *Muntakhab-u't-Tawārīkh* adds the names of Mullā Sherī, and Shaikh Faizī (the brother of Abu'l-Fazl).

"Badaoni translated," we are informed by Sir Jivanji,[4] on the author-

---

1 As is done also by the redactors of the Javanese *Bhāratam* ; cf. LABBERTON, *JRAS*. 1913. 7 : "The knotty points as to the more reliable of the two sets [of genealogies] is decided by our Old Javanese text in favour of the *second*, that being the only one it knows."

2 Cf. HOLTZMANN, *Das Mahābhārata*, 3. 110 ; and A. LUDWIG, "Das Mahābhārata als Epos und Rechtsbuch" (Review), pp. 66 ff., 93 ff.

3 Cf. vol. 6 (1924-25), pp. 84 ff.

4 *ABI*. 6, 95.

ity of contemporaneous chronicles, "two out of the eighteen sections. Mullā Sherī and Naqīb Khān did a part of the work and the rest was completed by Sulṭān Hājī of Thanessar. Shaikh Faizī converted their 'rough translation into elegant prose and verse, but he did not complete more than two sections.' Sulṭān Hājī then revised these two sections and verse. Not only did he do so, but he also revised his work which formed a large share of the work." Quoting Badāūnī, Sir Jivanji continues: "The Hājī aforesaid revised these two sections, and as for the omissions which had taken place in his first edition, those defects he put right, and comparing it word for word was brought to such a point of perfection that not a fly-mark of the original was omitted"! The preface to this translation was from the pen of that gifted courtier of Akbar who has left us such an admirable account of the Emperor's reign, Abu'l-Fazl. This Persian version appears to have been a free rendering of the original, made by Muslim poets and scholars at the Court of Akbar, to whom the sense of the original had been explained by Hindu pandits, under the orders of the Emperor.

There are numerous other vernacular abstracts of the Mahābhārata besides the Telugu abstract mentioned above, but most of them are of a late date. Moreover, they are all far too free to be of much use to us in reconstructing the text of the Mahābhārata.

Besides these abstracts and adaptations, there are parallel versions of certain passages or even of whole episodes to be met with in other works. Thus we have a parallel version of the Śakuntalā episode (adhy. 62 ff.), in the Padmapurāṇa;[1] of the Yayāti episode (adhy. 71 ff.), in the Matsyapurāṇa;[2] of the story of Ruru (adhy. 8 ff.), in the Devībhāgavata; of a portion of Samudramanthana (adhy. 16 f.), again in the Matsyapurāṇa; of a portion of a cosmogonic passage (1. 60. 54 ff.), in the Rāmāyaṇa. [29] There is more distant connection between our Sauparṇa (adhy. 14 ff.) and the peseudo-vedic Suparṇādhyāya.[3] Some of the stanzas of the Ādi are cited, with or without mention of the source, in the Tantravārttika of Kumārila Bhaṭṭa (e.g. our 1. 1. 209), as also in the Bhāṣyas of Ācārya Śaṁkara (e.g. our 1. 1. 37). A few of the sententious stanzas (e.g. our 1. 74. 1 ff.) recur, with variation, in Buddhist literature,[4] while stray stanzas are to be found again in the Khilas of the Ṛgveda (e.g. our 1. 53. 22 f.),[5] the Manusmṛti[6] (e.g.

---

1 Cf. BELLONI-FILIPPI, "La leggenda Mahābhāratiana di Śakuntalā nell' edizione critica di Poona," *Giornale della Società Asiatica Italiana* (NS). 2 (1932). 135-140.

2 Cf. Gaya Prasad DIXIT, "A Textual Comparison of the Story of Yayāti as found in the Mahābhārata and the Matsyapurāṇa," *Proc. Fifth Ind. Orient Conf.* (Lahore 1930), vol. 1, pp. 721 ff.

3 Cf. Jarl CHARPENTIER, *Die Suparṇasage*, Uppsala 1920.

4 FRANKE, "Jātaka-Mahābhārata Parallelen," *WZKM*. 20 (1906) 323, 357 f.

5 Cf. Max MÜLLER's edition of the Ṛgveda, vol. 4 (1892), p. 521, stanzas 5-8.

6 2. 111.

our 1. 3. 94) and the Bṛhaddevatā[1] (e.g. our 1. 59. 12). One of our stanzas (1. 119. 6) has been cited in the Dhvanyāloka of Ānandavardhana, as by Maharṣi Vyāsa. There are probably many stanzas which remain to be identified.

It is perhaps well to add in this place that a certain amount of caution is necessary in making any critical use of citations of stray Mahābhārata stanzas we meet with again in other works. We must, in the first place, bear in mind that most of the other works have yet to be properly edited. Even in critically edited texts we must take into account the various readings of the passage in question in the manuscripts collated. Then in the case of citations we must allow for failures of memory; since in ancient times the stanzas were almost invariably quoted from memory, and the quotation was never compared with the original. Moreover we must never forget that probably from time immemorial there have existed local versions of the Mahābhārata. The citations made even by very old writers were from these *local* versions. A citation by a writer of the eighth century or even the sixth century proves nothing for the Ur-Mahābhārata, that ideal but impossible desideratum; though the citation is far older than our manuscripts, it is evidence only for the text of the *local* Mahābhārata in the eighth, respectively the sixth century, notwithstanding that the differences between the various recensions and versions of the Mahābhārata must diminish as we go back further and further.

[30] PEDIGREE OF ĀDIPARVAN VERSIONS

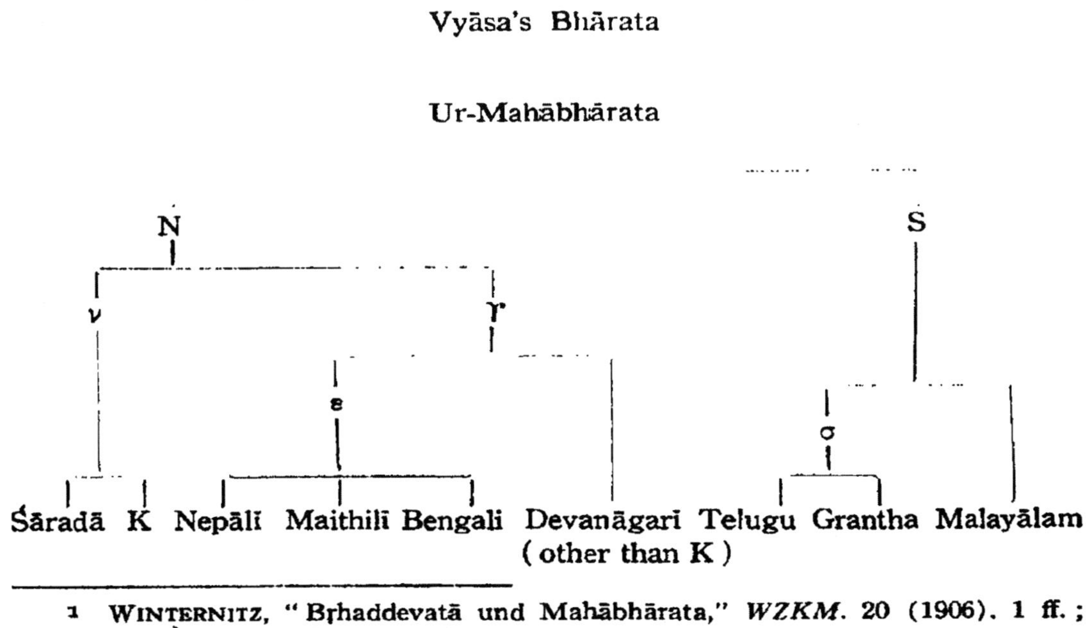

1 WINTERNITZ, "Bṛhaddevatā und Mahābhārata," *WZKM*. 20 (1906). 1 ff.; especially, pp. 10 f., 28 f., 31 ff., 34.

EXPLANATION OF THE SIGLA USED IN THE ABOVE PEDIGREE

N is the ultimate source from which all versions of the Northern recension are, directly or indirectly, derived.

ν is the lost archetype of the North-Western group, appreciably shorter than any of the other known versions (*textus simplicior*).

K is a specific Devanāgarī version allied to the Śāradā (or Kaśmīrī) version (sharply distinguished from other Devanāgarī versions), of which one MS. (K_1) is the direct copy of a Śāradā original. The version is largely contaminated from MSS. of the (central) sub-recension (γ), and in part, also from some unknown Southern sources. Exact provenance of the version is unknown.

γ is the intermediate (inflated) source from which all versions of the central sub-recension are derived (comprising the Eastern and Western groups), occupying a position intermediate between the North-Western and the Southern groups. It contains a considerable number of secondary additions (including repetitions), as also a very large number of verbal alterations and corruptions.

ε is the lost archetype of the Eastern group (comprising the Nepālī, Maithilī and Bengali versions), which is free from the additions and alterations made later in certain Devanāgarī MSS.

S is the ultimate source from which all versions of the Southern recension are, directly or indirectly, derived and which is appreciably longer than N, and far more elaborate (*textus ornatior*).

σ is the lost archetype of T G, containing a large number of corruptions and secondary additions, from which M is free.

[31] A CRITICAL SURVEY OF THE RECENSIONS AND THEIR VERSIONS

THE TWO RECENSIONS

The textual criticism of the Mahābhārata proceeds from the incontrovertible fact that the text of the Great Epic has been handed down in two divergent forms, a Northern and a Southern recension, texts typical of the Āryāvarta and the Dakṣiṇāpatha. With the realization of this patent contrast began the Mahābhārata textual criticism nearly fifty years ago, when Protap Chandra ROY brought out his popular edition of the Mahābhārata (1883-96), under the auspices of the Dātavya Bhārata Kāryālaya. A brief account of the controversy to which the publication of this edition of the Mahābhārata gave rise is to be found in ROY's writings.[1] We are told there

[1] Cf. the letter addressed by ROY to the Editor of *The Hindu* (Madras) and published on the cover of fascicule XXIX of his translation of the Mbh. (1887). See also HOLTZMANN, *Das Mahābhārata*, 3. 33.

that the appearance of his edition was hailed by *The Hindu* of Madras, that great bulwark of Dravidian Hinduism, in its issue dated November 22, 1885, with the publication of a bellicose letter, headed "Another edition of the *Mahabharata*", purporting to give an account of the proceedings of a public meeting held at Mayaveram, and containing an outspoken and trenchant criticism of ROY's edition by one Mr. Sreenivasa SASTRIAL. This worthy gentleman thought ROY's edition to be "sadly defective in the text and that this defect is detrimental to the religious interests as many portions supporting the *Advaita* and *Vāsishta-advaita* (sic) doctrines, but unfavourable to the Sakti worshippers of the North, have been omitted". "It was sad, therefore," bemoaned this aggrieved protagonist of the Southern Recension, "that the generous gentleman of the North, Protapa Chandra ROY, that undertook to edit the text, should decline the responsibility of editing the text as correctly as possible and to compare various manuscripts of the text from Southern India." Mr. Sreenivasa SASTRIAL, it is reported, "instanced one or two portions of the *Mahābhārata*, omitted in the Calcutta edition, which can be proved by indisputable testimony to have existed in the earliest copies of the work." One wonders, where and how this estimable gentleman could have got hold of "the earliest copies" of the work; or rather, just how early were the copies he was referring to. "Again, many verses", complained this Vaiṣṇava propagandist, "quoted by the great philosophers of the South in support of their respective doctrines, are not to be found in Mr. Protapa Chandra ROY's edition"!

The reply of Protap Chandra ROY is not altogether without interest. He ruefully admitted—what we must even now admit—that "there can be no edition of the *Mahabharata* how carefully edited soever, that would please scholars of every part of India..... Like other ancient works that have come down to us from century to century by the method of manual transcription, *large interpolations have been inserted in this great work.*[1] To settle, at this fag-end of the nineteenth century, what portions are genuine and what otherwise, is, except in a very few instances, simply impossible". With highly commendable [32] objectivity, ROY then proceeds to enunciate a critical principle, which, simple—nay, obvious—as it is, many a reputable scholar of India will find it difficult to appreciate even at the present day. "*I know of no method*", wrote ROY, nearly fifty years ago, "*except that of taking that only as undoubtedly genuine which occurs in all the manuscripts of the East, the North, the West, and the South*"! "As far as my edition is concerned", he continued, "it is substantially based on that of the *Royal Asiatic Society* of Bengal, published about forty-five years ago under the superintendence of a few learned Pandits of Bengal aided, as I believe, by an English orientalist of repute.... Manuscripts had been procured from all parts of India (the South unexcepted) and these were carefully collated. Although edited with

---

[1] Italics mine!

such care, I have not, however, slavishly followed the Society's edition. I have compared it carefully with the Maharājah of Burdwan's text in the Bengalee character which was edited with still greater care. About 18 manuscripts procured from different parts of India (the South not excepted) were carefully collated by the Burdwan Pundits before they admitted a single *sloka* as genuine. I have very frequently referred to this Burdwan edition also for checking the Society's text.... Besides the published texts, I have now and then referred to certain manuscripts. These, however, are all of Bengal. I am willing to consult any approved manuscript of Southern India.... I conclude by repeating that I have no complaint against Mr. Sreenivasa. On the other hand, I freely admit that an edition like the one projected by him will be a valuable accession to the libraries of all scholars in India and in countries out of India. Only the same remarks that he has applied to *my* edition will, I am confident, apply to *his*, when a Pundit of Northern or Western India takes it up for notice or review, unless, of course, the learned SASTRIAL includes, without critical examiation, *every* passage bearing on both the *Advaita* and the *Çākta* worship. I may assure Mr. SASTRIAL, however, that in that case, in his attempt to please everybody he will, like the painter in the fable, please none, particularly among readers of judgment and critical discrimination. The fact is, that the divergences of manuscripts are so great that it is perfectly impossible to produce an edition that could at once satisfy both *Aryāvarta* and *Dākshinātya*." That edition, alas, so bravely and enthusiastically planned by Mr. Sreenivasa SASTRIAL, to which reference is made in the above extract, appears never to have seen the interior of any printing establishment !

I have quoted Protap Chandra ROY *in extenso*, not merely because of the interesting sidelight his remarks throw on the question of the different editions of the Mahābhārata, projected or planned, in or just before his time, but also because of some remarkably sound principles of textual criticism, briefly, but clearly, propounded therein by him. Protap Chandra ROY had grasped the Mahābhārata Problem in all its essentials. But the time was not yet ripe for the actual preparation of a critical edition of the Mahābhārata.

The differences between the two recensions of the Mahābhārata must not be underrated. Between them there lies, to start with, the irksome barrier of scripts. It is no exaggeration to say that in India to the Northerners, the Southern versions written in Southern scripts, ordinarily speaking, were and are sealed books ; on the other hand, the Southerners, with the possible exception of a few learned Pandits—who, in fact, after a half-hearted admission of epic poetry into the realm of literature, cheerfully leave the [33] study of the bulk of the Mahābhārata text to their less gifted brethren—could not and cannot decipher the Northern scripts, perhaps with the exception of the Devanāgarī.

When one laboriously surmounts this initial obstacle, and starts to compare the two recensions, one finds, to one's surprise, that the difference between them begins, as a matter of fact, with the very division of the Mahābhārata into its various parvans! Against the commonly accepted, conventional division of the epic into eighteen books (parvans), there is the Southern division into twenty-four.[1] More surprising still is the fact that the Ādiparvan itself, the very *first* book of the epic (with which alone we are, in fact, here concerned), is sub-divided in Southern *manuscripts* into three (Ādi, Āstīka and Saṁbhava), or at least into two (Ādi and Saṁbhava) separate *major* parvans.[2] Let me emphasize that it is the main large divisions (parvans) of the epic I am here referring to, and *not* the hundred (sub-)parvans (also called upaparvans or antaḥparvans). The sub-parvans, in point of fact, could not come into question here at all. Only the Northern manuscripts, as a rule, mention *in their colophons* the names of the sub-parvans; the Southern manuscripts ignore (as far as I can say at present, uniformly) this detail, very rarely mentioning, in their colophons, the name of the corresponding sub-parvan.[3] We have, therefore, no means of knowing precisely the number and the limits of the sub-parvans in the Southern scheme, except, of course, the meagre and ambiguous data of the Parvasaṁgraha (Ādi 2) itself.[4]

It is true that the Southern (printed) editions (not excepting Professor P. P. S. Sastri's *critical* edition of the Southern recension, as far as it has gone) follow the division of the epic uniformly into the conventional eighteen books.[5] But in so far as they do that, the editors, it seems to me, must be overriding knowingly (but without giving the fact inexpedient prominence) the clear and unmistakable testimony of Southern manuscripts. They prefer to sacrifice the Southern manuscript tradition and make their editions harmonize with the data of the Parvasaṁgraha: always a grave blunder; because, clearly, the data of the Parvasaṁgraha can be manipulated far more easily than those of the manuscripts of the text. The Parvasaṁgraha, *if*

---

1 See the remarks of Burnell, *A Classified Index to the Sanskrit MSS. in the Palace at Tanjore* (London 1879), p. 180; and Winternitz, *Ind. Ant.* 1898. 122.

2 In most Southern manuscripts the adhyāyas of these different parts of our Ādiparvan are *separately numbered*. In our critical apparatus a new beginning is made with (our) adhy. 54 in all Southern MSS. except T_1 (which is a misch-codex), an adhyāya which marks the beginning of our Ādivaṁśāvataraṇaparvan; in the colophons of the Southern MSS. it is called the *first* adhyāya of the Saṁbhavaparvan.

3 On the other hand, the Southern MSS. (and in fact even most of the Northern MSS.) frequently mention the name of the Upākhyāna or the name of the adhyāya; but even this is never done regularly and systematically.

4 The Parvasaṁgraha gives only the names of the (100) sub-parvans, and the contents of the (18) major parvans. But from these data, we cannot say from what adhyāya to what adhyāya a particular sub-parvan extends.

5 Thus, from these Southern ed., one can never elicit the fact that in the Southern Recension our Ādi is divided into two parts (parvans) and that these parts have *separate numbering* of adhyāyas!

compiled, originally, on the basis of some Northern version,[1] would certainly not fit the Southern recension exactly, even when the Parvasaṁgraha was first compiled.

[34] The difference between the recensions does not end there by any means, unhappily. The manuscripts of the two recensions show numerous other, big and small, discrepancies : discrepancies in the spelling of most ordinary words (e.g. N व्रीडाः S व्रीला or व्रीळा), especially of proper names (e.g. N नैमिष : S नैमिश); in the readings of words, phrases, lines, stanzas, groups of stanzas (passim); in the sequence of all these elements (passim); in the relative position of single adhyāyas or of a small group of adhyāyas (passim); in the relative sequence of whole episodes (e.g. the Śakuntalā and Yayāti episodes, Ādi, 62 ff., and 70 ff.). What is more disconcerting still is that the recensions show also complicated displacements of portions of adhyāyas ; cf., for example, the long notes on 1. 106. 11 (p. 474 f.), and 1. 144. 20 (p. 624). Besides these variations in spellings, readings and sequences, there are additions (or omissions, just as one may happen to regard them) of single lines (often "inorganic", i.e. such as can be added or omitted with no effect upon the grammar or continuity), of short passages (passim) and long passages comprising more than a hundred lines (cf. App. I, No. 55, a passage of 125 lines, setting forth the story of the Kāśī princess Ambā). These additions (respectively omissions) and verbal variants sometimes go to such a length that, at times, there emerges in the end an entirely different story. Compare, for instance, the two versions of the highly popular episode "Rape of Subhadrā" (Subhadrāharaṇa) in adhy. 211-212 of our edition and passage No. 114 of App. I (comprising over 460 lines !).[2] We find that the Southern version of this story is enriched with many entirely novel and startling features, such as Arjuna's masquerading as a peripatetic monk (yati), or his fierce battle with the Yādava forces led by Viprthu, which he, of course, routs, alone and unaided, or rather merely with the help of his newly acquired, valiant and resourceful wife, who acts as his charioteer !

A notable feature of the Southern recension is that it is considerably *longer* than the Northern. The constituted text of the Parvasaṁgraha (1. 2. 96) gives 7984 "ślokas" (that is, probably, what is technically called *granthas*) as the extent of the Ādi :

सप्त श्लोकसहस्राणि तथा नव शतानि च ।
श्लोकाश्च चतुराशीतिर्दृष्टो ग्रन्थो महात्मना ॥

---

[1] This is clearly suggested by the fact that the longer Table of Contents (1. 2. 72-233) follows the eighteen-parvan division, which does not harmonize with the data of the colophons of the Southern MSS., which have the twenty-four-parvan division.

[2] Even the Śakuntalā episode gets a somewhat different colouring in the Southern recension.

The extent of the Vulgate is computed to be about 8460 "stanzas". The length of the Southern text of the Ādi edited by Professor P. P. S. SASTRI is given by himself as 9984 "stanzas", slightly in excess of his own Parvasaṁgraha figure (M. 1. 2. 102), which differs as regards this figure (as in many other figures in adhy. 2) from our edition. This latter figure (9984) is perhaps a trifle in excess of the presumable extent of the (normal) Southern recension, since P. P. S. SASTRI's text contains some clear instances of interpolation (from Telugu, Tamil and even Northern sources),[1] which need not necessarily be put down to the already swollen account of the Southern recension. The difference between the Vulgate and SASTRI's text is about 1524 "stanzas". But even the common Southern text, which will be appreciably shorter than SASTRI'S, may confidently be {35} reckoned to contain approximately 1300 "ślokas" (i.e. granthas) more than the longest Northern version of the Ādi!

This excess in the Southern recension is not due to the addition of any single lengthy passage or just a few of such passages even, though there are undoubtedly among them some fairly long passages. The excess is due to additions, large and small, distributed almost evenly throughout the parvan.

Not only is the Southern text thus appreciably longer than the other, the story itself of the Southern recension, as compared with that of the Northern, is, owing to many of these additions, much richer in details, leaving little or nothing to the imagination of the reader or the hearer. Thus, for example, in the Northern recension, the father of Satyavatī or Matsyagandhā (Vyāsa's own mother) is a nameless king of fisher-folk, making a living, on the banks of the Yamunā, by fishing. This is rather unsatisfactory. That the name of Matsyagandhā's father—he is really only her foster father—according to the fable—should not have been preserved, seems a shocking piece of negligence on the part of the historian, that is, the story-teller, since history as it is narrated (as has been well said) is a kind of *roman à thèse.* The Southern recension here comes to our help. It has carefully procured the name of the foster-father of Kālī Matsyagandhā *alias* Satyavatī : it was Uccaiḥśravas (a high-sounding Aryan name), if we are to believe the Southern recension. He was named after the great snow-white Stallion of the Gods, which came out of the ocean when it was being churned for Ambrosia by the Gods and the Titans.

Then again, the Purohita sent by the Yādavas to the forest retreat of Pāṇḍu in the Himalayas was a Kāśyapa. He was required, of course, to perform all the little Aryan rites for the Pāṇḍavas. Moreover, it is best that kings always have their Rājaguru by their side, to advise and help them on all occasions. The Nothern recension does not even tell us that the Yādavas

---

[1] For instance the Śvetaki episode (M. 1. 214, 29-98½), which, in the form printed there, is missing in *all* MSS. of his own critical apparatus!

had sent any Purohita at all to Pāṇḍu's hermitage ; so there, no question of his name arises.

But a really illuminating instance of the richness of information furnished by the Southern recension is supplied by an "additional" adhyāya[1] in this recension, which gives us some new and interesting *chronological* details about the Pāṇḍavas themselves. These details disperse that haze of uncertainty and vagueness which overspreads the ordinary account.

The Southern recension informs us that when the Pāṇḍavas first arrived at the Court of Hāstinapura from the forest retreat, after the death of their father, Yudhiṣṭhira was exactly sixteen years old, Bhīma fifteen, Arjuna fourteen, the twins thirteen. We are further told exactly how long the Pāṇḍu brothers stayed at the Kaurava Court, in the Lac House (Jatugṛha), in Ekacakrā, at the Court of the Pāñcāla King, then again at the Kaurava Court, then in Indraprastha, and so on. Yudhiṣṭhira died at the ripe old age of 108, which is a mystic number. Arjuna was younger than Kṛṣṇa by three months, which was also exactly the difference between the ages of Kṛṣṇa and Balarāma. And so on and so forth. Almost all these useful details are lacking in the Northern recension, and I doubt whether they can even be reconstructed from the meagre data of this recension on these points.

[36] The Southern recension impresses us thus by its *precision, schematization, and thoroughly practical outlook.* Compared with it, the Northern recension is distinctly vague, unsystematic, sometimes even inconsequent, *more like a story rather naïvely narrated,* as we find in actual experience.

The Southern recension of the Ādi at least is thus not merely longer, but also fuller, more exuberent, more ornate than the Northern. It may therefore be fitly styled, in relation to the Northern, the *textus ornatior*.

Notwithstanding these and other discrepancies, there persists throughout, between the recensions, a distinct and undeniable family resemblance, and there cannot be the slightest doubt that they both spring from a common source, albeit a distant and somewhat nebulous source. Follow the course of these divergent streams as far back as one will, the elusive source seems to recede still further and lose itself in the mists of antiquity.

It was pointed out above that a noteworthy feature of the Southern recension was that it was appreciably *longer* than the Northern. The character of the principal additions may be seen from the following list of some of the more important and lengthy passages peculiar to the Southern recension, whose texts are given in Appendix I.

(1) No. 9 (S except M_1) : God Śiva (Rudra) drinks up the poison (hālāhala) which exudes from the mouth of Vāsuki, while the Devas and Asuras are churning the ocean for Ambrosia (samudramanthana) ; comprising 19 lines.

---

[1] Cf. App. I, No. 67, lines 47-62.

(2) No. 45-48 and 51 : Additions to the Śakuntalā episode (together 231 lines).

(3) No. 52 : Mādhavī is introduced on the scene during the discourse between Yayāti and his grandsons, in the Yayāti episode (43 lines).

(4) No. 55 : Anticipation of the story of the Kāśī princess Ambā (125 lines).

(5) No. 59 : Sūrya persuades Kuntī to have sexual intercourse (21 lines).

(6) No. 67 : Details of the early life of the Pāṇḍavas in the Himalayan retreat (46 lines).

(7) No. 68-69 : Pāṇḍu's death and many funeral orations (together 123 lines).

(8) No. 78 (S, and by conflation K_4 Da_1 Dn $D_{2\cdot 4\cdot 5}$) : Details of a battle between the Kurus and the Pāñcālas, and capture of Drupada (119 lines).

(9) No. 79 : Anticipation of the account of the birth of Draupadī and Dhṛṣṭadyumna ; and account of the birth of Drupada (together 194 lines).

(10) No. 87-89 : Additions to the Hiḍimba episode (69 lines).

(11) No. 91-93 : Additions to the Bakavadha episode, including a detailed account of the fight between the two well-matched giants, Baka and Bhīma (106 lines).

(12) No. 95 : Drupada bemoans the loss of the Pāṇḍavas, and is consoled by his Purohita ; decides, at the advice of the Purohita, to celebrate the Svayaṁvara of Kṛṣṇā, in the hope that the Pāṇḍavas might turn up (74 lines).

(13) No. 100 : Story of Nāḷāyanī narrated by Vyāsa to the Pāñcāla king, to justify the polyandrous marriage of the Pāṇḍavas (118 lines).

(14) No. 101 : Story of Bhaumāśvi related on the same occasion (22 lines).

(15) No. 103 : Mimic warfare between the Kauravas and Pāṇḍavas aided by Pāñcālas (219 lines).

[37] (16) No. 108 : Dhṛtarāṣṭra crowns Yudhiṣṭhira king before despatching the Pāṇḍavas to Indraprastha (58 lines).

(17) No. 111 : Description of Nārada, who comes to visit Yudhiṣṭhira (55 lines).

(18) No. 113-115 : Expansion of the Subhadrāharaṇa (562 lines !).

(19) No. 116 : Arjuna's welcome on his return from exile (28 lines).

These passages alone comprise 2250 lines or 1125 stanzas approximately !

The discrepancies between the two recensions, as already observed, are so numerous and so multifarious, that any attempt to enumerate and classify them must remain incomplete and unsatisfactory. Nevertheless it may be useful to begin a cursory survey of the divergences, noting at the same time the typical characteristics of the Southern "additions", characteristics which recur with fair frequency in the Ādi, and which are likely to reappear in other parvans. These notes may prove useful for distinguishing between the different "hands" which have been at work in shaping this imposing monument of Indian antiquity, when the entire text has been treated in the manner proposed here, and we have sufficient data for undertaking a minute and systematic study of the variations and evaluating them.

The deviations of the Southern recension from the Northern (taking for purposes of exposition the latter to represent the norm) are of the following kind.

1. *Variants of isolated words or phrases,* (a) *unimportant and* (b) *important.*

(a) Unimportant, such as one comes across in line after line. They are far too numerous to be listed even approximately completely, but from among them we may single out these for specific mention :

(i) fluctuations in the spelling of proper names, e. g. S नैमिश (N नैमिष), रोमहर्षण (लोमहर्षण), अस्तीक (आस्तीक), इलिल (इलिन), हस्तिनपुर (हास्तिनपुर), उचथ्य (उतथ्य), महाभिषक् (महाभिष), त्रस्नु (तंसु), etc., etc.

(ii) variations mainly due to mere transpositions of words, e. g. S महर्षेः सर्वलोकेषु पूजितस्य महात्मनः (N °र्षेः पूजितस्येह सर्वलोके म°) 1. 1. 23; प्रतीपस्तु ततो राजा (ततः प्रतीपो राजा स) 92. 1; etc., etc.

(iii) unremitting variation of: monosyllabic particles and verse-fillers, which are among the most unstable elements of the received text, such as च, वै, तु, ह, हि, [अ]थ; common adverbs and conjunctions, such as ततः, तदा, तथा, तत्र, यतः, यदा, यथा, यत्र, अत्र, अतः, इतः, अथ, चापि, चैव ; and prepositions अधि–अभि–वि–अति, प्रति–परि, अनु–उप, etc., etc.

(iv) substitution of metrically equivalent synonyms, or words and phrases of similar significance; e. g. रोष–क्रोध–कोप; ऋषि–मुनि; प्रभु–विभु–(अ)भिभू; द्विज–विप्र; राज्य–राष्ट्र; पन्नग–भुजग; नरेश्वर–नरोत्तम–नराधिप–नरर्षभ; ब्रह्मवित्तम–द्विजसत्तम–वेदवित्तम–विप्रसत्तम; पन्नगेश्वर–पन्नगोत्तम (and similar compounds with ईश्वर and उत्तम); अस्त्रविशारद–शस्त्रविशारद–शास्त्रविशारद–धर्मविशारद–वाक्यविशारद; यशस्विन्–तरस्विन्–तपस्विन्; समरदुर्मदौ–समरदुर्जयौ; कथयिष्यामि–संप्रवक्ष्यामि–कीर्तयिष्यामि; अमिततेजसा–अमितबुद्धिना; महाबल–महाभुज–महारथ–महायशः; वराङ्गना–शुचिस्मिता; चारुदर्शना–चारुलोचना–चारुहासिनी–वरवर्णिनी–(अ)मरवर्णिनी; धर्मभृतां वर–शस्त्र(शास्त्र)विदां वर; असंशयं–न संशयः; etc., etc.

(v) substitution of equivalent epic iterata; e. g. उवाच तदनन्तरं, पुनरेवाभ्यभाषत; परस्परजिघांसया, परस्परवधैषिणः; निःश्वसन्तं यथा नागं, श्वसन्तमिव पन्नगं; etc., etc. For other examples, see [38] HOPKINS's collection of "Parallel phrases in the two Epics" in the *Great Epic*, pp. 403 ff. (Appendix A).

(b) Important variants, which make a considerable difference in the sense, and of which the critique must take account. Of such variants, relatively speaking, there are only a few ; e. g. discrepant divisions of the epic into parvans and adhyāyas ; variants of the titles of the sub-parvans (e. g. S प्रायोपवेशन: N मृगस्वप्नभय), of the numbers of adhyāyas and ślokas in the Parvasaṁgraha (the figures for ślokas differ, at times, by thousands).

— An example of a different character from another part of the Ādi is the variant वर्षः मास in the stanzas which refer to the duration of Arjuna's exile. According to the Northern recension it is thirteen *years*; according to the Southern, only thirteen *months*! Cf. 1. 204. 28. स नो द्वादश वर्षाणि (S वै मासान् , मासानि etc.) ब्रह्म(S व्रत)चारी वने वसेत् ; 205. 30 वने द्वादश वर्षाणि (S मासानां, मासानि,मासान् हि).[1] — Then we have in 1. 3. 21 the variant वर्द्धुं–वन्दं. How was the infinitive really made? — And so on.

2. *Larger variations between continuous passages, as a whole, the total extent remaining approximately the same.*

We find them (a) mostly in the long lists of names : e. g. of the hundred sons of Dhṛtarāṣṭra (adhy. 108), of ancient kings (1. 1. 166 ff.), or serpents (1. 52. 5 ff.), of kings present at Draupadī's svayaṁvara (adhy. 177) ; but (b) also when there are transpositions of whole or parts of adhyāyas (e. g. the prose genealogy, adhy. 90) ; or again (c) when there is free paraphrase of a passage (passim).

3. *Expansion of the text in S without materially altering the nature of the contents or the course of the narrative.*

(a) By multiplication of the items of a list. For instance :

In adhy. 20, S (with K_4 marg. Dn D_4 marg.) adds seven lines of praise to an existing hymn (स्तोत्र) addressed to Garuḍa. In these lines, Garuḍa is identified, in turn, with all the principal gods, and with everything that is pre-eminent in the world :

299* त्वं विभुस्तपनः सूर्यः परमेष्ठी प्रजापतिः ।
त्वमिन्द्रस्त्वं हयमुखस्त्वं शरस्त्वं जगत्पतिः ।
त्वं मुखं पद्मजो विप्रस्त्वमग्निः पवनस्तथा ।
त्वं हि धाता विधाता च त्वं विष्णुः सुरसत्तमः ।
त्वं महानभिभूः शश्वदमृतं त्वं महद्यशः ।
त्वं प्रभास्त्वमभिप्रेतं त्वं नस्त्राणमनुत्तमम् ।
त्वं गतिः सततं त्वत्तः कथं नः प्राप्नुयाद्भयम् ।

In adhy. 64, S (with K_4 Dn $D_{1\cdot5}$) gives an additional short list of sciences in which the Ṛsis in Kaṇva's penance grove were proficient :

586* शब्दच्छन्दोनिरुक्तज्ञैः कालज्ञानविशारदैः ।
द्रव्यकर्मगुणज्ञैश्च कार्यकारणवेदिभिः ।
जल्पवादवितण्डज्ञैर्न्यासग्रन्थसमाश्रितैः ।
नानाशास्त्रेषु मुख्यैश्च शुश्राव स्वनमीरितम् ।

---

1 Cf. HOPKINS, *Ruling Caste in Ancient India*, p. 342 (footnote).

[39] In adhy. 74 an additional passage (of 7 lines) in S (with D_3) harps on the well-worn theme of the evils that attend on anger :

745* तस्मादक्रोधनः श्रेष्ठः कामक्रोधौ न पूजितौ ।
क्रुद्धस्य निष्फलान्येव दानयज्ञतपांसि च ।
तस्मादक्रोधने यज्ञस्तपो दानं महत्फलम् ।
न पूतो न तपस्वी च न यज्वा न च धर्मकृत् ।
क्रोधस्य यो वशं गच्छेत्तस्य लोकद्वयं न च ।
पुत्रभृत्यसुहृन्मित्रभार्या धर्मश्च सत्यतः ।
तस्यैतान्यपयास्यन्ति क्रोधशीलस्य निश्चितम् ।

In adhy. 165, a Southern passage expands in *hyperbolic* language the list of edibles and other commodities (such as wines, clothes and blankets) furnished by Vasiṣṭha's Kāmadhenu, by the addition of 6 more lines :

1753* बाष्पाढ्यस्यौदनस्यैव राशयः पर्वतोपमाः ।
निष्ठान्नानि च सूपांश्च दधिकुल्यास्तथैव च ।
कूपांश्च घृतसंपूर्णान्भक्ष्याणां राशयस्तथा ।
भोजनानि महार्हाणि तत्र तत्र सहस्रशः ।
इक्षून्मधु च लाजांश्च मैरेयांश्च वरासवान् ।
वस्त्राणि च महार्हाणि कम्बलानि सहस्रशः ।

In adhy. 213, the Southern recension furnishes us with a supplementary list of items in Subhadrā's dowry, which, taken along with what has gone before, exhausts almost all the things worth possessing in this world :

2082* काम्बोजारट्टबाह्लीकसिन्धुजातांश्च भारत ।
सुवर्णकृतसंनाहान्घण्टानादविनादितान् ।
श्वेतचामरसंछन्नान्सर्वशस्त्रैरलंकृतान् ।
जात्यश्वानां सहस्राणि पञ्चाशत्प्रददौ तदा ।

2088* भूषणानां तु मुख्यानां शतभारं ददौ धनम् ।
मुक्ताहाराणि शुभ्राणि शतसंख्यानि केशवः ।
प्रवालानां सहस्रं च तथान्यानपि भारत ।
सुवर्णपादपीठानां महार्हास्तरणांस्तथा ।
पर्यङ्काणां सहस्रं च ददौ कन्याधनं तदा ।

(b) By anticipation or repetition of stories, motives or discourses. For example :

(i) the miraculous birth of Kṛṣṇā and Dhṛṣṭadyumna is narrated twice in S : in adhy. 155 and in App. I, No. 79 (after adhy. 128) ;

(ii) the theme of the amusing experience of a maiden, who, on praying to Mahādeva for one husband five times, was granted, as a boon, five husbands at one time—a story which seems to have been very popular in the South—is used, with variation, in S,' no less than *three* times in the course of the Ādi ; cf. adhy. 157, 189 and passage No. 100 (of App. I) ;[1]

(iii) account of the tragi-comic experiences of the Kāśī princess Ambā, who was passed on in turn by Bhīṣma to Śālva and Śālva to Bhīṣma, repeatedly, like a shuttle-cock, a story which is really the subject-matter of the Ambopākhyāna in Udyoga 173 ff. (Bom. [40] ed.), apparently a favourite piece, is anticipated in passage No. 55 of App. I (cf. adhy. 96) and forms a bulky addition of 125 lines !

(iv) the future of the royal family, which is the subject-matter of the additional dialogue between Bhīṣma and his step-mother, Satyavatī, in S, in passage No. 57 (of App. I) is only a continuation and *repetition* (with v. l.) of the discourse between the same parties in adhy. 99.

(v) Sūrya's warning to Karṇa about the designs of Indra to supplicate Karṇa in the disguise of a Brahman, in passage No. 60 of App. I, which is an anticipation of the story told in Araṇya 300 (Bom. ed.).

(c) Additions in S, due to the explicit mention of the observance of the correct and complete Brahmanic ritual and ceremonial on the proper occasions. Thus, in adhy. 68, at the birth of Bharata :

625* यथाविधि यथान्यायं क्रियाः सर्वास्त्वकारयत् ।

In adhy. 92, at the birth of Śaṁtanu :

921* तस्य जातस्य कृत्यानि प्रतीपोऽकारयत्प्रभुः ।
जातकर्मादि विप्रेण वेदोक्तैः कर्मभिस्तदा ।
नामकर्म च विप्रास्तु चक्रुः परमसत्कृतम् ।
शंतनोरवनीपाल वेदोक्तैः कर्मभिस्तदा ।

In adhy. 100, at the birth of Dhṛtarāṣṭra and Pāṇḍu :

1084* तयोर्जन्मक्रियाः सर्वा यथावदनुपूर्वशः ।
कारयामास वै भीष्मो ब्राह्मणैर्वेदपारगैः ।

In adhy. 115, we have, likewise, with reference to the Pāṇḍavas themselves (App. I, No. 67, lines 13-14, 20-27) :

न भवेरन्क्रियाहीनाः पाण्डोः पुत्रा महाबलाः ।
पाण्डोः प्रियहितान्वेषी प्रेषय त्वं पुरोहितम् ।

* * * * *

तमागतं द्विजश्रेष्ठं काश्यपं वै पुरोहितम् ।
पूजयामास विधिवत्पाण्डुः परपुरंजयः ।
पृथा माद्री च संहृष्टे वसुदेवं प्रशंसताम् ।
ततः पाण्डुः क्रियाः सर्वाः पाण्डवानामकारयत् ।
गर्भाधानादिकृत्यानि चौलोपनयनानि च ।
काश्यपः कृतवान्सर्वमुपाकर्म च भारत ।

---

[1] In SASTRI's edition these stories occur in adhy. 164, 189 and 191.

चौलोपनयनादूर्ध्वं वृषभाक्षा यशस्विनः ।
वैदिकाध्ययने सर्वे समपद्यन्त पारगाः ।

In adhy. 124, at the royal tournament :

1412* रङ्गमध्ये स्थितं द्रोणमभिवाद्य नरर्षभाः ।
चक्रुः पूजां यथान्यायं द्रोणस्य च कृपस्य च ।
आशीर्भिश्च प्रयुक्ताभिः सर्वे संहृष्टमानसाः ।
अभिवाद्य पुनः शस्त्रान्बलिपुष्पैः समर्चितान् ।
रक्तचन्दनसंमिश्रैः स्वयमर्चन्त कौरवाः ।

(d) Expansion in S of existing scenes by the addition of speeches or detailed descriptions and by other digressions. Examples :

[41] (i) in App. I, No. 9, in the account of the churning of the ocean (samudramanthana), we are incidentally told of the drinking of poison by Siva, which had exuded from the mouth of Vāsuki during the churning ;

(ii) in 998*, we have nine additional lines depicting the humiliating treatment meted out to Bhīṣma at the court of the king of Kāśi, during the Svayaṁvara of his daughters ;

(iii) passage No. 59 (of App. I) depicts the persuasion of the shy and reluctant Kuntī by Sūrya for intercourse, by alternate threats and promises, like a real Don Juan ;

(iv) in passages No. 68-69, the Southern recension has tried to develop a very pathetic scene indeed, depicting the death of the father of the heroes, Pāṇḍu : an incident which must have been considered as deserving fuller and more sympathetic treatment than the perfunctory notice we find preserved in the Northern recension. At the sight of the corpse of her husband, Kuntī falls to the ground in a swoon, like a felled tree. Then the five brothers come up in a single file, and in the order of their ages, and recite their little mournful dirges : Yudhiṣṭhira gets 8 lines, Bhīma 7, Arjuna 4, the twins (in chorus) only 3 lines together.[1] Then follow long-winded farewell orations by Kuntī, Mādrī and the rest of the company, which are followed by a touching scene describing Mādrī mounting the funeral pyre ;

(v) passage No. 78 gives, in 119 lines, the details of a fight, which, in the Northern recension, at least originally, is disposed of in two lines ! The latter I consider adequate treatment, taking everything into consideration ;

(vi) passage No. 93 is a Southern addition of 37 lines giving fuller details of the titanic struggle between Bhīma and the cannibal Baka ;

(vii) 1737* adds a hymn (in Triṣṭubh metre and pseudo-vedic style) by Vasiṣṭha, addressed to Sūrya, when Vasiṣṭha presents himself before that luminary on behalf of Saṁvaraṇa ;

(viii) 1828* ff. describe in turn the discomfiture of each of the suitors for the hand of Draupadī ;

(ix) passages No. 100-101 add to the existing stock two new anecdotes—alternative explanations—narrated by Vyāsa to prove to Drupada and his son, that

---

[1] This schematic treatment perhaps betrays the hand of the interpolator more clearly than anything else.

the polyandrous marriage proposed by Yudhiṣṭhira, though apparently immoral and illegal, is a most righteous and necessary union, being pre-ordained by the gods themselves for the accomplishment of their cosmic plans : these are the well-known legends of Nāḷāyanī and Bhaumāśvī ;

(x) passage No. 106 gives an almost complete inventory of the presents Drupada gave to the Pāṇḍu brothers when they left with Draupadī, for the Kaurava Court, at the invitation of Dhṛtarāṣṭra. The Northern recension ignores this huge mass of presents completely !

(xi) passage No. 110 is a farewell scene containing short orations by Kṛṣṇa, Yudhiṣṭhira and Kuntī, when Kṛṣṇa sets out for Dvārakā ;

[42] (xii) passage No. 112 contains the farewell of Arjuna to Citrāṅgadā, telling her that she must not give way to sorrow in his absence, as they would meet again soon at the Rājasūya, which is going to be performed by Yudhiṣṭhira : a prophetic utterance ! And so on and so forth.

(e) Additions of little ethical, moral and sententious maxims, to which S, permeated as it is by a conscious didactic purpose, is particularly partial. We meet with the same old proverbs over and over again in S :

595* अन्यथा सन्तमात्मानमन्यथा सत्सु भाषते ।
स पापेनावृतो मूर्खस्तेन आत्मापहारकः ।
605* पिता रक्षति कौमारे भर्ता रक्षति यौवने ।
पुत्रस्तु स्थविरे भावे न स्त्री स्वातन्त्र्यमर्हति ।

* * * * *

मन्युप्रहरणा विप्रा न विप्राः शस्त्रपाणयः ।
अग्निर्दहति तेजोभिः सूर्यो दहति रश्मिभिः ।
राजा दहति दण्डेन ब्राह्मणो मन्युना दहेत् ।
क्रोधितो मन्युना हन्ति वज्रपाणिरिवासुरान् ।

780* परभार्या स्वसा ज्येष्ठा सगोत्रा पतिता स्नुषा ।
अपरा भिक्षुकास्त्वस्था अगम्याः कीर्तिता बुधैः ।

782* क्वचिदाशीविषो हन्याच्छस्त्रमन्यं निकृन्तति ।
यदृच्छयाग्निर्दहति मनसा हन्ति वै द्विजः ।

804* पुत्रार्थं भर्तृपोषार्थं स्त्रियः सृष्टाः स्वयंभुवा ।
अपतिश्चापि या कन्या अनपत्या च या भवेत् ।
तस्या जन्म वृथा लोके गतिस्तस्या न विद्यते ।

833* गुरोर्वै वचनं पुण्यं स्वर्ग्यमायुष्करं नृणाम् ।
गुरुप्रसादात्त्रैलोक्यमन्वशासच्छतक्रतुः ।

856* न च कुर्यान्नरो दैन्यं शाठ्यं क्रोधं तथैव च ।
जैह्म्यं च मत्सरं वैरं सर्वत्रैतन्न कारयेत् ।
मातरं पितरं चैव विद्वांसं च तपोधनम् ।
क्षमावन्तं च देवेन्द्र नावमन्येत बुद्धिमान् ।

शक्तस्तु क्षमते नित्यमशक्तः क्रोशते नरः ।
दुर्जनः सज्जनं द्वेष्टि दुर्बलो बलवत्तरम् ।
रूपवन्तमरूपी च धनवन्तं च निर्धनः ।
अकर्मी कर्मिणं द्वेष्टि धार्मिकं चाप्यधार्मिकः ।

1019* वाचा दत्ता मनोदत्ता कृतमङ्गलवाचना ।
निर्दिष्टा तु परस्यैव सा त्याज्या परचिन्तनी ।

1101* बालो हि द्वादशाद्वर्षाज्जन्मनो यत्करिष्यति ।
न भविष्यत्यधर्मोऽत्र न प्रज्ञास्यति वै दिशः ।

1189* नाग्निस्तृप्यति काष्ठानां नापगानां महोदधिः ।
नान्तकः सर्वभूतानां न पुंसां वामलोचनाः ।
एवं तृष्णा तु नारीणां पुरुषं पुरुषं प्रति ।
अगम्यागमनं स्त्रीणां नास्ति नित्यं शुचिस्मिते ।

[43] 1423* अद्भ्योऽग्निर्ब्रह्मतः क्षत्रमश्मनो लोहमुत्थितम् ।
तेषां सर्वत्रगं तेजः स्वासु योनिषु शाम्यति ।

(f) Additional stanzas in S with, perhaps, a certain amount of sexual appeal, bearing the taint of later decadence. Examples :

App. I, No. 89 (lines 3-4) with reference to Hiḍimbā :

शुभं हि जघनं तस्याः सुवर्णमणिमेखलम् ।
न ततर्प मुदा मृद्नन्भीमसेनो मुहुर्मुहुः ।

No. 48 (lines 78-79), describing Śakuntalā :

करान्तमितमध्यां तां सुकेशीं संहतस्तनीम् ।
जघनं सुविशालं वै ऊरू करिकरोपमौ ।

No. 55 (lines 46-47), describing Ambā :

पीनोन्नतकुचद्वन्द्वा विशालजघनेक्षणा ।
श्रोणीभरालसगमा राकाचन्द्रनिभानना ।

Then also 929* स्नातमात्रामधोवस्त्रां गङ्गातीररुहे वने ।
प्रकीर्णकेशीं पाणिभ्यां संस्पृशन्तीं शिरोरुहान् ।

1189* पुत्रं वा किल पौत्रं वा कासांचिद्भ्रातरं तथा ।
रहसीह नरं दृष्ट्वा योनिरुत्क्लिद्यते ततः ।

More sentiments of this type, occurring in the Grantha version alone, are :

1937* राकाशशाङ्कवदनाः पद्मिनीजातिसंभवाः ।
पद्मगन्धाः पद्ममुखाः पद्मपत्रनिभेक्षणाः ।

मुक्तायुक्तसुकर्णाश्च सप्तबिन्दुललाटिकाः ।
पीवरस्तनभारार्ताः शङ्खकण्ठ्यः सुनासिकाः ।
कृष्णदीर्घसुकेशिन्यो मुष्टिग्राह्यसुमध्यमाः ।
भृङ्गालिरोमलतिका ह्यावर्तनिभनाभिकाः ।
विपुलश्रोणिफलका रम्भास्तम्भोरुयुग्मकाः ।

The lengths to which the Muses lead these Southern poetasters may be judged from the following interpolation in certain Grantha manuscripts of the Ādi. 1334* with 1335* reads :

व्यपकृष्टाम्बरां दृष्ट्वा रम्यगुह्यस्थलां नृप ।
पीनोत्तुङ्गकुचां दृष्ट्वा तामृषिश्चक्रमे ततः ।

Cf. also lines 73-74 of passage No. 100 (of App. I) :

मारो मां बाधतेऽत्यर्थमनुगृह्णातु मां भवान् ।
तर्पयस्व ममाक्षाणि गुह्यं मां बाधतेऽनिशम् ।[1]

4. *Southern additions which alter the purport of the fable as narrated in the Northern recension.*

Made apparently with the object of correcting the laxity of sexual relations implied in the old narrative. In adhy. 67, the royal Purohita, a handy person, quickly but surely and secretly, performed the marriage of Duḥṣanta and Śakuntalā, in order to legitimize Bharata, the eponymous ancestor of the Bhāratas, who has given his name to the country of his birth and to the Great Epic of India, altogether an important personage in ancient Indian history :

[44] 610* पुरोहितं समाहूय वचनं चेदमब्रवीत् ।
राजपुत्र्या यदुक्तं वै न वृथा कर्तुमुत्सहे ।
क्रियाहीनो हि न भवेन्मम पुत्रो महाद्युतिः ।
तथा कुरुष्व शास्त्रोक्तं विवाहं मा चिरं कुरु ।
एवमुक्तो नृपतिना द्विजः परमयन्त्रितः ।
शोभनं राजराजेति विधिना कृतवान्द्विजः ।
शासनाद्विप्रमुख्यस्य कृतकौतुकमङ्गलः ।

In adhy. 77, the marriage of Yayāti and Śarmiṣṭhā is celebrated semi-secretly, in a secluded corner of the Aśoka grove, in the palace grounds, with the usual *baksheesh* to the Brahmins, in the presence of counsellors, chaplains, priests and so on, but *unknown to Devayānī* ! All this was done to legitimize Puru, the eponymous ancestor of the Pauravas :

---

[1] These lines occur in three MSS. (क, ग, घ) of SASTRI's edition (vol. 2), p. 1209.

807* ऋत्विक्पुरोहिताचार्यैर्मन्त्रिभिश्चैव संवृतः ।
कृत्वा विवाहं विधिवद्दत्त्वा ब्राह्मणदक्षिणाम् ।
पुण्ये नक्षत्रसंयोगे मुहूर्ते द्विजपूजिते ।

In passage No. 114 of App. I, Subhadrā and Arjuna were likewise secretly and hastily married in the presence of gods, ṛṣis, and elders, *while Balarāma was away from the scene*, to legitimize Abhimanyu (the father of the famous Parikṣit and grandfather of Janamejaya, to whom the epic was narrated). Cf. lines 281-286 of the passage :

महेन्द्रशासनात्सर्वे सहिताश्च महर्षिभिः ।
विवाहं कारयामासुः शक्रपुत्रस्य शास्त्रतः ।
अरुन्धती शची देवी रुक्मिणी देवकी तथा ।
दिव्यस्त्रीभिश्च सहिताः क्रियां भद्रां प्रयोजयन् ।
महर्षिः काश्यपो होता सदस्या नारदादयः ।
पुण्याशिषः प्रयोक्तारः सर्वे ह्यासंस्तदार्जुने ।

Most Grantha manuscripts (G_{1-5} of our critical apparatus : क, ख and ग of SASTRI'S) have a passage to show that Parāśara and Matsyagandhā were secretly but regularly married. Cf. passage No. 36 of App. I, which is a somewhat lengthy passage describing with circumstantial detail the nuptial ceremony at which the ancestors of both the bride and the bridegroom are invoked, all the details of the regular Hindu marital rite are scrupulously gone through, and the marriage is solemnized in the presence of Vasiṣṭha, Yājñavalkya and other great Ṛṣis living in the Naimiṣa forest !

5. *Additions in S, due to the filling out of lacunae (real or imaginary).*

Examples of such additions are :

482* which gives a summary of the last five parvans of *our* Mahābhārata text, and passage No. 79 (of App. I) giving an account of Drupada's birth. It appears, from the latter account, that Drupada was born in the same miraculous way as two of his contemporaries Droṇa and Kṛpa, due to the perturbation of his father at the sight of a beautiful Apsaras. Ascetics involuntarily emitting semen at the sight of heavenly nymphs, broad-hipped, fat-breasted, fair-clad, pleasure-fraught, and the miraculous germination of the semen into human beings, is the regular Purāṇic apparatus for the generation of the great men of the past, about whose birth nothing exciting was specially known to the chronicler.

[45] 6. *Multiplication of fights and battle-scenes.*

I have drawn attention above to the expansion of the description of a battle (in which the Kurus and the Pāṇḍus capture Drupada), and of a fight (between Bhīma and Baka).[1] Analogous to it is a battle scene described in

[1] App. I, Nos. 78 and 92-93 respectively.

an *additional* adhyāya in the Southern recension (App. I, No. 103). This stages a little war between the cousins, a miniature replica of the Great War to come. Here also Kurus plan the destruction of the Pāṇḍavas, who are residing in Kāmpilya as the guests of Drupada. A regular council of war is held, in which Śakuni and Karṇa advocate hostilities, while the nameless son of Somadatta counsels peace and conciliation. The bellicose party has the upper hand in the council chamber. The Kuru army marches against the Pāṇḍavas with their allies, the Pāñcālas. The Kaurava forces are, of course, easily repulsed. No great damage is done. The status quo is immediately restored : things go on just the same as before, as though no battle had ever taken place. There is also no other reference to this battle in the whole of the Mahābhārata. The present parvan does not offer much scope for the full development of this tendency. We shall probably meet with it again in the battle-books (6-9).

7. *Omissions in S, as compared with N.*

These are quite numerous and scattered almost evenly over the whole parvan, but short and contextually unimportant, as a rule. An exception is the somewhat lengthy Śvetaki episode (App. I, No. 118). Since, on the one hand, all reference to the episode is missing in the whole of the Malayālam version, as also in some manuscripts of each of the remaining two versions (T G) of the Southern recension, while, on the other hand, those T G manuscripts that do contain some mention of it insert a *variant version at an entirely different place,* therefore the episode may legitimately be considered a Northern interpolation which has insinuated its way, by conflation, into some Southern manuscripts. It is a story in true Purāṇic style. King Śvetaki sacrificed with such phenomenal zeal and keenness that his priests, in the end, refuse to sacrifice any more ! Śvetaki practised penance on the Himalayas with the object of making Rudra his sacrificial priest. Rudra, however, excused himself, asking Śvetaki to apply to Durvāsas, who was his part-incarnation (*aṁśa*). Durvāsas completed the sacrifice, and Śvetaki poured libations of clarified butter into the fire for twelve years continuously. As a result, Agni had a severe attack of indigestion ! He refused after that every offering, and became enfeebled. At Brahmā's direction, he set the Khāṇḍava forest on fire, and tried his best to burn the forest down ; but the denizens of the forest put the fire out, over and over again. He reported his discomfiture to Brahmā, who then asked him to betake himself to Arjuna and Kṛṣṇa, the part incarnations of Nara and Nārāyaṇa, with whose help alone Agni would be in a position to burn the Khāṇḍava forest.

It should be made clear that the variants and passages cited here are merely *by way of illustration*, and comprise only a small fraction of the total number of deviations.

The presence of an astonishingly large number of additions, some of which are undoubtedly late and spurious, should not be allowed to impair our appreciation of some real merits of the Southern recension. It would be, in fact, a grievous error to ignore on that account the Southern recension or underestimate its value. This recension is an [46] indispensable aid for controlling the deviations of the Northern recension, both in point of readings and sequence. In comparison with γ it has unquestionably preserved a very large number of original readings, proved by actual agreements between S and ν, as well as by their intrinsic merits. The superiority of the Southern recension in comparision to the Vulgate may be said to be quite evident. It may, however, quite easily happen that in a particular instance, the *whole* of the Northern recension is corrupt, and the true reading is preserved only in the Southern recension.[1] An instance of this is 1. 214. 5. The Vulgate reads (B. 1. 222. 5):

अध्येतारं परं वेदान्प्रयोक्तारं महाध्वरे ।
रक्षितारं शुभाल्लँोकाल्लँेभिरे तं जनाधिपम् ॥

Nīlakaṇṭha's gloss is : परं अध्येतारं परस्य ब्रह्मणोऽधिगन्तारम् । वेदान् वेदानाम् ।

The stanza has been translated by Manmath Nath DUTTA as follows: "Having obtained him as their king, they obtained a monarch who was devoted to the study of the Vedas, who was a performer of great sacrifices, and who was the protector of all good works." Protap Chandra ROY's translation reads similarly : "And the subjects having obtained Yudhisthira as their king, obtained in him one that was devoted to the study of the Vedas, one that was a performer of great sacrifices, and one that was the protector of all good people."

But the translations of both these scholars are generally free and arbitrary. As it stands, the stanza can be translated only as follows :

"They, (i.e. the people) obtain for a king, one who studied Brahma (*para*), employed the Vedas in a great sacrifice, and protected the blessed words."

This pedestrian stanza will satisfy most people as it has satisfied a long succession of critics, commentators and translators in the past. About it one can only say that there are worse stanzas in the Mahābhārata. Only a reader endowed with a fine sensibility and critical acumen will feel that there is something amiss here. We are face to face with the danger of acquiescing in a sense which might satisfy us, but which would not have satisfied the ancient writer. The Northern variants do not offer much help ; even the Śāradā and K manuscripts have substantially the same readings. It would, consequently, not be easy to reconstruct from this sad wreck of a Dīpaka, the epigrammatic original, which is preserved intact only in the Southern recension, which the constituted text here follows (1. 214. 5):

---

[1] For examples from another parvan, see LÜDERS, *Grantharecension*, pp. 52 ff.

अध्येतारं परं वेदाः प्रयोक्तारं महाध्वराः ।
रक्षितारं शुभं वर्णा लेभिरे तं जनाधिपम् ॥

No glosses, translations, exegetical notes, and such other accessories are necessary for the elucidation of this stanza ; for it is self-luminuous. The correctness of the Southern reading is confirmed by the very next stanza (1. 214. 6), which is also an epigrammatic period of the same type :

अधिष्ठानवती लक्ष्मीः परायणवती मतिः ।
बन्धुमानखिलो धर्मस्तेनासीत्पृथिवीक्षिता ॥

It should thus seem that the infidelities of the Southern recension are confined mainly to a tendency to inflation and elaboration. In parts unaffected by this tendency, [47] it is likely to prove, on the whole, purer, more conservative and more archaic than even the best Northern version. The Southern variants, therefore, deserve the closest attention and most sympathetic study.

After this brief survey of the interrelationship between the two recensions, we shall proceed to the consideration of the various provincial versions, into which each of the recensions breaks up.

CHARACTER AND MUTUAL RELATIONS OF THE VERSIONS AND THEIR MANUSCRIPTS

THE ARCHETYPE ν

The Śāradā Version.

The archetype ν comprises the two versions : Śāradā and "K".

The Śāradā version is represented in our critical apparatus by the fragmentary codex $Ś_1$, belonging to the Bombay Government Collection (No. 159 of 1875-76), which seems to be the only extant genuine representative of the old version of Kaśmīr. The manuscript, which is undated, may be three to four centuries old. For reasons which will appear in the sequel, I have made the Śāradā version the norm to follow.

The text of the Ādi (as of other parvans of the Mahābhārata) according to the different printed editions, as is well-known, varies considerably, not merely as regards the readings, but also as regards the extent. The length of the Ādi, according to the Calcutta edition, as already observed, is estimated to be about 8460 "stanzas", of the Bombay edition, 8620,[1] of the Madras edition (i.e. SASTRI'S Southern Recension) 9984 (according to SASTRI'S data), of the Kumbhakonam edition 10889.[2] Now, in a statement following the colophon (or forming part of the long colophon) of our Śāradā manuscript, the length of its text is given as 7984 in a stanza cited from the

[1] This is the figure given in LELE'S edition of the text with Marathi translation (Wai, Śaka 1818).

[2] See the volume of Index etc., Descriptive Contents, p. 4.

Parvasaṁgraha ; cf. the accompanying facsimile of fol. 155 a of the Śāradā codex. To judge by the amount of textual matter which an average folio of the fragmentary Śāradā codex holds, this estimate of its extent appears to be approximately correct.* Assuming then that to be the length of the Śāradā version, it becomes the *shortest* known version of the Ādi, and may, therefore, appropriately be called the *textus simplicior*.

While it is the shortest extant version, it is a demonstrable fact that it contains relatively little matter that is not found, at the same time, *in all other versions of both recensions*. It is clear, therefore, that it must contain, relatively, *less spurious matter* than any other known version. That is precisely the main reason why it is taken as the norm for this edition.

Since our codex ($Ś_1$) is fragmentary, it must be considered a piece of singularly good fortune that there has been preserved at least one nearly complete Devanāgarī manuscript of the Ādi, namely, India Office No. 2137, that may, as will presently be shown, be used, without hesitation, to supplement the missing portions, since it undoubtedly is a moderately trustworthy, though comparatively late and slightly contaminated and incorrect transcript of a Śāradā exemplar.

[48] Further particulars of the Śāradā version will be found under the account of the "K" version.

The accompanying facsimile of a page of the Śāradā codex (fol. 155a) contains the end of the Ādi and the beginning of the Sabhā. The Parvasaṁgraha stanza, mentioned above, giving the extent of the Ādi, will be found in lines 2-3 of the facsimile.

The "K" Version.

This version, as already explained, is a specific Devanāgari version, closely akin to the Śāradā version and clearly differentiated from the (so-called) Devanāgarī version.

The affinity of the manuscripts comprising this version is illustrated by the following concordant readings, selected at random. The references are to adhyāyas and ślokas.

1. 2 $K_{0\cdot 2-6}$ महर्षीन् : rest (mostly) ब्रह्मर्षीन्.
1. 8 K V_1 लोमहर्षणिरुवाच : others सूत उ°, सौतिरु°, सूतः.
1. 49 K V_1 B_1 m संक्षेपतोऽब्रवीत् : others संक्षेपमब्र°, संक्षिप्य चाब्र.°
1. 51 K विचक्षणाः : rest (mostly) मनीषिणाः.
1. 192 K_{0-6} धुतपाप्मानः : rest शुभकर्माणः.
2. 76 K यक्षाणामथ रक्षसां : rest (mostly) यक्षाणां च महौजसां.
4. 10 K °पुरस्कृताः : rest °पुरःसराः.

* [Actual counts of the critical text give 7964¼ ślokas of 32 syllables each.]

8. 2 K D_2 शुनकस्त्वं यतोऽभवः : others शुनकं समजीजनत्, शुनकस्तु सुतोऽभवत्, etc.

8. 16 K अदृष्टोऽङ्गे : others भृशमङ्गे, etc.

10. 2 K $D_{2\cdot5}$ (by transp.) सदैव भुजगं हन्यां : rest हन्यां सदैव भुजगं.

13. 1 K $D_{2\cdot5}$ ब्रवीहि : rest वदस्व.

13. 25 K $D_{2\cdot5}$ बान्धवैः : others बन्धुभिः, etc.

17. 9 K $D_{2\cdot5}$ ततो नानाप्रहरणैः : others नानाप्रहरणैर्भीमैः, etc.

19. 4 K $D_{2\cdot5}$ संवृतं बहुसाहस्रैः सत्त्वैर्नानाविधैरपि : others सत्त्वैश्च बहुसाहस्रैर्नानारूपैः समावृतं, etc.

24. 1 K D_2 त्विच्छामि : rest om. तु.

24. 14 K $D_{2\cdot5}$ महाद्युतिः : rest महाबलः.

55. 8 K क्षुद्रः : others क्रूरः, क्रुद्धः.

55. 35 K जातवेदसं : rest हव्यवाहनं.

56. 14 K कीर्तयेत् : rest श्रावयेत्.

57. 2 K चेदिपतिर्नृप : rest पौरवनन्दनः.

57. 8 K D_5 रम्यश्च : others पुण्यश्च, etc.

57. 43 K D_5 गृहान् : rest गृहं.

58. 3 K D_5 कीर्तयिष्यामि : rest कथयिष्यामि.

58. 40 K D_5 समक्षं : rest संनिधौ.

59. 29 K D_5 वीर्यवान् : others दानवः, etc.

60. 6 K $\tilde{N}_3$ D_5 अत्रेः पुत्रास्तु बहवः (by transp.) : rest अत्रेस्तु बहवः पुत्राः.

60. 52 K संभूतः rest संजातः.

62. 6 K D_5 राज्यं प्रशासति : rest राजनि शासति.

64. 29 K. D_5 ददर्श : rest जगाम.

67. 30 K D_5 निधाय कायकं त्वच : others विनिधाय ततो भारं, etc.

[49] 68, 69 K D_5 ध्वस्ता (*or* °स्तां) : rest याता.

71. 41 K D_5 वत्स : rest विप्र.

74. 7 K *alone* transp. कुमाराः and कुमार्यः.

76. 33 K. D_5 शुचिस्मितां : rest सुमध्यमां.

150. 18 K वासस्य : rest विप्रस्य; etc., etc., etc.

Further examples of the concordant readings of the K version will be found below.

It was remarked above that K_1 (= India Office 2137) was a manuscript of Kaśmīrī origin, exhibiting specially near affinities with $Ś_1$, so much so that K_1 may be regarded as a copy of some Śāradā original. The Kaśmīrī character of K_1 was already fully recognized by Profesor LÜDERS, who had utilized it in the preparation of his specimen[1] of a critical edition of the epic men-

[1] *Druckprobe einer kritischen Ausgabe des Mahābhārata*, Leipzig 1908.

tioned above, although he had no genuine representative of the Kaśmīrī or Śāradā version to compare it with.

The affinity between Ś$_1$ and K$_1$ is documented by a mass of readings, of which the following (selected at random) will serve as illustrations. The references are to adhāyas and ślokas.[1]

27. 15 Ś$_1$ K$_1$ पुरंदरः : rest शतक्रतुः (synonym !).
28. 24 Ś$_1$ K$_1$ ततः : rest नदीः.
29. 4 Ś$_1$ K$_1$ अरा अरेण : others अरान्तरेण, etc.
30. 7 Ś$_1$ K$_1$ प्रदेह्येतत् : others प्रतिगृह्यतां, प्रगृह्य, संगृह्य, आगृह्य, etc. (original hypermetric !).
31. 6 Ś$_1$ K$_1$ पंजवकः (corrupt) : others पिंजरकः, पंजरकः, etc.
37. 25 Ś$_1$ K$_1$ रक्षितव्यः पिता त्विति (corrupt) : others रक्षितव्याः प्रजास्तथा etc.
42. 7 Ś$_1$ K$_1$ नेतरां रोचयाम्यहं : others न भरेयं च तामहं, etc.
44. 2 Ś$_1$ K$_1$ भयात् : others तदा, तथा, ततो, etc.
45. 5 Ś$_1$ K$_1$ अवदन् : rest अब्रुवन् (synonym).
45. 19 Ś$_1$ K$_1$ तथोदितं : others नराधिपं, etc.
131. 3 Ś$_1$ K$_1$ प्रभुमते, (corrupt) : rest पशुपतेः.
131. 13 Ś$_1$ K$_1$ चरन् : rest शनैः.
154. 24 Ś$_1$ K$_1$ जाह्नव्यां : rest भागीरथ्या (original has double crasis !).
206. 3 Ś$_1$ K$_1$ एकका: (corrupt ?) : rest कथकाः (G$_1$ श्रद्धकाः).
218. 48 Ś$_1$ K$_1$ मन्दराच्छिखरं महत् (= 47^b) : rest गिरेः शृंगं सहस्रधा. (*or* °शः).

The above are examples of concordant *readings* of Ś$_1$ and K$_1$. As instances of adhyāya division and numbering may be pointed out that adhy. 42-44 and 46 of the constituted text (comprising adhy. 46-48 and 50 of the Vulgate) are numbered in Ś$_1$ K$_1$ 54-56 and 59 respectively, and are so numbered in no other manuscript hitherto collated ; further, after only the *third* stanza of our adhy. 40, both manuscripts (Ś$_1$ K$_1$) interpolate the figure 51, Ś$_1$ marginally inserting, at that place, an additional colophon : इत्यादिपर्वण्येकपञ्चाशत्तमोध्यायः. Likewise, after 1.165.34, Ś$_1$ K$_1$ insert, an additional colophon, not found in any other manuscript.

Among "additional" passages peculiar to Ś$_1$ K$_1$ may be mentioned 1735*.

K$_1$ is, however, by no means, a direct copy Ś$_1$. There are numerous discrepancies between them. Notably, there is a big lacuna in K$_1$ in adhy. 47-48, where Ś$_1$ is intact. [50] Again at 1. 107. 26 ; 154. 10, 11 ; 175. 4 and other places : Ś$_1$, which generally omits the verbs उवाच (resp. ऊचुः) in the short prose formulae of reference to the speaker, does show these verbs,

---

[1] It should be noted that Ś$_1$ begins only at 1. 26. 10.

while they are lacking in K_1 ; 1. 208. 14 is an exception where both $Ś_1$ and K_1 have उवाच. $Ś_1$ K_1 exhibit also numerous minor differences in their readings ; e.g. 1. 36, 22 ; 38. 21, 36 ; 41. 29 ; 46. 11 ; 98. 9 ; 125. 3, 16 ; 128. 2 ; 138. 24 ; 195. 11 ; 200. 3. After 1. 144. 17, $Ś_1$ has a colophon which is missing in K_1.

These agreements and differences show that while $Ś_1$ and K_1 are closely akin, their text is not identical. Neither $Ś_1$ nor K_1 is a direct copy of the other. They are independent witnesses, a circumstance which adds greater weight to their arguments.

I shall now cite some readings (also selected at random) which $Ś_1$ shares with the K version, $Ś_1$ and K standing together against all other manuscripts (barring, of course, conflated specimens). The references are to adhyāyas and ślokas.

28. 18 $Ś_1$ K श्वसनेन : rest कथनेन.
29. 1 $Ś_1$ K ततो जाम्बूनदो भूत्वा : rest जाम्बूनदमयो भूत्वा
32. 3 $Ś_1$ K दशार्णे : rest गोकर्णे.
32. 12 $Ś_1$ K वा : rest मे.
33. 20 $Ś_1$ K °रुच्यते (K_3 °रिष्यते) : rest °रुत्तमा.
36. 21 $Ś_1$ K D_5 गवि जातो : rest तिग्मतेजाः.
38. 2 $Ś_1$ K D_5 कुतोऽन्यथा : rest कुतः शपन्.
38. 14 $Ś_1$ K गुणान्वितं : rest समाहितं.
42. 7 $Ś_1$ K हि : rest च.
94. 31 $Ś_1$ K D_5 गृहान्विभो : others गृहान्तिकं, गृहं विभो, etc.
94. 93 $Ś_1$ K सहिताश्च : rest समेताश्च.
118. 1 $Ś_1$ K यथा विधिः : rest विशेषतः.
124. 23 $Ś_1$ K D_5 मनुष्याः : rest मनुजाः.
128. 12 $Ś_1$ K D_5 जाह्नव्यामहमुत्तरे : rest भागीरथ्याह° (double crasis !).
128. 15 $Ś_1$ K D_2 कालिन्द्याः : others माकन्दीं, मागधीं, etc.
142. 23 $Ś_1$ K भुजाभ्यां साधु योक्त्रय : others भुजयोः सारमर्पय, etc.
155. 13 $Ś_1$ K पुनः परिचरन्मुदा : rest स तं पर्यचरत्पुनः.
162. 6 $Ś_1$ K सोऽमात्यस्तं : rest om. सः.
163. 7 $Ś_1$ K $D_{2.5}$ °कोभवत् : others °कं बभौ, etc.
168. 3 $Ś_1$ K D_5 पार्थिवं : rest भारत.
169. 18 $Ś_1$ K D_5 ते ततः कोपात् : others ते महेष्वासाः, etc.
170. 9 $Ś_1$ K D_5 सर्वलोकेषु सत्तमः : rest सर्वलोकपराभवं.
177. 5 $Ś_1$ K D_5 प्रकीर्तिताः : rest समागताः.
181. 37 $Ś_1$ K $D_{2.5}$ °ले च लंघिते : others °लेऽभिगच्छति, etc.
181. 40 $Ś_1$ K D_5 प्राविशत्तत्र बीभत्सुः : others ब्राह्मणैः प्राविशत्तत्र ; etc., etc.

These concordances are sufficient for postulating the archetype ν, comprising the versions Śāradā and K, a hypothesis which will be confirmed by further agreements which are mentioned below.

The K version, though comprising manuscripts akin to each other and clearly distinguishable from those of the Devanāgarī version, is by no means—as is natural—quite homogeneous. Only $K_{0.1}$ represent the version K in a comparatively pure form, while the [51] remaining manuscripts of the group (i.e. K_{2-6}) are really nothing more than misch-codices, being conflated either with γ or with S. On the other hand, just owing to this conflation, some of the other composite Devanāgarī manuscripts (particularly $D_{2.5}$) have so many features in common with K, that they may as well be separated from D and classed under K.

The contamination of K_{3-6} with γ is illustrated by the following passages: No. 14 of App. I (found in K_4 marg., and Ñ V_1 B D); No. 41 (in $K_{3.4}$ and $Ñ_{2.3}$ V_1 B D except D_5); No. 42-43 (in $K_{3.4}$ and Ñ V_1 B D except D_5). K_4 includes passage No. 61 (of App. I) and 1131*, like Ñ B D. The contamination of $K_{2-4.6}$ with γ is illustrated by 116*, 119*, 122*, 124*, 125*, 128*, 132*, 137*, 139*, 142*, 143*, 144*, 145*, 151*, 157*, 160*, 162*, 166*, 167*, 168*, 172*, 173*, 189*, 190*, 191*, 221*, 228*, 245*, 281*, 305*, 354*, 372*, 405*, 416*, 417*, 438*, 487*, 490*, 523*, 536*, 564*, 692*, 694*, 824*, 1000*, 1035*, etc., etc.

The contamination of K_{4-6} with S is exemplified by the following among other facts. $K_{5.6}$ contain 22*, $K_{4.6}$ 25*, K_4 49*, K_4 (suppl. fol.) passage No. 55 (125 lines) and No. 100 (118 lines), of App. I.: all of these are Southern passages.

K_{4-6}, moreover, contain the Brahmā episode[1] in adhy. 1 (a slippery passage, which migrates from place to place), while $K_{4.6}$ have found place even for the venerable elephant-headed Gaṇeśa, who is unquestionably a late Northern intruder. In K_4 these interpolations are written out on separate folios (called here क्षेपपत्र), and inserted at appropriate places, which shows the interpolations on the high road to recognition as genuine parts of the Mahābhārata.

Important omissions which distinguish ν (really only $Ś_1$ K_{0-3}) from all other manuscripts are these:

(i) the adhyāya giving a naïve account of the birth of Duḥśalā (Bom. adhy. 116), which uncommonly looks like being an afterthought (App. I, No. 63);

(ii) a passage of about 25 lines describing how Droṇa's son Aśvatthāman is given flour mixed with water, which he drinks in the belief that it is milk (App. I, No. 75);

---

1 See notes on passage No. 1 of App. I.

(iii) an adhy. (Bom. adhy. 139), in which there is an incidental allusion to the installation of Yudhiṣṭhira as Yuvarāja,[1] and which is repetitious and incoherent (App. I, No. 80);

(iv) the so-called polity of Kaṇi(ṅ)ka, Kaṇi(ṅ)kanīti (Bom. adhy. 140), which is a replica (naturally with many additions, omissions and variant readings) of the advice given by Bhāradvāja (apparently a gotra name of this very individual) to Śatruṁjaya, and duly communicated by Bhīṣma to Yudhiṣṭhira in the Śānti (App. I, No. 81);

(v) the crossing of the Ganges by the Pāṇḍavas (Bom. adhy. 149), a superfluous adhyāya, which only serves to confound the already confused geography of the narrative (App. I, No. 85).

These five passages are found in all manuscripts collated except $Ś_1$ K_{0-3}, but it is worthy of note that even apart from their omission in *v* the documentary evidence with regard to at least two of them, is confused and unsatisfactory. No. v (crossing of the [52] Ganges) is inserted in different groups of manuscripts at different points of the text. In No. iv (Kaṇikanīti), on the other hand, most of the Southern manuscripts repeat, after the interpolation, the immediately preceding portion of the original, apparently in order to restore the context broken by the intrusion of extraneous matter.[2]

Of *important* additions in *v*, I can recall only one, that of an adhyāya of 42 lines, at the very end of the Ādi (added probably as an Appendix), which is a variant, abbreviated version of the Śvetaki interpolation. It is found only in $Ś_1$ $K_{0.1.4}$ and therefore cannot even be said to be characteristic of the whole of *v* (App. I, No. 121). Instances of small additions are Nos. 349*, 449*, 451*, 516*, 565*, etc. etc. found in K with or without some Devanāgarī manuscripts; while 969*, 1855*, 2077*, etc., are found in $Ś_1$ K, with or without some Devanāgarī manuscripts: all these passages are missing in B. S.

That $Ś_1$ and K are not identical but independent (though allied) sources, may be concluded, for example, from 449*, 452*, 491*, 492*, 516*, 565*, 750*, 866* etc., which are found inserted in some or all manuscripts of the K version, but which are conspicuous by their absence in $Ś_1$ (sometimes with K_1).

It was remarked above that *v* is the shortest of the extant versions of the Ādi. Let us examine, without bias, this feature of *v*. Those passages that are lacking in *v* in comparison with the other versions, cannot ***all*** be omissions in *v* whether accidental or intentional.

---

1 Cf. remarks of HOLTZMANN, *Das Mahābhārata*, 2. 33.

2 The reason of these repetitions has been explained by JACOBI, *Das Rāmāyaṇa*, p. 34, with reference to the Rāmāyaṇa. The same explanation is applicable here, *mutatis mutandis*.

They cannot be *intentional* omissions, notwithstanding that these missing passages are mostly of inferior character, intrinsically worthless, repetitious, superfluous, or finally such as scholars have already (even before the discovery of this version) marked as likely interpolations.[1] For, this Śāradā (Kaśmīrī) version of the Ādi is *not* an abstract or an adaptation. It claims to be the unabridged text itself, in all its fullness, and I see no sufficient reason to doubt the *a priori* presumption that it is not an abridged version.

The explanation that primarily with the very object of excising what seems to us to be superfluous or repetitious matter, and abridgement might have been intentionally made in the past by some Kaśmīrī redactor or a syndicate of redactors, would be a grotesque distortion of Indian literary and religious tradition. No one in the past found the epic text too long. Far from it. It was perhaps not long enough.

Taking away something from the received text of the Mahābhārata and passing it off as the original work is a thing categorically different from *adding* something to it. To add small details here and there, embellishing and amplifying the original, would be merely a gentle and lowly service *ad majorem gloriam dei*. Even long pieces may sometimes be added, if they are actually found in other Mahābhārata manuscripts ; and occasionally, even if they are not found in the current manuscripts, provided there is at least oral tradition to support their claims.

[53] No doubt the received text contained difficulties and obscurities and repetitions. But they would be merely due to corruptions of the text ; the difficulties could be solved and the purpose of the repetitions explained by a really learned Pandit, who knows and understands everything.

That the omissions cannot be the result of a preconceived plan to shorten or to improve the text, follows further from two other facts : firstly, enough digressions and superfluities still remain in *v*, which would have all been swept away in pursuance of the alleged plan ; and, secondly, *v* has its own interpolations, albeit they are few in number and short in extent, such as 349* (in K V_1 Da D_{2-4}), 451* (K D_2), 516* (K except K_3 Dn D_1), 565* (K except K_2), 1499* ($Ś_1$ K D_5), 1735* ($Ś_1$ K_1 *only*), 1855* ($Ś_1$ K $Ñ_1$), 2077* ($Ś_1$ K except K_2 and $Ñ_{1-3}$ V_1 D_{2-5}), etc.

While these so-called "omissions" cannot be all intentional, they can also not be all *accidental*. The text is continuous and complete in itself. It has no apparent lacunae, as it surely would have had, if the omissions had been due to fortuitous loss or destruction of some intermediate folios of a parent manuscript.

---

[1] Cf. HOLTZMANN, *Das Mahābhārata*, 2. 33, on adhy. 139 of the Vulgate ; or the surmises of various scholars regarding the Gaṇeśa episode (for literature see the next footnote).

It may further be pointed out that many of the apparent "omissions" of *v*, in relation to *γ* or the Vulgate (i.e. Nīlakaṇṭha's text) are confirmed by the rival recension, the Southern recension; e.g. the Gaṇeśa episode (App. I, No. 1), or the anticipation of the list of the hundred sons of Dhṛtarāṣṭra (No. 41), or again the story of the birth of Abhimanyu (No. 42), or finally the anticipation of the story of the birth of Karṇa (No. 43) in the Saṁbhavaparvan. These passages are omitted in S no less than in K.

In these instances, moreover, the intrinsic probability is wholly on the side of those manuscripts that lack these accretions. It is unnecessary to dilate on the Gaṇeśa episode, which, on the face of it, is a later addition, and which has been dealt with so often by different critics.[1] As for the two passages, Nos. 42-43 of App. I, it is sufficient to observe that the adhyāya in which they occur is meant to be a mere list of the *dramatis personae*, in which each actor in the great drama is identified as the incarnation of some god, goddess, or titan, taking this or that part in one momentous phase of an all-embracing cosmic movement. The adhyāya being originally a mere (metrical) *list* (as it is in the constituted text and the Southern recension),[2] such *stories* as the account of the birth of Abhimanyu and Karṇa are wholly out of place here, and could not possibly have belonged to the original scheme of the adhyāya. The contrary supposition only stultifies the original writer, making him out to be an irresponsible lunatic, scarcely a desirable conclusion from the orthodox view-point.

Likewise many of the apparent omissions in *v* in relation to the Southern recension are confirmed by other Northern versions; e.g. the anticipation of the birth of Kṛṣṇā and Dhṛṣṭadyumna (App. I, No. 79), or the Nāḷāyanī episode (No. 100), or the account of a battle between the Kauravas and the Pāṇḍavas (No. 103), which are peculiar to S. In other words, these "omissions" are documented by the *whole* of N.

[54] One notable feature of *v* to which I must now draw attention is its frequent agreement with S against *γ*, especially in the matter of isolated and even unimportant readings, scattered throughout this parvan. I shall cite a few (out of the hundreds of possible) instances to exemplify this interesting and important characteristic of *v*. The readings of conflated manuscripts which serve only to confuse the issue, have been ignored; the references are, as usual, to the adhyāya and śloka.

1. 138 K V_1 S दुरुत्सहं (Text) : B D सुदुःसहं.
1. 144 K S पाण्डवं युध्यमानं : B D मण्डलशश्चरन्तं.
1. 208 K S चत्वार एकतो वेदाः : V_1 B D एकतश्चतुरो वेदाः

---

[1] WINTERNITZ, *JRAS*. 1898. 380 ff.; Venkatachellam IYER, *Notes of a Study*, pp. 23 f., 28 ff.; LÜDERS, *Deutsche Literaturzeitung*, 1929, 1143 f. Particularly, WINTERNITZ, *Ind. Ant.* 1898. 77 ff.

[2] See adhy. 58 of SASTRI's Ādiparvan in the Southern Recension.

20. 2 K S विनतां विषण्णवदनां (hypermetric !) others विषण्णरूपां विनतां, etc.
21. 10 K S °घन° : Ñ V$_1$ B D (mostly) °गण°.
26. 9 K S नदीजलविशोषणं : Ñ V$_1$ B D (mostly) समुद्रजलशोष(*or* °षि)णं.[1]
34. 13 Ś$_1$ K S उत्पत्स्यति महातपाः : Ñ V$_1$ B D (mostly) भविष्यति तपोधनः.
37. 5 Ś$_1$ K S पत्रिणा : Ñ V$_1$ B D (mostly) शीघ्रगं.
39. 16 Ś$_1$ K S गृह्णायोरगसत्तम : Ñ$_{1.2}$ V$_1$ B D स्वापतेयं प्रगृह्य वै.
41. 17 Ś$_1$ K S पुण्यं : Ñ$_{1.2}$ V$_1$ B D तीव्रं.
64. 10 K S स्वन्ति रावं (*or* रावैर) विहगाः षट्पदैः सहिता मृदु : Ñ V$_1$ B D (mostly) स्वन्ति रावान्मधुराण्षट्पदा मधुलिप्सवः.
68. 14 K S तरुणादित्यवर्चसा : Ñ V$_1$ B D (mostly) बालार्कसमतेजसा.
76. 22 K S पुरुषेण : Ñ B D (mostly) ज्ञेयः पुंसा.
77. 4 K S भृशं : Ñ B D (mostly) सुखी.
94. 12 Ś$_1$ K S सूर्यसंकाशो : Ñ V$_1$ B D (mostly) सूर्यकल्पोऽभूत्.
100. 6 Ś$_1$ K S रात्रौ : Ñ$_{1.2}$ V$_1$ B D (mostly) सार्धं.
119. 8 Ś$_1$ K S मा द्रक्ष्यसि (irregular) : Ñ$_{1.2}$ B D मा द्राक्षीस्त्वं (regular).
138. 17 K S प्रासादशयनां नित्यं : Ñ$_{2.3}$ V$_1$ B D तथैव चास्मज्जननीं.
141. 4 Ś$_1$ K S दुर्बुद्धे राक्षसानां : Ñ V$_1$ B D (mostly) दुर्वृत्त रक्षसां वै.
142. 18 Ś$_1$ K S प्रसुप्ताः : Ñ V$_1$ B D (mostly) रक्षसा.
143. 38 Ś$_1$ K S विनाशाय महात्मनः : Ñ V$_1$ B D प्रतियोद्धा महारथः.
159. 20 Ś$_1$ K S पृथिवीं नृपः : Ñ$_2$ V$_1$ B D भूतिमात्मनः.
176. 5 K S कुरुनन्दनाः : Ñ V$_1$ B D (mostly) पाण्डुनन्दनाः.
182. 9 Ś$_1$ K S माद्रीसुतः सहदेवो जघन्यः : Ñ$_{2.3}$ V$_1$ B D पश्चादयं सहदेवस्तरस्वी.
187. 20 K S ततस्तमब्रवीद्राजा : Ñ V$_1$ B D तमब्रवीत्ततो राजा.
189. 23 Ś$_1$ K S भगवन् : Ñ V$_1$ B D भुवनस्य.
193. 1 Ś$_1$ K S चिन्तयामि : Ñ B D चिकीर्षामि.
196. 4 Ś$_1$ K Ñ$_1$ S बहु : Ñ$_{2.3}$ V$_1$ B D वसु.
199. 12 Ś$_1$ K Ñ$_1$ S चोपस्थितान् : Ñ$_{2.3}$ B D चाप्यागतान्.
199. 19 Ś$_1$ K Ñ$_1$ S भर्तारः : Ñ$_{2.3}$ V$_1$ B D नगरं.

Such extensive agreements in *petty verbal details* must necessarily be, in the main, an *original inheritance*, and could never be, in their totality, the result of contamination or conflation, as one may vaguely imagine they are because to acheive them would necessitate more expenditure of energy than an ancient Indian redactor or reciter or commentator of the epic would bargain for. And even if one or the other of them had the requisite amount [55] of energy to use in this way, it would appear to him to be a ludicrous waste of it. We in the present century are apt to get nervous and irritable over misprints and *variae lectiones*. But an ancient Indian scribe, redactor

[1] Note that the fragmentary Śāradā codex begins at 1. 26. 10.

or even commentator, not to speak of the common reciter (*pāṭhaka*)—if I read aright Indian literary history—was not perturbed in the least by a little difference in wording or in sequence, especially if the variant did not give an appreciably better or appreciably worse sense. The enormous and complicated critical apparatus assembled here, moreover, can leave us in no doubt as to the attitude of the custodians of the epic tradition towards paltry verbal details : it was that of total indifference.

Addition or omission of *passages* is, I may add, a variation of an entirely different order. If a reciter or commentator came across, in another manuscript, an additional passage, there was every chance of his copying it down somewhere, either in the margin of his own copy, or on a supplementary folio ; for there would be, in his mind, always present the possibility that the passage in question was some part of the original that his own manuscript had unaccountably lost. How else, forsooth, could the passage get into the other manuscript ?

In my opinion, therefore, this fact of the concord between *v* and S in *small details*, coupled with the almost entire lack of agreement as regards the additions peculiar to *v* or S, is the strongest argument imaginable for the independence of these two versions, and consequently for the primitive character of their concordant readings. It is needless to point out that this is a factor of supreme importance for the reconstruction of the original.

The text of *v* is throughout of such a character as to inspire confidence. Its conservatism is proved by its preserving archaisms and the *lectio difficilior* (e.g. अभिभो: 1. 2. 144 ; श्लोकाग्रं[1] 1. 2. 177, 189 ; कामया adv. "frankly" 1. 10. 6 ; कन्यस 1. 98. 13 ; समुद्रे 1. 98. 18), often in a corrupt form, while other manuscripts have discarded them in favour of modern forms or easy paraphrases. It is well known that, for purposes of textual reconstruction, the mechanical corruptions of a stupid but faithful copyist are to be preferred to the intelligent copying of a less faithful one.

Again, *v* is often the only version that has preserved the correct reading : e.g. 1. 2. 102 :

> यत्र द्यूतार्णवे मग्नान्द्रौपदी नौरिवार्णवात् ।
> तारयामास तांस्तीर्णाञ्ज्ञात्वा दुर्योधनो नृपः ।
> पुनरेव ततो द्यूते समाह्वयत पाण्डवान् ॥ ;

where the Vulgate version reads (1.3.138 f.) :

> यत्र द्यूतार्णवे मग्नां द्रौपदीं नौरिवार्णवात् ।
> धृतराष्ट्रो महाप्राज्ञः स्नुषां परमदुःखिताम् ॥
> तारयामास तांस्तीर्णाञ्ज्ञात्वा दुर्योधनो नृपः ।
> पुनरेव ततो द्यूते समाह्वयत पाण्डवान् ॥ ;

---

1 Devabodha paraphrases the word with श्लोकसंख्या.

while SASTRI'S reading is (1. 2. 108 f.):

यत्र द्यूतार्णवे मग्ना द्रौपदी नौरिवार्णवे ।
गच्छतश्चातिसृष्टांस्ताञ् ज्ञात्वा दुर्योधनो नृपः ॥
पुनरेव ततो द्यूते समाह्वयत पाण्डवान् ।

[56] It is Draupadī who, like a canoe, rescues the Pāṇḍavas, who were submerged in the ocean of the dice-play. The correctness of the text reading, which is based on that of K, is proved by a stanza in the Sabhā (B. 2. 72. 3)*, which is the source of our stanza:

अप्लवेऽम्भसि मग्नानामप्रतिष्ठे निमज्जताम् ।
पाञ्चाली पाण्डुपुत्राणां नौरेषा पारगाभवत् ॥

Compare also the following three versions of 1. 166. 23 (=B. 1. 176. 27; M. 1. 174. 29):

K_2 $\tilde{N}_2$ V_1 B D=Vulgate	ν=Text	Southern Recension
ततो राजा परिक्रम्य	अन्तर्गतं तु तद्राज्ञः	अन्तःपुरं गतो राजा
यथाकामं यथासुखम् ।	तदा ब्राह्मणभाषितम् ।	श्रुत्वा ब्राह्मणभाषितम् ।
निवृत्तोऽन्तःपुरं पार्थ	सोऽन्तःपुरं प्रविश्याथ	सोऽन्तःपुरं प्रविश्याथ
प्रविवेश महामनाः ॥	संविवेश नराधिपः ।	न सस्मार नराधिपः ।

Obviously, the stumbling block was अन्तर्गतं of the constituted text, which is a *lect. diff.*; here it means "forgotten", a meaning cited in our dictionaries generally as an uncommon meaning given only by Indian lexicographers! Unless one here assumes ν to be original, it is impossible to explain this divergence of ν, γ and S, both of which give a possible though weak sense.

An unbiassed comparative survey of the different versions leads one to the conclusion that the Śāradā (Kaśmīrī) version is certainly the best Northern version, and probably, taken as a whole, the best extant version[1] of the Ādi, a conclusion not based on abstract considerations, but one that may be verified inductively and pragmatically. As is natural, this version is, not by any means, entirely free from corruptions and interpolations. These must be carefully corrected and controlled with the help of the other versions, particularly of those of the rival recension.

SUB-RECENSION γ.

This sub-recension comprises the four versions: Nepālī, Maithilī, Bengali and Devanāgarī, and is represented by a very large number of manu-

* [See now Crit. Ed. 2.64.3.]

[1] Cf. LÜDERS, *Deutsche Literaturzeitung*, 1929. 1141: "Das ist um so mehr zu begrüssen, als *die Kāśmīrī-Version den relativ ältesten Text des Epos bietet.*" (Italics mine!)

scripts; it is, in fact, the most numerous group. Instances of reading which distinguish γ from ν S, have been adduced above (p. LIV), to show the agreement between ν and S against γ. The versions comprising this sub-recension have, moreover, quite a considerable number of "additional" passages in common, which clearly differentiate it from other versions. Noteworthy is the substitution of a lengthy passage of 56 lines (App. I, No. 61) for 1. 105. 4-7, giving a detailed account of the marriage of Pāṇḍu with Kuntī and Mādrī. This detailed account is obviously secondary. On no other supposition can one, it seems to me, account for the circumstance that Ś$_1$ K$_{0-3}$ and S should agree in having a short version for the episode for which K$_4$ Ñ B D substitute a considerably longer and more elaborate version, *both versions being embedded in a portion of descriptive text with minimal variation.* For, while it is inconceivable that two (more or less) independent groups of manuscripts such as Ś$_1$ K$_{0-3}$ and S could arrive at the same short account *independently* of each other, it is, at the same time, extremely improbable that either group (Ś$_1$ K$_{0-3}$ or S) should have copied the short summary from the other, discarding altogether its own original detailed account.

[57] The secondary interrelationship of the various versions comprising subrecension γ is documented sufficiently clearly by their having in common quite a large number of lengthy passages which are missing in ν S, and which, on independent (intrinsic) grounds, have been or may be declared spurious. The following passages, given in App. I, are instances of such interpolations :

(1) No. 12 (Ñ$_{1\text{-}2}$ V$_1$ B D), a *duplicate* and superfluous description of the ocean, a similarly worded description having occurred only in the *preceding* adhyāya ;

(2) No. 14 (K$_4$ Ñ V$_1$ B D except D$_5$, D$_2$ on suppl. fol.), a short Purāṇic story relating how Sūrya resolves to burn the world down, whereupon Garuḍa, at Brahmā's behest, brings his brother Aruṇa, over the east that he might act as Sūrya's charioteer, shielding the world from the heat of the enraged Sun—a *digression* suggested by the casual mention of Aruṇa in adhy. 14 ;

(3) No. 41 (K$_{3\cdot 4}$ Ñ$_{2\cdot 3}$ V$_1$ B D except D$_5$), a list of the hundred sons of Dhṛtarāṣṭra—an *anticipation* of adhy. 108, whose occurrence here (like that of the two following interpolations in the same adhyāya), as has been explained above, is obviously contrary to the original plan of the adhyāya ;

(4) No. 42 (K$_{3\cdot 4}$ Ñ V$_1$ B D except D$_5$), an account of the scene which was enacted in heaven before the birth of Abhimanyu, a story which is really meant to explain the mystery of his premature death ;

(5) No. 43 (K$_4$ Ñ V$_1$ B D except D$_5$), the open secret of the mysterious birth of Karṇa, which is an *anticipation* of adhy. 104 ; and, finally,

(6) No. 81, lines 193-230 (K$_4$ Ñ V$_1$ B D T$_1$), meant to be a summary

of the Jatugṛha episode, which is, however, *a garbled and incoherent* version of the original story.

The view that ν and γ may stand in genetic relation to each other does not receive much support from the facts of the case. Neither ν nor γ can be derived from the other. Each possesses original features that the other lacks, as is evidenced by their *alternate agreement with* S, even in the matter of petty verbal details. All these coincidences need not, of course, be original. Some could be indeed secondary changes, made independently in the same direction; others again may possibly be explained as the result of contamination. There will remain still an obstinate residue of agreements between ν and S, or between γ and S, that *must* be set down as the expression of the ultimate connection of the respective concordant versions through the lost original source.

Contamination between ν and γ, owing to the contiguity of the areas in which the respective versions were current, was inevitable, and must, in any case, be assumed to have existed; on the other hand, contamination between γ and S cannot be altogether denied.

Particularly interesting is a small group of passages of doubtful character, to which reference has already been made. These are certain passages that are common to γ and S, and are missing in $Ś_1$ K_{0-3} only; in other words, they are found in all manuscripts collated except $Ś_1$ K_{0-3}; for example, the Kaṇikanīti. There is usually other evidence against the passages. Thus the secondary character of the Kaṇikanīti is quite unexpectedly confirmed; firstly, by the illogical repetition in certain Southern manuscripts (T_2 $G_{2\cdot4\cdot5}$) of two preceding adhyāyas (129-130); and, secondly, from the fact there is no reference to the Kaṇikanīti in Kṣemendra's *Bhāratamañjarī*, in the Javanese version, as also in Devabodha's [58] commentary. It may, of course, happen that in particular cases there is no collateral (confirmatory) evidence of this character available; e.g. in the puerile account of the birth of Duḥśalā (App. I, No. 63). Here the evidence of documentary and intrinsic probability is almost equally balanced; and documentary probability points in one direction, while intrinsic probability points in the other.

I have in such cases hesitatingly followed ν ($=Ś_1$ K), taking into account, on the one hand, the superiority of ν in general trustworthiness, and, on the other hand, the special characteristics of γ and S, which are versions rather of the *inclusive* than of the exclusive type, prone to amplification and elaboration. Fortunately for us such cases are comparatively rare.

The rejection, on the evidence of ν alone, of the whole of the incoherent adhy. 139 of the Bombay edition (our App. I, No. 80), an adhyāya which contains only some needless repetition, besides minor absurdities, would not have called forth any comment from me, but for the fact that with its omission disappears the only reference, I think, in the whole epic to this alleged installation of Yudhiṣṭhira as heir apparent to the throne of Hāstinapura. The Kaśmīrī version, which omits the entire adhyāya containing the reference, unexpectedly justifies the indignant outburst of HOLTZMANN (*Das Mahābhārata*, Bd. 2, p. 33) : "Geradezu Fälschung ist es, wenn 1, 139, 1=5517 behauptet wird, der blinde *Dhṛtarāshṭra* habe mit Uebergehung seiner eigenen Söhne den *Yudhishṭhira* zum Kronprinzen (*yuvarāja*) ausrufen lassen." One of the main objects in interpolating this adhyāya seems to have been to exonerate Arjuna from the blame or sin of fighting with his own guru (Ācārya Droṇa) in the Great War, by making the Ācārya himself exact from his pupil in the presence of all his kinsfolk—for no reason that is adduced or can be seen—the solemn but senseless promise that he (Arjuna), when challenged, would not refuse to fight with Droṇa. Cf. B. 1. 139. 13 :

आचार्यदक्षिणां देहि ज्ञातिग्रामस्य पश्यतः ।
ददानीति प्रतिज्ञाते फाल्गुनेनाब्रवीद्गुरुः ।
युद्धेऽहं प्रतियोद्धव्यो युध्यमानस्त्वयानघ ।
तथेति च प्रतिज्ञाय द्रोणाय कुरुपुंगवः ।
उपसंगृह्य चरणौ स प्रायादुत्तरां दिशम् ।

There is no reference to this alleged promise in the sequel. And originally a different solution of the dilemma was obviously imagined. To Arjuna's question (Gītā 2. 4) :

कथं भीष्ममहं संख्ये द्रोणं च मधुसूदन ।
इषुभिः प्रतियोत्स्यामि पूजार्हावरिसूदन ॥

the reply of Bhagavān Śrī Kṛṣṇa is (Gītā 2. 19, 32, 38) :

य एनं वेत्ति हन्तारं यश्चैनं मन्यते हतम् ।
उभौ तौ न विजानीतो नायं हन्ति न हन्यते ॥
अथ चेत्त्वमिमं धर्म्यं संग्रामं न करिष्यसि ।
ततः स्वधर्मं कीर्तिं च हित्वा पापमवाप्स्यसि ॥
सुखदुःखे समे कृत्वा लाभालाभौ जयाजयौ ।
ततो युद्धाय युज्यस्व नैवं पापमवाप्स्यसि ॥

[59] ARCHETYPE ε

This archetype is represented, in our critical apparatus, by the three closely allied versions Nepālī, Maithilī and Bengali ; probably together with Uriyā (belonging to Orissa), of which version, however, no manuscripts were available for collation.

The Nepālī Version.

The Nepālī version is represented in our critical apparatus by the three manuscripts $\tilde{N}_1$, $\tilde{N}_2$ and $\tilde{N}_3$.[1] The version is closely allied to the Bengali, with which the agreement of one or the other of the three manuscripts is almost constant. That even the manuscripts of distant Nepal are not wholly free from contamination from some Southern source or sources (direct or indirect) follows, for instance, from 224*, 263*, 819*, 991*, 998*, 1096*, 1246*, 1470*, 1569*, 1748*, 1768*, 1788*, 1828*, 1910*, 1957*, 2133*, etc., etc. as also passage No. 112 of App. I—interpolations common to S and some of the Nepālī manuscripts. One of these manuscripts ($\tilde{N}_3$) happens to be the *oldest* of the dated manuscripts (A.D. 1511) belonging to our critical apparatus.*

The Maithilī Version.

Of the Maithilī version, which is the version of North Bihar, only one manuscript (V_1) was collated for this edition. V_1 and K agree sporadically against all other manuscripts (cf. for instance, 1. 1. 8, 49, 162), but such agreements are few and far between, and it would not be safe to draw from them any far-reaching conclusion regarding the relationship of V_1 and K. As in 306*, 321*, 328*, 346*, 378*, 418*, 450*, 541*, V_1 agrees, on the other hand, with the typical Bengali-Devanāgarī group against all other manuscripts. V_1 contains 1548*, a Southern passage, found otherwise only in Dn $D_{1\cdot 4\cdot 5}$

The Bengali Version.

The Bengali version of sub-recension γ was studied more carefully than either the Nepālī or Maithilī. The study of this version was facilitated by the extreme courtesy and kindness of Pandit Vidhushekhara BHATTACHARYA, who has, now for many years, kindly and unselfishly supervised the work of our collation centre at the Visvabharati, a centre organised by Professor M. WINTERNITZ, when he was residing at Bolpur as a Guest Professor in Rabindranath TAGORE's University. With the co-operation of a select batch of advanced students, Pandit Vidhushekhara has been good enough to supply the Institute regularly with carefully prepared collations of a large number of valuable old Bengali manuscripts in the rich collection of the Visvabharati, as also of other manuscripts placed at his disposal by different Bengali Institutes and scholars, among the latter, my kind friend Professor Sushil Kumar DE, of the University of Dacca. Of the large number of manuscripts thus collated, ultimately five were selected for inclusion in the critical apparatus

---

[1] I may mention here that, unfortunately, in the footnotes to the constituted text, towards the end of this volume, the diacritical mark of Ñ has broken off in many places; but, on examining the passages carefully I found that the context almost invariably shows whether one has to read N or Ñ.

* [See now Epic Studies VII *infra.*]

of the edition. Notwithstanding considerable variation in these manuscripts as regards petty verbal details, the material appears sufficient to settle the text of this important version.

[60] The Bengali version is closely allied to the Vulgate, but is unquestionably superior to the latter in so far that it is happily free from a large number of late accretions which encumber the Vulgate. Of such "omissions", exhibiting the superiority of the Bengali version, the following will serve as illustrations :

(1) The *entire* Brahmā-Gaṇeśa complex in adhy. 1, of which the Bengali version contains not the remotest trace. The spurious character of this passage has been discussed and demonstrated so often that it is unnecessary to dilate upon it here.[1]

(2) The short dialogue of 8 lines (71*) between Paraśurāma and the shades of his ancestors, in the beginning of adhy. 2, which is *wholly unnecessary* here, and is, as a matter of fact, only an excerpt from a detailed description of the principal Indian tīrthas, which occurs in the Araṇya (B. 3. 83. 29 ff.).*

(3) A short passage of only six lines (cf. App. I, No. 13), which represents a somewhat feeble attempt (as unnecessary as it is unsuccessful) to fill out an *apparent* lacuna in the original.[2]

(4) A long interpolation (App. I, No. 78) of 119 lines in adhy. 138 (Bom. ed.), which gives an inflated account of the defeat and the ultimate capture of Drupada by the Pāṇḍavas. It is one of the miniature Bhārata-yuddhas—mere by-play for the benefit of the gallery—which expand and embellish the Southern recension and the Vulgate. The older version disposes of the battle in two lines, which, taking everything into consideration, is after all perhaps not a very inadequate treatment, as already remarked.

(5) More than usual interest attaches to another omission in the Bengali version, which concerns a well-known and popular scene describing the discomfiture of Karṇa at Draupadī's svayaṁvara, which is commonly believed to be one of the main reasons why he always entertained feelings of such deep and implacable hatred towards Kṛṣṇā (Draupadī), and lost thereafter no opportunity to hurt and humiliate her.

This passage deserves a detailed consideration. Ramesh Chandra DUTT, who had to make a very careful selection of the incidents of the epic in compressing the story, has made this scene the centre of his poetic account of

---

[1] Cf. p. LIII. footnote 1, above.

* [See now Crit. Ed. 3.81.24 ff.]

[2] See F. BELLONI-FILIPPI, "L'episodio di Kadrū e di Vinatā nell' edizione critica del Mahābhārata" (Traduzioni di epica indiana), published in the Ascoli Memorial Volume, *Silloge Linguistica* (Torino 1930).

the marriage of Draupadī, and given a vivid rendering of the passage in his *Epic of the Bharatas* :

> " Uprose Karna, peerless archer, proudest of the archers he,
> And he went and strung the weapon, fixed the arrows gallantly,
> Stood like Surya in his splendour and like Agni in his flame,—
> Pandu's sons in terror whispered, Karna sure must hit the aim !
> But in proud and queenly accent Drupad's queenly daughter said :
> ' Monarch's daughter, born a Kshatra, Suta's son I will not wed.'
> Karna heard with crimsoned forehead, left the emprise almost done,
> Left the bow already circled, silent gazed upon the Sun ! "

The situation is, undoubtedly, full of dramatic possibilities. Just at the moment when the prize was going to be snatched away from the heroes of the epic by an upstart, [61] the brave little Draupadī comes to the rescue and snubs openly, in the presence of the assembled princes, the semi-divine bastard, the understudy of the Villain of the piece, the unwanted suitor, who thereupon withdraws discomfited ; and everybody breathes a sigh of relief. A tense scene !

Unfortunately, this melo-dramatic interlude, to judge by the documentary evidence, appears to be the handiwork of a very late Vyāsaïd, as it is found only in K_4 $\tilde{N}_2$ Dn $D_{2.\ 4.\ 5}$, that is, one manuscript of the K group, one Nepālī manuscript, and three composite Devanāgarī manuscripts, besides the Nīlakaṇṭha version ! All of these are late and inferior or conflated manuscripts. It is missing, on the other hand, not only in the Śāradā version and the Southern recension (as in the case of many of the interpolations of the Vulgate), but for once, *also in the entire Bengali version* !

It might seem a piece of sheer vandalism or perverseness to omit this seemingly beautiful little passage, which has won its way into people's hearts, from any edition of the Great Epic of India, relying merely upon documentary evidence. A little reflection will, however, convince any one that the loss to the epic is not as serious as one might, at first, suppose, since it is a palpably *faked and thoroughly unreal* situation. If one thinks about it at all, one fails to understand how Draupadī, who was, after all, then only an unexperienced maiden in her teens, had recognized the King of Aṅgas (whom she had probably never seen before) and known him for the son of a coachman, unfit to wed a princess. He had been invited by her father. At least he was given a seat of honour among the princes. He is specifically named by Dhṛṣṭadyumna among the suitors (1. 177. 4). Moreover, it does not appear as if the bride elect had much choice or voice in the matter, at the time of these elaborate and formal state functions notwithstanding that they were called *svayaṁvaras*. She had to wed any competitor who excelled in the particular proficiency test which had been arranged by her father or guardian. She was *vīryaśulkā* : she was given by her guardian to the highest bidder, the price paid being heroism, or rather proficiency in marksmanship. This is quite evident from the words of Yudhiṣṭhira, addressed later to the Purohita of Drupada (1. 185. 23 f.) :

प्रदिष्टशुल्का द्रुपदेन राज्ञा सानेन वीरेण तथानुवृत्ता ।
न तत्र वर्णेषु कृता विवक्षा न जीवशिल्पे न कुले न गोत्रे ॥
कृतेन सज्येन हि कार्मुकेण विद्धेन लक्ष्येण च संनिसृष्टा ।
सेयं तथानेन महात्मनेह कृष्णा जिता पार्थिवसंघमध्ये ॥

We accordingly find, as a matter of fact, that without murmur or hesitation, she follows an unknown and apparently undistinguished Brahman boy—Arjuna in disguise—who happens to have hit the mark. She does not know him from Adam, but she makes no inquiries about his status or lineage. Even if this were regarded as a case of romantic love at first sight for the handsome and heroic bowman (which it certainly is not), she never opens her lips when Yudhiṣṭhira proposes that she should be the common wife of the five brothers, which must have shattered her romance to smithereens, but quietly submits to (what is made to appear) as a most unusual and unnatural, if not a shocking, proposal, and from which even her old father and brother recoil with perplexity and amazement. It seems to me, therefore, that the documentary evidence is amply supported here by intrinsic probability.

[62] Examples of other important "omissions" in the Bengali version which distinguish it from the Devanāgarī are : 54*, 60*, 71*, 152*, 171*, 274, 277*, 689*, 1171*, 1205*, 1270*, 1614* (proverbs, one of them being a citation from Manu), 1714* (a short list of sacred rivers), 1788*, 1827*, 1841*, all of which occur in the Vulgate, but are missing in the Bengali version.

Occasionally Bengali manuscripts agree in their readings with the Southern recension, standing in opposition to $Ś_1$ K (with or without D); e.g. :

1. 22 B S शुचिं : K (mostly) D (mostly) शिवं.
1. 42 B S आत्मवान् : $K_{0.2-4}$ D (mostly) एव च.
7. 3 B D (mostly) S परान् : K कुलान्.
39. 10 B D (mostly) S ततः : $Ś_1$ K (with a few D) पुनः.
64. 29 Ñ B D S जगाम : K ददर्श, etc., etc., etc.

Other examples have been cited under the description of the K version.

In these cases, I have, as a rule, given preference to the agreement between B and S, on the postulated principle of the originality of the agreement between independent versions, adopting in the constituted text, the concordant reading ; but owing to the circumstance, that sporadic contamination between B and S, as a whole, cannot be altogether denied and that there are, as a matter of fact, some Bengali manuscripts that stand, palpably, under the influence of the Southern tradition, even in the matter of minor readings, it is impossible to be perfectly certain about the originality of a reading common to B and S. I am, however, of opinion that the probability is always on the side of the concordant reading, though the evidence of this agreement may be rebutted by other considerations, such as intrinsic probability or the evidence of pertinent testimonia.

The Devanāgarī Version.

The Devanāgarī script plays in the Mahābhārata textual tradition the important rôle of being the commonest medium of the contamination of different Mahābhārata versions. A Devanāgarī manuscript of the Mahābhārata may, in fact, contain practically any version or combination of versions.

Of the four "Devanāgarī" scholiasts whose commentaries were collated for the Ādi, Arjunamiśra is certainly an Easterner, and bases his commentary on the Bengali text; Ratnagarbha appears to be a Southerner, and his text is evidently a blend between the Northern and the Southern texts; while Nīlakaṇṭha is quite definitely a Westerner, though he seems to have written his commentary in Benares. The provenance of the fourth and the last commentator mentioned above cannot be determined with certainty; but it might be surmised that Devabodha was a "Northerner"; in any case, his text (to judge by the *lemmata* in his commentary) shows remarkable affinities with the North-western or Kaśmīrī version (v).

Most of the Devanāgarī manuscripts, as already remarked, are eclectic on no recognizable principle: now they approach the Southern tradition (S), now the purer Northern (v). If any one were to maintain that just this composite text was the original, a patchwork of disjointed ancient passages, which had later split up into the Northern and Southern recensions (as might easily be implicitly assumed by the protagonist, say, of Nīlakaṇṭha's version), it would be a thesis difficult to substantiate. It [63] seems more natural to regard, as already observed, the Devanāgarī as a sort of "vulgar" script (like the Latin, in Europe), the script understood by the savants all over India, into which many of the local versions were, from time to time, transcribed, a circumstance which facilitated contamination and conflation.

It has been mentioned above that the Devanāgarī version contains many more interpolations than even the Bengali. It would be no exaggeration to say that the Devanāgarī manuscripts, which are by far the most numerous of Mahābhārata manuscripts, are, at the same time, the *least important* of them, with the possible exception of those of the adjoining version, Telugu.

The Devanāgarī Version of Arjunamiśra.

This is in a sense a misnomer, because this Devanāgarī version, as already remarked, is nothing but a Devanāgarī transcript of the Bengali version.

Instances of the concord of B and Da will be found under : 1. 4. 6 ; 7. 13 ; 8. 22 ; 10. 2 ; 11. 7 ; 26. 38 ; 33. 25 f. ; 111. 4 ; 141. 21 ; 143. 6 ; etc., etc.

The name of the commentary is variously given as (*Mahā*) *Bhāratārtha-(pra)dīpikā* and *Bhāratasaṁgrahadīpikā*.[1] The commentary on the different parvans has been handed down singly or in groups of a few parvans at a time. Complete manuscripts of the commentary are said to exist in Bengal, but even there they are not common. The manuscripts, which are written in Bengali or Devanāgarī characters, have various dates in the seventeenth or later centuries ; the earliest hitherto reported date is V. Saṁvat 1676 (ca. A.D. 1620). Arjunamiśra, who styles himself Bhāratācārya in the colophons of his commentary, was the son of Īśāna, who was a "Reciter" (pāṭhaka) or "Prince of Reciters" (pāṭhakarāja) of the Mahābhārata, and who appears to have borne, like his son, the title Bhāratācārya. Arjunamiśra is cited by name by Nīlakaṇṭha once in his commentary on the Mahābhārata (*ad* B. 3. 291. 70) and was, therefore, certainly anterior to Nīlakaṇṭha, who belongs to the last quarter of the seventeenth century. Arjuna, in turn, mentions, among his predecessors : Devabodha, Vimalabodha, Śāṇḍilya, Sarvajña-Nārāyaṇa (also known as Nārāyaṇa-Sarvajña or merely Nārāyaṇa). He appears to have based his scholium closely on that of Devabodha, from whose commentary Arjuna often cites, *verbatim* long extracts, without specifically naming the source. Arjuna wrote also a commentary on the Puruṣasūkta, to which he himself refers in the *Dīpikā* on B. 14. 25. 26. TELANG[2] surmises that he is posterior to the Vedantist Śaṁkarācārya ; and HOLTZMANN[3] assigns him to the thirteenth or fourteenth century, both without mentioning any cogent reasons for their assumptions. Arjuna has treated the Harivaṁśa as an integral part of the epic, elaborately defending this position ; his commentary, therefore, embraces the Harivaṁśa also.[4]

[64] Following the example of my predecessors, I have utilized Devanāgarī manuscripts of his commentary and treated his version as a sub-division of the Devanāgarī version. The two Devanāgarī manuscripts utilized by me are, however, extremely corrupt. Moreover, the text they contain is evidently contaminated from the Vulgate, as proved by the glaring discrepancies that exist between the readings of the text and the *lemmata* in the commentary

---

[1] See, for further details, Haraprasada SHASTRI, *A Descriptive Catalogue of Sanskrit Manuscripts in the Collections of the Asiatic Society of Bengal* (Calcutta 1928), Preface, pp. lxixff., HOLTZMANN, *Das Mahābhārata*, 3. 67 f. ; and SUKTHANKAR, "Arjunamiśra," *Dr. Modi Memorial Volume*, p. 565 f.

[2] *The Bhagavadgītā* (S. B. E. vol. 8), p. 204.

[3] *Das Mahābhārata*, 3. 67 f.

[4] Haraprasada SHASTRI, *op. cit.* p. xxxvi, wrongly assumes that it was Arjunamiśra who "boldly made the proposal of including the Harivaṁśa 12,000" in the Mbh. This fact is already implied in the Parvasaṁgraha, which calls Harivaṁśa the Khila and includes it in the list of the 100 sub-parvans !

6

(e. g. 1. 1. 17, 22). This corruption of the Arjunamiśra manuscripts, I could not explain at first, but now it is clear that it is due to their being faulty transcripts of Bengali originals. Two such Bengali manuscripts[1] (unaccompanied by the epic text) were sent to me subsequently by my kind friend Professor Sushil Kumar De of the University of Dacca from the collection of the Dacca University. These manuscripts are far superior, as is but natural, to the Devanāgarī manuscripts. It would seem, therefore, expedient to secure and use, whenever possible, good old Bengali manuscripts of Arjunamiśra's commentary, treating his version as an offshoot of the Bengali version (with the symbol Ba); or, still better, such Bengali manuscripts of his commentary as are unaccompanied by the epic text. The reason of the last precaution will be presently explained.

A word of caution is here necessary in regard to what are cited in the critical notes as the readings of Arjunamiśra. The readings found in the (epic) text accompanying the commentary have, as a rule, been taken to represent the readings of Arjunamiśra. The commentary was consulted by me only occasionally, in case of doubt or difficulty, or when a pāṭhāntara was noticed during a hurried perusal of the commentary. It is, therefore, more than likely that, since the (epic) text of our Arjunamiśra manuscripts is conflated with various types of texts, in particular with the Nīlakaṇṭha type, some errors in our readings have crept in.[2] Such errors can, however, be rectified only by carefully working through the whole commentary word for word, and comparing the *lemmata* with the (epic) text of the manuscripts. Even then one can, of course, be sure only of the words and passages actually cited by the scholiast.

In passing, it may be mentioned that the practice of combining text and commentary in one manuscript is probably not very old. It is almost certain that the autograph copy of the commentator was *not* made up on the tripartite system of combining the epic text and commentary in such a way that [the] text occupies a central strip of the folio, while the commentary is written in two narrow strips, one at the top and the other at the bottom of the folio, which is the prototype of the Bombay *pothi*-form editions. The scholiast must have written his commentary, certainly at first, on separate leaves, especially in the case of voluminous texts like those of the two epics. Accordingly the commentaries of Devabodha and Vimalabodha have been handed down always unaccompanied by the epic text. Those of Arjunamiśra and Nīlakaṇṭha, on the other hand, are generally accompanied by the epic text, but the two Dacca manuscripts (lent to me by Professor De), as was mentioned above, contained only the commentary. The two elements—text and

1 Dacca University Collection, Nos. 989 A, and 2318 (dated Śaka 1689).

2 Cf. Winternitz, *Indol. Prag.* 1. 65; and Sukthankar, "Epic Studies II," *ABI.* 11. 167 f.

commentary—appear to have been combined into the tripartite form by professional scribes. If this combination was done under the supervision of the commentator or at [65] least in his lifetime, there is some chance of the scribe's reproducing, in an approximately correct form, the text of the commentator. But if the combination is made independently of him and especially if made some time after the death of the commentator, there is every chance that the scribe would combine the commentary he was copying with some text known better to himself than to the scholiast. In the latter case, therefore, it must remain doubtful how far the epic text of such a manuscript resembles the text actually commented upon by the scholiast. It is consequently best to use always texts of the commentary unaccompanied by the epic text, though it is an extremely laborious process to collate such a manuscript with any given Mahābhārata text ; but we eliminate in this way automatically all chances of avoidable errors of commission and omission.

The Devanāgarī Version of Nīlakaṇṭha : the Vulgate.

Nīlakaṇṭha, considered until lately, at least in India, as the most trustworthy guide for the exposition of the Mahābhārata, was a Brahmin scholar of Mahārāṣṭra, with the surname Caturdhara (modern Chaudhari), son of Govinda Sūri and Phullāmbikā, residing at Kūrparagrāma (modern Kopargaon) on the Godavari.[1] Nīlakaṇṭha wrote his commentary on the Mahābhārata (and another work called the Gaṇeśagītā), in Benares, in the last quarter of the seventeenth century. He appears to be the author also of a work called *Mantrarahasyaprakāśikā.*

At the beginning of his commentary on the Great Epic, Nīlakaṇṭha tells us that before writing his scholium, the *Bhāratabhāvadīpa*, he had compared many copies of the Mahābhārata, collected *from different parts of India*, with a view to determining the "best" readings and even consulted the scholia of old authorities:

बहून्समाहृत्य विभिन्नदेश्यान्कोशान्विनिश्चित्य च पाठमग्र्यम् ।
प्राचां गुरूणामनुसृत्य वाचमारभ्यते भारतभावदीपः ॥

We accordingly find that he occasionally mentions (in about 125 places) variant readings and additional passages found in different provincial versions (most of which can be identified among the readings of the manuscripts comprising our critical apparatus), and cites (as a rule, without naming the source) the explanations given by other scholiasts — information, scanty though it is, yet of immense interest and value for the history of the received text. *Variants* cited by Nīlakaṇṭha will be found in the footnotes under : 1. 1. 1, 3, 4, 6, 8, 13, 19, 22, 41, 80, 100, 118, 129, 185, 188 ; 2. 6, 64, 243 ;

---

[1] See PRINTZ "Bhāṣā-wörter, in Nīlakaṇṭha's Bhāratabhāvadīpa," Einleitung, *KZ*. 44. 70 ff.

3. 19, 149, 189 ; 4. 1 ; 5. 9 ; 11. 1 ; 13. 2, 29 ; 14. 8, 16 ; 16. 10, 33 (found only in Cd !) ; 18. 11 ; 19. 6 ; 24. 9 ; 27. 35 ; 28. 24 ; 30. 5 (not found elsewhere !), 11; 32. 18 ; 33. 20 ; 38. 30 ; 39. 11 ; 46. 25, 29 (not found elsewhere !); 49. 4, 17 ; 50. 9-12, 17 ; 51. 4 (not found elsewhere !), 5 ; 53. 34 ; 54. 3, 8 ; 55. 3 ; 57. 21, 22, 78 ; 58. 35 f., 50 ; 59. 54 ; 62. 10 ; 68. 38 ; 69. 26 ; 70. 3, 19, 46 ; 71. 31, 51 ; 82. 8 ; 87. 12 ; 88. 22 ; 89. 51 ; 92. 43 ; 102. 23 ; 109. 10, 12, 15 (not found elsewhere !) ; 110. 33 ; 114. 2 ; 117. 9 ; 118. 9 ; 120. 10 (Nīlp समन्वयात् as in text ; om. through oversight ; cf. B. 1. 130. 10) ; 124. 32 ; 125. 2 ; 131. 8 ; 133. 18 ("Gauḍapāṭha") ; 141. 7 ; 143. 12 ; 148. 10 ; 150. 15 ; 153. 3 ; 154. 2, 13 ; 155. 28, 34, 49 ; 158. 14 (mentions Devabodha !), 46 ; 161. 4 (not found elsewhere !) ; 168. 25 ; 169. 20 ; 170. 21 ; 171. 7 ; 178. [66] 9 ; 186. 1 ; 188 colophon (mentions S interpolation, the Nāḷāyanī episode) ; 190. 5 ; 191. 18 ; 192. 10, 27 ; 197. 14 ; 199. 19, 30 ; 206. 2 ; 207. 23 ; 214. 9, 11 ; 218. 31, 33 (not found elsewhere !); 219. 3 ; 221. 5 (not found elsewhere !); 223. 17. The readings of Nīlakaṇṭha's own text are, as a rule, inferior ; our text readings will be found mostly among Nīlakaṇṭha's pāṭhāntaras.

Nīlakaṇṭha refers to Devabodha, Vimalabodha, Arjunamiśra, Ratnagarbha, and Sarvajña-Nārāyaṇa, in the course of his comments on the different parvans. Devabodha, who is one of the oldest (if not *the* oldest) commentators of the Mahābhārata hitherto known, he refers while commenting on 1. 158. 14 (= B. 1. 170. 15.) :

न नंहसाः शृङ्गिणो वा न च देवाञ्जनस्रजः ।
कुबेरस्य यथोष्णीषं किं मां समुपसर्पथ ॥

इति प्राचीनः पाठो देवबोधादिभिर्व्याख्यातत्वात् ।

Not a single word of this stanza, as cited here, is commented on, however, by Devabodha ! The only word in Devabodha's scholium which might possibly have been taken from some reading of the stanza before Devabodha is शकुनाः (= पक्षिणः) and that does not occur in the reading of the stanza cited by Nīlakaṇṭha. The mention of Devabodha by Nīlakaṇṭha here, is, therefore, surely *honoris causa*. Such mistakes by commentators are far too frequent to cause surprise or need comment.[1] It is, however, noteworthy that the reason Nīlakaṇṭha assigns for considering this as an *ancient* variant is that it had been commented on by Devabodha and others. This shows that Nīlakaṇṭha held Devabodha in high esteem, and reckons him among the *ancient authorities*. What Nīlakaṇṭha regards as "ancient" (prācīna) is of course a matter for speculation. Nevertheless I do not think that he would have called Devabodha a "prācīna" commentator, unless the inter-

[1] Cf. KIELHORN, "On the Jainendra Vyākarana", *Ind. Ant.* 10. 75 ; 16. 24 : and SUKTHANKAR, "Miscellaneous Notes on Mammaṭa's Kāvyaprakāśa", *ZDMG*. 66 (1912). 541 f.

val between them was at least four or five centuries. Nīlakaṇṭha refers to Devabodha again in B. 7. 82. 2 : मधुपर्किकाः मधुपर्कसमये पठन्त इति देवबोधः. Arjunamiśra he cites in his comment on B. 3. 291. 70 : जात्यान् त्रिगुणदक्षिणान् इत्यर्जुनमिश्रः.

Since Arjunamiśra also cites Devabodha, we can arrange the three commentators in an incontrovertible sequence ; Devabodha—Arjunamiśra—Nīlakaṇṭha.[1]

The text used or prepared by Nīlakaṇṭha is a smooth and *eclectic* but inferior text, of an inclusive rather than exclusive type, with an inconsiderable amount of Southern element.

As instances of simplification in the Vulgate, I may cite : 1. 2. 144 Text चाभिभोः (Vulg. वा विभो; cf. 1. 13. 20 ; 41. 21) ; 2. 189 श्लोकाग्र्यं (श्लोकानां); 10. 6 कामया (कामं मां; cf. 1. 187. 6); 37. 10 दिवं स्तब्ध्वेव विष्ठितः (शवं स्कन्धे प्रतिष्ठितं); 39. 16 दित्स (देहि); 45. 16 बाल एवाभिजातोऽसि (°भिषिक्तस्त्वं); 62. 12 त्सरु° (सर्व°); 96. 16 शुभ्राणां (सर्वेषां); 122. 5 प्रशृश्वति (हसन्निव); 122. 42 तद्दत्तं (तदेतत्); 139. 18 विलज्जमानेव लता (लज्जमानेव ललना); 150. 8 वसतीः (रजनीः); 221. 1 शुक्रे (वन्हौ); etc., etc.

[67] Instances of the correction of solecisms in the Vulgate are : 1. 2. 93 Text गृह्य (Vulg. गृहीत्वा); 9. 2 चिन्त्य (स्मृत्वा); 119. 8 मा द्रक्ष्यसि (मा द्राक्षीस्त्वं); 181. 25 अहनत् (अवधीत्); 184. 1 ब्रवीहि (वदस्व); etc., etc.

I add a selection of the Southern passages which were interpolated into the Northern recension by Nīlakaṇṭha or by one of his immediate predecessors in the field : 263*, 299*, 473*, 513*, 598*, 700*, 701*, 722*, 857*, 863* 963*, 977*, 1037*, 1054*, 1062*, 1066*, 1069*, 1100*, 1101*, 1169*, 1211*, 1548*, 1768*, 1828*, etc., etc., as also passage No. 56 of App. I.

Nīlakaṇṭha's text has acquired in modern times an importance out of all proportion to its critical value,[2] to the utter neglect of far superior texts, such as the Kaśmīrī or Bengali.

Nīlakaṇṭha's guiding principle, on his own admission, was to make the Mahābhārata a *thesaurus of all excellences* (culled no matter from what source). At the beginning of his commentary on the Sanatsujātīya, Nīlakaṇṭha naïvely remarks (Bom. ed. Udyoga 42) :

---

[1] Many of these facts were communicated by me in a paper read before the International Congress of Orientalists, Leiden (1931), and entitled "Miscellaneous Notes on Mahābhārata Commentators" ; cf. the summary in *Actes dus XVIIIe Congress International des orientalistes* (Leiden 1932), p. 156. [See now Epic Studies—III below.]

[2] Even HOLTZMANN, *Das Mahābhārata,* 3. 74 : "Für die Erklärung der Einzelheiten ist er von grosser Bedeutung".

उद्योगपर्वणि सनत्सुजातीये भाष्यकारादिभिर्व्याख्यातान्संप्रतितनपुस्तकेषु च स्थितान्पाठान् श्लोकांश्च गुणोपसंहारन्यायेनैकीकृत्य व्याख्यायते ।[1]

That Southern manuscripts were utilized by him is incontrovertibly proved, for instance, from the fact that he cites at the end of his comment on Ādi 196 (Bom. ed.), the Nāḷāyanī and Bhaumāśvī episodes (in two adhyāyas), which are *typical* Southern interpolations, not found in any Northern manuscript :

अत्र यत्तद्देवा ददुरित्यादिना त्रिपथगां नदीमिव्यन्तो नारायण्युपाख्यानग्रन्थोऽध्यायद्वयात्मकः क्वचित्पुस्तके पठ्यते ।[2]

Characteristically the scholiast speaks only in general terms (क्वचित्पुस्तके) without furnishing any further information about the manuscripts in question. But, fortunately, he is not always so reticent. Thus he mentions specifically the Bengali version, while commenting on B. 1. 145. 20 (अत्रोत्तरार्धं गौडपाठ एव दृश्यते) and elsewhere ; cf. his notes on B. 3. 119. 3, and on 6. 43. 1 (गीता सुगीता कर्तव्या इत्यादयः सार्धाः पञ्च श्लोकागौडैर्नपठ्यन्ते).

It must be said to his credit that there is at least *one* place where he honestly confesses his inability to understand the confused textual tradition, and that is in his comment on B. 1. 22. 1 :

नागाश्च संविदं कृत्वेति द्वादशश्लोकमध्यायं केचिन्न पठन्ति । कांश्चिदत्रत्यान् श्लोकान्पूर्वत्रैव च पठन्ति । अन्ये तु पञ्चषान्पठन्त्यपीत्यत्र कोशशुद्धिं न प्रतीमः ।[3]

The (printed) editions of Nīlakaṇṭha's version leave much to be desired. They have arbitrarily changed many of the readings and added a certain number of lines which are not found in the Nīlakaṇṭha manuscripts hitherto examined.

Instances of lines of stanzas with which modern Pandits have enriched most of our (printed) Northern editions and which are lacking even in the Nīlakaṇṭha manuscripts, are besides a (Southern) passage of 21 lines given in App. I (No. 112) and another of 9 lines (998*), the following short interpolations :

[68] 27* इदं शतसहस्राख्यं श्लोकानां पुण्यकर्मणाम् ।
उपाख्यानैः सह ज्ञेयं श्राव्यं भारतमुत्तमम् ॥ B. 1. 1. 101 f.

146* संशप्तकानां वीराणां कोट्यो नव महात्मनाम् ।
किरीटिनाभिनिष्क्रम्य गमिता यमसादनम् ॥ B. 1. 2. 261

---

1 Cf. TELANG, *The Bhagvadagitā*, p. 203 f. ; and WINTERNITZ, *Ind. Ant.* 27 (1898). 128.

2 Cf. our note on adhy. 188 (p. 757).

3 Cf. our note on adhy. 19 (p. 132).

148* धृतराष्ट्रस्य पुत्राश्च तथा पाषाणयोधिनः ।
नारायणाश्च गोपालाः समरे चित्रयोधिनः ॥ B. 1. 2. 262

224* शौनकस्तु महासत्त्वः सर्वभार्गवनन्दनः ।
जातस्तपसि तीव्रे च स्थितः स्थिरयशास्ततः ॥ B. 1. 8. 3

314* गुरुर्हि सर्वभूतानां ब्राह्मणः परिकीर्तितः । B. 1. 28. 4

752* मरणं शोभनं तस्य इति विद्वज्जना विदुः । B. 1. 79. 13

1048* उक्त्वा जन्मकुलं मह्य नासि दाशसुतेति च । B. 1. 105. 9

1099* स्वल्पमेव यथा दत्तं दान बहुगुणं भवेत् ।
अधर्म एव विप्रर्षे बहुदुःखफलप्रदः ॥ B. 1. 108. 12

1805* आहरिष्यत्ययं नूनं प्रीतिं वो वर्धयिष्यति । B. 1. 184. 19

1957* इत्युक्त्वा प्रययौ राजन्विदुरः स्वं निवेशनम् । B. 1. 200. 26

2043* आद्यं पशुपतेः स्थानं दर्शनादेव मुक्तिदम् ।
यत्र पापोऽपि मनुजः प्राप्नोत्यभयदं पदम् ॥ B. 1. 217. 35

It would, however, hardly repay, now, the trouble to re-edit, from manuscripts, the version of Nīlakaṇṭha, as there are far better versions that could be edited instead, for instance, the Kaśmīrī.

The manuscripts of the Nīlakaṇṭha version (which show among themselves slight discrepancies) contain a number of lines which are not found in any of the other versions (except occasionally in a few manuscripts of the composite Devanāgarī version) ; e.g. 102*, 147*, 276*, 412*, 493*, 574*, 699*, 765*, 838*, 1270*, 1457*, etc. They belong perhaps to the oral tradition which, at one time, had probably as great value and authority as the written text.

Nīlakaṇṭha has misunderstood the text, and given doubtful, far-fetched or fanciful interpretations at : B. 1. 1. 52 (मनुः=मन्त्रः !), 275 (नकल्कः); 2. 33 (शौनक = वृद्धतम ! ; 17. 12 (कलश); 23. 15 (Vedantic interpretation); 27. 8 (मनःसंहर्षजं); 37. 15 (the difference between हेतु and कारण); 43. 22 (गदैः) 47. 11 (श्वेतकाकीयैः); 50. 3 (ब्रह्माणं=आचार्यं !); 61. 11 (वृकोदरः); 63. 90 (संहिताः); 131. 52 (अवसीदेत); 164. 9 (context); 166. 10 (एकतमं); 232. 1–7, 19 (esoteric meaning) ; etc., etc.

Nīlakaṇṭha's stanza (B. 1. 145. 20) :

प्राज्ञः प्राज्ञप्रलापज्ञः प्रलापज्ञमिदं वचः ।
प्राज्ञं प्राज्ञः प्रलापज्ञः प्रलापज्ञं वचोऽब्रवीत् ॥

which appears to be sheer nonsense is so in fact. No other version, as far as I know, contains this mystifying repetition. The explanation of the stanza by Nīlakaṇṭha is childish, to say the least.

The stanza containing the unintelligible word कुलिङ्ग (v. l. कलिङ्ग) which Nīlakaṇṭha has great difficulty in explaining :

ततो दुर्योधनः शूरः कुलिङ्गस्य मते स्थितः ।
पाण्डवान्विविधोपायै राज्यहेतोरपीडयत् ।

looks uncommonly like one of the kūṭaślokas, said to be interspersed by Vyāsa at different places in his poem, in order to puzzle and confuse his divine amanuensis, but is, un-[69]-fortunately, nothing of the kind. The passage is only one of the common instances of "conflate" readings. The stanza cited above is the Southern variant (473*) of the Northern stanza, which, in our edition, reads (1. 55. 8) :

ततो दुर्योधनः क्रूरः कर्णश्च सहसौबलः ।
तेषां निग्रहनिर्वासान्विविधांस्ते समारभन् ॥

The कुलिङ्गस्य in the former stanza is only a *mislection* of the original कणिङ्कस्य (often mis-written कनिङ्कस्य, कलिङ्गस्य), which is the Southern equivalent कणिकस्य, the reference being, no doubt, to the minister or statesman (mantrin) Kaṇika (named after the famous authority Kaṇika or Kaṇiṅka cited in the Arthaśāstra of Kauṭilya), who appears only once in the epic, and that expressly for the purpose of expounding his political philosophy to the Kauravas.

As another instance of conflation which has had a rather disastrous effect on his text, I may cite Nīlakaṇṭha's version of the story of Dīrghatamas. The addition has been made in such a manner that *one sentence of the original has remained hanging in the air* and cannot be construed at all ! The story begins at B. 1. 104. 9. All goes well till stanza 28 :

अहोऽयं भिन्नमर्यादो नाश्रमे वस्तुमर्हति ।
तस्मादेनं वयं सर्वे पापात्मानं त्यजामहे ॥

Then we read 29 :

इत्यन्योन्यं समाभाष्य ते दीर्घतमसं मुनिम् ।
पुत्रलाभा च सा पत्नी न तुतोष पतिं तथा ॥

"Having spoken thus among themselves, they [*scil.* the inmates of the hermitage] to the anchorite Dīrghatamas. Then that wife also, having (already) obtained sons (?) (from him) did not (seek to) please the husband."

Bhīṣma, who is narrating the story, then goes on quite unconcernedly to speak about the wife (of Dīrghatamas) Pradveṣī or Pradviṣantī ; about the maryādā made by the exasperated Dīrghatamas, and so on. But what the inmates of the hermitage (āśramavāsinaḥ) did to Dīrghatamas, we never learn from the Vulgate. All modern translators try to eke out a sense by interpolating into the text some words to complete the sense. A reference to the constituted text and the critical notes will, however, show that the text of the Vulgate is *conflated ;* it is a most clumsy blend of interpolations *from two entirely different sources* (γ and S), which, as is but natural, alters the situation considerably and confuses the narrative hopelessly. By athetizing either passage we get a tolerable text ; by athetizing both we get the original, which is the constituted text.

The Devanāgarī Version of Ratnagarbha.

The critical notes contain only specimen collations of this version, which is a blend between the Northern and Southern recensions. Like the Telugu manuscripts, which will be described presently, it is eclectic, following now the Northern tradition, now the Southern. It seems to be an attempt to combine the two recensions *by superposition*, like the Kumbhakonam edition. Its composite character may be seen from 24*, 25*, 27*, 114*, 138*, 149*, 170*, etc., etc. It contains the additional passages of the Southern recension, as well as the Gaṇeśa episode, which latter is found only in late Northern [70] (Devanāgarī) manuscripts : exactly like the Kumbhakonam edition. The collation of this version was discontinued after the second adhyāya. The version may be safely ignored as useless for critical purposes.

The Devanāgarī Version of Devabodha.

A commentary older and more important than the *Arthadīpikā* of Arjunamiśra, and one more neglected still, is the *Jñānadīpikā* of Devabodha, cited here as Cd. Devabodha is certainly earlier than Vimalabodha, Arjunamiśra and Nīlakaṇṭha, all of whom cite him with great respect, and probably earlier than Sarvajña-Nārayaṇa and Vādirāja. He is, therefore, most likely, the *earliest commentator* of the Mahābhārata hitherto known, and, in my opinion, also the *best*. The commentary is in any case most valuable, and its evidence, both positive and negative, of supreme importance for the constitution of the text.

The *Jnanadīpika* is a concise ṭīkā ; that is, a running commentary, explaining, as a rule, only the difficult words and passages in the text. Occasionally it offers explanations of constructional obscurities and grammatical difficulties, and gives the gist of passages ; in the latter case, usually, under citation of entire verses (i.e. half ślokas) from the text. The extent of the commentary on the Ādi is given in one manuscript as 1400 granthas. The homage which Arjuna pays to Devabodha in the Introduction to his scholium is not a mere matter of form. Arjuna has in fact based his commentary largely on that of his predecessor. He has copied very large portions of Devabodha's commentary, sometimes *verbatim*, sometimes in extract. Moreover even when the two commentaries differ, the influence of Devabodha is plainly discernible. In fact, the *Arthadīpikā* may be considered as a *revised and enlarged edition* of the *Jñānadipikā.* The similarity of the names is suggestive and worthy of note.

Unlike the commentaries of Arjunamiśra, Nīlakaṇṭha and Ratnagarbha, that of Devabodha is unaccompanied by the epic text. The question what was Devabodha's text cannot, therefore, be answered with any high degree of certainty. The entire Southern recension and even the Vulgate may, however, be definitely ruled out. There remain the Bengali, Śāradā and "K" versions. With the latter two, the pratīkas of Devabodha seem to show greater affinity than with the Bengali version. For instance, Devabodha has no comment on any of the six adhyāyas (including the Kaṇikanīti) of the central subrecension (γ), which are missing in Śāradā and K. Worthy of special note is the absence of all reference to the Kaṇikanīti in Devabodha's commentary, since the passage has evoked lengthy comments from both Arjunamiśra and Nīlakaṇṭha. Still greater probative value has an addition which is peculiar to the Kaśmīrī version. This version adds at the very end of the Ādi a supplementary and superfluous adhyāya,—an addition which is only a variant of the well-known Purāṇic tale of Śvetaki's sacrifice, occurring earlier in the course of the same parvan. Curiously enough, the king who is called Śvetaki in the first version is here called Śvetaketu ! That the version of Devabodha contained this additional adhyāya is revealed by the concluding remark of Devabodha's commentary on the Ādi : श्वेतकिरेव श्वेतकेतुरिति नाम This remark will not apply to any version which has not the additional adhyāya peculiar to the Kaśmīrī version. These considerations tend to show that the version of Devabodha was of the Śāradā-K type. And the inference is confirmed by many minor agreements, which need not be cited here.

[71] *The Composite Devanāgarī Version.*

The fourteen manuscripts (D_{1-14}) comprising this version are *mischcodices* of small trustworthiness and of no special value for critical purposes. Consequently, half of them (D_{8-14}) were discontinued already after adhyāya 2. The characteristics of these manuscripts may be briefly noticed here.

D_1 is akin to Dn and looks uncommonly like a Nīlakaṇṭha manuscript *minus* the commentary. Yet it differs conspicuously from the ordinary Nīlakaṇṭha manuscripts by the unaccountable omission of the *entire* Brahmā-Gaṇeśa complex (that is, both the visit of Brahmā and the employment of Gaṇeśa as a scribe, which arises out of the visit) as well as the description of the battle in which the Pāṇḍavas capture Drupada and hand him over as gurudakṣiṇā to their preceptor, Ācārya Droṇa (App I, No. 78). The omission of these episodes points rather in the direction of Bengal, since Kaśmir is excluded by the mass of other interpolations which D_1 contains, as also by the almost complete lack therein of readings peculiar to $Ś_1$ K. The manuscript may be a blend of Bengali and some composite Devanāgarī manuscript or manuscripts.—D_2 (like D_5) is akin to K_{3-6} and might have been with advantage classed with them; see, for instance, the critical apparatus pertaining to the list of the contents of the Araṇyaparvan in adhy. 2.—D_3 is palpably under Southern influence, to prove which it is sufficient to point out that it transposes the Śakuntalā and Yayāti episodes, a transposition which is quite peculiar to the Southern tradition.—D_4 contains notably large additions from Southern manuscripts, additions which are either entered on the margin or, when the marginal space would not suffice, written on supplementary folios. The Southern influence is illustrated by the following passages. 587*, 594*, 596*, 598*, 599*, 602*, 603*, 604*, 605*, 609*, 610*, 611*, 612*, 613*, 617*, 621*, 623*, 624*, 628*, 629*, 630*, 633*, 634*, 635*, 637*, 670*, 671*, 713*, 715*, 1255*, 1256*, 1257*, and scores of others. Cf. also the following passages given in App. I : 35, 46-48, 52, 53, 55, 56, 59, 64, 67-69, etc., etc.—D_5 (like D_2) often stands in opposition to other manuscripts of this composite class, agreeing with K_{3-6}, with which it might have been with advantage classed. Like K_{4-6}, it contains Southern additions as well, e.g. 1565*, 1579*, 1580*, etc., and passage No. 89 of App. I.—The manuscripts $D_{6.7}$ were discontinued after adhy. 53. Frequently they are found to be in opposition to the Vulgate and agreeing with the manuscripts of the ε group. They also show 230*, which is a Southern passage.

D_{8-14}, as already remarked, were collated only *as specimens* for the first two adhyāyas and *discontinued* thereafter.—Of these, $D_{8-12.14}$ are palpably under Southern influence, as is evidenced by their containing one or the other of the following typical Southern insertions : 18*, 21*, 22*, 24*, 32*, 42*, 45*, 48*, 49*, 56*, 80*, 81*, 89*, 114*, 117*, 138*, 149*, 170*.—D_{13}, which is a fragmentary manuscript, beginning almost at the end of adhy. 1, is used in this edition practically only for adhy. 2, as it is discontinued at the end of that adhyāya. The text shows strong affinities with the version of Arjunamiśra.— The text of D_{14} is a complex. It contains some old readings such as are preserved only in the Kaśmīrī manuscripts, but also an extraordinarily large number of individual readings, not found elsewhere (cf. 1. 1. 50, 63 ; 2. 101, etc). At the same time, it is contaminated from some Southern source, perhaps the Malayālam version !

[72] The Devanāgarī manuscripts of the Mahābhārata in the Tanjore Library seem to have been all copied during the regime of the Maratha Chiefs of Tanjore, and are a blend of the Northern and Southern recensions, and as such, of little value for text-critical purposes.

The Telugu Version.

The Telugu version, situated as it is on the boundary line which divides the Northern from the Southern recension, was particularly open to contamination from the Northern tradition. We accordingly find that the majority of Telugu manuscripts are *eclectic on no recognizable principles*; presenting somewhat the aspect of a mosaic of the texts of the Northern and Southern recensions, not unlike the Kumbhakonam edition. T_1 is one of the extremely few Southern manuscripts which contain the (Northern) salutational stanza नारायणं नमस्कृत्य etc. For the Northern element in the make-up of T_1, cf. 29*, 30*, 96*, 97*, 98*, 106*, etc., etc. As compared with T_1, T_2 shows a *purer* Southern tradition and has distinct leanings towards the Grantha version.—T_3 only replaces the fragmentary manuscripts T_2, which breaks off at the end of adhy. 181.

Important variants of one other Telugu manuscript (Tanjore 11809) are now given by Professor P. P. S. SASTRI in his edition of the Southern recension. It does not differ appreciably from our Telugu manuscripts.

The Grantha Version.

The Grantha version is the version of the Tamil country, and is written in the so-called Grantha script. It is one of the two important Southern versions, the other being the Malayālam. The Grantha version—to judge by the manuscripts utilized for the Critical Edition, and for Professor P. P. S. SASTRI's Southern Recension— is more heavily interpolated than the Malayālam, and is also more influenced, on the whole, by the Northern recension.

For the beginning of the Ādi, we get, temporarily, the sub-groups G_{1-3} and G_{4-6}, but soon the configuration changes to $G_{1.\ 2.\ 4.\ 5}$ versus $G_{3.\ 6}$. The latter group ($G_{3\cdot6}$) represents the purer Southern tradition, agreeing with M against the other Southern manuscripts, whereas the four MSS. $G_{1\cdot2\cdot4\cdot5}$ are not merely heavily interpolated but stand palpably under Northern influence. All Grantha manuscripts are probably *contaminated* (*directly or indirectly*) *from Northern sources* in different degrees. G_6 shows, on the whole, little Northern influence, but 419*, 494*, 693*, 1310*, 1312*, 1885*, 1975*, and passage No. 73 of App. I, show that even G_6 is probably not entirely free from contamination, since all these (Northern) passages are missing in M.

SASTRI's edition of the Southern recension gives the (most important) variants of five Grantha manuscripts of which three, क, ख and ञ (the latter being SASTRI's "principal text") are identical with our G_4, G_5 and G_6 respectively. Extracts from a Grantha manuscript belonging to the Royal Asiatic Society of Great Britain and Ireland (Whish Collection, No. 65) have been given by Professor WINTERNITZ[1] and compared with the text of the Bombay edition (Śaka 1799). The passages which differ from the Bombay edition [73] have been underlined in his extracts, and the corresponding passages of the latter are given opposite each line : a convenient arrangement which shows, at a glance, the relation of the two texts to each other for the

[1] *Ind. Ant.* 1898. 69 ff., 92 ff., 124 ff.

passages excerpted.[1]

The clearest proof[2] of the contamination of $G_{1\cdot2\cdot4\cdot5}$ from some Northern source is furnished by 294*, a Northern passage, added in this sub-group *irrelevantly* before 1. 20. 1. The two lines comprising this passage must have been interpolated in a remote ancestor of $G_{1\cdot2\cdot4\cdot5}$ by a clumsy scribe, who had missed the right place by four stanzas, and have remained there ever since, fortunately. Another rather transparent interpolation in $G_{1\cdot2\cdot4\cdot5}$ from a late Northern source is a passage referred to already, No. 14 of App. I, which describes the circumstances under which Aruṇa becomes the charioteer of the Sun, an *irrelevant digression.* Cf. also 1373*, 1375*, 1377*, and passage No. 76 of App. I.

The sub-group contains an amazingly large number of interpolations, which have not been found, so far, elsewhere, and of which a few may be mentioned as illustrations: 320*, 322*, 326*, 330*, 337*, 345*, 351* (third line!), 357*, 363*, 364*, 368*, 371*, 373*, 382*, 386*, 387*, 388*, 406*, 519*, 584*, 636*, 705*, 706*, 741*, 755*, etc., etc.

But the Grantha version itself inclined to admit freely new lines. Instances of rather lengthy interpolations of G are furnished by passages No. 35-39, 73 and 93 of App. I. Most of the interpolations are however short, consisting, as a rule, of less than 10 lines, e.g. 500*, 501*, 502*, 504*, 507*, 509*, 510*, 511*, 520*, 552*, 569*, 570*, 693*, 814*, 841*, 897*, 1259*, 1268*, 1312*, 1313*, 1316*, 1319*, 1320*, 1372*, 1435*, 1441*, 1447*, 1448*, 1452*, 1453*, 1476*, 1489*, 1531*, 1541*, 1542*, 1543*, 1544*, 1545*, 1547*, 1550*, 1551*, 1596*, 1597*, 1604*, 1631*, 1658*, 1666*, 1707*, 1868*, 2009*, 2040*, etc., etc.

G_7, which is one of the few Southern manuscripts containing the (Northern) mantra नारायणं नमस्कृत्य etc. is, like T_1, a *typical* blend of the Northern and Southern tradition, and was, on that account, discontinued after adhy. 2. Its composite character may be seen from: 29*, 30*, 96*, 97*, 98*, 106*, 145*, etc., etc.

The Malayālam Version.

This is the version of Malabar, the Southernmost extremity of India. It is, in my opinion, *the best Southern version.* It is not only largely free from the interpolations of σ (=T G), but appears to be also *less influenced by N than σ,* wherein lies its importance for us.

---

[1] The collation of the text is accompanied by notes in which WINTERNITZ draws attention to the most striking points of difference between the two versions, without entering into a full discussion of all the various readings. The notes contain nevertheless many valuable text-critical observations.

[2] Cf. SUKTHANKAR, "Epic Studies III", *ABI*. 11. 269.

Instances of additional passages found in G (with or without T), but missing in M, are : 443*, 500*, 501*, 502*, 504*, 507*, 509*, 510*, 511*, 520*, 552*, 569*, 570*, 691*, 693*, 814*, 839*, 841*, 897*, 1259*, 1268*, 1310*, 1312*, 1313*, 1316*, 1319*, 1320*, 1447*, 1448*, 1452*, 1453*, 1476*, 1489*, 1523*, 1541*, 1542*, 1543*, 1544*, 1545*, 1547*, 1550*, 1551*, 1563*, 1566*, 1596*, 1604*, 1658*, 1666*, 1751*, 1868*, 1872*, 1893*, 1896*, 1935*, 2006*, 2007*, 2009*, 2021*, 2024*, 2032*, 2040*, 2052*, 2053*, 2062**, 2071*, 2106*, etc. ; and the following passages of App. I : 35-39 and 73.

[74] M_1 often stands in antagonism to M_{2-4}, sometimes agreeing with manuscripts of the Northern recension ; and is, therefore, an untrustworthy guide. $M_{1.2.4}$ are incomplete manuscripts, ending with adhy. 53 ; in other words, with the Āstīkaparvan. M_{6-8} replace these manuscripts in the Saṁbhavaparvan, which is the name under which the *remaining portion* of the Ādi is known in the Southern recension. This practice of writing the two portions of the Ādi in separate volumes is worthy of note, as an archaic survival. It is, in my opinion, the reflex of some half-forgotten factor connected with the compilation of the Ādi, and seems to me to be text-critically highly important. It should seem that *the South has never completely assimilated the (Northern) division of the epic into the conventional eighteen parvans.*

Instances of additional passages which distinguish M from all other versions are : 407*, 453*, 800*, 801*, 842*, 970*, 1051*, 1052*, 1278*, 1437*, 1438*, 1613*, 1678*, 1709*, 1871*, etc.

M_{6-8} constitute really one manuscript, as is proved, for instance by their repeating the following indubitable clerical errors : (i) in 1. 85. 25, M_{6-8} *repeat* inconsequentially the words पूजयन्तीह लोके नासाधवः; (ii) in 1, 154. 13, they omit 13^a and 13^d, transposing 13^b and 13^c, which they read as one line ; (iii) in 1. 193. 1, they all read the meaningless क्षत्तारं विश्रुतं दुरं (Text वाकारं विदुरं प्रति); (iv) they read 1. 213. 4^a-5^b erroneously after stanza 31 of adhy. 212 ; (v) in 1. 213. 6, $M_{6\cdot 8}$ omit the words च यशस्विनः of the text, for which M_7 shows a lacuna. Instances of readings peculiar to M_{6-8} are (reference to adhyāya and śloka) :

58. 6 M_{6-8} समाजग्मुः : rest समापेतुः.
106. 2 M_{6-8} समतोषयत् : rest समतर्पयत्.
157. 9 M_{6-8} शंकरस्तुष्टः : rest भगवांस्तुष्टः.

Conflation in M_{6-7} is suggested by 1. 209. 19, where $M_{6.7}$ have both the Northern reading and the Southern reading.

It may be added that the cases cited are merely by way of illustrations. A careful study of the critical apparatus would easily furnish scores of other instances.

This version has several *striking agreements with* Ś$_1$, a fact all the more impressive, because M, a Southern version, hails from the province at the opposite end of India from the province of Ś$_1$, a Northern version ; for instance, Malayālam supports Ś$_1$ (against T G) in omiting the spurious parts of adhy. 128-129 of the Bombay edition.

WINTERNITZ has published, in Devanāgarī transcript, portions of a fragmentary Malayālam manuscript belonging to the Royal Asiatic Society of Great Britain and Ireland (Whish Collection, No. 158), which contains twelve chapters of the Saṁbhavaparvan.[1] The extracts contain the beginning of the Pūruvaṁśānukīrtana (our adhy. 90), the passage referring to Śakuntalā and the birth of Bharata (our 1. 90. 27-34), and the end of the adhyāya (our 1. 90. 93-96). The manuscript correctly shows the Southern transposition of the Śakuntalā and Yayāti episodes. It is interesting to observe that this manuscript also further shows the *anticipation* of 1. 89. 1-16, before the Yayāti episode, which is found in our Malayālam manuscripts (cf. note on p. 282) and in the conflated MSS. G$_{4\cdot5}$ (cf. note on p. 992), and which is text-critically highly important.

[75] Readings or features which are peculiar to M or such as distinguish M from G (with or without T) will be found under : 1. 1. 3. 35, 45, 122, 128, 168, 176, 179, 184, 189 ; 2. 160 ; 4. 4 ; 7. 10 ; 24. 1 ; 36. 3 ; 39. 2, 16 ; 53. 31 ; 54, 6, 7 ; 57. 81 ; 61. 98 ; 67. 28 ; 68. 16, 51 ; 69. 9 ; 73. 33 ; 77. 9 ; 78. 23 ; 80. 2 ; 84, 14 ; 86. 1 ; 92. 45 ; 93. 14 ; 94. 9, 27, 32 ; 95. 8 ; 96. 2, 57; 98. 5, 12 ; 113. 22 ; 117. 5, 23 ; 119. 30 ; 123. 39 ; 129. 9-11 (om. in M) ; 132. 1 ; 136. 1 ; 138. 10 ; 139. 11 (om. in M) ; 142. 19 ; 150. 10, 26 ; etc., etc.

With regard to the versions described above, it must be frankly admitted that they do not, by any means, form water-tight compartments. The isolectional boundaries, as is natural, do not coincide, but are independent of each other ; in other words, the textual peculiarities, which are, in final analysis, the real basis of our classification, never have, as a matter of fact, an identical area of distribution. The manuscripts cannot always be squeezed into the same moulds consistently. Thus, for instance, in the beginning of the Ādi, the Grantha version, as already remarked, shows two sub-groups G$_{1-3}$ and G$_{4-6}$; but soon the configuration changes and, from about adhy. 25 onwards, we get the grouping G$_{1\cdot2\cdot4\cdot5}$: G$_{3\cdot6}$. Not only that. Individual manuscripts, groups, or even versions often overstep the boundaries of their particular recension. Thus, for example, on the one hand, G$_{1\cdot2\cdot4\cdot5}$. frequently agree with Ñ V$_1$ B D ; M agrees with Ś$_1$; Ś$_1$ and Dn agree with S ; against other manuscripts of their respective recensions.

These discrepancies, as is shown in the sequel, are due chiefly to two different causes : firstly, initial fluidity of the text ; and, secondly, subsequent

1 WINTERNITZ, *Ind. Ant.* 1898. 134 ff.

contamination or conflation. As regards fluidity : to conceive of the Epic of the Bhāratas—or for that matter, of any true epic—as a rigid or fixed composition like the dramas or poems of Goethe or Milton, or even of Kālidāsa or Bhavabhūti, would be manifestly grotesque. Such a view can originate only in a fundamental misconception of the origin, growth and function of epic poetry.

In the case of the Mahābhārata, we find, however, the fact of the fluidity of the original reflected in the tradition as preserved even to this day. Only a very late interpolation in some inferior Devanāgarī manuscripts speaks of the text as having been written down by Gaṇeśa to the dictation of Vyāsa, a fantastic story that we may ignore with an easy conscience. On the other hand, we are plainly told that the epic was *first* published, at an elaborate sacrificial session, in the form of a free *recitation* by Vaiśaṁpāyana, a direct pupil of the author, before king Janamejaya and the assembled guests. It was again *recited* by Sūta (or Sauti), who had heard it only at the first recitation, and somehow committed the whole poem to memory. After just one single hearing, he obviously could not reproduce such a voluminous text *verbatim et literatim*. In the beginning, therefore, it is clear that the poem, which was committed to memory, was recited freely, as faithfully as the particular reciter could contrive. This mode of transmission is not calculated to preserve rigid textual purity in any high degree, without stringent precautions, such as were adopted in the case of Vedic texts, but which never existed, as far as one knows, in the case of the epics. This fact also we find unexpectedly preserved by tradition (1. 57. 74 f.). Vyāsa, we are told, taught his Bhārata to his five pupils. Sumantu, Jaimini, Paila, Śuka, and Vaiśaṁpāyana. And the five rhapsodists—the direct pupils of the author—it is reported, published *five separate versions* of the epic :

[76] संहितास्तैः पृथक्त्वेन भारतस्य प्रकाशिताः ।

As is well known, there is preserved a work which actually passes for the Aśvamedhaparva of the Bhārata of Jaimini (whether it is actually so or not) and which is totally different from our Aśvamedhaparvan.

Here, I think, we have a clear glimpse of the early history of the text. Two facts emerge rather clearly out of the chaos : firstly, *the text was originally committed to memory and recited freely* ; secondly, *different rhapsodists recited differently*. This has indeed been assumed by many writers on the subject.[1] All that is quite natural and intelligible. As a matter of fact, from generation to generation, from place to place, from bard to bard, the wording, even the contents, would vary a little, until the text is committed to writing, which is the beginning of a different phase in its history. The view that the epic has reached its present form by a gradual process of addition and alte-

[1] For instance, WINTERNITZ, *Geschichte der ind. Litteratur*, 1. 396.

ration receives strong support from the fact that this *process is not stopped even by scriptal fixation.*[1] The study of the manuscripts themselves, which belong to a very late phase in the evolution of the text, shows that texts must have been constantly amplified and altered by conflation. Such derangements, it may be observed, do not totally destroy, as might be imagined, the value of our division of the manuscript material into recensions and versions, but merely complicate its use and interpretation.

CRITICAL PRINCIPLES FOLLOWED IN THE CONSTITUTION OF THE TEXT

As already remarked, the Mahābhārata versions when they first come within our ken appear already dispersed in several distinct groups. The original, from which all these versions are derived, is itself preserved in no authentic copy contemporaneous with, or even reasonably close to, its period of composition. We can only reconstruct the original, approximately, by comparative methods. We recognize today, as already explained, two recensions, descended from the original, each recension embracing a plurality of versions, each version being divided into a multiplicity of sub-groups. The ultimate problem is to unify, as far as possible, this manuscript tradition : to evolve, by comparative methods, a form of the text that will explain this phenomenal wealth of divergent and conflicting texts, and justify it.

Before I elucidate the critical principles followed in preparing the constituted text of the Ādi, I must review briefly other principles of textual criticism and textual reconstruction, and discuss the applicability of these principles to the Mahābhārata Problem.

THE CLASSICAL MODEL

The method that naturally presents itself first to our mind is the time-honoured method of Classical Philology.[2] The older school of classical philologists distinguished four stages in the work of preparing a critical edition of a classical text : (1) *Heuristics,* [77] i.e. assembling and arranging the entire material consisting of manuscripts and *testimonia* in the form of a genealogical tree ; (2) *Recensio,* i.e. restoration of the text of the archetype ; (3) *Emendatio,* i. e. restoration of the text of the author ; and, finally, (4) *Higher Criticism,* i.e. separation of the sources utilized by the author.

Excellent as this method is for the purpose for which it is devised, it should not be forgotten that it depends ultimately upon there being a more or less complete concatenation of copies and exemplars reaching finally back to a single authentic (written) archetype ; and, consequently, can be applied to

---

1 LÜDERS, *Deutsche Literaturzeitung,* 1929, 1143.

2 See RUBEN, "Schwierigkeiten der Textkritik des Mahābhārata", *Acta Orientalia,* 8. 240-256 ; and SUKTHANKAR, *ABI.* 11. 259 ff.

the Mahābhārata with great limitations.[1] Indeed our ideal is the same as that of the classical philologist : restoration of the text, as far as possible, to its original form. But the original of a Sanskrit poem and that of a classical poem : how entirely different they are ! Particularly, in the case of the Mahābhārata, where, one may well ask, is the original of a whole literature ?

In the Mahābhārata we have a text with about a dozen, more or less independent, versions, whose extreme types differ, in extent, by about 13,000 stanzas or 26,000 lines ; a work which, for centuries, must have been growing not only upwards and downwards, but also laterally, like the Nyagrodha tree, growing on all sides ; a codex which has been written in nearly a dozen different scripts assiduously but negligently copied, chiefly as a source of religious merit, through long vistas of centuries by a legion of devout and perhaps mostly uneducated and inefficient copyists, hailing from different corners of a vast sub-continent, and speaking different tongues ; a traditional book of inspiration, which in various shapes and sizes, has been the cherished heritage of one people continuously for some millennia and which to the present day is interwoven with the thoughts and beliefs and moral ideas of a nation numbering over 300 million souls ! The classical philologist has clearly no experience in dealing with a text of this description, an opus of such gigantic dimensions and complex character, with such a long and intricate history behind it.

THE DIFFICULTIES OF MAHĀBHĀRATA TEXTUAL CRITICISM

The capital difficulty of the Mahābhārata problem is just this that there are hardly any clear objective criteria which may enable us to discriminate with precision and certainty between the data of the rival recensions, to evaluate correctly and confidently the amazingly large mass of variants. Only an inconsiderable fraction of these variants represents clear "mistakes", which can be corrected with confidence. As a rule, the variant readings, if they are not mere synonyms, convey a slightly different meaning, but almost always a possible meaning. From the grammatical point of view also, they are both equally valid. One of the variants may be a trifle more suitable than the other ; for instance, in the discrimination between the Simple and the Periphrastic Future, or the Parasmaipada and the Ātmanepada. But can we legitimately premise that the original must necessarily have been quite flawless from the point of view of the Pāṇinian grammar ? Is it not at least likely that the supposed solecism may be a genuine *lapsus calami* of the author, or (should that supposition be considered inadmissible or unacceptable) that the usage fluctuated ?

Then again, as we have seen, there are numerous passages, short and long, that are found in one recension and are lacking in the other, what I call

---

[1] Cf. WINTERNITZ, *Indol. Prag.* 1. 61 ; and CHARPENTIER, *Orient. Literaturzeitung*, 1932, 276 f.

"additional" passages. No [78] convincing proof can *in general* be given to establish either the originality or the spuriousness of any given passage of this type. What may fairly be regarded as interpolations are in general so ingeniously fashioned and so cunningly fitted in that, except under very favourable circumstances, the intrinsic (contextual) evidence is inconclusive.

For these and other reasons it is not always easy to correlate the divergent recensions, to discriminate between the variants, and to constitute a wholly unobjectionable single text.

This difficulty has its origin in the circumstance that in the Mahābhārata manuscript tradition, perhaps as much as in any literary tradition, the textual critic is faced with a bewildering profusion of versions as also with an amazing mixture of versions. Contrary tendencies have been at work in the evolution of the text. While, on the one hand, some elements have been working, from the earliest times, for the development of different types ; on the other hand, there were not wanting elements that operated against the evolution of sharply differentiated types. To understand the phenomenon of this luxuriant growth and indiscriminate fusion of versions, one must appreciate certain details of historical moment, certain special factors in the transmission of the Mahābhārata, traits which distinguish our work from every other known text except the Rāmāyaṇa and perhaps other similar ancient epopees.

Let us examine closely the character of the differences between the two recensions to start with.[1] The differences are of three kinds. Broadly speaking, each recension differs from the other, firstly, in point of readings of the common stanzas ; secondly, in point of additions (or omissions) of short and long passages ; and, thirdly, in point of sequence of the text-units. How do these differences at all arise ?

Our first thought would be to attempt to explain the additions or omissions as the result of conscious editorial revision, or of clerical error, or partly of one and partly of the other. But the frequent differences in sequence, especially when no material gain is perceptible in either arrangement, rather support the explanation suggested above that both recensions are, in final analysis, *independent copies of an orally transmitted text.* The suggestion is confirmed by the consideration of the variation of the first type, namely, minor differences in the readings of the stanzas common to the two recensions, which confront us step by step throughout the parvan, nay, throughout the epic, as the partial collations of the other parvans now available at the Institute clearly show.

It will be found for one thing perfectly useless to try to derive *mechanically* one set of readings uniformly from the other. Hundreds and thousands

---

[1] The conditions are analogous to that of the Rāmāyaṇa recensions, as revealed by the researches of JACOBI ; see particularly, *Das Rāmāyaṇa*, pp. 3 ff, and LÜDERS, "Ueber die Grantharecension" (1901).

of the minor readings are nothing more than mere synonyms or paraphrases, grammatically and semantically equivalent, but graphically totally unrelated. They, therefore, cannot be all *corruptions*, in the ordinary sense of the word, of a *written* archetype. The vast majority of these variants cannot again be due to the zeal of a purist trying to correct the solecisms of the received text, or to the whim of a minor poet endeavouring to polish its diction or style. Had that been the case, we should find that the enthusiasm of the reformer had evaporated long before he had reached the middle or at least the end of the first parvan. The [79] Herculean task of cleansing the Augean stables would be child's play compared to a systematic purification of the Mahābhārata text, according to later standards. Under these circumstances, however great might be the divergence between the two recensions in the beginning, it is bound to vanish or at least diminish towards the middle or the end of the poem. We find, on the other hand, as already remarked, that the stream of variation flows with unabated volume from the beginning to the end of the epic. This fact can in no way be reconciled with the hypothesis of a single uniform revision (or a series of them either) of a fixed and rigid text.

All the difficulties in the explanation of this phenomenal variation vanish, however, as soon as we assume that the epic was handed down from bard to bard originally by *word of mouth*, as is clearly implied by tradition. That would explain, without any strain or violence, the existence of the mass of variants, of differences in sequence, and of additions or omissions. If the text has been preserved, for any considerable period of time, only in memory and handed down by word of mouth, those are just the changes that could not possibly be avoided. It is evident that no great care would be lavished on the text by these custodians of the tradition to guard it against corruption and elaboration, or against arbitrary emendation, and normalization : to reproduce the received text, which was not guarded by canonical authority or religious sanction, with any degree of precision would be neither attempted by the bards nor required of them. Whenever and wherever the text was then written down—and it was probably written down *independently* in different epochs and under different circumstances—these transmissions by word of mouth must have contaminated the written text and introduced innumerable variations in it. The assumption of some of such complicated derangement, beyond the normal vicissitudes of transmission, is necessary to account for the abnormal discrepancies and strange vagaries of the Mahābhārata manuscript tradition. In other words, we are compelled to assume that even in its early phases the Mahābhārata textual tradition must have been not uniform and simple, but multiple and polygenous.

Moreover, a study of the critical apparatus shows that there has intervened a long period in the history of the Mahābhārata in which there was a free comparison of manuscripts and extensive mutual borrowings. A natural and inevitable source of confusion of the tradition has always been the marginalia, comprising glosses, *variae lectiones* and additions. The copyist of a manuscript with such accretions copied sometimes the original readings and sometimes the marginal. It may be incidentally remarked that an examination of the marginalia shows that the variant readings are taken *mostly* from manuscripts belonging to the same version, or at least the same recension. But there is no reason, theoretical at any rate, why readings of the rival recension could not creep into a manuscript of the text by the medium, say, of a popular commentary such as Nīlakaṇṭha's. And, as a matter of fact, we do find, occasionally, readings of the opposite recension noted in the margins of manuscripts. Under these circumstances it was inevitable that the true reading, especially if it was a *lectio difficilior* or an archaism or a solecism, would be partly suppressed, being preserved to us in one or two manuscripts only.

Furthermore, the texts may be improved by a comparison of manuscripts is not by any means a modern discovery. The process has been known and practised for ages : [80] the difference is merely in our ideas of what is meant by "improvement" of the text. I have cited above the instance of Nīlakaṇṭha, who himself says that he had collected and compared Mahābhārata manuscripts from different parts of India in order to ascertain the "best" readings. The other commentators also, Devabodha, Arjunamiśra and Ratnagarbha, cite *pāṭhāntaras* and speak *apapāṭhas* ("bad readings"). These they could have got only from a comparison of different manuscripts.

The text favoured by the ancients appear to have been of the inclusive, rather than of the exclusive, type. This is proved in the case of Nīlakaṇṭha by a remark of his cited above, where, he naïvely admits that he had put together the stanzas which had been commented on by the ancient Bhāṣyakāras, and others he had found in modern manuscripts, with the idea of making a "thesaurus of excellences." The remark does not apply by any means exclusively to the Sanatsujāta episode, to which it is appended, at any rate as far as Nīlakaṇṭha is concerned. In the Ādi, we have abundant evidence that he has borrowed, according to his fancy, passages, short and long, from the Southern recension. The critical notes will show that his text includes a large number of Southern passages which are not found in any other Northern version, such as, for example, the catalogue of forest trees, which serves in a modest way for a description of the sylvan scenery amidst which Uparicara Vasu finds himself :

513* अशोकैश्चम्पकैश्चुतैस्तिलकैरतिमुक्तकैः ।
पुंनागैः कर्णिकारैश्च बकुलैर्दिव्यपाटपैः
पनसैर्नारिकेलैश्च चन्दनैश्चार्जुनैस्तथा ।
एतैरन्यैर्महावृक्षैः पुण्यैः स्वादुफलैर्युतम् ।

At one place, as was shown above, Nīlakaṇṭha has disfigured his text in his frantic attempt to squeeze into it a lengthy (Southern) passage containing some details which did not fit into his own text. This he has done, be it noted, at the risk of making his text wholly unintelligible, without a word of apology or explanation. Professor WINTERNITZ, while criticizing DAHLMANN'S *Das Mahābhārata*, has pointed out this incongruity[1] : "The story... which relates how Dīrghatamas is insulted by his wife Pradveṣī, and how he consequently establishes the fixed rule (*maryādā*) that henceforth a woman shall always have to adhere to one husband, whether he be alive or dead, and that a woman who goes to another man shall go to hell, thus forbidding any kind of remarriage of widows.....is *strangely out of place*[2] in a chapter treating of Niyoga." As was pointed out above, in consequence of the intrusion of this foreign matter, the first half of the stanza of the original text is separated from the second half by 27 lines ! That in itself is, however, not a very serious matter in Mahābhārata textual tradition, where such transpositions are a common occurrence. But in the present instance, this transfer has had the unexpected and undesirable result that the subject of the sentence, which was left behind in the first half of the stanza, *remains to the end without its predicate*, which latter, being shunted off to such a remote distance, was furnished with a new and entirely different subject ! The effect of this arrangement on the original story may be easily imagined.

[81] Conflation is in general not so easy to detect and prove as in the case of Nīlakaṇṭha. We can date Nīlakaṇṭha with fair accuracy. Again, Nīlakaṇṭha, who is one of the latest of our commentators, has himself vouchsafed some information as to how he has prepared his text. We have no such reliable data in the case of the majority of the manuscripts or versions of our critical apparatus.

Take, for instance, the case of the sub-group $G_{1.2.4.5}$ of the Grantha version. In opposition to other manuscripts belonging to the same recension and even the same version, $G_{1.2.4.5}$ contain, as shown above, an astonishingly large number of passages which are found otherwise only in some inferior manuscripts of the Northern recension. Now is this a case of contamination of the four MSS. $G_{1.2.4.5}$ from a Northern source ; or are the common passages a remnant of the lost archetype, which were somehow lost in the remaining manuscripts of the Southern recension ?[3] There is apparent agreement here between independent versions. But is this agreement original ? The clumsy interpolator of a remote ancestor of $G_{1.2.4.5}$ happens to have supplied us with the means of answering these questions. He has left behind, quite unintentionally, an impress of his "finger-prints," so to say, by which we can *easily* and *confidently* trace him and examine his handiwork. The said manus-

[1] *JRAS*. 1897. 723 footnote. [2] Italics mine !

[3] Cf. RUBEN, *Acta Orientalia*, 8. 250 ; SUKTHANKAR, "Epic Studies III", *ABI*. 11. 269 ff.

cripts contain a Northern stanza (belonging to manuscripts of class γ)—a mere string of attributes of Garuḍa—wedged in at a place where it can be construed neither with what precedes nor with what follows. This proves incontrovertibly that these four manuscripts $G_{1.2.4.5}$ have been compared with some Northern manuscripts, and makes it highly probable that the other doubtful stanzas, which they have in common with the Northern recension, have crept into their text in the same surreptitious way. At least this is the most plausible explanation of the anomaly. But even such confirmatory evidence is not always available.

The reader need not be sceptical about the possibilities of such indiscriminate conflation and addition. The critical apparatus, if closely scrutinized and properly understood, will reveal numerous instances of a similar character. Even a close study of the Kumbhakonam edition, prepared in our own times by two excellent Southern Pandits, will throw some light on the mentality of the old redactors of the Mahābhārata : parallel and even contradictory versions are placed quite unconcernedly side by side, regardless of the effect on the reader, regardless of the fact that sentences are left hanging in the air, that passages do not construe. Here one notices above all the anxiety that nothing that was by any chance found in the Mahābhārata manuscript should be lost. Everything was carefully preserved, assembled in a picturesque disarray.

Another important fact that must be kept in view in dealing with these interpolations is this. The older the borrowal and the more interesting the passage borrowed, the wider will be the area over which it will spread in its new habitat. It then becomes difficult to prove the borrowal.

Thus there is a certain group of passages which are found in all versions except in $Ś_1$ and K (that is, in the group ν), for example, the Kaṇikanīti.[1] In the particular case of the Kaṇikanīti, there appears to be sufficient extrinsic and intrinsic evidence to make it [82] highly probable that the passage is spurious, and the corresponding agreement between some of the (more or less) independent versions is unoriginal.

There are indeed yet more difficult cases, where the evidence *pro et contra* of documentary and intrinsic probability is equally balanced, as far as we can at present judge. In such cases we are forced to look for small things which look suspicious and lead us to probabilities, not facts.

The problem is clearly not solved by formulating *a priori* a hypothesis as to the interrelationship of the different versions and fix the text in terms of some preconceived formula ; for instance, by assuming as *absolutely* independent a certain number of these divergent versions, and laying down an arithmetical rule that whatever is common to two or more of such and such

---

1 App. I, No. 81.

versions *must* be original. In this method, we can easily deceive ourselves and others; for the results arrived at will appear sounder than in reality they are. Even though the formal operations may be a piece of flawless logic, nevertheless the results, being based on premises possibly unsound though apparently clear and definite, may be wholly fictitious. The study of the manuscripts themselves must first teach us what their interrelationship is. And they unmistakably indicate that their interrelationship is of most complex character. The critical apparatus is a veritable labyrinth of complicated and intermingled versions, each with a long and intricate history of its own behind it. We have unfortunately no single thread to guide us out of the maze, but rather a collection of strands intertwined and entangled and leading along divergent paths. With the epic text as preserved in the extant Mahābhārata manuscripts, we stand, I am fully persuaded, at the wrong end of a long chain of successive syntheses of divergent texts, carried out—providentially—in a haphazard fashion, through centuries of diaskeuastic activities; and that *with the possible exception of the Śāradā (Kaśmīrī) version*, which appears to have been protected by its largely unintelligible script and by the difficulties of access to the province, *all versions are indiscriminately conflated.*

Now it goes without saying that the genetic method (operating with an archetype and a *stemma codium*) cannot strictly be applied to fluid texts and conflated manuscripts; for, in their case, it is extremely difficult, if not utterly impossible, to disentangle completely, by means of purely objective criteria, their intricate mutual relationships. The documentary evidence is no doubt supremely important, but the results, arrived at from a consideration of the documentary probability, must be further tested in the light of intrinsic probability. No part of the text can be considered really exempt from the latter scrutiny, when we are dealing with a carelessly guarded text such as we have in the present instance. A careful study of the critical notes will show—if, indeed, the foregoing remarks have not made it abundantly clear—that all the problems which present themselves for solution in editing any text from manuscripts are present in the case of the Mahābhārata on a colossal scale and in an intensified form. We must, therefore, clearly recognize that a wholly certain and satisfactory restoration of the text to its pristine form—even the so-called *śatasāhasrī saṁhitā* form—may be a task now beyond the powers of criticism.

CRITICL EDITIONS OF THE DIFFERENT VERSIONS

No doubt, in view of some of these difficulties, one scholar has suggested that to expedite and facilitate the work, we should, as a first step, before any attempt is made [83] to constitute the final text of the Mahābhārata, critically edit all the different versions.[1] That, it must be said, is a

[1] Cf. LESNY, *Archiv Orientální*, vol. 5 (1933), p. 159.

rather tall order, as any one will admit, who has any practical experience of editing the Mahābhārata in any shape or form, critical or otherwise. But perhaps funds and workers—not to speak of patience—can be found to edit a dozen or more lakhs of stanzas comprising the dozen or more versions of the Great Epic. There remains, however, yet another and a more fundamental difficulty, which appears to have wholly escaped the attention of the learned critic. The difficulty is that it is practically impossible to edit even a single version of the Mahābhārata—or for that matter of any other text—wholly satisfactorily, without considering the entire evidence, that is, without, at the same time, consulting the readings of all other versions. Suppose we examine six manuscripts of a version (Grantha) in order to prepare a critical text of that version. It may happen that four of them ($G_{1\cdot 2\cdot 4\cdot 5}$), which are conflated manuscripts, have a "secondary" reading, while only two ($G_{3\cdot 6}$) have the correct reading. In these circumstances, the true character of the variants could never be inferred from the readings of this version (G) itself ; it would be shown only by other versions (T or M or N). In fact, there is no way of finding out whether any of the manuscripts of a particular version are conflated (if they happen to be conflated) without consulting the other versions. And, if for the editing of each of the indivual versions, we have to scrutinize and weigh the entire evidence, we might as well get busy with the work of preparing the final text, assuming of course that a final (critical) text has to be prepared.

That consideration apart, even if we assume, for the sake of argument, that all the dozen or more versions lie before us in a critically edited shape, our main task is not made any easier on that account. One has to go through the same mental processes in picking out or reconstructing the correct readings, whether, as at present, the *variae lectiones* are concentrated on a single page of the critical edition or have to be searched in a dozen or more different provincial editions, arranged round about the critic in a semi-circle. Preparing all these different editions would not by itself give us the correct readings. Some of them, moreover, would but slightly differ from each other, for instance, the editions of the Bengali and the Devanāgarī versions, and it would mean useless duplication of labour. All that is really needed to facilitate our work is a critical edition of the Southern recension. An attempt to supply that need is now being made by Professor P. P. S. SASTRI in his edition of the Mahābhārata, referred to already.

THE VULGATE AS BASE

Another high authority, while full of apparent admiration for the way in which the work is being done at present at the Institute, has with much pathos and eloquence deprecated this hastily prepared, eclectic text. All that we need to do at present, according to this scholar, is to reprint the Vulgate, giving merely the *variae lectiones* of the manuscripts collated and leaving each individual reader to constitute his own text, unhampered and uninfluenced by the obtrusive personality of some editor who stands like a monitor between the reader and his author. The learned critic is evidently of opinion that any average reader, who picks up an edition of the Great Epic for casual study is better qualified to reconstruct the text than the editor who has made a special study of the [84] problem! That is a paradox natural to the subtle mentality of the learned critic. But we need not take it too seriously. Whatever the Average Reader might or might not be able to do, I beg to submit that the Critical Reader, like the learned scholar whose opinion I am quoting, would not be any the worse off, if he is put in possession of this "Recension of Poona".[1] For, who and what is to prevent him from constituting his own text from this critical edition? Whoever makes the text—even if Bṛhaspati himself were to come down and constitute the text—the Critical Reader would undoubtedly reject it as it would surely not fit in with his ideas of what is right and what is wrong. The Critical Reader has the same freedom of action whether he has before him the critical text or the Vulgate. The Vulgate, as far as I can judge, is no better suited for serving as the base than the present text.

It may, however, be that the hesitation of the learned authority is really due to a categorical objection to interfering in so definite a manner with the received text. Should that be the case, it is certainly difficult to appreciate the veneration of this scholar for the form of a text which was made up, probably, also in great haste but with inadequate and insufficient materials, only in the last quarter of the seventeenth century, that is, only about 250 years ago. It is surely illogical to assume that a text which has been built up largely on unscientific conjecture is *now* beyond the reach of conjecture.

A simpler and more probable explanation still of the hesitating attitude of the learned critic might perhaps be that his theoretical misgivings are based on a rather hasty study of both the Vulgate and the critical text. For, the text of the Vulgate is so corrupted and so obviously contaminated that it would be a criminal neglect of his duty for any intelligent editor now to reprint the Vulgate, when he has at hand the material to control its vagaries and to correct its absurdities.

ONE SELECTED MANUSCRIPT AS BASE.

No doubt to remedy the inherent defects in the last method as also to avoid the dreaded *saṁkara* of *pramāṇas*, it has been suggested by other scholars that the best course would be to select *one* manuscript, the best manuscript extant (of any version presumably) and print it, with minimal change, correcting only the obvious and indispensable clerical errors and adding the variants of the collated manuscripts.[2] This expedient, though un-

---

[1] *Journal Asiatique*, Oct.-Dec. 1929, p. 347.

[2] C. V. Vaidya, *JBBRAS*. 1920. 367.

questionably simple and "safe", and in most cases indubitably effective, fails totally in the present instance, for two reasons: firstly and chiefly, owing to the negligible age of our manuscripts, which are barely five hundred years old; and, secondly, owing to the systematic conflation which has been carried on through ages of revisional and amplificatory activity. By following any manuscript—even the oldest and the best—we shall be authenticating just that arbitrary mixture of versions which it is the express aim of this method to avoid!

This suggestion, however, has special interest, because the principle underlying it has now been, partly and timidly, put into practice by Professor P. P. S. SASTRI, in preparing his edition of the Southern recension, whereas the three foregoing methods are mere castles in the air of theoretical critics.

[85] A CRITIQUE OF PROFESSOR SASTRI'S METHOD

Professor SASTRI's edition is an excellent demonstration of the inadequacy of the underlying principle, which has been repeatedly advocated, showing up its defects as nothing else could. What Professor SASTRI set out to do is (to quote his own words): "*to print the text as it is in the original palm-leaf, liberty being taken only to correct scriptorial blunders,*[1] to weigh the different readings in the additional manuscripts and choose the more important ones [*scil.* readings] for being added to the text by way of footnotes".[2] How difficult it is to carry this out *verbatim* in practice and at the same time to present a half-way readable text may be realized when we see how SASTRI has had to doctor his text. A few examples may be added to elucidate the point. To begin with, SASTRI does not follow the parvan division, nor the adhyāya division, of his basic manuscript, adding and omitting colophons arbitrarily, in order to reach some imaginary norm. Secondly, he adds an adhyāya of 40 lines after his adhy. 164, which is not found in his manuscript! Thirdly, he omits one whole adhyāya of 40 lines, after his adhy. 180, where *all* Southern manuscripts, without exception (including his own exemplar) have it, and is moreover unaccountably silent about the omission! Fourthly, in one place (his adhy. 122) he has omitted fourteen lines of the text of his manuscript and added instead thirteen lines which are not found in *any* Southern *manuscript*![3] Fifthly and lastly, in yet another place (his adhy. 214) he has added an interpolation (*upākhyāna*) of 114 lines of which *not a single line* (as actually printed in SASTRI's edition) is to be found in *any* of the six manuscripts utilized by him! These are some of the things that an extremely orthodox Southern Pandit actually does when he sets out with the avowed object of printing up a Southern manuscript *as it is*, correcting only "scriptorial blunders." I will not here speak of a certain number

---

1 Italics mine!

2 The Mahābhārata, Vol. I, Introduction, p. xiii.

3 SASTRI's ed. 1. 122. 2½-8½ (page 803 f.).

of spurious lines which appear to have crept insidiously into his text *from the Vulgate* and whose existence even he probably does not suspect.[1] The changes mentioned first are of a different order : they have been made by SASTRI consciously and intentionally.

Let me not be misunderstood. I do not blame SASTRI in the least for taking such liberties with his manuscript, which is a tolerably good manuscript (though probably not very old), but has its faults like any other manuscript. I myself have had to proceed similarly, only more thoroughly, more systematically. Our methods are similar in practice, though not in theory ; that is, in *his* theory. SASTRI's text is eclectic (an epithet often used by critics with a tinge of reproach, the ground of which it is not easy to perceive) : as *eclectic as any other Mahābhārata text,* printed or in manuscript, that I have seen. I have adduced the above instances chiefly to show what correcting merely "scriptorial blunders" in Mahābhārata textual criticism really ends in.

Thus it will be seen that the method of printing a Mahābhārata manuscript *as it is,* viewed as a rigid principle, is a deplorable failure. The lateness of our manuscript material [86] and the peculiar conditions of transmission of the epic are responsible for the defection. *They force upon us an eclectic but cautious utilization of all manuscript classes.* Since all categories of manuscripts have their strong points and weak points, each variant must be judged on its own merits.

WHAT IS THEN POSSIBLE ?

The Mahābhārata problem is a problem *sui generis.* It is useless to think of reconstructing a fluid text in a literally *original* shape, on the basis of an archetype and a *stemma codicum.* What is then possible ? Our objective can only be to reconstruct *the oldest form of the text which it is possible to reach, on the basis of the manuscript material available.*[2] With that end in view, we must examine as many manuscripts—and above all as many *classes* of manuscripts—as possible, and group them into families. We must try to ascertain and evaluate the tradition of each family, eschewing late and worthless material. We may then consider the relation of these traditions in regard to the *variae lectiones,* and the genuine and spurious parts of the text. Beyond that, we have to content ourselves with selecting the readings apparently the earliest and choosing that form of the text which commends itself by its documentary probability and intrinsic merit, recording again most carefully the variants, and the additions and omissions. A little critical *re-*

---

[1] e.g. 1. 22. 28^{ab} ; 58. 1^{cd} ; 82. 4^{ab} ; 184. 27^{ab} (S has v. l.); 194. 62½ (no Ms. has this line !); 203. 28^{ab} ; 212. 66½ ; 215. 54^{ab} ; 216. 41, 43 (found only in $Ñ_2$ Dn and printed editions) ; etc. References are to SASTRI'S edition of course. It must be admitted that, when compared with the mass of the text these interpolations are really negligible.

[2] Cf. LÜDERS, *Deutsche Literaturzeitung,* 1929, 1143.

maniement of the text need cause no alarm. For, as I have already observed, it is hardly logical to assume that a text which is largely based on conjecture is now beyond the reach of that principle. Of course there will always remain many doubts, but that consideration should not prevent us from correcting those parts which can be corrected with confidence; moreover, that limitation applies to our comparatively well preserved classical texts, despite the guarantee of the careful editings they have undergone. However, owing partly to the fluid character of the original and parly to the fragmentary and inadequate information we possess as regards the origin, growth and transmission of the text, it is incumbent on us to make *Conservatism* our watchword. We must abstain from effecting any change which is not in some measure supported by manuscript authority.[1]

THE METHOD OF RECONSTRUCTION EXPLAINED

The method I have followed in reconstructing the text cannot, unfortunately, be presented in the shape of short general rules. I shall endeavour, however, to explain it as briefly as possible.

The main principle underlying all speculation as to authenticity is the postulated *originality of agreement between what may be proved to be (more or less) independent* [87] *versions.* The principle I have tried to follow religiously—and I hope I have never deviated from it—is to accept as original a reading or feature which is documented uniformly by all manuscripts alike (N=S).

For instance, we frequently come across three-lined stanzas, one of whose lines is an "inorganic line", that is, a line which can be added or omitted without detriment to sense or grammar. These seemingly superfluous lines, if proved by both recensions, have *not* been deleted; they have been kept scrupulously intact. A more important instance is of the initial adhyāyas of this parvan. The connection between adhy. 1-3 and what follows, as also the connection between the three adhyāyas *inter se*, is of most loose character. There is further the suspicious circumstance that adhy. 4 begins precisely in the same way as adhy. 1; both adhyāyas have in fact the *identical* opening (prose) sentence:

लोमहर्षणपुत्र उग्रश्रवाः सूतः पौराणिको नैमिषारण्ये शौनकस्य कुलपतेर्द्वादशवार्षिके सत्रे ।

---

[1] Few scholars, I imagine, would endorse the view of Pandit Vidhushekhara BHATTACHARYA (*Modern Review*, Calcutta, for August 1928, page 176), that the first prose sentence of our Mahābhārata (लोमहर्षणपुत्र उग्रश्रवाः सूतः etc.), though found in *all* MSS. without exception, should be *deleted* from the Criticil Edition, because it is *intrinsically inappropriate* in the context. He writes: "They [*scil.* those lines] are to be found in *all* the different versions of which MSS. are collated for the present edition, though with some variant readings, but *can we be satisfied only with this ground as to their being genuine*"? That is a little too radical! This edition cannot and should not proceed so far.

In other words, adhy. 4 begins as though *nothing* had gone before! The prose sentence seems to fit better the context of adhy. 4 than the context of adhy. 1; but that is not material to my argument. It would have been possible to athetize the first three adhyāyas in order to remove this anomaly, relegating them to the Appendix. But as all the four adhyāyas are handed down in exactly the same form (with the usual amount of variants) in all manuscripts of both recensions, they were left perfectly intact. Here we have an *old conflation* of two different beginnings. They were not harmonious in juxtaposition, but each was too good to lose, in the opinion of the ancient redactors. They therefore put both in, making but a poor compromise.[1]

Another passage that may be thought to need some radical treatment is the account of the cremation of Pāṇḍu and Mādrī. We are first told that the king died in the forest, and Mādrī mounted the funeral pyre and was burned with him (1. 116. 31). After this we read that their "bodies" (*śarīre*) are brought to the capital of the Kurus (1. 117. 30), and an elaborate royal funeral takes place. In the account given in the following adhyāya (118), from the description of the annointing and dressing of the king's body, and from the remark that the king looked as if he were alive (1. 118. 20):

आच्छन्नः स तु वासोभिर्जीवन्निव नरर्षभः ।

it is clear that no former burning is imagined. After Pāṇḍu had been burned with his favourite queen Mādrī on the funeral pyre, there could not have been (as HOPKINS[1] has justly pointed out) much corpse left or not enough to dress and smear with sandal paste! But the manuscripts do not render us any help here. The passage is handed down in identical form in all manuscripts of both recensions.

The above examples will show that the diaskeuasts did not always employ any great art—I may add, fortunately—in conflating two discrepant accounts of an incident, which is by no means an easy task. To resolve such anomalies, however, is beyond the scope of this edition, since the entire manuscript evidence unanimously supports the conflation, which is too old and deep-rooted to be treated by the ordinary principles of textual criticism. If we went about, at this stage of our work, athetizing such passages as were self-contradictory or as contradicted the data of some other part of the epic, there would not be much left of the Mahābhārata to edit in the end.

[88] I give in a footnote[2] the text of a hundred selected stanzas for

---

[1] *Ruling Caste in Ancient India*, p. 172, footnote.

[2] Adhy. 1

आद्यं पुरुषमीशानं पुरुहूतं पुरुष्टुतम् ।
ऋतमेकाक्षरं ब्रह्म व्यक्ताव्यक्तं सनातनम् ॥ २०

Adhy. 26

ददर्श तं पिता चापि दिव्यरूपं विहंगमम् ।
तेजोवीर्यबलोपेतं मनोमारुतरंहसम् ॥ ६

तमागतमभिप्रेक्ष्य भगवान्कश्यपस्तदा ।
विदित्वा चास्य संकल्पमिदं वचनमब्रवीत् ॥ १०

प्रजाहितार्थमारम्भो गरुडस्य तपोधनाः ।
चिकीर्षति महत्कर्म तदनुज्ञातुमर्हथ ॥ १३

पक्षानिलहतश्चास्य प्राकम्पत स शैलराट् ।
मुमोच पुष्पवर्षं च समागलितपादपः ॥ २२

which no variants, or only unimportant variants, have been recorded in the

Adhy. 27

कश्यपस्य द्विजातेश्च कथं वै पक्षिराट् सुतः ।
अधृष्यः सर्वभूतानामवध्यश्चाभवत्कथम् ॥ २
विषयोऽयं पुराणस्य यन्मां त्वं परिपृच्छसि ।
शृणु मे वदतः सर्वमेतत्संक्षेपतो द्विज ॥ ४
यजतः पुत्रकामस्य कश्यपस्य प्रजापतेः ।
साहाय्यमृषयो देवा गन्धर्वाश्च ददुःकिल ॥ ५
एतस्मिन्नेव काले तु देवी दाक्षायणी शुभा ।
विनता नाम कल्याणी पुत्रकामा यशस्विनी ॥ २४
तपस्तप्त्वा व्रतपरा स्नाता पुंसवने शुचिः ।
उपचक्राम भर्तारं तामुवाचाथ कश्यपः ॥ २५

Adhy. 29

तमुवाचाव्ययो देवो वरदोऽस्मीति खेचरम् ।
स वव्रे तव तिष्ठेयमुपरीत्यन्तरिक्षगः ॥ १३

Adhy. 31

भुजंगमानां शापस्य मात्रा चैवसुतेन च ।
विनतायास्त्वया प्रोक्तं कारणं सूतनन्दन ॥ १

Adhy. 32

तमब्रवीत्सत्यधृतिं तप्यमानं पितामहः ।
किमिदं कुरुषे शेष प्रजानां स्वस्ति वै कुरु ॥ ६
जानामि शेष सर्वेषां भ्रातॄणां ते विचेष्टितम् ।
मातुश्चाप्यपराधाद्वै भ्रातॄणां ते महद्भयम् ॥ १३

Adhy. 35

ततः प्रभृति तां कन्यां वासुकिः पर्यरक्षत ।
जरत्कारुं स्वसारं वै परं हर्षमवाप च ॥ २

Adhy. 38

संदिश्य कुशलप्रश्नं कार्यवृत्तान्तमेव च ।
शिष्यं गौरमुखं नाम शीलवन्तं समाहितम् ॥ १४

Adhy. 39

एवमुक्तः स नागेन्द्रः काश्यपेन महात्मना ।
अदशद्वृक्षमभ्येत्य न्यग्रोधं पन्नगोत्तमः ॥ ४
भस्मीभूतं ततो वृक्षं पन्नगेन्द्रस्य तेजसा ।
भस्म सर्वं समाहृत्य काश्यपो वाक्यमब्रवीत् ॥ ७
विद्याबलं पन्नगेन्द्र पश्य मेऽस्मिन्वनस्पतौ ।
अहं संजीवयाम्येनं पश्यतस्ते भुजंगम ॥ ८

Adhy. 40

ततो नृपे तक्षकतेजसा हते
प्रयुज्य सर्वाः परलोकसत्क्रियाः ।
शुचिर्द्विजो राजपुरोहितस्तदा
तथैव ते तस्य नृपस्य मन्त्रिणः ॥ ५

Adhy. 41

वायुभक्षो निराहारः शुष्यन्नहरहर्मुनिः ।
स ददर्श पितॄन्गर्ते लम्बमानानधोमुखान् ॥ ३

Adhy. 42

पुत्र दिष्ट्यासि संप्राप्त इमं देशं यदृच्छया ।
किमर्थं च त्वया ब्रह्मन्न कृतो दारसंग्रहः ॥ ३
एवं दृष्ट्वा तु भवतः शकुन्तानिव लम्बतः ।
मया निवर्तिता बुद्धिर्ब्रह्मचर्यात्पितामहाः ॥ ५

Adhy. 45

चातुर्वर्ण्यं स्वधर्मस्थं स कृत्वा पर्यरक्षत ।
धर्मतो धर्मविद्राजा धर्मो विग्रहवानिव ॥ ७

Adhy. 46

ततस्तस्मिंस्तु दिवसे सप्तमे समुपस्थिते ।
राज्ञः समीपं ब्रह्मर्षिः काश्यपो गन्तुमैच्छत ॥ १४

Adhy. 48

तक्षकस्तु स नागेन्द्रः पुरंदरनिवेशनम् ।
गतः श्रुत्वैव राजानं दीक्षितं जनमेजयम् ॥ १४
अजस्रं निपतत्स्वग्नौ नागेषु भृशदुःखितः ।
अल्पशेषपरीवारो वासुकिः पर्यतप्यत ॥ १९

Adhy. 49

तत आहूय पुत्रं स्वं जरत्कारुर्भुजंगमा ।
वासुकेर्नागराजस्य वचनादिदमब्रवीत् ॥ १
ततः स वासुकेर्घोरमपनीय मनोज्वरम् ।
आधाय चात्मनोऽङ्गेषु जगाम त्वरितो भृशम् ॥२५
जनमेजयस्य तं यज्ञं सर्वैः समुदितं गुणैः ।
मोक्षाय भुजगेन्द्राणामास्तीको द्विजसत्तमः ॥ २६
स गत्वापश्यदास्तीको यज्ञायतनमुत्तमम् ।
वृतं सदस्यैर्बहुभिः सूर्यवह्निसमप्रभैः ॥ २७

Adhy. 53

स यज्ञः पाण्डवेयस्य राज्ञः पारिक्षितस्य ह ।
प्रीतिमांश्चाभवद्राजा भारतो जनमेजयः ॥ १०
ऋत्विग्भ्यः ससदस्येभ्यो ये तत्रासन्समागताः ।
[89] तेभ्यश्च प्रददौ वित्तं शतशोऽथ सहस्रशः॥ ११
पुनरागमनं कार्यमिति चैनं वचोऽब्रवीत् ।
भविष्यसि सदस्यो मे वाजिमेधे महाक्रतौ ॥ १५

Adhy. 54

तत्रोपविष्टं वरदं देवर्षिगणपूजितम् ।
पूजयामास राजेन्द्रः शास्त्रदृष्टेन कर्मणा ॥ १२

Adhy. 55

शृणु राजन्यथा भेदः कुरुपाण्डवयोरभूत् ।
राज्यार्थे द्यूतसंभूतो वनवासस्तथैव च ॥ ४

Adhy. 56

कथितं वै समासेन त्वया सर्वं द्विजोत्तम ।
महाभारतमाख्यानं कुरूणां चरितं महत् ॥ १
कथं धर्मभृतां श्रेष्ठः सुतो धर्मस्य धर्मवित् ।
अनर्हः परमं क्लेशं सोढवान्स युधिष्ठिरः ॥ ९
एतदाचक्ष्व मे सर्वं यथावृत्तं तपोधन ।
यद्यच्च कृतवन्तस्ते तत्र तत्र महारथाः ॥ ११
महर्षेः सर्वलोकेषु पूजितस्य महात्मनः ।
प्रवक्ष्यामि मतं कृत्स्नं व्यासस्यामिततेजसः ॥ १२

Adhy. 58

त्रिःसप्तकृत्वः पृथिवीं कृत्वा निःक्षत्रियां पुरा ।
जामदग्न्यस्तपस्तेपे महेन्द्रे पर्वतोत्तमे ॥ ४
कर्माणि च नरव्याघ्र धर्मोपेतानि मानवाः ।
धर्ममेवानुपश्यन्तश्चक्रुर्धर्मपरायणाः ॥ २१
इत्युक्त्वा स महीं देवो ब्रह्मा राजन्विसृज्य च ।
आदिदेश तदा सर्वान्विबुधान्भूतकृत्स्वयम् ॥ ४५
अथ शक्रादयः सर्वे श्रुत्वा सुरगुरोर्वचः ।
तथ्यमर्थ्यं च पथ्यं च तस्य ते जगृहुस्तदा ॥ ४८

Adhy. 59

ब्रह्मणो मानसाः पुत्रा विदिताः षण्महर्षयः ।
मरीचिरत्र्यङ्गिरसौ पुलस्त्यः पुलहः क्रतुः ॥ १०
प्रह्लादः पूर्वजस्तेषां संह्लादस्तदनन्तरम् ।
अनुह्लादस्तृतीयोऽभूत्तस्माच्च शिबिबाष्कलौ ॥ १८
अमृतं ब्राह्मणा गावो गन्धर्वाप्सरसस्तथा ।
अपत्यं कपिलायास्तु पुराणे परिकीर्तितम् ॥ ५०

Adhy. 60

क्रतोः क्रतुसमाः पुत्राः पतंगसहचारिणः ।
विश्रुतास्त्रिषु लोकेषु सत्यव्रतपरायणाः ॥ ८
द्वादशैवादितेः पुत्राः शक्रमुख्या नराधिप ।
तेषामवरजो विष्णुर्यत्र लोकाः प्रतिष्ठिताः ॥ ३५

Adhy. 61

तेषामन्यतमो यस्तु चतुर्थः परिकीर्तितः ।
श्रेणिमानिति विख्यातः क्षितौ राजर्षिसत्तमः ॥ ४९
बृहस्पतेर्बृहत्कीर्तेर्देवर्षेर्विद्धि भारत ।
अंशाद्द्रोणं समुत्पन्नं भारद्वाजमयोनिजम् ॥ ६३
शकुनिर्नाम यस्त्वासीद्राजा लोके महारथः ।
द्वापरं विद्धि तं राजन्संभूतमरिमर्दनम् ॥ ७२
अरिष्टायास्तु यः पुत्रो हंस इत्यभिविश्रुतः ।
स गन्धर्वपतिर्जज्ञे कुरुवंशविवर्धनः ॥ ७७

Adhy. 64

नरनारायणस्थानं गङ्गयेवोपशोभितम् ।
मत्तबर्हिणसंघुष्टं प्रविवेश महद्वनम् ॥ २४

Adhy. 71

तान्पुनर्जीवयामास काव्यो विद्याबलाश्रयात् ।
ततस्ते पुनरुत्थाय योधयांचक्रिरे सुरान् ॥ ७

Adhy. 73

कृतविद्ये कचे प्राप्ते हृष्टरूपा दिवौकसः ।
कचादधीत्य तां विद्यां कृतार्था भरतर्षभ ॥ १
दृष्ट्वा दुहितरं काव्यो देवयानीं ततो वने ।
बाहुभ्यां संपरिष्वज्य दुःखितो वाक्यमब्रवीत् ॥२८

Adhy. 76

इयं च मे सखी दासी यत्राहं तत्र गामिनी ।
दुहिता दानवेन्द्रस्य शर्मिष्ठा वृषपर्वणः ॥ ९

Adhy. 81

तस्य विस्तीर्णयशसः सत्यकीर्तेर्महात्मनः ।
चरितं श्रोतुमिच्छामि दिवि चेह च सर्वशः ॥ ८

Adhy. 91

अथ गङ्गा सरिच्छ्रेष्ठा समुपायात्पितामहम् ।
तस्या वासः समुद्धूतं मारुतेन शशिप्रभम् ॥ ४

Adhy. 93

स वारुणिस्तपस्तेपे तस्मिन्भरतसत्तम ।
वने पुण्यकृतां श्रेष्ठः स्वादुमूलफलोदके ॥ ७

अस्याः क्षीरं पिबेन्मर्त्यः स्वादु यो वै सुमध्यमे ।
दश वर्षसहस्राणि स जीवेत्स्थिरयौवनः ॥ १९

एतच्छ्रुत्वा तु सा देवी नृपोत्तम सुमध्यमा ।
तमुवाचानवद्याङ्गी भर्तारं दीप्ततेजसम् ॥ २०

Adhy. 94

स कदाचिद्वनं यातो यमुनामभितो नदीम् ।
महीपतिरनिर्देश्यमाजिघ्रद्गन्धमुत्तमम् ॥ ४१

ततः कदाचिच्छोचन्तं शंतनुं ध्यानमास्थितम् ।
पुत्रो देवव्रतोऽभ्येत्य पितरं वाक्यमब्रवीत् ॥ ५४

Adhy. 96

सुहृदां यतमानानामाप्तैः सह चिकित्सकैः ।
जगामास्तमिवादित्यः कौरव्यो यमसादनम् ॥ ५८

Adhy. 102

वाहनानि प्रहृष्टानि मुदिता मृगपक्षिणः ।
गन्धवन्ति च माल्यानि रसवन्ति फलानि च ॥ ३

Adhy. 117

तथा विट्शूद्रसंघानां महान्व्यतिकरोऽभवत् ।
न कश्चिदकरोदीर्ष्यामभवन्धर्मबुद्धयः ॥ १२

[90] Adhy. 125

अश्वत्थाम्ना च सहितं भ्रातॄणां शतमूर्जितम् ।
दुर्योधनममित्रघ्नमुत्थितं पर्यवारयत् ॥ ३१

Adhy. 127

तमालोक्य धनुस्त्यक्त्वा पितृगौरवयन्त्रितः ।
कर्णोऽभिषेकार्द्रशिराः शिरसा समवन्दत ॥ २

ततः पादाववच्छाद्य पटान्तेन ससंभ्रमः ।
पुत्रेति परिपूर्णार्थमब्रवीद्रथसारथिः ॥ ३

ततो दुर्योधनः कोपादुत्पपात महाबलः ।
भ्रातृपद्मवनात्तस्मान्मदोत्कट इव द्विपः ॥ ९

Adhy. 132

पाण्डवा धृतराष्ट्रेण प्रेषिता वारणावतम् ।
उत्सवे विहरिष्यन्ति धृतराष्ट्रस्य शासनात् ॥ ६

स त्वं रासभयुक्तेन स्यन्दनेनाशुगामिना ।
वारणावतमद्यैव यथा यासि तथा कुरु ॥ ७

Adhy. 138

तस्मान्मुक्ता वयं दाहादिमं वृक्षमुपाश्रिताः ।
कां दिशं प्रतिपत्स्यामः प्राप्ताः क्लेशमनुत्तमम् ॥२९

Adhy. 139

गच्छ जानीहि के त्वेते शेरते वनमाश्रिताः ।
मानुषो बलवान्गन्धो घ्राणं तर्पयतीव मे ॥ ८

Adhy. 152

स तदन्नमुपादाय गतो बकवनं प्रति ।
तेन नूनं भवेदेतत्कर्म लोकहितं कृतम् ॥ १७

Adhy. 158

शिरोरुहेषु जग्राह माल्यवत्सु धनंजयः ।
भ्रातॄन्प्रति चकर्षाथ सोऽस्त्रपातादचेतसम् ॥ ३०

अस्त्राग्निना विचित्रोऽयं दग्धो मे रथ उत्तमः ।
सोऽहं चित्ररथो भूत्वा नाम्ना दग्धरथोऽभवम् ॥३७

Adhy. 159

नक्तं च बलमस्माकं भूय एवाभिवर्धते ।
यतस्ततो मां कौन्तेय सदारं मन्युराविशत् ॥ ११

Adhy. 162

सहस्रांशुं ततो विप्रः कृताञ्जलिरुपस्थितः ।
वसिष्ठोऽहमिति प्रीत्या स चात्मानं न्यवेदयत् ॥१७

Adhy. 170

गर्भानपि यदा यूयं भृगूणां घ्नत पुत्रकाः ।
तदायमूरुणा गर्भो मया वर्षशतं धृतः ॥ ३

Adhy. 192

अथ दुर्योधनो राजा विमना भ्रातृभिः सह ।
अश्वत्थाम्ना मातुलेन कर्णेन च कृपेण च ॥ ९

Adhy. 194

विक्रमं च प्रशंसन्ति क्षत्रियस्य विशां पते ।
स्वको हि धर्मः शूराणां विक्रमः पार्थिवर्षभ ॥ १८

ते बलेन वयं राजन्महता चतुरङ्गिणा ।
प्रमथ्य द्रुपदं शीघ्रमानयामेह पाण्डवान् ॥ १९

critical notes ; of these about [91] thirty have no variants at all, while the remaining (seventy) show only insignificant variants, such as transposition, substitution of synonyms, and so on. The number of the latter class of stanzas could naturally be easily augmented, by increasing the latitude of permissible variation. Being handed down uniformly in all manuscripts alike, they may be regarded as authentic (as least as far as manuscript evidence goes), forming so to say, pieces of firm bedrock in the shifting quicksands of Mahābhārata poetry. As such they will be valuable for the study of epic style, diction, vocabulary and so on.

To return to the question of text reconstruction. The rule arising out of the agreement between independent recensions or versions is easy to comprehend and simple to apply ; only its sphere of operation is rather restricted. Difficulties arise when there is fluctuation ; and that is the normal state. When there was fluctuation, the choice fell, as a corollary of the previous rule, upon a *reading which is documented by the largest number of (what* prima facie *appear to be) more or less independent versions*, and which is

---

Adhy. 198

दिष्ट्या जीवन्ति ते पार्था दिष्ट्या जीवति सा पृथा ।
दिष्ट्या द्रुपदकन्यां च लब्धवन्तो महारथाः ॥ ५

Adhy. 199

यदा तु मन्यते वीरः कुन्तीपुत्रो युधिष्ठिरः ।
भीमसेनार्जुनौ चैव यमौ च पुरुषर्षभौ ॥ ३
रामकृष्णौ च धर्मज्ञौ तदागच्छन्तु पाण्डवाः ।
एतौ हि पुरुषव्याघ्रावेषां प्रियहिते रतौ ॥ ४

Adhy. 200

पाञ्चाली भवतामेका धर्मपत्नी यशस्विनी ।
यथा वो नात्र भेदः स्यात्तथा नीतिर्विधीयताम् ॥ १७

Adhy. 202

चन्द्रादित्यौ ग्रहास्तारा नक्षत्राणि दिवौकसः ।
जग्मुर्विषादं तत्कर्म दृष्ट्वा सुन्दोपसुन्दयोः ॥ २६

Adhy. 203

ततो ददृशुरासीनं सह देवैः पितामहम् ।
सिद्धैर्ब्रह्मर्षिभिश्चैव समन्तात्परिवारितम् ॥ ३
एवं चतुर्मुखः स्थाणुर्महादेवोऽभवत्पुरा ।
तथा सहस्रनेत्रश्च बभूव बलसूदनः ॥ २६

Adhy. 205

तेषां मनुजसिंहानां पञ्चानाममितौजसाम् ।
बभूव कृष्णा सर्वेषां पार्थानां वशवर्तिनी ॥ २

Adhy. 206

तत्राभिषेकं कृत्वा स तर्पयित्वा पितामहान् ।
उत्तितीर्षुर्जलाद्राजन्नग्निकार्यचिकीर्षया ॥ १२

Adhy. 210

प्रतिगृह्यार्जुनः सर्वमुपभुज्य च पाण्डवः ।
सहैव वासुदेवेन दृष्ट्वाभटनर्तकान् ॥ १०

Adhy. 211

पौराश्च पादचारेण यानैरुच्चावचैस्तथा ।
सदाराः सानुयात्राश्च शतशोऽथ सहस्रशः ॥ ६
एते परिवृताः स्त्रीभिर्गन्धर्वैश्च पृथक्पृथक् ।
तमुत्सवं रैवतके शोभयांचक्रिरे तदा ॥ १२

Adhy. 212

ते समासाद्य सहिताः सुधर्मामभितः सभाम् ।
सभापालस्य तत्सर्वमाचख्युः पार्थविक्रमम् ॥ १०

Adhy. 220

स गत्वा तपसः पारं देहमुत्सृज्य भारत ।
जगाम पितृलोकाय न लेभे तत्र तत्फलम् ॥ ७

Adhy. 225

यदा प्रसन्नो भगवान्महादेवो भविष्यति ।
तुभ्यं तदा प्रदास्यामि पाण्डवास्त्राणि सर्वशः ॥ १०

supported by intrinsic probability. Diagrammatically we might represent the types as follows :

(i) $N_1 = S =$ Text.	(ii) $N = S_1 =$ Text.	(iii) $N_1 = S_1 =$ Text.	
N_2	S_2	N_2	S_2
N_3	S_3	N_3	S_3
etc.	etc.	etc.	etc.

The presumption of originality in these cases is frequently confirmed by a lack of definite agreement between the discrepant versions. The commonest application of this rule is when Ś$_1$ K or B (with or without D) agree with S against their own agnates. Numerous examples of this type of agreement have been adduced above (pp. LIV, LXII).

Occasionally we get "double" agreement, that is, agreement between two or more groups of each recension ($N_1 = S_1$ and $N_2 = S_2$) ; for example, when

(1) Ś$_1$ K = M, and simultaneously B = TG,

or (2) Ś$_1$ K = TG, and simultaneously B = M.

Here one of the agreements must, generally speaking, be accidental, since both can hardly be original ; and either may be adopted, *if they have equal intrinsic merit*. Owing to the much greater correctness and reliability of Ś$_1$ K, I have, as a rule, adopted the readings of this group, other things being equal.

When the two recensions have alternate readings neither of which can have come from the other and *which have equal intrinsic merit* (N : S), I have, for the sake of consistency and with a view to avoiding unnecessary and indiscriminate fusion of versions, adopted, *as a stop-gap*, the reading of N. This rule is of very common application, since one constantly comes across readings which are but paraphrases of each other and between which it is impossible to discriminate. Examples of such alternative readings are :

	N	S	
1. 23	महर्षेः पूजितस्येह सर्वलोके महात्मनः ।	महर्षेः सर्वलोकेषु पूजितस्य महात्मनः ।	1. 23
1. 51	ग्रन्थं धारयितुं परे	केचिद्ग्रन्थस्य धारणे	1. 51
54. 3	सेतिहासान्महायशाः	इतिहासांश्च सर्वशः	54. 3
57. 30	पृथग्वंशाश्च शाश्वताः	सर्वे वंशकराः पृथक्	57. 30
60. 9	दक्षस्त्वजायताङ्गुष्ठाद्दक्षिणाद्भगवानृषिः ।	अङ्गुष्ठाद्दक्षिणाद्दक्ष उत्पन्नो भगवानृषिः ।	60. 9
60. 10	वामादजायताङ्गुष्ठाद्भार्या तस्य महात्मनः	महर्षेस्तस्य भार्या तु वामाङ्गुष्ठादजायत ।	60. 10
[92] 65. 20	सुभृशं तापयामास शक्रं सुरगणेश्वरम् ।	कम्पयामास देवेन्द्रं पुरा शक्रं महातपाः ।	65. 20
65. 35	एतानि यस्य कर्माणि तस्याहं भृशमुद्विजे ।	एतान्यन्यानि कर्माणि भृशं देव बिभेम्यहम् ।	65. 35
65. 35	तथाज्ञापय मां विभो	तथा पश्य सुरेश्वर	65. 35

N	S
66. 2 तपसा दग्धकिल्बिषम्	तपसोग्रेण कर्शितम् 66. 2
66. 3 अभिवाद्य ततः सा तं	ततोऽभिवाद्य सा तस्मै 66. 3
66. 9 कृतकार्या ततस्तूर्णमगच्छच्छक्रसंसदम्	शक्रसंसदमागच्छत्कृत्वा कार्यं शचीपतेः। 66. 9
73. 4 वने चैत्ररथोपमे	आरामे नन्दनोपमे 73. 4
106. 6 करेण्वोरिव मध्यस्थः श्रीमान्पौरंदरो गजः ।	गजराजः करेणुभ्यां यथा मध्यगतस्तथा। 106. 9
107. 20 इत्युक्त्वा भगवान्व्यासस्तथा प्रतिविधाय च ।	एवं संदिश्य कौरव्य कृष्णद्वैपायनस्तथा। 107. 20
जगाम तपसे धीमान्हिमवन्तं शिलोच्चयम् ॥	जगाम पर्वतायैव तपसे संशितव्रतः ॥
200. 9 नारदस्त्वथ देवर्षिराजगाम यदृच्छया।	आययौ धर्मराजं तु द्रष्टुकामोऽथ नारदः। 200. 9

When the above tests break down or when they give only a negative result, the expedient adopted by me was to find *a reading which best explains how the other readings may have arisen.* The true reading in this case has often proved to be a *lectio difficilior*, or an archaism or a solecism, the desire to eliminate them being the cause of the variation. Here follow some examples of variation due to the *lectio difficilior* :

57. 7 ऊधः "udder" (v. l. ऋद्धः, रूपं, ऊर्ध्वः, रम्यः Nil., श्रेष्ठः, उच्चैः, ऊढः, ऊधुः, गूढः)
57. 29 मच्छिल्लः proper name (v. l. मावेल्लः, सशेल्लः, माचेल्लः, etc)
96. 16 शुभ्राणां from शुभ्र "shining" (v. l. सर्वेषां, हैमानां)
98. 13 कन्यस (doublet of कनीयस्) "younger" (v. l. कमहं, मा गमः कनीयस्)
98. 18 समुद्रे (v. l. समुद्रे, समूहे, समृद्धे, etc.)
102. 18 चाभिभो (v. l. वा विभो, बोधिताः, चान्विताः)
103. 13 नात्यश्नीयां (v. l. नान्यधीयं, नान्यं श्रये, नाभ्यसूयां, नान्यश्रियां, etc.).

EMENDATION

Emendation has played a very inconspicuous rôle in the preparation of the constituted text. *Interpretation has in general been given preference over emendation.* Even in the case of corrupt passages, the reading of some manuscript or other gives sense, though it may not be the original sense, not even a wholly satisfactory sense. Precipitate emendation is, however, to be deprecated ; for experience has shown that but a small proportion of scholars' corrections are really amendments. Moreover, in this special case, we know, as yet, too little about the epic idiom and the epic world altogether ; as also about the vicissitudes of the epic text. Besides, who can say that the original was linguistically uniform, and conformed to any particular norm ? What would be the style of a work which in the main is obviously a compilation?

The text, as it has been fixed by me, contains about 35 emendations. The corrections are generally very slight, being concerned mostly with single isolated words, never with whole passages. Wherever even a single letter has been added, omitted or altered, without the authority of any of the manuscripts, I have inserted an asterisk (*) in the text.

Only in very few instances do the emendations effected in this edition make any difference to the sense, e. g. 1. 41. 5 गर्तेऽऽ*तांस्त्राणमिच्छतः, where the word (आ)तान् has been [93] added to the pāda, a word found only in D_2; the other readings are: गर्ते तत्त्राणं, गर्ते तांस्त्राणं, गर्ते स्वत्राणं, गर्तेषु त्राणं, गर्ते स्वशरण° (hypermetric!), गर्तेऽस्मिंस्त्राणं, गर्ते संत्राणं°, seven combinations, each having a different syllable between र्ते and त्रा! In a few cases the emendation affects merely some grammatical form of the stanza in question; e. g. 1. 86. 5 अशिल्पजीवी *नगृहश्च नित्यं, where the readings for नगृहश्च are विगृहश्च, अगृहश्च, ह्यगृहंश्च, व्यगृहंश्च (corruption of last?), गुणवांश्च, गुणवांश्चैव, न गृहस्थश्च (hypermetric!).

But the large majority of our emendations concern merely metre and sandhi. My study of the manuscript material led me to the conclusion that there was an ever growing antipathy, firstly, to hypermetric pādas, in fact to any form of metrical irregularity; and, secondly, to forms of sandhi not sanctioned or countenanced by Pāṇini's great grammar. In particular, there is noticeable a strong aversion to hiatus, *even where it was permitted by rules of grammar*. Hiatus between pādas also came to be disapproved and was removed by such expedients as that of adding a meaningless हि, तु or च at the beginning of the posterior pāda.

Manuscripts betray the surreptitious efforts of the scribes and redactors to eliminate hiatus (sometimes even when it is grammatically permissible) in the following instances among others: 1. 2. 91 (between pādas) वनवासश्च। उलूप्या पथि संगमः; 2. 130 पाण्डवा आयुधान्युत (8 readings); 2. 150 यत्र राज्ञा उलूकस्य; 2. 212 तत आश्रमवासाख्यं; 9. 11 (between pādas) °भरणा। उत्तिष्ठतु; 15. 2 हृष्टरूपा अपूजयन्; 21. 3 काल आहूय वचनं; 33. 18 भविष्यन्त्यस्य ऋत्विजः; 33. 22 वा अपरे and विप्र एवं; 36. 7 स ऊर्ध्वे (v. l. स ह्यूर्ध्वे, स तूर्ध्वे°); 41. 8 गर्ते अस्मिन्नधोमुखाः; 41. 21 गर्ते दीना अधोमुखाः (v. l. ह्यधोमुखाः); 45. 13 (between pādas) कुरुषु। उत्तरायामजायत (v. l. चोत्तरा°, सोत्तरा°, ह्युत्तरा°); 50. 17 राजा सदस्या ऋत्विजो (v. l. सर्त्विजो) हव्यवाहः; 60. 4 मरीचिरङ्गिरा अत्रिः (v. l. °राश्चात्रिः, °रा ह्यत्रिः, °राथात्रिः); 65. 24 (between pādas) सुदुर्धर्षं। उग्रे (S °र्धर्षश्चोग्रे); 72. 22 N देवा इन्द्र° (S देवाश्चेन्द्र°); 76. 18 ऋषिश्च ऋषिपुत्रश्च (v. l. °श्चास्यृषि°, °श्चाप्यृषि°, °श्चाहृषि°, °स्त्वमृषि°); 83. 3 °लोका अन्तवन्त (v. l ह्यन्त°, त्वन्त°, चान्त°); 84. 13 महतो अजयं वै; 85. 8 तथा अशीतिं परिवत्सराणि (v. l. तथाशीती च परि°); 94. 38 मेने आत्मानं (ह्यात्मा°, सोत्मा°, चात्मा°); 96. 42 (between pādas) कालेन। अत्यक्रामत् (v. l. त्वभ्याक्रा°, त्वत्यक्रा°, सोत्यक्रा°, त्यक्तकाम°, सोभ्यक्रा°); 98. 8 अन्तर्वत्नी अहं (v. l. त्वहं, ह्यहं, °त्यहं

°त्यस्मि ते); 99. 15 च अमितद्युते; 99. 39 (between pādas) °व्रतोपेता । उपेयात् (v. l. ह्युपेयात्); 100. 2 निशीथे आगमिष्यति; 101. 3 स आश्रम° (v. l. चाश्रम°, त्वाश्रम°); 103. 5 (between pādas) कन्या । अनुरूपा (v. l. सानु°, त्वनु°, स्वनु°, ह्यनु°, etc.); 107. 32 (between pādas) जनपदस्यार्थे । आत्मार्थे ($Ś_1$ K_1 स्वात्मार्थे); 109. 7 (between pādas) °तेजा । ऋषि° (M_{6-8} ह्यृषि°); 109. 21 (between pādas) च । अधर्मिष्ठं च; 110. 28 यदि आर्वा; 112. 31 वा ऋतुस्नाता; 114. 38 देवऋषीणां (v. l. °स्थानां, °गणानां, °निकायानां, °महर्षिणां); 116. 25 तज्ज्येष्ठा अनुमन्यतां; 148. 1 विदित्वा अपकर्षेयं; 152. 19 सर्वे आजग्मुः; 157. 13 त्वया उक्तः (6 readings); 183. 3 (between pādas) तांश्च । उपोपविष्टान् (N ins. अपि); 218. 11 (between pādas) वासुदेवश्च । अप्रतिष्ठो. — It is evident that sandhi was originally more flexible. It is only in later phases of literature that writers make a shibboleth of it.

Similar efforts to correct hypermetric lines may be seen from :

20. 2 विनतां विषण्णवदनां (v. l. विषण्णरूपां विनतां, विनता दीनवदनां, विषण्णवदनां कद्रूः)

78. 23 त्वरितं सकाशं काव्यस्य (v. l. शीघ्रं and द्रुतं for त्वरितं; also पितुः सकाशं त्वरितं, त्वरया काव्यसंकाशं)

92. 4. करवाणि किं ते कल्याणि, (v. l. किं ते करोमि कल्याणि, करवाणि किमद्याहं, किं ते कल्याणि करवै)

94. 74 बलवत्सपत्नतामत्र (सापत्न्यमत्र बलवत् , तव सापत्न°, अहं सपत्न°).

Owing to the increasing sensitiveness to solecism, we find likewise different efforts made, independently of each other, to purge the text of what came to be regarded as stylistic blunders or corruptions in the ancient text. Examples of attempts made to [94] remove solecisms are: 1. 1. 190 ये च वर्तन्ति (v. l. वर्तन्ते ये च, ये वर्तन्ते च); 2. 93 हरणं गृह्य संप्राप्ते (v. l. गृहीत्वा हरणं प्राप्ते, दत्त्वा चाहरणं तस्मै); 7. 26 पुलोमस्य (v. l. पुलोम्नस्तु, °म्नश्च, °म्नोथ); 9. 2 चिन्त्य (v. l. स्मृत्वा, मत्वा); 21. 6 पन्नगाभवन् (फणिनोऽभ°, चारयोऽभ°); 43. 14 इयात् (v. l. अगात् , अयात्); 46. 37 शृङ्गिवचनं (v. l. शृङ्गिणो वाक्यं); 48. 24 सा त्रायस्मान् (v. l. त्रायस्वास्मान्); 96. 44 यथा दुहितरश्चैव (v. l. यथावद्दुहितॄश्चैव); 123. 16 तत्रोपकरणं गृह्य (v. l. °करणग्राही); 124. 24 उह्यन्तो pass. pres. part. (v. l. उह्यन्ते); 141. 7 नयिष्यामि (v. l. हि *or* तु नेष्यामि), 151. 23 गृह्य वाससी (v. l. वाससी आदाय); 154. 24 भागीरथ्याहमुत्तरे (v. l. जाह्नव्यामहमु°); 165. 24 बलाध्द्रियसि मे नन्दि (v. l. ह्रियसे त्वं बलाद्भद्रे etc.); 169. 20 दाधार तैजसं (v. l. दध्रे महौजसं etc.); 184. 18 धरन्ति (v. l. वसन्ति, कदन्ति, चरन्ति, ध्रियन्ति; जीवन्ति, वदन्ति, हरन्ति !); etc., etc.

I add examples of *hypermetric* pādas (generally with the scheme ⏑⏑–⏑–⏑,–––), which are the result of emendation: 1. 30. 7 प्रतिगृह्यतामिदानीं मे*; 1. 155. 35 *अवलिप्तं मे मुखं ब्रह्मन्.

And, finally, examples of *hiatus* as the result of emendation :

51. 8 अथो* इन्द्रः स्वयमेवाजगाम
57. 20 क्रियते *उच्छ्रयो नृपैः
98. 8 अन्तर्वत्नी *अहं भ्रात्रा
99. 15 त्वया च *अमितद्युते
100. 2 निशीथे *आगमिष्यति
103. 5 श्रूयते यादवी कन्या *अनुरूपा कुलस्य नः ।
110. 20 नाहं श्वाचरिते मार्गे *अवीर्यकृपणोचिते ।
110. 28 यदि *आवां महाप्राज्ञ
116. 25 तज्ज्येष्ठा *अनुमन्यतां
119. 11 तथेत्युक्ते *अम्बिकया
147. 2 रोरवीथो *अनाथवत्
148. 1 विदित्वा *अपकर्षेयं
157. 13 पञ्चकृत्वस्त्वया *उक्तः
207. 17 कुले *अस्मिन्बभूव ह
214. 9 धर्मराजे *अतिप्रीत्या
224. 5 संतप्यमाना (sing.) *अभितो.

It is important to remember that emendation has been resorted to merely for the purpose of *unifying divergent and conflicting manuscript evidence*, never in opposition to clear and unanimous testimony of manuscripts. The emendations are thus not amendments of the text in the ordinary sense of the word, made in order to eke out a better sense when the manuscripts yield no sense or an unsatisfactory sense ; they are rather an effort to find, so to say, a hypothetical focus towards which the discrepant readings converge.

THE "ADDITIONAL" PASSAGES

The uniformity of the interrelationship of the different manuscripts, versions or recensions, as has been already explained, is disturbed chiefly by comparison and conflation of manuscripts. A constant and fruitful source of confusion, as was pointed out above, has always been the marginalia. A more dangerous and troublesome source was the practice of incorporating into one's text—without stating the source and without much explanatory comment—passages found in other versions. It may be surmised that celebrated places of pilgrimage like Ujjayinī,[1] Rāmeśvaram, Kāśī, and others, with recitations of the epics held periodically in their famous shrines, have played an important rôle in the dissemination of the knowledge of local versions among the pious visiting pilgrims, whose number undoubtedly included the bards and the professional reciters of the epics.

[95] Much light is thrown on the origin of these misch-codices by the MS. K_4, a manuscript belonging to the Bombay Government Collection deposited at the Institute. In this manuscript we find long extracts from other cognate versions (such as γ) as also from the Southern recension, written out on separate folios and inserted at appropriate places in the body of the manuscript, with the words अत्रशोधपत्रमेकं written on the margin of the original

1 Bāṇa's *Kādambarī* (ed. PETERSON, p. 61) refers to a recitation of the Mbh. on the fourteenth day of the half month in the temple of Mahākāla at Ujjain, which the queen attends.

folio, near the place where the passage is to be interpolated. Should this manuscript happen to be copied again and should the copyist insert the passage at the place indicated by the previous scribe, the interpolation would become an integral part of the new text which is *externally absolutely indistinguishable* from the rest of the text.

This leads us to the question of "additional" passages in general. Our attitude with regard to them is quite clear, in my opinion. The first and foremost source of our knowledge as to what the Mahābhārata comprises, is and must remain the manuscript evidence itself. For example, the question —which seems to trouble a great many people, judging by the inquiries on the point received at the Institute—whether the Uttaragītā, Gajendramokṣa and Anusmṛti are parts of the Mahābhārata, must be answered by the manuscripts themselves. If none of our manuscripts contain these passages, it is *prima facie* evidence that they are *not* parts of the Mahābhārata. There is nothing to suggest that our Mahābhārata manuscripts have suffered any serious loss at any time. There never was any lack of manuscripts, many of which were preserved carefully in temples, and which must have been copied repeatedly, for the enhancement of merit. There is no evidence of any break in the tradition at any time or any place, within the confines of India at least. The probable inference is that *our manuscripts contain all that was there originally to hand down,* and more. What late writers and commentators have said about passages not found in our manuscripts is always a matter of secondary importance; it cannot *ipso facto* nullify or override the primary evidence of manuscripts. Such extrinsic testimony has only local or personal value; it can always be rebutted by the evidence of the Mahābhārata manuscripts.

Likewise, whether an episode, adhyāya, passage, stanza or line may be regarded as belonging to the Mahābhārata or not must primarily depend upon whether the manuscripts contain it. Extrinsic evidence, in so far as it is valid, will principally hold good only for the period or locality to which it belongs. Intrinsic evidence may be considered; but, being of a subjective character, it must be used with caution. Our primary evidence being the manuscripts themselves, we are bound to view with suspicion, as a matter of principle, any part of the text which is found only in one recension, or only in a portion of our critical apparatus. Therefore, the evidence for such passages as are contained only in one manuscript, or a small group of manuscripts or versions, or even in a whole recension must be pronounced to be defective. Consequently, all lines belonging to one recension only, and *a fortiori* such as pertain to a combination of manuscripts amounting to less than a recension, for which there is nothing corresponding in the other recension and which are not absolutely necessary for the context—all lines, in short, with a defective title—have been placed in the footnotes or the Appendix, pending further inquiry regarding their credentials.

Such passages are not all necessarily spurious. There might be a hundred good reasons why the questionable passages are missing in a particular recension or version. It *might* conceivably be, for instance, that the shorter recension represents (as certain [96] scholar has said) "a mutilated and hastily put together composition of the Middle Indian Redactors, who could not lay their hands on all manuscripts of the Mahābhārata".[1] The shorter version *might* again be, theoretically, a consciously abridged or expurgated version. Or, more simply, the omission *might* be due to mere oversight of some scribe who had quite unintentionally omitted the defaulting passage and this mistake of the first scribe had been perpetuated by the other copyists. And so on and so forth. But all these are mere *possibilities*. All these reasons in general and particular must be adduced and proved, or at least made probable, in any given case. Moreover, the manuscripts clearly show that there has been in progress, through centuries, constant comparison of manuscripts. In view of this circumstance, the explanation that the omission of a passage *in a whole version* might be due to a scribe's omission loses much of its force. *Omission is as much a fact in Mahābhārata textual tradition as addition.* And it is fair to demand of a person who alleges the authenticity of such one-recension passages why the rival recension does not contain it.[2]

The general condemnation of a recension or version that it is mutilated, merely on the ground that it lacks certain passages that are found in a rival recension or version, is entirely meaningless; for the argument might easily be reversed, so that the controversy will resolve merely into mutual vituperation. What I mean is this. From the fact that one of the recensions, say N, does not contain a certain passage or a certain set of passages found in another, say S, it is illogical to argue that N is a mutilated version; because such an argument can with equal cogency be applied to S, in regard to certain other passages that are missing in S but found in N. The point is so important and at the same time so difficult to grasp that I shall endeavour to make my meaning clearer with the help of a concrete illustration. My contention is this. From the fact that the Southern recension contains, say, the Nāḷāyanī episode (App. I, No. 100), which is missing in the Northern recension, it would be illogical to argue that the Northern recension is defective

---

[1] P. P. S. Sastri, The Mahābhārata, Vol. 2, Introduction, p. viii.

[2] Cf. Lüders, "Zur Sage von Ṛṣyaśṛṅga", *Nachrichten von der königl. Gesell. der Wiss. zu Göttingen.* Phil-hist. Kl. 1901. 42: "Allein wie man über die Erklärung solcher Verschiedenheiten innerhalb der Nāgarīrecension auch denken mag, soweit es sich um die Verschiedenheiten zwischen N und G"—then, *a fortiori,* between N and S—"handelt, halte ich es für ein durchaus richtiges Princip, in den Abschnitten, die im allgemeinen Vers für Vers übereinstimmen wie z. B. der Text des Ṛṣyaśṛṅga-sage, einen Vers, der entweder in N oder in G fehlt, als verdächtig, und wenn sich ein einleuchtender Grund für seine Einfügung darbietet, als interpoliert zu betrachten. Wer solche Verse für echt hält, muss erklären, wie es kam, dass sie in der einen Recension fortgelassen wurden."

or mutilated; because one can, with equal cogency, seek to establish the mutilation or defection of the Southern recension by pointing, say, to the Gaṇeśa passage, which is found only in certain Northern manuscripts and is entirely missing in the Southern manuscripts. The argument could have been employed with greater semblance of reason and plausibility, had there been only a mere plus or minus on either side, but is entirely without cogency in the present instance where there are both additions and omissions on both sides.

[97] Originality and authenticity are, unfortunately, not the prerogative of any single recension or version or manuscript.[1] They must be established, laboriously, chapter by chapter, line by line, word by word, syllable by syllable.[2] The optimistic view that any extant manuscript, however old and trustworthy, of some favoured version or recension, could give us, with a few additions and alterations, the text of Vyāsa's Bhārata or Mahābhārata is the index of a naïve mentality and does not need any elaborate refutation.

The argument in favour of any particular recension or version or text is frequently sought to be strengthened by a reference to the authority of the Parvasaṁgraha (Ādi 2), a week reed on which every tyro leans rather heavily in the beginning, and it would be well to examine the argument here.

THE PARVASAṀGRAHA ARGUMENT

Until lately high hopes had been entertained that the Parvasaṁgrahaparvan (Ādi 2) would supply the clue to the solution of the perplexing question of the reconstruction of the original Mahābhārata. But the paradoxical situation created by the circumstance that two different editors of the Virāṭaparvan, both of whom rely mainly on the data of the Parvasaṁgraha for establishing the originality and authenticity of their respective texts, have produced critical editions of that parvan which differ by no less than 1467 stanzas,[3] has created grave misgivings in the minds of unbiassed critics as to whether the Parvasaṁgraha can render us any help at all in reconstructing the text of the Mahābhārata, and these misgivings appear justified by the facts of the case.

The exaggerated importance which the late Mr. UTGIKAR was inclined to attach to the numerical data of the Parvasaṁgraha, was, I believe, mainly, if not wholly, due to his mistaken belief that there was complete agreement between the two rival recensions in all material particulars as regards the text of this adhyāya. This erroneous and wholly unfounded notion seems to

---

1 LÜDERS, *op. cit.* p. 43, justly asks: "Wenn aber die Grantha-recension Zusätze erfuhr, warum sollen wir denn annehmen, dass die Nāgarī-recension von ihnen verschont geblieben sei?"

2 Cf. WINTERNITZ, *Geschichte der ind. Litteratur*, 1. 398 f.

3 Mr. UTGIKAR'S text contains only 2033 stanzas; while in Professor SASTRI'S Southern Recension, the Virāṭaparvan has 3500 stanzas! And both are said to be supported by manuscript authority.

have been induced by the ambiguous and thoroughly misleading character of the text of the Khumbhakonam edition, which claims to be an edition "mainly based on South Indian texts", but presents a version of this adhyāya which has been unblushingly copied from the Bombay and Calcutta editions, ignoring wholly the Southern divergences, which are quite considerable.

Not only are there discrepancies between the two recensions as regards the numbers of the adhyāyas and the ślokas in the various parvans, there is no complete agreement even between the different versions of the same recension. Take, for instance, the case of the Ādiparvan itself. Our constituted text (following the Śāradā codex) gives (1. 2. 96) the number of ślokas in the Ādi as 7884. But this is not the only reading of that number. For the digit representing the thousands alone, the choice lies between seven, eight, nine and ten! There can, therefore, be no doubt that the text of this adhyāya also has been tampered with and designedly altered, from time to time in various [98] ways, in order to make it harmonize with the inflated version of a later epoch. It will thus have to be admitted that the parvasaṁgraha argument is of secondary importance and must not be pressed too far.

Be that as it may, it is extremely problematic whether we could make any use whatsoever of the Parvasaṁgraha enumeration of ślokas in the case of the Ādi at least, because it will be difficult to compute the extent of this parvan and that for two reasons. Firstly, because this parvan, as is well known, contains two lengthy prose adhyāyas (3 and 90). Taking the figure of the Parvasaṁgraha to represent the exact extent of the *whole* of the Ādi, it is not clear how the prose portions were computed by the compilers of the Parvasaṁgraha. Most of the modern computers add the numbers of *stanzas* to the number of their respective prose *sections*, and arrive at the length of the Ādi in *ślokas*! But this is bad arithmetic. P. P. S. SASTRI offers a solution which is more ingenious than convincing. He holds the compiler of the Parvasaṁgraha down to the letter of his statement. The Parvasaṁgraha tells us, says SASTRI, merely the number of *ślokas* which the different parvans contain. Nothing is said about the prose sections. He therefore ignores the prose adhyāyas in computing the extent of the Ādi, and is satisfied that his text exactly agrees with the data of the Parvasaṁgraha!

The other difficulty in the way of using the Parvasaṁgraha figure in the case of the Ādi is that this parvan contains a large number of Triṣṭubh stanzas, which again introduce an element of uncertainty in the computation. Was each Triṣṭubh stanza counted as *one* śloka; or did the Bhārata-cintakas (mentioned in 1. 2. 172) compute the exact equivalent of the long-metre stanzas in ślokas? It is difficult to say. The difference in the reckoning will be, however, between 40 and 50 per cent. of the total! As a very rough estimate, the Ādi may contain something like 500 long-metre stanzas. This factor alone would introduce a difference of about 225 stanzas!

These are some of the obvious difficulties in the way of making any practical use of the figure recorded in the Parvasaṁgraha for text-critical purposes. The computation may have some value in the case of a parvan in which there is no prose at all, which is almost wholly in anuṣṭubh metre, and for which finally the Parvasaṁgraha figure is certain, the manuscript evidence being unanimous.

It is quite within the range of probability that the apparent extent of the critical text of a parvan may fall appreciably below or rise appreciably above the figure recorded in the Parvasaṁgraha, as is actually the case with other editions. Moreover, unless it can be made probable that the compilation of this "Table of Contents" is nearly contemporaneous with the present redaction of the Great Epic, *these discrepancies will be without much cogency* in matters relating to the constitution of the text. The value of a manuscript, version, or printed text of the Mahābhārata must not be thought to depend exclusively or even mainly upon its agreement with or discrepancy from the numerical data of the Parvasaṁgraha. It must in final analysis be regarded as depending upon the place it occupies in a logical and convincing scheme formulated to explain the evolution of the different extant versions and types of Mahābhārata manuscripts.

It should further be carefully borne in mind that even if there be exact agreement as to extent between the Parvasaṁgraha and any constituted text, this fact alone is no guarantee of the absolute correctness of the entire text, line for line, because the same [99] number of stanzas could be made up in innumerable different ways by accepting and rejecting stanzas of doubtful authenticity and uncertain documentation, of which there is always a plentiful supply in every parvan. The difficulty will finally not be solved even if we happen to light upon a unique manuscript which agrees with the Parvasaṁgraha exactly as to the number of stanzas in any particular parvan and we should adopt its *verbatim;* because there is every probability that while it satisfies the one criterion of extent given by the Parvasaṁgraha, it may not satisfy, in every respect, other and more exacting critical tests, when compared line by line and word by word with other extant manuscripts.

In the above discussion I have implicitly assumed, as is done by most writers on the subject, that the word *śloka* in the Parvasaṁgraha chapter has the usual meaning "stanza". This interpretation was called into question, by the late Mahamahopadhyaya Haraprasad SHASTRI, who offered a new interpretation, which I cannot but think is far more plausible, although I do not agree with all the conclusions he deduces therefrom.

The really valuable discovery of the Mahamahopadhyaya, in my opinion, is that the word śloka cannot mean here stanza or verse or anything of the kind, but must denote (as in the parlance of scribes and vendors of manuscripts) *a unit of measurement of written matter,* comprising 32 syllables of akṣaras.[1] The difficulty of computing prose passages and the long-metre-stanzas mentioned above finds a satisfactory solution at once in this interpretation of the word "śloka". And that is moreover the only interpretation of the word which, as far as I can see, can successfully solve that difficulty, in view of the circumstance that the text is heterogeneous, consisting of ślokas, prose, and long-metre stanzas. But in this supposition we shall have to count, not only the actual text (consisting of prose and verse), but the whole of the written matter. And that enumeration, whether it be 7884, 8884, 9884 or 9984, will include not only the text properly so called but also the colophons and the hundreds of the prose formulaic references (like वैशंपायन उवाच) besides perhaps the captions of adhyāyas, sub-parvans and parvans, and even the numerical figures denoting the numbers of ślokas, and so on.

The number of adhyāyas in our edition (225) does not tally with the number given in the Parvasaṁgraha (218), any more than in any of the previous editions : the Calcutta edition of the Ādi has 234 adhyāyas, the Bombay editions vary between 234 and 236, while the Kumbhakonam edition reaches the astonishing figure 260, though the Parvasaṁgraha figure in the case of each of these latter editions is the same, 227.

It may be pointed out that the adhyāya division in our extant manuscripts is extremely arbitrary. The average length of our adhyāyas should be about 35 stanzas ; but adhy. 12 and 22 of our edition contain only 5 stanzas each, while adhy. 57 (to mention only one instance) has over 100 stanzas. As regards the contents of the adhyāyas also there is much inconsistency. Thus we frequently find that one adhyāya ends with the remark that a certain person spoke as follows, and his speech, which may be quite short, forms the beginning of the following adhyāya. Then again the manuscripts are far from being unanimous in the matter of marking the colophons : they show in fact wild [100] fluctuations. Even the reading of the Parvasaṁgraha figure is not entirely free from doubt (e.g. our Śāradā codex gives the number of the adhyāyas as 230 !), though the reading 218 seems highly probable.

Under these circumstances, nothing would be easier than to manipulate the colophons, by arbitrarily combining the conflicting data of the different recensions or versions or even manuscripts and arriving at *any required* figure. This has actually been done by Professor P. P. S. SASTRI in his edition of the Southern Recension, which thereby achieves the dubious distinction of being the only edition of the Ādiparvan in which the adhyāya number agrees exactly with the Parvasaṁgraha figure but the colophons are mostly at the wrong places. This procedure is the less excusable in his case

---

[1] Cf. Haraprasada SHASTRI, *A Descriptive Catalogue of Sanskrit Manuscripts in the Collection of the Asiatic Society of Bengal*, Vol. 5, Preface, pp. xxxii, xxxv, xxxvii, XLII.

as he is at great pains to create the impression that he is just reproducing the text of one selected manuscript, correcting only "scriptorial" blunders. Now his basic manuscript (ञ = our G_6) divides the Ādi into two separate *major* parvans, Ādiparvan and Saṁbhavaparvan, with 40 and 200 numbered adhyāyas respectively, which makes a total of 240 adhyāyas, and which is nearer the Kumbhakonam figure (260) than the Parvasaṁgraha figure (218). While correcting "scriptorial blunders", Professor SASTRI has, so to say, spirited away 22 colophons before our very eyes

A more careful study of the manuscript evidence may tend to reduce the discrepancy between the constituted text and the data of the Parvasaṁgraha as regards the number of the adhyāyas, or at any rate may enable us to account for the difference, though at present it seems impossible to harmonize the manuscript evidence (consisting of the actual colophons) with the Parvasaṁgraha.

INTERPOLATION

There has been an extraordinary reluctance among scholars to face the fact that the Mahābhārata manuscripts may contain and do contain quantities of spurious matter. But there is now no excuse for such recalcitrance. The critical apparatus of this edition contains a unique record of hundreds of lines which are evidently and unquestionably spurious. Here is a list of passages from our Appendix, each found in *one* manuscript only : App. I, No. 2 (in K_6 marg. : containing 4 lines); No. 4 (K_3 : 14 lines); No. 5 (B_4 : 23 lines) ; No. 7 (G_1 : 4 lines) ; No. 16 (K_4 : 9 lines) ; No. 25 (D_5 : 4 lines) ; No. 26 (B_4 : 6 lines) ; No. 31 (K_4 : 27 lines) ; No. 34 (K_4 : 6 lines) ; No. 44 (D_2 : 24 lines) ; No. 49-50 Da_1 : 21 lines) ; No. 66 (D_4 : 47 lines) ; No. 70 (G_1 : 8 lines) ; No. 74 (B_1 : 9 lines) ; No. 94 (D_4 : 31 lines) ; No. 98 (D_4 : 50 lines) ; etc., etc. These are passages from the Appendix alone, to which many of them have been relegated on account of either their length or their irrelevancy ; but the foot-notes contain hundreds, nay thousands, of lines of precisely the same character. Then there are also lines which are found in only two or three manuscripts, of which I have counted some 300 instances. A number of new additions have been now given by Professor SASTRI, who has examined other Telugu and Grantha manuscripts for his edition of the Ādi in the Southern recension. And I am fully persuaded that if we examine yet other manuscripts, we shall still find fresh passages which had never been seen or heard of before. No sane person would maintain that these are all original passages lost in all manuscripts except the few late and inferior manuscripts in which they happen to occur.

[101] It is not always easy, as has already been remarked, to prove that these "additional" passages are interpolations. The epic metre is easy to imitate ; the epic grammar is flexible ; the epic style is nondescript. The additional lines are generally fashioned with skill, and fitted in with cunning.

The following interpolated stanzas, by a poet aspiring after higher things, in fancy metre and classical style are rather exceptional :

1859* भीम उवाच ।

रे भूभुजो यदि भुवोल्लसितं न किंचि-
त्तत्किं स्पृहाजनि सुतां प्रति पार्षतस्य ।
जज्ञे स्पृहाथ कथमागतमागतं वा
प्राणाधिके धनुषि तत्कथमाग्रहोऽभूत् ॥

कस्य द्रोणो धनुषि न गुरुः स्वस्ति देवव्रताय
मन्दाभ्यासः कुरुपतिरयं श्रीसमुत्थैर्विलासैः ।
रे कर्णाद्याः शृणुत मधुरां ब्राह्मणस्याशु वाणीं
राधा यन्त्रं रचयतु पुनर्विक्रमप्यस्त्वविक्रम् ॥

An interesting instance of a passage which is betrayed by its contents is an extravaganza in some Grantha manuscripts. This bizarre interpolation[1] describes among other things, with circumstantial detail, the marriage of Parāśara and Satyavatī (*alias* Matsyagandhā). At this ceremony, the shades of the ancestors of both the bride and the bridegroom are invoked, all the details of a regular Hindu marital rite are minutely observed, and the marriage is solemnized in the presence of Vasiṣṭha, Yājñavalkya and other great Ṛṣis living in the Naimiṣa forest, with the distribution of *baksheesh* to Brahmins. It is an interesting speculation whether credulity can go so far as to regard even such passages as an authentic part of the original Mahābhārata or Bhārata of Vyāsa, just because the passage is found in some Mahābhārata manuscripts.

The foot-notes contain a rare selection of passages that are either palpably absurd, sometimes contradicting the immediate context, or else have little connection with the context in which they lie embedded : quotations, glosses, fanciful additions of details, the jetsam and flotsam of Mahābhārata poesie.

These bewildering fluctuations in the text are quite unique, being peculiar to the Mahābhārata. They are not found in the manuscripts of the Vedic literature or in those of grammatical, philosophical, or rhetorical texts or of the works of the classical poets and dramatists. This only proves that the Mahābhārata was peculiarly liable to inflation and elaboration.

When I say that the Mahābhārata manuscripts contain quantities of spurious additions, I intend no disparagement or condemnation of the text or of the manuscripts. The process is normal, inevitable and in a wider sense wholly right. *If* the epic is to continue to be a vital force in the life of any progressive people, *it must be a slow-changing book!* The fact of expurga-

---

1 App. I, Nos. 35-36.

tion and elaboration is ony an outward indication of its being a book of inspiration and guidance in life, and not merely a book lying unused and forgotten on a dusty book-shelf. Those are probably just the touches that have saved the Mahābhārata from the fate of being consigned to the limbo of oblivion, which has befallen its sister epics like the Gilgamesh.

[102] To give only one illustration. The awkwardness of the sexual relations of some of those epic characters of bygone ages must have been indeed a puzzle and a source of constant tribulation to the *reciter* of the epics (Paurāṇika), who was called upon to narrate, explain and justify those old-world stories to his devout and impressionable audiences, in the course of his recitations, which were, in the post-epic period, nothing more than edifying popular sermons. It is then no wonder that the shrewd ones among these pastors of the people, these professional keepers of their morals, should have occasionally taken the bull by the horn, so to say, and boldly added or substituted, *bona fide*, details which harmonized better with their own conceptions of right and wrong or with those of their pious flock.

A PROBLEM IN "TEXTUAL DYNAMICS"

After what has been said above, it is needless to add that the constituted text is based on all versions of both recensions and prepared on eclectic principles. I have given in the text whatever in each case appeared to be supported by the balance of probabilities, but all important deviations in the manuscripts are noted in the critical apparatus, so that every reader has, at his disposal, the entire material for controlling and correcting the constituted text, where necessary. All important elements of the text—lines, phrases, significant words and even word-parts—that are less than certain, are indicated by *a wavy line* printed below them. Slight differences in the spellings of words, of proper names (e.g. नैमिष: नैमिश) and some minor details (such as the expletives or the prose formulae सूत उवाच सौतिरुवाच, सूतः etc.) are ignored for this purpose. This device is, by nature, hard to apply strictly, and there are bound to be many inconsistencies in its application. I have retained it all the same with the express object of obviating all false sense of security. This wavy line, running through the entire length of the text is, to my mind, the symbol and constant remembrancer of this essential fact in Mahābhārata textual criticism that the Mahābhārata is not and never was a fixed rigid text, but is fluctuating epic tradition, a *thème avec variations*, not unlike a popular Indian melody. Our objective should consequently not to be to arrive at an archetype (which practically never existed), but to represent, view and explain the epic tradition in all its variety, in all its fullness, in all its ramifications. ***Ours is a problem in textual dynamics, rather than in textual statics.***

To put it in other words, the Mahābhārata is the whole of the epic tradition : the *entire* Critical Apparatus. Its separation into the constituted text and the critical notes is only a static representation of a constantly changing epic text—a representation made for purpose of visualizing, studying and analyzing the panorama of the more grand and less grand thought-movements that have crystallized in the shape of the texts handed down to us in our Mahābhārata manuscripts.

WHAT IS THE CONSTITUTED TEXT?

To prevent misconception in the mind of the casual reader, it is best to state at first what the constituted text is *not*.[1] The editor is firmly convinced that the text [103] presented in this edition is *not* anything like the autograph copy of the work of its mythical author, Maharṣi Vyāsa. It is *not*, in any sense, a reconstruction of the Ur-Mahābhārata or of the Ur-Bhārata, that ideal but impossible desideratum. It is also *not* an exact replica of the poem recited by Vaiśaṁpāyana before Janamejaya. It is further wholly uncertain how close it approaches the text of the poem said to be recited by the Sūta (or Sauti) before Śaunaka and the other dwellers of the Naimiṣa forest.

It is but a modest attempt to present *a version of the epic as old as the extant manuscript material will permit us to reach* with some semblance of confidence. It is, in all probability, not the best text of the Great Epic, possible or existing, nor necessarily even a good one. It only claims to be *the most ancient one according to the direct line of transmission*, purer than the others in so far as it is free from the obvious errors of copying and spurious additions. It may be regarded, if the editor has dône his work properly, the ancestor of all extant manuscripts, or, to be precise, of the manuscripts examined and collated for this edition. The constituted text cannot be accurately dated, nor labelled as pertaining to any particular place or personality. Since our manuscripts are comparatively modern, our text cannot claim to be very old. It goes without saying that (precisely like every other edition) it is a mosaic of old and new matter. That is to say, in an average adhyāya of this edition (as of any other edition) we my read a stanza of the second century B.C. followed by one written in the second century A.D. Sometimes the gap will occur in the middle of a line, precisely as in every other edition. This unevenness and these inequalities are inevitable, conditioned as they are by the very nature of the text and the tradition.

The Vulgate text of the Mahābhārata is fairly readable and will appear in places, at first sight, to be even "better" than the critical text, because the

---

[1] Thus Professor SASTRI (Southern Recension, Vol. I, Introduction, p. xiii) writes about this edition: "Whilst the Poona edition *lays claim* to constitute the text of the Mahābhārata *as closely as* [103] *possible to Vyāsa's version* of the same, the principle underlying this edition" etc. Even Professor Sylvain LÉVI, in a review of this edition (*JA*. Oct.—Dec. 1929, p. 347) wrote: "Si j'osais me permettre une suggestion dans ce domaine, je conseillerais à l'éditeur de renoncer, par pitié pour nous, à la part même du travail qui lui tient le plus à cœur et qui apporte à son esprit le plus de satisfaction, *la reconstruction de "l'Ur-Mahābhārata"* comme il se plaît à dire", etc. (Italics mine!). Both statements are false!

former has been purged by the continuous emendations of scholars for centuries. A whole army of anonymous scholars and poets must have worked at the text to make it smooth and easy of comprehension, and to increase its popularity and usefulness by adding to it interesting anecdotes, incorporating into it current and popular versions and explanations, bringing it in a line with the ethical, moral, religious and political ideas of essentially different ages.

The reader will find that the constituted text is by no means smooth. It contains fresh instances of loose and archaic linguistic forms and constructions, anacoluthons and lack of syntactical concord. There remain many contradictions and superfluities. There is evident lack of finish in the hidden parts. These blemishes—if they be blemishes in epic poetry, which is dynamic poetry, with no necessary pretensions to niceties of style, in the narrower sense of the term—must have been inherent in the old poem. Where they are met with in the critical text, they are not speculative fiction ; they are documented by the manuscripts themselves or at least are inferable from them with a high degree of probability.

[104] For the shortcomings mentioned above, the constituted text has merits also. It cleanses the text of puerile modern accretions and obvious errors of repetition, which lengthen and weaken the text. It solves a certain number of textual riddles (bogus *kūṭas*), which were the outcome of long standing corruptions and unskilful conflation. It rescues from undeserved oblivion many an authentic archaism, which had been gradually ousted in the course of transmission of the text.

Sooner than print up the text of one manuscript, however reliable it may be, declining to shoulder the responsibilities attaching to the work of an editor, I have ventured on the perilous path of text reconstruction, in the hope and belief that it will present a more faithful picture of the original than any *extant* manuscript could do. That to prepare such a text is a phenomenally difficult task, no one can realize better than the editor himself. It is as certain as inevitable that in preparing a text like this the editor will frequently make blunders, even gross blunders.

It is to be feared that there is no royal road in this incomparably difficult field. The only path left open to us by which we may return to the original Mahābhārata or Bhārata is the rough, narrow, scientific foot-path of repeated trial and error. More than one attempt will probably have to be made before the ideal is attained. It will, therefore, be prudent not to claim too much for the *first* critical edition, nor to expect too much from it.

OTHER EDITIONS

Of the old editions it must be said that they are creditable performances, but they lack the critical apparatus. We do not know on what manuscripts they are based, according to what principles the editors have prepared the text, information essential on account of the wild fluctuations of the manuscripts. That is why they have been almost wholly ignored in the present edition.

The editio princeps (Calcutta 1836) remains the best edition of the Vulgate, after the lapse of nearly a century. The later text editions, as is unfortunately too often the case with our editions, add to the *editio princeps* only a fresh crop of spurious lines and misprints.

The well-known *pothī*-form Bombay editions (published by Ganpat KRISHNAJI in Śaka 1799, and Gopal Narayan in 1913, and others), which include Nīlakaṇṭha's scholium, are supposed to represent Nīlakaṇṭha's text; but they contain many readings and lines which are not to be found in the Nīlakaṇṭha manuscripts, and are therefore not wholly reliable.

The Kumbhakonam edition, which is said to be "mainly based on the South Indian texts", is a fine representative of the composite Telugu version; it has been of immense help to me in the study of what may be called "conflate" readings. In former years its chief value lay in that it gave the reader glimpses, however imperfect and confused, of the important Southern recension. It is now rendered obsolete and superfluous by P. P. S. SASTRI's new edition of the Mahābhārata, which will presently be described, and which is unquestionably a better representative of the Southern tradition.

[105] The Grantha edition (Sarfojirajapuram 1896) and the old Telugu edition (Madras 1855) were not examined: they are not likely to contain anything of high importance that is not found in the other editions or manuscripts collated for this edition.

The editions accompanied by vernacular translations, which form a very numerous class, are mostly bad reprints of one or the other of the earlier (printed) editions and may be completely ignored here; they are perfectly useless for critical purposes.

The new edition[1] of the Southern recension of the Mahābhārata by Professor P. P. Subrahmanya SASTRI of Madras, now in the course of publication, which has been referred to several times already, is a laudable attempt to supply a long-felt want. He deserves the cordial thanks of all lovers of Sanskrit literature in general and of the Great Epic in particular, for his courageously undertaking such a stupendous and exacting task and pursuing it steadfastly, single-handed, during the scanty leisure permitted by his official duties as Professor of Sanskrit in the Presidency College of Madras, and Editor of the Descriptive Catalogue of Sanskrit Manuscripts in the extensive library of the Saraswathi Mahal at Tanjore. The edition is in no

---

[1] The Mahābhārata, Southern Recension, critically edited by P. P. S. SASTRI, B.A. (Oxon.), M.A. Professor of Sanskrit, Presidency College, Madras, etc. V. Ramaswami Sastrulu & Sons, Madras, 1931 ff.

sense rendered superfluous by the Critical Edition, although most of the information it contains is or will be included, in some shape or other, in the present edition. The gulf between the Northern and the Southern recensions is so vast, that it is extremely difficult, if not practically impossible, to reconstruct the Southern text, completely and correctly, from the critical notes of this edition.

The principles on which the text of this edition of the Southern recension of the Mahābhārata is prepared have been set forth and briefly discussed above. The editor, it was pointed out, fondly cherishes the unfounded belief that he is printing a Grantha manuscript *as it is*, but consciously and unconsciously he has introduced so many important innovations, that the text, as a whole, must be pronounced to be *eclectic;* as eclectic as any text—at least as far as the Ādiparvan is concerned—published so far. For far less important deviations from the manuscripts have I condemned, above, the editions of the Vulgate. Judged as an *eclectic* edition, it must be pronounced to be inferior. The principle SASTRI has laid down is a simple one to follow ; in fact nothing could be simpler ; he is to print the text of a selected manuscript *as it is*, only correcting clerical errors. And it is to be greatly regretted that he does not follow *rigorously* this principle. He constantly flouts it, in pursuit of some imaginary norm. Clear as his principle is, his actual procedure is somewhat paradoxical. He has left innumerable minor " inferior " readings in possession of the text (when he could have with perfect confidence, if not certainty, put into his text the correct readings), because he ostensibly wants to present the text as it is in one selected manuscript ; on the other hand, he has light-heartedly, on utterly insufficient grounds, effected very substantial additions (in one instance extending to 140 lines), omissions and other unwarranted alterations (such as transpositions of adhyāyas), in the utterly mistaken (though unquestionably *bona fide*) belief that he is correcting only the " scriptorial blunders " of his exemplar, when they are in reality (as is shown by the evidence of cognate versions) nothing of the kind.

[106] The sub-title " Southern Recension " is perhaps a trifle ambitious, at least as far as the Ādi is concerned ; because, firstly, he has utilized only six Southern manuscripts (1 Telugu and 5 Granthas), even less than the number (18) of the Southern manuscripts collated for our edition ; and, secondly, he has completely ignored one whole Southern version, the important Malayālam version, in my opinion, the most important of Southern versions.

Further, it may be questioned whether the edition deserves to be called a critical edition at all, since, as was pointed out above, the editor is avowedly aiming only at *reproducing the text of one manuscript*, categorically renounicng the obligation of the textual critic to restore the text, as far as possible, to its original form.

The inclusion in SASTRI's text of a certain number of stray lines and even a few lengthy passages which are peculiar to the Northern recension and ***absolutely foreign*** to the Southern,[1] throws much light on the unconscious process of the growth of the epic and the irresistible influence which the Vulgate exerts on a text that is coming into being, in other words, on that subtle process of textual osmosis (if I may term it so) by which the epic texts have become conflated. SASTRI's explanations in his Introduction as well as his procedure elucidate much of the psychology for the ancient scribes and redactors, who have in the past shaped our Mahābhārata texts for us. Unconsciously he seems to have worked on the identical principles on which the ancient scribes have worked. His edition is a true *lineal descendant* of the Mahābhārata manuscripts of South India.

In preparing Appendix I of this edition (in which there is a strong preponderance of the Southern element), I had to go rather carefully over SASTRI's text of the Ādi, when I came across far too many inaccuracies in the passages for which I checked his text and critical notes with the collations of the manuscripts common to our critical apparatus. The critical notes of the edition leave much to be desired. He has mostly shown correctly the additional passages in the manuscripts examined by him ; but he fails, as a rule, to note the transpositions, omissions, and above all repetitions, which often are, critically, highly significant, probably again in the erroneous belief that they are negligible "scriptorial blunders." Some of them are undoubtedly so, but not all. Likewise he has not always shown correctly the additions and omissions of the colophons, and yet he is evidently most anxious to reach the number 218, given by the Parvasaṁgraha. All deviations, however trivial they may seem to him, he should have scrupulously noted, as a matter of principle, because he must realize that with his utterly negligible critical apparatus—comprising only five or six manuscripts out of a total of more than three hundred manuscripts of the Ādi—it is wholly impossible for him to understand and explain the full significance of all the textual features and anomalies of the manuscripts examined by him. I will not take him to task for the numerous wrong readings which have inadvertently crept into his text, because I know, from personal experience, that it would be a physical impossibility to combine any high degree of accuracy with the pace at which he is compelled to bring out the volumes. But it is inevitable that the discovery of such inaccuracies should give rise to a sense of insecurity and suspicion in the mind of the reader in respect of those matters that he has to take from the editor on trust.

[107] The minor deficiencies pointed out here do not, however, detract materially from the many merits of the work, from the incalculable advantage we derive from having a Southern version of an entire parvan in Deva-

---

[1] See above, p. 108 and foot-note 1.

nāgarī transcript, printed in handy volumes, because the Southern manuscripts are really most inconvenient for the purposes of rapid consultation. I should be indeed very ungrateful if I did not frankly admit that Professor SASTRI'S edition has been of immense help to me, personally, for the study of the Southern recension, and I have no doubt that it will also help other workers in the field in future.

There remains for me the pleasant duty of recording all the encouragement and assistance I and my colleagues on the Mahābhārata Editorial Board have received from different quarters in the course of our labours in this connection.

To Shrimant Balasaheb Pant Pratinidhi, B. A., Ruler of Aundh, whose liberality made it in the first instance possible for the Institute to undertake this ambitious project—the greatest philogical enterprise undertaken in India within living memory—I have to tender on behalf of myself and other people like myself interested in the study and regeneration of our great National Epic, our most sincere and cordial thanks. For the numerous marks of personal kindness with which the Chief Saheb has favoured me, in this connection, on all occasions, I have to offer him the expression of my profound gratitude. His unflagging zeal and irrepressible optimism have helped me to carry on the work in the face of heavy odds. The Chief Saheb has been pleased to enliven the dry and scientific character of the work by contributing to this edition excellent paintings of scenes selected from the Great Epic, paintings especially prepared under his expert guidance and supervision, for the purposes of this edition.

I have next to record the gratitude of the promoters of this scheme to various distinguished donors : the Imperial Government of India ; the Provincial Governments of Bombay, Madras and Burma ; the Governments of H. E. H. the Nizam of Hyderabad, H. H. the Maharaja of Mysore, H. H. the Gaekwad of Baroda ; the Chief of Phaltan and other enlightened and patriotic Rulers and Chiefs of Indian States ; the University of Bombay ; and diverse other generous donors : who have all rendered valuable financial assistance to the scheme and contributed their share to that measure of success which has already been achieved. In this connection I must not forget to mention the kind offices of my old friend the Honourable Mr. Mukundarao R. JAYAKAR, M. A., Bar-at-law, Member of the Legislative Assembly, whose selfless interest in the success of this project has moved him to exert his influence for enlisting the sympathy and securing the help of some of the distinguished donors mentioned above.

I must next record my grateful thanks for help of various kinds I have received from my colleagues on the Mahābhārata Editorial Board, namely : Prof. S. K. BELVALKAR, M. A., Ph. D., I. E. S.; Prof. A. B. GAJENDRAGADKAR, M. A., B. E. S. ; Mr. P. V. KANE, M. A., LL. M ; Principal R. D. KARMARKAR, M. A. ; Prof. V. G. PARANJPE, M. A., LL. B., D. Litt. ; Prof. V. K. RAJAVADE, M. A.; the late Mr. N. B. UTGIKAR, M. A.; [108] Prof. P. L. VAIDYA, M. A., D. Litt.; Mr. V. P. VAIDYA, J. P., B. A., Bar-at-law ; Prof. M. WINTERNITZ, Ph. D.; and the late Rev. Father R. ZIMMERMANN, S. J., Ph. D. No Board of which I have been a member has worked, ever since its inception, more smoothly and harmoniously.

But I desire to make a special mention of my indebtedness to Mr. V. P. VAIDYA, Bar-at-law, of Bombay, and the late Rev. Father R. ZIMMERMANN, S. J., whose advice and ready help accompanied my labours from the time I first undertook the responsibilities of the work. The interest of my late lamented fellow-student and friend Father ZIMMERMANN in this project did not flag even as he lay, in 1931, in a Nursing Home at Faldkirch, waiting prepared to meet his Maker! Nothing encouraged me more in the early stages of this arduous and fascinating work than the active and unwavering interest with which these two friends followed it.

Nepal and Kashmir in the North and Tanjore and Travancore in the South are known to contain vast treasures of unpublished and valuable Sanskrit manuscripts; and the course of Indological studies of the last two or three decades may be said to have been dominated by discoveries of outstanding importance made during that period in the three last mentioned centres. On the other hand, in regard to the large and well-stocked public and private libraries which are known to have been in existence in the country, Nepal decidedly appears not have contributed its quota to the stock of fresh material which is now required for unravelling further the tangled skein of the history of Indian literature. Satis Chandra VIDYABHUSHANA and Haraprasad SHASTRI among Indians, and Sylvain LÉVI and Giuseppe TUCCI among Europeans have undoubtedly done valuable pioneering work, but in view of the immense possibilities, what has been achieved thus far must be said to be tantalizingly little.

Under these circumstances, we cannot be sufficiently grateful to Rajaguru Hemaraj PANDIT, C.I.E., Director of Public Instruction, Nepal, through whose good offices the doors of the rich store-house of the Nepālī material were thrown open to us—material which is all but inaccessible to Indologists—and we have been placed in a position to publish, *for the first time in the history of Mahābhārata studies*, collations of valuable Nepālī manuscripts. This supremely unselfish and profoundly learned patron of Sanskrit studies has really done more than merely supplying to the Institute, free of cost, collations of Nepālī manuscripts available to him in local libraries. Realizng that there were valuable manuscripts to be had outside Kathmandu, the headquarters of the Rajaguru, he caused a search to be made, at his own expense, throughout that distant outpost of Hindu culture and civilization, for old Mahābhārata manuscripts, and the find of the valuable Ms. $Ñ_3$, the oldest of the dated manuscripts of our critical apparatus, is the unexpected and welcome fruit of the Rajaguru's exertions in the cause of Mahābhārata research. Only those who know the difficulties in the way of obtaining any manuscript from Nepal will be in a position to appreciate fully the debt which the editor and the other members of the Mahābhārata Editorial Board, and beyond that the whole world of Indologists, owe to the Rajaguru. Sanskritists have much to hope for from the dispassionate efforts of this truly patriotic and cultured Rajaguru, who loses no opportunity of placing his immense learning and unbounded resources freely at the disposal of all serious workers in the field of Sanskrit research.

[109] In connection with other help that has been received from extra-mural collaborators, I must put on record our special obligation to Pandit Vidhushekhara Sastri BHATTACHARYA of the Visvabharati, and to M. R. Ry. Rao Saheb T. Sambamurthi RAO Avl., B. A., B. L., of the Saraswathi Mahal, Tanjore. These gentlemen have been good enough to supply the Institute, for many years past, with carefully procured collations of manuscripts which are in their charge or which were kindly procured by them, on loan, for the purpose, unselfishly supervising the work of their collation centre, at great sacrifice of their time and labour. To Professor

K. Rama PISHAROTI, then Principal of the Sanskrit College at Trippunittura in Cochin State, I am indebted for the collations of Malayālam manuscripts for the first two adhyāyas of this parvan.

My special thanks are due to the Managing Committees and Trustees of the following libraries and institutions for supplying me with the manuscripts required by me and allowing me to retain them as long as necessary : the Adyar Library, the Baroda Oriental Institute, Benares Sanskrit College, Mysore Oriental Library, Shri Yadugiri Yatiraj Math (Melkote, Mysore) and the India Office (London). The latter deserves special mention as the only European library I know, which sends out freely its Indian manuscripts, on loan, back to India, for the use of Indian scholars. A few manuscripts were sent to me by my kind friends Professor Sushil Kumar DE, Head of the Department of Sanskrit and Bengali, Dacca University, and Professor BHAGAVADDATTA of the Dayananda Anglo-Vedic College, Lahore, to whom I wish to thank for this kind help. I am obliged also to Sardar KIBE of Indore for the loan of a Nīlakaṇṭha manuscript. The Chief of Idappalli, Mr. Anujan ACHAN, Mr. Kallenkara PISHARAM, all of Cochin, as also the Proprietors of the following estates in Cochin, Poomulli Mana, Avaṇapparambu Mana, Nareri Mana, have put me under heavy obligation by sending me freely Malayālam manuscripts in their possession, for collation, at a time when it was rather difficult for me to secure any Malayālam manuscripts at all.

I desire further to express my gratefulness to various scholars who have followed the publication of the fascicules of this volume with keen interest, periodically publishing reviews of them in the Journals of different learned Societies, reviews expressive of their interest and appreciation ; to wit, Professors BANERJI, SASTRI, BARNETT, BELLONI-FILIPPI, CHARPENTIER, S. K. DE, EDGERTON, R. FICK, JAYASWAL, KONOW, Krishnaswami AIYANGAR, LESNY, Kalidas NAG, WELLER, WINTERNITZ and others. These kind reviewers have adopted uniformly a most courteous and sympathetic tone in their reviews. Their sympathy and courtesy have always reminded me of those classic lines of Bhartṛhari :

परगुणपरमाणून्पर्वतीकृत्य नित्यं
निजहृदि विकसन्तः सन्ति सन्तः कियन्तः ।

I must next record my thanks for the ungrudging assistance I have uniformly received from the members of the permanent staff of the Mahābhārata Department of the Institute. Mr. S. N. TADPATRIKAR, M.A., Supervisor of Collations, was always by my side, helping me with useful suggestions, when I constituted the text of the Ādi. Mr. TADPATRIKAR has been associated with the work, in various capacities, since 1919. He has assisted my predecessor, the late Mr. UTGIKAR, in preparing the Tentative Edition of the Virāṭparvan and seeing it through the press. The compiling of the critical notes (printed at the foot of the page) was entrusted by me to Messrs. B. G. BHIDE and D. V. [110] NARAVANE. For the conscientious manner in which these two gentlemen have discharged their duty, I feel greatly obliged, since it is a most tedious and trying piece of work to collect the variant readings from the different collation sheets, and to arrange, in a prescribed form, according to stringent rules of sequence and enunciation, that ponderous mass of variants which is and will remain the unique feature and abiding achievement of this edition. The Śāradā codex was collated by the Head Shastri of the Mahābhārata Department, Shankar Shastri BHILAVADIKAR. The comparative paucity of printing mistakes in this volume is largely due to the vigilence and conscientiousness of the Collator and Reader, K. V. Krishnamurti SHARMA, Sastri, of Erode (South India).

Photo taken on the occasion of an *At Home* given by Dr. V. S. Sukthankar on 4th August 1937, after completing 12 years of work as General Editor.

Standing: **(left to right) Dr. S. M. Katre; Dr. H. D. Sharma; Prof. P. K. Gode; Dr. B. A. Saletore.**

Sitting: **(left to right) Dr. P. L Vaidya and Dr. V. S. Sukthankar**

B. O. R. Institute, Poona. MAHĀBHĀRATA DEPARTMENT 4th August 1934.

Sitting: (from left) S. R. Bhilavadikar; S. N. Tadpatrikar; P. K. Gode; V. S. Sukthankar; B. G. Bhide; K. V. Anantanarayana Sastri.
Standing: (from left) G. G. Soman; M. M. Patkar; K. V. Krishnamurti Sarma; D. V. Naravane; R. J. Joshi; K. S. Visvanatha Shastri.

These and other members of my staff have uniformly worked with exemplary zeal and untiring patience, to make a success of this edition, and I gladly take the opportunity of putting on record their loyal help and willing co-operation.

It is but right that I should also mention here that the Manager and the expert compositors of the renowned Niranaya Sagar Press have rendered ungrudgingly every assistance in carrying out the typographical arrangements which appeared to me best suited for the purpose of the work, meeting requirements that would have tried the patience and exhausted the resources of any other press in India.

Last but not least, I must express my profound gratitude to my revered Guru Geheimer Regierungsrat Professor Dr. Heinrich LÜDERS of the University of Berlin. What little merit there may be in the present work is due wholly to that excellent though somewhat rigorous and exacting training in philological methods which I had the benefit of receiving at his hands in the Indogermanisches Seminar, as a student in the University of Berlin. It is my firm conviction that there is no living scholar who has a deeper insight into the history of the Indian epic and the complicacies of its tradition than Geheimrat LÜDERS. It was, therefore, an unlucky day in the annals of Mahābhārata studies when, for lack of sympathetic co-operation and adequate financial support, he must have been compelled to abandon his epic studies, and our Great Epic lost the benefit of redaction at the hands of one of the greatest living philologists. His early Mahābhārata studies, *Ueber die Grantharecension*, *Die Sage von Ṛṣyaśṛṅga* and the *Druckprobe* have been to me like beacon lights in the perilous navigation of the Mahābhārata Ocean. May this work be to him a small recompense for the great trouble he has taken to initiate me in the mysteries of textual criticism!

August, 1933. V. S. SUKTHANKAR

[115] CONCORDANCE OF THE SCHEME OF ADHYAYAS

in the following three editions : the Critical Edition, the Bombay Edition (Ganpat Krishnaji, Saka 1799), and the Madras Edition (Southern Recension, 1931)

Crit. Ed.	Bom. Ed.	Mad. Ed.
1	1	1
2	2	2
3	3	3
4	4	4
5	5	
6	6	5
7	7	6
8	8	7
9	9	8
10	10	
11	11	
12	12	
13	13–15	9–10
14	16	11
15	17	12
16	18	13
17	19	14
18	20	15
19	21	16
—	22	—
20	23	17
—	24	—
21	25	18
22	26	19
23	27	20
24	28	
25	29	21
26	30	22
27	31	23
28	32	24
29	33	25
30	34	26
31	35	27
32	36	28
33	37	29
34	38	30
35	39	31
36	40	32
37	41	33
38	42	34

Crit. Ed.	Bom. Ed.	Mad. Ed.
39	43	35
40	44	36
41	45	37
42	46	38
43	47	39
44	48	40
45	49	41
46	50	42
47	51–52	43
48	53	44
49	54	45
50	55	
51	56	46
52	57	47
53	58–59	48–49. 1–10
54	60	49. 11–34
55	61	50
56	62	51
57	63	53–54
58	64	55
59	65	56
60	66	57
61	67	58
62	68	79
63	69	80
64	70	81
65	71	82
66	72	83
67	73	84
68–69	74	85–88. 1–46; 88. 103–105
70	75	59
71	76	60
72	77	61
73	78	62
74	79	63
[116] 75	80	64
76	81	65
77	82	66
78	83	67

Crit. Ed.	Bom. Ed.	Mad. Ed.
79	84	68
80	85	69
81	86	70
82	87	71
83	88	72
84	89	73
85	90	74
86	91	75
87	92	76
88	93	77
89	94	{ 78 88.$_{47-94}$
90	95	52
91	96	89
92	{ 97 98	{ 90 91
93	99	92
94	100	93–94
95	101	95
96	102	96-98.$_{9}$
97	103	98.$_{18}$ 99.$_{4}$
98	104	99.$_{5-50}$
99	105	100–101
100	106	102
101	107–108	103
102 103 }	109 110 }	104
104	111	105
105	112–113	106.$_{1-30}$
106	114	{ 106.$_{31-41}$ 107.$_{73-75}$
107	115	{ 108.$_{1-7}$ 110.$_{24-40}$ 110.$_{68-82}$
—	116	111
108	117	112
109	118	106.$_{42-72}$
110	119	107.$_{1-51}$
111	120	{ 107.$_{52-72}$ 108.$_{21-36}$
112	121	108.$_{37-71}$
113	122	109–110.$_{13}$
114	123	{ 110.$_{14-23}$ 110.$_{41-66}$ 113
115	124	114
116	125	115
117	126	116

Crit. Ed.	Bom. Ed.	Mad. Ed.
118	127	117
119	128–129	118–120
120 121 }	130	{ 121 122
122	131-132.$_{12}$	123–124
123	132.$_{20}^{cd}$–133	125–126
124	134	127
125	135	128
126	136	129
127	137	130
128	138	131
—	—	132–133
—	139	134
—	140	135
129	141	136
130	142	137
131	143	138
132	144	139
133	145	140
134	146	141
135	147	142
136	148	143
—	149	145.$_{2-21}$
137	150	{ 144 145.$_{1}$ 145.$_{22-28}$
138	151	146
139	152	147
140 141 }	153	{ 148 149
142	154	150
143	155	151–153.$_{40}$
[117] 114	156	153.$_{41-58}$
145	157	154
146	158	155
147	159	156
148	160	157
149	161	158
150	162–163.$_{3}$	159.$_{1-29}$
151	163.$_{4-28}$	159.$_{31}$–160
152	164	161
153 154 155 }	165 166 167 }	162
—	—	163
156 157 }	168 169 }	164
158–159	170	166–168

Crit. Ed.	Bom. Ed.	Mad. Ed.
160	171	169
161	172	170
162 163	173	171 172
164 165	174 175	173
166	176	174
167 168	177	175 176
169	178	177
170 171 172	179 180 181	178
173	182	179
174	183	180
175	184	165
176	185	181
177 178	186 187	182
179 180	188 189	183
181	190	184
182–183	191	185
184	192	186
185 186	193 194	187
187 188	195 196	188
—	—	189
189	197	190–191.$_{21}$
190	198	191.$_{22-45}$
191	199	192
192.$_{1-7}$	200.$_{1-7}$	193.$_{1-10}$
192.$_{8-29}$	200.$_{8-31}$	195.$_{1-27}$

Crit. Ed.	Bom. Ed.	Mad. Ed.
193 194 195	201 202 203	195.$_{28-95}$
196 197	204 205	196
198 199	206 207	197
200	208	199
201 202 203 204	209 210 211 212	200
205	213	201
206	214	202
207	215	203
208 209	216 217	204
210	218	205
211	219	206
212	220	207–209
213	221	210–212
214	222	213–214.$_{17}$
215–216	223–225	214.$_{18-146}$
217 218	226 227	215
219 220 221	228 229 230	216
222 223	231 232	217
224 225	233 234	218

INTRODUCTION[1]

THE CRITICAL APPARATUS

LIST OF MANUSCRIPTS FORMING THE CRITICAL APPARATUS

The manuscripts utilized for this edition of the Āraṇyakaparvan are as follows :

I. N(orthern) Recension.

(*a*) *North-western Group* (*v*).

Śāradā (or Kaśmīrī) Version (Ś).

$Ś_1$ = Poona, Bombay Govt. Collection (deposited at the BORI), No. 159 of 1875-76. (The Śāradā Codex.)

Devanāgarī transcripts of the Śāradā (or Kaśmīrī) Version (K).

K_1 = Poona, Bombay Govt. Collection (deposited at the BORI), No. 471 of Viśrāmbāg I.

K_2 = Poona, BORI, Mbh. Collection, No. 15 (= Institute's Collection, No. 246). Dated V. Saṁ. 1828 and Śaka 1693 (ca. A.D. 1772).

K_3 = Poona, Bombay Govt. Collection (deposited at the BORI), No. 184 of 1891-95.

K_4 = Poona, Bombay Govt. Collection (deposited at the BORI), No. 57 of 1882-83.

(*b*) *Central Group* (γ).

Bengali Version (B).

B_1 = Dacca, University Library, No. 495. Dated Śaka 1393 (ca. A.D. 1471).

B_2 = Santiniketan, Visvabharati Library, No. 781. Dated Śaka 1183 (ca. A.D. 1261).

B_3 = Dacca, University Library, No. 601. Dated Śaka 1678 (ca. A.D. 1756).

B_4 = Dacca, University Library, No. 728 B. Dated Śaka 1739 (ca. A.D. 1817).

Devanāgarī Versions *other than K* (D).

Devanāgarī Version of Caturbhujamiśra (Dc).

Dc_1 = Poona, Bombay Govt. Collection (deposited at the BORI), No. 32 of A 1879-80.

Dc_2 = London, India Office Library, No. 3170 (1908). Date A.D. 1765 (?).

Devanāgarī Version of Nīlakaṇṭha (Dn).

Dn_1 = Indore, Private Property of Sardar M. V. Kibe of Indore. Dated V. Saṁ. 1839 (ca. A.D. 1783).

Dn_2 = Poona, Bombay Govt. Collection (deposited at the BORI), No. 236 of 1895-1902.

Dn_3 = Poona, Bombay Govt. Collection (deposited at the BORI), No. 496 of Viśrāmbāg I.

Devanāgarī Composite Version.

D_1 = Poona, Bombay Govt. Collection (deposited at the BORI), No. 269 of Viśrāmbāg II.

---

1 [to *Āraṇyakaparvan*].

[2] D_2 = Poona, Bombay Govt. Collection (deposited at the BORI), No. 229 of 1895-1902. Dated V. Saṁ 1795 (ca. A.D. 1739).

D_3 = Poona, Bombay Govt. Collection (deposited at the BORI), No. 168 of 1887-91. Dated in year 1677, probably V. Saṁvat (then = A.D. 1620).

D_4 = Baroda, Oriental Institute Library, No. 767. Dated V. Saṁ. 1655 (ca. A.D. 1599).

D_5 = Pudukottah, State Library MS. (without number). Dated V. Saṁ. 1712 (ca. A.D. 1656).

D_6 = Madras, Adyar Library, No. 36 G. 15.

II. S(outhern) Recension.

Telugu Version (T).

T_1 = Lahore, D. A. V. College Library, No. 3908.

T_2 = Tanjore, Saraswathi Mahal Library, No. 11809.

Grantha Version (G).

G_1 = Melkote, Yadugiri Yatiraj Math Library MS. (without number).

G_2 = Poona, BORI, Mbh. Collection, No. 53 (= Institute's Collection, No. 266).

G_3 = Tanjore, Saraswathi Mahal Library, No. 11839.

G_4 = Pudukottah State Library, No. 322.

Malayālam Version (M).

M_1 = MS. (without number) belonging to Ponnokkoṭṭu Mana Nambudiripad, Alwaye, Travancore.

M_2 = Malabar, Poomulli Mana Library, No. 299.

DETAILED ACCOUNT OF THE MANUSCRIPTS

Ś$_1$

(The Śāradā Codex.)

Poona, Bombay Government Collection (deposited at the BORI), No. 159 of 1875-76. Total number of folios, for this parvan, 192 (some frayed and patched at ends), with about 24 lines to a page. Size 12″ × 19″. Clear Śāradā characters. Birchbark (bhūrjapatra).

The codex, which is unfortunately incomplete and fragmentary, must have originally contained at least the first three parvans (Ādī, Sabhā, and Araṇya or Āraṇyaka), written, as far as one can judge, by the same hand. The extant portion contains the Sabhā in its entirety, but only fragments of the other two parvans, the beginning of Ādi and the end of Āraṇyaka being lost. The text of Āraṇyaka begins on fol. 211a, line 1; and ends, or rather breaks off, at the end of a folio marked 194b (sic). The numbering of the pages is most erratic. There are in all 192 folios pertaining to this parvan. The fragment breaks off in the middle of our 3. 253. 18[d], ending with the words : वराज्यपूर्णामिव. The margins are mostly clean, and corrections are few and far between. Erasures have been made in a few places with green pigment.
[3] In good many places (e.g., folios numbered 156a, 185b, 186a, 193b, 194a, etc.) the scribe has written dots to denote portions of the text which were either lost or illegible to him : sign of a conscientious copyist. On fol. 220a, some stanzas which had been omitted (? hapl.) in the text have been written on the margin (*sec. m.*), in a different and inferior ink. The top

parts of the four folios numbered 89-92 are broken off and lost, involving a loss of from 5 to 8 top lines on each page. The names of sub-parvans have been sporadically mentioned. The manuscript has been fully described at p. x of the *Prolegomena* to Ādiparvan (q. v.)

K_1

Poona, Bombay Government Collection (deposited at the BORI), Viśrāmbāg I, No. 471, Folios 486 (numbered 55-540; first 54 folios missing), with about 10 lines to a page. Size 12½" × 5¼". Devanāgarī characters. Thin glazed superior Indian paper.

First 54 folios are lost; fol. 55 begins with 3. 32. 4^a. Number 237 is given to two consecutive folios, but the second folio thus marked is subsequently corrected (*sec. m.*) to 238. The missing portion of the text at the end of the first of the two folios marked as 237 is written out in small letters (? *sec. m.*) at the bottom of the page. Fol. 485 is written only on one side; and at the end of this folio is the remark : प्रभुतात्रो अग्रे पत्रं लिखितं ॥ विस्मृतं न ॥. the contents of this folio (485) have been copied out again *sec. m.* (on a separate sheet of modern paper with watermarks), including the final remark प्रभुतात्रो ...॥ विस्मृतं न ॥, with the addition, श्रीरस्तु । कल्याणमस्तू ॥ श्रीकृष्णजी सत्य छे ॥ श्री छ, which shows that the copyist of this sheet was some Gujarati scribe. The handwriting of the original, which is Kashmirian in style is not quite uniform : some folios show very thick, black, broad upright characters, while others are appreciably thinner and somewhat slanting. Frequently in the colophons, and the references to speakers, only alternate letters are written, blanks being left to be filled with red ink, which, however, has not been done. Mere folds, without vertical lines, mark the right and left margins of folios. The ink used is jet black and of a superior quality. The sub-parvan names are generally mentioned.

K_2

Poona, BORI, Mbh. Collection No. 15 (= Institute's Collection, No. 246). Folios 300, with about 14 lines to a page. Size 13¼" × 6⅗". Devanāgarī characters. Dated V. Saṁvat 1828 and Śaka 1693 (ca. A.D. 1772). Grey Indian paper.

This manuscript is described as D_1 at p. VII of the Introduction to the Udyogaparvan, for which parvan it was first used. The name of the scribe, which comes after the date (year) at the end of this parvan, appears as : उदैराम लिषायतं मिश्रजी । श्री सदानंदजी; the day and month come last : मिती आषाढ-प्रथमे १५ गुरौ संपूर्णम्. In the Udyogaparvan, the scribe's name is given as Kāśmīrīya Sadānanda. Very incorrect, containing numerous little errors of spelling, such as writing श for स. Adhyāya colophons and margins are marked with red pigment, corrections with yellow pigment. Marginal (vertical) lines of pages are in black and red, separated by a thick yellow line. The manuscript is almost without any marks of punctuation. The *daṇḍas* were probably to be marked with red ink, but the [4] revision was never actually carried out. It may be noted that this is a parvan from an almost complete manuscript of the Mahābhārata written by one hand, and as such important.

K_3

Poona, Bombay Government Collection (deposited at the BORI), No. 184 of 1891-95. Folios 285, with about 17 lines to a page. Size $10\frac{1}{2}'' \times 5\frac{1}{4}''$. Devanāgarī characters. Indian paper.

Total number of folios is 294, of which fol. 270, 272-279 are missing. Fol. 152a has only six lines of writing, the greater part of the folio being left blank, and the writing continued on the reverse, without any loss of text. In the references to speaker the word उवाच (resp. ऊचुः) is generally omitted; the name of the speaker to be generally given in some abbreviated form like युधि, वैशं, मार्कं The manuscript seems to be fairly old. The edges, especially of the last folios, are brittle and worn. Characters are short and broad, representing an old style of writing in. Writing is incorrect on the whole. There are occasional corrections in margin (*sec. m.*). Adhyāya colophons and names of speakers are generally coloured with red pigment. The manuscript mentions sub-parvans as a rule. It does not distinguish between ब and व; both are again often confused with च.

K_4

Poona, Bombay Government Collection (deposited at the BORI), No. 57 of 1882-83. Folios 370 (numbered 52-421), with about 10 lines to a page. Size $12\frac{3}{4} \times 5\frac{1}{2}''$. Devanāgarī characters. Old Indian paper.

First 51 folios are lost; fol. 52 begins with 3. 36. 1^a. The hand-writing of the manuscript, though it seems to be of one scribe, is not uniform. For some portion we have large round letters with flourishes, while for others the characters are thin and upright. Pṛṣṭhamātrās are almost invariably used. Marginal notes, especially variants, are written (*sec. m.*) with the clear remark that it is a pāṭha; there are explanatory notes also, written on the margins. Colophons, references to speakers, and śloka endings (the latter sporadically) are marked with red pigment.—The manuscript breaks off at the last folio (421), where it ends with the colophon of the last adhyāya of this parvan. There is no *phalaśruti*, nor the list of contents, which we often find at the end of Mahābhārata manuscripts.

B_1

Dacca, University Library, No. 495. Folios 1-323, and 325. Bengali characters. Dated Śaka 1393 (ca. A.D. 1471). Paper. Slightly damaged.

The manuscript contains two correction slips, one between fol. 163 and 164, and another between fol. 247 and 248.—*Collated at the Visvabharati.*

B_2

Santiniketan, Visvabharati Library, No. 781. Folios 264. Size $20'' \times 4\frac{3}{4}''$. Bengali characters. Dated Śaka 1183 (ca. A.D. 1261). Paper—*Collated at the Visvabharati.*

[5] The manuscript is written in one running hand, and has marginal corrections. It is described as "looking very old", and being extremely fragile. It was collated in 1931. With lapse of years its condition is said to have become steadily worse.—*Collated at the Visvabharati.*

B_3

Dacca, University Library, No. 601. Folios 326 (fol. 141 wrongly numbered as 142 and the mistake continued up to fol. 240; fol. 241 wrongly numbered as 231, and the mistake continued upto the end; fol. 227 duplicated). Bengali characters. Dated Śaka 1678 (ca. A.D. 1756). Paper.—*Collated at the Visvabharati.*

B_4

Dacca, University Library, No. 728 B. Folios 280 (fol. 185 wrongly numbered as 285, and 214 as 215). Bengali characters. Dated Śaka 1739 (ca. A.D. 1817). Paper.—*Collated at the Visvabharati.*

Dc_1

Poona, Bombay Government Collection (deposited at the BORI), No. 32 of A 1879-80. Folios 506, with about 11-13 lines to a page. Size 13¾″ × 6″. Devanāgarī characters. Indian paper.

Text with commentary of Caturbhujamiśra entitled *Vākyadīpikā.* The handwriting is not uniform: it begins with a longish upright style, which gradually becomes slanting towards right, up to fol. 164; fol. 165 begins with a broad, short, round, broken style up to folio 265; from the next fol. (266), the style of writing again becomes long, slanting and thin; and towards the end the lettering becomes a little thick and bold. Right and left margins are marked by double lines in red, and stops in the text and the commentary, are also marked by double daṇḍas in red. The lower borders of folios of this manuscript are a little soiled by damp.

Dc_2

London, India Office Library, No. 3170 (1908). Folios 502, with about 10-14 lines to a page. Size 15½″ × 6½″. Devanāgarī characters. Date of writing A.D. 1765 (?). Indian paper.

Text with commentary of Caturbhujamiśra, entitled *Vākyadīpikā.* 1765 is the date given by EGGELING in the *India Office Catalogue* (1899), though the manuscript itself appears to be undated.

Dn_1

Manuscript belonging to Sardar M. V. KIBE of Indore, on loan at the Institute. Folios 523, with about 11 lines to a page. Size 16″ × 6″. Devanāgarī characters. Dated V. Saṁvat 1839 (ca. A.D. 1783). Thick Indian paper.

[6] Text with the commentary of Nīlakaṇṭha, called *Bhāratabhāvadīpa,* The date of writing this parvan is noted on the back-cover as: सं० १८३९ प्रारंभ कार्त्तिक शुल्ध २ समाप्तिः फाल्गुणशुक्लनवम्यां ९ बुधवारे.—

The first part of this manuscript is described as Dn_1, at p. xvi of the *Prolegomena* to the Ādiparvan, and the details of that description apply to this parvan also.

Dn_2

Poona, Bombay Government Collection (deposited at the BORI), No. 236 of 1895-1902. Folios 768, with about 9 lines to a page. Size 15¼" × 7". Devanāgarī characters. Thick Indian paper.

Text with the commentary of Nīlakaṇṭha, called the *Bhāratabhāvadīpa*. The manuscript is written in a uniformly neat upright handwriting. Right and left margins are marked by two double lines in red. Double daṇḍas in red are used on some folios to mark the stops in the text as well as in the commentary. Adhyāya colophons in both the text and the commentary are also in red ink. On some pages, continuations are written on the right side along the marginal red lines.

Dn_3

Poona, Bombay Government Collection (deposited at the BORI), Viśrāmbāg I, No. 496. Folios 626, with about 12 lines to a page. Size 16" × 6½". Devanāgarī characters. Indian paper.

Text with the commentary of Nīlakaṇṭha, called the *Bhāratabhāvadīpa*. The manuscript has its right and left margins marked with close double lines in red as usual. The first three folios and the last folio have an illuminated border with floral designs. The writing, though incorrect, is bold and upright. Numerous corrections are made in the text by using yellow pigment. Fol. 401-439 are written with ink of a faint black colour. Subsequent portion is written in a shaky style, with short and round letters. There are also marginal corrections, entered *sec. m.*, throughout the manuscript. Adhyāya colophons are marked with red pigment. The last colophon in the commentary is left incomplete, and the last but one fol. (625) breaks off with : श्रीगोविंदसूरिसू. The first śloka of the Virāṭa too, is left incomplete, while the last folio is numbered 626 in one (right bottom) corner and 627 in the other (left top) corner. The usual table of contents is also wanting. All this suggests that the actual fol. 626 is lost.

D_1

Poona, Bombay Government Collection (deposited at the BORI), Viśrāmbāg II, No 269. Folios 225, with about 16 lines to a page. Size 18" × 6½". Devanāgarī characters. Old Indian unglazed paper.

A few folios of this manuscript are missing. This manuscript was written by the same scribe who wrote manuscript No. 266 of Viśrāmbāg II, which is described as D_{14} at pp. xx of the *Prolegomena* to the Ādiparvan. Most folios of this manuscript have a soiled appearance, while the last (225) reveals at its top left corner signs of burning by [?] fire; some folios are partly damaged. The manuscript is carefully written in a perfectly uniform style and the characters are short and round. The name श्रीनृसिंह is written at the lower right margin above the folio number. The corrections in the text are made by deleting the original incorrect reading with yellow pigment and putting in the correct one in black ink. Adhyāya colophons and references to speakers are marked with red pigment.

D_2

Poona, Bombay Government Collection (deposited at the BORI), No. 229 of 1895-1902. Folios 234, with about 15 lines to a page. Size 14¾" × 6¾". Devanāgari characters. Dated V. Saṁvat 1795 (ca. A.D. 1739). Old Indian paper.

This manuscript, which contains the first three parvans, is the same as manuscript K_0 of the Ādiparvan, described at p. xi of the *Prolegomena.* The date of the manuscript is recorded at the end of the Āraṇyakaparvan. The manuscript is very corrupt and full of spelling mistakes. It frequently writes व for च and sometimes च for व; in other words, it confuses च and व. It likewise confuses त and न. The date is given as : संवत् १७९५ वर्षे भातादपद (read भाद्रपद) वदि १३ इ (?) गुरू ॥

D_3

Poona, Bombay Government Collection (deposited at the BORI), No. 168 of 1887-91. Folios 240, with about 11 lines to a page. Size 13¾" × 5". Devanāgari characters. Dated in year 1677, probably V. Saṁvat (then = 1620 A.D.). Old Indian paper.

An old and valuable but fragmentary manuscript with many folios missing, some of which have been subsequently replaced, being written *sec. m.* Many of the folios are badly mutilated, carelessly copied and full of scribe's mistakes. The last preserved folio but one is numbered 372 and breaks off with our 3·278. 10[ab] ; while the last folio, which has its borders worn away and is pasted on to another sheet of paper, has the last three ślokas of the parvan, and the final colophon but no contents or *phalaśruti.* The date is given as : १६७७ शमए नाम आश्वनि शुदि त्रीदशी १३ वार गुरवाशर. The specification of the era is lost on a missing portion of the folio, but it is probably the Vikrama era (Caitradi). In that case it would, correspond to Thursday, the 28th September 1620 A.D. The edges of some folios are coloured yellow ; while for margins there are four close lines in black, on the right and left. Handwriting is uneven and there are many corrections. Single or double daṇḍas are used to mark the stops. There are corrections entered *sec. m.* on the margins and at some places in the text also by using yellow pigment. Colophons and references to speakers are marked by red pigment in many places. The scribe writes ब for व, and makes little distinction between च and व, as also between प and य.

D_4

Baroda, Oriental Institute Library, No. 767. Folios 437, with about 11 lines to a page. Size 12" × 4½". Devanāgari characters. Dated V. Saṁvat 1655 (ca. A.D. 1599). Old Indian paper.

[8] The characters are short and round, which later become thin and upright. Margins are marked by three close lines in red ; some pages have

black lines; while double daṇḍas, which mark the stops in the text, as also adhyāya colophons and references to speakers are marked by red pigment. There are no marginal corrections, and blanks are left in the text where the scribe could not read the exemplar correctly or the exemplar was defective. The following statement containing the date and some other details comes after the last colophon : संवत् १६५५ वर्षे माह सुदी ७ सोमवासरे वाई श्रीधनागोत गोलवाली। पुस्तकं वन प्रर्व (sic) दत्तं व्यास दामोदर है दीधो वासवुदीको ।। लीषतं जोसी लक्ष्मीदास वास पाटण जंबुदीपे ॥ ग्रंथाग्रंथः श्लोकः संष्या सहस्र १२६९५ प्रमाणं ॥ Then follows *sec. m.* : || राज्यश्रीभोज्यराज्यप्रवर्तते व्यासश्रीदामोदरपठणार्थे लीषाइतं राजश्री मह्वेराजी तस्यात्मजा उभयकुलआ-नंददायनि वाई श्रीधनाजी तया इदं पुस्तकं दत्तं।

D_5

Pudukottah, State Library Manuscript (without number). Folios 334, with about 10 lines to a page. Size 14¾″ × 5¼″. Devanāgarī characters. Dated V. Saṁvat 1712 (ca. A.D. 1656). Indian paper.

Many of the folios are coloured yellow on both the sides; margins are marked to the right and left, by two black lines with one red line in the middle. Double daṇḍas in red ink are used to mark stops in the text. There are a few marginal corrections, added *sec. m.* Those in the body of the text are made by using yellow pigment. The characters are uniformly longish and upright. The date is given at the end as : ॥ समाप्तेदं आरण्यपर्व संवत् १७१२ ॥. No name of the scribe or place of writing is mentioned.

D_6

Madras, Adyar Library, No. 36 G. 15. Folios 303 (including a *śodhapatra* bearing number 199), with about 12 lines to a page. Size 5½″ × 13¾″. Devanāgarī characters. Old Indian paper.

Style of handwriting is upright and narrow. Double daṇḍas in red ink are used to indicate stops. Margins have, in places, additional stanzas, glosses etc. added *sec. m.* Many pages are coloured yellow; the right and left margins are marked by fine double lines in black, the intervening space being coloured red. The manuscript has a very old appearance, with worn and frayed folios.—A separate additional folio, numbered 199, written (*sec. m.* ?) on both sides is inserted as a śodhapatra after fol. 199 with the remark :

इदं शोधपत्रमेकोनशतद्वयस्थमेकादशपंक्तावनंकपुटे द्रष्टव्यं ॥

T_1

Lahore, D. A. V. College Library, No. 3908. Folios 144, with about 13 lines to a page. Size 18¼″ × 1¾″. Telugu characters. Palm-leaf.

Incomplete, breaking off at 3. 297. 60[ab].

T_2

Tanjore, Saraswathi Mahal Library, No. 11809. Folios 146 (numbered 248-393), with about 12 lines to a page. Size 29½″ × 2¼″. Telugu characters. Palm-leaf.

[9] This manuscript contains the first five parvans and is the same as T_3 of the Ādiparvan. It is written in small clear letters of good style. The manuscript bears no date, but it appears to be old.—*Collated at Tanjore.*

G_1

Melkote, Yadugiri Yatiraj Math Library Manuscript (without number). Folios 130 (numbered 165-294), with about 15-21 lines to a page. Size 18¾" × 1¾". Grantha characters. Palm-leaf.

The manuscript contains the first four parvans and a part of the fifth.

G_2

Poona, BORI, Mbh. Collection, No. 53 (= Institute's Collection, No. 266). Folios 216 (two of which, namely 117 and 125, are missing), with about 12-14 lines to a page. Size 15½" × 2½". Grantha characters. Palm-leaf.

The manuscript contains parvans three and four. It belongs to the Institute and was purchased a few years ago from a South-Indian manuscript collector, the late Mr. Rangaswamy AIYANGAR of the Oriental Library, Mysore. It is in a very good state of preservation, only one folio (149) being broken. The manuscript is undated, but it does not appear to be very old. The margins are clean ; but there are a few interlinear corrections.

G_3

Tanjore, Saraswathi Mahal Library, No. 11839. Folios 277 (numbered 75-351), with about 9 lines to a page. Size 21" × 1½". Grantha characters. Palm-leaf.

The manuscript, which contains parvans two and three, seems to be old. At fol. 75, the Sabhāparvan ends and the Āraṇyakaparvan begins thereafter immediately. After the end of the Āraṇyaka, about five ślokas from the Virāṭa are written on the last folio (351), which indicates that the manuscript originally contained some more parvans.—*Collated at Tanjore.*

G_4

Pudukottah, State Library, No. 322. Folios 168, with about 10-14 lines to a page. Size 19" × 2⅛". Grantha characters. Palm-leaf.—The manuscript contains parvans Nos. 3 and 14-18.

M_1

Travancore, Alwaye. From the private Library of Ponnokoṭṭu Mana. Folios 300, with 8 or 9 lines to a page. Size 17½" × 2". Malayālam characters. Palm-leaf.

The leaves have been cut regularly and are of uniform size. The manuscript is undated and is probably not very old. It is in a state of good preservation, having a fresh and clean appearance. The margins are clean. No corrections are noticeable.

M_2

Malabar, Poomulli Mana Library, No. 299. Folios 259, with about 9 lines to a page. Size 21½" × 1¾". Malayālam characters. Palm-leaf.

[10] The numbering of the folios begins with the second folio, the first being marked श्री and not counted. The manuscript has an oldish appearance. The leaves are uneven and discoloured in places. The edges are

considerably worn and uneven ; the central holes are enlarged, apparently from constant use ; one corner of the last folio (numbered 258) is broken off and part of text is lost. The margins are clean ; corrections, which are interlinear, are few and far between.

MANUSCRIPTS NOT INCLUDED IN THE CRITICAL APPARATUS

Besides the twenty-eight manuscripts detailed above, the following two manuscripts were also examined by me, which deserve notice.

1. Calcutta, Royal Asiatic Society of Bengal Collection, No. 3312 (4065). Folios 166 ; size 13" × 10". Śāradā characters. Dated Śaka 1630 (ca. A.D. 1708). Kaśmīrī paper.

2. Bombay Branch of the Royal Asiatic Society's Collection, No. 966 (= B.D. 245). Folios 235, with about 15 lines to a page ; size 14½" × 6½". Old Devanāgarī characters. Dated Saṁvat 1573 (ca. A.D. 1516). Indian paper. *Illustrated.*

The dated Śāradā manuscript belonging to the Royal Asiatic Society of Bengal is a very fragmentary and fragile manuscript, in an extremely delapidated condition. The custodians of the manuscript would not part with it for collation at the Institute, but allowed it to be collated and photographed on the premises of the Society. The difficulty in the way of collating--as of photographing—it, was that many of the folios were stuck together and could be separated only at the risk of damaging the writing. A partial study of the manuscript showed that the basic text is probably Kaśmīrī, but it is contaminated deeply from the Mid-Indian versions (Bengali-Devanāgarī). The manuscript is briefly described in Haraprasada SHASTRI'S *Descriptive Catalogue*, Vol. 5, at p. 106. A facsimile of a page from this manuscript, containing the text from 3. 242. 20^{b} to 243. 15^{c}, is given at the end of Volume 4 of this edition. Note the bits of commentary (टीका), wrongly incorporated, in lines 9-10, and in lines 12-13.

The other manuscript, which belongs to the Bombay Branch of the Royal Asiatic Society, is, on the other hand, an extremely valuable old manuscript, dated in V. Saṁvat 1573 (= A.D. 1516). It would have been fully collated and used for our edition, but for the circumstance that it is also very fragmentary, nearly one-third of the number of folios being, unfortunately, irrecoverably lost. The original manuscript was written at Yoginīpura (modern Delhi) during the reign of "Sulitrāṇ Sikandara", who appears to be the famous Sikandar Shah Lodi, Sultan of Delhi, for Bhānudāsa Chaudharī—a resident of Kacchauvā (a "water-fortress", *jaladurga*).[1] The manuscript was constantly [11] consulted by me in case of doubt to see what help it could give. I have cited its evidence occasionally, in the "Critical Notes" at the

[1] This Kacchauvā may perhaps be identified with the modern "Kachola", a town in Udaipur State. *The Imperial Gazetteer* (1886) states that in former times the town, which stood on the western bank of a *large lake*, must have been a place of some importance ; for all around, the ground is strewn with fragments of extremely fine sculpture, and *half way up the hill* the ruins of a temple are visible.

end of this Book, on important matters. I append here in full the somewhat lengthy post-colophon statement, which is not without interest. The copyist was probably a Jaina. Here follows the statement :

शिवमस्तु सर्वजगतः परहितनिरता भवंतु भूतगणाः । दोषाः प्रयांतु नाशं सर्वत्र सुखी भवतु लोकः ॥ ॥ ॥ संवत् १५७३ वर्षे ॥ श्रावण वदि ९ सोमे ॥ ॥ तत्समये योगिनीपुरे । सुलित्राण-सिकंदरविजयराज्य प्रवर्त्तमाणे ॥ ॥ तत्स[म]ये कच्छौवाजलदुर्गे ॥ ॥ चंद्रापुरीनिवासिनः तत्र निवसः सन् । चौधरी विन । तस्य सुपुत्र चौधरी कण्हा । तस्य पुत्र वैष्णव (।) चौधरी श्रीभानदास । इदं महाभारत आरण्यपर्व आत्मश्रवणार्थं लिखापितं । लिखितं कायस्थगौडान्वय । (sign) श्रीलखणसीसुत (sign) । भवानीदास ॥ ॥ शुभं भवत् ॥ ॥ तैलाद्रक्षे जलाद्रक्ष्येद्रक्षेत् शिथिलबंधनं । परहस्तगतं रक्षे एवं वदति पुस्तकः ॥ ॥ संकोडिवि करचरणं । विमुक्कवयणाइ निम्मला (read णिच्चला) दिट्ठी । तं होउ तुम्ह रिउणा (read°णो) । जं सुक्खं पावए लेहो ॥ छ ॥ ॥ छ ॥ ॥

The manuscript is briefly described in H. D. VELANKAR'S *Descriptive Catalogue* of the Society's manuscripts, Vol. 2, p. 292.

TESTIMONIA

The testimonia of the Āraṇyaka consist of ancient commentaries and epitomes, of which there are not very many in the case of this parvan.

Devabodha's commentary on the Āraṇyaka has unfortunately been lost, or at least has not been recovered so far. The same is true of the Javanese version. This parvan thus unfortunately lacks two of the oldest—and the most important—of the testimonia of the Mahābhārata,—works which have rendered yeoman service in some of the parvans already edited.

As regards other works of that nature, there is, as far as I know, extant at least one complete manuscript of the commentary of Arjunamiśra on the Āraṇyaka. It belongs to the Government Sanskrit College Collection in Calcutta (No. 310); cf. *Catalogue,* Vol. 4, p. 190. There are also incomplete copies of the commentary in the Sanskrit College at Benares (MSS. No. 2279 ; and ग 16 पु 34). I had the use of a rough copy of the Calcutta Sanskrit College manuscript mentioned above, which was kindly supplied to me, at my request, by the Principal of the College. The copy was however found to be full of clerical errors and was not exactly suitable for collation. It was therefore used by me merely for occasional consultation. The text used by Arjunamiśra is, as usual, of a superior type, and his commentary would repay careful study, if good manuscripts of the commentary could be obtained. A facsimile of the single extant page of a paper manuscript of what proved to be Arjunamiśra's commentary on the Āraṇyakaparvan, written in Śāradā characters and included by chance in the Śāradā manuscript of this parvan belonging to the Royal Asiatic Society of Bengal, forms the frontispiece of the second part of the Āraṇyakaparvan (Vol. 4). The passage commented on is 3. 133. 20 to 134. 9. Note the consecutive numbering of the lines in the left margin.

Another useful testimonium of the Mahābhārata is the *Bhāratamañjarī* of Kṣemendra. Kṣemendra summarizes the Āraṇyaka in about 2000—to be precise 1964—stanzas, divided into the following 51 sections :

[12] (1) सूर्यस्तव ; (2) विदुरागमन ; (3) सुरभ्युपाख्यान ; (4) मैत्रेयशाप ; (5) किन्दीरवध[1]; (6) साल्ववध ; (7) कैरात ; (8) लोकपालास्त्रप्राप्ति ; (9) इन्द्रलोकगमन ; (10) नलोपाख्यान ; (11) पुलस्त्यतीर्थयात्रा ; (12) धौम्यतीर्थयात्रा ; (13) आगस्त्य ; (14) ऋश्यशृङ्गोपाख्यान ; (15) कार्तवीर्योपाख्यान ; (16) सौकन्य ; (17) मान्धात्रुपाख्यान ; (18) जन्तूपाख्यान ; (19) श्येनकपोतीय ; (20) अष्टावक्रीय ; (21) यावक्रीत ; (22) हनुमद्भीमसमागम ; (23) पुष्कराहरण ; (24) जटासुरवध ; (25) मणिमद्वध ; (26) वैश्रवणसमागम ; (27) निवातकवचवध ; (28) लोमशतीर्थयात्रा ; (29) आजगर ; (30) ब्राह्मणमाहात्म्य ; (31) वैन्योपाख्यान ; (32) सरस्वतीतार्क्ष्यसंवाद ; (33) मत्स्योपाख्यान ; (34) मार्कण्डेयसमस्या (sic); (35) भविष्यत् ; (36) मण्डूकोपाख्यान ; (37) इन्द्रद्युम्नोपाख्यान ; (38) धुन्धुमारोपाख्यान ; (39) पतिव्रतोपाख्यान ; (40) आङ्गिरस ; (41) द्रौपदीसत्यभामासंवाद ; (42) घोषयात्रा ; (43) दुर्योधनप्रायोपवेश ; (44) धार्तराष्ट्रयज्ञ ; (45) मृगस्वप्नप्रदर्शन ; (46) व्रीहीद्रौणिक ; (47) द्रौपदीप्रमाथ ; (48) रामोपाख्यान ; (49) साविश्र्युपाख्यान ; (50) कुण्डलाहरण ; (51) आरणेय.

From this list of contents, it can be seen that almost all the stories and episodes which we now find in our text of the Āraṇyaka were there already in Kṣemendra's time (ca. 1050 A.D.). The parvan must therefore have had then the same general form and appearance as now. More significant is the fact that all important passages—without exception—that are lacking in our manuscripts of the Kaśmīrī version are likewise missing in the *Mañjarī*. This fact alone cannot prove that these passages were lacking in the Kaśmīrī version of the eleventh century. Some or even all of them could have been omitted by a poet who was making an epitome of an extensive work like the Āraṇyakaparvan : he would be within his rights in doing so. But the *Mañjarī* does not omit any important episode or passage which is not omitted at the same time in the Kaśmīrī version of the Great Epic. Consequently, unless the version of the Āraṇyakaparvan used by Kṣemendra was nearly indentical with *our* Kaśmīrī version, the coincidence that our Kaśmīrī manuscripts omit just those passages which Kṣemendra had considered not worth including in his epitome, *and no other*, would be extremely curious, if not miraculous. It seems accordingly most probable that the episodes which are not found in Kṣemendra's *Mañjarī* were already lacking in the Kaśmīrī version of the Mahābhārata *in the eleventh century*. I think, therefore, that with the help of this testimonium, we can establish for the omissions of the Kaśmīrī version an antiquity much higher than that vouchsafed solely by the age of our manuscripts, which are later by some centuries than the period of the composition of Kṣemendra's *Bhāratamañjarī*.

Noteworthy among such omissions of the *Mañjarī* are the following three

[1] It is worth noting that our Śāradā Codex *uniformly* writes किन्दीर for our किर्मीर.

lengthy passages : (1) the Temptation of Arjuna by Urvaśī (App. I, No. 6); (2) Karṇa's Conquest of the World (App. I, No. 24); (3) the Visit of Durvāsas to Yudhiṣṭhira (App. I, No. 25). The first of these three interpolations has insinuated itself in the manuscripts of almost all versions and is now lacking only in some manuscripts of the Kaśmīrī version.[1] The second among them is documented only by Devanāgarī manuscripts, excepting a few conflated manuscripts of other versions ; consequently its claim to be recognized as an authentic passage is not very substantial. Finally, the last passage introducing Durvāsas into the story, a passage which is really restricted to the Nīlakaṇṭha version, with the casual support of a few Devanāgarī and some conflated manuscripts, does not really come into question ; because its spurious character is very [13] evident and does not need an elobate proof.[2]

The versions of the commentators Caturbhuja and Nīlakaṇṭha are described below under the Devanāgarī version.

PEDIGREE OF THE ĀRAṆYAKAPARVAN VERSIONS

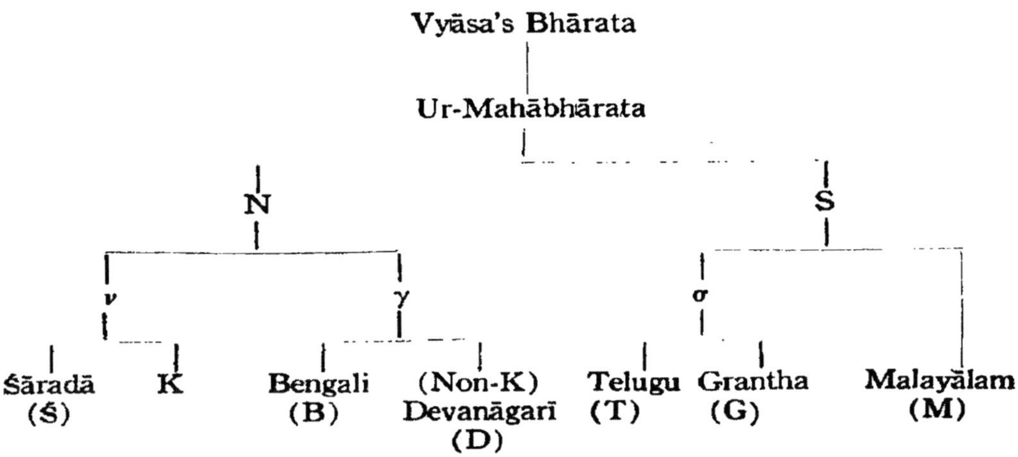

---

1 See below, p. 160.

2 With this story disappears one of the very few episodes in the Mahābhārata in which Śri Kṛṣṇa is represented as hearing from a distance, as it were by clairaudience or divine omniscience, the prayers of his distressed devotees and as either coming instantly to their help in person or providing invisibly the means of their rescue or safety. The other episode I had in mind, which has likewise proved to be an interpolation, is the well-known scene, in the Sabhāparvan of the disrobing of Draupadī (Draupadī-vastra-haraṇa), when, according to the Vulgate version, Draupadī prays to Śrī Kṛṣṇa, who hears her prayer and comes running to her rescue. (त्यक्त्वा शय्यासनं पद्भ्यां कृपालुः कृपयाभ्यगात् । B. 2. 68. 45), and she is clothed again and again, miraculously, but presumably by the intervention and grace of Śrī Kṛṣṇa. They undoubtedly represent a later phase of Kṛṣṇa worship.

A CRITICAL SURVEY OF THE RECENSIONS AND THEIR VERSIONS

GENERAL SURVEY

A description of the forest life of the Pāṇḍavas constitutes the topic of the Third Book, the Āraṇyaka—(Āraṇya—or Araṇya—) parvan, commonly called (for short) the Vanaparvan, whose extent is between 11,000 and 12,000 ślokas (i.e. "granthas"). The actual incidents narrated, pertaining to the life-history of the heroes in this parvan, are indeed few and unimportant compared to the size of the book. The entire narrative has been condensed by Kṣemendra in his *Bhāratamañjarī* into less than 2,000 stanzas, without omitting any of the main incidents. The great extent of the parvan has been made up by the inclusion of episodes of the most diverse kind : stories of ancient kings, sages, and virtuous women ; description of places of pilgrimage (*tīrtha-yātrā*); discourses [14] on moral, ethical and philosophical topics, ancient gāthās and anuvaṁśa stanzas. It was a fashion for some time to obelize this episodic matter as late interpolation. But that is a misguided view, originating with a certain type of critics who have exhibited a uniform lack of understanding of the meaning of the Mahābhārata and of the basic plan and aim of the creators of our great epic. The episodical material in the Mahābhārata is, in general, not secondarily introduced ; it belongs to the original plan and serves a distinct purpose. As PISANI has pointed out in his paper on the "Rise of the Mahābhārata", the bulk of didactic and episodic matter has been used to fill up the great "temporal hiatuses" in the narrative, viz, in the first place, the twelve years of exile in forest (Āraṇyaka), and then the long interval between the end of the Bhārata War and the last adventure of the Pāṇḍavas (Śānti and Anuśāsana). "This distribution", remarks PISANI, "to fill up temporal hiatuses has not only the scope of not disturbing the course of narration, but also that of helping the reader to pass over irrelevant years without striking against too strong a contrast between periods minutely narrated and others rapidly surpassed. In a not different manner Homer introduces often dialogues and episodic stories when he must conceal the flowing of times without noteworthy events."[1]

The episodic material is largely Purāṇic in character. Many of the Purāṇic stories we find here narrated over again. Moreover, as the references given in the foot-notes to the text and the critical notes at the end of this Book (pp. 1091-1109) will show, there is considerable verbal agreement between the epic and Purāṇic versions of the stories. The Purāṇas which show the closest contact and widest parallelism are the Skanda, Padma and Brahma. The entire story of Skanda (adhy. 213-221), together with the passage containing the 108 names of the Sun (our adhy. 3, stanzas 18-28), recurs

---

[1] *A Volume of Eastern and Indian Studies presented to Prof. F. W. Thomas,* etc. (1939), p. 170.

almost verbatim in the Skanda Purāṇa. The story of the Bhārgava sage Cyavana and the princess Sukanyā, the prose story of the Frog-girl, and a considerable portion of the Rāmopākhyāna are also to be met with in the Skanda, worded almost identically with the Mahābhārata. The 108 names of the Sun recur besides in the Brahma Purāṇa, which, moreover, has a portion of the story of Mārkaṇḍeya in common with the Āraṇyakaparvan. Furthermore, sections of our tīrthayātrā are to be met with again in the Padma and Matsya. A Bengali manuscript[1] of the Padma Purāṇa contains besides a version of the Ṛśyaśṛnga legend. In all these cases, the parallelism of verbal expression of the epic and the Purāṇic narratives is so complete and striking, that the possibility of their having originated independently of each other is at once ruled out. Many stray stanzas from our parvan are found in the Kūrma, Varāha, Vāyu, Viṣṇu, Viṣṇudharmottara, and in the Harivaṁśa.

Our recensions of the Purāṇas are admittedly of a very late date, and it is not to be expected that the Mahābhārata would have borrowed any of its material from our Purāṇas. The claim that the the Mahābhārata owed certain geographical and cosmographical sections of the Bhīṣmaparvan to the Padma Purāṇa, preferred by Luise HILGENBERG,[2] [15] has been answered and liquidated by Rao Bahadur Professor Dr. S. K. BELVALKAR, who has shown that in reality the converse of this proposition is true.[3] This scholar has now shown from internal evidence that the Padma Purāṇa must have written up its geographical section from the information supplied by the Mahābhārata. Similarly, the question of relationship between our Pulastya Tīrthayātrā and a very similar episode in the Padma Purāṇa has been discussed by my assistant, Mr. M. V. VAIDYA, M.A., who has likewise shown from intrinsic evidence that the Mahābhārata passage is the source of the Padma Purāṇa version.[4]

It must, however, be admitted that although in most cases the compilers of our Purāṇas appear to have drawn their material from the Mahābhārata, there may be—indeed there *must* be—a few cases in which both the Mahābhārata and the Purāṇas may have drawn independently upon a third common source. We can also say this with regard to episodes like the Sāvitrī episode, which likewise occurs in the Matsya Purāṇa, where it is narrated in an entirely different manner from that in the epic, and where all traces of

[1] The Bodleian MS., Wilson 111-116, mentioned by LÜDERS in "Die Sage von Ṛṣyaśṛṅga." *Nachrichten von der Königl. Gesell. der Wiss.* zu Gottingen, Phil. hist. Kl., 1897, pp. 88, 94.

[2] *Die Kosmographische Episode im Mahābhārata und Padmapurāṇa* (= Bonner Orientalistische Studien, Heft 4), Bonn 1934.

[3] S. K. BELVALKAR, "The Cosmographical Episode in Mahābhārata and Padmapurāṇa", *A Volume of Eastern and Indian Studies presented to Prof. F. W. Thomas* etc. (1939), pp. 19 ff.

[4] M. V. VAIDYA, "Tīrtha-yātrā in the Āraṇyakaparvan and the Padmapurāṇa", *A Volume of Studies in Indology presented to Prof. P. V. Kane* etc. (1941), pp 530 ff.

mutual relationship are absent or obliterated, except for two or three common stanzas and stray pādas.

The reference in our parvan to Vāyu, वायुप्रोक्तमनुस्मृत्य (3, 189. 14), is worth considering in this connection. Nothing corresponding to the general contents of the passage where it occurs is to be found in the extant Vāyu Purāṇa, as is remarked by HOPKINS,[1] or for the matter of that in any other Purāṇa proclaimed by Vāyu. There are, however, a few stanzas in the Vāyu describing the dissolution of the world where verbal similarity with some stanzas of this passage is pronounced, even though they are introduced in the Vāyu in a different context. The Mahābhārata, as mentioned in it (3. 189. 14), draws upon a Purāṇa of Vāyu—and indeed, the topic narrated belongs properly to a Purāṇa in its right, a Purāṇa which is older than the extant Purāṇas and which must be presumed to be now irretrievably lost. The evidence for establishing a relationship between the extant Vāyu and its old namesake to which the epic is indebted is lacking, barring these few stray stanzas.

Our parvan also contains an epitome of the legend of Rāma, son of Daśaratha, the hero of the Rāmāyaṇa, which is known as Rāmopākhyāna (adhy. 258-275); but in the Parvasaṁgraha this passage is called रामायणमुपाख्यानं (1. 2. 126). Does this name imply any connection with our "Rāmāyaṇa"? JACOBI has tried to show that the Rāmopākhyāna is indeed an epitome of the work commonly known as Vālmīki's Rāmāyaṇa, a conclusion which has been confirmed by subsequent researchers.[2]

This book, as already observed, is particularly rich in legends of ancient India. Among them are three worthy of special mention, viz., the Tale of Nala, the Ṛśyaśṛṅga Legend and the Story of Sāvirtrī which have been critically edited here for the first time. The first of these, the Tale of Nala, has by way of translations into English, [16] French, German, Dutch, Italian and other European languages, passed into the great stream of world literature. The second, the Ṛśyaśṛṅga Legend, though not so well known, has yet a long and interesting history and shows many modulations and ramifications, as has been convincingly shown by Professor Heinrich LÜDERS in his well-known monograph on the subject, "Die Sage von Ṛṣyaśṛṅga."[3] The story of Sāvitrī portraying woman in the rôle of the saviour of man, which represents the high-water mark of epic poetry, is in a class by itself, and deserves to be more widely known. It is to be hoped that this first critical edition of the three of the most famous episodes of the Mahābhārata will evoke the interest of Indologists and encourage further study of them.

[1] *The Great Epic of India*, p. 48 f.

[2] Cf. V. S. SUKTHANKAR, "Epic Studies VIII", in *A Volume of Studies in Indology presented to Prof. P. V. Kane etc.* (1941), pp. 472 ff.

[3] *Nachrichten von der Königl, Gessell, der Wiss.* zu Göttingen, Phil-hist. Kl., 1897, pp. 87-135; see also *ibid.* 1901, pp. 28-56.

THE TWO RECENSIONS

The text of the Āraṇyakaparvan is, relatively speaking, remarkably smooth, offering no special difficulties for textual reconstruction. There are of course, as usual, discrepancies between the Northern and the Southern recensions, and between the various versions comprising these two main recensions. But it is noteworthy that in the whole of this big parvan, comprising between 11,000 and 12,000 "ślokas", there are not many transpositions of any consequence and there are also remarkably few "substitute passages". By the latter I mean parallel versions of fairly long passages in two or more conflicting recensions which agree in general sense but are worded differently in different groups of manuscripts, so that they cannot be co-ordinated line by line,—passages which we find in large numbers in some of the other parvans, notably in the Virāṭaparvan. These substitute passages are very clear evidences of textual corruption—or, shall we say, derangement?—and indeed very embarrassing to the textual critic. As for the transpositions, there is only one that is worth noting here, and that is of the last adhyāya of this parvan. The whole of this adhyāya is bodily transferred in the Southern recension to the *next* parvan and appears there incorporated in the first adhyāya of that parvan! It is not possible to say with certainty whether this chapter, which in all probability is itself an interpolation, belongs legitimately to our parvan or to the next; but it appears to be distinctly more appropriate in its Northern setting, as its intrusion in the Virāṭaparvan seems to lead to some obvious repetitions as well as disturbance of context.[1]

There are naturally quite a number of large and small insertions in the various versions. But in this matter also the present parvan prepares a surprise for us. From the experience gained from our critical editions of the Ādi, Sabhā, and Virāṭa parvans especially, we are inclined to regard the Southern recension as a highly inflated version of the text. Now, in this parvan—strange to say—the Vulgate version, which is based on the late Northern tradition, is actually considerably longer than the Southern, as may be seen from the extent of this parvan according to the existing printed editions of the Vulgate and the Southern recension: the Calcutta edition has 12,848 ślokas (corrected figure) as against 11,138 ślokas in SASTRI's Southern Recension.

[17] The large excess in the Calcutta-Bombay editions compared with SASTRI's is explained by the fact that the Vulgate text contains about a dozen adhyāyas which are lacking entirely in the Southern recension; whereas the Southern recension contains only two passages of any considerable length (App. I, Nos. 4 and 23), which are not found in representative manuscripts of the Northern recension, they being peculiar to the Southern,—with the result that the Calcutta edition has 1710 ślokas in excess of SASTRI's edition

---

1 See H. LÜDERS, "Über die Grantharecension des Mahābhārata", *Abhandlungen der Königl. Gesell. der Wiss. zu Göttingen* (1901), p. 53 f.

of the Āraṇyaka-parvan. Thus we see that though, as a whole, the Southern recension is unquestionably inflated, yet the process of inflation, as is evident from this parvan, is not uniform throughout the epic,—which is a very important and significant fact.

Though the best version of the Northern recension—namely, the Śāradā-K version—and the Southern recension agree remarkably well as regards the general extent of the parvan, there are nevertheless numerous specific individual readings, characterizing the two recensions—Northern and Southern—and distinguishing them sharply from each other. Here is a selection of readings peculiar to the two main recensions, the references being to adhyāyas and ślokas.

	Northern Recension	Southern Recension
1. 37	घोरं	सर्वाः
1. 41	शुशुभे	शुश्रूषुर्
2. 13	धिक्पापान्	द्विषतो (text)
2. 31	न लिप्सेत	स्वपक्षेभ्यः (text)
2. 34	स्मृता	नृणाम् (text)
2. 45	ऐश्वर्यं	आरोग्यं
2. 50	ब्रह्मन्	विप्र
2. 74	°संबन्धात्	°योगाच्च
5. 8	एवं शेषं यदि	एतच्छ्रेयस्तव
8. 2	वचनं राजा	मधुरं वाक्यं
12. 16	न्यमीलयत लोचने	विषादमगमद्भृशं
12. 59	गृह्य मध्ये वृकोदर	भीमसेनो महाबलः
13. 13	अप(*or* अव)कृष्टोत्तरासङ्गः	कृष्णाजिनोत्तरासङ्गः
13. 28	महिषीं	रुक्मिणीं
13. 50	दश	तथा
13. 78	पुनः सुप्तान्	ततः पुनर्
13. 83	राजानं दक्षिणेन च	दक्षिणेन युधिष्ठिरं
48. 4	सिंहविक्रान्तौ	युधि विक्रान्तौ
101. 11	परमेष्ठिनमाज्ञाप्य अगस्त्यस्याश्रमं ययुः ।	समनुज्ञाप्य ब्रह्माणं वारुणिं समुपस्थिताः ।

I may add here examples of short passages found in the Southern Recension which are lacking in the Northern, and thus distinguish it from the latter : 6*, 17*, 18*, 100*, 118*, 176*, 197*, 201*, 207*, 208*, 209*, 217*, 236*, 237*, 239*, 241*, 246*, 273*, 289*, 304*, 306*, 314*, 315*, 331*,

341*, 347*, 351*, 367*, 383*, 385*, 386*, 407*, 425*, 471*, 474*, 475*, 481*, 489*, 491*, 496*, 497*, 500*, 503*, 506*, 507*, 509*, 513*, 515*, 518*, 519*, 520*, 523*, 524*, 525*, 526*, 527*, 533*, 534*, 573*, 594*, 598*, 606*, 612*, 615*, 626*, 634*, 645*, 650*, 653*, 709*, 721*, 739*, 740*, 742*, 745*, 751*, 756*, 759*, [18] 781*, 782*, 807*, 808*, 816*, 854*, 935*, 941*, 950*, 954*, 975*, 988*, 995*, 997*, 1002*, 1006*, 1030*, 1092*, 1093*, 1102*, 1114*, 1204*, 1206*, etc. etc., etc.

It may be observed that all these additions in the Southern recension (with the exception of only one or two), numerous as they are, are uniformly short, each usually consisting of not more than a couple of lines.

As remarked already, the text of this parvan is remarkably smooth, not presenting any unusual difficulties in the way of restitution. When the Śāradā-K version (which is the best Northern version) and the Southern recension are placed *vis-à-vis*, we can in general reconstruct the original with confidence, barring a certain number of minor verbal fluctuations in the shape of synonymous phrasings, which remain indeterminate without affecting the construction or obscuring the sense. The concord between the Śārada-K version and the Southern recension in point of general content is striking, and forms a sure basis for constituting a single text. Contamination between the Kaśmīrī version and the Southern recension cannot be proved, but contamination between the Bengali-Devanāgarī version and the Southern recension is not impossible. The agreements between the Bengali-Devanāgarī and the Southern recension have nevertheless been as a rule utilized to arrive at a tentative stop-gap, based on the indications of documental evidence. But it should be noted that the Kaśmīrī-Southern agreements have for greater documental authority and probative value than the Bengali-cum-Devanāgarī and Southern agreements.

Let me put the matter in a slightly different way. The highest documental probability we can demand and expect is when all manuscripts of our critical apparatus—which is the same as saying, all our different versions—agree on a reading or a feature. We must accept this as the original; at least we do not want to question it, at present. In the absence of such complete concord, the next best combination is the agreement between the Śāradā version and the Southern recension (against Bengali-Devanāgarī). Third in importance is, in my opinion, the concord between the Southern recension and the Bengali-cum-Devanāgarī version (against the Śāradā). Fourth in order stands the agreement between only Northern versions or only Southern versions *inter se*, which I consider, in general, as of equal value. With the proviso that a passage or a stanza or even a line, which is not *necessary* to the context, may be rejected, if it is actually omitted entirely in even *one* of the important versions, since—as experience has shown—the chances of conflation are always very much greater than those of accidental or intentional omission.

CHARACTER AND MUTUAL RELATIONS OF THE VERSIONS AND THEIR MANUSCRIPTS

The Śāradā (or Kaśmīrī) Version.

We are fortunate in possessing for this parvan also, a genuine Kaśmīrī manuscript written, in old Śāradā characters, on folios prepared from the Himalayan birch-bark (*bhūrjapatra*). The manuscript is no other than the now world-famous "Śāradā Codex", the unique birch-bark manuscript of the Mahābhārata belonging to the Bombay Government Collection, now deposited at the Bhandarkar Oriental Research Institute, with identification No. 159 of 1875-76, which is the only extant genuine representative of the old [19] version of Kaśmir.[1] Our manuscript is, in other words, the continuation of the Śāradā manuscript used for the Ādi and Sabhā. The manuscript is fragmentary, breaking off in the middle of 3. 253. 18^{d}, thus lacking unfortunately the last 46 adhyāyas of our text. For this lacuna we have to depend upon the "K" version, some manuscripts of which have proved to be moderately good copies of the Śāradā version, especially K_3, which is described below.

It is now recognized by the competent authorities on the subject that the Śāradā version is, in many respects, the most faithful representative of the original now extant; and the text of the Āraṇyakaparvan as preserved in our Śāradā Codex only confirms this view.

The Śāradā text of the Āraṇyaka is of a piece with the texts of the Ādi and the Sabhā. The stanzas comprising the text have not been actually counted—it would not be easy to compute its exact extent, as the text comprises ślokas, triṣṭubhs and two lengthy prose passages—but it is, in all probability, the shortest version of the parvan now extant, since it omits many passages which are found in other versions and manuscripts, while it does not contain new additions of any consequence. The text includes many archaic survivals in point of linguistic usage and shows what may fairly be regarded as "difficult readings" (*lect. diff.*), in comparison with those of other manuscripts.

The most striking omission of the Kaśmīrī version is the story of Urvaśī (adhy. 45-46 of the Vulgate=passage No. 6 of our App. I), which relates how Arjuna is tempted by Urvaśī during his sojourn in Indra's heaven, and

---

[1] The Kaśmīrī character of the text of our Śāradā manuscript, which is suggested by the script (Śāradā) and the writing material (bhūrjapatra), is confirmed not only by the reading व्यासं in the third pāda of the introductory mantra नारायणं नमस्कृत्य etc.; but also by the regular omission of the word उवाच in such reference as वैशंपायन उवाच; and further by such Kaśmīrī spellings of names like चारुदोष्ण (for चारुदेष्ण) in 3. 17. 22. corresponding to सुदोष्णा (for सुदेष्णा) in the Virāṭa; cf. RAGHU VIRA, Introduction to the Virāṭaparvan, p. xi. The *Bhāratamañjarī* has चारुदोष्ण in 3. 159 and सुदोष्णा in 4. 36, etc. That is a real Kaśmīrī trait.

how he refuses her advances on the ground that she is an ancestress of his. Although this piquant story has permeated all versions of the epic except the Kaśmīrī ($Ś_1$ and some K), there is no reason to doubt that it is a late addition. The highly erotic description of the voluptuous hetäre of the gods, Urvaśī, with its pronounced sex appeal, is in my opinion totally incompatible with the epic setting, which lacks all "feminine" interest and eschews all erotic topics as such. The stanzas I refer to are (App. I. No. 6. lines 50-57=Bombay ed. 3. 46.8-11 = Calcutta ed. 3. 1824-1827) :

दिव्याङ्गरागौ सुमुखौ दिव्यचन्दनरूषितौ ॥
गच्छन्त्या हारविकचौ स्तनौ तस्या ववल्गतुः ।
स्तनोद्वहनसंक्षोभान्नम्यमाना पदे पदे ।
त्रिवलीदामचित्रेण मध्येनातीव शोभिना ।
अधोभूधरविस्तीर्णं नितम्बोन्नतपीवरम् ।
मन्मथायतनं शुभ्रं रसनादामभूषितम् ।
ऋषीणामपि दिव्यानां मनोव्याघातकारणम् ।
सूक्ष्मवस्त्रधरं रेजे जघनं निरवद्यवत् ।

[20] The spurious character of this lengthy erotic interlude seems to me to be further revealed by two stanzas of *phalaśruti* with which the passage ends (App. I, No. 6, lines 157-162=Bomb. ed. 3. 46. 62-63=Cal. ed. 3, 1877-1878) :

य इदं शृणुयान्नित्यं वृत्तं पाण्डुसुतस्य वै ।
न तस्य कामः कामेषु पापकेषु प्रवर्तते ।
इदममरवरात्मजस्य घोरं
शुचि चरितं विनिशम्य फाल्गुनस्य ।
व्यपगतमददम्भरागदोषा-
स्त्रिदिवगताभिरमन्ति मानवेन्द्राः ।

The object of the interpolations seems to be also clear. It is primarily intended to motivate Arjuna's masquerading as the dancing master to Princess Uttarā in the harem at the court of Virāṭa, which is narrated in the next parvan. The devout see in it a trial, a test, to see if Arjuna's mind was as pure as his body was strong. Arjuna withstands the test successfully. But the reward he gets for his patience and self-control is a curious one; he is *cursed* by the angry and disappointed nymph that he would live as a eunuch among women! This apparent curse is, however, looked upon as a blessing in disguise, for it was to take effect and serve its purpose in the thirteenth year of the exile through which Arjuna along with his brothers must remain unrecognized (*ajñatavāsa*).

This jejune invention creates, however, many complications not foreseen by the interpolator, as it is unfortunately contradicted by Arjuna himself in the very next parvan, when he confesses to Uttara, that though he has been telling people that he is a eunuch (4. 10. 8-9), ***he is in reality nothing of the kind***, and that he has only been practising strict continence, having taken the vow of rigid celibacy for one full year by order of his eldest brother, Yudhiṣṭhira (4. 40. 12-13) :

भ्रातुर्नियोगाज्ज्येष्ठस्य संवत्सरमिदं व्रतम् ।
चरामि ब्रह्मचर्यं वै सत्यमेतद्ब्रवीमि ते ॥
नास्मि क्लीबो महाबाहो परवान्धर्मसंयुतः ।
समाप्तव्रतमुत्तीर्णं विद्धि मां त्वं नृपात्मज ॥

If that be so, then we must assume that either Urvaśī's curse had failed to materialize or—what is more plausible—that Arjuna was never under any curse such as the one implied in this interpolation. Such an interpolation could have been made only when it was considered necessary that Arjuna ought in reality to have been a eunuch to be admitted into the ladies' apartments at the Virāṭa court, or at least to justify his specific statement to the effect that he was a eunuch. But this appalling realism is as clumsy as it is unnecessary. The original conception was obviously quite different. At the end of the twelfth year of their exile Dharma tells Yudhiṣṭhira that they could go to Virāṭa's kingdom in any capacity or with any profession, and no one would recognize them under any circumstances. Their *saṁkalpa* would be so strong that they would appear to others in any shape or form desired by themselves, without any external aid or make-up (3. 298. 17, 19) :

यद्यपि स्वेन रूपेण चरिष्यथ महीमिमाम् ।
न वो विज्ञास्यते कश्चित्त्रिषु लोकेषु भारत ।
[21] यद्वः संकल्पितं रूपं मनसा यस्य यादृशम् ।
तादृशं तादृशं सर्वे छन्दतो धारयिष्यथ ॥

In these circumstances I think there is not much doubt that the suspected episode is in fact a clumsy interpolation, and the circumstance that the Śārradā version lacks is only an additional proof of the superiority of this version.

I may add here that the whole story is likewise missing not only in the *Bhāratamañjarī* but also in the fragmentary but excellent Devanāgarī manuscript of the Āraṇyakaparvan belonging to the Bombay Branch of the Royal Asiatic Society (No. 966, fol. 43b), which I have occasionally consulted in doubtful cases.[1]

Further particulars of the Śāradā version will be found under the account of the "K" version, which follows next, and with which the Śāradā version is intimately connected.

---

[1] See above p. 150 f.

A facsimile of a page of the "Śāradā Codex" ($Ś_1$) appears as the frontispiece of this volume. The text is 3. 45. 1-25.

The "K" Version.

This version, as is the case of the other parvans, is a specific Devanāgarī version, closely related to the Śāradā, and clearly differentiated from the so-called Devanāgarī version. The manuscripts comprising this version must in part be merely Devanāgarī copies of Śāradā originals and may in part represent the version of a province or a region adjoining the Śāradā zone, which it has not been possible to localize more precisely.

That the manuscripts of the K version are akin to and cognate with $Ś_1$ may be seen from the numerous readings common to S_1 and K (with or without some other Devanāgarī manuscripts). But it is demonstrated especially forcibly by their common *omission* of certain important and well-known passages found in all other manuscripts, or at least in all other manuscripts of the Northern recension. Of such passages, given in our App. I, the most important are numbered 16-18, 22, 27 and 31.

Of these passages No. 16, which forms a separate adhyāya of about 130 lines, and is a medley of legends—among them the story of Narakāsura and the legend of the rescue of the Earth by Viṣṇu in the Boar incarnation,—is omitted in all five manuscripts of the group $Ś_1$ K, besides D_{1-3} of the Northern recension. It is, in other words, characteristic of the Mid-Indian group, Bengali and late Devanāgarī.—Passage No. 17 (42 lines), describing the return of the Pāṇḍavas to the hermitage at Badarī, has permeated more widely, and is now found not only in the entire Southern recension but also in all manuscripts of the Northern recension except $Ś_1$ K (with $D_{1-3\cdot5}$). Here also we notice that the group $Ś_1$ K is clearly distinguished from the typical Central sub-recension B Dc Dn $D_{4\cdot6}$.—No. 18 is a short passage of 24 lines of exactly the same type ; that is to say, it is omitted in $Ś_1$ K (with some other allied Devanāgarī manuscripts) in opposition to the typical Mid-Indian group B Dc Dn $D_{4\cdot6}$. K_3 secondarily incorporates in its text only the first four lines of the passage, which is as indication of the manner in which the additions of the Central sub-recension (B D) have contaminated the Śāradā-K version.—Another passage of that type is No. 22 (giving the names of Skanda); which is omitted in the whole group ($Ś_1$ K), with [22] the single exception of the conflated manuscript K_2.—The next passage of that kind is No. 27, a lengthy passage of 87 lines describing in detail how Jayadratha, after being released from captivity by Yudhiṣṭhira, seeks the help of the god Mahādeva in order to avenge himself ; it is found in all Northern manuscripts except $Ś_1$ K D_1.—The last passage in our list is No. 31, a long spun out lament by Yudhiṣṭhira on seeing his brothers lying on the ground as if dead near the Enchanted Lake, a passage which is also found in all Northern manuscripts except $Ś_1$ K (with $D_{1\cdot3\cdot5}$).

The contrast between Ś$_1$ K and the Mid-Indian group is well brought out by two different single-line insertions, which are nothing but two different attempts to fill out a supposed lacuna after 3. 107. 18. After this stanza,

Ś$_1$ K D$_5$ ins.:	B Dc Dn D$_{3.4.6}$ ins.:
531* तावत्स्वर्गे न वत्स्यन्ति मम पूर्वपितामहाः ।	532* तावत्तेषां गतिर्नास्ति सागराणां महानदि ।

Both of these, as shown by S (which our constituted text here follows), are superfluous, as will be clear from a perusal of the text (3. 107. 18-19) :

तेषामेवं विनष्टानां स्वर्गे वासो न विद्यते ।
यावत्तानि शरीराणि त्वं जलैनाभिषिञ्चसि ॥
स्वर्गं नय महाभागे मत्पितॄन्सगरात्मजान् ।
तेषामर्थेऽभियाचामि त्वामहं वै महानदि ॥

Notwithstanding the fact that the manuscripts comprising the K version show many striking agreements which distinguish them from other groups, the K group itself cannot be said to be quite homogeneous. Of these K$_2$ is distinctly conflated and rather more deeply contaminated than the others. While preserving a large number of Kaśmīrī readings, it sides frequently (especially in the early adhyāyas) with the Bengali-Devanāgarī group ; at times even showing readings peculiar to the late Nīlakaṇṭha tradition. K$_1$ is really a manuscript of the same type, though the degree of contamination is considerably less. K$_3$, on the other hand, shares with Ś$_1$ many unique readings, coming closest to it. Indeed I am inclined to regard the concordant readings of Ś$_1$ and K$_3$ as the specific Kaśmīrī readings. In K$_4$ the last manuscript of the K version, the contamination has gone yet further than in any other K manuscript, K$_4$ incorporating occasionally not merely Southern readings, but sporadically even what are characteristic Southern insertions.

I append here examples of readings showing special affinity between Ś$_1$ and K$_3$ (references are to adhyāyas and ślokas) :

	Ś$_1$ K$_3$		Other MSS.
7. 10	जगाम संजयस्तूर्णं		संजयो बाढमित्युक्त्वा
	यत्रास्ते विदुरो वने ।	:	प्राद्रवत्काम्यकं वनं (*or* प्रति) ।
7. 15	त्वच्छोकाकुलितेंद्रियं	:	संजीवय च पार्थिवं (*or* नराधिपं)
,,	धर्मज्ञ	:	त्वं क्षिप्रं (text), त्वरितं, सुक्षिप्रं, etc.
7. 16	(with D$_{1-3}$) भारत	:	मानद (text), सत्तम
7. 18	आगतं विदुरं ज्ञात्वा	:	तमब्रवीत् महाप्राज्ञं (*or* महाराजः, °तेजाः, °प्राज्ञः)
,,	राजा वचनमब्रवीत्	:	धृतराष्ट्रोंबिकासुतः °राष्ट्रः प्रतापवन्
9. 5	(with D$_{1-3}$) अपि	:	तान.

[23] Here follow examples showing the contamination of K_2 with B D; and especially with the group B Dc Dn $D_{4,6}$:

	K_2 B + some D		Other MSS.
2. 6	देवता ह्यपि	:	दैवतान्यपि
2. 9	दुःखार्दितान्	:	दुःखान्वितान्
2. 10	चान्नानि	:	वन्यं तु, वन्यास्त्वां, वन्यानि
2. 32	युक्तेषु	:	मुख्येषु (text), सिद्धेषु
13. 54	शोणितेन	:	रुधिरेण
13. 98	परंतपाः	:	यशस्विनः
17. 3	चैत्यवृक्षांश्च	:	चैव चैत्यांश्च
25. 15	तपःसिद्धा महात्मनः	:	तपस्विनः सत्यशीलाः
34. 11	दुर्बला°	:	अवीरा° (text), अधीरा°.

The contamination of K_2 is further proved by the circumstance that it has incorporated in its text the following insertions of the Central sub-recension : 10*, 14*, 16*, 22*, 50*, 52*, 55*, 76*, 91*, 97*, 107*, 126*, 184*, 192*, 215*, 249*, 390*, etc., etc., etc.

Examples showing specially close contact between K_2 and Dn are as follows :

37. 9 K_2 Dn तं प्रति : rest सांप्रतं (text) संप्रति etc.
37. 10 K_2 Dn संगरे : rest रक्षणे
37. 26 K_2 Dn धनुर्धरः : rest धनंजयः (text), युधिष्ठिरः
37. 38 K_2 Dn °विशारदाः : rest °विदस्तथा
38. 5 K_2 Dn तम् (Dn_2 ते) : rest च
38. 8 K_2 Dn भवानेव प्रियोस्माकं : rest त्वयि व्यपाश्रयोस्माकं, etc.
44. 16 K_2 Dn देवेशं : rest देवेंद्रं
52. 5 K_2 Dn त्वं : rest स
54. 3 K_2 Dn transp. महा — and नृपाः
61. 82 K_2 Dn D_5 रम्यं : rest पुण्यं
61. 111 K_2 Dn D_5 जग्मुः : rest तस्थुः
81. 68 K_2 Dn D_5 [अ]नुत्तमान् : rest दुर्लभान्.

Examples of insertions almost restricted to K_2 Dn are : 50*, 55*, (both very clear interpolations), 326 * (with K_4) 390* (with $D_{2.5}$), 412* (with D_5); and passage No. 12 of App. I (also found in D_6, but with a different point of insertion).

The contamination of K_2 from Dn is especially noticeable in the Nala Episode. Its Kaśmīrī character, however, again comes to the surface in such wrong transcription from the Śāradā as तत्पादय (for उत्पादय) in 3. 97. 17.

Sporadic contamination of K_4 from S is seen in the insertion 159*, and in passage No. 4 of App. I (cf. v. l. 3. 38. 18).

Manuscripts D_{1-3} of the Devanāgarī version show pronounced affinities with the K version, often supporting the specific readings and omissions of the latter, and they might have been classed under the K version.

The Bengali Version.

Our four Bengali manuscripts form on the whole a very homogeneous group, presenting generally a single common reading. The version has very close affinities with [24] a particular type of Devanāgarī manuscripts represented by our Dn $D_{4\cdot6}$ (with or without Dc). These two groups—B and Dc Dn $D_{4\cdot6}$—show as a rule the same readings, and contain the same insertions. A notable exception is 939*, which is a specific Bengali insertion lacking even in Dc $D_{4\cdot6}$ and found only in Dn of the Devanāgarī manuscripts.

The affinity of B (Dc) Dn $D_{4\cdot6}$ (often with the conflated manuscript K_2) is exemplified by the following readings :

11. 27 K_2 B Dn $D_{4\cdot6}$ मन्यु° : rest मृत्यु°
28. 32 K_2 B Dc Dn $D_{4\cdot6}$ वै : rest ते
32. 13 B Dn $D_{4\cdot6}$ [अ] नघे : rest मम
34. 11 K_2 B Dc Dn $D_{4\cdot6}$ दुर्बला° : rest अवीरा° or अधीरा°
91. 2 B Dn $D_{4\cdot6}$ ऋषिणा चैव : rest देवर्षिणा च
93. 10 B Dn $D_{4\cdot6}$ नगो : rest सरो
104. 9 B Dn $D_{1\cdot6}$ तप्यते : rest (mostly) तताप.

Similarly B (Dc) Dn $D_{4\cdot6}$, differing from most other manuscripts, have the following short additions : 446*, 448*, 455* (also in two Southern MSS.) 466*, 467*, 477*, 498*, 512*, (with K_1), 532*, (with D_3), 540*, 541*, 684*, 806*, (with K_3), 844*, etc., etc.

The Devanāgarī Versions (other than K).

I have divided the Devanāgarī Versions into three groups : (1) the Version of Caturbhuja ; (2) the Version of Nīlakaṇṭha ; and (3) the Composite Version. The first two are the versions respectively of the commentators Chaturbhuja and Nīlakaṇṭha, being accompanied by their glosses ; the third is a group of Devanāgarī manuscripts not associated with any commentary.

The Devanāgarī Version of Caturbhuja.

The version of the commentator Caturbhuja has little to recommend for itself. It generally sides with the BD group, showing a slight preference for B ; thus B and Dc have a common insertion 415*, not found in other manuscripts of our critical apparatus. But it is definitely superior to the version of Nīlakaṇṭha, in so far that it lacks many of the very clearly spurious additions of the latter. The best known of such additions is a passage of 39 lines (App. I, No. 12) inserted in the Nala Episode after our 3. 62. 10, which is found only in K_2 Dn D_6 and is comparable to the passage substituted in K_4 D_{1-3} for stanzas 1-17 of our adhy. 62 (cf. App. I, No. 10). Especially in the later adhyāyas of this parvan, Dc and D_2 go together, showing numerous agreements peculiar to themselves. Dc shows some unique additions, though their number is small; examples are 129* and 402*, both being one-line insertions.

Manuscripts of Caturbhuja's commentary on different parvans are available; that on the Virāṭa has been published by the Gujarati Printing Press (Bombay 1915). It is not unlikely that Caturbhuja had written a commentary on the whole of the Mahābhārata, though it is doubtful whether complete manuscripts of the whole of his commentary are now extant. The manuscripts I have hitherto seen were invariably of individual parvans separately handed down.

[25] Very little is known about this scholiast. He bore the surname or title Miśra, like his fellow commentator Arjuna Miśra. It is therefore likely that he hails from Eastern India. It has not been possible to fix his chronology with precision even in relation to the five major Mahābhārata commentators, Devabodha, Vimalabodha, Sarvajña-Nārāyaṇa, Arjunamiśra and Nīlakaṇṭha. But it is most unlikely that he is a very early commentator.[1] In our manuscripts the commentary is called *Vākyadīpikā* (fol. 1):

श्रीचतुर्भुजमिश्राणामारण्ये वाक्यदीपिका ।

This name is analogous to the titles of the commentaries by Devabodha and Arjunamiśra, *Jñānadīpikā* and *Arthadīpikā* respectively; compare also the title of Nīlakaṇṭha's commentary *Bhārata-bhāvadīpa*.

The Devanāgarī Version of Nīlakaṇṭha: the Vulgate.

The version of Nīlakaṇṭha has never inspired confidence, and in the case of the present parvan, it is singularly disappointing. It contains (along with some other manuscript groups) fourteen additional adhyāyas, some of which are palpably very late interpolations. Notable among the latter are adhy. 262-263 of the Vulgate (our App. I, No. 25), which relate how Duryodhana sends the Ṛṣi Durvāsas, with 10,000 disciples, to Yudhiṣṭhira at a moment when the latter would not be able to feed such an alarming crowd of hungry mendicants. In answer to Draupadī's prayers, however, Śrī Kṛṣṇa appears, all of a sudden, from Dvārakā, and so contrives it that the mendicant fraternity, without having eaten a morsel of food, inexplicably feels all of a sudden completely satiated and slinks away in fear and trepidation. They vanish without even making an effort to explain the situation and express

[1] Mr. P. K. GODE, the Curator of the Institute, tentatively assigns him to the period A.D. 1350-1550.

their apologies to Yudhiṣṭhira, who had managed in the meantime to cook food enough to feed that astonishing large troop of beggars. This naïve story, which is not without an element of humour, is found only in Dc_1 $D_{1.2.6}$ G_3 besides Dn, a very poor collection of manuscripts, and is therefore obviously a *very* late interpolation. Its omission from our text, I feel sure, will not be regretted.

The Vulgate contains many lines which are extremely weakly supported, at least by manuscripts of our critical apparatus. Thus, besides Dn, 5* is found only in D_5 ; 25* only in $Ś_1$ K_3 ; 30* only in K_2 D_6 ; 48* only in D_6 : 50* and 55* only in K_2 ; 874* only in D_6 ; 1193* only in D_3 ; and passage No. 32 of App. I (a long interpolation of 72 lines) only in D_6 G_3 !

Dn also shows a surprisingly large number of unique readings, not found in *any other* manuscript, a few of which are noted below as illustrations :

32. 31 Dn आप्नोति : rest अस्तीति
33. 13 Dn °दुर्बुद्धिः : rest °बुद्धियैः
43. 28 Dn धर्मचारिणां : rest भूमिचारिणां
60. 14 Dn अतीव : others सा तीव्र (text), सातीव
82. 5 Dn पुण्या देवी : rest महापुण्या
82. 33 Dn च गच्छति : rest महीपते
84. 11 Dn °ज्वलनो : rest °जलदो
87. 1 Cn आनर्तेषु : rest अवन्तिषु
93. 4 Dn कौरवाः : rest पाण्डवाः
[26] 100. 4 Dn आश्रमे : rest आश्रमं
145. 1 Dn मा चिरं : rest मातरं
146. 53 Dn तीरात्तीर° : rest तीरान्तर
167. 8 Dn शान्ता : others तदा (text), तथा, ततो
195. 14 Dn °वारयन् : rest °वाकिरन्.

Other *specific* readings of Dn, not supported by any other manuscript, will be found in : 3. 33. 35 (एवात्मा), 36 (एव), 46 (न मे), 52 (विवासं); 81. 21 (संमितं), 156 (गतः); 82. 46 (मानवः); 85. 1 (तथा), 10 (तत्र), 16 (अ [or आ]गस्त्यपर्वतो रम्यः); 86. 13 (शुभः); 178. 25 (सा ज्ञेया); 198. 15 (इदम्), 19 (पदं *or* परं); 200. 54 (निबोध मे); 229. 16 (सहस्रशः); 230. 23 (एकैकश्च); 235. 3 (दुरात्मनः); 244. 13 (स्थानं); etc. ; etc.

In his commentary on 3. 291. 70 (Bombay ed.), Nīlakaṇṭha mentions Arjunamiśra : जारूथ्यान् त्रिगुणदक्षिणानित्यर्जुनमिश्रः, showing that Arjunamiśra is prior to Nīlakaṇṭha, as has been proved by me elsewhere on other grounds also.[1]

---

[1] Cf. SUKTHANKAR, "Epic Studies (V)", *Annals of the Bhandarkar Oriental Research Institute*, vol. 17 (1935), p. 189 f.

In commenting on 3. 33. 59 (Bombay ed.):

जिह्वां दत्त्वा बहूनां हि क्षुद्राणां लुब्धचेतसाम् ।
निकृत्या लभते राज्यमाहारमिव शल्यकः ॥,

Nīlakaṇṭha notes certain commentators (प्राञ्चः).

शल्यकः श्वावित् क्षुद्रान् मधुमक्षिकाविशेषान् जिह्वां दत्त्वा बहिर्निःसार्य भक्षयति तद्वज्जिह्वां वाचं दत्त्वा शत्रून् जहीति प्राञ्चः ।

Owing to the ambiguity of the word प्राञ्चः, it is not possible to say for certain whether Nīlakaṇṭha is here referring to eastern commentators or merely to old commentators, but he probably means the latter, as he calls easterners "Gauḍas."

Nīlakaṇṭha appears to have been an adept in the Kāma-śāstra also. In the course of his commentary on the chapter describing the general degeneracy of the Kali age, he discusses certain pornographic details with a frankness which is as astonishing as it is disconcerting. The stanza in question is 3. 186. 35 (= Bombay ed. 3. 188. 41):

बहुप्रजा ह्रस्वदेहाः शीलाचारविवर्जिताः ।
मुखेभगाः स्त्रियो राजन्भविष्यन्ति युगक्षये ॥,

on which Nīlakaṇṭha has the gloss: मुखेभगाः स्त्रियो वङ्गेषु प्रसिद्धाः । प्रथमं मुखेनैव भगकार्यं कृत्वा पुरुषस्य काममुद्दीपयन्त्यः । अत्यन्तं रतार्तत्वात् ।

In the beginning of his commentary, Nīlakaṇṭha mentions his guru Lakṣmaṇārya, Nārāyaṇa-tīrtha and Dhīreśamiśra of Hamīrapura:

प्रणम्य नारायणतीर्थवर्यान् धीरेशमिश्रांश्च हमीरपुर्यान् ।

Nīlakaṇṭha's guru Nārāyaṇa-tīrtha—not to be confused with the Mahābhārata commentator Nārāyaṇa-Sarvajña or Sarvajña-Nārāyaṇa—has been identified by Mr. P. K. GODE with the author of the Mīmāṁsā work *Bhāṭṭa-bhāṣā-prakāśikā* (c. A.D. 1650).[1]

Variants cited by Nīlakaṇṭha will be found in his commentary on the following stanzas (references to the adyhāya and śloka of the *Bombay ed.*): 2. 37; 3. 63; 4. 19; 6. 3 (अपपाठः) 7. 5; 8. 11-12; 9. 15; 10. 24, 32, 37; 11. 4, 8 (अपपाठः); 12. 23, 35, 36, [27] 80; 15. 7; 20. 10; 22. 4; 23. 8; 25. 1 29. 8, 22 (गौडपाठः), 29; 30. 23, 41; 31. 8; 32. 13, 38, 59; 33. 8, 59 (प्राञ्चः) 63, 68, 72; 35. 3 (अपपाठः); 37. 34; 40. 4; 43. 6 (अपपाठः); 71. 16 (इति

[1] Cf. P. K. GODE. "Date of the Bhāṭṭabhāṣāprakāśikā and identification of its author with the Guru of Nīlakaṇṭha Caturdhara", *Mīmāṁsā-Prakāśa*, vol. 3 (1938), pp. 65 ff.—For further particulars about the life and family of Nīlakaṇṭha, see now: P. K. GODE, "Nīlakaṇṭha Caturdhara, the Commentator of the Mahābhārata—His Genealogy and Descendants," *Annals of the Bhandarkar Oriental Research Institute*, vol, 23 (*Silver Jubilee Volume*), 1942, pp. 146-161,

श्लोकः क्वचिन्न दृश्यते); 82. 36, 38 (इति न पुस्तकान्तरेषु दृश्यते); 84. 9 ; 110. 3, 23 (मूर्धन्यादिपाठः प्रामादिकः); 117. 12 (प्रमादपाठः); 119. 13 (गौडपाठे); 120. 2 ; 125. 18 (गौडास्तु ...... इति श्लोकमत्रापि पठन्ति); 129. 9 (प्राञ्चः, अर्वाञ्चः); 147. 8 ; 161. 20 (गौडपाठे); 162. 28 ; 169. 8 ; 172. 9 ; 176. 9 ; 177. 22; 179. 15; 207. 49, 97 (गौडपाठे); 211. 9, 16 ; 219. 22 ; 222. 1 ; 233. 8 ; 236. 31 ; 264. 12 ; 269. 3, 10 ; 297. 24, 36 ; 315. 9 ; etc.

The Composite Devanāgarī Version.

The Devanāgarī has always been found to be a composite version. Our composite Devanāgarī manuscripts may be roughly divided into three groups. (1) The best group, from our view-point, is D_{1-3} which frequently agrees with $Ś_1$ K (but especially K_4) in opposition to other D manuscripts and might have been classed under the K version. Of these D_2 agrees, however, frequently—especially in later adhyāyas—with Dc, the version of Caturbhuja. (2) Then there is the group $D_{4.6}$, which generally agrees with B Dc Dn. (3) The remaining manuscript D_5 is in a class by itself, presenting a text which is, for large parts, almost the same as that of the Nīlakaṇṭha version, but which shows exceptionally some noteworthy discrepancies. Groups 2 and 3 are frequently seen in combination, and we accordingly very often get a wider group B Dc Dn D_{4-6} (sometimes joined by K_2).

The affinity of the group D_{1-3} is exemplified by the following concordant readings of these three manuscripts.

1. 3 D_{1-3} वने विजह्रु : (Parasm.) पार्थास्ते : rest वने विजह्रिरे (Atm.) पार्थाः
1. 5 D_{1-3} परघातिनां : other MSS. अरिघातिनां (text), अनिवर्तिनां
1. 13 D_{1-3} नार्थकामः सुखं कुतः : other MSS. न धर्मो(*or* र्मा)र्थः कुतः सुखं
1. 14 D_{1-3} सदामर्षी : other MSS. गुरुद्वेषी(text), गुणद्वेषी
1. 15 D_{1-3} गच्छामः (Parasm.) सहिताः rest साधु गच्छामहे (Atm.)
1. 34 D_{1-3} सेवनीयाः : rest पालनीयाः
2. 5 D_{1-3} या गतिः : rest गतिर्या (by transp.)
6. 22 D_{1-3} भविष्यामि : rest करिष्यामि
48. 29 D_{1-3} यथा : other MSS. मया (text), तथा
167. 19 D_{1-3} गांधर्वं : other N MSS. माधवं (text) etc., etc.

Examples of insertions, almost peculiar to D_{1-3} and showing the close affinity between these three manuscripts, are : 182* (with K_4), 288*, 334* (with K_4), 1025*, 1186*, 1188*, 1190*, 1194* (latter four with K_4), etc., etc.

As remarked above, the group D_{1-3}, differing from other Devanāgarī manuscripts, frequently agrees with $Ś_1$ K. Examples of insertions common to $Ś_1$ K and D_{1-3} (often with D_5) are : 640*, 707*, 711*, 715*, etc. etc.

Group D_{1-3} is important for the reason that it lacks (like $Ś_1$ K) many of the interpolations of the B D group ; e.g. 44*, 128*, 130*, 131*, 133*, 162*,

163*, 166*, 167*, 168*, 178*, 184*, 185*, 187*, 188*, 189*, 193*, 195*, 224*, 238*, 240*, 244*, 245*, 247*, 248*, 249*, 540*, 541*, 895*, 985*, etc., etc., etc.

The Telugu Version.

Only two manuscripts of the Telugu version were collated, of which one (as is often the case with these manuscripts) is certainly contaminated, to a very high degree, from [28] Northern sources. In such conflated parts, T_2 is generally associated with G_3. Examples of such contamination will be found below, under the Grantha version.

T_1, differing from T_2 often sides with G_1 M_1 (with or without M_2), giving what appears to be the real Southern reading.

For examples of contamination of T_2 through the Northern recension, cf. 174*, 248*, 484*, 563*, 570*, 572*, 577*, 661*, 673*, 932*, (with M_1). 991*, etc., etc. Many of these are marginal insertions, added *sec. m.*

The Grantha Version.

Most of our Grantha manuscripts are unfortunately contaminated from the Northern recension. The contamination is particularly noticeable in the case of G_3, and it increases towards the end of the parvan ; so much so that in the final chapters G_3 often omits the specific insertions of the Southern recension, absorbing at the same time the characteristic insertions of the Northern ! Such manuscripts are valuable for a study of the fusion of recensions.

Examples of *omission* in G_3 of specific Southern insertions are : 1050*, 1059*, 1060*, 1061*, 1062*, 1069*, 1071*, 1077*, 1082*, 1085*, 1086*, 1091*, 1092*, 1093*, 1102*, 1114*, 1137*, 1138*, 1139*, 1142*, 1146*, 1148*, 1149*, 1152*, 1154*, 1326*, 1343*, 1372*, 1373*, etc.. etc.—Examples of the *incorporation* of Northern insertions in G_3 (sometimes with T_1) are : 1046*, 1048*, 1063*, 1065*, 1066*, 1067*, 1073*, 1074*, 1088*, 1103*, 1120*, 1126*, 1131*, 1134*, 1167*, 1203*, 1224*, 1226*, 1227*, 1229*, 1230*, 1279*, 1331*, 1337*, 1358*, 1365*, 1382*, 1385*, etc., etc. ; and passages Nos. 24, 27, and 32 of App. I.

But the most striking instance of conflation is the inclusion in G_3 of our final adhyāya (299), which is regularly transposed in all *genuine* Southern manuscripts to the beginning of the Virāṭaparvan. The evidence of G_3 is thus seen to be fully inconclusive and therefore untrustworthy for the constitution of the Grantha version and the Southern recension.

The Malayālam Version.

While forming an integral part of the Southern recension, the Malayālam version has its own peculiarities, which distinguish it clearly from the T G version, as regards both readings and insertions. Here is a list of T G insertions, which are lacking in the Malayālam version : 183*, 218*, 232*, 243*, 286*, 356*, 620*, 667*, 674*, 685*, 802*, 803*, 805*, 824*, 856*, 859*, 867*, 868*, 869*, etc., etc.—On the other hand, M also shows a certain number of *specific* insertions which are not known to the Telugu and Grantha versions, such as 307*, 494*, 560*, 581*, 949*, 1028*, 1041*, 1083*, 1158*, 1262*, 1336*, etc., etc.—Nearly all of these insertions (of both types) are single-line insertions ; a few are of two lines.

But our M is not homogeneous, M_1 and M_2 exhibiting among themselves numerous differences. M_2 shows clear signs of contamination from Northern sources, and is by no means a good representative of the Malayālam version. Examples of Northern accretions in M_2 are 96*, 99*, 466*, 516*, 796*, 955*, etc. etc. M_2 is again often excepted from the common Southern reading, as in 3. 41. 24 : S (except M_2) स्वर्गंच्छेत्यभ्यनुज्ञातः against N (with M_2) [29] स्वर्गं गच्छेत्यनुज्ञातः, where M_2 agrees with N. M_2 (like G_3) also omits a few of the typical Southern insertions ; e.g., 102*, 723*. M_1 is not altogether free from contamination from some Northern source or sources as is indicated by 629*, 677*, 932* (with T_2 marg. *sec. m.*), etc., etc.

A very good example of the contamination of M_2 from N is furnished by the conflated reading of M_2 in 3. 22. 8. N reads विस्रवत्यसृगुल्बणं as opposed to S, which has व्यसृजद्रुधिरं बहु ; but M_2 reads व्यसृजच्चसृगुल्बणं, which is very evidently a result of the conflation of the Southern and Northern readings : व्यसृजत् (S) च [अ]सृगुल्बणं (N). But the most convincing proof is furnished by a palpable mistake in M_2. The manuscript inserts line 1 of a Northern additional stanza (95*), after 3. 28. 16^{ab}, but line 2 of that stanza after 16^{cd}. The two lines of the stanza, though superfluous, do convey some meaning when read together ; but arranged as in M_2, they serve no useful purpose except to betray the conflated character of the manuscript in question.

With regard to the status and merit of the Malayālam version in general, I am glad to cite here an observation of Professor P. P. S. SASTRI, which I am able to confirm from my own experience. In the course of his remarks on the Southern recension in the Introduction to his edition of the Āraṇyakaparvan, Professor SASTRI writes : "Not having been subject to Nāyak influence in any manner whatsoever, the tradition handed down by the Malayālam manuscripts preserved the Grantha text, in a purer and more unmixed form than even some comparatively early Grantha manuscripts, as the Malayālam Mss. do not at all seem to have come into contact with the Northern Recension till very recent times".[1] This is in substantial agreement with what I had stated in my *Prolegomena* to the Ādiparvan regarding the Malayālam

---

[1] The Mahābhārata (Southern Recension), Vol. IV (1933), Introduction, p. iii f.

version, namely, that it is "*the best Southern version*."[1] I am happy to find that this cautious remark of mine has subsequently been confirmed by the editor of the Southern Recension himself in a clear and unambiguous manner.

THE PARVASAMGRAHA

The number of adhyāyas and ślokas of the Āraṇyaka, according to the Parvasaṁgrahaparvan, in our edition, and in the current editions, can be seen in the following table.

COMPARATIVE TABLE OF THE NUMBER OF ADHYĀYAS AND ŚLOKAS IN THE ĀRAṆYAKAPARVAN

	Parva-saṁgraha	Crit. Ed.	Cal. Ed.	Bomb. Ed. (Śaka 1799)	Kumbh. Ed.	South Rec. (SASTRI)
Adhyāyas	269	299	314	315	315	269
Ślokas	11,664	? *	12,848	12,002	12,476	11,136

[30] With regard to the above figures the following particulars may be noted. According to the count of the Calcutta edition the number of ślokas in this parvan is 17,478. But this calculation misses the correct figure by several thousands. The Calcutta Pandits responsible for the edition, who were apparently not very good mathematicians, have made repeated mistakes in the counting of the lines, being evidently baffled by the complicacies of calculation at the turn of the century! They have numbered the lines, by fives, without committing any mistake up to 3095. They make their first mistake by putting down the next figure (after 3095) as 4000, in place of 3100; and this is followed by several other lapses of that type! The correct total as computed by JACOBI[2] is 12,848 as shown above.—The figure for the ślokas of the Bombay edition has been taken from the edition of text and Marathi translation by Kashinath alias Bhau Shastri LELE of Wai (Śaka 1821), who has counted the stanzas in his edition, adhyāya by adhyāya; and, after correcting his own errors in three different places, gives the correct figure, according to him, at the end of the Vanaparvan volume (p. 1344) as 12,002.[3] —The figure for the stanzas of the Kumbhakonam edition has been taken from the Index Volume (p. 5) of that edition.—The extent of Professor

[1] *Prolegomena*, p. LXXIII.

* [By actual counts, 11,421 ślokas of 32 syllables each.].

[2] *Das Mahābhārata, Inhaltsangabe, Index, etc.*, p. 257.

[3] According to another computation, that of the Chitrashala Edition (Poona 1930), the correct number is 11,859, as given in the footnote on p. 500 of its edition of the "Vanaparvan."

P. P. S. SASTRI'S *Southern Recension* has been given by himself in the Introduction to the second part of his Āraṇyakaparvan (vol. 5, p. xiv).—The figure for the critical text has been intentionally left blank by me, since the parvan contains two prose adhyāyas, in addition to a large number of Triṣṭubh stanzas, and it is difficult to compute their equivalent in ślokas. Indeed the figures given for the other editions are all defective for the same reason. In fact they are all *purely fictitious*, being obtained by *the addition of figures for the stanzas and prose sections*, but may be taken to represent a *very rough* approximation of the extent. It will thus be realized that it is futile to compare these figures with the Parvasaṁgraha figures, which are often themselves doubtful. It has been the general experience that ancient figures, when at all complicated, seldom come out quite right. And there is no reason to think that the Parvasaṁgraha figures for the number of stanzas are an exception to the rule.

We do not expect strict agreement between our figures and the Parvasaṁgraha figures in respect of the number of stanzas in such a voluminous work but we do expect some agreement as regards the number of *adhyāyas*. It is, therefore, surprising to find that almost all extant manuscripts contain about 30 adhyāyas at least more than the figure given by the Parvasaṁgraha ! This discrepancy is the more striking, as the manuscripts of the Parvasaṁgraha, of all versions and recensions without exception, agree—for a change—in giving the same figure for the number of adhyāyas, namely, 269. As regards the manuscripts of the Āraṇyaka, the Kaśmīrī (Śāradā) and the Southern manuscripts agree in having about 300 adhyāyas, while the Central Sub-recension (Bengali-Devanāgarī group) show in fact about 315 adhyāyas. The former may be taken as the more reliable figure. Professor P. P. S. SASTRI'S device of arriving at the Parvasaṁgraha figure (269), by omitting arbitrarily about 31 colophons actually contained in all of his manuscripts is hardly commendable.

[31] Due to these discrepancies between the data of the Parvasaṁgraha and the manuscripts, which are patent, two probabilities are presented to us : either, the compiler of the Parvasaṁgraha had made a mistake in counting the adhyāyas, or some thirty adhyāyas have been added to our parvan since the time of the Parvasaṁgraha count. No third explanation is possible, and both these are significant alternatives. If we admit that there has been an original error in the counting of adhyāyas, it is roughly a mistake of 30 in 300, that is 10 per cent., which is indeed a very high percentage of error. If we could prove even two or three such errors, the value of the figures in the Parvasaṁgraha will dwindle down to an insignificant quantity. If, on the other hand,—as is more likely—our critical text contains about 30 adhyāyas (equivalent to about 1500 stanzas) more than the text which was the basis of the Parvasaṁgraha calculation, then even in the matter of general contents

it is nowhere near the Parvasaṁgraha standard and must be very far removed from the hypothetical archetype of the Mahābhārata ; for it is hardly credible that as many as thirty colophons could get displaced or lost in a mere aggregate of 300 colophons. There are moreover no means to excise these spurious accretions except by methods of higher criticism, which owing to the peculiar character of our work would be a very delicate operation indeed, and withal one of doubtful utility. We thus see how easy it would be to delude ourselves that just by collating a small fraction of the extant manuscripts, we could arrive at the archetype.

The passage in the Parvasaṁgraha giving the *contents* of this parvan exists in two versions (1. 2. 111-126) : the longer version of the Vulgate being based on the Central Sub-recension (the Bengali-Devanāgarī), the shorter version on the Kaśmīrī-Southern tradition. I have adopted the latter in this edition, relying mainly on the superiority of the agreement between what appear *prima facie* to be independent versions. But I think it is possible to fortify the argument in the present case from intrinsic considerations. It will be seen that in the shorter version, the sequence of the incidents mentioned in the list of contents *does not tally* with the actual sequence in the original text of the parvan, given uniformly by all extant manuscripts ; the sequence of the longer version on the other hand tallies exactly with the present text. Moreover, the latter—namely, the longer version—is much fuller, containing as it does far more details. Is it now likely that the Kaśmīrī and Southern traditions had independently—or in collusion with each other—discarded the original fuller and more correct version in favour of a shorter and defective version ? It seems far more probable that the defects of the original short version, which has been preserved independently by the Kaśmīrī and Southern traditions, had been noticed early, and that had led to its being modified and corrected by the revisers of the Central Sub-recension, which then adopted the revised version of the contents.

The Parvasaṁgraha mentions sixteen sub-parvans, which is also our number, but the Vulgate has twenty-two ; that is six more. The latter number is obtained by adding to the list the names of certain episodes like the Nalopākhyāna, Rāmopākhyāna, Sāvitryupākhyāna, which originally did not form separate sub-parvans at all, as will be seen from the following table.

[32] Critical Edition (and old Parvasaṁgraha)	Vulgate Editions (and revised Parvasaṁgraha)
1 आरण्यक (adhy. 1–11)	1 अरण्य (adhy. 1–10)
2 किर्मीरवध (12)	2 किर्मीरवध (11)
	3 अर्जुनाभिगमन (12–37)
3 कैरात (13–42)	4 कैरात (38–41)

Critical Edition (and old Parvasaṁgraha)	Vulgate Editions (and revised Parvasaṁgraha)
4 इन्द्रलोकाभिगमन (43–79)	5 इन्द्रलोकाभिगमन (42–51)
	6 नलोपाख्यान (52–79)
5 तीर्थयात्रा (80–153)	7 तीर्थयात्रा (80–156)
6 जटासुरवध (154)	8 जटासुरवध (157)
7 यक्षयुद्ध (155–172)	9 यक्षयुद्ध (158–164)
	10 निवातकवचयुद्ध (165–175)
8 आजगर (173–178)	11 आजगर (176–181)
9 मार्कण्डेयसमास्या (179–221)	12 मार्कण्डेयसमास्या (182–232)
10 द्रौपदीसत्यभामासंवाद (222–224)	13 द्रौपदीसत्यभामासंवाद (233–235)
11 घोषयात्रा (225–243)	14 घोषयात्रा (236–257)
12 मृगस्वप्नभय (244)	15 मृगस्वप्नोद्भव (258)
13 व्रीहिद्रौणिक (245–247)	16 व्रीहिद्रौणिक (259–261)
14 द्रौपदीहरण (248–283)	17 द्रौपदीहरण (262–271)
	18 जयद्रथविमोक्षण (272)
	19 रामोपाख्यान (273–292)[1]
	20 पतिव्रतामाहात्म्य (293–299)
15 कुण्डलाहरण (284–294)	21 कुण्डलाहरण (300–310)
16 आरणेय (295–299)	22 आरणेय (311–315)

The limits of these sub-parvans can be fixed, as a rule, with tolerable certainty with the aid of the colophons of our manuscripts, which give indications sufficient for purposes of approximate identification.

OTHER EDITIONS

Of the numerous printed editions of the Āraṇyaka-parvan (almost uniformly passing under the name Vanaparvan), I have consulted the following :

(1) The *editio princeps* of the Mahābhārata printed in Calcutta between 1834 and 1839. Its Vanaparvan comprises, according to its own data, 17478 ślokas in 314 adhyāyas. It gives in general the Nīlakaṇṭha version, which we have called the Vulgate and which has been reproduced in many subsequent editions, sometimes accompanied by translation and commentary. The *editio princeps* still remains the best edition available of the Vulgate version of the Āraṇyakaparvan, though that is not saying very much.

(2) The oblong pothī-form edition, published by Ganapat KRISHNAJI in Śaka 1799 in Bombay (hence commonly known as the Bombay edition). It is accompanied by Nīlakaṇṭha's commentary, *Bhārata-bhāvadīpa*, and should therefore represent the [33] Nīlakaṇṭha tradition. But it contains as a matter of fact

[1] The Parvasaṁgraha of the Vulgate cites Nos. 19 and 20 in reverse order, that is, the Pativratāmāhātmya precedes the Rāmopākhyāna.

quite a large number of lines and readings not countenanced by Nīlakaṇṭha himself. The text is divided into 315 adyhāyas, and contains (according to some editions which give the aggregate number of stanzas in the parvan) 12,002 stanzas.[1]

(3) The Kumbhakonam edition published by T. R. KRISHNACHARYA and T. R. VYASACHARYA, and described on its title-page as " A New Edition, mainly based on the South Indian Texts ". Its Vanaparvan comprises (according to the Index Volume) 12,476 ślokas and 315 adhyāyas, but contains like our misch-codices a good number of specific Northern passages unknown to the true Southern recension.[2]

(4) Professor P. P. S. SASTRI'S Southern Recension, Volumes 4-5, comprising (according to his own count) 11,136 ślokas divided into 269 adhyāyas.

As these old editions contain nothing of any serious importance which is not to be found in the different manuscripts already collated for this edition, they have been only sparingly used and cursorily studied by me. The following observations may be of use to those who may wish to consult these editions.

As remarked above, there are some grave mistakes in the numbering of the stanzas of the Calcutta edition. The first mistake occurs after stanza 3095, where the next number suddenly jumps up to 4000 (when it should be 3100). Similarly after 8895, the following number jumps up to 9900 (when it should be 8900). For the third time, after 10,095, the following number is given as 11,000 (instead of 10,100). For the fourth time, after 11,095, the next number jumps up to 12,000, when it should be 11,100. At the next step, however, the number equally suddenly jumps back to 10,200 ! Thus at one place three successive numbers (which are supposed to increase by five at each step) are 11095, 12,000, 10,200 ! ! After adhy. 117, there appear to be no new mistakes, and from that point onwards the numbering may be taken to be continuous and correct. But the result of these earlier miscalculations is that the extent of the parvan appears to be 17,478, when it should in reality be (according to JACOBI'S computation) 12,848, the Parvasaṁgraha figure being 11,664 ! Several numbers occur twice, and in giving reference to the Calcutta edition, it is advisable to cite the adhyāya number as well.

The Bombay edition, like the Calcutta, is based on the Nīlakaṇṭha version but (like yet other editions of the Mahābhārata prepared in the same fashion, e.g., the Chitrashala edition) does not represent the Nīlakaṇṭha tradition very faithfully. In the footnotes to the text, and the critical notes at the end, I have frequently drawn attention to unwarranted departure from Nīlakaṇṭha's original text. The vagaries are small and of no great consequence, but they are there nevertheless. They prove very clearly that *with-*

1 According to the Chitrashala Edition the number is 11,859, though the text is precisely the same in both editions.

2 It seems not to have been noticed that in the old printed editions though the name of this parvan is given on the title-page and in the captions as " Vanaparva " the colophons invariably give the name correctly as Āraṇya-or—Āraṇyakaparvan

out any conscious effort at alteration or emendation—and perhaps, notwithstanding the half-hearted efforts to preserve intact the received text—discrepancies do arise in course of time, and the text does drift away from the norm, imperceptibly, within a relatively short period of time. Thus in 3. 9. 7 for our प्रतिपद्यथाः (which is documented [34] uniformly by almost all our manuscripts), the different editions printed in the Bombay province, and examined by me, all have the reading प्रतिपद्यतां, a reading which has not been found in a single manuscript ! In 3. 83. 30, the Bombay edition (with the Kumbhakonam and some other editions) reads गवां मेधम्, when the Nīlakaṇṭha manuscripts themselves (along with a host of other manuscripts) have the correct reading गवामयम् (*lect. diff.*), which is the reading of the constituted text ! Likewise in 3. 249. 8, out edition reads सुबलस्य which is the reading offered by all manuscripts collated for our edition, except one inferior Grantha manuscript (G_3), which reads सुभवस्य, and yet this latter reading (सुभवस्य) has been adopted in many of the Bombay editions.

Professor SASTRI's edition is based chiefly on *four* manuscripts, of which one (ख) is in Telugu script, two (अ, घ) in Grantha, and one (क) in Malayālam. For adhyāyas 67-130, that is, for about 64 adhyāyas out of his total of 269 adhyāyas, a fifth manuscript (ग) was partly utilized. According to the editor, manuscript अ (Grantha) "represents the Principal Text printed". It bears a date corresponding to A.D. 1795, that is, it is less than 150 years old. As an edition of the Southern recension, Professor SASTRI'S edition is preferable and indeed much superior to the Kumbhakonam edition. But it seems to me that in its preparation the manuscript material has not been as fully and carefully utilized as it should have been. Judging by the Southern manuscripts collated for our edition and examined by me, which cannot be very different from his, it should seem that too often SASTRI's edition agrees in its mislections and other short-comings with the Kumbhakonam edition to the exclusion of the genuine Southern tradition. I miss in his critical apparatus many of the readings which are given uniformly by all Southern manuscripts. Even if the editor, for some occult reasons, did not wish to adopt in his text these perfectly good and authenticated Southern readings, they should have appeared in the footnotes as discarded readings. Instances of Northern readings having contaminated his text will be found in the following stanzas (reference is to ślokas and adhyāyas of *his* text) :

1. 27^b, 28^b; **2.** $13\frac{1}{2}^d$, 22^a, 46^c, $71\frac{1}{2}^b$, $80\frac{1}{2}^b$; **4.** 8^a, 8^c, 15^b; **5.** 1^b, 6^c, 7^c, 22^d; **7.** 2^b, 2^c, 9^b, 23^b ; **8.** 17^c ; **10.** 49^d, 55^d, 66^a ; **11.** $60\frac{1}{2}^c$, $72\frac{1}{2}^c$; **12.** $23\frac{1}{2}^a$, 41^b ; **13.** 1^b ; **14.** 6^d, 16^c **17.** $10\frac{1}{2}^a$, $11\frac{1}{2}^a$; **18.** 5^b ; etc., etc. These examples have been selected at random from the first 18 adhyāyas only ; but such lapses keep turning up on page after page up to the end of the book.

As his edition is based on four manuscripts only and even these manuscripts appear not to have been rigorously collated and fully utilized, I should hesitate to accept his text as a true representative of the Southern recension, even ignoring the deficiencies of the critical apparatus.

In the division into adhyāyas, Professor SASTRI seems to have followed the Grantha edition of Sarabhojirajapuram (Tanjore District) printed in 1895. The reason given by Professor SASTRI for following the edition instead of the manuscripts is that the division of the Tanjore edition "accords exactly with the enumeration of the number of chapters for the Vana Parvan (sic) in the Anukramaṇikādhyāya of both the Northern and the Southern Recensions".[1] This is a dangerously vicious circle! As the Tanjore edition does not pretend that it has followed any manuscript tradition, the adhyāya division of both these editions (Tanjore and SASTRI) remain unsupportel by manuscript authority [35] and therefore perfectly arbitrary. Adopting the Parvasaṁgraha figure, SASTRI has divided the parvan into 269 adhyāyas, while the actual numbering of the adhyāyas in Southern manuscripts reaches the figure 300 approximately, the number according to our Southern manuscripts varying between 299 and 302.

While SASTRI by arbitrary elimination of colophons, has equated his adhyāya-number to that given by the Parvasaṁgraha, he could not make the figures for the ślokas tally! According to the Parvasaṁgraha the number of ślokas should be 11,664. "The total number of stanzas," says Professor SASTRI, "printed in the Text of the Southern Recension comes to 11,136, which is short by 528".[2] As his text is short by over 500 stanzas, his equation of the number of adhyāyas with the Parvasaṁgraha figure, by arbitrary omission of about thirty colophons, which are found in all Southern manuscripts, has no significance, and remains a piece of useless and unmeaning manipulation.

It is exactly seventeen years since I took over charge of the Mahābhārata work, and reorganized, on somewhat different lines, this Department of the Institute, having profited by the experiments and experiences of my predecessor, the late lamented Mr. N. B. UTGIKAR, M.A. During this interval the Mahābhārata Department of the Institute has prepared and published critical editions of four whole parvans (in this sequence) : the Ādi (1933), the Virāṭa (1936), the Udyoga (1940), and now the Āraṇyaka (1942). These four parvans comprise, according to the data of the Parvasaṁgraha-parvan, about 28,400 "ślokas". In addition to this : the Sabhāparvan, which is being edited by Professor Franklin EDGERTON of the Yale University (U.S.A.) and which has been ready for some time, has been taken up for printing, and its printing has made considerable progress ; nearly the whole of the text, along with the critical apparatus pertaining to it, has been printed off, and the printed portion may even be issued, in the near future, as a separate fascicule. Furthermore, the press-copy of the Bhīṣmaparvan, which is being edited by Rao Bahadur Dr. S. K. BELVALKAR, I.E.S (Retd.), is almost ready and is now undergoing final revision at the hands of its editor. Funds permitting, it will be sent to the press in the not very distant future. Thus, during these seven-

[1] The Mahābhārata (Southern Recension), vol. 5, Introduction, p. xiii.

[2] *Op. cit.* p. xiv,

teen years the Institute has critically dealt with the first six parvans of the Great Epic : the Ādi, Sabhā, Āraṇyaka, Virāṭa, Udyoga and Bhīṣma. These six parvans make up a total of about 36,800 "ślokas", out of the aggregate of about 82,150 "ślokas" comprising the entire Mahābhārata, a portion which is approximately 45 per cent. of the aggregate, excluding of course the "Supplement", Harivaṁśa, which, for the time being, we have placed aside. This is no mean achievement, we think. The part of the epic critically dealt with so far is, I imagine, in bulk, about four times as great as the Iliad and the Odyssey put together, and one and a half times as great as our Rāmāyaṇa.

That a work of this nature and these dimensions is not one man's job is very evident. Many collaborators, sympathisers, friends, benefactors and patrons have contributed to such measure of success as has been achieved so far, and they include among them, princes and potentates, persons owning manuscripts, curators and librarians, printers and parvan-editors, not to speak of the General Editor and his modest staff in [36] the background. Surely the most potent among these multifarious contributory factors have been—

अर्थस्य पुरुषो दासो दासस्त्वर्थो न कस्यचित् ।

—the generous patrons of learning, who out of regard for this venerable monument of Indian antiquity, this great and lustrous heritage of Bhāratavarṣa, have liberally supplied the Institute, all through these years, with funds to carry on this costly but very vital work.

First among these generous patrons stands in our estimation Shrimant Balasaheb Pant Pratinidhi, B.A., RAJASAHEB of Aundh, whose princely liberality made it, in the first instance, possible for the Institute to think of undertaking this ambitious project. The RAJASAHEB has already paid up a large part of the Foundation Grant of a lakh of rupees promised by him, and thus placed under his obligations not only the Institute but all those who love the Great Epic of India.

I have next to record the gratitude of the promoters of this scheme—which has now become nothing less than a great national undertaking—to a number of other distinguished and generous donors, scattered all over India, who have contributed liberally to our Mahābhārata Publication Fund, the chief among them being : The Imperial Government of India, the Provincial Governments of Bombay, Madras, Burma and United Provinces ; the Gwalior, Hyderabad (Deccan), Baroda, Bhavnagar, Phaltan, Mysore, Porbunder, Kolhapur, Patiala, Sangli, Ichalkaranji, Ramdurg, and other Indian States. The Trustees of the Sir Dorab Tata Trust, the Savitribai Bhat Trust, and the Tulsidas Charities also deserve a grateful mention here for their kind help to our finances. We must gratefully think also of those persons less gifted by Fortune, who have contributed smaller sums—with the one idea of helping on this great cause—each according to his ability.

The Institute is indebted, for subsidies to its Mahābhārata work, to the Trustees of the Mahābhārata Fund of Great Britain in London ; and indebted also for a token grant, in appreciation of this work, to the British Academy of London.

And last, but not least, I must mention, in this connection, our Alma Mater—The University of Bombay—who has been exceptionally generous and appreciative of our endeavours in this field, supply us with funds, lending us manuscripts, and generally taking a very keen and active interest in the welfare and rapid progress of our project.

In connection with further assistance rendered by extra-mural collaborators and helpers, I must put on record our special obligations to Pandit Rajaguru HEMRAJ,

C.I.E., of Nepal ; as also to Professor Kshitimohan SEN, who has succeeded Professor Vidhushekhar BHATTACHARYA as Principal of the Viśvabharati ; further to Mr. S. GOPALAN, B.A., B.L., who has succeeded the late Raosaheb Sambamurthi RAO, as Honorary Secretary of the Saraswathi Mahal Library of Tanjore. Both these latter gentlemen have been kind enough to carry on, in a purely honorary capacity, the onerous and responsible task of supervising the Mahābhārata collations done in their respective institutions.

The thanks of the Institute are also due to the Curators, Trustees, and Custodians of the following libraries and institutions for keeping us equipped with the manuscripts required for our Mahābhārata work, during almost two decades : the Bombay Branch of the Royal Asiatic Society, the Royal Asiatic Society of Bengal, the Bangiya Sahitya Parishad, the Adyar Library, the Oriental Institute of Baroda, Madras Government [37] Library, Mysore Oriental Manuscripts Library, Sri Yadugiri Yatiraj Math (Melkote, Mysore), Cochin State Library, Pudukkottah State Library, and the India Office Library (London). The Institute has also received manuscripts or photo-copies or hand-made copies of manuscripts from the Bombay University, the Viśvabharati, Dacca University, Dayananda Anglo-Vedic College of Lahore (Research Department), Benares Sanskrit College, and Calcutta Sanskrit College—all of whom I wish to thank on behalf of the Institute very cordially for their kind help in the matter. The Institute is, moreover, obliged to Sardar M. V. KIBE, M.A. of Indore for the loan of a complete Nīlakaṇṭha manuscript of the Mahābhārata. It is further indebted for the free loan of Southern manuscripts of the Mahābhārata to the Chief of Idapalli, Mr. Kallenkara PISHARAM, Mankavu Padinnare KOVILAKAM, Killimangalam NAMBUDIRIPAD, and to the proprietors of the following Malabar estates : Poomullimana, Avaṇapparambu Mana, Nareri Mana, Ponnokkottu Mana, Paliyam Estate, Channamangalam.

Once more I would fain express my gratitude for help of various kinds from my colleagues on the Mahābhārata Editorial Board, who have throughout reposed, very generously, full confidence in me, and helped and supported me invariably in the true spirit of *camaraderie*. It is sad to reflect that before we are even halfway through our work, several members of the old Editoial Board, formed in 1925, are no longer with us ; from among whom I remember particularly my friends Father R. ZIMMERMANN, S.J., Professor M. WINTERNITZ, and Mr. Vishvanath P. VAIDYA.

I have to record here my keen appreciation of the willing compliance and ungrudging assistance I have uniformly received from members of the Permanent Staff of the Mahābhārata Department of this Institute. Mr. S. N. TADPATRIKAR, M.A., Supervisor of Collations, who is in special charge of the collations, has been moreover, as usual, always by my side, helping me with useful suggestions, when I was engaged in constituting the text of this extensive parvan. The critical notes were compiled from the collation sheets by Mr. B. G. BHIDE SHASTRI, Mr. D. V. NARAVANE, and Mr. G. G. SOMAN. We shall miss, in future, the expert assistance of Mr. BHIDE in several fields, who having served the Institute in the Mahābhārata Department since 1921, has now owing to old age, retired from service. The Śāradā manuscripts have been invariably collated by our Śāradā expert, Shankar Shastri BHILAVADIKAR, Head Shastri of the Mahābhārata Department. The proof-reading has been done by the Collator and Reader Pandit K. V. Krishnamurti SHARMA SHASTRI, of Erode (South India), who is now helped in that work by Mr. M. V. VAIDYA, M. A., both of whom have worked with praiseworthy diligence, exemplary zeal, and signal devotion to their work. Collations of Southern manuscripts have been done at the Institute uniformly by the Pandits K. V. Anantanarayan SHASTRI of Erode, and K. S. Vishvanath SHASTRI of Kolengode (South India), both of whom also are very accurate and conscientious workers, exhibiting characteristically a single-minded devotion to duty.

The superior finish of the Āraṇyakaparvan Volumes, from the typographical viewpoint, is due solely to the care and thought personally bestowed on them by my indefatigable friend Professor Dr. Raghu VIRA of the International Academy of Indian Culture, who, as part of a programme of multifarious activities for the regeneration of our culture, has equipped at Lahore a small but efficient printing establishment—the [38] Arya Bharati Press—which is solely devoted to the cause of the service of the *ārya-bhāratī* for endowing Sarasvatī with better vestments than she grudgingly receives in India at the hands of very mercenary printers and publishers. At great trouble and inconvenience to himself—and, I fear, even at the risk of pecuniary loss—he undertook and has carried out successfully the printing of these two big tomes, and thus led us safely out of the first big forest our little party of explorers had encountered on our way to the yet distant Utopia of a complete critical edition of the Mahābhārata.

If Maharṣi Kṛṣṇa Dvaipāyana Vyāsa tells us that he has cried himself hoarse, urging people to follow the Path of Duty :

ऊर्ध्वबाहुर्विरौम्येष न च कश्चिच्छृणोति माम् ।
धर्मादर्थश्च कामश्च स किमर्थं न सेव्यते ॥

his shouting with uplifted arms has *not* been entirely in vain. He has *not* failed in his mission. Across the reverberating corridors of Time, we his descendants can still hear dimly his clarion call to Duty. It is in response to that call and in a spirit of reverent homage to that sage of unfathomable wisdom—that embodied Voice of the Collective Unconscious of the Indian people—we offer this work, pledged to broadcast to mankind, in this hour of its need and its peril, the luminous message of the Maharṣi :

न जातु कामान्न भयान्न लोभाद्
धर्मं त्यजेज्जीवितस्यापि हेतोः ।
नियो धर्मः सुखदुःखे त्वनित्ये
जीवो नित्यो हेतुरस्य त्वनित्यः ॥

August 1942. V. S. SUKTHANKAR.

[39] CONCORDANCE OF THE SCHEME OF ADHYAYAS

in the following three editions: the Critical Edition, the Bombay Edition (Ganapat KRISHNAJI, Śaka 1799), and the Madras Edition (P. P. S. SASTRI's Southern Recension, 1931).

Crit. Ed.	Bom. Ed.	Mad. Ed.	Crit. Ed.	Bom. Ed.	Mad. Ed.
1	1	1	37	36	32
2	2	2	38	37	33
3.$_{1-14}$	3.$_{1-12,\ 32-35}$	3.$_{1-14}$	39	38	34
3.$_{15-33}$	3.$_{13-31}$	3.$_{28-47}$	40	39	35.$_{1-69}$
—	3.$_{35-70}$	—	41	40	35.$_{70-96}$
4	3.$_{70-86}$	3.$_{15-26}$	42	41	36
5	4	4	43	42	37
6	5	5	44	43	38
7	6	6	—	45–46	39
8	7	7	45.$_{1-8}$	44	40.$_{1-8}$
9	8	8.$_{1-12}$	45.$_{9-38}$	47	40.$_{9-38}$
10	9	8.$_{13-35}$	46	48–49	41
11	10	9	47	50	42
12	11	10	48	51	43
13	12	11	49	52	44
14	13	12.$_{1-17}$	50	53	45
15	14	12.$_{18-41}$	51	54	46.$_{1-29}$
16	15	13.$_{1-23}$	52	55	46.$_{30-56}$
17	16	13.$_{24-56}$	53	56	47
18	17	14	54	57	48
19	18	15.$_{1-33}$	55	58	49.$_{1-15}$
20	19	15.$_{34-60}$	56	59	49.$_{16-35}$
21	20	16	57	60	50.$_{1-25}$
22	21	17	58	61	50.$_{26-61}$
23	22	18	59	62	50.$_{62-86}$
24	23	19	60	63	51
25	24	20	61	64	52
26	25	21	62	65	53
27	26	22	63	66	54
28	27	23	64	67	55
29	28	24	65	68	56.$_{1-39}$
30	29	25	66	69.$_{1-28}$	56.$_{40-68}$
31	30	26	67	69.$_{29-50}$	56.$_{69-90}$
32	31	27	68	70	57.$_{1-28}$
33	32	28	69	71	57.$_{20-64}$
34	33	29	70	72	58
35	34	30	71	73	59
36	35	31	72	74	60.$_{1-31}$

Crit. Ed.	Bom. Ed.	Mad. Ed.	Crit. Ed.	Bom. Ed.	Mad. Ed.
[40] 73	75	$60._{32-60}$	121	121	97
74	$76._{1-25}$	$61._{1-24}$	122	122	98
75	$76._{26-53}$	$61._{25-51}$	123	123	99
76	77	62	124	124	$100._{1-25}$
77	78	$63._{1-32}$	125	125	$100._{26-50}$
78	79	$63._{33-64}$	126	126	101
79	80	$64._{1-30}$	127	127	$102._{1-21}$
80	81–82	$64._{31}$—$65._{130}$	128	128	$102._{22-42}$
81	83	66	129	129	103
82	84	67	130	130	104
83	85	68	131	131	105
84	86	69	132	132	106
85	87	70	133	133	107
86	88	71	134	134	108–109
87	89	72	135	$135._{1-42}$	$110._{1-42}$
88	90	73	136	$135._{43-60}$	$110._{43-60}$
89	91	$74._{1-23}$	137	136	111
90	92	$74._{24-47}$	138	137	112
91	93	75	139	138	113
92	94	76	140	139	114
93	95	77	141	140	115
94	96	$78._{1-29}$	142	141	116
95	97	$78._{30-53}$	—	142	—
96	98	79	143	143	117
97	99	80	144	144	118
98	100	$81._{1-25}$	145	145	119
99	101	$81._{26-47}$	146	146	120
100	102	$81._{48-74}$	147	147–148	121–122
101	103	$81._{75-98}$	148	149	123
102	104	82	149	150	124
103	105	$83._{1-21}$	150	151–152	125
104	106	$83._{22}$—$84._{25}$	151	153	126
105	$107._{1-29}$	$84._{26-55}$	152	154	127
106	$107._{30-70}$	$84._{56-100}$	153	155	128
107	108	85	—	156	129
108	109	86	154	157	130
109	$110._{1-21}$	$87._{1-21}$	[41] 155	158	131
110	$110._{22-58}$	$87._{22-58}$	156	159	132
111	111	88	157	160	133
112	112	$89._{1-18}$	158	161	134
113	113	$89._{19-43}$	159	162	135
114	114	90	160	163	136
115	115	91	161	164–165	137
116	116	92	162	166	138
117	117	93	163	167	139
118	118	94	164	$168._{1-61}$	$140._{1-60}$
119	119	95	165	$168._{62-86}$	$140._{61-86}$
120	120	96	166	169	141

Crit. Ed.	Bom. Ed.	Mad. Ed.	Crit. Ed.	Bom. Ed.	Mad. Ed.
167	170	142	213	223–224	183
168	171	143	214	225	184
169	172	144	215	226	$185._{1-25, 56}$
170	173	145	216	227	$185._{26-42}$
171	174	146	217	228	$185._{43}$—$186._{47}$
172	175	147	218	229	$186._{48-57}$
173	176	$148._{1-22}$	219	230	187
174	177	$148._{23-46}$	220	$231._{1-27}$	$188._{1-26}$
175	178	149	221	$231._{28-113}$	$188._{27-115}$
176	179	150	—	232	—
177	180	151	222	233	189
178	181	152	223	234	190
179	182	153	224	235	191
180	$183._{1-52}$	154	225	236	192
181	$183._{53-95}$	155	226	237	193
182	184	156	227	238	194
183	185	157	228	239	195
184	186	158	229	240	196
185	187	159	230	241	197
186	188	160	231	242	198
187	$189._{1-57}$	161	232	243	199
188	$189._{58}$–$190._{97}$	162	233	244	200
189	191	163	234	245	201
190	192	164	[42] 235	246	202
—	193–198	—	236	247	203
191	199	165	237	248	204
—	200	—	238	249–250	205–207
192	201	$166._{1-32}$	239	251	208
193	202	$166._{33-64}$	240	252	209
194	203	167	241	253–255	210
195	204	168	242	256	211
196	205	169	243	257	212
197	206	170	244	258	213
198	207	171	245	259	214–215
199	208	172	246	260	216
200	209	173	247	261	217
201	210	174	—	262–263	—
202	211	175	248	264	218
203	212-213	176	249	265	219
204	214	177	250	266	220
205	215	$178._{1-32}$	251	267	221
206	216	$178._{33-69}$	252	268	222
207	217	$179._{1-21}$	253	269	223
208	218	$179._{22-29}$	254	270	224
209	219	$179._{30-55}$	255	271	225
210	220	180	256	272	226
211	221	181	257	273	227
212	222	182	258	274	228

Crit. Ed.	Bom. Ed.	Mad. Ed.	Crit. Ed.	Bom. Ed.	Mad. Ed.
259	275	229	280	296	251
260	276	230	281	297	252
261	277	231--232	282	298	253
262	278	233	283	299	254
263	279	234	284	300	255
264	280	235	285	301	256
265	281	236	286	302	257
266	282	237	287	303	258
267	283	238	288	304	259
268	284	239	289	305	260
269	285	240	290	306	261
270	286	241	291	307	262
271	287	242	292	308	263
272	288	243	293	309	264
273	289	244	294	310	265
274	290	245	295	311	266
275	291	246	296	312	267
276	292	247	297	313	268
277	293	248	298	314	269
278	294	249	299	315	Trans. to Virāṭa p.
279	295	250			

EPIC STUDIES

I. Some Aspects of the Mahabharata Canon.*

The problem of the Mahābhārata textual criticism is a problem *sui generis.* Here the principles of textual reconstruction must first be evolved from an intensive study of the manuscript material and the manuscript tradition.[1] They can be finally considered as settled only after prolonged and considerable discussion and exchange of ideas and opinions.

The vulgate text of the Mbh. is fairly readable and appears, in places, to be even " better " than the critical text, because the former has been purged by the continuous emendations of scholars for centuries. The reader is consequently apt to prefer, at first sight, the readings of the vulgate text, but a thorough and sympathetic study of the author's language and thought and a critical evaluation of the variants would show him that the constituted text is sound.

Of the many reviews of the first fascicule of the critical edition of the Mahābhārata that have appeared during the past year there are two that deserve my special attention : the review by Dr. Hermann WELLER in the *Zeitschrift für Indologie und Iranistik* (vol. 6, pp. 166 ff.), and that by Professor EDGERTON in the *Journal of the American Oriental Society* (vol. 48. pp. 186-190). Both reviews are evidently products of a very close study of the text and the critical apparatus. Particularly valuable is the review by Prof. EDGERTON, who can appreciate the difficulties of the problem I have had to confront perhaps better than most scholars, since he has had to struggle with problems of a like nature in his valuable work on the Pañcatantra and the Vikramacarita.

In the succeeding pages I have endeavoured to set forth my reasons for adopting in the text the readings that have commended [158] themselves to me, in those cases which have been discussed by WELLER and EDGERTON in the reviews mentioned above. They concern the readings of 1. 1. 19, 42, 49, 62, 201, and of the identification of the hundred sub-parvans of the Mbh. enumerated in the second adhyāya of the Ādiparvan, that is, in the Parvasaṁgrahaparvan.[2]

* * * *

* [*JBBRAS* (NS) 4. 157-78].

1 Valuable hints are to be found especially in the writings of Prof. LÜDERS.

2 As most of the references in these studies will be to the Mahābhārata, all numbers without alphabetical prefix refer to the *critical edition* of the epic. When a reference is made to other editions of the epic, I have prefixed to the reference an indicatory letter enclosed within parantheses : thus (C.) denotes the Calcutta edition, (B.) the Bombay edition, and (K.) the Kumbhakonam edition.

1. 1. 19 :

vedaiś caturbhiḥ samitām (v. l. *saṁmitam*).

WELLER suggests an emendation—in fact, two alternative emendations. He first proposes to read *saṁmitām* for my *samitām*. The former variant is found only in one MS. which besides transposes the first two words of the pāda. His alternative suggestion is more radical. Seeing that the variant preferred by him yields a pāda metrically defective, he proposes to mend matters by recasting the pāda thus : *caturbhiḥ saṁmitāṁ vedaiḥ*. This pathyā he thinks, must have been the original reading of the pāda. The only reason WELLER has adduced for rejecting the text reading is the supposed intrinsic fitness of the alternate ; it suits the context much better, he believes. K_5, the solitary MS. which contains the reading preferred by WELLER, stands sixth on my list of K MSS., whose relative value diminishes in the order there given ; it is full of clerical mistakes, due probably to the difficulty experienced by the copyist (either of this MS. or of one of its ancestors) in deciphering the (? Śāradā) exemplar. I consider it an inferior codex. With WELLER'S reading we get a prior pāda with the scansion — — ⌣ — / — — ⌣ —. HOPKINS' statistical study of the relative frequency of the different forms of the pādas (*Great Epic*, p. 236) shows that this is a "rare" combination. Even WELLER realizes that the line does not read smoothly and calls therefore the length of the sixth syllable a "metrical archaism." Now *samitām* (of the text, [159] without the anusvāra) recurs in a similar context, also at the end of a prior pāda, and apparently in the same sense in (B.) 1. 95.90 : *idam hi vedaiḥ samitām*. It also occurs, in a different context, in Suśruta 2. 346. 3 : *anguṣṭhaparvasamitam*. If we read *saṁmitām* in the passage under discussion, we should have *pari passu* to read it in the two latter passages also, both of which then would be metrically defective ; the scansion of the first would be nearly the same as that of the pāda in question, the second would end with three consecutive iambs. Are these all instances of "metrical archaisms" ? For that, it seems to me, the documental probability of the reading perferred by WELLER is not strong enough. The text reading, which is mentioned by Nīlakaṇṭha as a variant, is supported indirectly by K_2 (*samatām*) and directly by $K_{0.3.4.6}$ $M_{1.3.4}$. On the other hand, WELLER'S reading, as has already been remarked, is found only in one inferior MS. Worthy of note is Nīlakaṇṭha's gloss : *samitām iti pāṭhe tulyām ity arthaḥ*. The initial mistake of WELLER lies in supposing that *saṁmitām* suits the context better than *samitām*, whereas, in point of fact, *saṁmmitām* is nothing more than a doublet of the other word. WELLER does not realize that his attempt to substitute an "easier reading" has been anticipated by the scribe of K_5, who *likewise* finding the emended line (metrically) unreadable has transposed the words of the pāda, reaching a new combination : *caturbhir vedaiḥ saṁmitām*, which according to HOPKINS (*loc. cit.*) is of "very rare, sporadic" occurrence. The word *samita* has been perfectly correctly explained in PW. : *samita* (*sa* + *mita*) = *saṁmita*, "gleiches Mass habend, gleich." The relation between the two words is clearly revealed by the more familiar doublets *satata* : *saṁtata*, *sahita* : *saṁhita* and so on, *sa*-and *sam* being the unaccented and accented forms of one and the same prefix. When the accentual factor became inoperative, the choice was conditioned solely by metrical considerations. The identification in the case of *samita* may have been helped by contamination with *sam* + *ita* (= *saṁgata*), "conformable to, in harmony with" (a meaning not unsuitable even here), or by its supposed connection with *sama*, "equal" (cf. WACKERNAGEL, *Altind. Gramm.* II, 1. § 30 bβ). The semantic values of the words in question being the same, the combined [160] force of documental probability and metrical preference decides the question of choice incontestably in favour of the adopted text.

The text reading really needs some further justification. WELLER'S misunderstanding of the text is, in my opinion, a direct confirmation of my remark in the Foreword (p. VI) that it is a *lectio difficilior*. The word was, I suppose, early misunderstood. To judge by the character of the variants, it was commonly, though erroneously, interpreted as *sám* + *ita*, "united, combined with." In this sense, in course of time, it must have been ousted by its easier synonyms *saṁyukta* (substituted for it in V_1 B D) and *sahita* (mainly in T and G). Both these readings are inadequate. Nīlakaṇṭha's explanation *caturvedārthavatīm* is inadmissible ; the phrase can at best mean *caturvedavatīm* ("possessing the four Vedas"), which is of course sheer nonsense. ROY'S "comprehendeth the sense of the four Vedas" and DUTT'S "contains the sense of the four Vedas" are equally inaccurate paraphrases (based upon the explanation furnished by the scholiast), because the passage in the vulgate cannot bear the meaning here forced upon it. On the other hand, the *literal* meaning of *saṁyukta* or *sahita* is, as already remarked, wholly unsuitable. For what could the assembled sages mean by saying that they wished to hear the (Mahābhārata) Saṁhitā "combined with the four Vedas"?

To return to the manuscript evidence. The K group is partly corrupt and indecisive though the majority has the text reading : $K_{0, 3, 4, 6}$ as in text; K_1 *sahitām* ; K_2 *samatām* ; K_5 *saṁmitām*. All these stand resolutely against *saṁyuktām* of the vulgate ; but, from the point of view of transcriptional probability, none of them is wholly incompatible with *samitām* of the text. Three out of the four Malayālam MSS. have also preserved the true reading ; the remaining Malayālam MS. has *sahitām*, the reading of the T G group. With this data I should explain the genesis of the variants thus. The text reading is a *lectio difficilior*, preserved in the majority of K intact, and in the remaining MSS. of the K version in a corrupt condition. The K reading being partly supported by M, there is a partial agreement between two more or less independent versions, a condition almost wholly absent in the case of the rejected variants. Being a difficult and unfamiliar word, it was [161] early misunderstood and finally dropped—independently in certain groups of the Southern and Northern recensions—in favour of such words as were thought to be its equivalents in sense but which do not fit the context and are wholly inadequate.

After what has been said above, it is hardly necessary to consider the alternative proposed by WELLER. But in passing it may be pointed out that it is methodologically wrong to expect to find the original reading by picking out a stray variant which appears to give a better meaning, and shuffling the words of the pāda until the pathyā form turns up. For one thing, it is by no means certain that the original must be a pathyā ; the MS. evidence, so far as I have examined it, is all in favour of the hypothesis that originally the vipulās were far more numerous than what one is led to suppose from the study of the vulgate text, which has modernized many of the archaic lines of the original and successfully covered up the traces of the metamorphosis.

* * * *

1. 1. 42 :

daśajyotiḥ śatajyotiḥ sahasrajyotir ātmavān (v. 1. *eva ca.*)

Here the situation is much clearer. According to WELLER the variant *eva ca* is not quite wrong ("abwegig"). Quite true. But about the text reading, I think we can say much more than that. In point of grammar, metre or even sense, there is not much to choose between the variants. But in point of documental probability, their values are totally different. *eva ca* is the variant offered by $K_{0.2.4.}$ Da Dn Dr D_{1-12} ; the text, on the other hand, is documented by a much stronger group, $K_{1.5.6}$ V_1 B Da_1 (marg.). D_{14} S. It is further attested by another good MS. of a different category, I have since compared : a Nepālī MS. belonging to the Benares Sanskrit College Manuscripts Library. The text reading figures also in GOLDSTÜCKER'S collations from European codices, of which I have photo copies.[1] The position them, is this. On the [162] one hand the K version is indecisive, agreeing partly with D, which is the main witness for the rejected variant ; on the other hand B S (probably together with the Nepālī Maithilī version) form a solid group in favour of the text, further attested by three K MSS, including the important India Office codex K_1. It will be seen that the documental authority is almost wholly on the side of the text. For a contamination between Devanāgarī transcripts of Kāśmīrī MSS. and Devanāgarī MSS. must be postulated to be far more likely than a contamination between the entire Bangālī version and the entire Southern recension. The different Indian scripts being

[1] The photographs were kindly presented to the Bhandarkar Institute by the University of Strassburg, through the kind offices of the late Prof. Emile SENART. I take this opportunity to thank the University publicly for this service.

all but unintelligible outside the provinces where they were developed, there is already a *prima facie* reason for assuming the independence of B and S. This principle was long ago recognized and enunciated by Prof. LÜDERS, than whom no scholar has a profounder acquaintance with and a clearer insight in the problem of Mahābhārata textual criticism. In *Die Grantha-recension des Mahābhārata* (Berlin 1901), Prof. LÜDERS has said : "Das beweist, dass die Grantha-handschriften nicht etwa auf Bengali-Handschriften zurückgehen, —etwa, was von vornherein nicht gerade wahrscheinlich ist,—sondern dass in den Fällen wo B und G zusammengehen, ihre Lesarten als alt zu sehen sind." Now what is true of the consensus of B and G is *a fortiori* true of the consensus of B and S. This presumptive independence is wholly confirmed by my intensive study of the first 3,000 stanzas of the Ādiparvan from the extensive collations at my disposal, during which study I have not been able to detect the slightest trace of "secondary interrelationship" between the Bangālī version *as a whole* and the Southern recension *as a whole*. Equally fundamental in character is the agreement between K and S, the only difference between K and B being that K is comparatively purer and freer from interpolation than the other. The canon of Mbh. textual criticism, in its simplest form, may therefore be said to be the fundamental character of the consensus of K and S on the one hand, and of B and S on the other, provided of course the concordant reading is of such a nature that it could not be the result of a fortuitous coincidence.

Doubt can, and frequently, does arise when K B (then generally [163] with D ; in other words the whole of N) stands against S. Here each case must be judged and decided on its own merits. It may sometimes be possible to adduce evidence of a decisive character on one side or the other. Such evidence may be intrinsic ; one reading may be intrinsically better than the other. Or it may be extrinsic ; when it is possible to supplement the evidence of MSS. from other ancient and independent sources. But as a rule, when there is a conflict between N and S, the evidence is so nicely balanced that no definite decision is possible.

To return to the instance under consideration. The agreement between B and S raises such a strong presumption in favour of the text reading that its evidence cannot be rebutted by the *possibility* conceived by WELLER that *ātmavān* might have crept into the text secondarily, under the influence of *ātmanaḥ* and *ātmajāḥ* in the following lines.

In this particular instance, I think, intrinsic probability is, to some extent, also on the side of the text. It is a feature of epic technique that out of three consecutive proper names occurring in the same hemistich, the last name is very frequently accompanied by a qualifying adjective. Scores of illustrations may be produced ; here are thirteen selected at random.

1. 31. 14. *Virajāś ca Subāhuś ca Śālipiṇḍaś ca vīryavān,*

(K.)	1. 88. 9 :	*Ṛceyur atha Kakṣeyuḥ Kṛkaṇeyuś ca vīryavān*
		Staṇḍileyur Vaneyuś ca Jaleyuś ca mahāyaśāḥ
(K.)	6.25.4-5 :	*Yuyudhāno Virāṭaś ca Drupadaś ca mahārathaḥ*
		Dhṛṣṭaketuś Cekitānaḥ Kāśirājaś ca vīryavān
		Purujit Kuntibhojaś ca Śaibyaś ca narapuṅgavaḥ
	17 :	*Dhṛṣṭadyumno Virāṭaś ca Sātyakiś ca parājitaḥ*
(K.)	8. 83. 9 :	*Kṛpaś ca Kṛtavarmā ca Drauṇiś caiva mahārathaḥ*
(K.)	9. 2. 17 :	*Aśvatthāmā ca Bhojaś ca Māgadhaś ca mahābalaḥ*
		Bṛhadbalaś ca Krāthaś ca Śakuniś cāpi Saubalaḥ
(K.)	9. 3. 12 :	*hate Bhīṣme ca Droṇe ca Karṇe caiva mahārathe*
(K.)	9. 5. 2 :	*Śalyaś ca Citrasenaś ca Śakuniś ca mahārathaḥ*
(K.)	9. 24. 40 :	*Aśvatthāmā Kṛpaś caiva Kṛtavarmā ca sātvataḥ.*

[164] The practice being the outcome of a natural desire to avoid the monotony of a bald enumeration of names, it is not surprising to find that even the Homeric epics furnish ample illustrations of it ; here is one with the trick repeated in consecutive hemistiches (Illiad, 24.250-1) :

> Πάμμονά τ', Ἀντίφονόν τε, βοὴν α'γαθόν τε Πολίτην,
> Δηίφοβόν τε, καὶ Ἱππόθοον, καὶ Δῖον α'γαυον.

After having proved that the text reading is not only better documented but in itself very plausible, we may proceed to consider whether any reason can be suggested how the variant *eva ca* may have arisen. Two explanations—both mere possibilities—occur to me. It is for one thing possible that the original *ātmavān* may have been deliberately suppressed in order to avoid the monotonous reiteration of *ātma* at the end of three consecutive verses. A more likely reason for the suppression may have been the lack of a copula in the original line, which had been crowded out by the succession of three unusually long names (two of four syllables each, and the third one of not less than five), taking up by themselves 13 syllables out of an aggregate of 16 of the śloka line.

* * * *

1.1.49 :

vistīryatan mahaj jñānam ṛṣiḥ saṁkṣepam abravit
(v. l. *saṁkṣepato 'bravīt*).

The two rejected variants are : *saṁkṣepato 'bravīt* K V_1 B_1m D_{14} and *saṁkṣipya cābravīt* B Da Dn Dr $D_{1,12}$ S (except $G_{1,3}$ M_3). WELLER finds *saṁkṣepato* satisfactory ("befriedigend"). As a matter of fact, of the rejected variants, the reading *saṁkṣipya cābravit* is far superior to the other. In it the sense is clear ; grammatically it is correct, metrically flawless. It is moreover the reading indicated by the principle of agreement between independent versions. being supported by the Bangālī and Devanāgarī versions on the one hand and by one section of the Southern recension on the other. But the compelling power of this agreement is weakened by the circumstance that one Malayālam MS. and three (out of the seven) Grantha MSS. are outside the group. Had the whole of B agreed with the whole of S, it would have been difficult, if not impossible, for reasons explained in the previous section, [165] to reject the concordant reading. The weak point of this variant lies in the fact that it does not at all explain, as far as I can judge, how the other readings may have arisen. There is the same flaw in the other rejected variant, though not in the same degree. The text reading, though weakly supported by MSS, serves admirably, in my opinion, to account for the existence of the variants, especially if *saṁkṣepam* is taken as an adverbial gerund in-*am* (Pāṇini's *ṇamul*), as I think it should be ; *cf.* WHITNEY, *Sanskrit Grammar*, § 995. For there would then be an inherent tendency to substitute for it simpler readings. *saṁkṣipya ca* and *saṁkṣepataḥ* would be very neat paraphrases of the awkward adverbial gerund : the second (*saṁkṣepataḥ*) preserving nearly intact the original akṣaras, the first (*saṁkṣipya*) involving a more radical change from the view-point of form, but closely following the original in sense. The latter may, moreover, have been directly suggested by *vistīrya* in the first pāda which it nicely balances. I assume, of course, that *saṁkṣipya* was introduced independently in B D on the one hand and S on the other. In other words, I think that the concordance between certain sections of the Northern and the Southern recensions is purely accidental, and it is unquestionable that it *could* be that. I must frankly admit, however, that there is a strong element of subjectivity in this choice, which can in no way be said to be compelling. I prefer the text reading, fully realizing that others may prefer either of the other two readings ; but that is precisely why a wavy line has been printed in the text below *saṁkṣepam*. I doubt very much whether any compelling reason can be advanced to prove the absolute superiority of any one of the variants over the others.

* * * *

1.1.62 :

anukramaṇim adhyāyam (v.l. *anukramaṇikādhyāyam*)

This again is a somewhat difficult and complicated case. The text reading is perhaps less than certain, as has been indicated by the use of the wavy line ; but it can, I think, claim for itself greater certitude than the reading in the preceding case. The apparatus contains five variants for this pāda. They are :

$K_{0, 2-6}$ V_1 B_3 Da Dn Dr $D_{1-4, 6-12-14}$ D_4	*anukramaṇikādhyāyam*
K_1	°*kramāṇimādhyā*°
[166] T_1 G_{5-7}	°*krāmiṇam adhyā*°
T_2	°*krāmikam a*°

$G_{2.3}$	*°kramaṇam a°*
$B_{1.2-4}$ D_5	as in text

Along with this passage, we must consider 1.1.199, where the pāda recurs and where again there are five variants, in part different from those of the passage under discussion. The second set of variants is :

$K_{0,\ 2-4.6}$ V_1 Dn Dr $D_{1.2.4.6-12-14}$		*anukramaṇikādhyāyam*
T G_{4-6} $M_{1-2.4}$	(S Recension)	*°krāmiṇam a°*
G_1	(S Recension)	*°krāmaṇim a°*
$G_{2.7}$ M_3	(S Recension)	*°krāmaṇam a°*
G_3	(S Recension)	*°kramaṇam a°*
$K_{1.5}$ B Da $D_{3.5}$		as in text.

We have here very remarkable vascillation for a perfectly simple pāda. Every textual variation presupposes a cause. Therefore that reading is best which best explains how the various different readings may have arisen. The variant preferred by WELLER, which is also the reading of the vulgate text, though perfectly satisfactory in itself, fails wholly to explain why there are so many variants. What is wrong with *anukramaṇikādhyāyam* ? Nothing apparently, if taken by itself. But let us have a closer look at the variants and try to understand the cause of the variation. We shall first consider the variants at 1.1.199, where the situation is slightly clearer. The text reading is supported by $K_{1.5}$ B Da $D_{3.5}$; that is, two of the K MSS. (including the important K_1) together with the whole of Bangālī and Arjunamiśra and two Devanāgarī MSS., a combination not to be despised. The rejected variants fall into two natural groups ; on the one hand we have the majority of K and Devanāgarī (with the notable exception of Arjunamiśra MSS., which, as remarked in the Foreword, p. v, frequently side with Bangālī) having *anukramaṇikādhyāyam ;* on the other hand we have the Southern MSS., which show *anukrāmiṇam adhyāyam,* with some unimportant variations. The case is somewhat similar at 1. 1. 62, the difference being that the manuscript support for the text reading is slightly weaker. The two sets of variants, it may be remarked, have this noteworthy feature [167] in common that in both places there is partial agreement between K B on the one hand and S on the other, in so far that they both have as the first part of the pāda, a word uncompounded with *adhyāyam*. The explanation of this chaos is, I think, furnished by 1.2.34, where the name of the adhyāya (or rather of the parvan) is found to be *anukramaṇī* (and not *anukramaṇikā*) :[1]

parvānukramaṇī pūrvam.

Here the reading is certain, the variants (mainly in G) being negligible.

---

1 Accordingly I have called the parvan Anukramaṇī-parvan, differing from the Calcutta, Bombay and Kumbhakonam editions, in which it is called Anukramaṇikā-parvan.

All printed editions of the text without exception have the same reading, an indication that the large majority of all reliable MSS. hitherto examined read the name of the adhyāya as in text. The name in this form occurs at 1.1.200 :

anukramaṇyā yāvat syād ahnā rātryā ca saṃcitam,

where again the variants though numerous, do not concern us since they are also mainly restricted to a single version, the Grantha.

As remarked already there is partial agreement between K B Da and S in so far that they break up the compound of the vulgate text into words, one standing in epithetical or appositional relation to the other. A little reflection will show that, used by a writer familiar with the older name of the adhyāya, the first word *uncompounded* with adhyāya could be no other than *anukramaṇīm*. With this word, however, we should get the awkward prior pāda ⏑ — ⏑ ⏑ — —́ — — —, which, according to HOPKINS (*op. cit.* p. 236), is a " very rare, sporadic " combination. Now it is well known that, in the epic, grammatical accuracy is often sacrificed to the observance of preferred vipulā forms. The awkwardness of the pāda was removed by the (anomalous) shortening of the troublesome long ī in the final syllable of the word. Examples of shortening metri causâ, cited from the epics by HOPKINS (*op. cit.* p. 246) are : *svadhā ca svadhabhojinam,* Rām. 7. 23. 23 (again in the *fifth* syllable) ; *apakramat,* (B.) 9. 11. 62 ; *sakhigaṇāvṛtā,* Nala 1. 24 ; *na śrīr jahati vai tanuḥ,* (B.) 11. 25. 5. The examples, as is well known, can be very easily multiplied.

[168] The assumption of an original *anukramaṇim adhyāyam* could, as far as I can judge, satisfactorily explain all the different variants of this pāda. It accounts for the neat bifurcation of the manuscript evidence into the vulgate text (with partial reflexes in the K version) and the Southern group. The vulgate text may be seen to have successfully overcome the difficulty of the anomalous shortening by substituting in the lame foot a form with a legitimate short vowel where required by the (later) stringent rule : *pañcamam laghu sarvatra* ; it had to sacrifice the original appositional construction and substitute for it a compound. The Southern editors, on the other hand, adhered firmly to the appositional construction, and eked out a tolerable pāda with various synonyms having a short vowel in the fifth syllable such as : *krāmiṇam, °kramikam, °krāmaṇam, °krāmaṇim.*

It may be argued that even *anukramaṇikādhyāyam* as the original reading might likewise furnish reasons for the growth of this singular crop of various readings, because the name *anukramaṇikā* here given to the adhyāya was felt to be inappropriate, the correct name being *anukramaṇī* as given in 1. 2. 34. But such an interpretation would not be valid, because the original postulated here would at best serve to explain only one variant, namely, *anukramaṇim adhyāyam ;* it fails wholly to account for the vascillations of the entire Southern recension, since nothing would have been gained by substituting *anukramaṇam*, °*kramikam* and so forth, which all equally fall short of reproducing the original name of the adyhāya. So at least it seems to me must the variants be interpreted. I consider the text reading all but certain. A comparison of the extant manuscript material should show that, clerical errors and occasional anomalies apart, the Bangālī MSS. uniformly, Arjunamiśra (? together with Devabodha) MSS. frequently, and K MSS. sporadically will have the text reading ; MSS. of the vulgate text and other MSS. contaminated from this source will have the compound ; while MSS. of the Southern recension will mostly have synonyms of *anukramaṇim* such as °*kramaṇam* °*kramikam* and so on.

* * * *

1. 1. 201 :

[169] *bhāratasya vapur hy etat satyam cāmṛtam* (*v.l. cānṛtam*) *eva ca.*

EDGERTON discusses at some length the variation *amṛtam* : *anṛtam* and decides emphatically in favour of *anṛtam*. EDGERTON'S arguments are briefly these : first and foremost, the text reading does not do justice to the emphatic particle *eva* in the same line, which is a "crucial word ;" secondly, *anṛtam* is intrinsically far superior to the innocuous *amṛtam*, which has been substituted for the original *lectio difficilior* by ignorant copyists who, missing the "paradox" intended, "naturally gagged at attributing 'falsehood' to the epic." In the first place I differ from EDGERTON radically as to the value and importance of the word *eva* in the sentence. It is unquestionably true that *eva* does emphasize the preceding word or words, but this is neither necessarily nor universally true. Very frequently, especially in the epics and the Purāṇas, the emphasis is so slight that it is almost negligible, and the word is nothing more than an expletive. My experience fully corroborates P. W., which has the following note s. v. *eva* : "Nicht selten, namenlich nach einigen Partikeln, ist die Bedeutung von *eva* abgeschwacht, dass wir auch den Nachdruck aufgeben." But the best answer to EDGERTON'S contention as to the value of *eva* is to show that it figures very frequently at the end of the pāda, in long enumerations of names and attributes where no emphasis could be intended whatsoever. Here are some examples chosen at random :

(K.) 1. 68. 95.: *Durmarṣaṇo Durmukhaś ca Duṣkarṇaḥ Karṇa eva ca*

(B.) 2. 100. 2 : *Droṇam Kṛpam nṛpāṁś cānyān Aśvatthāmānam eva ca*

(B.) 13. 254. 17 : *avyayaḥ puruṣaḥ sākṣī kśetrajño 'kṣara eva ca*
120 : *yajñāntakṛd yajñaguhyam annam annāda eva ca*

Brahma Pur. 182. 7 : *tvam svāhā tvam svadhā vidyā sudhā tvam jyotir eva ca*

Bhaviṣya Pur. 10. 8. 38 : *jyotiś cakram jalam tejo nabhasvān vidyud eva ca*

It would be clearly preposterous to see in these *eva ca* "emphatic particles" or "crucial words" emphasizing paradoxes; [170] they are nothing more than copulative expletives. My impression is that the epic "poets" use the conjunctions *ca*, *caiva* or *eva ca* according as they require one, two or three syllables to fill their line! This, I hope, will suffice to dispose of the alleged necessity of looking for and finding any striking paradox in this line.

But I think EDGERTON is making another and a graver mistake. His remark that "the panegyrist of the *epic* [italics mine] starts out to claim that it contains everything" makes me suspect that EDGERTON has possibly misunderstood the hemistich in question. Here the subject matter of glorification is not the *epic* at all, but merely the first adhyāya thereof. The hemistich occurs in a passage at the end of the first adhyāya, and the passage is evidently of the nature of a *phalaśruti*. The hemistich says: "This is the body of the (Mahā-)Bhārata." Here "this" refers not to the whole epic but merely to the Anukramaṇī chapter mentioned in the previous stanzas. The whole line is a subordinate (*hi*) clause depending upon the main clause contained in the immediately preceding stanza. "(200) He who repeats (in an undertone, even) a little of the Anukramaṇī at both twilights is freed immediately from as much sin as has been accumulated during the day and the night; (201) for, this is the body of the (Mahā-)Bhārata (that is) Truth and also Immortality!" It is owing to its partaking of the qualities of (or, as the panegyrist of the adhyāya will have it, owing to its being) Truth and Immortality that it is able to absolve the devout reciter of the adhyāya immediately from sin. The emphasis, if any, is on *hi* ("for"), not on *eva*. Objection may be taken to the neuter gender of *etat*, since it is made to refer the Anukramaṇī (f.) chapter as I do here. The gender may be explained either as a case of attraction by the gender of the predicate (*vapus*, n.) or as referring indiscriminately to *anukramaṇī* (f.) or *adhyāya* (m.). But if EDGERTON does not like that, I have no great objection to his translating: "For this form of the (Mahā-)Bhārata is Truth and Immortality." According to this interpretation, the variant *anṛtam* is wholly inappropriate and inadmissible; and in fact on second thoughts I am inclined even to dispense with the wavy line under *amṛtam*.

[171] The paradox conceived by EDGERTON might apply fitly to the whole epic, which may be said to mirror all phases of life, "Truth,—yes, and Falsehood too!" but it is clearly unreasonable and even impossible to say that the Anukramaṇī chapter by itself could be "Truth,—yes and Falsehood too." Furthermore, even if this wonderful chapter be the Truth as well as Falsehood, I fail to see how it should follow that such a chapter could on that account be able to give absolution to a sinner. If one bears in mind that the subject matter of the panegyric is the Anukramaṇī chapter (and *not*

the epic), one cannot, I think, come to any other conclusion than that the true reading is *amṛtam*.

It may be added that EDGERTON's mistake is quite natural and is caused primarily by the misleading division of the passage (stanzas 200-202) into distiches, which suggests that the subject matter of the *praśasti* is the Mahābhārata. The first half of stanza 201 is logically and grammatically connected with the preceding stanza (200); on the other hand the second half is part and parcel of the following stanza (202). The first half clearly refers to the Anukramaṇī chapter, the second half equally clearly to the epic as a whole. Could I have foreseen the confusion it is apt to cause, I would certainly have joined the first half of stanza 201 to 200 and the second half to stanza 202, notwithstanding that this arrangement yields two consecutive three-line stanzas. In such cases I have mostly made three distiches, sometimes, I fear, as in this instance, clouding the sense.

There remains now only one point to be considered. By saying that *amṛtam* is a *lectio difficilior*, EDGERTON implies that the change from *amṛtam* into *anṛtam* is ordinarily inconceivable, since any copyist would have fought shy of attributing falsehood to the epic. Such a view would, in my opinion, be entirely incorrect. The distinguishing feature of scribes' emendations is that it is superficial. The scribe does not stop to think very deeply about the consequences of the change. Here, I fancy, the variant has arisen merely because, in entirely different contexts, *satyam* and *anṛtam* are found frequently combined into a phrase, sometimes even combined into the compound *satyānṛta* (e.g. *satyānṛte yo vivinakte loke,* 1. 3. 152; *satyānṛte avapaśyañ janānām* RV. 7.49.3). I [172] therefore hold that the substitutions of *anṛtam* for *amṛtam* is wholly within the range of probability and even quite natural for an Indian scribe.

* * *

1.2.70:

etat parvaśataṁ pūrṇaṁ Vyāsenoktaṁ maharṣiṇā.

Although it is prefectly true that all previous efforts to make the text of the Mbh. agree with the numerical data of its extent and size have ended in dismal failures, EDGERTON is needlessly nervous about my attempt to reduce the number of the (sub-)parvans exactly to one hundred. EDGERTON's view is that the traditional hundred should be regarded as an approximate or "round" number. This is the explanation given also by C. V. VAIDYA in his *Epic India* (p. 189) when he is faced with the anomaly that his list of "hundred parvans" contains 107 titles. In support of the view, one might cite the use of the word *śataka* in titles of anthologies like the *Śṛṅgāraśataka*, which frequently, if not uniformly, contain more than 100 stanzas. The parallelism would, in my opinion, be not quite exact, because, I think, here the suffix *ka* (miscalled *svārthe* by Indian grammarians) probably suggests, if it does not actually connote, the approximate character of the denomination. Less convincing still is the analogy (mentioned by C. V. VAIDYA, *loc. cit.*) of the appellation *śatasāhasrī* of the Mbh. This expression is admittedly *not* intended to mean exactly one hundred thousand, whatever else it may mean. But the latitude implicitly allowed in the use of the expression *śatasahasra* in stating the number of stanzas which are approximately a lakh cannot, it seems to me, be claimed by a person giving the number of chapters which are approximately only one hundred. That question apart, when the old experts of the Great Epic (*bhāratacintaka*, 1. 2. 172) had calculated and stated the exact number of adhyāyas and ślokas, parvan by parvan for all the eighteen parvans, apparently correct to the last digit, would it not be exceedingly strange if the number of the chapter-groups alone, given in the very same adhyāya, in the same context, were to be only approximate? A few stanzas more or less in an aggregate of several thousand stanzas, or a few adhyāyas more or less [175] in an aggregate of several hundred adhyāyas would not have mattered very much one way or the other; but a few parvans more or less when the total was only in the neighbourhood of hundred! So careless I suppose even the careless custodians of the fifth Veda were not. Their calculations may have been wrong, but their intention is perfectly clear. They say and mean that the number was exactly one hundred: notice the *pūrṇam* in the first pāda of the hemistich. In fact, the amazing difference in the lengths and characters of these chapter-groups—there are some containing only 1 adhyāya and less than 70 stanzas, there are others which contain more than 70 adhyāyas and considerably more than 3,000 stanzas!—could, I think, only have been the result of an over-mastering desire on the part of some old editor or editors to reach, by hook or crook, some such predetermined "round" number.

EDGERTON is perfectly right when he says that the attempt to reconstruct the original text of this passage presents some very serious textual difficulties. Whether my text will finally prove correct in every respect or not remains of course to be seen. I hope it will fit the constituted text of the whole epic; but I shall not be greatly shocked if it does not. The texts of the present editions, Calcutta, Bombay or Kumbhakonam, do not conform to the details given in the "Table of Contents." There are all kinds of discrepancies between them: the śloka numbers do not agree; the same is true of the adhyāya and the parvan number. These discrepancies cannot be helped,—so long as we do not know who had done the counting and when it was done. As for the constituted text of the passage in question, I will only say that I have formed it rigidly on the principles of textual criticism worked out by me and followed elsewhere in the course of my work on the edition. These principles have been applied independently of the question of the past, present or future form and divisions of the epic. The constituted text is based mainly on documental and intrinsic probability. It is more than likely that it contains some slight errors ; the different versions are interwoven in such an intricate manner that to disentangle them with complete assurance or to one's complete satisfaction is not yet possible, or perhaps is no longer possible. I honestly believe that the discrepancies between the constituted [174] text and the present "Table of Contents," will be very considerably diminished. But about one thing I feel perfectly confident and that is that the number is intended to be e x a c t l y one hundred. EDGERTON himself would probably have been less sceptical had he known that both Arjunamiśra and Nīlakaṇṭa have left behind them in their scholia mnemonic stanzas, stating the exact number of (sub-)parvans in each of the eighteen (major) parvans. In both cases the total is exactly one hundred ; besides that, the individual figures tally exactly in the two lists.

Here are the stanzas themselves.

Arjunamiśra[1] towards the end of the second adhyāya (Da_1 fol. 45)

ekonaviṁśati *tu parvabhir Ādiparva*
khyātam, Sabhā navabhir, aṣṭabhir aṣṭayuktaiḥ
Āraṇyakam, nanu Virāṭakathā caturbhir,
ekādhikair daśabhir *Udyamam āmananti* || 1 ||
Bhaiṣmam ca pañcabhir, *atho Gurur* aṣṭasaṁkhyair
ekena *Karṇam, atha Madrakathā* caturbhiḥ
Sauptam tribhis, *tad anu* pañcabhir *Aṅganānām*
Śāntis caturbhir,-*Anuśāsanam* ekakena || 2 ||
dvābhyām *uṣanti Hayamedham, ath-Āśramākhyam*
āhus tribhir, *Muśalaparva* tathaikakena
ekaikaśo *gamana-Nākagatī*, ubhābhyām
Vaṁśo Harer, iti kṛtā śata *parvasaṁkhyā* || 3 ||

Nīlakaṇṭha (*ad* 1. 2. 396) :

Ādi-dhyā[19]na-*Sabhā*-dha[9]naṁ *Vana*-ca[16]yaṁ *Vairāṭa*-bhū[4]*dyoga*-yu[11]k,

Bhīṣma Droṇa-ma[5]jaṁ[8] *ca Karṇa*-ku[1] *tathā Śalye*-bha[4] *Sauṣuptaga*[3]m

Strī-saṁ[5] *Śānti*-bha[4] *Dānadharma*-ku[1] *Hayejyā*-r[2]-*Āśramāvāsa*-gaṁ[3]

kaṁ[1] kaṁ[1] *Mausala-Yānayor Dyugati*-kaṁ[1] *Vamśe*-kha[2]m *etac* chatam ||

[175] According to my list the various sub-parvans are distributed among the eighteen major parvans as under :

---

[1] The *a priori* attempt of BROCKHAUS (*ZDMG* 6. 528-532) to identify the hundred parvans from these stanzas of Arjunamiśra was premature and doomed to fail.

I. Ādi (19) :	1 Anukramaṇī.[1] 2 Parvasaṁgraha. 3 Pauṣya. 4 Pauloma. 5 Āstīka. 6 Ādivaṁśāvataraṇa. 7 Saṁbhava. 8 Jatugṛhadāha. 9 Haiḍimba. 10 Bakavadha. 11 Caitraratha. 12 Svayaṁvara. 13 Vaivāhika. 14 Vidurāgamana. 15 Rājyalambha. 16 Arjunavanavāsa. 17 Subhadrāharaṇa. 18 Haraṇahārika. 19 Khāṇḍavadāha.
II. Sabhā (9) :	20 Sabhā. 21 Mantra. 22 Jarāsaṁdhavadha. 23 Digvijaya. 24 Rājasūyika. 25 Arghābhiharaṇa. 26 Śiśupālavadha. 27 Dyūta. 28 Anudyūta.
III. Āraṇyaka[2] (16) :	29 Āraṇyaka. 30 Kirmīravadha. 31 Kairāta. 32 Indralokābhigamana. 33 Tīrthayātrā. 34 Jaṭāsuravadha. 35 Yakṣayuddha. 36 Ājagara. 37 Mārkaṇḍeyasamasyā. 38 Draupadī Satyabhāmāsaṁvāda. 39 Ghoṣayātrā. 40 Mṛgasvapnabhaya. 41 Vrīhidrauṇika. 42 Draupadīharaṇa. 43 Kuṇḍalāharaṇa, 44 Āraṇeya.
IV. Virāṭa (4) :	45 Vairāṭa. 46 Kīcakavadha. 47 Gograhaṇa. 48 Vaivāhika.
[176] V. Udyoga (11) :	49 Udyoga. 50 Sañjayayāna. 51 Prajāgara. 52 Sanatsujāta. 53 Yānasaṁdhi. 54 Bhagavadyāna. 55 Vivāda. 56 Niryāṇa. 57 Rathātirathasaṁkhyā. 58 Ulūkadūtāgamana. 59 Ambopākhyāna.
VI. Bhīṣma (5) :	60 Bhīṣmābhiṣecana. 61 Jambukhaṇḍanirmāṇa. 62 Bhūmi. 63 Bhagavadgītā. 64 Bhīṣmavadha.

[1] This is the correct name of the first (sub-)parvan, miscalled Anukramaṇikā in modern editions. See above, the discussion on 1. 1. 62.

[2] This is the orthodox name of the third parvan, miscalled Vanaparvan in most Northern MSS., and modern editions. The Southern MSS. generally adhere consecutively to the older names.

VII. Droṇa (8) : 65 Droṇābhiṣeka. 66 Saṁśaptakavadha. 67 Abhimanyuvadha. 68 Pratijñā. 69 Jayadrathavadha. 70 Ghaṭotkacavadha. 71 Droṇavadha. 72 Nārāyaṇāstramokṣa.

VIII. Karṇa (1) : 73 Karṇa.

IX. Śalya (4) : 74 Śalya. 75 Hradapraveśa. 76 Gadāyuddha. 77 Sārasvata.

X. Sauptika (3) : 78 Sauptika. 79 Aiṣīka. 80 Jalapradānika.

XI. Strī (5) : 81 Strī. 82 Śrāddha. 83 Abhiṣecanika. 84 Cārvākanigraha. 85 Gṛhapravibhāga.

XII. Śānti (3) : 86 Rājadharma. 87 Āpaddharma. 88 Mokṣadharma.

XIII. Anuśāsana (2) : 89 Ānuśāsanika. 90 Bhīṣmasvargārohaṇa.

XIV. Aśvamedhika (2) : 91 Aśvamedhika. 92 Anugītā.

XV. Āśramavāsika (3) . 93 Āśramavāsa. 94 Putradarśana. 95 Nāradāgamana.

XVI. Mausala (1) : 96 Mausala.

XVII. Mahāprasthānika (1) : 97 Mahāprasthānika.

[177] XVIII. Svargārohaṇa (1) : 98 Svargārohaṇa.

(Khila) Harivaṁśa (2) : 99 Harivaṁśa. 100 Bhaviṣyat.[1]

My series differs from that of the mnemonic stanzas only as regards the two (consecutive) parvans Śānti and Anuśāsana. The aggregate number of the two parvans is the same in our lists ; the discrepancy is only with regard to the division of the five sub-parvans between the two major parvans. My figures for these parvans are 3 and 2 ; those given by the scholiasts in their stanzas are 4 and 1 respectively, differing only by one each from mine. I am unable to account for this discrepancy at present.

These stanzas, it will have to be admitted, make the case for the exactitude of the figure 100 very much stronger. Is it conceivable that two different scholiasts would make up two different mnemonic stanzas, each giving a perfectly fictitious series of figures, with the total exactly hundred,

1 It will be noticed that 17 (out of the aggregate of 19) names of the (major) parvans, in this scheme, are identical with the names of the *initial* (sub-)parvan of each group. This is valuable because it suggests how the names of the 19 (major) parvans were obtained from the (older) list of the hundred (sub-)parvans.

for the number of chapter-groups in each of the eighteen books of the epic? These stanzas establish, in my opinion, irrefutably that as late as the time of Arjunamiśra the total number of (sub-)parvans was believed to be *exactly* one hundred, and (what is much more important) the exact number of (sub-)parvan in *each* of the (major) parvans was also believed to be *accurately* known. Whether or not these figures tallied exactly with the actual divisions of the version of the text prepared by these commentators is an entirely different question, which I am not yet prepared to answer in the affirmative. These stanzas stand, in my opinion, for an effort to save from the limbo of oblivion some precious fragment of traditional knowledge regarding the epic. Like fossils these skeletons of the old Parvasaṁgraha-parva have survived, despite the frantic efforts of centuries of editors and critics to make the "Table of Contents" agree with the form of the text known to them.

Many of EDGERTON'S suggestions and queries relate to the uses of the wavy line: mostly cases where he has either less or [178] more confidence in the readings I have adopted. This device, as EDGERTON himself admits, is "by its very nature hard to apply strictly and consistently." Moreover, most of the words cited by him are merely commonplace adverbs, conjunctions and other expletives like *caiva, āhuḥ* (v. l. *viduḥ*), *iha, vai, tv-atra, cāpi, kim-vā* (v. l. *vā kim*) and so on. I will therefore forbear from entering into a detailed discussion of the relative merits of the variants, especially as, in the majority of the cases, the manuscript evidence is so conflicting that absolute certainty is impossible.

I cannot conclude this paper without expressing both to Professor EDGERTON and to Dr. WELLER my cordial thanks for the very kind remarks they have to make regarding the work in general, and my keen appreciation of the uniformly courteous tone of their very sympathetic reviews.

II. Further Text-critical Notes.*

The organizers of the new Indian project of preparing a critical edition of the Mahābhārata are deeply indebted to both Geheimrat LÜDERS and Professor WINTERNITZ not merely for their taking personally a keen interest in the scheme, but for their bringing the project formally to the notice of the savants assembled at the historic XVIIth International Congress of Orientalists held at Oxford in August 1928, and moving resolutions conveying messages of appreciation and congratulation.[1] A singularly happy feature of this event was that this gesture of cordial sympathy and willing co-operation should have proceeded spontaneously from just those two

* [*ABORI*, 11. 165-191].

[1] The text of the resolution moved by Geheimrat LÜDERS and adopted unanimously by the Indian Section of the Congress has been published by WINTERNITZ in *Indologica Pragensia*, 1, 63.

veteran scholars who not merely enjoy the greatest amount of respect and confidence in the world of Indologists but whose names are most intimately connected with the earlier scheme of the International Association of Academies of publishing a critical edition of our Great Epic. It is a matter of high gratification to the members of the Mahābhārata Editorial Board that their modest efforts in the cause of Mahābhārata studies are being so keenly appreciated by their fellow workers in Europe, just as it is a matter of relief to the responsible editors that the general method and principles underlying the preparation of this edition have won the warm approval of the two eminent European critics[1] who have themselves made the closest study of the central textual problem and enriched the literature on the subject by the contribution of several valuable papers and monographs.

At the said session of the Congress of Orientalists, WINTERNITZ read a paper entitled "The Critical Edition of the Mahābhārata", dealing with the history of the project from its early beginnings. Much of what WINTERNITZ says in this [166] memorable address of his bears the unmistakable stamp of being personal reminiscences, because he was the first scholar who more than thirty years ago, at the XIth International Congress of Orientalists held in Paris (1897), emphasized the superlative importance of a critical edition of the Mahābhārata and proposed measures for its preparation.[2]

After nearly thirty years of restless endeavour, he is again one of the small group of the first collaborators of the great and ambitious project. During 1922-3 he used his opportunities as a Guest Professor at the University of the poet philosopher Rabindranath TAGORE to train some of his advanced pupils at the Viśvabhāratī to do collation work, thus helping to establish there a centre for the collation of Bangālī MSS. of the Mahābhārata,[3] a centre which is still doing excellent work under the supervision of the Principal, Pandit Vidhushekhara BHATTACHARYA. Finally, WINTERNITZ has taken over some of the editorial burden on his own shoulders by kindly agreeing to edit for the Institute one Parvan, the Sabhāparvan. This is indeed a very happy augury for the continued success of our cherished project.

To the text of his Congress address, which he has published in the first issue of his Journal, *Indologica Pragensia*, Vol. 1 (1929), pp. 58-63, WINTERNITZ has appended (pp. 64-68) some critical remarks on my edition of the Ādiparvan. While expressing his whole-hearted agreement with the general principles underlying my reconstruction of the text, he has given a long list of passages in which he differs from me with respect to the readings of the constituted text. With unerring judgement he has picked out those

---

1 Cf. WINTERNITZ, *ABI*. 5. 24, 30, and *Ind. Prag.* 1. 62, 67; LÜDERS, *Deutsche Literaturzeitung*, 1929 (Heft 24), Sp. 1137-1146.

2 Cf. also *ABI*. 4. 145 ff.

3 Annual Report of the B. O. R. I. for 1922-23, p. 11 f.

passages in the first two adhyāyas that had given me most trouble, and he has criticized the readings of the constituted text, weighing the pros and cons with great acumen, and pointing out the errors and imperfections with much delicacy and courtesy. While tendering him my cordial thanks for the honour he has done me by making so close and penetrating a study of my critical work, I shall endeavour here briefly to answer his queries and criticism. I write these notes not so much to justify my selection and establish the readings of the critical edition as [167] to set forth the reasons that have guided me in the choice of the readings in question and that may not have occurred to my critic—remarks which will not fail to throw some fitful light on the obscure and complicated processes which go to make up Mahābhārata textual criticism.

* *

MINOR QUESTIONS.

1. 1. 30 : WINTERNITZ observes that "in the notes the interesting remark of Arjunamiśra is given ; *parameṣṭhy atha iti prāyaśaḥ pāṭhaḥ*, but the actual reading of the Da MSS. is not given". The reading of the Da MSS. not being *specifically* mentioned, it must, in conformity with a tacitly assumed Paribhāṣā, be taken to be the same as the text reading, namely, *parameṣṭhy atha*. In that sense the reading of the Da MSS. (i.e. of Arjunamiśra) *has* been given, and my note is both complete and correct, because both the Da MSS. collated for the passage do, in point of fact, read *parameṣṭhy atha*.[1] Nevertheless, as I discovered on referring to the commentary once more, the note does not represent the facts fully and correctly, because the MSS. which are corrupt, being contaminated from the vulgate, had succeeded, for the time being, in completely misleading me.

That the true Arjunamiśra reading must, against the testimony of MSS., be assumed to be *parameśvaraḥ* (agreeing then with B_2 $D_{0\text{-}8}$ C_d) follows, with certainty, from the commentary itself, a fact I had overlooked when I wrote the note. The commentary runs thus :

मनुः प्रसिद्धः। कः वसिष्ठः। तस्य विशेषणं परमेश्वरः प्रजापतित्वात्। परमेष्ठ्यथ इति प्रायशः पाठः। परमेष्ठी कश्यपः।

In the Foreword to Fascicule 1 (p. 1), I have already drawn attention to the fact that "the (epic) text in the Arjunamiśra codices is frequently contaminated from the "vulgate" and has to be corrected with the help of Arjunamiśra's commentary." The examples cited there are 1. 1. 17*b* and

---

1 A reference to Prof. LÜDERS' *Druckprobe* (p. 6) will show that the (Devanāgarī) MSS. of Arjunamiśra's commentary collated by him for his Specimen edition read likewise *parameṣṭhy atha ;* only in one instance has the reading been corrected (by a later hand) to *parameśvaraḥ*. Accordingly Prof. LÜDERS has also taken *parameṣṭhy atha* as the reading of the version of Arjunamiśra.

22*b*. In the former case, the Da MSS. read *puṇyāṁ* (like the vulgate, with which the constituted text here agrees; the true Arjunamiśra [168] reading is, however, *puṇya-*, as follows clearly from Arjunamiśra's own observation :

पुण्यमन्थार्थसंयुताम् । पुण्यौ मन्थार्थौ श्रुतमात्रस्य ज्ञातमात्रस्य च पुण्यहेतुत्वात् । मन्थो मथ्यमानः शब्दसमूहः । अर्थो वाच्यादिरेव ।

In the latter case (1. 1. 22 *b*), likewise, the Da MSS. read *śivam*, agreeing with many K and D MSS.; but the commentary shows (as I have pointed out in the notes) that the true Arjunamiśra reading is *śucim*, agreeing with the constituted text, *śivam* being only a variant mentioned by the scholiast :

अनर्घं निष्पापमनवद्यं वा । अनुपाधि विश्वोपकारकत्वात् । अत एव शुचिम् । शिवमिति पाठे शिवं कल्याणं महेश्वरं वा ।

I must here add, therefore, a word of caution. In the critical notes published with the text, the readings as actually found in the (epic) *text* (in contradistinction to the commentary) of the Arjunamiśra codices have, as a rule, been taken to represent the readings of Arjunamiśra; the commentary was consulted by me only occasionally, in case of doubt or difficulty, or when a *pāṭhāntara* was noticed. It is, therefore, more than likely that, owing to the fact our Da MSS. are conflated by contamination with various types of MSS., in particular with the Nīlakaṇṭha type, a few errors of the kind pointed out by WINTERNITZ may have inadvertently crept in. Such errors can be rectified only by working through the whole commentary, word for word, and comparing the lemmata with the (epic) text of the MSS.; even then one can of course be sure only of the words and passages actually cited and explained by the scholiast.

The version of Arjunamiśra, as I pointed out in the Foreword to Fascicule 1 (p. v), is closely allied to the Bangālī version. The reason for this affinity (as I have stated elsewhere) appears to be that Arjunamiśra was a native of Bengal.[1] Following the example of my predecessors, I have utilized, for the critical edition of the Ādiparvan, Devanāgarī MSS. of Arjunamiśra's commentary. The two MSS. I am using are extremely corrupt. In fact, all the MSS. of Arjunamiśra's commentary I have seen—and they are all Devanāgarī MSS.—have been remarkably corrupt. Not only that, the text they offer is, as already remarked, obviously contaminated from the [169] vulgate. This corruption of the Devanāgarī MSS. I could not account for at first; but it must be due, I cannot but think now, to their being copies of Bangālī or Maithilī originals. It would, therefore, be expedient to procure and use, whenever possible, Bangālī[2] or Maithilī MSS. of Arjuna-

---

[1] See my note on Arjunamiśra in the *Dr. Modi Memorial Volume*, p. 565 ff.

[2] The Asiatic Society of Bengal does contain some Bengali MSS. (Descrip-

miśra's commentary, treating his version as an offshoot of the Bangālī (respectively Maithilī) version.[1]

* * *

1. 1. 62 : WINTERNITZ points out that the lengthy interpolation App. I, No. 1 = (B.) 1. 1. 55*cd*—93 is inserted in the R. A. S. Whish MS. No. 65 after 62*ab*, and not after 62, as in most of the Southern MSS. used by me. But two of my MSS. (T_1 G_7) also insert the passage in question after 62*ab*, like the Whish MS.; only between 62*ab* and the Appendix passage, my MSS. further interpolate 29*, 64 and 30*, as stated in the very note cited by WINTERNITZ. The point of insertion of this interpolation varied in the different MSS. Thus of the MSS. collated by Prof. LÜDERS for his *Druckprobe*, two G_2 [? read G_3] T_2 read it after 62*ab*, while two others (G_2 T_1) read it after 62 ; moreover, in T_2 (of the *Druckprobe*) the inserted passage is preceded by 29*, 64 and 65 (somewhat like T_1 G_7)[2]

* * *

1. 1. 131 : The printer's devil, I regret to say, is responsible for the erroneous spelling *Saṁsaptaka*—(with dental *s*) in this stanza ; the correct spelling *Saṁśaptaka*—(with palatal *ś*) is given at 1. 2. 56 and 160. Moreover, the various readings have been given only at 1. 2. 56, and, through some unfortunate oversight, omitted at 1. 1. 131 and 1. 2. 160. I make good the omission here. At 1. 1. 131 the various readings are as follows . $K_{0.\ 2-4.6}$ B_4 Da Da_1. n_3 Dr_1 r_3. r_4 $D_{1-4.\ 6.\ 7.\ 10.\ 14}$ T_1 *Saṁsapata*°; K_1 B_{1-3} Dn_2 Dr_2 $D_{5.\ 8.\ 9.\ 11.\ 12}$ T_2 G (G_1. 2 om.) M *Saṁśapta*° ; V_1 *Śaṁsapta*° ; K_5 D_{13} missing. At 1. 2. 160 they are: $K_{0.\ 2-4.\ 6}$ V_1 Da_2 Dn Dr_1. r_4 $D_{2-4.\ 7.\ 10-14}$ [170] T_1 G_7 *Saṁsapta*° ; K_1 B Da_1 Dr_2. r_3 $D_{1.\ 5.\ 6.\ 8.\ 9}$ T_2 $G_{1.\ 3-6}$ *Saṁśapta*° ; G_2 *Śaṁsapta*° ; K_5 missing ; M om.

From the readings of the three passages in question, it should seem that, anomalies apart, K_1 (or the India Office Codex), Bangālī and Southern MSS. read it correctly (that is, with the palatal *ś*), while the rest of K agrees with the commentators in reading it with the dental *s*. The balance of probability inclines to the side of the palatal, I think, even if we restrict ourselves to the MS. evidence. C. V. VAIDYA (*The Mahābhārata : A Criticism*, p. 159) speaks of them as the "7 clans who came probably from the Afagan (*sic*) borders," but it seems to me more likely that they got their nickname from the fact that they had bound themselves by an oath to kill Arjuna or die in the great Bhārata battle (Droṇap. 17).

* * *

---

tive Catalogue, vol. 5, Nos. 3371-3374, 3422), but it is very difficult to move the Society to send out its MSS. on loan.

1 That would also account for the frequent divergence of Da from the D class.

2 The passage is found inserted not only after 62*ab* and 62, but also after 26, 53*ab*, 59*ab* (according to the *Druckprobe*), and 60.

1. 2. 85 : The spurious line (102*) *kūṭasya Dhārtarāṣṭreṇa preṣaṇaṁ Pāṇḍavān prati* stands in the MSS. *not* before 97* (as WINTERNITZ imagines and very naturally), but after 101*, as correctly stated in the critical notes. I have re-examined the MSS. concerned on the point and find that my note is perfectly correct. One cannot be dogmatic about the Mahābhārata MSS.; there is no knowing what they may or may not contain. The line was found only in six Nīlakaṇṭha MSS. in Devanāgarī or Bangālī characters, collated for the first two adhyāyas. In all these six MSS. the line is found interpolated at the same place, the place mentioned in the critical apparatus (namely, after 101*), although all printed editions without exception place it elsewhere (namely, before 97*), which is no doubt the reason of WINTERNITZ's remark. A note drawing attention to this patent discrepancy might have been usefully added in the critical notes. But I have found the printed editions so arbitrary and unreliable[1] that I have almost [171] completely ignored them in the foot-notes, which have necessarily to be rather brief and to the point. The meaning of this enigmatic line found in Nīlakaṇṭha MSS. is as obscure to me as the cause of its transposition in the first printed edition. We need not inquire why the line occurs in the wrong place in the other editions as well, since the subsequent editors appear to have studiously and uniformly avoided consulting MSS. WINTERNITZ could easily convince himself of the correctness of my statement regarding the point of insertion of this line in the MSS. by referring to the superb complete copy of the Mahābhārata in Śāradā characters, with Nīlakaṇṭha's scholium, he purchased in Kaśmīr during his stay there.

* * *

1. 2. 102 : Da Dn Dr do have *magnām* and *Draupadīm*, as found in the printed editions and as rightly surmised by WINTERNITZ. This group has, through oversight, completely dropped out of the long list of MSS. that read *Draupadīm*, and I am thankful to WINTERNITZ for drawing my attention to it. The correction will be duly notified in the list of Errata, which will be added at the end of the volume. In passing I may draw attention to the superiority of the K MSS., the only group which, as WINTERNITZ rightly remarks, gives the undoubtedly correct rendering of the whole stanza ; all other MSS.—even such as do not contain the interpolated line 112*—are in utter confusion.

* * *

---

1. The Kumbhakonam edition contains a misleading colophon after its adhyāya 100, which is not found in *any* MS. and is, moreover, unnecessary.—All printed editions contain the line (B.1.28.4*cd*=K. 1.28. 5*cd*)

gurur hi sarvabhūtānāṁ brāhmaṇaḥ parikīrtitaḥ |

which is not found even in Nīlakaṇṭha MSS. The note on 1.74.12 mentions a line (B. 1. 79. 13 *ef* = K. 1. 73. 23 *ab*)

maraṇaṁ śobhanaṁ tasya iti vidvajjanā viduḥ |

which was not found in any of the 60 MSS. collated for that adhyāya !

MAJOR QUESTIONS.

1. 1. 129 : *yadāśrauṣaṁ Śukrasūryau ca yuktau*
Kaunteyānām anulomau jayāya |
nityaṁ cāsmāñ śvāpadā vyābhaṣantas
tadā nāśaṁse vijayāya Saṁjaya ||

This is indeed a difficult case, and I for my part doubt whether any definite decision can be reached as to how the stanza originally read. I must say, I cannot share the confidence with which WINTERNITZ decides for the reading :

yadā Vāyuḥ Śakrasūryau ca yuktau,

which is mentioned as a pāṭha by Nīlakaṇṭha and was adopted in the *editio princeps*. It is one of the eight rival readings and is found chiefly in the Bangālī version, and in MSS. and editions allied to or influenced by it. The combinations found [172] in the different MSS. may be arranged schematically as follows :

	Vāyu	*Śakra*		*Sūrya* :	Majority of N
	Vāyu	*Śukra*		*Sūrya* :	K_1 + some D
	Vāyu		*Candra*	*Sūrya* :	Dn
(a)śrauṣam		*Śukra*		*Sūrya* :	Text (T $G_{1.5.6}$)
(a)śrauṣam		*Śakra*		*Sūrya* :	Majority of M
(a)śrauṣam			*Candra*	*Sūrya* :	A few G
(a)śrauṣam	*Vāyu*			*Sūrya* :	D_5 (inferior MS.)
(a)śrauṣam	*Vāyu*	*Śakra*		*Sūrya* :	M_1 (conflated)

According to WINTERNITZ, the stanza refers to (B.) 7. 7. 34 ff. "where the line *vātoddhūtaṁ rajas tīvram* etc., also testifies to the reading *vāyuḥ*, while *śakra* (= Indra) probably refers to the rain of pieces of flesh, bones and blood." To start with I doubt whether Śakra could be held responsible for the "rain" of flesh, bones, and sundry other articles ; but that is a minor point, immaterial to the present discussion. In believing, however, that our stanza refers to (B.) 7. 7. 34 ff., WINTERNITZ is partly mistaken, as will presently appear. The important point is that in the opinion of WINTERNITZ the stanza alludes to certain forces of Nature, certain elements, such as wind, rain and so on, which were favourable to the Pāṇḍavas and unfavourable to the Kauravas. The commentators Nīlakaṇṭha, Arjunamiśra and Devabodha (with the readings which they had adopted or which were before them) have explained the stanza in a similar way. I hold a different view, however. When I selected the reading of the constituted text, I thought—and I still think—that in this stanza there is allusion not to the elements, but to some *astrological* factor or constellation—an allusion which was not understood by commentators and which I could not then fully explain. On reading the criticism of Prof. WINTERNITZ, I therefore made a reference to my friend Prof. Jyotish Chandra GHATAK, M. A., of Calcutta University, who has made a special study of Indian Astrology and allied sciences and is rightly regarded as an authority on these topics ; and I was not disappointed. Having already worked through the whole of the Mahābhārata in special search of references which have a bearing on Astrology, Augury and kindred subjects, he could at once lay his fingers on the right passage, the prototype of our stanza, which throws a flood of light on the question, without however fully solving the riddle of the stanza, so far as I can judge. The said stanza, (B.) 6. 20. 2, reads :

[173] [Dhṛtarāṣṭra to Saṁjaya]

केषां जघन्यौ सोमसूर्यौ सवायू
केषां सेनां श्वापदा व्याभषन्त ।
केषां यूनां मुखवर्णाः प्रसन्नाः
सर्वं ह्येतद् ब्रूहि तत्त्वं यथावत् ॥

While the connection between the two stanzas is patent and indeed unquestionable, the discovery of the prototype leaves, unfortunately, most of our real difficulties unsolved. The reading which agrees closest with that of the Bhīṣmaparvan stanza is that of the vulgate text and is found *only* in the MSS. of Nīlakaṇṭha. These latter have Vāyu-Chandra-Surya (lacking Śakra or Śukra altogether) like Soma-Sūrya-Vāyu of the Bhīṣmaparvan. Is the Nīlakaṇṭha reading then the *original* reading? As I have pointed out elsewhere, we are apt to prefer, at first sight, the readings of the vulgate, which appear to be better than those of the critical text ; but that is only because the text of the vulgate has been arrived at by the purging of the original by the continuous emendations of scholars for centuries.[1] It seems to me that there is a long history behind the reading of the vulgate in the present case also. Nīlakaṇṭha had evidently arrived at it by an emendation, by collation with the prototype, because there is no indication of there being any MSS. before him which could have contained that particular combination. This fact may, perhaps, supply us with a clue to the labyrinth of the readings recorded in the critical notes for the line in question. An important factor is that Śukra (or Śakra), which persistently occurs in all the various categories of our MSS. and which must, therefore, be regarded as an essential feature of our stanza, is entirely lacking in the later stanza. This proves irrefutably that the combination of the former was not *identical*, in every respect, with that of the latter originally. That is an important point to remember. WINTERNITZ is emphatic in asserting that *yadā Vāyuḥ* of the original was changed in S into the usual *yadāśrauṣam*. This assumption does not seem to me to

---

1 See my Epic Studies (I), *JBBRAS*. (NS.) 4 (1928). 157. A patent example of correction is *gṛhitvā haraṇaṁ prāpte* (in Devanāgarī MSS.) for *haraṇaṁ gṛhya saṁprāpte* (1. 2. 93).

be at all well founded, because the very next stanza (130) begins *yadā Droṇo vividhān astramārgān*, and here no attempt has been made in S (or anywhere else) to change the beginning into *yadāśrauṣam*. There are a few more stanzas (133, 140, 145) in [174] this series which do not begin with the oft-repeated formula. It seems to me much more likely, therefore, that Vāyu was introduced into our passage, secondarily, by some early Northern redactor who knew the prototype and had noticed the omission of one of the elements in the prior stanza ; precisely as Nīlakaṇṭha, much later, appears to have further altered the line by changing the difficult Śakra (or Śukra) to Candra, thus equating the combination to that of the prototype. I therefore adhere to my original choice, explaining the genesis of the variants as follows. The stanza in question, which was suggested to the author of the *yadāśrauṣam* section by the Bhīṣmaparvan stanza but was composed from a vague recollection of the original, began like the other stanzas of the series, and contained, moreover, an allusion to an *astrological* situation. Some Northern redactor (who had known the Bhīṣmaparvan stanza and noticed that the first stanza did not contain Vāyu) then deleted *(a)śrauṣam* and substituted for it the missing Vāyu, retaining, however, the original feature Śukra. The corruption of Śukra into Śakra must be judged as easy and even natural (in juxtaposition with Sūrya), in view of the famous episode of the Mahābhārata which narrates how Indra, disguised as a mendicant Brahman, begs for the miraculous ear-rings and the armour which had been Karṇa's from his birth and which had made him invincible. The emendatory activity of the early Northern redactor was continued by Nīlakaṇṭha, who expunged the Śakra (or Śukra) which he found in his MSS. (and perhaps did not fully understand) and substituted for it Candra, thus equating the two combinations.

I am confirmed in the supposition that the original line contained only two agencies instead of three by the fact that no MSS. hitherto collated show *yuktāḥ* (plu.) for *yuktau* (dual) in the first line, as they certainly would have done, had there been three names in the original instead of two, as I have given.[1]

The question then arises whether Śukra and Sūrya, as *grahas*, were at that time favourable to the Pāṇḍavas or, what comes to the same thing, adverse to the Kauravas. About [175] Sūrya I cannot say. But as far as Śukra is concerned, we may safely answer the question in the affirmative. My friend Prof. GHATAK has kindly drawn my attention to a stanza in Varāhamihira's *Bṛhatsaṁhitā* which, if *dyūtajīvin* may be taken to apply to the

[1] It should be noted that even in the explanation of WINTERNITZ, Śakra and Sūrya do not make any *combined* effort. If the three elements wind, rain and sun operate all together for the success of the Pāṇḍavas, then *yuktāḥ* is indeed the correct word. What is the point of the dual, when the plural form would be even metrically equally suitable ?

Kauravas, would indicate that at the time of the Bhārata battle the planet Śukra, which was then in the Pūrvābhādrapadā (cf. 6. 3. 15), was in a position which augured disaster to the Kauravas and was therefore favourable (*anuloma*) to the Pāṇḍavas. The *Bṛhatsaṁhitā* reference (9. 34) supplied to me by my friend runs.

शतभिषजि शौण्डिकानामजैकपे द्यूतजीविनां पीडा ।
कुरुपाञ्चालानामपि करोति चास्मिन्सितः सलिलम् ॥

As Vāyu is missing in the whole of S except M_1 (which latter is a conflated MS.), it can never be established that Vāyu is an *essential* element of the original stanza ; on the other hand, (*a*)*śrauṣam*, though of course no less doubtful because it is documented also by only half of the entire evidence, is rendered probable, if not required, by the context. But I am prepared to leave the line as "less than certain," as indicated by the wavy line below the words in question.

* * *

1\. 1. 180 : *tava putrair mahattamāḥ.*

WINTERNITZ complains that the sentence is "very awkward grammatically". To have called forth no less than nine attempts at emendation, the original must indeed have been most awkward. WINTERNITZ prefers to read *tava putrair mahattarāḥ*, pointing out that there is not much evidence for the text reading. It is quite true that the text is weakly supported ; but so are almost all the readings except that of the vulgate, which certainly cannot be considered the original reading, as it is palpably an emendation. The text is based on $K_{1.6}$ $G_{5.6}$ only. But WINTERNITZ's reading is not much better supported ; in its entirety it is found only in K_3 M ; because, of the MSS. which do contain the questionable *mahattarāḥ*, K_0 begins the pāda with *tvatputrair ye* and K_4 with *tvatsutebhyo*. I submit, therefore, that the reading preferred by WINTERNITZ is not better documented than mine. That is the first point. WINTERNITZ then seeks to explain the variation on the ground that the scribes must have found difficulties with the [176] instr. *putraiḥ*. Now the so-called *instr. comparationis* is very common in both epics and, I submit, that alone would not account for this plethora of readings in the case of a simple line with a perfectly obvious meaning. I know instances in the Mahābhārata text where this *instr. comparationis* has called forth no variants at all in the MSS., no doubt because it was felt to be quite normal by the copyists, editors and readers alike. The cause of disturbance in this case must, therefore, be looked for elsewhere, and that was principally, I think, the use of the superlative joined to the instrumental.

In settling the original reading, the question is primarily one of fact, of the actual MS. evidence, not of grammar. The Shakespearean "This was the most unkindest cut of all" cannot be judged and emended by modern standards of grammar. It sounds harsh to our ears; but there is, I suppose, sufficient documentary evidence to prove or make it probable that the line as I have quoted it was in point of fact written by the author of *Julius Cæsar* (who knew his English quite as well as, if indeed not better than, we do), consciously or unconsciously using what our purists stigmatize as vulgarism. The argument that a dramatist like Shakespeare could not commit such a blunder (if blunder it be) would be without cogency, when the MS. evidence supports the questionable reading.

The Mahābhārata, I may point out here, has suffered from the great misfortune of being always edited by learned Paṅdits, who were concerned more about the purity of diction than with the determination and preservation of the words of the author or the authors of the epic. One of the very worst offenders in this way was Pandit BÖHTLINGK who, in the passages edited by him in his *Sanskrit-Chresthomathie*, has "corrected" away the few oddities of idiom and style of the original which had escaped the vigilence of mediaeval Indian scholiasts and editors and found their way stealthily into our printed editions ![1]

[177] The nine variants mentioned in the critical notes may be classified as follows. Readings

(1) in which the comparison is emphasized

(a) by change of the superl. to the comp.:

त्वत्पुत्रैर्ये महत्तराः । K_0
तव पुत्रैर्महत्तराः । K_3 D_{14} M

(b) by a double change of superl. to comp. and of instr. to abl. (the "correct" construction):

त्वत्सुतेभ्यो महत्तराः । K_4 (inferior MS.);

(2) in which the awkward instr. is done away with

(a) by changing the instr. into abl.:

त्वत्पुत्रेभ्यो महत्तमाः । K_2
तव पुत्रान्महत्तमाः । V_1

---

1 In the Pauṣyaparvan (Adip. 3), especially, his editorial activities are very much in evidence. He has not only introduced, with scrupulous care, the correct Sandhi wherever it was at all possible, he has substituted the correct *bandhum* for the (irregular) *baddhum* (1. 3. 21), found even in the printed editions and made many similar "corrections" independently of the MS. evidence. Most amusing, however, is his regular and systematic substitution of the correct form, as required by the Sūtra of Pāṇini, out of *etad* and *enad*, a rule probably unknown at any time to anybody outside a select coterie of Ācāryas of Vyākaraṇa.

(b) by using the adj. predicatively (mostly in G) :

तत्पुत्राश्च महत्तमाः । T_2 $G_{1-3.\ 4m.7}$

तव पुत्रा महत्तमाः । G_4 ;

(3) in which the line has been recast (the vulgate) :

तव पुत्रा इव प्रभो । K_6 B D (mostly) T_1 ;

and (4) corrupt :

तव पुत्रैर्महात्मनोः । D_{10}.

It is an admittedly sound principle of textual criticism to give preference to a reading which best suggests how the other readings may have arisen, and it would be hard, I think, to find another reading which could explain all these nine variants more satisfactorily. WINTERNITZ's choice, for instance, does not at all explain the origin of any of the readings which contain *mahattamāḥ* (superl.) such as 2 (a) and (b) and the text reading ; because there is in that case nothing to be gained by changing the (supposed) original comparative into superlative.[1]

En passant it may be pointed out that the so-called *instr. comparationis* is not a distinct category of the comparative at all ; it is only a special case of the (Prakritic) coalescence of the instr. and abl. pl. (*metri causa*), an equivalence which comes out very clearly in such parallel phrases as :

नरः पापात्प्रमुच्यते । 1. 1. 198

[178] and

सर्वपापैः प्रमुच्यते ।[2] 1. 1. 209 and 494 *.

The latter does not mean "he is *left by* all sins" but "he is *freed from* all sins."

That the superlative is used in the epic in the sense of the comparative[3] may be seen from :

तेषां के योगवित्तमाः । Gītā 12. 1

न च तस्मान्मनुष्येषु कश्चिन्मे प्रियकृत्तमः । ibid. 18. 69

"Of these which are *more versed in Yoga?*" "Nor among men shall there be any whose service is *dearer* to me than his."

The superlative is normally construed with the gen. or loc.; but that it is

---

1 Unless it be a scribe's error perpetuated through centuries or repeated independently in different places and times.

2 This pāda recurs frequently in the Rāmāyaṇa also.

3 These derivative forms have probably a merely intensive value, and do not necessarily and invariably connote comparison. The Prakrits frequently confuse the *tara* and the *tama* endings. It is further worth noting that a separate formation of the comparative and superlative is unknown to the Modern Indian dialects. The epics also sporadically furnish instances of the use of the *positive* in the sense of the comparative.

construed sometimes also with the abl. may be seen not merely from the example last cited but also from :

अपि चेदसि पापेभ्यः सर्वेभ्यः पापकृत्तमः । ibid. 4. 36

"Though thou art of all sinners the most sinful."

Then the above-mentioned equivalence of the instr. and abl. pl. ushers in finally the construction of the superlative with the instr., which we find in the passage in question.

Formally the two constructions *tava putrair mahattarāḥ* and *tava putrair mahattamāḥ* are almost equivalent ; but there *may* be just a slight difference of meaning between the two locutions. While *tava putrair mahattarāḥ* (comp.) evidently means only "greater than thy sons", the other clause (*tava putrair mahattamāḥ*) may have been intended to convey some such sense as "*far, very much,* greater than thy sons."

It may be finally observed that in dealing with the first two adhyāyas of the Ādiparvan (as in fact with the whole of the earlier portion of this Parvan) the critic should never forget that he has before him what HOPKINS has justly called the "pseudo-epic" : the poetasters responsible for the compilation of these passages are capable of the worst blunders of every description.

* * *

[179] 1. 1. 209 : *mahattvād bhāravattvāc ca.*

As WINTERNITZ rightly observes, here the MS. evidence is almost evenly balanced. Moreover, graphically there is so little difference between the rival readings that we cannot expect much help from the side of the MSS., though it may be pointed out that their evidence inclines, if at all, just a trifle to the side of the text reading. WINTERNITZ (*Ind. Ant.* 27. 93) admits that the lines (69*) *caturbhyaḥ* etc. and *tadā prabhṛti etc.* are "quite superfluous." When these lines are expunged from the text, as has been done by me, the line *mahattve ca gurutve ca* of 208*e*) stands adjacent to *mahattvād bhāra°* (of 209*a*). The idea of 208*e* is evidently reflected and repeated in 209*a*. Just as *mahattvāt* corresponds to *mahattve,* so *bhāra°* should correspond to *gurutve.* This clearly shows, as far as I can judge, that the doubtful word (*bhāra°*), which should be a paraphrase of *gurutve,* must be *bhāravattvāt* and not *bhāratatvāt.* The latter seems to be an emendation made by some revisor who wanted to squeeze in somehow the significant word *Bhārata* into the context ; and, it must truthfully be confessed, it is a very ingenious emendation indeed. But as to which is the orginal reading there cannot be much doubt. The importance that WINTERNITZ (like BÜHLER, *Ind. Stud.* 2. 9 f., before him) attaches to the circumstance that the verse is quoted in (our edition of) Kumārila's Tantravārtika with the reading *bhāratatvāt* is wholly unjustifiable, and that for two reasons : firstly, because we have no critical edition of the Tantravārttika, and so we cannot be wholly sure of what the

MSS. actually read at that place; and secondly, because, even if Kumārila should, in point of fact, have quoted the verse with *bhāratatvāt*, it does not at all follow that this is *ipso facto* the *original* reading, notwithstanding that Kumārila's work is far older than the extant Mahābhārata MSS; because Kumārila may have cited the stanza from one or the other of the versions which contained (and still contain) that reading. Or again he may have known both variants and preferred, for reasons similar to those adduced by BÜHLER and WINTERNITZ, the variant rejected by me.

The situation is somewhat clearer and the facts better capable of demonstration in the case of the other great mediaeval commentator Śaṁkarācārya. In many cases when the readings of the Mahābhārata verses and stanzas cited by him [180] differ from those of the Bombay and Calcutta editions, I was able to identify Śaṁkarācārya's readings in the Southern MSS. Being a Southerner, he had naturally studied and cited from the Southern recension of the Mahābhārata. It is quite clear that he was not going to work through all available MSS. and establish the original reading of the numerous Mahābhārata stanzas cited by him in the course of his voluminous commentaries. Therefore his citations, although of far greater antiquity than the oldest of our extant Mahābhārata MSS., do not necessarily give us in every case the "original" readings. Saṁkara's testimony applies to and affects mainly the version or the recension used or cited by him; and that was probably the Southern recension in its Malayālam version. Even in the time of the Ācārya the Northern MSS. must have read differently in places, as they do now, because the divagation of the recensions must be assumed to be far older than the epoch of the great Vedantist.

I shall give only one example in order to clarify my meaning. 1. 1. 37 of the critical edition reads *yathartāv ṛtuliṅgāni*, agreeing with other printed editions and with the majority of the MSS. of the Northern recension. Śaṁkarācārya in his Bhāṣya on the Brahmasūtra (1. 3. 30; Ānandāśrama ed., p. 313) cites, however, the verse with the reading *yathartuṣv ṛtuliṅgāni*.[1] Now this reading is found only in Southern MSS. and in such of the Northern MSS. as can be shown to be contaminated from the Southern source, but not in any Kaśmīrī or Bangālī MSS. collated so far. Here it would be clearly wrong to cite the Bhāṣya as an authority older than our MSS. to establish the text reading as *yathartuṣv ṛtuliṅgāni*. The Bhāṣya citation affects directly the Southern version only, documenting that the divergent reading of our Southern MSS. is as old as (or rather older than) the time of Śaṁkarācārya; and that is all. It does not take us beyond the Southern recension, much less beyond the two rival recensions to the archetype.

When WINTERNITZ further observes that "from the etymologizer's point of view" *bhāratatvāt* is a "better" etymology, since with the other reading

1 Only one of the Bhāṣya MSS. has our text reading.

the *ta* of the Bhārata remains unexplained, he is bringing into the discussion an element of finesse that is quite foreign to the view-point of [181] the Purāṇic writers, as will be evident from the following specimens of "etymologische Spielerei" culled from the earlier adhyāyas of the Ādiparvan:

(B.) 1. 30. 7 = line 3 of 343* (Garuḍa):

गुरुं भारं समासाद्योड्डीन एष विहंगमः ।

1. 36. 3 (Jaratkāru):

जरेति क्षयमाहुर्वै दारुणं कारुसंज्ञितम् ।

1. 56. 31 (Mahābhārata):

भारतानां महज्जन्म महाभारतमुच्यते ।

1. 69. 33 (Bharata):

भर्तव्योऽयं त्वया यस्मादस्माकं वचनादपि ।
तस्माद्भवत्वयं नाम्ना भरतो नाम ते सुतः ॥

In view of these bizarre specimens, it would be extremely strange should a Purāṇic "etymologizer" fight shy of sacrificing a *ta*, if he, for the moment, could not think of anything better.

* * *

1. 2. 2: *śuśrūṣā yadi vo viprā bruvataś ca kathāḥ śubhāḥ.*

I admit that my reconstruction of the line is not wholly satisfactory. The reading preferred by WINTERNITZ may also not appeal to other scholars, as it does not wholly appeal to me. I therefore cite here the 15 different readings found in the 48 MSS. collated for this passage, of which one (D_3), unluckily or luckily, omits the line altogether. The lines containing *ca* (to which WINTERNITZ takes exception in particular) have been underlined for the sake of ready identification.

1. शुश्रूषध्वमथो विप्रा श्रूवतो मे शुभाः कथाः । K_1
2. शुश्रूषध्वं वचो विप्रा ब्रुवतो मे कथाः शुभाः । $K_{2.3}$
३. शृणुध्वं मम वो विप्रा ब्रुवतश्च कथां शुभाः । K_4
4. शुश्रूषो मम वो विप्रा ब्रुवतश्च कथाः शुभाः । K_5 (corrupt)
5. शृणुध्वं मम भो विप्रा ब्रुवतश्च कथाः शुभाः । K_6 V_1 Dn $D_{1.5.\ 8-11}$
6. शुश्रूषा मम वो विप्रा ब्रुवतश्च कथाः शुभाः । B Da (Da_1 corrupt) D_{13}
7. शृणुध्वं मम वो विप्रा ब्रुवतश्च कथाः शुभाः । Dr D_4
8. शृणुध्वं मम वै विप्रा ब्रुवतः सत्कथां शुभां । D_2
9. शृणुध्वं मम भो विप्रा ब्रुवंतश्च कथाः शुभाः । D_6
10. शुश्रूषाम वचो विप्रा ब्रुवतश्च कथाः शुभाः । $D_{7.\ 12}$
11. शुश्रूषा यदि वो विप्रा ब्रुवतश्च शुभाः कथाः । T G_6
12. शुश्रूषा यदि वो विप्रा प्रवक्ष्ये निखिलाः कथाः । $G_{2.\ 3.\ 7}$
1 . शुश्रूषा यदि वो विप्रा ब्रुवंतो मे कथाः शुभाः । $M_{2.\ 4}$

14. शुश्रूषा यदि वो विप्रा ब्रुवतो मे कथाः शुभाः । M_8

15. शुश्रूषा यदि वो विप्रा ब्रुवतश्च कथाः शुभाः । Text (K_0 D_{14} $G_{1.\ 4.5}$ M_1).

[182] As for the doubtful *ca*, I may remark that, besides its normal use as a conjunction meaning "and", *ca* is very frequently used in the Mahābhārata (and the Rāmāyaṇa) as an expletive, a pure and simple verse-filler (*pādapūraṇa*), without restriction of position, like *hi* and *vai*. It may occasionally have served as a particle of emphasis, stressing the previous word like *eva*. The second use is somewhat doubtful ; but of the first, one can find scores of perfectly clear and certain instances in any portion of the epic, even in the printed editions. In the line in question, I consider, *ca* has been used in the first sense, as a mere verse-filler. Sporadically *me*, which improves this awkward line ever so slightly, appears to have been substituted for it, independently in both recensions. The first half of the line was so uncouth that it was recast in the vulgate. There are numerous instances of lines being recast in the vulgate, as a careful study of the critical apparatus will show.

* * *

1. 2. 29 : *yat tu Śaunakasatre te Bhāratākhyānavistaram* |
ākhyāsye tatra Paulomam ākhyānaṁ cāditaḥ param ||

This is again a most difficult case, and, as WINTERNITZ rightly remarks, "full of almost hopeless editorial cruces". The reconstruction would be, therefore, almost entirely a matter of speculation. WINTERNITZ has rightly surmised that I regard the Parvasaṁgraha as an accretion later than this stanza, which, in my opinion, belongs to a much earlier stratum of the text of the Mahābhārata. That *Śaunakasatre* in line 1 is a regular trap for the unwary. Misled by the printed editions, I had myself treated the words as separate at first, realizing only much later that in this adhyāya the Sūta is addressing not Śaunaka but the Ṛṣis, among whom Śaunaka is not yet present. Śaunaka is not mentioned in the foregoing portion of the text except once, in connection with his twelve-year sacrifice in 1. 1. 1. In adhyāya 4, moreover, it is plainly stated that the Sūta first approaches the Ṛṣis assembled in the Naimiṣa forest and asks them what he should narrate. The Ṛṣis request him to await the arrival of Śaunaka. The latter, *as soon as he arrives*, asks the Sūta to relate the history of the Bhārgavas (adhy. 5). If Śaunaka was not among the audience in adhyāya 4, I do not see how he could have been there in adhyāya 2. Moreover, in the latter adhyāya the interlocutors are throughout stated as being the Ṛṣis, while it is only from adhyāya 5 onwards that Śaunaka appears in this [183] rôle. It should, therefore, seem that the reading *Śaunaka satre* is not easy to understand or explain by any means. Or does WINTERNITZ mean that it should be adopted as the *lectio difficilior* ? It would be admissible, in my opinion, only on the supposition (which is not as improbable as it may at first sight appear) that the compiler of adhyāya 2, when he wrote stanza 29, had overlooked the fact that Śaunaka was not then among the audience. I have preferred to give the "poet" the benefit of the doubt and assume that the remark is addressed to one of the Ṛṣis present.

WINTERNITZ has misunderstood my reconstruction in some other particulars as well. *yat*, at the beginning of the stanza, is not a neuter pronoun but an adverb = *yadā*. The words *āditaḥ param* offer no difficulties at all for interpretation ; *āditaḥ* does not mean "*from* the beginning," but "*at* the beginning" (= *ādau*) ; *param* = excellent." *ākhyāsye* must of course be supplied in the first line ; but that is not difficult as it is the very first word of the second line. Therefore I translate :

"But when, during Śaunaka's (sacrificial) session, I (shall narrate) to thee the very extensive Bhārata Story, then shall I narrate, to begin with, the excellent Story of Pauloma."

Even a cursory examination of the variants given in the critical notes is sufficient to convince anybody that the stanza has been recast over and over again. With its history is bound up the history of the successive additions of the three episodes Āstīka, Pauloma and Pauṣya, which appear to have been appended successively to the main text in this order. The stanza in question seems to have been written at the time of or soon after the addition of the Pauloma, but before the addition of the Pauṣya. The purpose of the line was originally not—as WINTERNITZ imagines—to state all the episodes with which the Mahābhārata begins, but to *authenticate the latest interpolation then made*, namely, the Pauloma, by making the Sūta declare beforehand his intention of narrating that ākhyāna at the beginning of the Mahābhārata. The Āstīka must have formed at that time the recognized beginning of the epic (cf. *Manvādi Bhāratam kecid Āstīkādi tathā pare* 1. 1. 50), and the Pauṣya had not yet been added. This is the state of things the constituted text envisages.

A study of the critical apparatus of this adhyāya shows that the adhyāya is best preserved in the Southern recension ; [184] in the MSS. group on which the vulgate is mainly based (namely, BD) numerous additional stanzas are found which are missing in S and $K_{0.\ 1.\ 2}$; but even the three latter MSS. occasionally include some of such additional stanzas, which also nevertheless, since they are missing in S, may safely be regarded as interpolations. Of this character is interpolation 74*, which is found in almost the whole of N and which must have been made with a view to documenting the fact—or rather the fiction—that the Mahābhārata as narrated by the Sūta to Śaunaka was *identical* with that narrated by Vaiśampāyana to Janamejaya (cf. Nīlakaṇṭha *ad loc.*). $K_{0.\ 1}$ agree with S on the reading of this stanza except for the inclusion of 74* in the one and the addition of the name of the Āstīka to the other. The text is formed by collating S with the inferable version of K before the addition in the latter of 74*. The subsequent steps leading towards the reading of the vulgate consisted in the addition of the name of the Āstīka episode (which intervenes between the Pauloma and the beginning proper of the Mahābhārata), of a statement of the identity of the Sūta-version and the Vaiśampāyana version, and finally of the name of the Pauṣya interlude, all these changes being made in our stanza with a view to setting the seal of authenticity on the three spurious additions. That adhyāya 3 must be an interpolation follows from the fact that it is wholly unconnected with the previous adhyāya and only loosely connected with what follows. Noteworthy is also the fact that adhyāyas 1 and 4 have the same beginning : *Lomaharṣaṇaputra Ugraśravāḥ sūtaḥ paurāṇiko Naimiṣāraṇye dvādaśavārṣike satre* ! And in the text itself there is no explanation why after the Sūta has finished his narration of the Pauṣya episode, it is necessary to reintroduce the Sūta in the same words as approaching the same Ṛṣis assembled at the same twelve-year sacrificial session of Śaunaka in the Naimiṣa forest. There is clearly a *new* beginning made in one of the two adhyāyas.

Since many of the intermediate links are missing in the MS. evidence, it is not possible to reconstruct the history of this portion of the text fully and satisfactorily ; but that it must be reconstructed on the lines sketched above, I have no doubt. Accordingly the successive stages in the development of the reading of the vulgate (which is the reading preferred by WINTERNITZ) I would arrange in a scheme like the following, in which the innovations have been printed in black type. [185] It will show among other things that the *vistaram* of the text and of the Southern recension is not "a remnant of *vistarārtham*" of the vulgate ; on the contrary, in the latter the first line was filled up with *uttamam* when the original *vistara* was used in the interpolated stanza. The view of WINTERNITZ that at least *Āstīkam* must remain in the text is quite untenable ; because if the stanza had *Āstīkam* there is no reason why it should not have *Pauṣyam* as well. On the other hand, if *Pauṣyam* is not indispensable, then *Āstīkam* could go with it as well.

Stage 1 (Constituted Text)

यत्तु शौनकसत्रे ते भारताख्यानविस्तरम् ।
आख्यास्ये तत्र पौलोममाख्यानं चादितः परम् ॥

Northern recension.

Stage 2 (K_1) : by addition of 2 lines to the original.

यत्तु शौनकसत्रे ते भारताख्यानमुत्तमम् ।
जनमेजयस्य तत्सत्रे व्यासशिष्येण धीमता ॥
कथितं विस्तरार्थं च यशो वीर्यं महीक्षिताम् ।
आख्यास्ये तत्र पौलोममाख्यानं चादितः परम् ॥

Stage 3 (Da $D_{2-4,\ 18}$) : by addition of आस्तीकं to stage 2.

यत्र शौनकसत्रे तु भारताख्यानमुत्तमम् ।
जनमेजयस्य तत्सत्रे व्यासशिष्येण धीमता ॥
कथितं विस्तरार्थं च यशो वीर्यं महीक्षिताम् ।
आख्यानं तत्र पौलोममास्तीकं चादितः स्मृतम् ॥

Stage 4 (Dn Dr $D_{1,5-12}$) : by addition of पौष्यं to stage 3.

यत्तु शौनकसत्रे ते भारताख्यानमुत्तमम् ।
जनमेजयस्य तत्सत्रे व्यासशिष्येण धीमता ॥
कथितं विस्तरार्थं च यशो वीर्यं महीक्षिताम् ।
पौष्यं तत्र च पौलोममास्तीकं चादितः स्मृतम् ॥

Stage 5 (B) : by addition of 1 line to stage 4.

यत्र शौनकसत्रे तु भारताख्यानमुत्तमम् ।
जनमेजयस्य तत्सत्रे व्यासशिष्येण धीमता ।
आख्यानं कथितं कृत्स्नं महाभारतमुत्तमम् ॥
[186] कथितं विस्तरार्थं च यशो वीर्यं महीक्षिताम् ।
पौष्यं तत्र च पौलोममास्तीकं चादितः स्मृतम् ॥

Southern recension.

Stage 2 (S) : by addition of आस्तीक to the original.

यत्तु शौनकसत्रे ते भारताख्यानविस्तरम् ।
आख्यास्ये तत्र पौलोममास्तीकं च ततः परम् ॥

* * *

1. 2. 46 : *mṛgasvapnabhayaṁ tataḥ*

Here again WINTERNITZ prefers the reading of the vulgate (*mṛgasvapnodbhavaṁ*). It is clearer but, I must say, I am very doubtful about its originality. The MS. support for this variant is only slightly stronger than that for the reading of the constituted text. It is worthy of note that B, which generally sides with the vulgate, has here a third and entirely different reading : *mṛgasvapno 'bhavat tataḥ* ! How would WINTERNITZ account for that ? I explain the compound of the constituted text as an irregular compound with inverted sequence, common in Prakrit (PISCHEL, *Gramm. der Prakrit-Sprachen*, § 603) and not unknown to the Low Sanskrit of the epics. HOPKINS, *JAOS*. 20 (1899), 223, has cited two instances from the Rāmāyaṇa : 7.22.36 *dṛṣṭvā daṇḍodyataṁ Yaman* (for *udyatadaṇḍam*) "like Yama with upraised staff" ; and ibid. 7. 26. 2 *tulyaparvatavarcasi* (for *parvatatulyavarcasi*) "glorious like the mountain (Kailāsa)." I accordingly take the compound in question as equivalent to *svapna (dṛṣṭa) mṛgabhayam* "(Parvan) in which there is the fright of the deer (seen) in a dream" (cf. the compound *Svapnavāsavadattam*). Yudhiṣṭhira, in any case, was *not* frightened : that is certain ; but that the deer were, follows from (K.) 3. 259. 8, which WINTERNITZ himself cites :

तान्वेपमानान्वित्रस्तान्बीजमात्रावशेषितान् ।
मृगान्दृष्ट्वा सुदुःखार्तो धर्मराजो युधिष्ठिरः ॥

The readings of the vulgate and the Bangālī version seem to represent different attempts at emendation of the irregular compound which stood originally in the Northern recension and which was perhaps misunderstood, if it was not totally unintelligible. The wavy line below the pāda was called for also by the variant reading of S, which has *parva* or *tataḥ*) *prāyopaveśanam*. This refers to an entirely different section of [187] the narrative, the name being derived from the vow of fasting taken by Duryodhana.

* * *

1\. 2. 89 : *tathā rājyārdhaśāsanam.*

The variants are °*śāsanam*, °*lambhanam*, °*sarjanam* (vulgate), °*mārgaṇam*, °*pādanam*, °*dāpanam* ! If *rājyārdhasarjanam* corresponds better to one portion of the contents of Ādip. 207, °*śāsanam* may be said to correspond better to a subsequent portion of the same adhyāya : °*sarjanam* was followed by °*śāsanam*. Intrinsically there is not much to choose between the two. The sub-parvan name is really something quite different : *rājyalambha* or °*lābha*, which has given rise to the reading of K_3 *rājyārdhalambhanam*. The reading preferred by WINTERNITZ is found only in the vulgate group supported by four Southern MSS. $G_{4.\ 5}$ $M_{1.\ 3}$. The text reading was adopted on the direct testimony of $K_{0.\ 6}$ D_2 $G_{1.\ 6}$, but it has partial support of T_2 and of two K MSS. ($K_{1.\ 2}$), one of which is the important India Office codex (K_1). These MSS. ($K_{1.\ 2}$) read as a matter of fact *rājyānuśāsanam*, but the *nu* of these MSS. is obviously wrong (perhaps representing a mislection of the ligature *rdha*), being opposed by the remainder of the MS. material collated and conveying no satisfactory sense. There appears to be an agreement between independent versions on the reading °*sarjanam*, but the concord, I believe, is only apparent, being due to the conflation of MSS. That $G_{4.\ 5}$ are contaminated from some late Northern source, I think, I have established with tolerable certainty in the note on 1. 20. 1 ; the conclusion is corroborated by many less certain instances where these MSS. (along with $G_{1.\ 2}$) agree with Northern MSS. against other Southern MSS., and the agreement cannot be regarded as one derived from their connection through the archetype.[1] That further G_7 and M_1 are not reliable representatives of the Grantha and the Malayālam versions respectively, I have already pointed out in the Foreword to Fascicule 1 (p. v). There remains only one other MS. (M_3), which represents a moderately pure (Malayālam) tradition and must

[1] For instance, cf. v. l. 1. 5. 26 (220*) ; 13. 34 (255*) ; 20. 15.

have acquired its °*sarjanam*, secondarily, through some complicated infiltration of the reading of the vulgate.

[188] In this instance, we have, moreover, a complex cross-agreement between the different versions.

°*śāsanam* : $K_{0.\ 1-2}$ D_2 + T_2 $G_{1.\ 6}$
°*sarjanam* : Vulgate (B D) + $G_{4.\ 5}$ $M_{1.\ 3}$

Graphically there is no connection between the conflicting readings. The reading of the vulgate is found in only one MS. of the K group (K_4), an inferior conflated MS. It will thus be seen that the MS. evidence is utterly confused. That being so, I have adopted the reading °*śāsanam*, giving preference to the side on which the majority of K stand, according to a principle enunciated in the Foreword to Fascicule 1 (p. VII).

* * *

1. 2. 96 : In the Editorial Note appended to Fascicule 3, I have given my reasons for selecting 7984 as the figure representing the number of ślokas in the Ādiparvan. That is the figure given by the India Office MS. (K_1) and corroborated by the Śāradā codex ($Ś_1$). It may, therefore, be regarded as the extent of the Śāradā version at any rate. I consider, as I have frequently stated, the Śāradā (Kaśmīrī) version the best version now preserved, and my edition of the Ādiparvan is based mainly (though not wholly) on this version.

I fully agree with WINTERNITZ (*op. cit.* p. 61) that the Parvasaṁgraha argument is necessarily of secondary importance and should not be pressed too far.[1] Be that as it may, it is extremely problematic whether we could make any use whatsoever of the Parvasaṁgraha enumeration in the case of the Ādiparvan at least, because it will be difficult to compute the *exact* extent of this Parvan, and that for two reasons. Firstly, because this Parvan, as is well known, contains two lengthy prose adhyāyas (3 and 90) ; and it is difficult to say [189] now how the extent of the prose sections was computed by the compilers of the Parvasaṁgraha ; our section-numbers certainly can give no indication of the extent in "Ślokas."[2] Secondly, this Parvan also contains

---

1 The exaggerated importance UTGIKAR attached to the data of the Parvasaṁgraha was, I believe, mainly due to his erroneous belief (induced probably by the misleading character of the text of the Kumbhakonam edition) that the Northern and Southern MSS. agreed completely with each other in all material particulars for this adhyāya. The Kumbhakonam edition, which claims to be an edition "mainly based on the South Indian texts", presents a text of this adhyāya which is almost identical with that of the Calcutta and Bombay editions, taking no notice of the Southern divergences, while in other sections of the epic it introduces numerous innovations which are based on the Southern tradition.

2 The lengths of the prose sections must have been computed on the basis of 32 *akṣaras* to a śloka, but such a computation in the case of long prose sections can be only approximate.

a large number of Triṣṭubh-Jagatī stanzas, which again introduce an element of uncertainty in the computation. Was each Triṣṭubh-Jagatī stanza counted as one "Śloka" or did the Bhāratacintakas compute the exact equivalent of these long-metre stanzas in "Ślokas"? No definite answer is possible as yet. The difference in the reckoning will be, however, between 40 and 50 per cent of the total. As a very rough estimate, the Ādiparvan may contain something like 500 long-metre stanzas. This factor alone would then introduce a difference of a little less than 250 "Ślokas" in the total!

We must, moreover, not lose sight of the fact that the reading of the number itself is never entirely free from doubt, since the MSS., as WINTERNITZ remarks, differ sometimes quite essentially in the Parvasaṁgraha itself; the figures differ not by units or tens, but by hundreds, and even thousands in extreme cases.[1] There can be no doubt, as I have pointed out elsewhere, that the text of the Parvasaṁgraha has been tampered with and designedly altered, in various ways, in order to make it harmonize with the inflated versions of a later epoch.[2]

These are some of the difficulties in the way of making any practical use of the figures recorded in the Parvasaṁgrahaparvan for fixing the text of the Mahābhārata. The computations may have some value for a Parvan in which there is no prose at all, which is almost wholly in Anuṣṭubh metre, and for which finally the Parvasaṁgraha figure is tolerably certain.

It is quite within the range of probability, as far as I can judge now, that the extent of the critical text of a parvan may [190] fall appreciably below or rise appreciably above the figure recorded in the second adhyāya, as is actually the case with about half the number of Parvans in the Calcutta, Bombay and Kumbhakonam editions when checked up with the figures given in their respective Parvasaṁgrahas.[3] Moreover, unless it can be made probable that the compilation of this "Table of Contents" is nearly synchronous with the final redaction of the Great Epic, this discrepancy will be without any cogency in questions relating to the constitution of the text. The value of a MS. or a version cannot be said to depend exclusively or even mainly upon its agreement with or discrepancy from the data of the Parvasaṁgraha. It must, in the first analysis, be regarded as depending upon some intrinsic criteria, upon the place it occupies in a logical and convincing scheme formu-

---

1 Thus for the Virāṭaparvan, the Northern figure is 2050, the Southern 3500; the difference therefore is 1450 ślokas.

2 Cf. the Editorial Note (2) appended to Fascicule 3 (p. iii).

3 The actual number of ślokas falls *below* the Parvasaṁgraha figure in the following 10 Parvans: Ādi, Udyoga, Bhīṣma, Sauptika, Śānti, Anuśāsana, Aśvamedhika, Āśramavāsika, Mausala and Mahāprāsthānika; while it rises *above* the other figure in the following 8 Parvans: Sabhā, Araṇya, Virāṭa, Droṇa, Karṇa, Śalya, Strī, and Svargārohaṇa.

lated to explain satisfactorily the evolution of the different extant versions and types of Mahābhārata MSS.

It should further be carefully borne in mind that even if there is an exact agreement as to extent between a constituted text and the Parvasaṁgraha, this fact alone is no guarantee of the originality and the absolute correctness of the entire text, line for line ; because the same number of stanzas could be made up in innumerable different ways by accepting or rejecting, hesitatingly, stanzas of doubtful authenticity and uncertain documentation, of which there will always be a plentiful supply in every Parvan.[1] The difficulty will finally not be solved even if we happen to light upon a unique MS. which agrees with the Parvasaṁgraha exactly and we should adopt its text verbatim ; because there is every probability that while it satisfies the one criterion of extent given by the Parvasaṁgraha, it may not satisfy, in every respect, other and more exacting critical tests when compared, line by line and word by word, with other extant MSS.

* * *

[191] 1. 2. 105 : *paurānugamanaṁ caiva dharmaputrasya dhīmataḥ.*

WINTERNITZ is mistaken in thinking that the line is missing in the *whole* of K : it is missing in only two MSS. of the group, albeit the best MSS. These MSS. ($K_{0, 1}$) are, however, by no means infallible, as a careful study of the apparatus will show. Their evidence is, therefore, rebuttable and not conclusive. In this instance, not only does the line occur in the rest of N, but there is a corresponding line in S. I cannot think that the two lines :—

Text. *paurānugamanaṁ caiva dharmaputrasya dhīmataḥ*
S (except M_1) : *paurānukampā nirvedo dharmarājasya dhīmataḥ*

could have arisen *wholly* independently of each other. Even though the purport of the lines is different, the *construction* is identical, which is a very important point in its favour. Either these lines are connected through the archetype, or else there is wholesale contamination between S and N except $K_{0, 1}$. The latter contingency being improbable in the extreme, we are led to conclude that there must have been a line of that description in the original ; only its precise reading is doubtful ; the doubtful words have accordingly been indicated in the usual manner.

* * *

The problem of the Mahābhārata textual criticism, as I have pointed out already, is a problem *sui generis*. Here the principles of textual reconstruction, which must first be evolved from a study of the MS. material and the MS. tradition, can be considered as finally settled only after considerable discussion and exchange of ideas on the subject. I would, therefore, earnestly request Prof. WINTERNITZ to continue his searching and exhaustive

---

[1] See WINTERNITZ, *ABI*, 5. 25.

examination of the fascicules as they are issued and publish periodically the results of his scrutiny, a proceeding which cannot but throw much-needed light on at least some of the difficult problems the editors have to face, and thus advance the cause of Mahābhārata studies.

III. Dr. Ruben on the Critical Edition of the Mahābhārata *

I am bound to form and express an opinion on the issues raised in the article "Schwierigkeiten der Textkritik des Mahābhārata" published in the current issue of the *Acta Orientalia* (vol. 8, pp. 240-256), in which the author, Dr. Walter RUBEN of the University of Bonn, has reviewed Fascicules 1-3 of my edition of the Ādiparvan, criticizing at considerable length and in great detail the principles underlying the preparation of the edition and the constitution of the text.

From his discursive remarks it is indeed hazardous to say what precise opinion RUBEN has formed of the critical edition. But it seems to me that his general verdict is anything but favourable.

It is not my intention to scrutinize every statement of the writer and answer all his queries and criticisms ; nor is it incumbent on me to do so ; nor even necessary, as will appear from the sequel. I shall confine my remarks to a few points of outstanding importance in RUBEN's paper which might mislead the casual reader, creating an erroneous impression regarding the value of the results achieved by the critical edition.

* * *

The Bogey of Classical Philology

At the beginning of his paper (p. 241), the learned reviewer from Bonn formally recites the canon of the *caturvarga* of the Classical Philologist. The Classical Philology, we are explained, distinguishes : 1. Heuristics, i.e. assembling and arranging the entire material consisting of MSS. and *testimonia* in the form of a genealogical tree ; 2. *Recensio*, i.e. restoration of the text of the archetype ; 3. *Emendatio*, i.e. restoration of the text of the author ; 4. " Higher Criticism," i.e. separation of the sources utilized by the author.

[260] Tested on this touchstone of the classicist, the critical edition of the Mahābhārata is found wanting in no less than three items, namely, Nos. 1, 3 and 4. The third and the fourth items of the programme, R. points out, have been left wholly untouched ; even the first has by a long way not been done full justice to by the hapless editor ![1] But as one reads on, one finds that the dereliction is after all not as serious as one might be led to

---

* [*ABORI* 11. 259-283].

1 R. has inadvertently omitted the mention of the 23 Devanāgarī MSS. in the description of my critical apparatus ; cf. *op. cit.* p. 241, lines 3-6 from the bottom.

suppose at first. For, as regards No. 1 (Heuristics), R. himself admits that it is not yet possible to concentrate the entire material, and that in all likelihood it will be for ever impossible to prepare a genealogical tree of the Mahābhārata MSS.—As for No. 3 (*Emendatio*), I must plead guilty to having perpetrated so far, perhaps somewhat unnecessarily, minor emendations in 13 instances[1] in about 3800 stanzas; that is, on an average 1 emendation in a little under 300 stanzas. R. has not taken any notice of my conjectural corrections; I take it that he approves of them. I feel greatly flattered, I must confess, by R.'s (implied) suggestion that I should have gone in more systematically and vigorously for emendation. Most scholars will, I fancy, be sincerely grateful that I have been so moderate and that I have declared it as my policy to give preference to interpretation over emendation.[2]—In speaking at all of "Higher Criticism" (No. 4 on the programme) in this connection, R. seems to show a lamentable lack of understanding of the objective of the edition, having mistaken evidently the beginning for the end of the critical work on the Mahābhārata. Higher Criticism can begin only after Lower Criticism has done its work, and not until then. And our critical edition is just laying the foundation of the Lower Criticism of the Great Epic. But I imagine, R. does not want to say anything special at all, when he mentions his "Höhere Kritik". In the 1833 ślokas of the constituted text (=2161 of the Bombay edition and 2208 of the Calcutta edition) so closely investigated by R. in the preparation of his erudite paper, he does not mention even a single passage where the "Höhere Kritik" could have [261] earnestly and usefully "functioned". The item is probably introduced here merely *pro forma*, as the fourth and last stage of the *ariya-magga*.

But R. might have mercifully spared us this learned *prooemium* on the aims and methods of the Classical Philology and their application to the problem of the Mahābhārata textual criticism. The same thing has been said by others before R., more simply but with ample clearness and emphasis. In the paper[3] he read at the XVIIth International Congress of Orientalists (Oxford 1928), WINTERNITZ remarked: "The general principles followed in critical editions of classical texts, Greek or Latin or Sanskrit, can be applied to a critical edition of the Mahābhārata only with great limitations and modifications. It is simply impossible to trace a genealogical tree of all the MSS. of the Ādiparvan, and only in some cases are we able to state how MSS. are related to one another. On the whole, we have to be satisfied with a classification of the MSS. according to script, and the provinces to which they belong. And we have more often to refer to classes of MSS., than to

---

1 In the first 86 adhyāyas, the following stanzas contain conjectural readings: 1. 14. 15; 30. 7; 37. 10; 41. 5; 45. 15; 48. 9; 51. 8; 57. 20; 68. 25; 71. 36; 84. 3, 13; 86. 5.

2 Cf. Foreword to Fasc. 1, p. vi, column 2.

3 *Indol. Prag.* vol. 1 (1929), pp. 58-68.

individual MSS."[1] I had myself pointed out in the Foreword (p. ii) to Fascicule 1 that "it is impossible to apply to the Mahābhārata the special canons of textual criticism which are derived from a study of classical (Greek and Latin) texts and which depend ultimately upon there being a more or less complete concatenation of copies and exemplars reaching finally back to a single authentic (written) archetype".

And how would it be possible to apply to the Mahābhārata the canons of the Classical Philology *in toto*? Where has the Classical Philology, I should like to know, the necessary experience of dealing with a text with about a dozen recensions whose extreme types differ in extent by something like 13,000 stanzas (or 26,000 lines); a work which for centuries has been growing not only upwards and downwards but also laterally, like the Nyagrodha tree, growing on all sides; a codex which has been written in seven or eight different scripts, assiduously and lovingly copied through a long vista of centuries by a legion of devout—and perhaps mostly ignorant [262] and inefficient[2]—copyists speaking different tongues; a traditional book of inspiration which, in various shapes and sizes, has been the cherished heritage of one people continuously for several millennia and which to the present day is interwoven with the thoughts and beliefs and moral ideas of a nation numbering over two hundred million? No, the Classical Philology has no experience in dealing with a text of this description, a work of such colossal dimensions and complex character, with such a long and intricate history behind it. That is why I have elsewhere also said that the problem of the Mahābhārata textual criticism is a problem *sui generis*.[3] The method of the Mahābhārata textual criticism must be evolved from a special study of the Mahābhārata manuscripts and of the Mahābhārata manuscript tradition. Its results and achievements can be judged only by a standard of its own.

RUBEN'S *Exaggerations and Generalizations*

In his endeavour to maintain consistently an attitude of dogmatic doubt, R. has been unconsciously led to make wild exaggerations and rash generalizations, which such a meticulous and captious critic as R. should have taken pains to avoid.

Thus in one place (p. 242), R. observes that the Śāradā MS., as a matter of fact, does not differ at all from other MSS.! As a matter of fact, this statement of R. is demonstrably false. If a difference of something like 1000 stanzas (which is probably the difference between the Śāradā and the

---

[1] See *op. cit.* p. 61.

[2] The critical note on 1. 85. 20 mentions an instance whether the scribe (of K_1) has first copied the reverse of the folio of his exemplar and then the obverse!

[3] See my "Epic Studies I" (*JBBRAS.* vol. 4), p. 157.

Grantha versions of the Ādiparvan), not to speak of innumerable minor variants, is no difference, I should like to know what, in the opinion of R., would constitute a difference. Did R. expect that the Kaśmīrī Mahābhārata would be a poem of 8800 ślokas in Old Prakrit in which Kṛṣṇa was still a tribal hero?

On p. 253, R. remarks that *every* contextual criterion is problematic.[1] This is a rash generalization. In the Editorial Note (3) appended to Fascicule 4, I have now pointed out (p. ii f.) three passages for which there is the strongest in- [263] -trinsic probability, amounting to certainty, that they are interpolations in the recension in which they are found. All three are instances in which according to the Northern recension the parties to be married were united only by a shadowy and clandestine form of marriage known as the Gāndharva-vivāha, which is no marriage at all, while according to the Southern recension (respectively, in one case, the Grantha version only) the same parties were married, so to say, in church, in due form, with great pomp and ceremony. I maintain that at least in these three instances the criterion of the intrinsic probability is not at all problematic. I challenge R. to prove the contrary.

I shall mention only one other interesting instance of intrinsic probability. In the Paulomaparvan, Ruru, while praying for the life of his wife who has just died from the bite of a venomous serpent, says (1. 9. 4-5) :

"If I have (practised) charity, (if I have) practised penance, if I have duly served (my) Gurus, then on account of that (merit of these virtuous acts) let my beloved be restored to life! As from (the moment of) my birth I have restrained myself and maintained my vows, so let the beautiful Pramadvarā even now arise!"

The fulfilment of Ruru's fervent utterance is thought to be due merely to the efficacy of his pious acts in the past : they by themselves operate as a charm or spell to restore to life the dead Pramadvarā. This is a form of an "impersonal" prayer belonging to a comparatively older stratum of religious life and thought, which would never occur to an ordinary interpolator. At this place, $G_{1.\ 2.\ 4.\ 5}$ have some additional lines including the following prayer (233*).

"If my faith in Kṛṣṇa, Viṣṇu, Hṛṣīkeśa, the Lord of the Worlds, the Foe of the Asuras, unshakable, then let this beloved of mine be restored to life!"

This belongs to a later stratum, the period of the Bhakti cult. This is just the thing that would be interpolated by a devout Vaiṣṇava, to whom the former prayer would be meaningless and unintelligible.

I maintain that here also the intrinsic probability as to what is original

---

[1] Cf. also RUBEN, *op. cit.* p. 244.

and what is interpolation is so strong as to be conclusive in favour of the text and against $G_{1, 2, 4, 5}$. No [264] one with a modicum of the historical sense can doubt it. Can R. adduce even a shadow of a reason to show that the intrinsic evidence in this instance is in any degree problematic? Scores of illustrations of this character may be produced where the contextual evidence is not problematic at all, but quite definite and conclusive.[1]

R. (p. 254) has magnanimously set the seal of his approval on "Die Sage von Ṛṣyaśṛṅga" by Professor LÜDERS,[2] citing it approvingly as a piece of investigation that belongs to the coveted domain of *emendatio*. It is unquestionably that. Had R. now thought over the question a little more deeply than he appears to have done, he would have easily perceived that the whole thesis of "Die Sage von Ṛṣyaśṛṅga" rests on the exploitation of intrinsic probability. There was, in fact, nothing else except the vulgate text before Prof. LÜDERS when he framed his brilliant hypothesis about the different strata and the cross-currents in the Mahābhārata version of that legend. If now *every* contextual criterion is so very problematic, then what is the value, may I ask, of Prof. LÜDERS's monograph, which R. professes to admire so fervently? R. has been contradicting himself in one and the same paragraph (p. 253 f.).

Theoretically considered also, R.'s proposition is untenable. When a text has been tampered with *on a large scale,* however careful and however accomplished the interpolator may be, it is inconceivable that all the frills, patches and paddings added by the interpolator should remain for all time incapable of detection. It is inevitable that the interpolator should bungle something somewhere, produce a misfit, leave raw edges which do not meet. Therefore R.'s dictum (p. 253) "ebenso problematisch ist schliesslich *jedes*[3] inhaltliche Kriterium" is, in the form in which he has put it, fundamentally wrong and is to be unhesitatingly rejected.

Here is another instance of R.'s misstatements. On p. 242 he observes that among the fifty MSS. collated for the Ādiparvan [265] there are not even *two* that may be directly connected with each other. This is of course a wild exaggeration. The two Arjunamiśra MSS. show *inter se* no more difference than any two (carelessly made) copies of an original would show; as a matter of fact—but this could not have been known to R.—they agree almost page for page. If they were not copied from the same original, their respective exemplars could not have differed from each other very consider-

---

1 For instance, it is on grounds of intrinsic probability that Prof. LÜDERS (*DLZ*. Heft 24, Sp. 1142 f.) decides for and defends the reading *amṛtam* of the constituted text (1. 1. 201). Here the documentary evidence is inconclusive, but Prof. LÜDERS is on that account in no doubt as to which the true reading is.

2 *Nachr. d. Ges. d. Wiss. z. Göttingen,* 1897, pp. 87ff.

3 Italics mine.

ably. The same is the case with the three Nīlakaṇṭha MSS. The MSS. of the text as fixed by commentators (like Arjunamiśra and Nīlakaṇṭha) are, in general, as like as two peas. The number of such replicas can be increased almost indefinitely. I have intentionally restricted their number to the minimum necessary for fixing the text of the respective versions, always giving preference to a divergent type. But even apart from such texts with commentaries, there is considerable similarity and kinship to be noticed among the different MSS. In the Editorial Note (2) appended to Fascicule 3 (p. ii), I have demonstrated the kinship between $Ś_1$ and K_1. I pointed out there that "the India Office codex must be a transcript not merely of *a* Śāradā codex, but, as a careful comparison with $Ś_1$ would show, of an exemplar very closely allied to *our* Śāradā codex". This conclusion is supported by numerous other agreements throughout the Ādiparvan. That the three new Malayālam MSS. $M_{6.\ 7.\ 8}$ again go back to the same original follows not merely from the numerous readings these MSS. have in common, but conspicuously from one particular mistake where they *repeat* inconsequentially, at the same point, a fragment of a stanza (1. 85. 25): *pūjayantīha loke nāsādhavaḥ*. Further the four Grantha MSS. $G_{1.\ 2.\ 4.\ 5.}$ (which will come up for detailed discussion below) must go back to a not very distant common original. This group has not only numerous readings in common, but it contains quite a considerable number of interpolations peculiar to itself.[1] Their close affinity is, however, placed beyond the pale of reasonable doubt by the fact that they all contain a stanza (294*) interpolated at a place where it is, as will presently be shown, so thoroughly irrelevant that with it the passage does not construe even!

It will thus be seen that these generalizations of R. are absolutely unwarranted. They appear to have been introduced [266] by R. merely for the satisfaction of having made some pointed and effective little statement.

The Four Types of Variants.

After pointing out that no pedigree of the Mahābhārata MSS. is possible, R. proceeds (p. 243) to consider the different types of characteristic combinations among the variants, whose consideration must take the place of the formation of the usual genealogical tree. He distinguishes four different types of constellations. They are as follows: 1. *Complete Agreement*, where the two recensions N and S register one concordant reading; 2. *No Agreement*, where N and S stand opposite to each other with two divergent readings; 3. *Cross-Agreement*, where a part of N agrees with a part of S against the rest of N, which latter agrees with the rest of S; 4. *Partial Agreement*, where a part of N stands against S and the rest of N (or *vice versa*).

---

[1] See *infra* p. 273.

Diagrammatically the four types of constellations may be represented thus.

Type No. 1 : *Complete Agreement* : $N = S$

Type No. 2 : *No Agreement* : $N \neq S$

Type No. 3 : *Cross-Agreement* :

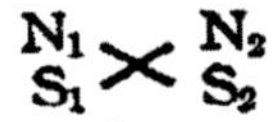

Type No. 4 : *Partial Agreement* :

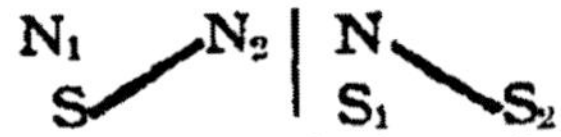

Type No. 1 (N=S). In this case I have assumed that the concordant reading of N and S must be postulated as having already belonged to the archetype. To my proposition R. adds the rider that there is a possibility that even such a concordant reading (or feature) might have been an innovation made in one recension and then borrowed *in toto* by the other recension. He cites (p. 244) Rāmāyana, Ayodhyā 6 (Bombay ed.), which (according to R.) is an interpolation in one recension, which had been borrowed *en bloc* by the other (independent) recension. R.'s proposition would be a contradiction in terms ; only he takes care not to put forward the proposition in this form.

If the two recensions N and S of the Mahābhārata should have an interpolation in common, they would not be (truly) independent. But these recensions must be assumed to be independent, and R. would not be able to prove any "second-[267]ary interrelationship" between N as a whole and S as a whole, at least for the Ādiparvan. Should there be found a passage which stands in such an apparent disagreement with the context that it may (*a priori*) be regarded as an interpolation, it would be no more difficult—in fact it would be, in my opinion, far easier and much more natural—to assume that the contradiction was already present in the "archetype," before the bifurcation of the recensions than to premise that one independent recension had borrowed it from another independent recension.

For example, adhyāyas 1 and 4 of the Ādiparvan begin with the identical sentence, depicting the identical situation, that the Sūta approaches the Ṛṣis assembled in the Naimiṣa forest at the twelve-year sacrificial session of Śaunaka. This implies that a new beginning is made at adhyāya 4, totally ignoring whatever has gone before it in the text as it now stands. Both passages occur with minimal variations in both recensions. It is evident that this double beginning (adhy. 1 and 4), as we find it in our version of the Mahābhārata, was not conceived and depicted by one and the same poet. But it does not at all follow therefore that the interpolation was first made in one recension of our text and was subsequently borrowed by the other from this recension. There are various possibilities.[1] Perhaps both versions

1 Cf. Holtzmann, *Das Mahābhārata*, 2. 12.

of the beginning lay before the diaskeuasts of the last redaction of the Mahābhārata : one giving the very useful table of contents, the other containing some interesting old tales of gods, Ṛṣis and serpents. They were not consistent in juxtaposition, but each was too good to lose. The redactors put both in, making but a poor compromise. This is one possibility. The other possibility is that one of these sections was composed and tacked on to an existing version of the beginning by the diaskeuasts of the last redaction themselves, using the same opening device. That would only show—as R. himself concedes in another connection (p. 254)—that though we might regard the original epic as a more or less homogeneous [268] work, the archetype of our MSS. already contained some inconsistencies and contradictions.[1]

Type No. 2 (N≠S). I agree with R. that when there is a conflict between N and S and they stand opposite to each other with two divergent readings, no definite decision is, in general, possible as to which is the original ; the versions should *a priori* be placed on an equal footing and treated with impartiality.[2] Accordingly, in such cases, I have adopted as stop-gap the reading of N, placing a wavy line below it, to show that the reading is uncertain. R. mentions an exception to this procedure of mine, but the exception is only apparent. R. has failed to understand my motives in departing from my usual practice in the solitary instance of the benedictory stanza with which the epic begins (*Nārāyaṇaṁ namaskṛtya* etc.). I have printed it above the line not because it is found in $K_{0.1}$ or in K or even in N, but simply as a maṅgala. I am aware that the stanza is missing in S. There is, therefore, every probability that it did not belong to the archetype. I am also fully aware that the stanza is a characteristic mark of the works of the Bhāgavata sect and not peculiar to the Mahābhārata.[3] There is, however, the fact that all our MSS. of the Ādiparvan begin with some benedictory stanza. These stanzas have probably usurped now the place of some simpler maṅgala with which the epic once began. No orthodox Hindu work can begin without a maṅgala ; and this edition of the Mahābhārata, critical though it be, is and remains a Hindu work, which could not dispense with

---

1 For instance, the story of the birth of Bhīṣma contains a patent contradiction. The reason why the Vasus were cursed by Vasiṣṭha as given in adhy. 91 (= 96 of the Bombay text) is quite different from and inconsistent with that given in adhy. 93 (=99 of the Bombay text). Both versions occur, in substantially identical form, in both recensions.— Cf. also the passage regarding the eight forms of marriage (1. 67. 8-12) in the Śakuntalā episode. The passage is made up of two different and mutually inconsistent systems of rules, taken from two different sources. 11*cd* and 12*ab* have been borrowed from a context which mentions only five forms of marriages ; cf. (K.) 13. 79. 9 and DAHLMANN, *Das Mahābhārata* pp. 203 ff. The same passage, with some variation, but with the same inconsistency, occurs in Manu (3. 21-26).

2 See my "Epic Studies 1" (*JBBRAS* Vol. 4), p. 163.

3 BÜHLER, *Indian Studies*, 2. 4 (footnote 2).

a maṅgala. My recognition of the unoriginal character of the stanza is, however clearly implied by the fact that I have omitted to give the [269] stanza a number, differing in this respect conspicuously from the earlier editions, which treat it as the first stanza of the epic and an integral part of the text.

The Position of $G_{1.2.4.5}$.

One of the most perplexing forms of variation in the Mahābhārata text is Type No. 4, namely, Partial Agreement. The critical apparatus is a veritable labyrinth of complicated and intermingled versions, each with a long and intricate history of its own behind it. We have unfortunately no single thread to guide us out of the maze, but rather a multitude of strands intertwined and entangled and leading along divergent paths. How difficult it is to find one's way in this maze may be realized from the fact that so painstaking and able a critic as R., despite his close and conscientious study of the critical apparatus, could totally lose his bearings the moment the network gets a little more complicated than usual.

The really perplexing part of the whole tangle is that while the agreements of $Ś_1$ K_1 with S are mostly authentic and fundamental, those of $G_{1.\ 2.\ 4.\ 5}$ with N are mostly secondary and spurious. Let us first consider the position of the group $G_{1.\ 2.\ 4.\ 5}$. which appears to have caused R. most trouble. I shall state the case as it has been put forward by R. himself (p. 249 f.).

Suparṇādhyāya 19 contains a conversation of Garuḍa with his father Kaśyapa. Garuḍa introduces himself as *patatāṁ variṣṭha* and makes some polite inquiries regarding his father (*kaccid vas tāta kuśalaṁ gṛheṣu*) and his mother (*kaccit...mātā na śocati*). The father replies that they are doing well at home (*vedāham etat kuśalaṁ gṛheṣu*) and then pronounces a blessing on Garuḍa (*...tvā rakṣatu...ṛco yajūṁṣi*; then *svastyayanam*). This conversation assumes in the Mahābhārata (1. 25. 7-25) the following form. Garuḍa asks his father for some new and substantial food and the father recommends the mammoth elephant and tortoise (as in Suparṇa 13. 1 f. Garuḍa's mother does) and proceeds to relate their history. In this scene the contents of the Suparṇ. are to be found in the "interpolated" verses (here adapted to the new contents). In the beginning (324*: $K_{0.3.4}$ Ñ V, B D T_1), the father asks Garuḍa if he is doing well "in respect of food"[1] (*kaccid vaḥ kuśalaṁ* [270] *nityaṁ bhojane*); the three lines of this N interpolation (says R.) correspond to the equally long S interpolation (326*:

---

[1] This is R.'s rendering ("fragt nach seinem Wohlergehen 'in Bezug auf das Essen'"); but he has evidently misunderstood the line, which may be translated thus: "Have you (all) been doing well? (have you had) always plenty of food?".

$G_{1.\ 2.\ 4.\ 5}$), in which Garuḍa introduces himself as *patatāṁ śreṣṭha*. In both these N and S groups there follows a common interpolation (327*) in which Garuḍa says that his mother is well (*mātā me kuśalā*), etc. At the end of the scene follows in these MSS. (Ñ V₁ B D T_1 $G_{1.\ 2.\ 4.\ 5}$; in $K_{2.\ 4}$ only partly) the blessings of the father (335* ....*svastyayanam*...*ṛco yajūṁṣi*).

Garuḍa has stolen the Amṛta ; Indra hurls at him his Vajra ; Garuḍa shows his strength and drops just one feather (Mbh. 1. 29. 19 = Suparṇ. 27. 6). Mbh. 1. 29. 23 is similar to Suparṇ. 28. 2 (Indra then tries to make friends with Garuḍa); Suparṇ. 28. 3 is similar to Mbh. 1. 30. 4 ff. (Garuḍa boasts about his great strength).[1] In Suparṇ. 28. 1 it is narrated that out of Garuḍa's feather, which had split in three parts (*chinnaṁ tridhā tat kuliśena patram*), there sprang the peacock, the "two-mouthed serpent-lords" and the mongoose. The last three pādas of this stanza are interpolated at this place in $K_{0.\ 4}$ (358*); the first finds an echo in 361*, an interpolation of T_2 $G_{1.2,4.5}$ (*tridhā kṛtvā tadā vajram*). $K_{0.4}$ has then further actually cited *verbatim* Suparṇ. 28. 3 in 365*.

R. admits that in the *second* scene $K_{0.4}$ unquestionably cite Suparṇ. Further 361*, according to R again, is to be judged similarly. That is an interpolation in the S MSS., the same stanza of the Suparṇ. (28. 1) having hovered before the eyes of the interpolators as in the case of those who interpolated 358* in $K_{0.4}$. After pointing out all this R. asks : "Should one now regard the first scene also as an interpolation made independently in N and S? Consider that $G_{1.\ 2.\ 4.\ 5}$ agree quite frequently in this episode with N (1. 20. 15 ; 301* ; 329*; 343*), that they alone have a remarkably large number of interpolations, and that 340* is found only $G_{1.\ 2.\ 4.\ 5}$ M and corresponds to Suparṇ. 13. 4....Has the G group then [271] interpolated the passage under the influence of the Suparṇ. and in its turn influenced the N groups? SU[KTHANKAR] gives in 1. 20. 1 the diametrically opposite answer with an assurance which is out of place in such difficult passages. It cannot even be strictly proved that these "interpolations"[2] in the first scene, which are common to N and S, are not an old remnant of the archetype."

There are in the Ādiparvan far more complicated passages than this : this is one of the simpler complications. I shudder at the thought of what

---

[1] It is by no means certain that (as R. says, p. 249) the stanzas which are common to the Mbh. and the Suparṇ. have been borrowed by the Suparṇ. from the Mbh. I believe, on the contrary, that the Suparṇ. has to be looked upon here as the source from which the stanza in question have been taken over by the epic. Four of the stanzas are nearly identical in the two works, because they occur as ślokas in the Suparṇ, and could be utilized by the redactors of the epic version without change of metre and with some trifling change of language.

[2] R. means the passages which have been regarded as interpolations by me and excluded from the text.

R. would have done if he had to handle one of the really difficult cases of conflation.[1] In the present case, it can, as it happens, be *strictly* proved that the doubtful passages of the first scene, which are common to certain N *groups* and S *groups*, are interpolations and no rest of the archetype. Also I may repeat here most emphatically what I have said in the note on 1. 20. 1 that the irrelevant insertion of 294* in $G_{1, 2, 4, 5}$ is *irrefutable* evidence of the contamination of these four Grantha MSS. from late Northern sources.

We shall consider the second point first. I imagine, R. has misunderstood or overlooked the little word "irrelevantly" in my note on 1. 20. 1. Otherwise he would have tried to visualize the passage, by reconstructing it carefully from the critical notes, and then he would have surely come to the same conclusion as I. All that is necessary in order to prove that 294* is an interpolation in the Grantha group is to cite the passage *in extenso*. Here is a transcript of the passage as it is found in G_2, the better preserved of the two Grantha MSS. belonging to the Bombay Government collection, collated for the Ādiparvan.

App. I, No. 13[2] : सूतः ।
नागास्तु सहिताः कृत्वा कर्तव्यमिति तद्वचः ।
[272] विस्नेहा विदहेन्माता ह्यसंप्राप्तमनोरथा ।
प्रसन्ना मोक्षयेदस्मान्तस्माच्छापाच्च भामिनी ।
कृष्णं पुच्छं करिष्यामस्तुरगस्य महात्मनः ।
तथेति तस्य ते तस्य कृष्णवाला इव स्थिताः ।
एतस्मिन्नन्तरे ते तु पत्न्यौ वै पणिते तदा ।
294 * : महासत्त्वबलोपेतः शशिवत् द्योतयन्दिशः ।
कामरूपः कामगमः कामरूपो वियत्तमः ।
1. 20. 1: तं समुद्रमविक्रम्य कद्रूर्विनतया सह ।
न्यपतत्तुरगाभ्याशे न चिरादिव शीघ्रगा ।
2: निशाम्य च बहून्वालान्कृष्णान्पुच्छमुपाश्रितान् ।
विनतां विषण्णवदनां कद्रूर्दास्ये न्ययोजयत् ।

Even a cursory reading of the passage will show that lines 7-8 of this passage (which constitute 294*) are *thoroughly* irrelevant here. The lines comprise merely a string of attributes of Garuḍa. There is no finite verb in

1 That would happen when the interpolation may have filled out a factitive lacuna or what looks like a lacuna in the archetype. Cf. the case discussed by BELLONI-FILIPPI in his paper in the next footnote.

2 In the stimulating article entitled "L'episodio di Kadrū e d Vinatā nell' edizione critica del Mahābhārata" (Traduzioni di epica indiana II) published in the Ascoli Memorial volume *Silloge Linguistica* (Torino 1930), F. BELLONI-FILIPPI justifies the excision of passage No. 13 of App. I (Bombay text 1. 22. 1-3), showing that the lacuna is only apparent and the *textus simplicior* is quite in order.

the sentence and there is no reference to Garuḍa in the foregoing or following lines. The only *rational* explanation of this state of things is that the lines were interpolated in an ancestor of $G_{1, 2, 4, 5}$ by a clumsy copyist, who had missed the right place by four stanzas. Such mistakes occur frequently in Indian MSS. because the additional lines were, as a rule, first written in the narrow margin of the MS. and a small mark was made to indicate the point of insertion. Should the mark get obliterated, the lines would be inserted by the next copyist wherever he considered they belonged or fitted best. If those lines (294*) belonged to the archetype of our MSS. we should have to assume that they were accidentally mis-placed in a sub-group of the Grantha version, omitted (for an unknown reason) in another group of MSS., $K_{1.3}$ D_2 $T_{3.6}$ M and are found in their correct place only in $K_{0.2.4}$ Ñ V_1 B D (except D_2). Is this plausible? I can hardly think that R. would say so. I am inclined to believe that R. had failed to realize how the passage actually read in this particular sub-group of the Grantha version. Taking all things into consideration, it is difficult to escape from the conclusion that an ancestor of the Grantha sub-group had been compared with some MS. or MSS. of the Northern recension which contained the spurious passage 294*. This is the first important fact to remember with regard to this interesting sub-group of the Grantha version. It is quite in harmony with [273] the other fact that this group contains 25 interpolated passages in 52 adhyāyas (24-75) or about 2000 stanzas, which have not been found so far anywhere else. They are: 320*, 322*, 326*, 330*, 337*, 345*, 351* (third line!), 357*, 363*, 364*, 368*, 371*, 373*, 382*, 386*, 387*, 388*, 406*, 519*, 584*, 636*, 705*, 706*, 741*, 755*. This group moreover contains in the same section the following 10 passages which it shares only with two or three other MSS. (in some written only on the margin) : 312*, 348*, 353*, 399*, 404*, 421*, 423*, 442*, 469* (phalaśruti!), 831*. How these passages originate is somewhat of a mystery. But as no one would be so inane as to maintain that these are rests of the archetype preserved only in a sub-group of the Grantha version and lost without a trace elsewhere, not only in the remaining MSS. of the Grantha version but in all other versions of both recensions as well, we are inevitably led to the conclusion that this sub-group of the Grantha version must present a text exceptionally heavily padded with indiscriminate additions. *This noteworthy fact renders its agreements with N immediately suspect.* And *a priori* also it is more likely that, when there is agreement between a sub-group of one version and some entirely different version or versions, the sub-group is the borrower. It may further be pointed out that 294* is by a long way not the only passage which this sub-group of the Grantha version shares with the vulgate text, against the rest of the Grantha version together with the Śāradā-Kaśmīrī and the Malayālam versions. Here is a list of these passages (in adhyāyas 20-43), which must all be assumed to be interpolated in the sub-group in question under the influence of some MS. or MSS. on which the text of the vulgate is based, that is, of some late Northern sources.: 294*, 301*, 307*, 327*, 329*, 335*, 341*, 343*, 355*, 385*, 392*, 393*, 396*, 402*, 411*, 419*, etc.

After this preamble we may proceed to consider the case of the Suparṇ. passage. Here the indebtedness of $G_{1.\ 2.\ 4.\ 5}$ to the Northern recension is equally clear and would have been manifest to R., had he but attempted to visualize the whole passage as it stands in the sub-group instead of contenting himself with merely counting the number of lines. R.'s initial mistake lies in thinking that 324* and 326* are equivalent passages, whereas the passages, although of the same length and inserted at the same point, are utterly different in contents and have an entirely different significance. The passage 324* [274] contains a kuśala-question and an inquiry as to whether Garuḍa gets enough to eat ; 326*, on the other hand, contains a question as to where Garuḍa is going in such hurry ! Remembering this and reading the various passages together, the relationship between the MSS. will be clear. It is again a case of *irrelevant* insertion in the conflated group. The passage in question reads in the different MS. groups as under.

$K_{0.3.4}$ Ñ V_1 B D T_1

(7*ab* and 324*)

ततोऽपश्यत्स पितरं पृष्ठश्चाख्यातवान्पितुः ।
यथान्यायममेयात्मा तं चोवाच महानृषिः ।

कश्यप उवाच ।

कच्चिद्वः कुशलं नित्यं भोजने बहुलं सुत ।
कच्चिच्च मानुषे लोके तवान्नं विद्यते बहु ।

$G_{1.\ 2.\ 4.\ 5}$

(7*ab* and 326*)

ततोऽपश्यत्स पितरं काश्यपं दीप्ततेजसम् ।
ववन्दे पततां श्रेष्ठो ब्रह्म ब्रह्मविदां प्रभुम् ।
पृष्टश्च पित्रा बलवान्वैनतेयः प्रतापवान् ।

(काश्यप उवाच ।)

क्व गन्तासीति वेगेन मम त्वं वक्तुमर्हसि ।

$K_{0.\ 3.\ 4}$ Ñ V_1 B D T_1 $G_{2.\ 4.\ 5}$

(327*)

गरुड उवाच ।

माता मे कुशला शश्वत्तथा भ्राता तथा ह्यहम् ।
न हि मे कुशलं तात भोजने बहुले सदा ।

Placed in this way, the reader will see at a glance that while 327* is a proper rejoinder to the query in 324,* it is totally irrelevant after 326*; because in $G_{2.\ 4.\ 5}$, in reply to Kaśyapa's question where Garuḍa is going, Garuḍa says "My mother is well, so is my brother, and so am I" etc. This clearly shows that in $G_{2.\ 4.\ 5}$, 327* is a *secondary* interpolation. Then the question arises whether 326* could be a rest of the archetype. The probability of this being so is reduced to nil not merely by the fact that the passage is found only in the highly inflated group $G_{1.\ 2.\ 4.\ 5}$, but also from the noteworthy circumstances (which I fear has escaped the vigilant R.) that in

$G_{1.\ 2.\ 4.\ 5}$, *7ab* has been altered from *pṛṣṭaś cākhyātavān pituḥ* to *Kāśyapaṁ dīptatejasam* in order to accommodate the additional lines. In any case these interpolations are *not* common to N and S, as erroneously believed by R.

The history of these interpolations must be something like the following. The question (which is missing in S except T_1) and the answer (which is found only in T_1 $G_{2.\ 4.\ 5}$ of the S MSS.) regarding Garuḍa's gastronomic requirements (324* and 327*) were interpolated in a part of N (namely, the base of the vul-[275]gate), inspired by Suparṇ. 19. 2. Independently there was inserted in $G_{1.\ 2.\ 4.\ 5}$ a question by Kāśyapa ("Where are you going with such speed?") in anticipation of the reply of Garuḍa in 1. 25, 7 *cd*, an interpolation which probably has nothing to do with the Suparṇ. Subsequently, after comparison with some MS. or MSS. of the N recension, the answer of Garuḍa 327* (which, as I have remarked above, fits only to the question in 324*) was irrelevantly added in an ancestor of $G_{1.\ 2.\ 4.\ 5}$ by an ignorant copyist after 326*, where it does not fit in the least! This *second* mistake of the copyist of an ancestor of $G_{1.\ 2.\ 4.\ 5}$ is another valuable piece of *irrefutable* evidence of the contamination of these four G MSS. from some late Northern source.

I have remarked above that the māṅgalya or svastyayana (335*) before 1. 25, 26 must also be regarded as an interpolation. This follows for one thing from the MS. evidence, and is corroborated by the fact that the words of the sūta : *sa tac chrutvā pitur vākyam* refer clearly to Kaśyapa's directions as to what Garuḍa should next do and ignore the intervening the long māṅgalya altogether. That is why the vulgate alters *śrutvā* to *smṛtvā*!

The reader need be not sceptical about the possibilities of such indiscriminate conflation and addition. The critical apparatus, if closely scrutinized and properly understood, will reveal numerous instances of a similar character. Even a close study of the Kumbhakonam edition, prepared in our own times by two excellent Southern Pandits, will throw some light on the mentality of the old redactors of the Mahābhārata : parallel and even contradictory versions are placed quite unconcernedly side by side, regardless of the effect on the reader, regardless of the fact that sentences are left hanging in the air, that passages do not construe. Here one notices above all the anxiety that nothing that was by any chance found in a Mahābhārata MS. should be lost. Everything was carefully preserved, assembled in a picturesque disarray. The guiding principle was to make the Mahābhārata a "thesaurus of all excellences," culled no matter from what source. At the beginning of his commentary on the Sanatsujātīya,[1] Nīlakaṇṭha naively remarks :

[276] उद्योगपर्वणि सनत्सुजातीये भाष्यकारादिभिर्व्याख्यातान्संप्रतितनपुस्तकेषु च स्थितान्पाठान् श्लोकांश्च गुणोपसंहारन्यायेनैकीकृत्य व्याख्यायते ।

1 Cf. Udyoga 42. See also TELANG, *Sacred Books of the East*, vol. 8, p. 203 f.; and WINTERNITZ, *Ind. Ant.* 27 (1898). 128.

That is why it is safe to assume that far more stanzas must have been added to the Great Epic than omitted from it. It follows from this as a corollary that the archetype must almost completely—if not quite completely—be contained in the extant MSS.[1]

It will thus be seen that the assurance with which I have spoken (in the note on 1. 20. 1) of the contamination of $G_{1.\ 2.\ 4.\ 5}$ from late Northern sources is amply justified ; and that the passages common to this sub-group and the vulgate text (324*, 326*, 327*) mentioned by R. are in fact interpolations and no remnants of the archetype.

The Position of K.

If I understand R. (v. 248, lines 1-3) right—his remarks are somewhat confused—he questions the propriety of my treating the concordant readings of the Southern recension and the Kaśmīrī (Śāradā) version (against the rest of N) as original readings. But in the course of the same paragraph, he expresses his unqualified approval of the procedure of Prof. LÜDERS in accepting as original the consensus of G and B (against the rest of N). Now, as a matter of documentary probability, there is no difference whatsoever between the consensus of K and S against B D on the one hand and the consensus of B and G against D on the other ; because the relationship between the different versions must be one of the following type :

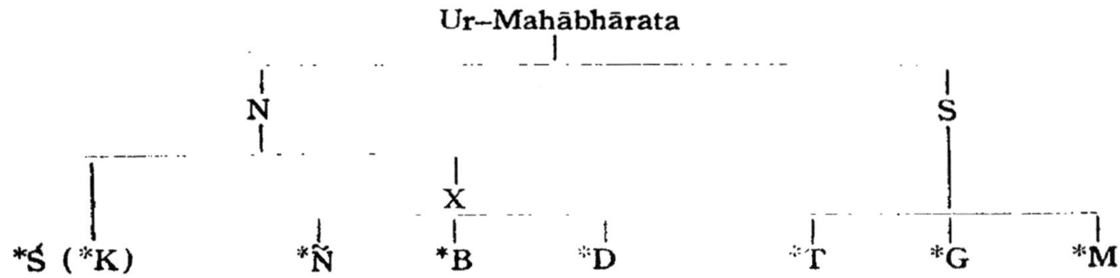

where X is the intermediate archetype of the vulgate, and *K, *B, etc. are the (uncontaminated) archetypes of K, B, etc.

[277] If Prof. LÜDERS gives preference to the consensus of B and G against the D MSS., it is to be presumed that he would likewise give preference to the consensus of K and S against B (with or without D). Let us see what Prof. LÜDERS himself has to say on the point :[2]

" . . . . Dagegen ist es sehr erfreulich zu hören, dass von Adhy. 26 an noch ein altes Śāradā-Manuskript auf Birkenrinde zu Gebote steht, voraussichtlich der einzige vollkommen echte Vertreter der Kāśmīrī-Version.

" Das ist um so mehr zu begrüssen, als die Kāśmīrī-Version den relativ ältesten Text des Epos bietet. Mit keiner der übrigen nördlichen Versionen

---

1 Cf. RUBEN, *op. cit.* p. 245.

2 *Deutsche Literaturzeitung*, 1930, Heft. 24, Sp. 1141,

stimmen aber die südlichen Handschriften so genau überein wie mit der Kāśmīrī-Version. Andererseits zeigt diese keine der offenkundigen Zusätze der südlichen Rezension. Die räumlich weite Getrenntheit der beiden Handschriftengruppen schliesst die direkte Abhängigkei der südlichen Rezension von der Kāśmīrī-Version nahezu aus. *Es ist daher anzunehmen, dass da, wo die beiden in Lesarten zusammenstimmen, die Lesungen des ältesten Textes, der erreichbar ist, vorliegen. Zu dieser Beurteilung des Verhältnisses der Kāśmīrī und der südlichen Handschriften, die Sukthankar vertritt, war auch ich bereits bei der Herstellung der Druckprobe gelangt,*[1] wenn mir auch von der Kāśmīrī-Version nur die ziemlich nachlässig geschriebene Handschrift der Bibliothek des India Office 2137 vorlag. . . . Selbstverständlich kann auch die Kāśmīrī-Version Textänderungen enthalten, und der Herausgeber ist meines Erachtens im Rechte, wenn er gelegentlich der Bangālī-Version, mit der die Maithilī-Version und der Text des Arjunamiśra in allgemeinen zusammengehen, da wo sie mit den südlichen Handschriften übereinstimmt, den Vorzug gegeben hat."

Prof. LÜDERS, in other words, unhesitatingly endorses my procedure. Herr Dr. RUBEN dissents ! I am content to leave it at that.

The Extent of the Virāṭaparvan

When I adopted 2050 as the figure[2] representing the extent of the Virāṭaparvan, I did not do so, as R. says (p. 251), [278] under the influence of UTGIKAR or anybody else. My chief reason for adopting the figure was that it represents the reading of the *majority* of K supported by the Maithilī MS. (V_1) and Nīlakaṇṭha version (Dn). When Nīlakaṇṭha adopts it, there is a certain amount of probability of its being well represented in the old Northern MSS. of his time. I cannot say whether R. knows that it is the reading of *all* printed editions as well ; it looks as though he does not.

Now let us consider the claims of the other variants. S has an obviously inflated text.[3] This inflated text appears to have been recounted in the South by the diaskeuasts and the Parvasaṁgraha figure altered accordingly to 3500.[4] So the reading of S may be left out of consideration altogether. The other Northern variants are as follows :

2015 :	श्लोकाः पंचदशैव तु	K_3
2300 ·	त्रीणि श्लोकशतानि च	K_1 V_1m $B_{2.\,3.\,4}$m $D_{7.\,12.\,14}$
2500 :	पंच श्लोकशतानि च	B_4 D_2

---

1 Italics mine !

2 See my remarks in "Epic Studies II", pp. 188 ff. *supra*, on the value of the figures in the Parvasaṁgraha.

3 See LÜDERS, "Ueber die Grantharecension des Mahābhārata", *Abh. d. Ges. d. Wiss. z. Göttingen*, 1901, p. 52.

4 See Editorial Note (2) to Fasc. 3, p. iii.

: तथा पंच शतानि च K_0 B_1 Da D_{13}

श्लोकाः पंच शतानि च Dr D_1

Only one thing that is plain in the midst of the prevailing confusion is that the text has been counted and the figure adjusted more than once. The *pañcadaśaiva* of K_3, however, is obviously only a corruption of *pañcāśad eva* of the text.[1] Thus the text reading represents the reading of K except $K_{0.1}$. There is no adequate reason for giving preference here to the readings of K_0 or K_1, because they not only disagree among themselves, but each finds only desultory support from other Northern MSS. What could the editor do under these circumstances but leave the reading of the vulgate (supported by the majority of K) in possession and mark it as doubtful? The text figure appears, however, in a certain measure, to be supported and even made probable by the facts of the case; because there are in existence, as a matter of fact, a few MSS. of the *textus simplicior* (F A M)[2]—and with the constantly operating [279] urge towards inflation their number will be necessarily small --which are approximately of that length.

The figure 2500, I must confess, I cannot adequately explain.[3] But as regards 2300, which approximately represents the extent of the vulgate text and which is documented by $B_{2.\ 3.\ 4}$ m among others, one may hazard the guess that it represents the measure of the text of that section of the Bangālī version in which the Kālī (or Durgā) hymn had been first interpolated along with some other accretions. All things considered, I think I was perfectly justified in adopting in the Parvasaṁgraha the reading which I did adopt.

What R. means[4] by saying (p. 251) that the reading of the archetype might have been :

सहस्रमेकं श्लोकानां सप्त श्लोकशतानि च ।

is beyond my comprehension. Does he mean that I should have set this (imaginary) line in the constituted text in place of the one which I have, or does he only want to show that he can compose an Anuṣṭubh line? If it is the latter, I will readily admit that the line is metrically, grammatically and stylistically impeccable, and does him credit. As we do not, however, want to rewrite the Mahābhārata, such manufactured lines have no value for us. The only sound test of the correctness of a reading is the evidence

1 The only difference between K_3 and the text is that the former has °*cadaśai*° for °*cāśade*° of the latter

2 UTGIKAR did not realize it, but I surmise that his F A M are also MSS. of the K version, that is, Devanāgarī transcripts of Śāradā originals.

3 I surmise that it is the extent of some composite text (like that prepared by the scholiast Ratnagarbha), comprising the vulgate text plus some interesting additions gleaned from the Southern recension.

4 A line made up by R. on the basis of UTGIKAR'S statement that there are 1729 stanzas common to N and S.

of MSS. In overriding this evidence, R. is unguardedly opening wide the door to a subjective "Höhere Kritik", which is the only thing that we must rigorously avoid doing at this stage of the Mahābhārata studies and which R. would be the first to deprecate if any one else were to attempt it.

Ruben constitutes the Text

At the end of his paper R. has appended, as a specimen, the text of 3 stanzas (1. 26. 1-3), as it should be constituted. The reader who has waded through 15 pages of R.'s disquisition on the complicacies of the Mahābhārata textual criticism will be amazed to discover that notwithstanding the overwhelming mass of variants and "additional" lines which stand at the [280] disposal of the exacting critic and despite the alarming theoretical doubts and scruples expressed by R. in the earlier part of his paper, his constituted text differs from mine principally in the readings of two *akṣaras*, and the addition of a line which he himself subsequently (p. 256) admits to be a probable interpolation ! The difference between our readings is as follows. In line 1 he ***hesitatingly*** sets °*mātre*[1] for my °*mātrā*, and in line 3 *bhaṅktvā* for my *bhagnāṁ*. R. (doubtfully) decides in favour of °*mātre* on the ground that it is a *lectio difficilior* and according to R. himself—of course in another place (p. 253)—the criterion of the *lect. diff.* is problematic and proves nothing. Here is a neat little paradox : R. prefers the *lect. diff.* and sets it in the text, because the criterion of the *lect. diff.* is problematic and proves nothing !—As regards the second word, R. admits that though he prefers *bhaṅktvā*, the differentiation from (an original) *bhagnāṁ to bhaṅktvā* may be an innovation (p. 256).

The other difference in the text as constituted by R. and by me lies in the underlining of the uncertain parts of the text. Let me at once admit that I have been rather remiss in showing the uncertain portions in this passage. The device is a practical makeshift and by its very nature hard to apply strictly and consistently. But the difficulty is not solved by R.'s marking below the text wavy and straight, single and double lines, in season and out of season, as soon as he espies a variant in the critical apparatus. An edition prepared on R's plan would be indeed not critical but hypercritical. Even a constituted text is after all a text, meant to be read like any other text, and not a chart of the aberrations of careless copyists of the last two millennia. While it would be foolish to underline *bhagnām* (line 2) merely on the

---

1 Even with his reading, R.'s translation is inaccurate. The translation should be : "Aber kaum hatte der übermächtige Garuḍa (den Baum) mit seinen Füssen berührt, als der Ast des Baumes abbrach", etc. and *not* "Nachdem (der Baum) von Garuḍa berührt war, brach von ihm ein Ast," etc. R.'s translation omits *tu*, *padbhyām* and *balīyasā* and ignores the force of °*mātra*—(ifc.) !—With R.'s reading °*mātre*, the word *sā* in line 1 (for which there is no variant even in TGM_1) remains unclaimed and has to be forcibly connected with *śākhā* in the middle of the following line. Altogether the reading adopted by R. is unsatisfactory.

ground that three (inferior) MSS. $D_{3.6.7}$ read for it *lagnām*, which is obviously a clerical error, it is fatuous to underline text-words merely because some MS. [281] or other has a divergent reading, as R. does in the case of *balīyasā* (K_1 *mahātmanā*), *sa tad-* (G_3 *sarṣiḥ*), *teṣām evā°* ($Ñ_3$ *teṣām caivā°*), etc.

With regard to the short explanatory notes (p. 255 f.) added by R. below the specimen of the text, I have to make the following comments.

The participle *smayamāna* is not "episch", but *smayan* (of the text) may be, since the root *smi* is commonly used with middle endings.—The line 340* being an interpolation (even R. admits, p. 256, the possibility of its being that), the *adhomukhān* of the text is opposed virtually only by the *avāṅmukhān* of the *two* Grantha MSS. $G_{3.6}$, because the remaining adverse MSS. ($G_{1.2.4.5}$ M), while trying to interpolate the Vaikhānasas (under the influence of Suparṇ. 13.4), have obviously altered the last foot of the line (*2d*);[1] therefore the text reading *adhomukhān* is hundred per cent. certain and in need of no underlining, straight or wavy.—In view of the fact that 340* is missing even in T $G_{3.6}$ and in regard to the general character of $G_{1.2.4.5}$ explained above, there cannot be the slightest doubt about the spuriousness of 340*; the line was probably first inserted in M and copied thence by the highly inflated group $G_{1.2.4.5}$.—The form *jagṛhe* is found only in five Devanāgarī and two Southern MSS. (one Malayālam and one Grantha). In old Devanāgarī MSS. (written with pṛṣṭhamātrās), *jagṛhe* would be all but indistinguishable from *jagrāha* of the text. So the reading of these Devanāgarī MSS. may be ignored in this case. The Bangālī and the Southern MSS., which would carefully distinguish between the two words, have *jagrāha*, with two insignificant exceptions in the Southern recension. It is on that account that *jagrāha* was adopted in the text, and it is *not* doubtful.—3*ef* is certainly a third line, but is in spite of that quite certain. The line is not missing in any MS., and as for its reading there is agreement on all material points between all versions of both recensions. Thus K and S agree *completely* with each other as far as *e* is concerned, which is a very significant fact in its favour and should not be lightly ignored. The variations concern mainly *f*. The difficult *praviśātayat*, a *lect. diff.*, preserved only in K, was the cause of the remodelling of the pāda in S and the vulgate. Of [282] course all guesses as to how the variants have actually arisen must be more or less problematic. I would, however, hazard the conjecture that the way to the variant *pravicālayan* was virtually paved by the southern tendency to confuse the palatal sibilant (*ś*) and fricative (*c*): the successive steps in the corruption would be *praviśātayan*, corrupted to *°cātayan* and

[1] $G_{1.2.4.5}$ have used their *adhomukhān* in 340*. They therefore substitute *tapodhanān* in its place in the original line. M has worked out another combination (*tapodhanān-avāṅmukhān*).

then "corrected" to * °*cālayan*. The *vināśayan* of K_3 D_2 is perhaps an original gloss; or (more probably) a wrong correction of an original mislection, the successive steps being *viśātayan*, **viśānayan* (*ta* and *na* being written almost alike in old Devanāgarī MSS), and *vināśayan*. The difficulty with the word *praviśātayan* may be realized when it is remembered that the Dhātupāṭha knows no root like *śat* or *śāt*; it cites only *śad*!

* * *

RUBEN's long disquisition on the difficulties of the Mahābhārata textual criticism boils down to this: only that portion of the text which is documented by both recensions, in identical terms, is *tolerably* certain; the rest is doubtful in varying degrees, there being no criterion whatsoever which can enable us to discriminate with complete confidence between the variants; even the concordance between K and S (against B D)[1] is not conclusive evidence of the originality of the common reading. This is a more or less obvious standpoint, though partly erroneous and distinctly timid and conservative. It was hardly necessary for the "Referent" to write so much in order to say so little. His attitude of dogmatic doubt has caused him to make unwittingly some wild exaggerations and unwarranted generalizations as I have shown above. His perfunctory study of the manuscript evidence has led him occasionally to make gross blunders in the estimation of the relationship of the different manuscript groups and versions, some of which have been pointed out above. Many of the difficulties of the Mahābhārata textual criticism of which he speaks in his paper are [283] due to his failure to understand the *modus operandi* of the redactors and copyists of the epic and his lack of insight into the character of the different manuscripts—an insight which can be acquired only after a long familiarity with the manuscripts themselves and a close and patient study of their tendencies and idiosyncracies. RUBEN's paper is, in general, quite intelligent, but not at all important for the Mahābhārata textual criticism.

IV. More Text-Critical Notes.*

The Mahābhārata Textual Criticism is unquestionably making progress: slow but steady progress. There are many things in it still that are obscure, but some things have undoubtedly been cleared up. Thus there seems to be consensus of opinion among scholars now on the following points.

---

1 R. seems to have somehow a lurking partiality for the consensus of B and S (or even B and G). If he only knew, the agreements between K and S are likely to prove much sounder than those between B and S; for, while there are indications that there may be *sporadic* contamination between B and G (and perhaps even between B and S), the (genuine) Kaśmīrī version (Ś) and S as a whole have certainly the appearance of being almost wholly independent of each other throughout the Ādiparvan.

* [*ABORI* 16. 90-113].

The Mahābhārata textual tradition, as we know it, is far from being quite uniform. There are now two main streams of tradition, the Northern Recension and the Southern Recension. Each recension is further sub-divided into a number of provincial versions, which differ *inter se* in many particulars. But the text of the Mahābhārata must have been in a fluid state for a very long time, almost from the beginning. Clearly therefore a wholly satisfactory restoration of the text to its pristine form—even the late so-called *śatasāhasrī saṁhitā* form—would be a task now beyond the powers of criticism. All that we can attempt now is to reconstruct the oldest form of the text that is possible to reach on the basis of the MS. material available. The peculiar conditions of the transmission of the epic necessitate an eclectic but cautious utilization of all MS. classes. The Kaśmīrī version (*textus simplicior*) has proved itself so far to be unquestionably the best Northern version; and the Malayālam, which in many respects is superior to the Grantha, is likewise the best Southern version (*textus ornatior*). The agreement between the Kaśmīrī version and the Southern recension (or sometimes even merely the Malayālam version) can be taken as an indication of originality. But contamination between the different versions was inevitable and must be admitted. The Telugu MSS. are generally and the Grantha MSS. frequently contaminated from Northern sources. Even the Malayālam version, which is on the whole free from Northern influence, may show some contamination, in unexpected places. [91] In fact, all versions, with the possible exception of the Kaśmīrī, are contaminated in various degrees. It is, therefore, often a very ticklish question to decide which agreements are original and which secondary. Notwithstanding these difficulties, experience has now shown, the case is not as desperate as it might at first appear. For one thing, there is a considerable bulk of text where the Northern and Southern versions are in full agreement, where there are no variants at all, or—more frequently—only unimportant variants : this part of the text is fortunately certain. There is then the question of the "additional" passages, that is, passages found in only one of the rival recensions. There is only one rational way of dealing with these "additional" passages : they must be carefully segregated from the rest of the text, and examined individually. The onus of proving the originality of these "additional" passages will naturally rest on him who alleges the originality : the documents speak naturally against them, but their evidence is not by any means conclusive.

These are some of the principal findings of the Prolegomena. It is assuring to find that these conclusions have been restated and endorsed emphatically by so cautious and judicious a critic as Prof. M. WINTERNITZ in his recent review of the Ādiparvan volume, in the pages of these *Annals* (Vol. 15, pp. 159-175). The outlines of the reconstruction may, therefore, be taken to be correct, and the method of reconstruction sound. There is bound to be difference of opinion as regards details. When there are hundreds of thousands of readings to be considered and weighed, it is natural that all the selections would not satisfy all readers; and there are bound to be small slips in so enormous and difficult a work as this. But the reader has the advantage of having the full critical apparatus before him, prepared with all possible care and presented in a convenient manner. The reader may easily substitute in the text any reading that appeals to him better. Prof. WINTERNITZ has thus shown his preferences, in the article mentioned above, in a certain number of cases, where he differs from me as regards the choice of readings. They are passages, as he tells us, which he came across in reading parts of the Critical Edition with his pupils in the Indologisches Seminar at Prag. He has thus published these criticisms after much thought and discussion with [92] other scholars. I gladly take this opportunity, therefore, to present my view of the case, setting forth the reasons which have guided me in the choice of the readings adopted by me in the Critical Text.

1. 3. 60 : *girā vā śaṁsāmi*.

I have indeed assumed that agreement between K (strictly speaking, between the original Kaśmīrī version, or at least the Śāradā MS. $Ś_1$) and S is a sufficient though not a neecssary proof of originality. But there is no agreement here between K and S. K_0, it is true, represents the version K in a comparatively pure form (Prolegomena, p. L.); but K_0 is not K; and K_1 is, on the whole, decidedly a better representative of the Kaśmīrī version than K_0 (Prolegomena, p. XLIX). Now here K_0 and K_1 have different readings : K_0 agrees with S, and K_1 with the rest of N! This fact has been ignored by WINTERNITZ. As for the agreement of $Ñ_1$ and S, I have pointed out in the Prolegomena (p. LIX), that "even the manuscripts of distant Nepal are not wholly free from contamination from some Southern source or sources (direct or indirect)." Thus the agreement between $Ñ_1$ and S cannot be considered as compelling evidence, by any means. Moreover, it should be borne in mind that this agreement between K_0 $Ñ_1$ and S concerns merely the *omission of one syllable*; and it is clear that this trifling omission could quite easily take place *utterly independently* in the respective groups. Therefore, even the documental probability in favour of the reading preferred by WINTERNITZ is not at all strong. It is, in fact, considerably weakened by the following (intrinsic) consideration. N has *vā* and a dodeka (hypermetric) line; S omits *vā* and has the eleven-syllable (normal) line. This is a circumstance suspicious in itself. It is by no means certain or necessary that all the pādas of our Triṣṭubhs should be of the eleven-syllable pattern. Some of these hypermetric pādas can indeed be made normal by the omission of one or more of the additional syllables, often merely of an expletive. But there are many lines which defy such athetization; for instance, the second pāda of the very *next* stanza (1. 3. 61 ; *nāsatyadasrau sunasau vaijayantau*). Such lines ought to [93] warn us against giving hasty preference to these normalizing readings. I have cited elsewhere (Prolegomena, p. XCIII) clear instances of efforts made by redactors to correct hypermetric pādas of Ślokas. Similar efforts are to be found among the variants of our Triṣṭubhs. But as the scheme of the Triṣṭubh is more variable and arbitrary, or at least more complicated and obscure, it is difficult to prove the alterations made by the different scribes or editors. In this particular instance, however, it seems to me, there is no reason to assume that the original pāda was *not* hypermetric, because our pāda is a standard hypermeter—a type of which HOPKINS has cited numerous instances. Cf. No. 6 of the typical, oft-recurring varieties (mentioned by HOPKINS in *The Great Epic*, p. 275):

— ⏓ ⏓ — — ⏓ | ⏑ ⏑ — ⏑ — — .

The scansion of *our* line is :

⏑ — — — — ⏑ | ⏑ ⏑ — ⏑ — —,

which, it will be seen, is a pāda of the identical pattern.

From the examples given by HOPKINS, I will cite here only the following :

3. 13. 193 *mamaiva* (*tau*) *vāmyau parigrahya rājan*
5. 42. 9 *tatrānu* (*te*) *yānti na taranti mṛtyum*
5. 48. 77 *vegena* (*iva*) *śailam abhihatya Jambhaḥ*
13. 94. 13 *na* (*hy*) *utsahe draṣṭum iha jīvalokam*
Hari. 2, 72. 44 *vi-añjano jano* (*'tha*) *vidvān samagraḥ*

Are we to omit the bracketed syllables—or some similar syllable—in each case, on the ground that they disturb the metre, if not the sense ? We do not possess yet the collations of all these passages, but I am confident that there will always be some MSS. if not versions (or even a whole recension), which omit these extra syllables, for one reason or other. There is this other consideration. The ancients had as good an ear for the rhythm of their Triṣṭubhs as we have, if not better. Why and how was the offending syllable first inserted, and then tolerated by generations of editors ? All N MSS. except D_2 contain the hypermeter. Is it not, under these circumstances, more probable that the *original* was a hypermetric line, which was emended by some redactors in conformity with the later ideas of the regular Upajāti metres ? [94] This particular hypermeter is moreover antique, for we find (as HOPKINS has pointed out) already an example of it in Muṇḍ. Up. 3. 1. 6 :

yatra (*tat*) *satyasya paramaṁ nidhānam,*

with the scansion — ⏑ — — — ⏑ | ⏑ ⏑ — ⏑ — — , which differs from our line as regards the quantity of the first two syllables only ; ours has an iambic opening, the Muṇḍaka line trochaic. Here, also, we can with impunity omit the bracketed syllable (*tat*), and get a line which is metrically a "better" line, but obviously not the original one. I am, therefore, fully persuaded that in all such cases we have original hypermeters. These old stanzas were not built at all on the pattern of the later, more regular, classical metres, but followed some other finer rhythmic principle, which escapes our methods of rough analysis by syllable-counting.—Now as regards the sense. The exact explanation of the phrase *girā vā śaṁsāmi* is, I admit, difficult. Nīlakaṇṭha offers the facile explanation : *vāśabdaś cārthe* (i.e. *vā* = *ca*), which can hardly be considered satisfactory. Devabodha analyses the phrase into *girāv*+*ā*=*śāṁsāmi* (with *girau*, loc. of *giri*), but that hangs together with his interpretation of the Aśvins as the Sun and the Moon, which is not very convincing. It is possible to interpret the words as '*girā vā*' *śaṁsāmi* (i.e. *vai*+*āśaṁsāmi*), as is done by some editors. On the other hand, it is also possible to emend *vā* to *vāṁ* ("ye two," acc. dual), which would give a satisfactory sense. This reading, which is mentioned as a pāṭha by Arjunamiśra, is found in only one of our inferior MSS. (D_2). It seemed to me such an obvious emendation that I did not like to adopt it on such slender MS. evidence, and I have hesitatingly (as shown by the wavy line) set in the text the old Northern reading *vā*, which is unquestionably a *lectio difficilior*. The whole hymn is, however, obscure and full of interpretative and other difficulties. It will have to be studied and dealt with more minutely before we can be sure of its text and meaning. But I am fully persuaded that *vā* (or some such word) did form part of the original line, and it would be a mistake to omit it.

1. 3. 145 *Kurukṣetre nivasatām.*

Why WINTERNITZ should have any doubts about *nivasatām*, I fail to understand. It is merely an augmentless imperfect, and [95] augumentless imperfects are most common in the Mbh., especially in the case of verbs with prepositions, as in this case. Even WHITNEY (*Sanskrit Grammar*, § 587d) remarks : "Besides the augmentless aorist-forms with *mā* prohibitive, there are also found occasionally in the later language augmentless imperfect-forms (very rarely aorist-forms), which have the same value as if they were augumented, and are for the most part examples of metrical license. They are *especially frequent in the epics*[1] (whence some scores of them are quotable)." To this, in 1884 (that is now more than fifty years ago), HOLTZMANN added the note :

"Beispiele von fehlendem Augmente des Imperfects sind ziemlich häufig, besonders in Compositum und hier wieder in solchen, die mit auf *a* auslautenden Präpositionen, *ava, upa, apa*, zusammengesetzt sind : aber nicht ganz vereinzelt ist der Mangel nur bei *bhavan* sie wurden 3, 110, 3 = 9970. 11, 27, 14 = 813. 16, 1, 9 = 9 u. a."

He has given the following examples : *pṛcchat, patan, cintayan ; manyadhvam, budhyetām ; vyapagacchatām ; adhyavasyan, avabudhyata, avatiṣṭhata, avekṣetām, avapadyanta, paryavasthāpayat ; abhyupamantrayat, upa-*

[1] Italics mine.

tiṣṭhetām, upanṛtyanta; abhiṣṭuvan, abhidhāvetām, abhyarcayat; samuttiṣṭhan, utthāpayan, uccārayan; paripālayan, nivartayetām, nirjayat; saṁgṛhṇītām; svīkarot. The Critical Ed. has, besides *nivasatām*, the following: *ṛdhyata* 1. 58. 8, *avabudhyata* 120.11, *avatiṣṭhat* 189.11, *avamaṁsthāḥ* (no. v. 1. !) 189. 21, *samabhidravat* 218. 28. There are many others, less certain. A number of instances will be found in the Tentative Edition of the Virāṭaparvan by Mr. UTGIKAR; the Critical Edition of this parvan, I may add, will again contain quite a few instances of this particular solecism. How many examples are really needed before it is admitted that augmentless imperfect forms occur regularly in the Mbh., and we cease to talk of "correct" and "incorrect" forms? The augmentless forms are quite as "correct" as the other as far as the Mbh. is concerned. WINTERNITZ points out that the "correct" form "is given by the Kaśmīrian transcript K_1, by the Maithilī and Bengali MSS., by Arjunamiśra, and by some Southern MSS.," and therefore he prefers it. It is a wonder that [96] it is not given by more MSS.; because the tendency is always to change an "incorrect" form into the "correct" one. We have here to look not to the MSS. which have the "correct" form, but to those which have not the "correct" form! Let us look at it in another way. If *nivasatām* be the original reading, then there are two ways of improving the text: (i) keep *vasatām* of the original and change the word to *nyavasatām* and thus make it "correct" (Central sub-recension and Malayālam, *independently*), or (ii) keep *ni-* intact, and change the word to the present *nivasataḥ* ("K" version); both are represented here. If, on the other hand, *nyavasatām* were the original reading, no one would think of changing it later to *nivasatām*; and *nivasataḥ* of K would also be quite unintelligible. The text reading *nivasatām* thus explains, to a certain extent, how the other readings may have arisen and has therefore been preferred. And I think there cannot be much doubt about its correctness and originality.

1. 3. 183 *prabrūhi vā kiṁ kriyatām dvijendra.*

If WINTERNITZ prefers *me kim*, he must, at the same time, also prefer *karaṇīyam adya | yenāsi kāryeṇa* etc., found in N (except K B_4 $D_{2.5}$); but he did not realize it. The *me kim* of the Vulgate cannot be joined to *kriyatāṁ dvijendra* of K B_4 $D_{2.5}$ S. There is no MS. which reads *prabrūhi me kiṁ kriyatāṁ dvijendra | śuśrūṣur asmy adya vacas tvadīyam.* The reading of the line proposed by WINTERNITZ will be like an animal with the head of a horse and tail of a donkey! The text reading of the entire line—nay, of the entire stanza—occurs *verbatim* in $K_{1.\ 3.\ 4.}$ I think, the original *Northern* reading was probably *prabrūhi vā kim*, as in text. If *vā* be useless after *prabrūhi*, it is more than useless after *kim*, where WINTERNITZ would have it. It is conceivable that the (original) Northern reading (preserved in $K_{1.\ 3.\ 4.}$ is corrupt, and we ought to give here preference to S. That is another matter. Not being convinced that *vā kim* of $K_{1.\ 3.\ 4}$ was "secondary" or corrupt from *kiṁ vā* of S, I have adopted, in the text, *vā kim* underlining it to show that it is less than certain. But *māṁ kim, māṁ yat, me kim, me tvam, vākyam* of the Northern MSS. are clearly all secondary, and need not be considered at all.

[97] 1. 55. 3 *śrotuṁ pātraṁ ca rājaṁs tvam.*

I have taken the Śāradā MS. only as the *norm* for my edition ; I have not undertaken to reproduce its text *verbatim*. The *śrotṛpātraṁ ca rājaṁs tvām* of $Ś_1$ K is opposed by *all other* MSS. And, moreover, as there is agreement between B D and S—more or less independent versions—on the reading *śrotuṁ pātraṁ ca rājaṁs tvam*, this reading is indicated as the original, and has been adopted, without wavy line ; a procedure quite in accord with the principles of text reconstruction laid down in the Prolegomena (p. XCI). WINTERNITZ finds *śrotṛpātraṁ ca rājaṁs tvām* of K "better Sanskrit," but I must frankly confess that I could not make head or tail of it, and I cannot understand it even now. The text reading is the same as the reading of the Vulgate and of the Southern recension, and is besides quite clear, and, as far as I can judge, flawless Sanskrit. It may be translated : "And thou art, O King, a fit person to hear (Vyāsa's Bhāratī Kathā)," a sense which suits the context admirably. Furthermore, K has here an entirely different reading for the whole stanza. If we adopt the reading preferred by WINTERNITZ, then we must read the stanza as :

śrotṛpātraṁ ca rājaṁs tvāṁ prāpyeyaṁ Bhāratī śubhā |
guror vaktraparispandaṁ mudā protsāhatīva mām ||,

which is apreciably different from the text. But the variants of the other versions do not at all suggest that this is the *original* reading. Our text represents the reading of the Southern recension, which has here, in my opinion, the greatest probability.

1. 56. 8 : *kathaṁ vyatikraman dyūte.*

It is natural that W. should demand wavy lines for this verse. I admit the line is most puzzling, and I only lighted upon the solution of the puzzle by accident, after prolonged wrestling with it. An explanatory note was really called for, because the first line is absolutely unintelligible unless one knows the particular meaning of the root *vyatikram* intended here, which is "to wrongly submit or surrender oneself to, wrongly take to (a thing or person, acc.)". It is a rare meaning, but not unknown. It is given in the dictionaries of MONIER WILLIAMS (ed. 1899, s. v. [98] *vyatikram*), and MACDONELL (s. v. *kram*). It appears not to be given in PW, but pw has (s. v. *kram*) : "verkehrter Weise sich einer Sache (Acc.) hingeben". One example of the use is (B.) 12. 174. 36 :

atha ye buddhim aprāptā vyatikrāntāś ca mūḍhatām
te 'tivelaṁ prahṛṣyanti saṁtāpam upayānti ca ||

Here *vyatikrāntāś ca mūḍhatām* must mean "those who have surrendered themselves (wrongly) to folly"; no other meaning will fit, as far as I can judge. Our stanza is, therefore, to be traslated thus:

"How (indeed) did the two sons of Pṛthā, as well as the two sons of Mādrī, (tamely) surrender themselves to the tiger among men (Yudhiṣṭhira), who was being cheated at dice by those wicked men, and (how did they) follow him?"

This strange submission consists in their consenting, in the first instance, to be used as pledges or stakes in that dire game of dice, and acquiescing dumbly to everything that Yudhiṣṭhira did. The Southern recension is unanimous on the point that the doubtful word was some form of *vyatikram*; and the eight readings recorded in our crit. app. show that it must have been some word which was as unintelligible to the scribes and editors as it is to WINTERNITZ. WINTERNITZ is again mistaken in thinking that the S reading is *vyatikramadyūte*. This is the reading not of S but of only *two* MSS. ($G_{2.6}$) out of the thirteen Southern MSS. of our crit. app. I myself have followed S in reading *vyatikraman dyūte*, which is the reading of *five* of the Southern MSS. In fact, my text represents the reading of the *majority* of the Southern MSS., and is, therefore in a sense, the true S reading. It is needless to add that *vinirjitam* of "K" and *vyasaninam* of the Central subrecension, are emendations, made by those who could not make head or tail of the original. For it is clear that no one would change *vinirjitam* or *vyasaninam* to any of the Southern readings, while the reverse would be the most natural thing in the world. It is further worthy of note that while the Northern MSS. have the easier reading, there is no agreement between the Kaśmīrī and the Central sub-recension. They must therefore represent independent alterations of a third original.—Following certain other S MSS. P. P. S. SASTRI has adopted the reading [99] *vyatikramaṁ dyūte* (without recording any v. l.); but I am inclined to think that this is a wrong analysis of °*kramandyūte* which in S MSS. stands for both °*kramaṁ dyūte* and °*kraman dyūte*.—Now that I have explained how the awkward word is to be interpreted, I have no doubt that WINTERNITZ will agree with me that the text reading is correct.

1. 57. 20 : *kriyate *ucchrayo nṛpaiḥ*.

There has been extraordinary reluctance among scholars to face the fact that the Mbh. text once contained far more examples of hiatus than what one deems right or reasonable for such an ancient and venerable text. But there is hardly any excuse now for such hesitation. On p. xciii of the Prolegomena, I have given numerous instances of the surreptitious efforts of scribes and redactors to eliminate hiatus, which show that hiatus was an anathema to them. It is well known that the Sandhi is not rigidly observed in the Vedic Saṁhitās, the Brāhmaṇas, and the Upaniṣads, in Pali, and in Prakrit works.

Why must the Śandhi then be rigidly observed in the popular epic, a work which has its roots firmly embedded in the soil of the heroic poetry of the Sūtas, and which has throughout preserved vestiges of its humble origin? The only reference (so far as I know), in the poem itself, to the Mbh. being a Kāvya (*kṛtaṁ mamedaṁ bhagavan kāvyaṁ paramapūjitam*) has now disappeared with the Brahmā-Gaṇeśa interpolation in the Ādi, and we are thus left only with a Purāṇa, Itihāsa or Ākhyāna. A specimen of this class of work may surely contain sporadic instances of hiatus, without our being scandalized. It is futile, I may add, to try to apply to this category of *popular* literature the rules of the dialect of the high-brow Śiṣṭas. We may expect every conceivable solecism in the language of the Mbh., and we find, in fact, an amazing variety of them; the hiatus, which was extremely common, is only one of such so-called irregularities. But for this strange modern antipathy towards hiatus, WINTERNITZ would have recognized that the emendation is quite legitimate and certain. WINTERNITZ considers the Northern readings but wholly ignores the Southern, which is fatal to his argument. S does not contain either *ati* (or *abhi*) which is found only in certain N MSS., and is besides superfluous. [100] TG have recast the line: *kurvanty ete dhvajocchrayam*, with *kurvanti* (note the *active* voice!), that is, a form of the root *kṛ* (like *kriyate* of N) at the head of the pāda. All these versions have the verb, it may be noted, in the *beginning* of the pāda. M contains the same three words as our *kriyate*, *ucchrayaḥ* and *nṛpaiḥ*, but transposes *kriyate* and *ucchrayaḥ*, reading *ucchrayaḥ kriyate nṛpaiḥ*. This is the key-reading, which gives a clue to the original. You can explain everything else, but you cannot explain the *transposition* in M (*which normally ought to agree with TG*), unless you start from the hypothetical *kriyate *ucchrayo nṛpaiḥ*. If you argue, on the other hand, that the reading of M is an arbitrary variant, which is in no need of a special explanation by means of an emendation, then there is no need of a critical edition either; because all MSS. contain approximately the same text and the same story, and the few differences could be regarded as arbitrary variations which needed no explanation. With this reading, containing the opprobious hiatus, you can explain *all* the variations. N inserts a futile and innocuous *abhi* (corrupted in some MSS. to *ati*) to destroy the hiatus. M transposes the *ucchrayo*, which is the chief cause of the trouble; TG recast the original, and substitute a reading which fits badly in the context, with an active *kurvanti* (having no proper subject), after *kriyate* in stanza 19. That is how I regard this little complex of readings, and hence the emendation, of whose correctness I myself have no doubt whatsoever.

1. 57. 21 : *hāsyarūpeṇa śaṁkaraḥ*.

This reading is undoubtedly, as WINTERNITZ rightly observes, the *lectio difficilior*, but there is not the slightest doubt about its being the original reading, judging by *documentary evidence*, and therefore, there is absolutely no need of underlining it. It is, in the first instance, the reading of the *whole of M*, which WINTERNITZ appears not to have realized. I have stated, as my opinion, that the Malayālam version is the best representative of the Southern recension (Prolegomena, p. LXXIII). I am glad to note that WINTERNITZ (*Annals*, Vol. 15, p. 170) agrees with me, and that even my learned friend Vidyāsāgara Prof. P. P. S. SASTRI now endorses it. In the introduction (p. iii) to Vol. IV of his edition [101] of the Southern Recension, SASTRI writes : "Not having been subject to Nāyak influence in any manner whatsoever, the tradition handed down by the Malayālam Manuscripts preserved the Grantha text, *in a purer and more unmixed form than even some comparatively early Grantha manuscripts, as the Malayalam MSS. do not at all seem to have come into contact with the Northern Recension till very recent times*."[1] Now this reading of the Malayālam version is supported by the reading of the Kaśmīrī version ; for though $Ś_1$ is missing, yet K_1 (India Office 2137) has the corrupt *hāmyahāmya°* (for *haṁsa°* of the rest of N), and it is well known that in Nāgarī copies of Śāradā MSS., *s* is frequently transcribed wrongly as *m* ; so that we have to read *hāsyahāsya* (dittography). The reading is further borne out by Devabodha's gloss (the MS. reads *hāsa°* for our *hāsya°*) : *hāsarūpeṇa krīḍāvatārarūpeṇa* (cf. p. 990 of the Crit. Ed. for the gloss), where *haṁsa*, in any case, would not fit, for it is not clear how *haṁsarūpa* would be *krīḍāvatārarūpa*. Further, *śaṁkaraḥ* is the reading of all MSS. except B_5 Dn, which have *īśvaraḥ* (an obvious emendation) and TG which has *vāsavaḥ* (which must likewise be an emendation), originally, perhaps, only a gloss. Here practically the whole of N is supported by M. *śaṁkaraḥ* is here not a *name* of Indra, but only an epithet, an attribute meaning 'auspicious, beneficent'. Thus in (B.) 3. 229. 6 *śaṁkara* is used with reference to Skanda : *lokānāṁ śaṁkaro bhava*. In (B) 3. 201. 29 the epithet *maheśvara* ("great lord") is applied to Viṣṇu *tvayi nityaṁ maheśvara*. Further in 1. 58. 43, the epithet *īśa* ("lord") and *śaṁbhu* ("auspicious") are applied to god Brahmā : *prabhavaḥ sarvabhūtānām īśaḥ śaṁbhuḥ prajāpatiḥ*. This shows that the words *śaṁkara, śaṁbhu, īśa, maheśvara*, and so on, which are now generally regarded as proper names of Mahādeva, were still not specialized, but were applied to other gods as well, as mere epithets, descriptive of their beneficence or omnipotence.

1. 57. 58 : *āvayor dṛśyator ebhiḥ*.

Here it is not difficult to see on what authority the adopted reading rests. The footnotes give here the reading of Ñ V_1 B D [102] (except D_5) of the Northern, and of G of the Southern recension. The adopted reading (which is partly supported by the *dṛśyayor* of B_3) is, therefore, the reading of the remaining MSS. K D_5 T M (since $Ś_1$ is missing, as mentioned on p. 244, at the beginning of the adhy., or as may be seen from the table on

[1] Italics mine.

p. XXIV of the Prolegomena). The Vulgate lacks here the support of the Grantha version, which has an enitrely different reading :

āvayoś ca kathaṁ brahman bhaviṣyati samāgamaḥ |

The Grantha version dispenses altogether with the troublesome *dṛśyatoḥ* of the original (or the unsuitable v. l. *dṛṣṭayoḥ* of the Vulgate), thus revealing its secondary character. The line was recast in the archetype "Sigma" (see the pedigree in the Prolegomena, p. XXX). The textual relations here are ideal, being clear as crystal. WINTERNITZ is right in regarding it as pass. part. praes. with active ending. Passive forms with active endings are quite common in the epic. I adduce a few examples to dispel the remaining doubts of sceptics : 1. 11. 15 *iṣyati* (v. l. *iṣyeta, arhati* etc.) ; 16. 15 *ākṣipyataḥ* (no. v. l. explanation); 34. 13 *mokṣyanti* (v. l. *mokṣyante*); 47. 9 *saṁbhriyantu* (v. l. °*bharantu*, °*bhavantu*); 48. 12 *dahyatām* (no. v. l. !) 48. 13 *pacyatām* (v. l. *jvalatām, dahyatām*) ; 48. 22 *dīryati* (v. l. *śīryati*) ; 53.6 *vidūyatā* (no. v. l. !) ; 71. 44 *dṛśyet* (v. l. *paśyet*) ; 124. 24 *uhyantaḥ* (v. l. *uhyante*) ; 147. 8 *vyucchidyet* (v. l. *ucchindyāt, chidyeta*) ; 165. 24 *hriyasi* (v. l. *gṛhyase, hriyase, prayāsi*) ; 202. 19 *adṛśyadbhiḥ* (v. l. *adṛśyaiś ca, adṛśyau tau*) ; 217. 13 *mathyataḥ* (v. l. *manthane*); 218. 49 *praviśīryataḥ* ; 219, 5 *adṛśyan* (v. l. *adṛśyā, nyapatan*).

1. 92. 2 : *Gaṅgā śrīr iva rūpiṇī.*

The configuration of the MSS. as well as the intrinsic merit of the readings are different in the two lines. That is how Ś$_1$ K$_1$ appear to be of greater authority in the first line than in the second. The *salilāt* of the text is found in *all* MSS. except Ś$_1$ K$_1$ (S only transposing the word : Text *salilāt tasmāt*, S *Gaṅgā salilāt*), and is, therefore, for one thing, obviously far better documented than *śayanāt* of Ś$_1$ K$_1$ only. In the second line, therefore, we have, practically, only two readings : *śayanāt* of Ś$_1$ K$_1$, against *salilāt* of the rest ; therefore the reading of Ś$_1$ K$_1$ has been rightly re-[103]-jected. Such is not the case in the first line. Here we have *three* nearly independent readings (Ś$_1$ K$_1$ *Gaṅgā śrīr iva rūpiṇī* : Vulgate G. *strīrūpadhāriṇī* : S *lobhanīyatamākṛtiḥ*, which latter is our *fourth pāda*). Here, while the two Northern readings are somewhat allied to each other, the Southern reading is entirely different, having very little connection with the Northern. None of the readings can be mechanically derived from the other, and intrinsically they are all more or less of the same value. Such being the case, the Northern tradition was, as usual, followed. WINTERNITZ does not say why he thinks *strīrūpadhāriṇī* is better than the other. The reason why I chose *śrīr iva rūpiṇī* ("beautiful like Lakṣmī") is that it is nearer in sense to *lobhanīyatamākṛtiḥ* ("with a most enticing form") of S, than *strīrūpadhāriṇī* ("assuming the form of a woman") of the Vulgate. I have here explained in detail the exact reasons which have weighed with me in making the difficult choice, but as a matter of fact, they are all three epic *iterata* and these *iterata* keep alternating with each other indiscriminately. In such cases, it is impossible to decide, with certainty, which is original and which is secondary, and the matter is also of no great consequence. The uncertainty of the text tradition has been duly indicated by a wavy line.

1. 92. 7 : *rājan kanyāṁ varastriyam.*

I am glad WINTERNITZ has drawn my attention to a wrong reading which has crept in here, through oversight, and I gladly take this opportunity to publish a correction. The reading I had intended to adopt, or at least I should have adopted, is precisely the one advocated by WINTERNITZ : *rājan kāmyāṁ vara°*, that of the Kaśmīrī version (Ś$_1$ K$_{0-2.4}$). The fact is that just for first two words of the last pāda of this stanza, there is a confusing array of readings in Northern MSS., all meaning, more or less, the same thing : *rājan kāmyām* (Ś$_1$ K$_{0-2.4}$), *rājan divyām* (K$_3$), *divyāṁ kanyām* (Vulgate), *kāmyāṁ divyām* (B), *divyāṁ kāmyām* (Ñ$_{1.3}$). Under these circumstances, clearly, the Kaśmīrī reading should have been adopted, according to the principles enunciated in the Prolegomena, but through a clerical error *kanyām* (of the Vulgate) [104] has crept in, in place of *kāmyām* (of the Kaśmīrī), which was intended.—I do not agree with WINTERNITZ however when he says that the epithet *kanyā* is "not very appropriate for Gaṅgā". It would be quite appropriate, as far as I can see. It would imply that she was an unmarried virgin, which is the regular meaning of *kanyā* ; compare :

1. 57. 63 *uvāca matpriyaṁ kṛtvā kanyaiva tvaṁ bhaviṣyasi*
1. 104. 12 *prādāc ca tasyāḥ kanyātvaṁ punaḥ sa paramadyutiḥ*
(B) 3. 307. 16 *sā mayā saha saṁgamya punaḥ kanyā bhaviṣyasi*

It would then answer Pratīpa's objection (1. 92. 6) :

nāhaṁ parastriyaṁ kāmāt gaccheyaṁ varavarṇini.

But *kanyām* is not supported by the MS. evidence, and *kāmyām* is : that is the main point. The constituted text should therefore be corrected accordingly by changing *kanyāṁ* to *kāmyāṁ*.

1. 92. 45 : *na ca tāṁ kiṁcanovāca.*

Here I do not agree with WINTERNITZ. I am fully persuaded that the text is quite in order. The first mistake WINTERNITZ makes is in thinking that *sa* is the reading of Ś$_1$ K ; it is actually given in the crit. app. as the reading of Ś$_1$ K$_{0.3.4}$ D$_5$. WINTERNITZ has overlooked the fact that Ś$_1$ differs from K$_1$, which is in itself suspicious ; and K$_2$ is also excluded from the group. If *ca* has to be translated by "but", there is no help for it ; for *ca* has frequently to be rendered in that way. For the Mbh., I may add, *ca* and *tu* are almost synonymous, *tu* having entirely lost the specific adversative force. It is quite clear that there must have been a period in the history of Sanskrit, as it was spoken, in which the two small particles *ca* and *tu* were confused in the mouths of the common people, and were used indiscriminately. That is, in fact, the only explanation of the curious particle *cu* one comes across in certain Aśoka inscriptions, which is evidently a combination of *ca* and *tu*. The Śāradā MS. undoubtedly offers a "better" reading, but, as a comparison of the different versions shows, it is a clear *innovation* or emendation. That the original had something like *na ca* (of the text) is proved by TG, which has *na tu*, only in a slightly different combination : [105] *uvāca kiṁcin na tu tām*. M differs from TG, and has a third combination, with a new word *vacanaṁ*, not found in the other versions : *novāca vacanaṁ kiṁcit*, which has neither *na ca* nor *na tu*, and which does not help to solve our difficulty. The *sa* of some of the Kaśmīrī MSS. is not necessary for the context, as the subject *mahīpatiḥ* ("the king") occurs in the same line.

1. 92. 50 : *aṣṭeme Vasavo devāḥ*.

Practically all the MSS. except those of the D version begin with *aṣṭau*, which makes it probable (if it does not directly prove) that the original must have begun with *aṣṭau* ; therefore *imeṣṭau* (one of the readings preferred by WINTERNITZ) must be ruled out, as an emendation, probably of a *lectio difficilior*. The (final) *me* of $Ś_1$ K_1 and the initial *ime* of some Nāgarī MSS. suggest that the original was the conjectural * *aṣṭeme*, which combines the characteristics of these groups, and which is very close to the *aṣṭa me* of $Ñ_2$. It is also suggested, to a certain extent, by the Bengali *aṣṭau ye*. The conjectural *aṣṭeme*, is in fact,, the hypothetical form to which the various readings *aṣṭau me*, *aṣṭa me*, *aṣṭau ye*, *aṣṭau hi*, and *imeṣṭau* seem to converge. The convergence is not a matter of which a mathematical proof can be supplied. If WINTERNITZ does not see the convergence, he may substitute for the text reading any of the five readings found in the MSS. I did not know which to choose ; hence the emendation. The change is not quite unmotivated. The motive appears to have been the seemingly irregular Sandhi (double crasis) : *aṣṭau* + *ime* = *aṣṭā* + *ime* = *aṣṭeme*. But as a matter of fact, there need not have been any irregularity at all in the Sandhi, for *aṣṭeme* may simply be resolved into *aṣṭā*+*ime*, or *aṣṭa*+*ime*, since besides the heavier *aṣṭau*, both the forms *aṣṭā* and *aṣṭa* were in use, of which the latter (*aṣṭa*) particularly was used, I think, in all periods of the language (cf. WHITNEY, *Sanskrit Grammar* § 483). The translation of WINTERNITZ is not quite accurate ; at least it is not literal. The stanza has no word for "obtained birth," which WINTERNITZ interpolates into it, in order to justify the reading *me*, "of me," which he has further to explain as "in my body". Translate : "Those gods, the Eight Vasus, had on account of Vasiṣṭha's curse become men (lit. attained the state of men)."

[106] 1. 93. 1 : *mānuṣīṁ tanum āgatāḥ*.

The agreement between S and Ñ V_1 Dn D_1 signifies absolutely nothing for the *original* reading ; it is purely the result of conflation. V_1 is, moreover, not a *version* ; it is merely a single MS., written in Maithilī script, and as such, capable of showing any reading at random. Again, the agreement of ÑV_1 with Dn and S against B Da is most unnatural and thoroughly suspicious. In other words, the MS. evidence here is extremely confused. Ordinarily I would have adopted the Ś$_1$ K reading *mānuṣatvam upāgatāḥ*, which has occurred already in the previous adhy. (1. 92. 50), and occurs again in (B) 3. 83. 66 ; but owing to the *mānuṣīm* of B, which recurs in S, I have given here preference to the reading of the Bengali version. I may point out that it is the reading of the entire Bengali version, and not of a few unimportant MSS., as WINTERNITZ imagines. The readings are these :

Ś$_1$ K *mānuṣatvam upāgatāḥ*
B *mānuṣīṁ tanum āgatāḥ*
S *mānuṣīṁ yonim āgatāḥ*,

This being the constellation of the readings, *mānuṣīm* and *āgatāḥ* are as good as certain, as suggested by the agreement between B and S. Therefore the real variant is only *tanum* : *yonim*. It is likely that the *original* was *yonim* which was corrupted, in N, to *tanum*, and then the original pāda *mānuṣīṁ tanum āgatāḥ* (preserved in Bengali only) was replaced by the recurrent tag *mānuṣatvam upāgatāḥ* ; but it is most unlikely that the latter was the original which was changed in B to *mānuṣīṁ tanum ā°*, and in S to *mānuṣīṁ yonim ā°*. In any case, the Kaśmīrī reading must be rejected here as secondary (cf. Prolegomena, p. LXII), as shown by the evidence of B and S. Dn D_1 appear to have got their *yonim* from *S* (ibid. p. LXVII), and Ñ V_1 possibly from Dn.

1. 93. 11 : *devadevarṣisevitam*.

WINTERNITZ is mistaken in thinking that the hermitage in question was frequented by Ṛṣis *only*, and not by gods as well. In fact, the talk is not about a hermitage at all, but about the [107] forest (*vanam*) containing the hermitage. Moreover, it was not an ordinary hermitage, but the hermitage of Vasiṣṭha, situated on the slopes of the celestial mount Meru (1. 93. 15 f.) :

Vasiṣṭho nāma iti sa khyāta āpava ity uta || 15
tasyāśramapadaṁ puṇyaṁ mṛgapakṣigaṇānvitam |
Meroḥ pārśve nagendrasya sarvartukusumāvṛtam || 16

The forest, therefore, in which Vasiṣṭha's hermitage was situated, was inhabited and frequented by divine ṛṣis (like Vasiṣṭha) *and by gods* (like the Vasus). That is how, in fact, the Vasus found themselves in that hermitage on that fateful day. If the forest were not frequented by gods, the Vasus would not have come there at all. If we adopt the reading *devā devarṣisevitam* (which is plausible) then the compound must be taken to mean "frequented by *gods and ṛṣis*" (and *not* by divine ṛṣis, as WINTERNITZ understands it). According to our text, the forest was frequented by gods and divine ṛṣis. As will be seen, there is not much to choose between the readings, but I prefer the text, because only the divine ṛṣis like Vasiṣṭha could reach those regions, not ordinary ṛṣis. Moreover, such adjectives (forming the entire second half of the line) are extremely common in the descriptions of sacred forests, hermitages, tīrthas, with many variants, as may be seen from the following examples from the Āraṇyaka (Bom. Ed.) :

3. 82. 41 *devarṣipitṛsevita*
84. 46 *siddhagandharvasevita*
87. 5 *rājarṣigaṇasevita*
89. 7 *devagandharvasevita*
89. 8 *devarṣigaṇasevita*
90. 21 *brahmarṣigaṇasevita*
156. 10 *siddhacāraṇapūjita*
and 145. 41 *devadevarṣipūjita*,

which latter has our combination *devadevarṣi*, and in which *deva* cannot be separated from *devarṣi*, for the stanza reads :

tatrāpaśyata dharmātmā devadevarṣipūjitam |
Nara-Nārāyaṇasthānaṁ Bhāgīrathyopaśobhitaṁ ||

The adjective *devadevarṣisevitam* (or °*pūjitam*) is used with reference to the most sacred and inaccessible regions like the [108] penance groves on Meru or Gandhamādana, or on the Himālayan peaks. I do not wish to suggest that the simple phrase *devarṣisevitam* would not have sufficed here. I only want to show that there is nothing wrong with the text reading, which is proved by the Kaśmīrī version ($Ś_1$ K). From the graphical point of view, the difference between the readings (*devā* and *deva-*) is so slight that the documentary evidence actually counts here for very little. It is just owing to this uncertainty that the reading has been underlined in the critical text.

1. 214. 9 : *Dharmarāje * atiprītyā.*

Here again we notice WINTERNITZ'S prejudice against hiatus, to which I had drawn attention in the discussion on 1. 57. 20, above. But here my case is stronger still. As far as the Vedic tradition is concerned, *e* (like *o*) remained unchanged before *a* which was generally elided in the written text, but, according to the evidence of metre, must almost invariably in the Ṛgveda and generally in the Yajurveda and Atharvaveda, be pronounced whether written or not. According to the statistics prepared by Vedic scholars, it must be pronounced in the Ṛgveda in 99 per cent of the cases, in the Atharvaveda and the metrical portion of the Yajurveda, in about 80 per cent of its occurrences. This shows that in the older stages of the language, at any rate, any Sandhi between final *e* (or *o*) and initial *a* was rare. The rule becomes more and more rigid as we advance, until with classical authors, ignorance or violation of the rule came to be regarded as a capital blunder. Now the Mbh., whatever its age be, stands unquestionably midway between the Vedic and the classical epoch, and therefore partakes naturally of the linguistic characteristics of both. In the Vedic literature, where the scribes or editors did not dare to add even a single syllable to the received text, the later antipathy towards hiatus shows itself in the efforts to coalesce, in the written text, the adjoining vowels, according to rules of (Sanskrit) grammar, leaving a correct but unmetrical and unreadable line. The subterfuge is however so obvious that no one hesitates to dissolve the Sandhi automatically and restore the hiatus. Much reluctance is felt, on the other hand, by scholars [109] in admitting that the epic text likewise contained originally many instances of hiatus, though of course they are not as frequent as in the Veda. The reluctance is due to two causes. Firstly the Mbh. text looks on the surface so like a classical text that scholars, who have so far studied the text mainly from printed editions, insist on applying rules of classical grammar to the text. The second reason is that the ancient redactors who had not the same compunction about making small alterations in the epic text (as is evident from our critical apparatus) as they had in the case of the Vedic texts, have not resorted to coalescence in order to remove the hiatus, but have boldly added little expletives like *ca, tu, hi* for saving their precious rules of grammar, a procedure which, as it leaves the line metrically intact, makes the detection of their nefarious interference difficult, if not impossible. Now though the Mbh. looks on the surface like a classical text, there are many peculiarities of Sandhi and grammar—even in the printed editions and the Vulgate—which distinguish it from a classical text. Coalescence unknown to classical usage is seen in *amale 'tmānam* (1. 68. 64), *te 'jñayā* (1. 70. 41), *manyate 'tmānam* (1. 198. 19). We have hiatus in a compound in *Nārāyaṇa-urogataḥ* (1. 16. 35) ; Pragṛhya Sandhi in *samupete 'dbhute 'naghe* (fem. du. 1. 14. 5), *jajñate 'stravi śāradau* (1. 57. 88) etc. Double crasis in *pannagābhavan* (1. 21. 6), *Vasumanābravīt* (1. 87. 18), *jāyateti* (1. 11. 13). Hiatus between pādas, caused by the change of *as* to *o* (1. 76. 35) : *jagāma svapuraṁ hṛṣṭo anujñāto mahātmanā.* Frequently we come across Prakritic Absolutives like *gṛhya* (1. 2. 93 ; 9. 19 ; 39. 23, 30 ; 119. 16 ; 123. 12, 16, 50 ; 124. 20 etc.), *toṣya* (1. 1. 109), *cintya* (1. 9. 2), *uṣya* (1. 71. 58), etc. etc. ; and the converse (*tvā* for *ya*) in *sam-pūjayitvā* (1. 54. 15), *ā-nayitvā* (1. 66. 12), *ni-ṣṭanitvā* (1. 85. 18), *anu-śiṣṭvānugatvā ca* (1. 133. 24), *prāpayītvā* (1. 189. 25) etc., some of which may however, be explained as absolutives of verbs with *separable* prepositions. Such a separable preposition we have in 1. 65. 34 :

prati śravaṇapurvāṇi nakṣatrāṇi sasarja ha |,

where *prati* is to be construed with *sasarja*, as *pratisasarja* : a line often misunderstood by editors, commentators and translators alike. These violations of (Sanskrit) grammar are not so rare that one has to hunt for them with a microscope. There is an endless list of [110] them. One meets with them at every step. If these and scores of other irregularities do occur as a matter of fact, why could there not be *hiatus* as well? Scholars are not yet familiar with this phenomenon, because they have been dealing, so far, with the clarified text, from which most of these irregularities have been carefully expunged, as is evident from our critical apparatus, by purists who have had the handling of the epic text during a long succession of centuries. I have noted that even BÖHTLINGK, who was otherwise a careful and conscious editor, has in editing Mbh. passages for his *Chresthomathie*, rigidly enforced Sandhi rules, even in prose passages, with a zeal which was worthy of a better cause, where there was not the slightest manuscript authority for doing so. My study of the Mbh. MSS during the last ten years has convinced me now that it is the grammatical and material irregularities of the original that are responsible for quite a large fraction of the mass of variations which we come across in the MSS. The correctness of my reconstructions can be proved only by adducing the entire evidence, which it is not possible to do here, but which may be undertaken later on, when a large part of the text has been dealt with in a like manner. I am fully persuaded that the Critical Edition, as it advances, will supply material for confirming most of my conclusions.—To return to the case under consideration. WINTERNITZ points out that *hi* is found in all N MSS., including Ś$_1$, but he ignores that K$_1$ shows here *tu*, not *hi*? Now K$_1$ is a *clear* transcript of *a* Śāradā MS., and agrees with our Ś$_1$ to such an extent that I have expressed it as my opinion that it is a copy of a Śāradā original very similar to *our* Śāradā MS. It is, no doubt, a very small and insignificant variation, but how would WINTERNITZ explain it all the same? *hya* cannot be misread as *tva*, even in the Śāradā script. Why should just K$_1$ show here *tva*? Is it not, perhaps, because a not very distant ancestor of our Ś$_1$ and K$_1$ *had* still the obnoxious hiatus, as in our text? The Kaśmīrī version does contain many original features and archaisms.

1. 215. 2 : *ekāṁ tṛptiṁ prayacchatām.*

prayacchatām of the text, I may point out, is not entirely wrong; it may be construed with *bhavantau*, understood, a more [111] respectful form of address than the second person. In stanza 5, however, the reading *saṁprayacchatam* has been accepted, because the subject in the second person (*yuvām*) is expressed. We cannot argue that since in 5 we have *saṁprayacchatam*, therefore in 2 we *must* have also *prayacchatam*. Because in the Mbh., which is not and never was polished literature, we do come across such strange yoke-fellows. Changes of subject and changes of construction are frequent. That is the view I had taken when I adopted the text reading.

But on second thoughts I decided that *prayacchatam* would nevertheless be a better reading, and the correction now proposed by WINTERNITZ had been already published by me, in the "Addenda et Corrigenda," at the end of the volume (p. 996).

1. 216. 10

sasarja yat svatapasā Bhauvano bhuvanaprabhuḥ |
prajāpatir anirdeśyaṁ yasya rūpaṁ raver iva ||

The matter is not simple as WINTERNITZ imagines. Of course, with the reading *yaṁ*, any one can see that the relative may be construed with *ratham* in 8. We then get two sentences: "Which (scil. chariot of Arjuna) was fashioned by Bhauvana....by (the power of) his austerities," and "whose beauty was like that of the sun." But the reading *yat* is actually found in $Ś_1$K (except K_0) V_1G (except G_1); i.e. in the Kaśmīrī version (except K_0), agreeing with the Grantha version (except G_1), plus the Maithilī MS. How is it that so many MSS. give what WINTERNITZ considers, an "impossible" reading? The reading is, in fact, not impossible at all; only the construction is a little involved and difficult to understand. By reading *yat* we actually get better sense. Construe: *yasya, raver iva, yat anirdeśyaṁ rūpaṁ,* (*tat*) *Bhauvanaḥ....svatapasā sasarja,* "whose indefinable (or incomparable) loveliness (or splendour), like that of the Sun, Bhauvana had fashioned by (the power of) his austerities." This construction avoids the two disjointed and halting sentences *yam anirdeśyaṃ Bhauvanaḥ....svatapasā sasarja,* and *yasya rūpaṁ raver iva* (or *yaṁ Bhauvanaḥ....svatapasā sasarja,* and *yasya anirdeśyaṁ rūpaṁ raver iva*), which result from the wrong reading *yaṃ* for [112] *yat, yat* is almost a perfect example of the *lectio difficilior,* and a regular trap for unwary editors.

1. 218. 14 : *jaladhārāmuco 'kulān.*

WINTERNITZ is here again mistaken in thinking that °*mucotulān* is the reading of S. It is the reading of only five of the thirteen Southern MSS. (T_1 $G_{1.2}$ $M_{3.5}$); three others (T_3 $G_{3.4}$) read °*muconilān,* three more (M_{6-8}) read *mumocivān,* two ($G_{5.6}$) read as in text (°*mucokulān*). The question is, in fact, what *was* the original reading of S. That question I have not been able to answer definitely, and I have, therefore, put in, *as a stop-gap,* the reading of $G_{5.6}$ which seemed to me not improbable, since initial *ā* is curiously enough, sporadically treated in the Mbh. text, like *a.* The reading °*samākulān* is useless; it is obviously a substitute for some reading which was difficult to understand or explain.

I have underlined *muco* in the text, but I now think that it is as good as certain. It is documented not only by the whole of S, but also by $K_{0.2.3}$ Ñ V_1D_1. If *muco* be admitted, then *samākulān* of the Northern group becomes secondary, but with an important residue in the shape of the final *kulān,* agreeing with the final of °*mucokulān* of $G_{5.6}$, rhyming with °*muco-*

tulān of $K_{0.3}$ T_1 $G_{1.3}$. $M_{3.5}$, and finally reflected faintly in *muconilān* T_3 $G_{2.4}$. The documentary evidence, therefore, points unmistakably to a reading *jaladhārāmuco(x)lān*. Query, what is the value of *x* ? The adjective *ākulān* ("confused") qualifying *meghān* would be not inappropriate, referring to the condition of masses of clouds confusedly hurled about by a cyclonic wind ; not so appropriate, to my mind, the *atulān* ("incomparable") preferred by WINTERNITZ, and adopted by P. P. S. SASTRI, against the evidence of his basic MS. ग्र, which has our text reading. In SASTRI's adoption of *atulān* and his ignoring of variants, which must have appeared to him meaningless corruptions or clerical mistakes, we have an illuminating example of how the readings get indiscriminately distributed, disturbing the relationships established by the *stemma codicum*, and how the *lectio difficilior* is gradually effaced.

[113] 1. 218. 27 : *vyātiṣṭhanta mahaujasaḥ*

The text reading *vyātiṣṭhanta,* it must be confessed, has not been adopted because it is the reading of S_1 K_1 ; it is a mere slip. I am thankful to WINTERNITZ for drawing my attention to it. The reading *vyatiṣṭhanta* should be adopted without doubt.

* * *

I may repeat here what I have stated elsewhere that the problem of the Mahābhārata Textual Criticism is a problem *sui generis*. Here the principles of textual reconstruction, which must be first evolved from a study of the MS. material and the MS. tradition, can be considered as finally settled only after considerable discussion and exchange of ideas on the subject. I would, therefore, repeat my request to Prof. WINTERNITZ, made some years ago, to continue his searching and exhaustive examination of the fascicules or volumes as they come out, and give us the benefit of his ripe experience and valuable opinions and findings. His publications on a subject which has engaged his attention, off and on, for the last forty years cannot but throw some much-needed light on the obscure question of the Mahābhārata Textual Criticism (which has unfortunately not received much attention so far from scholars), and thus advance the cause of Mahābhārata studies.

In conclusion, I must express my grateful thanks to Prof. WINTERNITZ for the very kind and encouraging remarks he has made regarding the work in general as also my keen appreciation of the uniformly courteous tone of his sympathetic and appreciative review.

V. Notes on Mahabharata Commentators *

§ 1. CHRONOLOGICAL NOTES.

A necessary complement to a critical study of the Mahābhārata is an intensive study of the commentaries of the Mahābhārata, of which there is

* [*ABORI* 17. 185-202].

quite a large number preserved still, mostly in manuscript form. Among the scholiasts who have written commentaries on the Mahābhārata—either on the whole, or only on selected parts of the Great Epic—are : (1) Anantabhaṭṭa, (2) Arjunamiśra, (3) Ānanda, (4) Caturbhuja(miśra), (5) Jagadīśacakravartin, (6) Devabodha, (7) Nīlakaṇṭha, (8) Mahānandapūrṇa, (9) Yajña-Nārāyaṇa, (10) Ratnagarbha, (11) Rāmakiṁkara, (12) Rāmakṛṣṇa, (13) Rāmānuja, (14) Lakṣmaṇa, (15) Varada, (16) Vādirāja, (17) Vidyāsāgara, (18) Vimalabodha, (19) Śaṁkarācārya, (20) Śrīnivāsa, (21), Sarvajña-Nārāyaṇa, and (22) Sṛṣṭidhara. Very little is at present known about these commentators : only very few of them have been, so far, published. The only collective study made of these commentaries is by HOLTZMANN in *Das Mahābhārata*, Vol. 3, p. 67 ff., and that was in 1897, that is, nearly forty years ago. The material at his disposal was very scanty, and so are his notes.

But the study of these commentaries must be now taken up more seriously, not so much for the sake of the explanations contained in the commentaries—though even the glosses of a commentator like Devabodha are extremely important—as for the readings and pāṭhāntaras recorded in them ; because, most of [186] the commentaries are older—some very much older —than our manuscripts ; and therefore the documentation of these readings by the commentators takes us back a stage further in our investigation of the history of the epic.

The usefulness of these commentaries is, however, considerably diminished by the fact that we know next to nothing about these commentators themselves. In particular, we lack information about their dates, which are not easy to fix in Indian literature. Even if the dates cannot be determined, it would be a great help if we could fix their relative chronology. An attempt is made in the following pages to fix, to start with, the relative chronology of some of the more important Mahābhārata commentators.

A fixed point in the exegetical literature centering round the Mbh. is furnished by Nīlakaṇṭha, who until lately was considered, at least in India, as the most trustworthy guide for the exposition of the Great Epic, and about whose date there is not much doubt. The available personal data about him has been put together by Wilhelm PRINTZ in the biographical note on Nīlakaṇṭha appended to his Berlin dissertation entitled *Bhāṣāwörter in Nīlakaṇṭha's Bhāratabhāvadīpa und in anderen Sanskritkommentaren.*[1] Nīlakaṇṭha, according to his own statements, was a Mahārāṣṭra Brahmin of the Gautama Gotra, with the surname Caturdhara (modern Chaudhari), eldest son of Govinda Sūri and Phullāmbikā, residing at Kūrparagrāma (modern Kopargaon) on the Godāvarī. Nīlakaṇṭha wrote his commentary

---

[1] *Zeitschrift fur vergleichende Sprachforschung*, Vol. 44, pp. 69-109 ; see particularly p. 70 f.

on the Mbh. and on the Gaṇeśagītā (a section of the Gaṇeśapurāṇa) in Benares, in the last quarter of the seventeenth century,[1] the latter (Gaṇeśagītā) being composed in A.D. 1694.[2]

In the beginning of his commentary on the Mbh. Nīlakaṇṭha tells us that before writing his commentary, the *Bhāratabhāvadīpa*, he had compared many (*bahūn*) copies of the Mbh., collect-[187]-ed together from different parts of India (*vibhinnadeśyān*) in order to ascertain the correct reading (*pāṭham agryam*) and also consulted older commentaries.[3] We accordingly find that he frequently mentions variant readings and "additional" passages found in the versions consulted by him, and he cites the explanations given by older scholiasts;[4] information, scanty though it be, of immense interest and value for the history of the received text.

(*i*) *Devabodha and Sarvajña-Nārāyaṇa.*

In marked contrast to Nīlakaṇṭha stands Devabodha, whom I regard as probably the oldest and therefore the most important commentator of the Mbh. He is extremely reticent about himself and his predecessors, but is cited or mentioned by several commentators, who must therefore have lived after him. One of such successors of Devabodha was Sarvajña-Nārāyaṇa. Sarvajña's *Bhāratārthaprakāśa* has fortunately been preserved, though it is not definitely known whether his commentary on all the eighteen parvans of the Mbh. is now available. His commentary on the Virāṭa and the Udyoga has already been published by Mahadeva Shastri BAKRE.[5] The Bombay Government MSS. Collection (No. 180 of 1891-95) contains a fragment of his commentary on the Ādi, comprising merely the first adhyāya with the beginning of the second; while the Madras Government Collection (No. 2169) contains another fragment which lacks the beginning. In the colophon of the latter MS., Sarvajña is styled *paramahaṁsa-parivrājakācārya*; he was therefore a saṁnyāsin.

Now Sarvājña explicitly refers to Devabodha in the beginning of his commentary on the Udyoga:

उद्योगे देवबोधस्य वाग्वाडवमरीचयः ।
पिबन्तु[6] ज्ञानदुर्ज्ञानवक्षोरक्तमहार्णवम् ॥

---

[1] He was apparently a protégé of Anūpasiṁha, who was a contemporary of Shah Jahan.

[2] The year of composition is given as Saṁvat 1750. The name of the commentary is *Gaṇapatibhāvadīpikā*. Cf. the name of his Mbh. commentary, *Bhāratabhāvadīpa*; see next note.

[3] बहून्समाहृत्य विभिन्नदेश्यान्कोशान्विनिश्चित्य च पाठमग्र्यम् ।
प्राचां गुरूणामनुसृत्य वाचमारभ्यते भारतभावदीपः ॥

[4] Cf. my Ādiparvan (Poona 1933), Prolegomena, pp. LXV ff.

[5] The Virāṭaparvan was published in 1915, and the Udyogaparvan in 1920, by the Gujarati Printing Press of Bombay.

[6] Read पिबन्त्वज्ञानं ?

[188] This stanza is curiously enough not found in the commentary of Sarvajña as printed in the Gujarātī Press edition of the Udyoga, but occurs in both the MSS. of the work in the Bombay Government Collection (deposited at the Institute), bearing Nos. 33 of A 1879-80 and 168 of 1884-87 respectively. The priority of Devabodha is, however, independently established by another direct reference to Devabodha in the body of the published commentary itself, to which my attention was recently drawn by my friend and colleague Professor Sushil Kumar DE of Dacca University, who is editing the Udyoga for the Institute. In Sarvajña's comment on B. 5. 96. 41 (on p. 327 of the Gujarati Printing Press edition), we find :

देवबोधपादास्तु ।

कामक्रोधौ लोभमोहौ मदमानौ तथैव च ।
मात्सर्याहंकृती चैव क्रमादेते उदाहृताः ॥

इति । केचित्तु काकुत्स्थीकं युधिष्ठिरं... ।[1]

This quotation can unfortunately not be verified ; for in the very old Bengal Asiatic Society's palm-leaf MS. (No. 3399) of the unpublished commentary on the Udyoga by Devabodha the corresponding folio is missing ! But there is no reason to doubt its authenticity.

This establishes Devabodha's priority to Sarvajña. We therefore get

Series 1: Devabodha—Sarvajña

Now this Sarvajña-Nārāyaṇa must be identical—as has indeed been assumed by JOLLY,[2] BÜHLER,[3] HOLTZMANN,[4] and others[5]—with the Sarvajña-Nārāyaṇa (also called Nārāyaṇa-Sarvajña) the author of the *Manvarthavṛtti* or *Manvarthanibandha*, a [189] well-known commentary on the Manusmṛti, published by V. N. MANDLIK.[6] The assumed identity of the two commentators at present rests, it is true, merely on the identity of the names, but can scarcely be regarded on that account as doubtful. It is hardly conceivable that there were two different Sarvajña-Nārāyaṇas, both commentators of well-known works on Dharmaśāstra like the Mahābhārata and the Manusmṛti.

The date of Sarvajña has been fixed on the basis of certain quotations[7]

---

1 This important passage was verified by me in a MS. of Sarvajña's commentary deposited at the Institute, namely, Bombay Government Collection No. 33 of A 1879-80 (fol. 194°).

2 *Tagore Lectures*, p. 11 ; passage cited in BURNELL'S *Tanjore Catalogue*, p. 126. Cf. also *Recht und Sitte*, p. 31.

3 *The Laws of Manu*, S. B. E., vol. 25, p. CXX.

4 *Das Mahābhārata und seine Theile*, Kiel 1894, 3. Band, p. 71 f.

5 Cf. KANE, *History of Dharmaśāstra*, Poona 1930, vol. I, pp. 157, 708.

6 *Mānava-Dharma-Śāstra*, Bombay 1886.

7 Cf. R. G. BHANDARKAR'S *Report on the Search for Skt. MSS.* for 1883-84, p. 62.

BÜHLER cautiously remarks that Sarvajña-Nārāyaṇa "cannot have written later than in the last half of the fourteenth century,"[1] but the recent researches of KANE tend to show that Sarvajña flourished between A.D. 1100 and 1300.[2]

(ii) *Arjunamiśra.*[3]

Both Devabodha and Sarvajña are mentioned and cited several times by the Bengali commentator Arjunamiśra, the manner in which Arjunamiśra refers to Devabodha suggesting that in his time Devabodha's commentary possessed an established reputation. These references are as follows :

(a) In the foreword to his scholium (Bombay Govt. Coll. No. 30 of A 1879-80 = Da_1 of the Critical Edition), Arjuna pays homage to his predecessors, citing by name several of them. Devabodha, he mentions with special reverence, whose commentary (among others) he had carefully studied before writing his own commentary on the Mbh.:

वेदव्यासवैशंपायनदेवबोधविमलबोधसर्वज्ञनारायणशाण्डिल्यमाधवपितृभ्यो नमः

श्रीदेवबोधपादादिमतमालोक्य यत्नतः ।
क्रियतेऽर्जुनमिश्रेण भारतार्थप्रदीपिका ॥

Worth noting is the fact that in the long series of names of Bhāratācāryas cited by Arjuna at the beginning of the above extract, the first four names Vyāsa and Vaiśaṁpayāna, Devabodha [190] and Sarvajña have been recited in the correct order of precedence and chronology, a point to which we shall return in the sequel.

(b) Arjuna mentions the Ācāryas again in the list of his (immediate and remote) "Gurus", placing this time Devabodha at the head of the list, which ends with the name of his father, who (as we know from other sources) was a well-known reciter (*pāṭhaka*)[4] of the Mbh.

श्रीदेवबोधविमलबोधशाण्डिल्यमाधवाः ।
नारायणश्च सर्वज्ञः पिता च गुरवो मम ॥

(c) In the short introduction which prefaces his commentary on the Virāṭa,[5] Arjuna twice mentions Devabodha, once to give expression to the high esteem in which Arjuna holds him and again to record his gratefulness to his illustrious predecessor :

वेदव्यासमुखाम्भोजगलितं वाङ्मयामृतम् ।
संभोजयन्तं भुवनं देवबोधं भजामहे ॥

... ...

---

[1] BÜHLER, *op. cit.* p. cxxix.

[2] KANE, *op. cit.* p. 157.

[3] See also my paper on Arjunamiśra in the *Sir J. J. Modi Commemoration Volume*, p. 565.

[4] See my "Arjunamiśra," p. 566.

[5] Gujarati Printing Press edition, p. 1 (right column).

श्रीदेवबोधपादादितातोपदेशसेविना ।
क्रियतेऽर्जुनमिश्रेण विराटपर्वदीपिका ॥

(d) Finally, while commenting on 1. 143. 34 (a difficult stanza, giving a fanciful derivation of the name Ghaṭotkaca), Arjuna mentions two readings which had both won the approval of Devabodha :

शेषपाठद्वयं देवबोधपदिनी (sic) संमतम् ।[1]

These two readings are *in fact* mentioned by Devabodha : vide fol. 37[b] of the Baroda MS. of Devabodha's commentary on the Ādi.

The above extracts taken together indisputably prove that Arjunamiśra was posterior to both Devabodha and Sarvajña-Nārāyaṇa. Adding the name of Arjunamiśra to Series 1, we get

Series 2: Devabodha—Sarvajña—Arjunamiśra.

Some faint light on the question of the age of Arjunamiśra is thrown by a dated MS. of Arjuna's commentary listed by the late M. M. Haraprasada Sāstri in his *Notices of Sanskrit MSS.*, Second [191] Series, Vol. I (Calcutta 1900), p. 298 (MS. No. 295). The late Mahamahopadhyaya reported that it was a carefully written palm-leaf MS. of Arjuna's commentary on the Mokṣadharma, called *Mokṣadharmārthadīpikā* written in archaic Bengali characters and belonging, apparently, to Babu Saradaprasanna Ghose of Kelomal, Tamluk. The MS. gave the date of writing as Śaka 1456 (ca. A.D. 1534).[2]

I may here draw attention to some stanzas added by the copyist, which are to the effect that already at the time when the copy was made, correct MSS. of Arjuna's commentary were a rarity even in Bengal, the home of the commentator, which can only be explained by assuming, as pointed out already by Mahadeva Shastri Bakre that there was a considerable interval of time between the two. The stanzas I am referring to are :

पितुः सदुपदेशेन विद्वद्भ्रात्रनुरोधतः ।
प्राङ्निबन्धस्य संशुद्धौ कृता यत्नोऽधुना मया ॥
अल्पाधीतीलिपिग्रन्थशुद्धाक्षरसमुच्चयः ।
विदुषां हेलया प्राच्यग्रन्थो नाशमुपेयिवान् ॥

The date Śaka 1456 (ca. A. D. 1534) is then the lower limit of the age of Arjuna, but the date of Arjuna, if we rely on the information vouchsafed by the copyist, must be long prior to A. D. 1534.

(iii) *Nīlakaṇṭha.*

We return to Nīlakaṇṭha, who is the next great Mbh. commentator, and who cites or mentions Devabodha, Sarvajña-Nārāyaṇa and Arjunamiśra, not

---

1 Read देवबोधपादानां संमतम् ?

2 The reference is given in the Gujarati Printing Press edition of the Virāṭaparvan, Introduction, p. 6.

indeed in the introduction to his commentary on the Mbh., where he mentions a number of his "Gurus", but elsewhere in the course of his well-known scholium. Here are the references.

(a) While commenting on 1. 158. 14, a stanza with numerous variants, Nīlakaṇṭha cites an old variant of the entire stanza, mentioning Devabodha in that connection.

न नंहसाः शृङ्गिणो वा न च देवाञ्जनस्रजः ।
कुबेरस्य यथोष्णीषं किं मां समुपसर्पथ ॥
[192] इति प्राचीनः पाठो देवबोधादिभिर्व्याख्याततत्वात् ।[1]

It is worthy of note that Nīlakaṇṭha regards the variants as *ancient*, owing to its having been explained by "Devabodha and others". He must therefore consider Devabodha as an ancient authority.

What Nīlakaṇṭha regards as ancient is of course a matter for speculation. Nevertheless I do not think that Nīlakaṇṭha would have used the word *prācina* in connection with Devabodha unless the interval between them was at least three or four centuries.

In passing it may be mentioned that this reference to Devabodha by Nīlakaṇṭha is yet another instance of the practice of mentioning names of Ācāryas *honoris causa* (pūjārtham),[2] because the reading cited by Nīlakaṇṭha is probably not that of Devabodha at all, who to judge by the lemmata in his commentary must have had before him a stanza differing from the corresponding stanza of the Critical Edition merely in reading *śakunāḥ* for *kuṇapāḥ* of the Critical Edition (1. 158. 14). The third pāda of the stanza as cited by Nīlakaṇṭha is certainly the reading of the T G version, found otherwise only in three conflated N MSS., and in a fourth one written in the *margin*; while the last pāda was found by me only in four MSS. (K_2 B_3 $M_{3.5}$) of my critical apparatus, one of them (B_3) having as a matter of fact the reading of our text in the *margin*! It is therefore most improbable that Devabodha had commented on the particular variant version cited by Nīlakaṇṭha, and it is really doubtful to me whether Nīlkaṇṭha had at all Devabodha's commentary before him. Devabodha is referred to by Nīlakaṇṭha merely as one of the ancient Ācāryas.

(b) While commenting on B. 7. 82. 2, Nīlakaṇṭha notices a variant interpretation of *madhuparkika* given by Devabodha :

मधुपर्किकाः मधुपर्कसमये पठन्तीति देवबोधः ।

(c) Nīlakaṇṭha's reference to Sarvajña will be found in his comment on B. 5. 40. 10 (Gujarati Printing Press ed., p. 131) :

[193] विषं लोहमिति सर्वज्ञः । स्वर्णनाभः शालग्रामः । दक्षिणावर्तः शङ्ख इति नारायणः ।

---

[1] This passage was already cited by me in the Critical Edition of the Ādiparvan, p. 666.

[2] Cf. *ZDMG.* Vol. 66 (1912), p. 541 f.

and again in the same adhyāya, a few stanzas further on (B. 5. 40. 26), we find :

परिसंस्तीर्याग्नीन् परिस्तरणैः । एतेनाग्निहोत्रमुपलक्षयतीति नारायणः । परिसंस्तीर्य वितत्य । स्वे स्वे स्थाने आधायेत्यर्थः ।

A reference to Sarvajña's commentary printed in the same work (p. 131 f.) will show that all these explanations do *as a matter of fact* occur in the commentary of Sarvajña, while they are *not* met with in any of the three other commentaries printed there.

(d) For Nīlakaṇṭha's mention of Arjunāmiśra, I may draw attention to Nīlakaṇṭha's comment on B. 3. 291. 70, a stanza at the end of the Rāmopākhyāna, where he mentions various explanations of the word *jārūthya*, among them the one given by Arjunamiśra, whom he mentions by name :

जारूथ्यान् त्रिगुणदक्षिणानिति अर्जुनमिश्रः ।

These various extracts establish the posteriority of Nīlakaṇṭha to Devabodha, Sarvajña-Nārāyaṇa and Arjunamiśra. Adding Nīlakaṇṭha to Series 2, we get

Series 3 : *Devabodha—Sarvajña—*
Arjunamiśra—Nīlakaṇṭha.

It will be remembered that as each member of this series of four names clearly *cites* one or more of his predecessors, this is a chronological sequence whose correctness is *absolutely* incontrovertible.

(*iv*) *Vimalabodha.*

There is moreover a subsidiary series connected with a Mbh. commentator called Vimalabodha,[1] to which we shall now turn our attention.

It will be recalled that in the excerpts given above from the commentary of Arjunamiśra, the commentator twice mentions Vimalabodha in close proximity to Devabodha. Therefore it is evident that Arjunamiśra is posterior to Vimalabodha, whose commentary (ṭīkā) variously known as *Durghaṭārthaprakāśinī* [194] or *Viṣamaślokī* has fortunately been preserved. In the introduction to this unpublished commentary, a copy of which is to be found in the Bombay Government Collection (No. 84 of 1869-70), while speaking of his predecessors, Vimalabodha says (fol. 1) :

निघण्टुभाष्यनिगमनिरुक्तानि विशेषतः ।
वैशंपायनटीकादि देवस्वामिमतानि च ।
वीक्ष्य व्याख्या विरचिता दुर्घटार्थप्रकाशिनी ॥

Again while giving the etymologies of the name of the Sūta, Loma- (or Roma-)harṣaṇa, Vimalabodha observes (fol. 2) ;

पश्यतां मुनीनां अतिविस्मयमुत्पादितवान् इति लोमहर्षणनामाभूदिति देवबोधपादा आहुः ।

---

[1] See HOLTZMANN, op. cit. vol. 3, p. 72.

Undoubtedly the Devasvāmin mentioned in the first excerpt is the same as the Devabodha (who in the colophons of his commentary is styled *paramahaṁsa-parivrājakācārya*) in the second. Incidentally it may be pointed out that the etymology of Loma- (or Roma-)harṣaṇa mentioned by Vimalabodha is actually to be found in Devabodha's scholium. In the Baroda MS. (11372) of the unpublished commentary of Devabodha, we read (fol. 3 b, line 1 f.) :

पश्यतां मुनीनामतिविस्मयात् रोमाञ्चमुत्पादितवानिति लोमहर्षणनामाभूत् । ,

which substantially agrees with the excerpt in the commentary of Vimalabodha.

Since Arjunamiśra mentions Vimalabodha, and Vimalabodha cites Devabodha, we get a subsidiary series, namely,

Series 4: Devabodha—Vimalabodha—Arjunamiśra.

Thus far we have been treading on solid ground and the correctness of Series 1-4 is, as far as I can judge, absolutely unimpeachable.

In trying to combine Series 3 and 4, however, there arises the difficulty that no cross reference has hitherto been found in the works of Vimalabodha on the one hand and Sarvajña-Nārāyaṇa on the other. Their relative chronological position is, therefore, a matter for speculation. It is possible, however, to combine the two series *tentatively*, on the equivocal testimony of Arjunamiśra, which we shall proceed to examine more closely.

[195] In one of the lists of the Ācāryas cited by Arjunamiśra, we have the sequence, Veda-Vyāsa, Vaiśaṁpāyana, Devabodha, Vimalabodha, Sarvajña-Nārāyaṇa, Śāṇḍilya Mādhava. Here the first two pairs, as was pointed out above, have been named in the correct chronological order, the earlier author being placed first, in conformity with the rule governing the sequence of the members of a Dvandva compound (P. 2.2.34 Vā.). Devabodha is, as we have seen, prior to Vimalabodha as surely as Vyāsa, the reputed author of the Great Epic, is prior to Vaiśaṁpāyana. Further in both lists the father of Arjunamiśra is mentioned last. These facts suggest the surmise that the whole series is arranged in the strict chronological sequence. If this surmise be correct, then Sarvajña-Nārāyaṇa would be posterior to Vimalabodha, and we get, tentatively, the sequence : Vimalabodha—Sarvajña.

It may, however, be noted that such names are often found arranged on the diametrically opposite principle of *uttarottaragarīyastva*, i.e., naming the more important persons later, which is however not admissible in the particular instance ; or even arranged on no principle at all ; or at least on some principle which it is difficult for us to comprehend. In fact a subsequent enumeration of these same Ācāryas by the same Arjunamiśra is in partial conflict with the earlier list ! There the sequence (already given above) is

Devabodha, Vimalabodha, Śāṇḍilya Mādhava, Nārāyaṇa-Sarvajña. Here Sarvajña-Nārāyaṇa has been placed *after* Śāṇḍilya Mādhava, while in the former list he is placed *before* them! This irregularity apart, the lists tally with each other.

It is not, however, impossible to resolve this contradiction and harmonize the data. There is a notable difference between the two lists. The first one is in prose, the second is an anuṣṭubh stanza. I am disposed to attach more importance to the sequence of the prose enumeration, and to regard the change of sequence in the other as due to the exigencies of metre. The first again is a formal expression of homage (*namaskriyā*), where the principle of priority has been, it seems, rigidly observed; on the other hand, the second is merely a collective metrical list of the author's "Gurus," where the consideration of rank and precedence did [196] not perhaps prevail so much. I may also point out that the first list is in the form of a Dvandva compound, while in the second the persons have been all *independently* mentioned. If these considerations have any value, then we may postulate, at least tentatively, another series,

Series 5: Devabodha—Vimalabodha—Sarvajña—Arjuna—Nīlakaṇṭha,

where the relative position of Vimalabodha and Sarvajña alone is open to doubt.

Of these five commentators, as was mentioned above, Sarvajña could not have lived later than the latter half of the fourteenth century and flourished probably between A. D. 1100 and 1300; while Arjunamiśra lived some time prior to A. D. 1534.[1] Moreover, if the position assigned in Series 5 to Sarvajña be correct, then both Devabodha and Vimalabodha must have lived long prior to A. D. 1300.[2]

* * *

§ 2. What was Devabodha's Version of the Mahābhārata Like?

The only commentary of the Mahābhārata completely printed so far is

---

1 Since the above was written, two efforts have been made to fix the date of Arjunamiśra. Mr. Jogendra Chandra Ghosh (*Indian Culture*, Vol. I, p. 706 ff.), working on the data supplied by certain ancient pedigrees preserved in Bengal, arrives at the date *ca.* A.D. 1300 for Arjunamiśra; but it may be pointed out that the method of *fixing* precise dates on the basis of pedigrees alone never gives *entirely* reliable results. On the other hand, Mr. P. K. Gode of the Bhandarkar Institute (*Indian Culture*, Vol. 2, p. 141 ff.), relying on his identification of the Satya-Khāna, who was a patron of Arjunamiśra (see *Sir J. J. Modi Commemoration Volume*, p. 566), argues for a date between A.D. 1450 and A.D. 1500. There is thus a difference of about 200 years between the two computations. But the matter is still *sub judice*, and more light on the question may be expected from further investigation of the question which is being carried on by these two scholars.

2 See further the Appendix at the end of this paper (below, p. 202).

the *Bhāratabhāvadīpa* by Nīlakaṇṭha. The Gujarati Printing Press of Bombay has done, however, inestimable service to the cause of Mahābhārata studies by publishing other commentaries at least on the Virāṭa and Udyoga, edited by Mahadeva Shastri [197] BAKRE. The Virāṭaparvan Volume (published in 1915) contains, besides (1) the *Bhāratabhāvadīpa*, the commentaries of (2) Arjunamiśra, (3) Caturbhuja, (4) Vimalabodha, (5) Rāmakṛṣṇa, (6) Sarvajña-Nārāyaṇa and (7) Vādirāja, as also a commentary called (8) the *Viṣamapadavivaraṇa* of unknown authorship. The Udyogaparvan Volume (published in 1920) includes, on the other hand, besides (1) the *Bhāratabhāvadīpa*, the commentaries of (2) Arjunamiśra, (3) Vimalabodha, (4) Sarvajña-Nārāyaṇa and (5) Vādirāja.[1] A commentary more important than any of these and one more neglected still is the *Jñānadīpikā* of Devabodha. Until recently nothing was in fact known about Devabodha or his commentary on the Mahābhārata save what is contained in perfunctory notices of Sanskrit MSS., which has been summarized in HOLTZMAN's meritorious work *Das Mahābhārata* (Vol. 3, section 14, para 3, p. 70 f.). A selection of Devabodha's readings and glosses was for the first time published by me in the critical notes of the Ādiparvan Volume.[2]

I have shown in the previous section that Devabodha is indubitably earlier than Nīlakaṇṭa, Arjunamiśra, Sarvajña-Nārāyaṇa or even Vimalabodha, and is therefore in all probability the earliest commentator of the Mahābhārata hitherto known. It is therefore needless to add that the commentary is most valuable and its evidence, both positive and negative, of supreme importance for the constitution of the text.

The MS. of the commentary (which is *unaccompanied* by the epic text) utilized by me for the Ādi belongs to the Baroda Central Library (Sanskrit Section) and was kindly placed at my disposal by Dr. Benoytosh BHATTACHARYA, Director of the Oriental Institute of Baroda, to whom my sincere thanks are due for the kind loan.[3] This paper MS. which bears the identification No. 11372, contains the commentary on Ādi only and is written in [198] Devanāgarī characters of about the seventeenth century. The bulk of the MS. is in a fair state of preservation, though in many places the text is extremely corrupt. In our MS. the name of the commentary is given as *Jñānadīpikā*; but, according to HOLTZMANN (*op. cit.* Vol. 3, p. 71), it is also known as *Mahābhārata-tātparyaṭīkā* or *tātparyadīpikā*. MSS. of this commentary are rare, and no complete copy has yet been found.

---

1 Vādirāja's commentary on the Sabhā has been published by Prof. P. P. Subrahmanya SASTRI as an Appendix to his edition of the Sabhā according to the Southern recension (Madras 1932). For Vādirāja's date see further below (pp. 203-210) the note on the subject by Mr. P. K. GODE.

2 See also my Prolegomena, p. LXX.

3 There is another MS. of the commentary in the Asiatic Society of Bengal, which was also consulted by me.

In the colophon the author is described as *paramahaṁsa-parivrājaka*. He must therefore have belonged to an order of Saṁnyāsins. The name of his Guru is given as Satyabodha. This is all the personal data we have at present about Devabodha.

The *Jñānadīpikā* is a concise ṭīkā, that is, a running commentary paraphrasing the difficult words of the epic text and occasionally explaining the gist or purport (*tātparya*) of the original. The extent of the text of the commentary on the Ādi is given at the end of our MS. as 1,400 granthas.

The homage which Arjuna pays to Devabodha in the Introduction to his scholium is by no means a matter of mere form. Arjuna appears to have made a very close study indeed of the scholium of Devabodha, and based his own commentary, on the Ādi at least, largely on that of his predecessor. He has copied very large portions of Devabodha's commentary, sometimes *verbatim*, sometimes in extracts. Moreover, even when the commentators differ, the influence of Devabodha is plainly discernible. In fact, Arjuna's *Arthadīpikā* may be considered, as I have remarked elsewhere,[1] as a revised and enlarged edition of Devabodha's *Jñānadīpikā*. Unlike the commentary of Nīlakaṇṭha, that of Devabodha is unaccompanied by the epic text. The question, therefore, naturally arises what was Devabodha's text like?

When we read the commentary along with any of the old printed editions of the Mahābhārata, like the Calcutta or the Bombay or the Kumbhakonam editions, we are at once struck by the singular disparity between the text and the commentary. Not only does Devabodha's commentary contain many words or expressions which do not occur at all in the Vulgate, but it also cites, at times, verses or stanzas which read differently in the
[199] Vulgate. One also comes across passages and even adhyāyas of the Vulgate on which one expects some comment but which are left wholly uncommented by Devabodha.

The Southern recension may be categorically ignored in our search for the prototype of Devabodha's commentary, as this commentator does not know even a single one of the many passages peculiar to the Southern recension. He further does not show the typical Southern transposition of the Śakuntalā and Yayāti episodes, nor the characteristic position of the prose genealogical adhyāya (called *pūruvaṁśānukīrtana*), after the chapter containing the eulogy of the epic (*Bhārataprasaṁsā*).

The vulgate (with the Bengali) may likewise be excluded. It agrees with Devabodha's text up to a certain point; but the divergences, which are numerous, remain inexplicable. There remain then only the Śāradā and the "K" versions. And with them, the version of Devabodha does, as a matter of fact, show very close affinity.

It is worthy of note that Devabodha has no commentary on any of the

---

[1] Ādiparvan, Prolegomena, p. LXX.

six adhyāyas of the Vulgate which are completely missing in the Śāradā and the K MSS. and which have also been completely omitted in the Critical Edition of the Ādi. They are the following adhyāyas of the *Vulgate* : (i) adhy. 22 (duplicate description of the ocean) ; (ii) adhy. 24 (Aruṇa is appointed charioteer of the Sun, an evident digression and interpolation) ; (iii) adhy. 116 (birth of Duḥśalā : a fairy tale of questionable authenticity) ; (iv) adhy. 139 (an absurd chapter describing further exploits of the Pāṇḍavas and containing a reference to Yavana kings) ; (v) adhy. 140 (Kaṇikanīti) ; and finally, (vi) adhy. 149 (Pāṇḍavas' crossing the Ganges, a passage of doubtful value).

But on principle, we cannot attach very great importance to such *omissions*, as a commentator is apt to skip in the Mahābhārata any adyhāya which he thinks too simple to need any comment. This explanation will apply to most of the omissions mentioned above, but will *not* hold good in the case of the Kaṇikanīti an adhy. of 140 stanzas, which has evoked lengthy comments from both Arjunamiśra and Nīlakaṇṭha ; we expect some comment on this adhyāya by a commentator like Devabodha.

[200] Much more important from our point of view is an *addition* characteristic of the Kaśmīrī version. This version adds at the very end of the Ādi a supplementary (and entirely superfluous) adhyāya, which contains merely a *variant* version of the well-known Purāṇic tale of Śvetaki's sacrifice, occurring earlier in the course of this very parvan, and which was known to Kṣemendra. Curiously enough the king who is called Śvetaki in the first version is here called Śvetaketu ! That the version of Devabodha contained this interpolated (supplementary) adhyāya is proved by the concluding remark of Devabodha on this adhyāya (fol. 48) :

श्वेतकिरेव श्वेतकेतुरिति नाम ।

This remark, as I have pointed out elsewhere, will not apply to any version which did not have the supplementary adhyāya containing the story of Śvetaketu, which in fact is peculiar to the Śāradā and the K versions. These facts demonstrate that the version of Devabodha agrees with the Śāradā and K versions with respect to both addition and omission of whole adhyāyas.

The conclusion regarding the affinity between the two versions is fortified by many minor agreements in point of shorter passages and even readings of individual stanzas.

For example, Devabodha has no comment on any portion of the Brahmā-Gaṇeśa episode (40 stanzas in the Vulgate), which is missing in its *entirety* only in the Kaśmīrī and the Bengali versions. Again, for 1. 105. 4-7 of the Critical Edition the Vulgate substitutes a lengthy passage of 56 lines, which is entirely ignored in the commentary of Devabodha, who on the other hand *cites* 7^{ab} (a line not known to the Vulgate), in exact agreement with the

Śāradā and K versions (besides the Southern recension), but in direct opposition to the Bengali and the Devanāgarī versions. In connection with the omission of adhy. 139-140 of the Vulgate mentioned above, the Śāradā and K versions omit the first 19 stanzas of the following adhyāya (namely, adhy. 141 of the Vulgate). In conformity with that, the first 19 stanzas of adhy. 141 are ignored completely in the scholium of Devabodha. It may be noted that the omission of adhy. 139-140 together with the first 19 stanzas of adhy. 141 of the Vulgate [201] makes an aggregate and continuous omission of 139 (= 27 + 93+19) stanzas of the Vulgate, a not inconsiderable portion of the text. Likewise there is no commentary on nearly 70 stanzas of adhy. 128 and 129 of the Vulgate, which are omitted only in the Śāradā-K group and the Critical Edition.

This affinity is further borne out by agreements as regards minor readings too numerous to mention.

These considerations make it, in my opinion, perfectly clear that the version of Devabodha is closely allied to the Śāradā and K versions.

Though the Śāradā version and what I have called the "K" version run for the most part parallel to each other, there are in fact minor discrepancies between the MSS. of these versions, which indicate different sources. But as, on the one hand, we have for the Ādi a solitary MS. ($Ś_1$) of the genuine Śāradā (or Kaśmīrī) version, and on the other hand we do not know the provenance of the Devanāgarī MSS. which I have denoted by the symbol "K" (on account of their affinity to the version of Kaśmīr), it is at this stage not easy to explain these discrepancies between Śāradā and Ḳ. It would be also premature to say whether Devabodha's version was more akin to Śāradā or the K version.

I may, however, draw attention to one instance which suggests to my mind and affinity with K rather than with the Śāradā version. In 1. 68. 72 the text reading is *asatyavacanā nāryaḥ* (nom. plu.), "women (are) perfidious," a general statement. Only $K_{1.2}$ B_1 (m as in text) have, on the other hand, *asatyavacane 'nārye* (voc. sing.), "O thou perfidious (and) dishonourable (woman)!" $K_{0.4}$ appear to have corrupt forms of the same. The vocative appears to be, therefore, peculiar to the K version, which differs here from the Śāradā, and which latter has the nom. plu. *as in all other MSS.* Now in agreement with K, Devabodha has *anārye* = *vakre*! One instance of an agreement like this is, I will readily admit, wholly inadequate to prove the point. It can only give an indication and may perchance give wrong indication. The question may, therefore, be left over for future investigation.

[202] APPENDIX.

List of five major Mahābhārata commentators arranged according to the probable chronological sequence, with the names of their commentaries, approximate date, and sundry data about them.

No.	Commentator	Commentary	Age	Remarks
1	Devabodha	Jñānadīpikā, Mbh.—tātparya-ṭīka, Tātparyadīpikā		Saṁnyāsin : pupil of Satyabodha, mentioned or cited by Vimala, Arj., Nīl.
2	Vimalabodha	Viṣamaśloka-ṭīkā, Durghaṭārtha-prakāśinī, Durbodhapa-dabhañjinī		Mentions Vaiśampāyana's Ṭīkā and cites Devabodha (once as °svāmin).
3	Sarvajña Nārāyaṇa	Bhāratārtha-prakāśa	Ante 1300	Mentions Dev. and is cited by Arj. and Nīl., as also by a lexicographer Rāyamukuṭa. (A.D. 1431).
4	Arjunamiśra	Mahābhāratārtha(pra)dīpikā, Bhāratasaṁgrahadīpīkā	Ante 1534	Mentions Dev., Vimala, S. Nārāyaṇa, Sāṇḍilya Mādhava. Belongs to Eastern (or Gauḍa) school. Cited by Nīl. One MS. of his comm. dated Śaka 1456 (=ca, A.D. 1534)[1]
5	Nīlakaṇṭha Caturdhara	Bhāratabhāva-dīpa.	ca. 1700	Maharāṣṭra Brahmin. Son of Govindasūri and Phullāmbikā, resident of Kopargaon on the Godavari. Mentions Dev., S. Nārāyaṇa, Arj. Ratnagarbha and others.

[1] For Arjunamiśra's date, see also Mr. J. C. GHOSH'S recent paper in *Indian Culture*, vol. 2 (1936), p. 585 ff.

* VI. The Bhṛgus and the Bharata : A Text-Historical Study[1].

The Bhṛgus are unquestionably an interesting old clan.[1] Tempted by the tantalizing affinity between the Sanskrit name Bhṛgu and the Greek φλέγυ in the name of Φλεγύας and of the Φλεγύαι, A. WEBER[2] postulated a genetic connection between the Indian and the Greek names, and even ascribed Indo-germanic antiquity to a certain legend about Bhṛgu Vāruṇi preserved in the Śatapatha Brāhmaṇa (11. 6. 1), a legend of which he thought he had discovered a parallel in Greek mythology. The facile phonetic equation put up by WEBER has not, however, commended itself to other scholars, and we are not specially concerned with it either. But it cannot be gainsaid that the clan is very ancient and that some of their legends are of hoary antiquity. There are scattered notices about the Bhṛgus to be found from the Vedic Saṁhitās onwards through the Brāhmaṇa, Āraṇyaka and Upaniṣad literature up to the Epics and the Purāṇas, steadily growing in volume and importance.

[2] Not only is the clan ancient, its legends also are highly interesting. So suggestive in fact are the early myths of this clan that they had in former years engrossed the attention of many a student of Indian mythology, and called forth a variety of interpretations. Thus, A. BERGAGNE[3] looked upon the Bhṛgu myth of the Ṛgveda as merely a more developed form of the early tradition about the descent of fire and identified Bhṛgu with Agni. A. KUHN[4] and A. BARTH[5] agreed in regarding the Bhṛgus as personifications of the lightning flash, and KUHN[6] tried to harmonize the Greek myth regarding the descent of fire with the Vedic. A. WEBER,[7] as already remarked, saw in a legend preserved in the Śatapatha Brāhmaṇa a relic of primitive Indo-germanic mythology. But even the later legends of these people are not without a

---

* [*ABORI* 18. 1-76.]

[1] The best general account of the Bhṛgus has been given by SIEG in the *Encyclopaedia of Religion and Ethics* (edited by HASTINGS), s. v. "Bhṛgu," from which the following details regarding previous work on this subject have been mainly extracted. For Vedic references see also MACDONELL and KEITH, *Vedic Index of names and Subjects,* s. v. "Cyavana", "Bhṛgu", etc.

[2] *ZDMG* 9 (1855), 237-243 ; "Eine Legende des Śatapatha Brāhmaṇa über die strafende Vergettung nach dem Tode."

[3] *Religion Védique* (1878-83) I, 52-56.

[4] *Herabkunft des Feuers und des Göttertranks* (1859) 8 ff [[2]Mythologische Studien, Vol. I. (1886), 10 ff.]

[5] *Les Religions de l'Inde* (Paris 1885), 8.

[6] *Op. cit.* 13 ff.[[2]14 ff.].

[7] *ZDMG* 9 (1855), 242.

certain amount of grandiosity and ostentation. Just consider the figure of Paraśurāma : a matricide, annihilator of the Kṣatriyas and finally an *avatāra* of Viṣṇu (the "Preserver") all in one.

The popularity of the Paraśurāma legend in India is attested by the number of places, scattered all over India, which are associated with his name and his exploits and held sacred to his memory.[1] Near the Kangra District[2] of the Punjab there is a very ancient temple dedicated to Paraśurāma, (a name not yet applied to him in our epic), in which is deposited a copper-plate grant recording the gift of a village to a Brahmin studying the *A. V.* In the State of Udaipur[3] there is a sacred pool called Markundiaḥ where Rāma is said to have bathed and atoned for his sins; likewise in Cape Comorin. In the Bijapur District[4] of the Bombay Presidency, an axe-shaped rock situated on a riverbank marks the spot where Rāma is represented as having washed his famous axe (*paraśu*), which has given him his nick-name Paraśurāma, Rāma-with-the-Axe; a stone boulder situated in the river bed has preserved Paraśurāma's foot-prints. Even this irresistible axe of his has been deified, and there is in Mysore State[5] a temple dedicated to it. Gokarṇ[6] shows a sacred pool dedicated to Mahādeva, which is said to have been built by the son of Jamadagni. Even the Lakhīmpur District[7] of distant Assam has a pool to show to which, according to popular belief, Paraśurāma had surrendered his dreaded axe, and which attracts pilgrims from every part of India.

Notwithstanding the absorbing interest of the Bhārgava myths, it is primarily not their interpretation that is attempted here. [3] That is a task fraught with difficulties and uncertainties, as also one which would call for a range of knowledge and a compose of mind to which the present writer can lay no claim. The modest aim of this paper is to collect and collate the Bhārgava references in the Mahābhārata, in other words, to give a succinct account of all that the Great Epic of India has to say about the Bhṛgus. The choice of the source-book is, I think, abundantly justified, because the Mahābhārata, as I believe, is the richest mine for the exploration of the Bhārgava material, a veritable thesaurus of Bhārgava legends, containing as it does the largest number and the greatest variety of such legends. Even this material is naturally not entirely new, having already attracted the attention of scholars, but it seemed to me that it has not been studied with that degree of attention to details which it deserves. It is a trite observation but never-

---

[1] Cf. ANUJAN ACHAN. *Paraśurāma Legend and its Significance*, p. 8 f. citing the *Imperial Gazetteer of India.* The paper was read at the Eighth Session of the All-India Oriental Conference (Mysore 1935) and has since been published separately with the special sanction of the Government of Cochin.

[2] *Imp. Gaz.* 19. 124.

[3] *ibid.* 16. 26.

[4] *ibid.* 5. 129.

[5] *ibid.* 13. 148.

[6] No reference given by ACHAN.

[7] *Imp. Gaz.* 9. 8.

theless true that even what appears on the face of it to be a most insignificant detail might yield a valuable clue if looked at from the correct angle, which is often difficult to get.

My intention is to pass under review here all the important myths and legends relating to the different Bhṛgus, which occur in the Mahābhārata, subjecting them to a critical analysis : to study the manner in which they are presented, to investigate their repetitions and even to examine their discrepancies. We shall find that there are many more Bhārgavas mentioned in our epic than commonly known and many more references to Bhārgavas than commonly suspected.

In essence, it must be admitted, this is merely a text-critical study, a subject which, having engaged my attention for a number of years, has acquired considerable fascination for me. But at the end of the paper it is shown that the investigation might at the same time yield results which are not without general value for a partial elucidation of the obscure history of this venerable old text.

The Bhārgava references could have been presented here in many different ways, but it appeared best to take them up for study in the sequence in which they appear in our epic, to examine the material book by book and chapter by chapter. The total number of passages of the Mahābhārata in which the Bhārgavas are mentioned is astonishingly large. Exigencies of space, [4] however, compelled the writer to restrict himself to the discussion of only the more important of the references.

I add here a genealogical table which will enable the reader to follow the legends of the Bhṛgus and the discussions about them with greater ease. The table is made up from the data of the Mahābhārata itself, but it is undoubtedly incomplete ; it appears to be very much abridged, lacking many details and intermediate links.

GENEALOGICAL TREE OF THE BHṚGUS (ABRIDGED)

- Bhṛgu (m. Pulomā)
  - Kavi
    - Śukra
      - Devayānī (m. Yayāti)
        - Yadu
          - Kṛṣṇa
        - Turvasu
  - Cyavana (m. Sukanyā & Āruṣī)
    - (by Āruṣī) Aurva
      - Ṛcīka (m. Satyavatī)
        - Jamadagni (m. Reṇukā)
          - Rāma Jāmadagnya
    - (by Sukanyā) Pramati (m. Ghṛtācī)
      - Ruru (m. Pramadvarā)
        - Śunaka

ĀDIPARVAN[1]

Strangely enough, already in the *second* chapter of the Ādiparvan, the Parvasaṁgraha, which is in fact, for the greater part of it, something like a Table of Contents, we make our acquaintance with one of the Bhārgavas, the most famous of them, Rāma Jāmadagnya,[2] not yet a full-fledged *avatāra*,[3] a character which *in reality* has no connection whatsoever with the action of the sublime tragedy which is going to be unfolded in the epic. That comes about in this way. The place where the Mahābhārata war was fought, as everybody knows who knows anything at all about the war, was called Kurukṣetra (Gītā 1. 1) :

[5] *dharmakṣetre Kurukṣetre samavetā yuyutsavaḥ |*
māmakāḥ Pāṇḍavāś caiva.....

But the Sūta Ugraśravas, son of Lomaharṣaṇa, who recites the epic at the twelve-year sacrificial session held in the Naimiṣa Forest under the auspices of Śaunaka, gives the name of the place as Samantapañcaka and is careful enough to add that he had visited that sacred spot (*puṇyaṁ deśam*) and was as a matter of fact just returning from it (1. 1. 11 f.):

Samantapañcakaṁ nāma puṇyaṁ dvijaniṣevitam |
gatavān asmi taṁ deśaṁ yuddhaṁ yatrābhavat purā ||
Pāṇḍavānāṁ Kurūṇāṁ ca sarveṣāṁ ca mahīkṣitām |
didṛkṣur āgatas tasmāt samīpaṁ bhavatām iha ||

That obviously needed a little explication. Accordingly we find in the beginning of the second chapter a query about this Samantapañcaka from the sages who formed the audience. They want to know all about this new place of pilgrimage (1. 2. 1) :

Samantapañcakam iti yad uktaṁ sūtanandana |
etat sarvaṁ yathānyāyaṁ śrotum icchāmahe vayam ||

And from the story narrated by the Sūta it proves to be a Bhārgava place of pilgrimage, situated probably somewhere in the neighbourhood of or within the limits of Kurukṣetra.[4] It was in fact, as the Sūta proceeds to explain,

---

1 In the Ādiparvan, the references are to the *Critical Edition* of that book published by this Institute (Poona 1933); elsewhere to the *Vulgate*, the edition used being the Chitrashala edition (Poona 1929-1933). References to the Vulgate are distinguished by prefixing "B." to them.

2 Special studies on Paraśurāma : Irawati KARVE, "The Paraśurāma Myth" in the *Journal of the University of Bombay*, vol. 1 (1932), pp. 115-139; and the paper by ANUJAN ACHAN cited above, *Paraśurāma Legend and its Significance* (1935), and Jarl CHARPENTIER, Paraśu-Rāma, *Kuppuswami Sastri Comm. Vol.* (1937) pp. 9-16.

3 Cf. HOPKINS, *Epic Mythology* (Grundriss d. indo-arischen Phil und Altertumskunde III. Bd., 1. Heft B), p. 211.

4 In the Śalyaparvan it is said that it is a holy place of pilgrimage situated on the Sarasvatī C. 9. 2136.

the sacred spot where the Bhārgava Rāma, the foremost of weapon-bearers (*śastrabhṛtāṁ varaḥ* 1. 2. 3), after extirpating the warrior race during the interval between the Tretā and the Dvāpara Ages, had made five pools of blood, probably forming a circle (hence obviously Samantapañcaka), and standing in the middle of the pools the terrible man offered the uncanny oblation of congealed blood to his forefathers, until the shades of the departed ancestors appeared before him and pacified him, giving him the boon that those sanguinary pools of his would become holy places of pilgrimage (1. 2. 3 ff.):

Tretādvāparayoḥ saṁdhau Rāmaḥ śastrabhṛtāṁ varaḥ |
asakṛt pārthivaṁ kṣatraṁ jaghānāmarṣacoditaḥ || (3)
sa sarvaṁ kṣatram utsādya svavīryeṇānaladyutiḥ |
Samantapañcake pañca cakāra rudhirahradān || (4)
sa teṣu rudhirāmbhaḥsu hradeṣu krodhamūcchitaḥ |
pitṝn saṁtarpayāmāsa rudhireṇeti naḥ śrutam || (5)

[6] A few stanzas later we read that the Kuru-Pāṇḍava war was also fought at this Samantapañcaka (1. 2. 9):

antare caiva saṁprāpte Kali-Dvāparayor abhūt |
Samantapañcake yuddhaṁ Kuru-Pāṇḍavasenayoḥ ||

Samantapañcaka is thus made out to be only another name of Kurukṣetra: evidently a Bhārgava name.[1] The people of India have forgotten this Bhārgava synonym: they remember only Kurukṣetra, a name which has struck deep root in the memory of the people. Even now at every solar eclipse there is held at Kurukṣetra, a mammoth fair, which attracts hundreds of thousands of devout pilgrims,[2] hailing from the different corners of India, who reverently visit the spot hallowed by the blood of their beloved kings of yore, those shining examples of knighthood and chivalry, who counting their lives as straw fell fighting, waging a holy war (*dharmayuddha*), which has made the Kurukṣetra a *dharmakṣetra*.

In passing, it may be mentioned that this short account of the annihilation of the Kṣatriyas by the Brahmin Rāma Jāmadagnya—a very popular theme, as will be seen later on, with the redactors of our Mahābhārata—has been even amplified in later times by the interpolation of a short dialogue

---

[1] Samantapañcaka mentioned in Parvans 1, 3, 6, 7 and 9 only. That the war took place at Samantapañcaka is also mentioned in:

B. 6. 1. 6: SAMANTAPAÑCAKĀD bāhyaṁ śibirāṇi sahasraśaḥ |
kārayāmāsa vidhivat Kuntiputro Yudhiṣṭhiraḥ ||
C. 7. 2725: śvaḥ śroṣyate śiras tasya Ṣaindhavasya raṇe hatam |
SAMANTAPAÑCAKĀD bāhyaṁ viśokā bhava mā rudaḥ ||
C. 9. 3032: etat Kurukṣetra-Samantapañcakam |
Prajāpater uttaravedir ucyate ||
C. 9. 3620-21: Samantapañcake puṇye triṣu lokeṣu viśrute |
ahaṁ nidhanam āsādya lokān prāpsyāmi śāśvatān ||

[2] *Imperial Gazetteer of India*, (1886) vol. 8, p. 374 f.

(of eight lines) between Rāma Jāmadagnya and his Bhārgava ancestors (Ādi 71 * ; cf. B. 3. 83. 29 ff.) :

Rāma Rāma mahābhāga prītāḥ sma tava Bhārgava |
anayā pitṛbhaktyā ca vikrameṇa ca te vibho |
varaṁ vṛṇīṣva bhadraṁ te kim icchasi mahādyute |
Rāma uvāca |
yadi me pitaraḥ prītā yady anugrāhyatā mayi |
yac ca roṣābhibhūtena kṣatram utsāditaṁ mayā | etc.

This passage, which is an abridged version of a dialogue occurring in the Tīrthayātrāparvan, a sub-section of the Āraṇyakaparvan, is found at this point only in certain Devanāgarī MSS. (including those of the "K" Version), and is missing in the Bengali MSS. as well as in the entire Southern recension, and therefore certainly suspect. We shall have occasion to mention other similar enlargements of Bhārgava anecdotes.

[7] The next reference to the Bhārgava Rāma occurs in adhy, 58 of the Ādi. and the theme is the same. The chapter, as a matter of fact, describes the circumstances which led to the incarnation of the gods and goddesses of the Purāṇic pantheon on this earth of ours. But the account begins with an allusion to the great exploit of the Bhārgava Rāma, his total extirpation of the bad old kings of yore (1. 58. 4) :

triḥsaptakṛtvaḥ pṛthivīṁ kṛtvā niḥkṣatriyāṁ purā |
Jāmadagnyas tapas tepe Mahendre parvatottame || (I)

The first line of this stanza is worthy of special note. It occurs, with slight variations, over and over again in our Mahābhārata, its exultant note ringing like a distant echo in the remotest corners and crevices of this huge epos, which was composed by Kṛṣṇa Dvaipāyana to spread in this world the fame of the high-souled Pāṇḍavas and of other puissant *Kṣatriyas* (1. 56. 25 f.) :

Kṛṣṇa-Dvaipāyanenedaṁ kṛtaṁ puṇyacikīrṣuṇā ||
kīrtiṁ prathayatā loke Pāṇḍavānāṁ mahātmanām |
anyeṣām kṣatriyāṇāṁ *ca bhūridraviṇatejasām* ||

When the Bhārgava Rāma, after making a clean sweep of the Kṣatriyas, retired to Mount Mahendra, on the eastern coast of India, to practise austerities, there remained of the warrior caste only the females, and the Kṣatriya race was in imminent danger of becoming totally extinct (Ādi. 58). When the earth was thus bereft of Kṣatriya manhood, the Kṣatriya women, casting aside their pride, approached the Brahmins for offspring. With these Kṣatriya women cohabited the Brahmins of rigid vows of those times, in pity for their sad plight. They cohabited with the Kṣatriya women, not from passion, only in season, never out of season. Thus thousands of Kṣatriya women conceived from their intercourse with pious Brahmins. Their children were the virtuous Kṣatriyas, who ushered in again the Golden

Age. Thus sprang up a second Kṣatriya race from the surviving Kṣatriya women, owing to their intercourse with ascetic Brahmins. The new generation, blessed with long life, throve in virtue. And there were again established the four castes, having Brahmins at their head (1. 58. 8. 10);

[8] *evaṁ tad brāhmaṇaiḥ kṣatraṁ kṣatriyāsu tapasvibhiḥ |*
jātam ṛdhyata dharmeṇa sudīrgheṇāyuṣānvitam |
catvāro 'pi tadā varṇā babhūvur brāhmaṇottarāḥ ||
... ...
tāḥ prajāḥ pṛthivīpāla dharmavratāparāyaṇāḥ |
ādhibhir vyādhibhiś caiva vimuktāḥ sarvaśo narāḥ ||

Later the Asuras, defeated by the gods and expelled from heaven, in order to continue their fight for supremacy, took birth in royal families, among animals and elsewhere on this earth, and so again godless kings were born here on the earth. The goddess Earth, oppressed by this vicious and godless creation, lodged a complaint with Brahmā, who, with a view to freeing her from the tyranny of her oppressors, ordains that the various gods and goddesses, *gandharvas* and *apsarases* incarnate themselves, in different forms and shapes, to wage war with the Asuras, and annihilate them.

In this legend, which is here skilfully interwoven with the much lauded exploit of the Bhārgava Rāma, the Brahmin appears in the rôle of the *de facto* Creator of the Later Kṣatriyas. But in a variant version of the same incident, which occurs in the Śānti (adhy. 48-49 of the Vulgate) and which will be discussed in due course, the narrator, Śrī-Kṛṣṇa himself, while admitting that there was a general slaughter of the Kṣatriyas, allows that some Kṣatriyas had escaped death at the hands of the Bhārgava Rāma and, after his retirement to the forest, emerged from their places of concealment and resumed sovereignty. But in this prologue to the Ādiparvan, however, Vaiśaṁpāyana, as we have seen is quite certain that the Kṣatriyas were *totally* annihilated by Rāma and the race was *entirely* regenerated by Brahmins.

Another little digression, adhy. 60, which explains the origin and genealogy of the different orders of beings, from the gods downwards, contains also a genealogy of the Bhārgavas, the only Brahmanic genealogy, besides that of the Aṅgirasas[1] (a clan closely connected with the Bhṛgus) considered by the epic bards worthy of inclusion in this chapter.

This confused cosmogonic account (1. 60. 1 ff.) begins with the enumeration of the six mind-born (*mānasa*) sons of Brahmā and the eleven sons of Sthāṇu, namely, the eleven Rudras. The six mind-born sons of Brahmā are : Marīci, Aṅgiras, Atri, Pulastya, Pulaha and Kratu, which list does not include Bhṛgu.[2] Dakṣa [9] was born from the right thumb (*aṅguṣṭha*)

1 Even the Aṅgirasas are shown scant courtesy. Only one generation of the family is mentioned : the sons of Aṅgirasas were Bṛhaspati, Utathya and Saṁvarta ; they had a (nameless) sister.

2 These six "mind-born" sons are mentioned again in 1. 59. 10.

of Brahmā, and Dakṣa's wife from his left thumb. Dakṣa begat fifty daughters on his wife, of whom he gave away thirteen, in a lot, to Kaśyapa, son of Marīci. Kaśyapa's offspring were the gods and the titans.[1] The list of gods and demi-gods closes with the progeny of Kaśyapa (1. 60. 39) :

eṣa devagaṇo rājan kīrtitas te 'nupūrvaśaḥ |
yaṁ kīrtayitvā manujaḥ sarvapāpaiḥ pramucyate ||

Immediately, after this list of celestials, come Bhṛgu and his descendants (1. 60. 40) :

Brahmaṇo hṛdayaṁ bhittvā niḥsṛto bhagavān Bhṛguḥ |

The close proximity to the gods is perhaps intended to be an indication of the high position of the Bhṛgus in the Precedence List. The genealogy given here is short and mentions only the well-known descendants of one branch of the Bhārgava clan, the branch made famous by Rāma Jāmadagnya. The pedigree begins with Bhṛgu, who also was a son of Brahmā, being born by piercing his heart (*hṛdaya*).

But this ancestry of Bhṛgu is in conflict with another account found in the epic (Anuśāsana 85 of the Vulgate), according to which Bhṛgu was born from the *seed* of Prajāpati which had fallen in the fire.

The latter account has partial Vedic support, for we read in the Aitareya Brāhmaṇa (3. 34) that the *seed* of Prajāpati became divided into three parts, from which were born Āditya, Bhṛgu and Aṅgiras. On the other hand, in the Pañcaviṁśa Brāhmaṇa (18. 9. 1),[2] the paternity of Bhṛgu with two others is attributed to Varuṇa. Further in the Śatapatha Brāhmaṇa (11. 6. 1. 1), Jaiminīya Brāhmaṇa (1. 42) Taittirīya Upaniṣad (1. 3. 1. 1), Taittirīya Āraṇyaka (9. 1) also, Bhṛgu is said to be the son of Varuṇa; from Varuṇa, it is said, he obtained the knowledge of Brahma.

There seems to be partial synthesis of some of these divergent versions in the confused Anuśāsana account cited above, according to which, while Mahādeva, *in the form of Varuṇa*, was performing a sacrifice, *Brahmā* was presiding and all the gods and the goddesses were present. Seeing that assemblage of celestial damsels of exceeding beauty, desire sprang up in the mind of Brahmā, and he had an emission. As soon as the seed came out, Brahmā took it up with the sacrificial ladle and poured it, like a libation of clarified butter, with the necessary *mantras*, on the burning fire. Thereupon [10] three beings emerged from the sacrificial fire. One arose from the flames (*bhṛk*) and *hence* he was called Bhṛgu ; another came out of the burning charcoals (*aṅgāra*) and hence he passed by the name of Aṅgiras ; the third originated from a heap of extinguished coals and was called Kavi. This tradition we find faintly reflected in a stanza (Ādi. 216*), interpolated

---

1 1. 60. 33 : *Kaśyapasya surāsurāḥ.*

2 Cf. Maitr. Saṁhitā 4. 3. 9 ; 49. 4 ; Jaim. Brāhmaṇa 2. 202.

in most MSS. of the Northern recension after 1. 5. 6 :

Bhṛgur maharṣir bhagavān Brahmaṇā vai svayaṁbhuvā |
Varuṇasya kratau jātaḥ pāvakād iti naḥ śrutam ||

Here we see that the great seer, "Bhagavān" Bhṛgu is said to have been produced by the self-create Lord Brahmā during Varuna's sacrifice from Fire.

However, to return to the pedigree of the Bhṛgus given in Ādi 60, we find the statement that Bhṛgu had two sons, Kavi (whose son was Śukra) and Cyavana. About both Śukra and Cyavana, we hear a great deal in our Mahābhārata. From Cyavana the short pedigree runs as follows: Cyavana-Aurva-Ṛcīka-Jamadagni-Rāma. About Kavi and Ṛcīka alone the epic has not very much to narrate, but it is full of the amazing powers and the wonderful exploits of the remaining Bhārgavas mentioned here, for whom our epic shows great predilection.

Thus we find, only a few chapters later, the epic relating at great length the well-known story of Yayāti (Yayātyupākhyāna, Ādi. 71-80), in which Śukra, the Asura priest, and his haughty and ambitious daughter Devayānī play a prominent rôle, and which probably contains a solid substratum of historic truth. Between Yayāti and the Pāṇḍavas there intervene, according to the computation of PARGITER, nearly ninety generations. And thus although the connection of this episode with the main epic story is of most slender character, it possesses considerable Bhārgava interest, which is probably the main reason why it has been excerpted here from some Purāṇic source.[1] The story of Yayāti is introduced in the epic in the following manner.

In adhy. 70, Vaiśaṁpāyana briefly sketches the early history of the Lunar Dynasty, incidentally mentioning Yayāti and his five sons. Janamejaya is not satisfied with this sketchy account and requests Vaiśaṁpāyana to relate in detail the story of Yayāti, a remote ancestor of the Pāṇḍavas, "tenth in descent from Prajāpati" (*daśamo yaḥ Prajāpateḥ* 1. 71. 1). The story of Yayāti is as follows.

[11] Bṛhaspati, son of Aṅgiras, was the preceptor of the Devas, the Bhārgava Śukra (Kāvya Uśanas) that of the Asuras. Śukra, a powerful sorcerer, like all the other Bhārgavas, had the knowledge of the secret of reviving the dead (*saṁjīvanī vidyā*); not so Bṛhaspati. The Devas were therefore handicapped in their wars with the Asuras. So at the instance of the Devas Bṛhaspati's son Kaca goes to Śukra, who was then the priest sorcerer of the Asura king Vṛṣaparvan and lives with him as his disciple in order to obtain from him a knowledge of the art of reviving the dead. Śukra's beautiful daughter Devayānī falls headlong in love with Kaca, son of Bṛhaspati, and boldly proposes marriage, an honour which Kaca politely but firmly declines. Subsequently one day when Devayānī and Śarmiṣṭhā,

---

1 It recurs almost *verbatim* in the Matsya Purāṇa (adhy. 25-42).

the daughter of the Asura Vṛṣaparvan, are having a bath in a neighbouring river, Indra tossed their clothes about, which had been left by the girls on the river bank, so that Śarmiṣṭhā by mistake took up the dress of Devayānī. There ensues a hefty quarrel between the girls, and Śarmiṣṭhā throws her rival into a dry well overgrown with grass. And there she remains until she is seen and pulled out of the well by the gallant king Yayāti, whom she promptly woos and who with the approval of her father, Śukra, marries her. Previously, as a recompense for her overbearing conduct towards Devayānī, Śarmiṣṭhā, the Asura princess, had become Devayānī's slave. She now accompanies Devayānī to the capital of Yayāti and the three people live in happiness together for some time. Yayāti has been warned beforehand by the Asura priest Śukra that he must on no account call Śarmiṣṭhā on to his bed : she was only a slave-girl belonging to Devayānī's entourage. But Śarmiṣṭhā prevails upon the soft-hearted and indulgent Yayāti, by dint of importunity and feminine logic to act so that her menstrual period will not be wasted, " for the husband of one's friend is as good as one's own husband ". Yayāti moved by her importunities admits the logic of Śarmiṣṭhā's requisition and begets on her secretly three sons, while Devayānī has only two. Devayānī learns the truth of the whole affair one day by accident, and goes in a huff to her father, complaining bitterly of the perfidy of her husband. The enraged Asura priest Śukra curses Yayāti that he would instantly suffer the effects of premature decrepitude, and so it happens. Śukra relents, however, and adds that, as Yayāti had acted from pure motives he might transfer his premature old age at will to any one who is willing to take it on in his stead. Accordingly Yayāti exchanged his decrepitude for the youth of his youngest son, [12] Pūru son of the Asura princess Śarmiṣṭhā, who was the only one of his five sons willing to take on his old age and to whom he subsequently handed over his vast kingdom as a reward for his filial affection.

In this version of the Yayāti legend, the Bhārgavī Devayānī has it all her own way and poor Śarmiṣṭhā, the Asura princess has been thrust in the background except in the finale, which raises Śarmiṣṭhā's youngest son to the throne and the tables are turned on Devayānī, the daughter of the Asura priest, Śukra. In spite of the Yayātyupākhyāna, Indian tradition honours Śarmiṣṭhā as the pattern of a wife most honoured by her husband ; for in Kālidāsa's famous drama, when Kāśyapa gives his parting blessing to his beloved daughter, Śakuntalā, he could think of no better boon than to wish that she might be like Śarmiṣṭhā :

Yayāter iva Śarmiṣṭhā bhartur bahumatā bhava |

" Be thou highly honoured of thy husband, as was Śarmiṣṭhā of Yayāti ! "

The extermination of the Kṣatriyas by the Bhārgava Rāma and the subsequent regeneration of the Kṣatriya race by pious Brahmins find a mention already for the third time in adhy. 98 of the Ādi : this time in the course of a conversation between Bhīṣma and Satyavatī. The continuance of the royal family of Kurus was sorely jeopardized by the untimely death of both the sons of Śaṁtanu, Citrāṅgada and Vicitravīrya. Satyavati asks Bhīṣma to marry the young and beautiful widows of his half-brother Vicitravīrya and beget children on them for the continuation of the race of the Kurus, a proposal which Bhīṣma firmly rejects as that would mean a deliberate breaking of his vow of celibacy. He proposes instead that a Brahmin be called to officiate (*niyoga*) and do the job. He cites a precedent for this *āpaddharma*. It is no other than the story of the Bhārgava Rāma and its sequel. To avenge the death of his father, Bhīṣma relates, the Bhārgava Rāma slew Arjuna, the son of Kṛtavīrya, king of the Haihayas. Then he set out on his war chariot to conquer the world. And taking up his *bow*, he hurled his mighty magical missiles (*astras*) and exterminated the Kṣatriyas more than once. In days of yore this illustrious descendant of Bhṛgu annihilated the Kṣatriyas thrice seven times (1. 98. 3) :

triḥsaptakṛtvaḥ pṛthivī kṛtā niḥkṣatriyā purā | (II)

Then from a high sense of duty, the virtuous Brahmins of the [13] day, skilled in the Vedas, co-habited with the widows of the Kaṣtriyas massacred by the Bhārgava Rāma and begat on them offsprings and thus revived the almost extinct race of the Kṣatriyas. Satyavatī should unhesitatingly follow this excellent precedent and arrange for the revival of the dying race of the Kurus.

So far we have come across only legends of the past achievements of the Bhārgavas. The first reference to a direct contact between a Bhārgava and one of the epic characters occurs in adhy. 121 of the Ādi. In this pseudo-historical epic, the myth may not be properly regarded as concerned with events in time. Therefore the Bhārgava Rāma, who only a few chapters previously is said to have lived in the interval between the Tretā and the Dvāpara Ages is here represented as the teacher (*guru*) of Ācārya Droṇa, who lived in the interval between the Dvāpara and the Kali Ages. The pupilship is only symbolical, but the basis of the symbolism is significant. Ācārya Droṇa is the *guru* of the Kauravas and the Pāṇḍvas and of all the other valiant Kṣatriyas of the time, and he was also one of the greatest warriors on the side of the Kauravas in the Bhārata War. But Ācārya Droṇa must also have a *guru*. And who would be more suitable as *guru* than the Bhārgava Rāma, who is the foremost of all weapon-bearers (*sarvaśastrabhṛtāṁ varaḥ*) ?

Once the symbol has been accepted, it is treated as real, and the myth is worked out in great detail. Thus we are told that when Droṇa had finished his studies and taken up the duties of a house-holder, he began to feel the pinch of poverty. He then happened to hear that the Bhārgava Rāma was bestowing wealth on Brahmins. No inconsistency or anachronism is felt, because Rāma is assumed to be "ever-living" (*cirañjīvin*). So Droṇa presented himself before the great Bhārgava, who was about to start for the forest, and asked for some wealth for himself. Rāma ruefully confessed to him that whatever wealth he at one time possessed he had freely presented to the Brahmins; he had even presented the earth to Kaśyapa, his sacrificing priest. And now he had nothing left except his mortal body and his weapons and magical missiles (*astras*). He asked Droṇa to choose what he wanted. Droṇa of course chose the famous missiles with which Rāma had conquered the whole earth. Rāma accordingly gave all his [14] weapons to Droṇa, instructing him at the same time fully in the science of arms.

This story of Droṇa and Rāma was apparently popular, for we find it repeated in an abridged form in adhy. 154, it being related there to the Pāṇḍavas by a Brahmin, who was urging them to proceed to the capital of Drupada to attend the *svayaṁvara* of Draupadī.

We learn another fragment of Bhārgava history from adhy. 169 to 172 of the Ādi, the Aurvopākhyāna, which is, as a matter of fact, a digression within a digression.

While the Pāṇḍava brothers were proceeding by slow stages to the capital of king Drupada to attend Draupadī's *svayaṁvara*, they are opposed on the way by Citraratha Aṅgāraparṇa, king of the Gandharvas, whom Arjuna after a brief fight overcomes. Citraratha and Arjuna soon become close friends. This sudden friendship gives the necessary opportunity to the skilful *raconteur* to smuggle in some stories. Citraratha, as a matter of fact, relates to Arjuna a number of interesting but flimsily motivated anecdotes, which are a pure and unadulterated digression, among them the well-known story of Vasiṣṭha. It is related how Viśvāmitra, king of Kanyakubja, tried to seize Vasiṣṭha's sacred cow (*kāmadhenu*) and, failing, turned ascetic and in the end became a Brahmin; how king Kalmāṣapāda Saudāsa was cursed by Vasiṣṭha's son *Śakti* (or Śaktri)! to become a cannibal and how he began his career as a cannibal by devouring Vasiṣṭha's own sons including Śakti; how Vasiṣṭha subsequently freed the king from the effects of the curse. Then finally to dissuade his enraged grandson Parāśara, son of Śakti, from destroying the whole creation in his frenzy, Vasiṣṭha relates to him the story of the Bhārgava Aurva. It will thus be seen that the Bhārgava legend is emboxed within the Vasiṣṭha legend, which is itself an episode of the Caitraratha section. This story of Aurva is as follows.

Once upon a time there was a king by name Kṛtavīrya of the Haihyas, whose family priests were the Bhṛgus. On them he bestowed great wealth. After his death the princes of his family, for some reason or other, demanded it back. The Bhṛgus came out with some of it, but not all. It then happened that one of the Kṣatriyas, accidentally digging the ground in the settlement of the Bhṛgus, came upon a large store of wealth buried under [15] ground. Enraged at what they naturally considered deceitful conduct on the part of the Bhṛgus, the Kṣatriyas used violence to the Bhṛgus, and slew them all indiscriminately. The Kṣatriyas even hunted down the women of the Bhṛgus, and with a view to exterminating the race killed all those that were pregnant. Pursued by the Kṣatriyas, some of the Bhṛgu women took shelter in the inaccessible fastnesses of the Himalayas. One of these women[1], in order to perpetuate the race of the Bhārgavas, had concealed her embryo in her thigh. The Kṣatriyas, when they came to know of it, pursued her with the intention of decimating her embryo ; when, lo and behold, the child was born from his mother's thigh, blinding the Haihayas with his lustre. Bereft of sight, they roamed about in the forest, and, meekly approaching the faultless Brahmin lady, prostrated themselves before her, begging that their eyesight might be restored. "My good sirs", said the Brahmin lady, "I have not robbed you of your eyesight, nor am I angry with you. But this scion of the Bhṛgus seems certainly to be angry with you. Your eyesight has no doubt been destroyed by this high-souled Bhārgava, whose wrath has been kindled by the massacre of his kinsmen. When you took to destroying even the embryos of the Bhṛgu race, the child was held by me concealed in my thigh for one hundred years. That he may do good to the Bhṛgu race, the entire Veda with its six *aṅgas* revealed itself to him when he was still in the womb. Being enraged at the slaughter of his kinsmen, he desires to kill you. It is by his divine effulgence that your eyesight has been destroyed. Pray therefore, my good sirs, to this excellent son of mine, born of my thigh (*ūru*) ; and pacified by your humbly prostrating yourself before him, he may restore your eyesight". Thereupon all those Kṣatriyas on their bended knees said to that high-born child, "Forgive us", and the high-born child forgave them. But that descendant of the Bhārgava race did not forget that outrage and resolved in his mind upon destroying this wicked world. With that object in view he started performing the most severe austerities. By the intensity of his austerities he afflicted all the worlds. On learning what Aurva was doing to avenge the wrong done to them by the Kṣatriyas, the shades of his ancestors came to him and addressed his as follows : [16] "O Aurva, O child, the prowess of thy fierce austerities has been seen by us. Control thy anger and forgive the people." They explain to him that the Kṣatriyas were really *not* to blame for the slaughter of the Bhṛgus ! How could those puny Kṣatriyas ever hope to kill the Bhārgavas? That *contretemps* was a little contrivance of the Bhārgavas themselves. The fact was that the Bhārgavas were tired of their lives and longed to die, but death dared not touch them, those sinless effulgent specimens of humanity, and suicide was a cowardly act and a sin. They had therefore staged that little quarrel with those foolish and arrogant Kṣatriyas, so that the Kṣatriyas might get en-

---

1 According to C. 1.2610 her name was Āruṣī :

Āruṣī tu Manoḥ kanyā tasya patnī manīṣiṇaḥ ||
Aurvas tasyāṁ samabhavad Ūrum bhittvā mahāyaśāḥ ||

raged and kill them, as they did. Of what use could wealth be to those emancipated souls, whose sole desire was to obtain heaven? Aurva replies that they may be all true, but he had made a vow to destroy the world in order to calm his own anger and he must destroy it, or else he would be destroyed himself by the fire of his uncontrollable wrath. And so the world was in imminent danger of being totally destroyed! But the ancestors of Aurva show him a way out of the dilemma. They wisely advise him to fling the fire of his wrath in the waters, which are the primeval source and support of the world, and Aurva does so. And now, in the shape of horse's head (*hayaśiras*), his wrath dwells in the ocean, consuming its waters, which are the world (*lokā hy āpomayāḥ smṛtāḥ*. 1. 171. 19).

In the above legend we may notice some of the repeated motives of Bhārgava stories. There is first of all the feud with the Kṣatriyas, which finally develops into the creation of the figure of the Bhārgava Rāma, "the foremost of all weapon-bearers," who single-handed, with the aid of his magical weapons, the *astras*, conquers the whole earth, annihilating the Kṣatriyas thrice seven times. Then there is the motif of the opportune birth of a miraculous child, whose effulgent lustre either blinds the oppressor (as here) or consumes him (as in the case of Cyavana). There is, lastly, the appearance of the shades of the ancestors, who step in to stop the carnage either contemplated (as here) or actually perpetrated (as in the case of Rāma), to avenge some private wrong done with reference to the family.

[17] SABHĀPARVAN

The short Sabhā, which is a compact little book with 81 chapters and about 2700 stanzas (in the Vulgate), begins with the Erection of the Darbar Hall and ends with the Second Gambling Match. Here the story marches forward by rapid strides, consisting as it does mainly of spirited dialogue and dramatic action. The digressions are few and far between, and of *upākhyānas* as such there are none. The real important digressions, which occur early in the beginning, are two: firstly, the somewhat lengthy and imaginative descriptions (*ākhyānas*) by Nārada of the halls of the celestials Indra, Yama, Varuṇa, Kubera, and Brahmā, preceded by a short Nīti tractate (adhy. 5-12); and, secondly, the previous history of Jarāsaṁdha, narrated by Kṛṣṇa (adhy. 17-19). Consequently, in this parvan, the Bhārgava material is extremely scanty.

The Bhārgavas are nevertheless briefly mentioned several times. Thus, naturally, many of the Bhārgavas, to wit, Bhṛgu, Mārkaṇḍeya, Rāma, Jāmadagnya, are several times mentioned as being present, along with other famous sages and seers of the past, in the halls of the celestials mentioned above, as also as a matter of course in the newly erected hall of Yudhiṣṭhira. In adhy. 8, Rāma has been placed by mistake among the royal sages (*rājarṣis*). They are likewise present at the coronation of Yudhiṣṭhira. These static figures are like mural decorations, and of no special interest to us. We shall therefore ignore them.

Rāma's extermination of the Kṣatriyas, which is really never quite forgotten by our bards, is mentioned in adhy. 14. Kṛṣṇa prefaces his long reply to Yudhiṣṭhira regarding the prerequisites of the Rājasūya sacrifice by pointing out, quite irrelevantly, that the contemporary Kṣatriyas were far inferior to that old race of Kṣatriyas that was exterminated by the Bhārgava Rāma (B. 2. 14. 2) :

Jāmadagnyena Rāmeṇa kṣatraṁ yad avaśesitam |
tasmād avarajaṁ loke yad idaṁ kṣatrasaṁjñitam ||

It was mentioned above that the high esteem in which our epic bards held Rāma Jāmadagnya had led to his being represented as the teacher of Ācārya Drona in the science of arms. The same ideology is responsible for the sedulously fostered belief that Rāma was the teacher of Bhīṣma also, an idea which is taken hold of [18] and further developed in that late addition to the Udyoga, the Ambā episode (Ambopākhyāna). Rāma is represented as standing in the same relation to Karṇa, the protégé and ally of Duryodhana. So, in his denunciation of Kṛṣṇa, Śisupāla mentions Karṇa's pupilship under Rāma as one of Karṇa's qualifications entitling him to receive the *argha* (B. 2, 37. 15 f.) :

ayaṁ ca sarvarājñāṁ vai balaślāghī mahābalaḥ |
Jāmadagnyasya dayitaḥ śiṣyo viprasya Bhārata ||
Yenātmabalam āśritya rājāno yudhi nirjitāḥ |
taṁ ca Karṇam atikramya kathaṁ Kṛṣṇas tvayārcitaḥ ||

ĀRAṆYAKAPARVAN

This book is a veritable thesaurus of ancient Brahmanic myths and legends. We accordingly find that a fair amount of Bhārgava material has been incorporated in it. We further find that one Bhārgava takes a considerable share in the story-telling that is done here.

The first important deference to the Bhṛgus is in the Tīrthayātrā section. The list of *tīrthas* given in adhy. 82 ff (of the Vulgate) is said to have been first communicated by the sage Pulastya to Bhīṣma and then repeated by Nārada to Yudhiṣṭhira. It is in reality a material compendium of *tīrthas*, which gives, in the space of a stanza or two, the necessary details about the particular *tīrtha* : the name of the *tīrtha*, the ritual acts to be done there, and finally the merit (*puṇya*) accruing from these acts. Thus, for example, we read (B. 3. 83. 13 ff.):

"O king, going to Śālūkinī and bathing in the Daśāśvamedha, the pilgrim obtains the merit of performing 10 *aśvamedha* sacrifices.—Then going to Sarpadevī, that excellent *tīrtha* of the Nāgas, one obtains the merit of performing 1 *agniṣṭoma* sacrifice and goes to the world of the Nāgas.—One should then proceed, O virtuous man, to (the shrine of) Tarantuka, the gatekeeper. Staying there only for one night, one obtains the merit of giving away 1000 kine.—Then going to the Pañcanada, with regulated diet and subdued soul, and bathing in the Koṭitīrtha, one obtains the merit of performing 1 *aśvamedha* sacrifice. Going to the *tīrtha* of the Aśvins, a man is born handsome (in a future birth, of course).—One should then go, O virtuous man, to the excellent [19] *tīrtha* called Vārāha, where Viṣṇu in times of yore appeared in the form of a boar. Bathing there, O foremost of men, one obtains the merit of performing 1 *agniṣṭoma* sacrifice.—O king of kings, one should then visit Somatīrtha, situated in Jayanti. Bathing in it, one obtains the merit of performing 1 *rājasūya* sacrifice.—Bathing in Ekahaṁsa, one obtains the merit of giving away 1000 kine.—O ruler of men, going to the Kṛtaśauca, the pilgrim becomes purified, and obtains the merit of performing 1 *puṇḍarīka* sacrifice.—Then going to Muñjavaṭa, the place sacred to Sthāṇu, and fasting for one night, one acquires the position of *gāṇapatya* ".— And so on and so forth.

Only very rarely is this dreary enumeration interrupted by a brief account of some myth or legend connected with the place of pilgrimage in question. Now we find embedded in this list the legend connected with the Rāmahradas (B. 3. 83. 26 ff.), which appears to have considerably roused the interest of the compiler and to which he has devoted not less than 32 lines. The story is of course no other than that of the extirpation of the Kṣatriya race by the Bhārgava Rāma, of which this is already the *fourth* repetition in some form or other. The story is as follows.

The greatly effulgent and heroic Rāma, after exterminating the Kṣatriyas with great valour, formed five lakes filled with the blood of the slaughtered warriors. And he offered that blood as oblation to his forefathers, who were most gratified by this supreme act of filial piety. The shades of these ancestors appeared before him and addressed him as follows : " O Rāma, O Rāma, O fortunate one ! We are pleased, O Bhārgava, with thy filial piety and with thy great valour. Ask for a boon, O greatly effulgent one. What dost thou wish to have ? " Having been thus addressed by his ancestors, Rāma, that foremost of smiters (*Rāmaḥ praharatāṁ varaḥ* B. 3. 83. 31), thus spoke with joined hands to his ancestors : " If you are pleased with me and if I have deserved your favour then by your grace I desire that I may again derive pleasure in asceticism. By your power, may I be freed from the sin I have incurred by killing these Kṣatriyas in a fit of wrath. Also may these sanguinary lakes become holy places of pilgrimage celebrated throughout the world ". Hearing these righteous words of Rāma, his ancestors were highly pleased, [20] and filled with joy they thus replied to Rāma : " Let thy austerities prosper, especially by virtue of thy filial piety. Forsooth thou hast exterminated the Kṣatriyas in a fit of wrath, but thou art already freed from that sin, for they have fallen owing to their own misdeeds. These lakes of thine shall without doubt become places of pilgrimage. He who will bathe in these lakes and offer here oblations to his ancestors will please his manes and they will gratify all his heart's desire, and lead him to the eternal celestial regions". Having granted these boons to Rāma and affectionately taken leave of him, the shades became invisible. It was thus that the bloody lakes of that illustrious descendant of Bhṛgu became sacred places of pilgrimage.—Leading the life of a student of the sacred lore and observing sacred vows, if a person bathes in the Lakes of Rāma (Rāmahrada) and worships Rāma, he will obtain much gold.

The reader will easily recognize this as the story which was briefly related already in connection with Samantapañcaka. In fact Rāmahrada appears to be only another name of Samantapañcaka, one of the *tīrthas* explicitly mentioned as having been visited by the Sūta (that is, the putative narrator of the Mahābhārata), before he came to Śaunaka's sacrifice. It will be recalled that some information was asked then about Samantapañcaka in adhy. 2 of the Ādi, and in that connection this story was briefly narrated by the Sūta to the sages of the Naimiṣa Forest. There the story was originally summarized in four stanzas, but some subsequent reviser, apparently not satisfied with such a cursory allusion to this epoch-making feat of Rāma, had interpolated at that place the dialogue between Rāma and his ancestors (compressed into eight lines) made up mostly of bits and pieces of verses borrowed from the present context, and like all interpolations proving itself to be somewhat of a bad fit.

A few chapters later, we have a strange story of a conflict between two different *avatāras* of the same god, Viṣṇu, between the Jāmadagnya Rāma and the Dāśarathi Rāma, told in connection with a Bhṛgutīrtha, "celebrated in the three worlds, which Yudhiṣṭhira and his party are said to have visited (B. 3. 99. 34 ff). Once upon a time, the story goes, Rāma Jāmadagnya went to Ayodhyā to meet Rāma Dāśarathi and to test his strength. [21] Rāma D. was sent by his father to the boundary of his kingdom to receive Rāma J. hospitably, but was flagrantly insulted by the latter. Rāma D. nevertheless bends the bow given to him by Rāma J. to test his strength and shoots an arrow which convulses the whole world, astounding Rāma J. Rāma D. further confounds Rāma J. completely by showing him his cosmic form (*viśvarūpa*), made popular by the Gītā (adhy. 11), and rebukes him for his overweening conduct. Abashed, Rāma J. returns to Mount Mahendra, having lost his lustre (*tejas*), which he regains later at some *tīrtha* or other. Yudhiṣṭhira is asked to bathe in the same *tīrtha* that he might regain the lustre he had lost in his conflict with Duryodhana.

This grotesque story, composed probably with the object of glorifying the Kṣatriya Rāma at the cost of the Brahmin Rāma, must be quite a modern interpolation, in the Mahābhārata. Contextually it is an obvious misfit, being incongruously wedged in between two halves of the Agastya legend, with which it has absolutely no connection. Not only is this bizarre story contextually a misfit, it is a very poor piece of composition, and it strikes moreover a discordant note, involving disrespect towards the Bhārgava Rāma, who in our epic is otherwise throughout held up for our admirations as the foremost of weapon-bearers and fighters. Fortunately we are not left to deduce the spuriousness of this passage merely from intrinsic arguments, which are apt to be discredited; for, the passage is missing entirely in the Southern recension, an omission supported by the Kaśmīrī version and even by some ancient Devanāgarī MSS. The story, which is narrated at some length in the Rāmāyaṇa, is not even alluded to in the Rāmopākhyāna of our epic and belongs evidently to a different complex of legends, quite inharmonious with the Mahābhārata context. It appears to have been smuggled into the capacious folds of the Āraṇyakaparvan in quite recent times by some well-meaning but ignorant Northern interpolater anxious to vindicate the claim of the epic to be a complete encyclopaedia of the Hindu legendary lore.[1]

But the next chapter (100) again contains a Bhārgava story, the legend of Dadhīca. Lomaśa relates how the Kālakeyas under the leadership of Vṛtra persecuted the celestials, who betook them-[22]-selves to Brahmā asking for his protection. The latter advises them to go to the (Bhārgava) Dadhīca and ask for his bones. The sage magnanimously gives up his body for the good of the three worlds. The celestials took the bones of Dadhīca to Viśvakarman, the architect of the gods, who fashioned out of his bones the thunderbolt, with which Indra vanquished the enemies of the gods. The story is repeated in the account of the pilgrimage of Baladeva (Śalya 51 in the Vulgate), where it is said of Dadhīca that he was the strongest of all creatures, tall as the Himalayas and that Indra was always mightily afraid of him on account of his lustre.

Yet again, a few chapters later, the arrival of Yudhiṣṭhira and his party at Mount Mahendra, the headquarters of Rāma, now a *saṁnyāsin*, affords a welcome opportunity to the bard for the presentation of a full-length portrait of the hero of the Bhārgavas, Rāma, son of Jamadagni (Āraṇyaka 115-117 in the Vulgate).

The Pāṇḍavas bathe at the mouth of the Ganges and proceed to the river Vaitaraṇī in Kaliṅga, where the altar of Kaśyapa is. They rest on Mount Mahendra and hear there from Akṛtavraṇa, a disciple of the Bhārgava Rāma, the well-known story of Rāma, which may be summarized as follows.

Gādhi, king of Kanyakubja, had retired to the forest to practise religious austerities. There a most beautiful daughter was born to him, Satyavatī, whom the Bhārgava Ṛcīka wooed. Gādhi perhaps did not relish his suit and tried to evade it by demanding a present of a thousand peculiarly coloured horses, but Ṛcīka supplied them and gained her. Then a Bhṛgu (perhaps, Aurva is meant), who was a great sorcerer, visits the newly married couple and gives his young

---

[1] *Yad ihāsti tad anyatra yan nehāsti na tat kvacit.*

daughter-in-law the boon that she would give birth to a gifted son, and so would her mother. To fortify the boon, he prescribes that she should embrace an *udumbara* tree, her mother an *aśvattha*, and both should partake of different dishes of some special *caru* prepared by him with powerful incantations and endowed with magical potency. These good ladies go and exchange the trees as well as the dishes of *caru* which were apportioned to them by the great sage, with the result that the daughter was about to give birth to a Brahmin son with Kṣatriyan qualities and the mother a Kṣatriya son with [23] Brahmanic qualities. But the Bhṛgu, who comes to know of this interchange by occult means, comes rushing to the hermitage and tells his daughter-in-law what was going to happen. Moved by her entreaties, he gives a further boon to the young woman who had really been deceived by her mother, postponing the action of the potent charm. Thus her son Jamadagni was saved from the taint of Kṣatriyahood, which ultimately fell upon her grandson Rāma, who turned out to be, as prophesied, a revengeful and bloodthirsty warrior, perpetrator of cruel and sanguinary deeds. Jamadagni, though a peaceful Brahmin who excelled in the study of the Vedas, as desired by his mother, was not without martial equipment, for "the entire science of arms with the four kinds of magical missiles spontaneously came to him, who rivalled the sun in lustre, without any instruction from anybody" (B. 3. 115. 45). Jamadagni married Reṇukā, daughter of king Prasenajit. She gave birth to five sons : Rumaṇvat, Suṣeṇa, Vasu, Viśvāvasu, and last but not least Rāma. The family lived happily for some time. Then one day when Reṇukā of rigid vows happened to see Citraratha, the handsome king of Mārttikāvataka, sporting in water with his numerous wives, her fortitude forsook her and she felt the pangs of desire. When she returned to the hermitage, Jamadagni noticed her pollution and guessed her secret. In a fit of rage he called in turn upon each of his sons to kill their unchaste mother. Four of them refused to do the atrocious deed and were cursed by the angry and disappointed father for their disobedience. Then came the last of all that "slayer of hostile heroes," Rāma Jāmadagnya. A military type, accustomed to receive and obey orders, Rāma, when sternly commanded by his father to slay his mother, took his axe and without hesitation chopped off his mother's head ! Jamadagni, mightily pleased with the instant obedience of his son, granted Rāma several boons, among them the boon that the mother whom Rāma had decapitated might be restored to life. And the family lived again happily for some time. Then one day Arjuna Kārtavīrya Sahasrabāhu came to the hermitage and was hospitably received by the Bhārgavas. The ungrateful king, intoxicated with the pride of power, not heeding the hospitality, seized and carried off by force from the hermitage the calf of the sacred cow of the sage (a variant of the *kāmadhenu* motif of the Vasiṣṭha-[24]-Viśvāmitra legend), and spitefully broke the big tree in the hermitage grounds. This was the beginning of a terrible feud. Rāma first slew the arrogant Arjuna Kārtavīrya, and Arjuna's sons then slew the unresisting Jamadagni. Then Rāma slaughtered the sons of Arjuna K. and finally destroyed all Kṣatriyas off the earth thrice seven times and made five pools of blood in Samantapañcaka (B. 3. 117. 9) :

triḥsaptakṛtvaḥ pṛthivīṁ kṛtvā niḥkṣatriyāṁ prabhuḥ |
Samantapañcake pañca cakāra rudhirahradān || (III)

Standing in the middle of these pools of blood—as has already been narrated several times above—Rāma offered oblations to the manes until at last his ancestor Ṛīcka appeared and stopped him. Rāma then performed a great sacrifice to gratify Indra, in which he bestowed the earth upon Kaśyapa, his priest. Then this annihilator of the Kṣatriya race was at last satisfied and retired to Mount Mahendra, engaging himself in austerities of a rather severe type. "Thus did hostility arise between Rāma and Kṣatriyas of this earth, and the entire earth was conquered by Rāma of immeasurable lustre" (B. 3. 117. 15). It is then narrated that the Bhārgava Rāma appeared there in person on Mount Mahendra to meet the Pāṇḍavas. He was duly received and honoured by Yudhiṣṭhira and his party, and he honoured them in turn.

This account has been amplified in later times—like several other Bhārgava episodes—by the addition of a passage of 23 lines (B. 3. 115. 9-19), which is prefixed to it and which is chiefly of interest on account of the vague suggestion it contains to the effect that Bhārgava Rāma was an *avatāra* of Viṣṇu. This interpolation begins with the previous history of Arjuna Kārtavīrya, king of Haihayas. He is represented here as a worshipper of Dattātreya, by whose favour he had obtained a golden *vimāna* and a wonderful chariot. Intoxicated with the pride of power, Arjuna Kārtavīrya insulted Indra, trampled upon the sages and even upon the celestials, and persecuted all creatures. Thereupon the celestials and the sages met together and went in a body to Viṣṇu to ask for his protection. Then the exalted god (Viṣṇu) held a consultation with Indra. The god of gods (Indra) told Viṣṇu what had to be done. Thereupon the exalted god, promising to do the needful, went to Badarī, his [25] favourite retreat.—Here the introduction suddenly breaks off, and the story narrated about Gādhi and Ṛcīka begins (B. 3. 115-20). The suggestion probably is that at the consultation between Indra and Viṣṇu it was decided that Viṣṇu should incarnate himself on the earth as the son of Jamadagni, as Rāma Jāmadagnya, who should, in the fulness of time, slay Arjuna Kārtavīrya, but that is left unsaid. The passage is missing in the entire Southern recension and in some Northern manuscripts including those of the Kaśmīrī version. There can therefore be no doubt about its being a comparatively recent interpolation.

As already remarked above, Rāma Jāmadagnya and the other Bhārgavas such as Cyavana, Ṛcīka and so on are generally used as static figures, along with other ancient sages like Nārada, in the description of largely attended and important meetings and state functions, and such treatment of these characters is quite intelligible, if not natural. But the Bhārgavas—and especially the Bhārgava Rāma—are accorded a somewhat different treatment; they are represented as taking part in the action more definitely and more frequently. We have seen that the Bhārgava Rāma is said to have given all his *astras* to Droṇa. He is also said to have taught Bhīṣma and Karṇa. Here he is represented as having shown himself to the Pāṇḍavas, as a special favour. In another context Rāma is said to have fought with Bhīṣma, a fight which lasted for twenty-three days but was absolutely barren of any consequence. Elsewhere also we shall find Rāma and some of other Bhārgavas represented as taking some innocuous part in the action, which in no way affects the course of events but which serves to establish and maintain contact between the Bhārgavas and the epic characters.

The above story of Rāma, which is miscalled the Kārtavīryopākhyāna, ends at adhy. 117 of the Vulgate. At adhy. 122, we have another Bhārgava story, which covers adhy. 122-124 and about half of adhy. 125 : the story of the great wizard Cyavana, son of Bhṛgu.

The Pāṇḍavas reach the Payoṣṇī and the Narmadā rivers and hear from Lomaśa the story (*upākhyāna*) of Cyavana : how he demanded in marriage a young princess, by name Sukanyā, who [26] had innocently and unwittingly blinded him ; how he recovered his sight by the grace of the Aśvins and how he gave them on that account that Soma libation, paralyzing the arm of Indra, who would have prevented it. The story runs thus.

Cyavana, son of Bhṛgu, practised austerities in a forest so long that an ant-hill was formed round him. There came one day to that place king Śaryāti, acompanied by his daughter Sukanyā, with beautiful eyebrows and tapering thighs. The sage imprisoned within the ant-hill gazed longingly at the youthful princess, clad in a single garment and adorned with costly ornaments, and addressed some words to her which she did not hear. Sukanyā saw, however, the gleaming eyes of the sage, engaged in self-mortification in the ant-hill, and mistaking them for a species of glow-worm, in youthful heedlessness, pierced the eyes of the sage with a thorn. Little did she think of the dire consequences of her childish act. For through the anger of the offended sage, smarting with the pain thoughtlessly inflicted on him by the heedless princess, the king's entire army suffered suddenly from a complete stoppage of urine and excreta. The bewildered king inquired about the cause of this strange mishap, but none of his soldiers and companions could enlighten him. The occurrence remained a mystery until the guilty princess confessed her misdemeanour. Śaryāti forthwith set out to pacify the irate sage. The sage would relent only if the mischievous but fascinating princess is given to him in marriage. Without reflecting, the king agreed to bestow his beautiful daughter on the high-souled Cyavana and returned to his own city. Some time later the Aśvins saw the faultless Sukanyā bathing in the lake adjoining the hermitage of the sage. They also were smitten by her ravishing beauty and asked her to accept one of them for her husband instead of the blind old sage. As she would not consent, they propose that they would rejuvenate Cyavana, and then she should choose. With the permission of her husband she consents to the second proposal. Cyavana had to dip into the waters of the lake, into the primordial element, the womb of all creation, along with the Aśvins (Fountain of Youth motif).[1] The three of [27] them came out of the water, all looking exactly alike. Here is a dilemma (Nala-Damayantī motif). By virtue of her unswerving loyalty to her husband, Sukanyā is however able to choose the right man. In gratefulness for the gift of youth and beauty, Cyavana promises the Aśvins a draught of the Soma juice during a regular sacrifice. Soon afterwards, Śaryāti comes to visit his son-in-law Cyavana and the latter arranges a great sacrifice for Śaryāti, at which he offers the first draught of Soma to the Aśvins, who used to be altogether excluded on these festive occasions on account of their being medicine-men. Indra tries to stop the sacrilegious act ; but as Cyavana will not heed, Indra then attempts to hurl the thunderbolt at him. But Cyavana was too quick for him. Instantly Cyavana paralyzed Indra's arm and brought him to his knees. At the same time the great sorcerer created by his magic a terrible demon (*kṛtyā*) called Mada (Intoxication). When Mada rushes towards Indra to slay him, Indra grants the wish of Cyavana, who triumphantly continues the sacrifice and gives the Aśvins, the promised libation of Soma. Since that time the Aśvins participate regularly in the sacrificial offerings on a basis of equality with the other gods. Indra at the same time apologizes and explains that he had opposed Cyavana merely to spread the fame of Cyavana and his father-in-law Śaryāti throughout the world : a significant and prophetic utterance.

Bhṛgu, the father of Cyavana, had only cursed Agni, a minor god, in fact, merely the " mouth " of the gods, to be *sarvabhakṣa*, devourer of all things, good and bad (1. 6. 13). Cyavana did even better. He thoroughly humbled Indra, the king of gods, who had to submit to the will of Cyavana.

In the next chapter again we have a passing allusion to a Bhārgava, who remains unnamed. The background is a Bhārgava hermitage, though the main actors are not Bhṛgus. The pious Yuvanāśva Saudyumni is practising austerities for the sake of progeny. One night he became very thirsty. Searching for water, he enters the hermitage of the Bhārgava who was engaged in performing some magical rites in order to make Yuvanāśva's queen give birth to a son. This sorcerer had actually prepared a potion, endowed with magical efficacy, for administering it to the queen and kept the jar containing the dose in a corner of the [28] hermitage. The thirsty king found it, and, not knowing that the water was charmed and intended in fact

---

[1] An alluring explanation of the idea underlying this intriguing motif has been given by H. ZIMMER in his *Maya, Der indische Mythos* (Stuttgart 1936), pp. 42 ff.

for the queen, drained the potion to the dregs. Here was a mess. But the potion prepared by a Bhṛgu is infallible in its effect. Whoever drinks it must give birth to a son. Consequently the king became himself pregnant, and a son, Māndhātṛ, was born to him, ripping open his left side, but owing to some propitiatory rites performed by the Bhṛgu, Yuvanāśva himself escaped unhurt.

It is interesting to compare this version of the story of Māndhātṛ with the one which occurs in the Droṇaparvan (adhy. 62 of the Vulgate). There we are told that once upon a time king Yuvanāśva, when out hunting, became thirsty, and his steed was exhausted. Seeing at a distance a curl of smoke, the monarch guided by it reached a sacrificial enclosure and found there some sacrificial butter (*ājya*), which he greedily swallowed. Thereupon the king became pregnant and was delivered of a son (Māndhātṛ) by the Aśvins. The rest of the story is nearly the same.

In this version, king Yuvanāśva was not practising austerities for securing the birth of a son, but had gone out hunting. Nor did he partake of the magical preparation at night in the dark, but presumably in full daylight, when the smoke from the sacred hearth could yet be seen by him. The second version moreover makes no mention of any Bhṛgu, playing the rôle of the officiating priest and saviour of Yuvanāśva, like the first, which is an important discrepancy. The second story is sketchy and lacking in definition, and appears to be the older version. In the first the details are filled out, by adding a Bhṛgu as an officiating priest and generally making the picture more vivid and realistic.

The next Bhārgava of importance we meet with in the Āraṇyaka is the sage Mārkaṇḍeya, whose discourses on the most divers topics extend over 51 chapters (182-232) in the Vulgate, containing about 2200 stanzas (Mārkaṇḍeya-samāsyā), which he delivers for the delectation and edification of the Pāṇḍavas. This is not his first visit to the Pāṇḍavas by any means. For early in the beginning of their exile, when the Pāṇḍavas had settled in the Dvaitavana Forest, Mārkaṇḍeya had paid a flying visit [29] to them (adhy. 25). He turns up again, as a matter of fact, also towards the end of their exile, without notice or warning, to console Yudhiṣṭhira and relates to him the Rāmopākhyāna, the popular story of Rāma and Sītā, as well as the Sāvitryupākhyāna, that immortal story of a wife's splendid devotion. These two *upākhyānas*, narrated by Mārkaṇḍeya, together comprise about 1060 stanzas. Thus the Mārkaṇḍeya-samāsyā together with the two latter *upākhyānas* comprise 3260 stanzas, which is nearly one fourth of the entire extent of this extensive *parvan*.

Mārkaṇḍeya was one of the *cirajīvins* : eternally youthful though many thousand years old. How he was exactly connected with the two well-known Bhṛgu families of our Mahābhārata (Bhṛgu-Cyavana-Rāma and Bhṛgu--Cyavana-Śunaka) is not exactly known ; but that he was a Bhārgava is beyond doubt. He is referred to as *Bhārgava* in B. 3. 183. 60 ; 189. 97 ;

190. 2. 13. 22. 15 : as *Bhārgava-sattama* in B. 3. 201. 7 ; 217. 5 : as *Bhṛgu-nandana* in B. 3. 205. 4 : as *Bhṛgukula-śreṣṭha* in B. 3. 205. 15. Moreover Mārkaṇḍa is explicitly declared to be a *gotra* founder of the Bhṛgu clan in the Matsya Purāṇa (195. 20).

Some of the subjects of Mārkaṇḍeya's discourses to the Pāṇḍavas are the following : great power of Brahmins ; merit of benevolence to Brahmins ; wife's duty to her husband ; and different forms of Agni. He relates, among others, stories of Manu, Yayāti, Vṛṣadarbha, Śibi, Indradyumna (father of Janaka), Kuvalāśva and of Skanda Kārttikeya. He is also responsible for the famous story of the Righteous Hunter (*dharma-vyādha*) of Mithilā. Besides these, there is, as is well known, a whole Purāṇa named after him, the Mārkaṇḍeya Purāṇa.

The most interesting of Mārkaṇḍeya's stories, however, is how he actually witnessed the act of creation and dissolution in progress. We have here in fact in Mārkaṇḍeya a Brahmanic counterpart of the Kṣatriya Manu, that distant cousin of the Semitic Noah with his ark, seeds and so on.

The legend of Manu, like that of Noah, is a childish story. According to this legend (Matsyopākhyāna, also related by the same sage Mārkaṇḍeya, Āraṇyaka 187 in the Vulgate), Manu, son of Vivasvat, while saying his usual prayers on the bank of a river, sees a tiny little fish, which asks the sage to protect it. [30] Manu rears the fish in a small earthern vessel, which the fish soon outgrows. The fish keeps on growing larger and larger. Manu places the fish successively in a tank, in the river Ganges, and in the ocean. Before parting from Manu, the fish warns him of the impending catastrophe and advises him to build an ark and keep carefully a store of *seeds* of all kinds. When the deluge comes, Manu gets into the ark with the Seven Sages. The ark is towed by the horned fish on the ocean, which during the deluge flooded everything. The ship, "like a drunken wench", staggered from side to side on the bosom of the agitated ocean. In the end the ship is fastened on to the peak of the Himalayas, called Naubandhana, which is projecting out of the water. When the flood subsides, Manu quietly gets out of the ark and, as he has all the necessary seeds with himself in the ark, there would be no difficulty in creating the world anew. Before parting again from Manu and the Seven Sages, the Fish says, "I am Brahmā, the lord of creatures. None is greater than I. In the form of a fish I have saved you all from this peril. Manu will create all beings : gods, *asuras* and human beings, the mobile and the immobile creation."

This story, which appears to belong to a different complex of myths and does not at all fit well in the Mahābhārata cycle, is, as has been surmised, probably of Semitic origin.[1] If Manu creates all beings, Brahmā is thrown

[1] Cf. WINTERNITZ, "Die Flutsagen des Altertums und der Naturvölker", in *Mitteilungen der Anthropologischen Gesellschaft in Wien*, vol. 31 (1901), pp. 321f., 327 ff.

out of employment. The Purāṇic theory of creation is that there is a deluge ; nothing remains of the universe except Viṣṇu-Nārāyaṇa, reclining on the coils of the Eternal Serpent (Śeṣa-Ananta) floating on the waters. Then out of Nārāyana's navel emerges Brahmā, seated on a lotus, the creative aspect of the deity. From Brahmā are born his mind-born sons (*mānasa-putrās*). Then other beings, male and female, emerge from his heart, breast, thumbs and so on. These are the Prajāpatis. They propagate this world of ours. The process is repeated at each dissolution : it is an eternal recurrence. In this complex there is clearly no room for the Semitic legend, which would imply a parallel creation by Manu, a state of things which is not at all what is intended by the legend. Since a [31] variant version of this legend is found even in the Śatapatha Brāhmaṇa (1. 8. 1), it should seem that the Semitic legend was introduced into India at a fairly early date but has remained unassimilated. Its exotic character, however, appears to me to be clearly betrayed by the *phalaśruti* at the end of the chapter, an addition which accompanies all late accretions to the Great Epic (B. 3. 187. 58 *emended*) :

ya idaṁ śṛṇuyān nityaṁ Manoś caritam āditaḥ |
sa sukhī sarvasiddhārthaḥ svargalokam iyān naraḥ ||

The Indian Noah is a man of a very different character. He requires neither boat nor horned fish to save him ; nor does he keep a store of seeds with himself. The man who could live through the dissolution of the world can only be a perfect Yogi ; and a perfect Yogi is deathless. "There is none equal to you in years save Brahmā Parameṣṭhin," says Yudhiṣṭhira to the Bhārgava Mārkaṇḍeya. But he requires neither food nor drink to live. He can walk on water as easily as on land. So when the world was overwhelmed with floods and the creation was gradually submerged, Mārkaṇḍeya found himself alone, walking on the waters of the ocean. After some time Mārkaṇḍeya, being human after all, begins to feel a little tired and lonely, tramping about all by himself on the surface of the endless ocean. He also felt inexpressibly sad at that awful destruction. Then all of a sudden he noticed a little child resting on the extended branch of a huge banyan tree (*nyagrodha*). Mārkaṇḍeya could not at all imagine how that little helpless child could have survived all that cataclysmal devastation, and he kept pondering over that matter, standing near the child. Seeing his confusion, the child softly told him to go into his body and rest there, and the child opened its little mouth and drew him gently inside. And, lo and behold, inside the child he found the world whose destruction he had seen with his own eyes. The sun, the moon and the stars, all the oceans, seas and rivers of the world, all the men, women and children whom he had known, all animals, gods and demons,—they were all there, inside the little stomach of that wonderful little child. He wandered about inside for hundreds of years and still he could not find the end of it all, when he suddenly found [32] himself outside the child, blown out by his gentle exhalation. Then the child spoke to the sage, and then it suddenly dawned on Mārkaṇḍeya who the Child was. He sees and recognizes God.[1]

As this Brahmin Noah had no need for the ark, he had no need for any seeds. The seeds are there permanently. There had been in fact no destruction at all : that destruction was an illusion. There was only an involution : the world had been only withdrawn into the interior of God. Creation, moreover, was not Mārkaṇḍeya's concern : it was the business of Brahmā. Like the seed which has been well planted, the universe will grow of itself, putting forth in due time blossoms and fruits and other seeds. Mārkaṇḍeya, the Yogi, is interested only in knowing and understanding things. He had seen God, but that is not sufficient for him. He wants to know God, know about His nature and character, His Māyā, that Māyā which had not been understood even by the gods themselves (B. 3. 188. 135):

Jñatum icchāmi deva tvāṁ māyāṁ caitāṁ tavottamām |

The divine Child declares itself to be Nārāyaṇa, the indestructible source of the world, and reveals to Mārkaṇḍeya His real nature and character.

The Bhārgava Mārkaṇḍeya is, according to this account, the only man who had survived the last deluge, witnessed the act of dissolution and creation in progress, stood in his own person face to face with Nārāyaṇa in the utter solitude of total annihilation, but it is nowhere made clear why Mārkaṇḍeya was singled out for this unique honour : it is an unmotivated theme. It is left to us to infer that the Bhārgava Mārkaṇḍeya is the only perfect Yogi that ever lived.

A little later, as already mentioned, Mārkaṇḍeya relates to the Pāṇḍavas the famous Rāmopākhyāna (Āraṇyaka 273-292 in the Vulgate), an abridgement of the Rāma story in about 750 stanzas. The occasion for relating the story arises in the following way.

Jayadratha, a near relative of the Kurus and the Pāṇḍavas tries to carry off Draupadī, but is defeated and captured, and ultimately pardoned and released. Yudhiṣṭhira mourns his fate [33] and asks Mārkaṇḍeya, who seems to be rather abruptly introduced for the purpose of the story, if there is any mortal more unfortunate than himself. Thereupon Mārkaṇḍeya relates the story of the Dāśarathi Rāma. Now the entire story of the attempted rape of Draupadī by Jayadratha is so ill conceived and unconvincing that it appears to have been invented solely for the purpose of introducing a summary of the Rāmāyaṇa. Who could be now a better narrator of the story of Rāma than the Bhārgava Mārkaṇḍeya, age-old and yet eternally young, the only man who had witnessed the happenings in this world in all the different ages, witnessed even the dissolution and creation of the world?

---

[1] An illuminating commentary on a different version of this same myth is given by H. ZIMMER, *Maya, Der indische Mythos*, pp. 52 ff.

After hearing the story of Rāma, Yudhiṣṭhira, the "dummy" of the bard, says that he did not grieve so much on his own or his brothers' account as he did on account of the daughter of Drupada; and then asks Mārkaṇḍeya if he had ever seen or heard of a woman as devoted to her husband as Draupadī. To console Yudhiṣṭhira, Mārkaṇḍeya then relates the well-known story (*upākhyāna*) of Sāvitrī, who rescues her husband from death by the insistent importunity of her pleading, by her deep feminine intuition and by her unflinching devotion to her husband (Āraṇyaka 293-299 in the Vulgate). And that is the last episode of the Āraṇyaka narrated by the Bhārgava Mārkaṇḍeya and in fact the last episode of this *parvan* in which a Bhārgava is concerned.

VIRĀṬAPARVAN

In the short Virāṭaparvan, as is in the Sabhā, the narrative is plain and straightforward, unembellished by any episodic enlargement, and the story marches rapidly forward. This book contains consequently no *upākhyānas* and there is no room for any Bhārgava digression. The references to the Bhārgavas are few and far between, and they are incidental allusions to the greatness or heroism of the Bhārgavas. One of these may be adduced for the purpose of illustration. Addressing Duryodhana, Bhīṣma asks: "Who is superior to Droṇa except Rāma, the son of Jamadagni?" (B. 4. 51. 10).[1]

[34] UDYOGAPARVAN

The Udyogaparvan furnishes its quota of references to the Bhārgavas, at least to the Bhārgava Rāma. Here again Rāma Jāmadagnya emerges from the obscurity of myth and legend, and we find him coming into direct contact—and in one case, actual conflict—with some of the epic characters.

In adhy. 72 ff. of the Vulgate version of the Udyoga, we have an account of a council held by the Pāṇḍavas, where Kṛṣṇa is commissioned to go and treat with Dhṛtarāṣṭra, which is followed in adhy. 83 ff. by a description of Kṛṣṇa's journey to Hāstinapura. On the way he meets a company of ancient sages, whom he duly honours. On his asking them whither they were bound, the Bhārgava Rāma, who is apparently their spokesman, explains that they were on their way to attend the council meeting which was going to be held at Hāstinapura in order to witness the proceedings and listen to the discussion. The sages then take leave of him and proceed on their way. Led by Rāma Jāmadagnya, they arrive in due course at the capital of the Kurus and present themselves in the darbar hall, where they are received with due honours by Bhīṣma (adhy. 94). The proceedings begin with a long peroration by Kṛṣṇa, in which he announces that the Pāṇḍavas were ready to obey implicitly the commands of Dhṛtarāṣṭra, provided

---

[1] But this is 852* of our edition, and it was found only in Dn $D_{4,12}$; that is, it was added perhaps within 3 or 4 centuries!

they were assured that they would be treated with fairness and given what is theirs by right (adhy. 95). The Bhārgava Rāma, taking advantage of the spell of silence which followed Kṛṣṇa's diplomatic speech, gets up and, advising peace, relates, unasked, the story of Dambhodbhava (adhy. 96). The foolish king Dambhodbhava, who wants to be acknowledged the unconquered and unconquerable hero, challenges in his cupidity the sages Nara and Nārāyaṇa (who were then practising penance at Badarī) to fight with him. The ascetics meekly decline, but Dambhodbhava is importunate. So in the end Nara takes up a handful of grass and, charging the blades in his hand with mystic potency, flings them at the enemy. They change into deadly missiles, overpowering the soldiers of Dambhodbhava, and compel him to surrender and acknowledge his defeat. Nara reads Dambhodbhava a sermon on self-control, on kindness to all creatures and humility towards Brahmins. The Bhārgava Rāma appearing here in the rôle of a [35] peace-maker concludes by advising conciliation and pointing out that Nara is Arjuna, while Nārāyaṇa is Kṛṣṇa. The story is an unnecessary digression, with the very obvious object of reiterating and emphasizing the identity between Nara-Nārāyaṇa and Arjuna-Kṛṣṇa.

The Udyogaparvan closes with a story (Ambopākhyāna), in which the Bhārgava Rāma plays a very active and prominent part (adhy. 173-196 of the Vulgate). Bhīṣma explains to Duryodhana that, because of a vow he had taken, he would not fight with Śikhaṇḍin, who at birth had been a girl, and then relates the whole life history of Śikhaṇḍin, who in a previous birth was Ambā, the daughter of the king of Kāśī. Bhīṣma narrates how Ambā, having been disappointed of marriage through Bhīṣma's action, vowed to compass his death and how the Bhārgava Rāma, having promised to help her, fought with Bhīṣma at Kurukṣetra for twenty-three days, a fight which ends in a stalemate. The story is developed in this way.

When Ambā was repulsed by Śālva, to whom she was engaged and who subsequently refused to marry her on account of her abduction by Bhīṣma, she left him and wandered about alone in a neighbouring forest, nursing her grief and vowing vengeance. There she meets a company of ascetics, who sympathize with her and devise means to help her. While the ascetics are cogitating as to how they should help her, there comes along by chance Ambā's grandfather, the royal sage Hotravāhana, who advises her to seek the help of his *friend* Rāma Jāmadagnya. While these deliberations are proceeding, Rāma's disciple and faithful follower Akṛtavraṇa appears on the scene. Hotravāhana tells him the previous history of Ambā and also her future plans. Akṛtavraṇa decides that Bhīṣma is certainly responsible for Ambā's misfortunes, and is the party deserving punishment. By a fortunate accident Rāma—on the war-path, armed with a bow and a sword and his famous axe (*paraśu*)—comes there the following morning. Ambā again relates the whole story of her unfortunate life to the Bhārgava Rāma and beseeches him to slay the offending Bhīṣma. But since Rāma has taken the vow that he would on no account take up arms except at the bidding of the twice-born, he has to be persuaded by the sages to espouse Ambā's cause. [36] He then proceeds with Ambā and all the assembled sages to the banks of the Sarasvatī and from there sends a message to Bhīṣma, who meets him at the boundary of the Kuru kingdom. Rāma orders Bhīṣma to take back Ambā or failing that fight a duel with him. Since Bhīṣma cannot do the former, he decides to fight, goes back to the city and returns, furnished with all arms and accoutrements, in a chariot made of silver, drawn by white horses. Bhīṣma's mother Gaṅgādevī (identified with the river Ganges) tries to stop the impending fight but without success. The fight lasts for several days, when at last Rāma wounded by an arrow of Bhīṣma falls down in a swoon. Bhīṣma stops fighting : it is a gentlemanly duel, following minutely all the strict rules of chivalry, and unlike the deadly combats of the Bhārata war. The fight is continued on the following days, with varying luck. Even after many days of constant fighting, in which millions and billions of arrows are showered by each combatant and cut up by the opponent, various magical missiles are flung by which alternately the combatants get wounded, fall down, recover and resume the fight, the grim contest continues indecisively. Then one night Bhīṣma, who was one of the Vasus, saw in a dream a group of eight Brahmins (the Eight Vasus), who had supported him and encouraged him that same day while he was lying wounded and unconscious on the battlefield. They remind him of a magical missile of his, by discharging which he could put the Bhārgava Rāma to sleep on the field of battle. Next day the fight began again and the combatants hurled at each other simultaneously the terrific Brahma missile, which is capable shattering the earth. The two missiles clash in the middle and neutralize each other. During the commotion caused by these weapons, Bhīṣma thinks of the sleep missile. As he is about to discharge that missile, the gods intervene. With Bhīṣma's mother, Gaṅgā, the gods go from one to the other of the combatants, trying to pacify them. Seeing that neither of them is prepared to yield and be the first to retire from the field of battle, the gods stand between the combatants and make the fight impossible. Still the combatants are not pacified and will not leave the field. Finally the shades of his ancestors persuade Rāma to lay aside his weapons, which he then reluctantly does. That is sufficient for Bhīṣma. He puts down his bow and arrow, goes to Rāma, his *guru*, and prostrates [37] himself at his feet. They soon forget their quarrel and become friends again. Thus this titanic conflict between Bhīṣma and the Bhārgava Rāma, which is said to have lasted for three and twenty days, is utterly barren of any result beyond adding a few hundred lines to the text !

One peculiar thing we notice about this story is the sudden change of heart on the part of the Bhārgava Rāma. While in all other accounts of him he is represented as the inveterate foe of the Kṣatriyas and the epic bards are never weary of telling us that he had exterminated the Kṣatriyas thrice seven times, here we find him befriending the royal sage Hotravāhana and championing the lost cause of an unhappy Kṣatriya damsel ! The episode shows another inconsistency in the behaviour of Rāma ; for, here we are surprised with the statement that in Bhīṣma Rāma had taken a *Kṣatriya* pupil and had apparently taught him so well that the pupil knew not only as much as the *guru* but perhaps even more. This does not prevent him subsequently from cursing Karṇa, who had learnt the secrets of the science of arms from Rāma in the guise of a Brahmin but later had to confess that he was a Kṣatriya. There Rāma is reported to have said to Karṇa that the Brahma weapon can never be learnt by one who is not a Brahmin (B. 12. 3. 31), though Bhīṣma had used the Brahma missile successfully against Rāma in the combat mentioned above.

BHĪṢMAPARVAN

With the Bhīṣmaparvan begin what may be called the "battle books," which in some shape or other must have formed the kernel of the Mahābhārata, which kernel has served as a nucleus for the growth of a vast amount of secondary material, cohering together so as to form a more or less harmonious whole. A rough sketch of the original plan of the epic is preserved in a stanza occurring in one of the chapters of the first book (1. 55. 43) :

evam etat purāvṛttaṁ teṣām akliṣṭakarmaṇām |
bhedo rājyavināśaś ca jayaś ca jayatāṁ vara ||

The Bhārata, according to this statement, was a trilogy consisting of the story of the dissension, loss of the kingdom, and victory, among some descendants of Bharata.

[38] The Bhīṣmaparvan, according to the Vulgate, is divided into four sections (*upaparvans*). Of these the first two are mainly geographical tractates : Jambūkhaṇḍa-nirmāṇa-parvan and Bhūmi-parvan. The third is the famous philosophical discourse, the Bhagavadgītā, which is, so to say, the keystone of the whole new superstructure of the remodelled Bhārata and which has passed into world literature. The fourth and last section of this book is a lengthy account in eighty chapters (or about 4300 stanzas) of the fight of the first ten days of the Great War, up to the fall of Bhīṣma. After the Bhagavadgītā, the account of the fight runs on smoothly and is not allowed to be interrupted by any digressions. Consequently this sub-section also contains no Bhārgava episode or for that matter any other episodic narrative at all. But passing allusions to the Bhārgavas are not by any means wanting even in this final section of the Bhīṣmaparvan. They are, however, for the most part trivial and confined to the glorification of Rāma Jāmadagnya, playing on the theme of his encounter with Bhīṣma. The Bhārgava

Rāma is subtly praised by saying that Bhīṣma was a hero whom even Rāma could not defeat.

But the Bhagavadgītā itself contains an interesting allusion to the Bhṛgus and that is in the tenth chapter, in the enumeration of the so-called *vibhūtis* of Śrī-Kṛṣṇa. The *vibhūtis* are said to be infinite (*nāsty anto vistarasya me*, Gītā 10. 19 in the Vulgate version), but about sixty of them have been specifically enumerated and they are worthy of close study. Some of these *vibhūtis* are pure and simple gods, such as Indra, Viṣṇu, Śiva and so on. Some are yet other supernatural beings, such as Kubera, Citraratha and others. Some are celestial luminaries such as the Sun, and the Moon. Some are merely terrestrial features such as mountains, rivers, the ocean and so on. Some are even animals such as the serpent (Śeṣa), elephant (Airāvata), eagle (Garuḍa) and so on. There are mentioned among these *vibhūtis* only nine human—or at least semi-human, that is, semi-divine—beings, whom we may regard as historical or semi-historical personalities. Three of them, Vāsudeva, Arjuna and Vyāsa, are well-known and important epic characters, and as such their inclusion in this list is expected and may be said [39] to be quite natural. They may therefore be ignored. Then, further, of divine sages (*devarṣis*), Śri-Kṛṣṇa declares himself to be Nārada, the official messenger between the gods and the men. Of perfected beings (*Siddhas*), Śrī-Kṛṣṇa says, he is Kapila, a celebrated sage, probably the codifier of the Sāṁkhya, the system most popular with the epic bards. Of household priests, Śrī-Kṛṣṇa identifies himself, quite naturally again, with Bṛhaspati, the priest of the gods, one of the Aṅgirases, a clan closely connected with the Bhṛgus from very ancient times. There remain three; of these all—or at least two—are clearly Bhārgavas. Of Kavis, Śri-Kṛṣṇa says, he is Śukra, the Bhārgava priest of the Asuras, the asuric counterpart of Bṛhaspati. Of weapon-bearers (*śastra-bhṛt*), Śrī-Kṛṣṇa declares himself to be Rāma, who is identified by some authorities as Rāma son of Daśaratha, but who in my opinion is meant to be no other than the much lauded hero of the Mahābhārata poets, Rāma son of Jamadagni, the Bhārgava Rāma. Lastly, of great sages (*maharṣis*), Śrī-Kṛṣṇa says he is Bhṛgu (*maharṣīṇāṁ Bhṛgur aham*, Gītā 10. 25).[1] All other *vibhūtis* are more or less intelligible; for each *vibhūti* is or may be regarded, more or less, as the foremost or the first of a class; but why Bhṛgu should be considered as the *greatest of the great sages* (*Maharṣis*) is somewhat enigmatic. He is not reckoned among the Seven Sages (*saptarṣis*). He is no doubt said to be a son of Brahmā, but Brahmā had nearly a dozen sons of that kind, who all became Prajāpatis and founders of *gotras*. And about Bhṛgu's greatness even the Mahābhārata has nothing to narrate beyond the

[1] C. V. VAIDYA, *Proc. & trans*: 1st Or. Conf. (1922), p. 39 ("Gotra and Pravara" p.p. 34-45) explains it differently. He is of opinion that of all Ṛṣis Bhṛgu was actually considered as the foremost.

fact that his wife Pulomā was abducted by a cannibal called Puloman (Ādi) or Daṁśa (Śānti), and that he had cursed various people.

DROṆAPARVAN

The Droṇaparvan supplies what is for our purpose one of the most interesting of Bhārgava references in the Mahābhārata.

On the thirteenth day of the Great War during Arjuna's temporary absence, Abhimanyu with a small following pierces the Kaurava ring-formation (*cakra-vyūha*), but Jayadratha intercepts his followers and isolates him, and Abhimanyu is slain after a brave fight; one of the most tragic episodes of the Great Epic. [40] To console Yudhiṣṭhira for the untimely death of Abhimanyu, Vyāsa tells him many stories illustrating the transitoriness of human life. At that time he relates how Nārada comforted Sṛñjaya in a time of bereavement by telling him of the sixteen kings of great merit, who nevertheless all died when their time came (adhy. 55-71 of the Vulgate). These kings were, as a matter of fact, all *cakravartins,* sovereigns who had conquered surrounding kingdoms or brought them under their sway and established a paramount position on more or less extensive regions around their own kingdoms. The episode, which is known as the Ṣoḍaśarājakīya, recounts the heroic deeds and the meritorious actions of sixteen of such famous kings of antiquity. The sixteen kings are these: (1) Marutta, son of Avikṣit; (2) Suhotra Ātithina; (3) Paurava (Bṛhadratha, king of Aṅga); (4) Śibi, son of Uśīnara; (5) Rāma, son of Daśaratha; (6) Bhagiratha, son of Dilīpa; (7) Dilīpa Ailavila; (8) Māndhātṛ, son of Yuvanāśva; (9) Yayāti, son of Nahuṣa; (10) Ambarīṣa, son of Nābhāga; (11) Śaśabindhu, son of Citraratha; (12) Gaya, son of Amūrtarayas; (13) Rantideva, son of Saṁkṛti: (14) Bharata, son of Duḥṣanta; (15) Pṛthu, son of Veṇa; and, last but not least, (16) the Bhārgava Rāma, son of Jamadagni.

Accordingly we have here a vivid and colourful description of that great feat of the Bhārgava Rāma, the extirpation of Kṣatriyas, an account which courts mistrust by its appalling exaggeration and staggering figures (adhy. 70 of the Vulgate). We are told how Rāma took a vow to relieve the Earth of her burden of Kṣatriyas. Thereafter he first slew Kārtavīrya, who was never before defeated in battle. Then of Kṣatriyas he slaughtered 64,000, cutting off their ears and noses and breaking their teeth, besides stifling in smoke 7000 Haihayas (the clan to which Arjuna Kārtavīrya belonged) and torturing them, and butchering 10,000 with his own axe.... Then the puissant son of Jamadagni, marching against the Kaśmīras, the Daradas, the Kuntis, the Kṣudrakas and Mālavas, the Aṅgas, Vaṅgas and Kaliṅgas, the Videhas, the Tāmraliptakas, the Rakṣovāhas, the Vītihotras, the Trigartas, the Mārttikāvatas, the Śibis and other warrior races, thousands in number, slew them all with arrows of exceeding sharpness. Going from country to country, he slew [41] thousands and hundreds of thousands of Kṣatriyas, creating a veritable deluge of blood and filling many lakes with it....Then bringing under his sway all the eighteen divisions of the earth, that descendant of Bhṛgu celebrated a hundred sacrifices, like a second Indra, when he gave away costly gifts (*dakṣiṇā*) to Brahmins. The sacrificial altar, full eight *nalas* high and made entirely of gold, embellished with hundreds of gems and adorned with thousands of banners, as also this earth abounding in domestic and wild animals, was accepted by Kaśyapa from the Bhārgava Rāma as his sacrificial fee for performing the sacrifice. Rāma also gave him many thousands of huge elephants adorned with golden ornaments. Freeing the earth of robbers that infested her, making her full of righteous and amiable people, Rāma gave the earth to Kaśyapa at his great horse sacrifice. Then comes the Bhārgava slogan (B. 7. 70. 20) :

triḥsaptakṛtvaḥ pṛthivīṁ kṛtvā niḥkṣatriyāṁ prabhuḥ | (IV)

Having cleared the earth of Kṣatriyas thrice seven times, having celebrated a hundred sacrifices, Rāma gave the earth to the Brahmins. When the earth with her seven grand divisions was bestowed by him upon Kaśyapa, then the latter said to Rāma, "Go thou out of this earth at my command !" Hearing these words of Kaśyapa, that foremost of weapon-bearers, obedient to the command of a Brahmin, caused the ocean to roll back and to give him a new strip of land to live in, and Rāma took up his abode on Mount Mahendra.

It is instructive to compare this Story of Sixteen Kings with a variant version of it in the Śānti (adhy. 29 of the Vulgate), as related to the same Yudhiṣṭhira by Śrī-Kṛṣṇa. After the battle the month of mourning is spent outside the capital on the banks of the Ganges. Yudhiṣṭhira, very dejected, proposes to renounce the kingdom and retire to the forest. At Arjuna's request, Kṛṣṇa tries to console him and so relates to him the Story of Sixteen Kings, which Nārada had once related to king Sṛñjaya. The stories are naturally almost the same as those related to Yudhiṣṭhira by Vyāsa after the death of Abhimanyu. There is, however, one very striking difference. Fifteen of the kings in the list are the same ; the sixteenth "king" of the Droṇa list, namely, the Bhārgava Rāma, is conspicuous by his absence in the Śāntī [42] list ! He is replaced by a real king, Sagara son of Ikṣvāku, who was indeed a very famous king, fully deserving to be included in this list of the celebrated sixteen kings of antiquity, whereas the Bhārgava Rāma was no king at all and does not properly fall into this enumeration. His "extermination" of the Kṣatriyas was merely an act of vendetta. And although he is said to have conquered the whole earth, he never was crowned a king. Therefore the propriety of including his exploits in the Ṣoḍaśarājakīya is more than questionable. In fact it would never strike anybody except an unscrupulous Brahmin redactor—with strong Bhārgava leanings—to perpetrate such a tendentious perversion and father it upon Vyāsa.

KARṆAPARVAN

Karṇa is represented in our epic as a pupil of the Bhārgava Rāma, like Bhīṣma and Droṇa. So there are several casual references—in his capacity as the *guru* of Karṇa—to Rāma Jāmadagnya in the course of this parvan.

In adhy. 31 (of the Vulgate), we have a reference to the bow (Vijaya) which Karṇa had received from the Bhārgava Rāma, who in his turn had obtained it from Indra himself. Indra had used it in his fight with the Daityas: Rāma had used it in his campaign against the Kṣatriyas of the earth, which he had conquered thrice seven times (B. 8. 31. 46):

triḥsaptakṛtvaḥ pṛthivī dhanuṣā yena nirjitā | (V)

On the seventeenth day of the war, Duryodhana persuades Śalya to be Karṇa's charioteer and to encourage him tells the story how Karṇa had become possessed even of celestial weapons through the Bhārgava Rāma.

To emphasize further the great importance of Karṇa, Duryodhana then narrates a story which shows the greatness of Karṇa's *guru*, Rāma Jāmadagnya (adhy. 34 of the Vulgate). Rāma is generally represented in the Mahābhārata as a man—or rather a Superman—who had fought his battles on this earth with other human beings like himself. Here we are told that he had fought with and vanquished even the Daityas. The story is this. To obtain celestial weapons from Mahādeva, Rāma (like the Pāṇḍava Arjuna later) was practising terrible austerities. At that time [43] the Asuras had become so powerful that even all the gods together could not subdue them, and so Mahādeva asks the Bhārgava Rāma to fight with them (as Arjuna later fought with the Nivātakavacas and other demons). Rāma went up to the Asuras and said to them, "Most invincible in battle as you are, O Daityas, give me battle". Then the Daityas began to fight with Rāma. Then that delighter of the Bhārgava clan slaughtered those Daityas, on the battle-field by strokes that were like the strokes from Indra's thunderbolt. After Rāma had vanquished the invincible Asuras without the use of any special weapons, then Mahādeva gave him those celestial missiles for which Rāma was practising the terrible austerities. Perhaps feeling that the story might be disbelieved, Duryodhana hastens to add that he had heard it himself from the lips of a pious and truthful Brahmin while the latter was relating it to king Dhṛtarāṣṭra, Duryodhana's father.

Then in adhy. 42 (of the Vulgate), Karṇa relates that under the guise of a Brahmin he had been a disciple of the Bhārgava Rāma in order to learn from him the secret of certain magical missiles known to Rāma alone. One day while Rāma was sleeping with his head resting in the lap of Karṇa, the thigh of the latter was bored through by Indra (Arjuna's *de facto* father) in the form of a ferocious centipede, and Karṇa was weltering in blood but did not move a muscle, for fear of disturbing the sleep of his *guru* and thus incurring his displeasure. When Rāma woke up and saw this state of things, he concluded that his disciple was no Brahmin, as only a Kṣatriya could suffer such agony and keep still. Then Karṇa confesses his guilt and begs Rāma's pardon. Rāma pronounces a curse on Karṇa, saying that at the critical moment the magical missiles of which he had obtained knowledge from Rāma by such a dastardly trick—even the great Yogi could not see through it—would fail him. Brahma could never reside firmly in one who is not a Brahmin : *abrāhmaṇe brahma na hi dhruvaṁ syāt* (B. 8. 42. 9.) And so it happened, needless to say.

In a variant version of this tale (Śānti 3 in the Vulgate) the worm which had bored through Karṇa's thigh is said to have been not Indra in disguise, but a demon suffering the effects of a curse pronounced on him by Bhṛgu !

[44] ŚALYAPARVAN

In the Śalyaparvan there are only stray references to the Bhārgavas, especially in the account of Balarāma's pilgrimage—another very obvious digression—during which Balarāma visits of course all the places sacred to the Bhārgavas such as Rāmatīrtha, Samantapañcaka and so on, which lay on his way.

At Rāmatīrtha we have a repetition of the story that Kaśyapa officiated at the sacrifice celebrated by Rāma Bhārgava after conquering the whole earth and annihilating the Kṣatriyas (B. 9. 49. 7 f.) :

yatra Rāmo mahābhāgo Bhārgavaḥ sumahātapāḥ ||
asakṛt pṛthivīm jitvā hatakṣatriyapuṁgavām |
upādhyāyaṁ puraskṛtya Kaśyapaṁ munisattamam ||
ayajad vājapeyena so 'śvamedhaśatena ca |
pradadau dakṣiṇāṁ caiva pṛthivīṁ vai sasāgarām ||

SAUPTIKAPARVAN

The Sauptika is one of the few books of the Mahābhārata which are entirely, or almost entirely, free from reference to the Bhārgavas. The book is short, consisting of 18 chapters and about 800 stanzas in the Vulgate version, and comprises only two *sub-parvans* : the Sauptika and the Aiṣīka. The first *sub-parvan* describes the slaughter of the sleepers in the camp of the Pāṇḍavas, while the second gives an account of the use of the world-destroying dart Aiṣīka by Aśvatthāman.

STRĪPARVAN

In the next book, the Strīparvan, which like the former is short, consisting of 27 chapters and about 800 stanzas in the Vulgate version, there are only three incidental references to the Bhārgavas. The *parvan* consists almost wholly of the description of the obsequial ceremonies of the warriors killed in the war and lamentations of women over their dead kinsfolk, which is fortunately held free from digressions and interpolations. The tragedy also does not permit the development of any other sentiment. The absence of reference to the Bhārgavas, who, as already remarked, had strictly speaking no connection whatsoever with the Kuru-Pañcāla heroes, is not only thoroughly [45] appropriate, but is an omission for which we may be truly grateful to the redactors of our Mahābhārata.

ŚĀNTIPARVAN

The Śānti, which is in essence a manual of instruction in king-craft (*rājadharma*), conduct in time of calamity (*āpaddharma*) and emancipation (*mokṣadharma*) compiled in the peculiar pedagogic technique developed by the redactors of the Great Epic for the edification of the people combined with their entertainment, supplies its quota of Bhārgava material, making up in some measures for the deficiency of the last three books.

Already in adhy. 2 f. (of the Vulgate) we hear of the Bhārgava Rāma. The month of mourning is spent by the Pāṇḍavas outside the capital on the banks of the Ganges. There Nārada relates to Yudhiṣṭhira the story of the early career of Karṇa, which is here said to be a secret of the gods (*devaguhya*). In the course of the narrative Nārada repeats with more details the story we have already noticed as to how Karṇa had easily deceived the Bhārgava Rāma and obtained from him the carefully guarded secret of the famous Brahma missile (*brahmāstra*) under the false pretence of being a Bramin, and a Bhṛgu too. An interesting point of difference between this version of the story and that given in the Karṇaparvan is, as mentioned already, that the worm which bites Karṇa and bores a hole through his leg is not Indra but a demon called Daṁśa, who had tried to carry off Bhṛgu's wife. If this wife be Pulomā, then her ravisher's name was given as Puloman in adhy. 4 of the Ādi, where, however, there is no mention of Bhṛgu's curse ; but we are told on the other hand that the ravisher of Pulomā was reduced to ashes by Bhṛgu's son Cyavana. But perhaps this demon Daṁśa is some other ravisher of Bhṛgu's wife.

In any event the happy result of this discourse of the sage was that Yudhiṣṭhira, casting off grief, enters the capital in state, is installed on the throne and performs the obsequial ceremonies of his departed kinsmen. Later Kṛṣṇa in an ecstatic trance communes with the distant Bhīṣma, who remains lying on the battlefield on a bed of arrows and who in a long hymn of adoration invokes Kṛṣṇa. Kṛṣṇa then sets out with the Pāṇḍava brothers and his followers [46] to visit Bhīṣma on his death-bed. The arrival of the party at the battle-field, which it will be remembered has been identified by the redactors of the epic with the Bhārgava *tīrtha* Samantapañcaka, affords an easy opportunity for another repetition of the legend of Rāma's heroic exploit. That was the very spot where the Bhārgava Rāma had established those five lakes of blood. Śrī-Kṛṣṇa in passing points to those lakes and says (B. 12. 48. 9) :

triḥsaptakṛtvo vasudhāṁ kṛtvā niḥkṣatriyāṁ prabhuḥ |
ihedānīṁ tato Rāmaḥ karmaṇo virarāma ha || (VI)

Yudhiṣṭhira, the "dummy" of the rhapsode, has an insatiable longing to hear all about the extermination of the Kṣatriyas by the Bhārgava Rāma though he had heard it all before from other story-tellers, and he has besides some doubts which he forthwith refers to Kṛṣṇa (B. 12. 48. 10) :

triḥsaptakṛtvaḥ pṛthivī kṛtā niḥkṣatriyā purā |
Rāmeṇeti tathāttha tvam atra me saṁśayo mahān || (VII)

To solve this doubt of Yudhiṣṭhira Kṛṣṇa gratuitously volunteers to repeat the whole story of Rāma from the very beginning, a full-size account of the birth of the Bhārgava Rāma, of the extirpation of the Kṣatriyas and of the subsequent regeneration of the race. Here we have now an attestation of the entire story by Śrī-Kṛṣṇa, a variant of the story told by Akṛtavraṇa, a disciple of Rāma, to Yudhiṣṭhira himself in the Āraṇyaka. There are naturally several discrepancies between the two versions, two of which are noteworthy. In the first version it was Satyavatī's father-in-law who prepares the magical *carus*, which were subsequently exchanged by the good ladies who were to partake of them ; here it is Satyavatī's husband himself, Ṛcīka, who prepares them. The other is a somewhat more serious discrepancy. In the Āraṇyaka version, Jamadagni was robbed of his calf by Arjuna Kārtavīrya himself, who is represented there as a perfect fiend. In the story as told by Śrī-Kṛṣṇa, Arjuna is a perfect angel of a man, always devoted to peace, ever obedient to Brahmins and ready to protect all classes ; he had given away the earth to Brahmins in a horse sacrifice which he had performed. His sons on the other hand were "proud and cruel", and it was they who brought away the calf of Jamadagni's sacrificial [47] cow. As it is difficult, at this distance of time, in the absence of independent evidence, to say whether Akṛtavraṇa or Śrī-Kṛṣṇa was more truthful, it must remain a moot point whether the guilty party is Arjuna Kārtavīrya or his sons. Then Śrī-Kṛṣṇa goes on to tell Yudhiṣṭhira that the Kṣatriyas were annihilated by the Bhārgava Rāma thrice seven times, speaking exactly like a Bhārgava (B. 12. 49. 64) :

triḥsaptakṛtvaḥ pṛthivīm kṛtvā niḥkṣatriyāṁ prabhuḥ |
dakṣiṇām aśvamedhānte Kaśyapāyādadat tataḥ || (VIII)

The matter being now attested by Śrī-Kṛṣṇa himself, it cannot be described by revilers of Brahmins as a fabrication made by the Brahmins themselves.

It must always have been something of a puzzle to all thoughtful persons where Kṣatriyas like the Kauravas and the Pāṇḍavas and even Śrī-Kṛṣṇa himself came from after the Kṣatriya race had been wiped out thrice seven times by the Bhārgava Rāma, and that was in fact Yudhiṣṭhira's doubt, which he had expressed to Śrī-Kṛṣṇa. Various explanations of the mystery have been propounded. In the earlier chapters of the epic, as we have seen several times, it was the pious Brahmins who procreated children on the widows of the Kṣatriyas slain by Rāma and they became Kṣatriyas by the Vedic rule *pāṇigrāhasya tanayaḥ* (1. 98. 5) : the child belongs to him who has gone through the form of marriage with the mother. That was however not the view of Śrī-Kṛṣṇa. His explanation was that the Earth had concealed some Kṣatriyas.[1] She had concealed some Haihayas among women, some Pauravas among the bears of Mount Ṛkṣavant. Some other Kṣatriyas were brought up in the forest among the kine, some in the cowpens among the calves. Some were protected by the Ocean, some by the wolves[2] on Mount Gṛdhrakūṭa. These had all escaped destruction at the hands of the formidable Bhārgava. And the old Kṣatriya dynasties were resuscitated by Kaśyapa, who first ordered Rāma to clear out from the earth which he had given to Kaśyapa as a part of the sacrificial fee and restored by and by those scions of the old Kṣatriya families to their rightful heritage. Śrī-Kṛṣṇa evidently did not know anything about the procreation of Kṣatriyas by pious Brahmins on the widows of the Kṣatriyas slaughtered by the bloodthirsty Bhārgava. He con-[48]-cludes by remarking that the present Kṣatriyas are the legitimate offsprings of those ancient Kṣatriyas (B. 12. 49. 88 f.) :

tataḥ pṛthivyā nirdiṣṭāṁs tān samānīya Kaśyapaḥ |
abhyaṣiñcan mahīpālān kṣatriyān vīryasaṁmatān ||
teṣāṁ putrāś ca pautrāś ca yeṣāṁ vaṁśāḥ pratiṣṭhitāḥ |

At the beginning of the third great sub-division of the Śānti, the Mokṣadharma, we have a lengthy discourse attributed to Bhṛgu, called the Bhṛgu-Bhāradvāja-saṁvāda (adhy. 182-192 of the Vulgate), which summarizes in the form of questions and answers almost the entire Brahmanic teaching on the subject of (1) the elements, (2) life and death, (3) caste distinctions, (4) good and evil, (5) the four stages of life, and finally, (6) the other world. It will be seen that it is a complete tractate on Hindu Ontology, Sociology, Eschatology and Ethics that is here attributed to Bhṛgu, the eponymous ancestor of the Bhārgavas.

The oft-cited stanza B. 12. 339. 103 f. :

Haṁsaḥ Kūrmaś ca Matsyaś ca prādurbhāvād dvijottama |
Varāho Narasiṁhaś ca Vāmano Rāma eva ca |
Rāmo Dāśrathiś caiva Sātvataḥ Kalkir eva ca |

from the Mokṣadharma is important as containing one of the two actual references in our Mahābhārata to the Bhārgava Rāma as an *avatāra* of Viṣṇu, one of his ten *avatāras* ; but the passage is suspect, as it is missing in some Grantha MSS. and some old Devanāgarī MSS. which have been

---

[1] The relevant passage is cited and translated by J. C. GHOSH, in an article which has appeared in the *Annals* (Vol. 12, pp. 168 ff.) entitled "Some additional notes on 'Foreign elements in the Hindu Population'."

[2] Monkeys? [MON. WILL.]

collated by the Bhandarkar Oriental Research Institute for a critical edition of that book. The other reference is in the same chapter, a few stanzas earlier (B. 12. 339. 84) :

> *Tretāyuge bhaviṣyāmi Rāmo Bhṛgukulodvahaḥ* |
> *Kṣatraṁ cotsādayiṣyāmi samṛddhabalavāhanam* ||

This stanza cannot be impugned on the score of documentary evidence, which is unanimous in its favour. But both references occur in the Nārāyaṇīya section of the Mokṣadharma, which is notoriously a late addition to our Mahābhārata. This shows that the theory of *avatāras* is still developing in the epic and their number is not yet fixed, nor are the *avatāras* fully canonized. It should thus seem that the Mahābhārata does not [49] necessarily presuppose the Bhārgava Rāma to be an *avatāra* of Viṣṇu.

ANUŚĀSANAPARVAN

The Anuśāsana, for some reason that is not yet quite clear, is the richest in Bhārgava material.

Early in the beginning of this book (adhy. 4), we have the *third* repetition of the legend of the birth of Jamadagni. The previous chapter (3) relates the mighty deeds of the Kṣatriya Viśvāmitra, which led to his attaining the coveted status of a Brahmin. In adhy. 4, Bhīṣma explains how it came about that Viśvāmitra who was of mingled Brahmin and Kṣatriya parentage was born in the Kṣatriya caste with Brahmanic qualities, while his nephew Jamadagni, under similar conditions, was born in the Brahmin caste with Kṣatriyan qualities. We have here a repetition of the old story how Ṛcīka married Gādhi's daughter Satyavatī, who obtained some boons for herself and her mother. The mother and the daughter exchange the trees they had to embrace and *carus* of which they had to partake. The wise Ṛcīka had purposely made the prescriptions differently. He had in fact put the entire accumulated energy of Brahmanism in the *caru* of his wife, while he had put the entire accumulated energy of Kṣatriyahood in the *caru* intended for her mother. The consequence of the exchange slyly effected by the mother was that the son of Gādhi's wife turned out to be a man with Brahmanic propensities, while the son of Ṛcīka's wife would have been a model Kṣatriya ; but, owing to the pleadings of Satyavatī, the great sage graciously gives his consent to the postponement of the doom to Satyavatī's grand-son.

This story we have had at Āraṇyaka 115 and Śānti 49 of the Vulgate. In passing it may be mentioned that the present version agrees with the Śāntiparvan version in making Ṛcīka the giver of the boons, whereas in the Āraṇyaka version this person is some ancestor of Ṛcīka, either Ṛcīka's father or perhaps Bhṛgu himself.

The mere mention of Bhārgava Rāma in B. 13. 14. 273 at once calls forth the reaction :

[50] *triḥsaptakṛtvaḥ pṛthivī yena niḥkṣatriyā kṛtā |*
Jāmadagnyena Govinda Rāmeṇākliṣṭakarmaṇā || etc. (IX)

In adhy. 30 (of the Vulgate) we are told how a Kṣatriya Vītahavya was made a Brahmin by the mere word of a Bhṛgu. The story is as follows.

Vatsa, a descendant of Śaryāti had two sons, Haihaya and Tālajaṅgha. The hundred sons of Haihaya attacked and killed Haryaśva, king of Kāśī, whose son Sudeva succeeded him on the throne. Sudeva was likewise defeated and killed by the Haihayas. Sudeva was succeeded by Divodāsa, who built Vārāṇasī, on the northern bank of Ganges and the southern bank of the Gomatī. Likewise defeated by the Haihayas, he fled to his priest Bharadvāja, who obtained for him, through sacrifice, a son Pratardana. The son of Divodāsa defeated in turn all the Haihayas, when Vītahavya pursued by Pratardana, fled to the hermitage of Bhṛgu. When Pratardana demanded from Bhṛgu the surrender of Vītahavya, who was hiding in Bhṛgu's hermitage, Bhṛgu in order to save the life of Vītahavya said that there were only Brahmins in the hermitage. Through that declaration of Bhṛgu, who could not tell a lie, Vītahavya actually became a Brahmin. His descendants are set out for fifteen generations. His son was Gṛtsamada, whose eleventh descendant was Pramati : his son was Ruru ; his son was Śunaka, from whom came the Śaunakas.

In adhy. 40, Bhīṣma expatiates on the fascination and frailty of women, the root of all evil, and to support his statement he relates the story of Vipula, another Bhārgava, an interesting story in which mesmerism or hypnotism plays some part (Vipulopākhyāna, adhy. 40-43 in the Vulgate).

The sage Devaśarman, the story goes, had a beautiful wife Ruci (Beauty) by name, who had attracted the attention of the gay king of the gods, Indra. Once upon a time it so happened that Devaśarman had to go away from his hermitage on some sacrificial business. Not feeling quite sure about his little Ruci, the old sage taking into his confidence his disciple, the Bhārgava Vipula, told him to protect his slender-waisted wife, especially against the amorous advances of Indra, who was an adept at assuming different forms at will. Devaśarman pathetically en-[51]-joined his disciple to take every care and see that the lascivious king of the celestials did not defile that frivolous wife of his, like a wretched dog licking the *havis* placed near the sacrificial altar. To protect the virtue of Ruci, who was peerless on earth in beauty, Vipula decided to enter into her by his yogic power and live in her without her being conscious of it, until the critical moment was passed. Indra comes as expected and makes overtures to the beautiful Ruci, who had captivated his mind. Ruci, though anxious to reciprocate, remains externally indifferent to the blandishments of Indra, through the influence of Vipula, who was living within her and guiding her actions. Indra, puzzled by the behaviour of Ruci, reflects and realizes how matters stand. At that moment Vipula leaves the body of Ruci and re-enters his own body. Then Vipula faces the philanderer and soundly rebukes him, and Indra slinks away abashed. Only *one* man had been able to protect a woman and that was the Bhārgava Vipula (B. 13. 43. 27):

> *tenaikena tu rakṣā vai Vipulena kṛtā striyāḥ |*
> *nānyah śaktas triloke 'smin rakṣituṁ nṛpa yoṣitam ||*

This story was told by the Bhārgava Mārkaṇḍeya to Bhīṣma (B. 13. 43. 18) and repeated by the latter to Yudhiṣṭhira.

A few chapters later we have again a Bhārgava story, the Cyavanopākhyāna in seven chapters (50-56), which is divided into two parts : the first two chapters (50-51) illustrate the sanctity of cows, the last five deal really with that topic of perennial interest, the mingled Brahmin and Kṣatriya parentage of the Bhārgava Rāma.

The first story, in which a cow was found to be the only equivalent possible for the ransom of the sage Cyavana, may be passed over.

In the second story (adhy. 52-56), we come back to the anecdote of Rāma Jāmadagnya, and we have here practically a repetition of the explanation given above (in adhy. 4 of this very *parvan*) of the circumstances under which Viśvāmitra, who was of mixed Brahmin and Kṣatriya parentage was born in the Kṣatriya caste with Brahmanic qualities, while Rāma under similar conditions was born in the Brahmin caste with the oppo-[52]-site qualities. The repetition comes about in this way. Yudhiṣṭhira, whose curiosity about the Bhārgava Rāma is, as already remarked, never satisfied, says to Bhīṣma (B. 13. 52. 1 ff.) : "I have a great curiosity, O Lord, about Jamadagni's son Rāma, that foremost of all righteous persons. You should satisfy that curiosity. How was Rāma born, that truly valorous hero? He belonged by birth to a family of Brahmin sages. How did he become a follower of Kṣatriyan practices? Relate to me in detail the circumstances of Rāma's birth. Also how did a man born in the family of the Kuśikas, who was a Kṣatriya, become a Brahmin? Great indeed was the power of the high-souled Rāma as also that of Viśvāmitra!"

The answer is given by Bhīṣma by relating the prophecy which had been made by Cyavana, an ancestor of the Bhārgava Rāma. Cyavana wants to prevent the harm that will come to his clan by Rāma's adopting the practices of the Kṣatriyas, a danger of which he has *prophetic* knowledge. He repairs to Kuśika, through whose descendant the harm was to happen, in order to vex him, and, if he finds a favourable opportunity to pronounce a malediction on Kuśika, damning him and his descendants to eternal perdition. When the sage presents himself before the king and says that he wants to observe a certain vow while living in the palace with the king, he is warmly welcomed with unfeigned joy, and also served with meticulous care and obsequiousness by the king and the queen. The sage has a meal and he then sleeps for twenty-one days, during which the king and the queen wait upon him without food or drink, gently massaging his legs. Suddenly the sage wakes up and goes out, followed with trepidation by the king and the queen, and as suddenly vanishes! The king looks for in vain, and, returning in a dejected mood to the room set apart for the sage, finds him again, stretched as before on his luxurious bed! The sage practises many tricks of this type, calculated to try the patience of the unfortunate couple, and ultimately yokes them to a heavily laden war-chariot. During the drive through the city, the sage gives the royal couple vicious digs with a heavy iron goad, distributing all the while in charity the entire wealth of the king. Still the sage finds no change in their behaviour. So in the end he has to [53] express himself as satisfied with their treatment of him and he goes back to the forest, asking the royal couple to come there on the following day. The king and queen take a little rest for the first time after forty-two days of trial and spend the night happily in each other's company. The next morning the king and the queen go to the forest to pay their respects to the sage and see there a magnificent palace standing in a big park, a fair imitation of Indra's paradise. After a short while, the magical palace and the park vanish, and there sits in the solitude of the forest the sage who had yoked them to the chariot and ill-treated them in other ways. Then the king feels that Brahmic power was the *summum bonum* of life. When he approaches Cyavana, the sage gives him a boon. Kuśika wants to know why Cyavana had come to live with him and what all those incidents implied. Cyavana tells him frankly what his intention was and also prophesies that Kuśika's wish would be fulfilled in so far that a descendant of Kuśika's (Viśvāmitra) would become a Brahmin. *Through the lustre of the Bhṛgus,* Kuśika's grandson (Viśvāmitra) would be an ascetic endowed with the splendour of fire (B. 13. 55. 32) :

Bhṛgūṇām eva tejasā |
pautras te bhavitā vipras tapasvī pāvakadyutiḥ ||

Then follows in the final chapter Cyavana's prophecy about the persecution of the Bhṛgus, about Ūrva (or Aurva), about Ṛcīka, and Jamadagni, who will marry Gādhi's daughter, that is, Kuśika's grand-daughter. Of the boons that will be given to the two ladies by Bhṛgu, the exchange of the trees and the *carus* by the mother and the daughter, about Viśvāmitra, and so on and so forth. Incidentally it may be mentioned that this is the *fourth* occurrence of this interesting story of the birth of the Bhārgava Rāma, it having occurred already at adhy. 4 of this very *parvan*, and before that in the Śānti (adhy. 48) and the Āraṇyaka (adhy. 115-117).

Some chapters later we again meet with the Bhārgava Rāma when Bhīṣma tells Yudhiṣṭhira about the merit of the gift of gold. The shades of his ancestors had appeared to Bhīṣma and told him that the gift of gold purifies the giver. Now it happens that the same advice had been given to the Bhārgava Rāma by Vasiṣṭha and other sages. In this connection we have again an [54] allusion to the extirpation of the Kṣatriyas and the conquest of the earth by Rāma (B. 13. 84. 31) :

triḥsaptakṛtvaḥ pṛthivī kṛtā niḥkṣatriyā purā |
tato jitvā mahīm kṛtsnāṁ Rāmo rājīvalocanaḥ || etc. (X)

The next chapter (85), a long rambling chapter with 168 stanzas, deals with the mystery, already alluded to above, of the birth of Bhṛgu, Aṅgiras and Kavi. They are said to be *prajāpatis* and progenitors of many tribes and clans, 'in fact of the entire mankind.

It will be a surprise to many that our sandals and umbrellas we also owe to a Bhṛgu. Chapter 95 relates how the practice arose of giving umbrellas and sandals to Brahmins at *śrāddhas* and other religious rites. Once upon a time Jamadagni was amusing himself by shooting arrows at a distant target, and his wife Reṇukā was fetching the arrows shot by him. Sorely afflicted by the scorching heat of the midday sun, she rested just for a moment under the shade of an umbrageous tree. Being kept waiting, the irascible Bhṛgu scolded his wife for her tardiness, but on learning the real cause of the delay, wanted to shoot down the offending sun from his high position in the heavens. The frightened luminary comes to him in the guise of a poor Brahmin, who tries to dissuade him from carrying out his terrible threat, but is recognized by the Bhṛgu and reprimanded. In the end Jamadagni is pacified and receives from the sun the first umbrella and the first pair of leather sandals. To make a gift of them to Brahmins is highly meritorious. This account of the origin of shoes and sandals is, I believe, not found outside the Mahābhārata.

In adhy. 98 (of the Vulgate) we have a report by Bhīṣma of a discussion between the Bhārgava Śukra and Bali about flowers, lamps, aromatics, appropriate to be offered to gods on diverse occasions and the merit accruing from the presentation.

Above, while discussing the Droṇaparvan version of the Ṣoḍaśarājakīya, I had referred to palpable evidence of the "bhṛguization" of a legend. We have another illuminating instance of the process in the next story (adhy. 99-100 of the [55] Vulgate) told by Bhīṣma to Yudhīṣṭhira. It is another version of the well-known legend of Nahuṣa's fall from heaven.

Nahuṣa, when king of the gods, neglected the daily offerings to the gods including the *bali*, losing thereby some of his spiritual power. Subsequently, having oppressed the sages, he was hurled down from heaven and turned into a boa by the curse of a Brahmin sage, Bhṛgu.

A similar version of this legend occurs in the Udyoga (adhy. 11-17) and is again alluded to in the Śānti (adhy. 342). There it is related that Nahuṣa became extremely arrogant and caused the sages to carry his palanquin. While being carried about in this way, his foot touched the head of Agastya, who by his curse turned him into a boa. The defect in the construction of this naïve story is very obvious and must have been early noticed by the diaskeuasts themselves. Nahuṣa, by the terms of the boon which

Brahmā and the gods had foolishly given him, could absorb the power of any being on whom he set his eyes. Under these circumstances, even the resourceful Agastya could not effectively curse Nahuṣa, because Agastya, when kicked by the tyrant, being in full view of the other, was *ipso facto* deprived of all his spiritual power, like all the gods and sages who had been oppressed by Nahuṣa and were utterly powerless before him.

The revised version of the legend in the Anuśāsana stages beforehand a confabulation between Bhṛgu and Agastya. Agastya wants to damn Nahuṣa but does not know how to. Bhṛgu befriends him and gives him the assurance that he (Bhṛgu) would somehow bring about the downfall of the tyrant. Bhṛgu, who knows beforehand, by spiritual prevision, that Nahuṣa was going to kick Agastya, proposes to Agastya, in anticipation of it, that on a certain day he would sit *hidden* inside the matted locks of the sage and from that position he would curse Nahuṣa. So when the opportune moment came, Bhṛgu, possessed of great lustre, addressed Agastya as follows : "Do you shut your eyes, Agastya, while I enter into the matted hair of your head". Having said this, Bhṛgu of unfading glory and great energy entered into the locks of Agastya, who stood still like a wooden post. Soon after, Nahuṣa saw Agastya approached for being yoked to his chariot. Bhṛgu, who was sitting in the matted locks of Agastya, took [56] care not to look at Nahuṣa. Fully acquainted with the power which the illustrious Nahuṣa had acquired on account of the boon which Brahmā had given him, Bhṛgu had acted thus. Agastya though thus treated by Nahuṣa did not yield to anger. Then Nahuṣa urged Agastya with his goad. The pious sage Agastya still did not yield to anger. The lord of celestials, himself enraged at this pusillanimity, then struck Agastya on the head with his left foot. When the sage was thus struck on the head, then Bhṛgu, who was sitting within the matted locks of Agastya, became incensed and cursed the sinful Nahuṣa saying, "Thou hast kicked the head of the great sage, fall down therefore on the earth, changed into a boa!" Thus imprecated by Bhṛgu, *who had not been seen*, Nahuṣa forthwith became transformed into a boa and in that form dropped down on the earth.

Yudhiṣthira, who had heard a different version of the story from Śalya, as narrated in the Udyoga, maintains naturally a discreet silence about these discrepancies and proceeds to question Bhīṣma about some other matters on which he wanted information.

Next, in the course of a long passage devoted to the praise of Brahmins, showing that the Brahmins are mightier than even the gods, the story of Cyavana is repeated (adhy. 156).

Cyavana, who had been rejuvenated and cured of blindness by the Aśvins, had, as we have seen, promised them that they should drink Soma with Indra and the other gods. The gods were wavering in their mind, but Indra was adamant. He refused to accept the Soma libation in Cyavana's sacrifice, if those low-caste Aśvins were invited at the same time. When Cyavana was going to put his magic in operation, Indra rushes on him with a mountain and thunderbolt, but is instantly paralyzed by Cyavana and brought to submission. Then Cyavana creates a fearsome monster, Mada, who is about to gobble up all the gods. Beseeched by the gods, who were frightened to death by this terrible apparition, Indra apologizes to Cyavana; and the Aśvins, patronized by the great wizard, are allowed to share the Soma libation with the other gods. This story was already narrated to Yudhiṣṭhira by the sage Lomaśa in the Âraṇyaka (adhy. 123 of the Vulgate).

[57] Aśvamedhaparvan

An echo of the above story we find early in the course of the Aśvamedhaparvan. In adhy. 9 we find Agni taunting Indra about the humiliation of the latter at the hands of Cyavana, which has been just described (B. 14. 9. 31):

yatra Śaryātiṁ Cyavano yājayiṣyan
sahāśvibhyāṁ somam agṛhṇād ekaḥ |
taṁ tvaṁ kruddhaḥ pratyaṣedhīḥ purastāc
Charyātiyajñaṁ smara taṁ Mahendra ||

Agni might have added the story of his own humiliation at the hands of another wizard of the same clan, Bhṛgu, when he was indiscreet enough to divulge some secret to Puloman, the seducer of Bhṛgu's wife Pulomā, but for obvious reasons he does not do so.

In another digression, the Anugītāparvan, we have an allusion to the annihilation of Kṣatriyas by the Bhārgava Rāma, used this time for a different purpose (adhy. 29-30 of the Vulgate). It is here made the basis of a homily on the vanity of life. After the murder of Arjuna Kārtavīrya and the extermination of the Kṣatriyas, the Bhārgava Rāma was taught by the shades of his ancestors that greater than any victory over kings was the conquest of one's own self: the ascetic ideal. This conquest is made by self-mortification. Thus admonished by his departed ancestors, the Bhārgava Rāma practised the most austere penances, and as a consequence of this exercise of self-control, that highly blessed one acquired that supreme felicity which it is so difficult to obtain.

The last Bhārgava story of the Mahābhārata is the Uttaṅkopākhyāna of this *parvan* (adhy. 53-58 of the Vulgate), which we shall next consider.

After the death of Bhīṣma, Kṛṣṇa returns to Dvārakā. On his way he meets in a desert the sage Uttaṅka, who is ready to pronounce a malediction on Kṛṣṇa when he learns that the latter had not brought about peace between the contending Kauravas and Pāṇḍavas. Śrī-Kṛṣṇa pacifies Uttaṅka by enlightening him about his divine nature and divine mission, complaining that the Kurus, intoxicated as they were by the pride of pomp and power, had not listened to the wholesome advice he had given [58] them for their welfare. At Uttaṅka's request, Śrī-Kṛṣṇa shows him his cosmic form (*rūpam aiśvaram*), made popular by the Gītā, giving him rare boons.

This story impels the intelligent Janamejaya to ask Vaiśampāyana what penances the great Uttaṅka had practised so that he had the temerity to threaten even Viṣṇu (Śrī-Kṛṣṇa). Vaisampāyana replies that it was his supreme devotion to his *guru* that had endowed him with this great spiritual power, and he proceeds to relate the story of Uttaṅka. He relates how Uttaṅka had escaped being eaten by the cannibal king Saudāsa and obtained the ear-jewels of Saudāsa's queen Madayantī as fee for his *guru* Gautama, how on the way the ear-jewels were stolen by a snake (*nāga*), and how Uttaṅka recovered them from the subterranean world of the Nāgas.

It will be noticed that this Uttaṅkopākhyāna is but a variant (metrical) version of Pauṣyaparvan, a (prose) sub-section of the Ādi (adhy. 3), but with some significant differences in the details. The *dramatis personæ* are in part different. The preceptor is not Veda, as in the Ādi, but Gotama, the husband of Ahalyā; likewise the king from whom Uttaṅka gets the ear-jewels is here not Pauṣya but Saudāsa (Kalmāṣapāda), who had become a cannibal by the curse of some great sage, whom the arrogant king had belaboured with a hunter. Moreover, in the first version, the name of the snake is given as Takṣaka, the snake which had bitten king Parikṣit and been the cause of his premature death; in the second he remains nameless. The only reason for citing the story of Uttaṅka here, in this paper, is that in the Aśvamedha version of the story Uttaṅka is several times called a Bhārgava, a fact which does not appear from the Ādiparvan version. We have thus here a documentation for a Bhārgava, who by the power of his austerities—devotion to one's *guru* is a kind of *tapas*—was in a position to curse an *avatāra* of Viṣṇu himself for his apparent fault in not conciliating the Pāṇḍavas and the Kauravas and preventing the fratricidal war, and who had to be gently pacified by the great god by showing him his cosmic form to support his assertions.

If we now go back to the Ādi. we shall find that this figure of Uttaṅka has been further deftly woven into the fabric of [59] the epic and not allowed to remain merely as a loose appendage. For, in the short *metrical* tail of the (prose) Pauṣyaparvan, it is narrated that, after his adventure in the world of the Nāgas Uttaṅka betakes himself straight to the Pāṇḍava Janamejaya in Hāstinapura and prevails upon the king to punish Takṣaka for causing the death of Parikṣit. At Uttaṅka's instance Janamejaya instituted the snake sacrifice; and at this sacrifice Vaiśampāyana first recited the Mahābhārata. Now the Mahābhārata that we *now* possess is said to have been recited by the Sūta Ugraśravas before Śaunaka exactly as he had heard it during the recitation of the poem by Vyāsa's own pupil Vaiśampāyana at the famous snake sacrifice which was instituted by king Janamejaya at the instigation of Uttaṅka. Our debt to this Bhārgava is therefore very obvious.

This Uttaṅkopākhyāna contains the last important reference in the Mahābhārata to the Bhārgavas, linking up with that in adhy. 3 of the Ādi.

There are still a few more Bhārgava stories in the Mahābhārata, the consideration of which I had intentionally postponed and to which we shall now turn.

We run into a nest of Bhārgava legends, as a matter of fact, already in the fourth sub-section of the Ādi, the Paulomaparvan, which have not been discussed above.

The Mahābhārata, as is well known, has two variant openings. In the first (Ādi. 1), when the Sūta (or, according to some editions, Sauti) Ugraśravas, who is to recite the Mahābhārata, presents himself at the hermitage of Kulapati Śaunaka, during the twelve-year sacrificial session inaugurated by the sage in the sacred Naimiṣa Forest and offers to recite stories for the edification and entertainment of the guests, the sages assembled there express their desire to hear the celebrated Mahābhārata (1. 1. 18 f.) :

Janamejayasya yāṃ rājño Vaiśaṁpāyana uktavān |
yathāvat sa ṛṣis tuṣṭyā satre Dvaipāyanājñayā ||
vedaiś caturbhiḥ samitāṁ Vyāsasyādbhutakarmaṇaḥ |
saṁhitāṁ śrotum icchāmo dharmyāṁ pāpabhayāpahāṁ ||

The Sūta accordingly commences with some *maṅgala* stanzas (1. 1. 20):

[60] *ādyaṁ puruṣam īśānaṁ puruhūtaṁ puruṣṭutam |*
ṛtam ekākṣaraṁ brahma vyaktāvyaktaṁ sanātanam || etc.,

which are followed by a sort of prologue, which latter languishes and breaks off somewhere.

In adhy. 4 of the Ādi, we come upon another opening, which totally ignores the first ! The Sūta is re-introduced. The scene is the same, but the programme is changed. Here the assembled sages do not themselves order the entertainment, but ask the Sūta to wait until the Kulapati Śaunaka comes. When in the next chapter (5), the Kulapati joins the company, after having duly performed his round of daily duties, he instead of asking the Sūta to narrate the Mahābhārata, as the sages in the first instance had done, tells him, strange to say, to relate first the history of the *Bhārgavas* (1. 5. 3).

tatra vaṁśam ahaṁ pūrvaṁ śrotum icchāmi Bhārgavam |
kathayasva kathām etāṁ kalyāḥ sma śravaṇe tava ||

The Sūta obediently proceeds to relate the history of that "most illustrious family of the Bhṛgus, which is honoured even by the celestials with Indra, Agni and the Maruts" (1. 5. 5). Here the Bhārgava interest is very clear and unmistakable. Accordingly eight chapters (5-12), which form the Paulomaparvan, are *entirely* consecrated to an account of the wonderful deeds of some of the Bhārgavas, an account which is not even remotely connected in actual fact with the incidents or characters of our epic. It is a digression pure and simple, introduced with the very obvious object of glorifying the Bhārgavas and giving a permanent form to some of the Bhārgava myths and legends. These chapters are a short history of one special branch of the Bhārgava clan, represented by : Bhṛgu, Cyavana, Pramati, Ruru and Śunaka. The significance of this branch and its connection with our version of the Mahābhārata will become apparent presently.

Bhṛgu, a sage of almost mythical character, the eponymous ancestor of the family, is here said to have been created from Brahmā from the sacrificial fire during Varuṇa's sacrifice (216*):

Bhṛgur maharṣir bhagavān Brahmaṇā vai svayaṁbhuvā |
Varuṇasya kratau jātaḥ pāvakād iti naḥ śrutam ||

[61] This interpolated stanza (found only in N) contradicts the statement in the main body of the text (documented jointly by N and S) to the effect that Bhṛgu was born by piercing the heart of Brahmā (1. 60. 40):

Brahmaṇo hṛdayaṁ bhittvā niḥsṛto bhagavān Bhṛguḥ |

While Bhṛgu's wife Pulomā was pregnant, the story continues (adhy. 5-6), there came to Bhṛgu's hermitage, during his absence, a demon (*rākṣasa*), Puloman, who became enamoured of her and wanted to carry her off. To make sure of his facts, however, the demon asked Agni whether she was really Bhṛgu's wife. The fact was that this Pulomā was first betrothed to Puloman and afterwards given by her father to Bhṛgu, and Puloman wanted to have his Pulomā back. On getting from Agni an answer in the affirmative, the demon, assuming the form of a boar, carried her off. On the way Cyavana is born. His lustre instantly reduces to ashes the demonic ravisher of his mother and saves her from a very awkward predicament. Pulomā returns home safely with the baby. Bhṛgu only learns of this incident after his return to the hermitage. Incensed at the outrage, he curses the god Agni, whom he regards as the prime cause of the disaster, saying that Agni would be an eater of all things, good and bad (*sarva-bhakṣa*).

There follows in adhy. 8 the story of Ruru, son of Pramati. Menakā an *apsaras*, abandons her beautiful daughter near the hermitage of the sage Sthūlakeśa. She is called Pramadvarā. Pramati arranges her marriage with his son Ruru, who has fallen in love with her. Shortly before the celebration of their marriage Pramadvarā is bitten by a venemous snake and dies, leaving Ruru disconsolate. By the miraculous powers of his austere penance, this Bhārgava gives up half of his life to Pramadvarā and revives her, and ultimately marries her. Ruru takes a vow to destroy all the snakes in the world, like Janamejaya before him, whose father Parikṣit had died as the result of a snake-bite. One day Ruru comes across a harmless old snake of the variety known as *ḍuṇḍubha* (adhy. 9). The snake begs to be spared and so Ruru does not kill it. The serpent body only concealed the metamorphosed soul of a sage, who was suffering the effects of a curse pronounced on him in a previous birth (adhy. 10). The [62] sage declares *ahiṁsā* to be the highest duty of a Brahmin. Janamejaya had once tried to destroy the race of snakes by performing a snake sacrifice ; they were saved by the Brahmin Āstīka (adhy. 11). Ruru subsequently hears the story of Janamejaya's snake sacrifice from his father Pramati (adhy. 12). This story of the snake sacrifice as told by Pramati to his son Ruru was repeated verbatim by the Sūta to Śaunaka and forms in our version of the Mahābhārata the Āstīka-parvan, the fifth sub-section of the Ādi. (adhy. 13-53).

It will be noticed that from adhy. 4 to adhy. 12 of the Ādi, a section which, as already mentioned, is entirely concerned with the history of a branch of the Bhārgava clan, there is no mention of the Mahābhārata at all. Nor is there, as a matter of fact, any mention of the epic in the immediate sequel up to adhy. 53 of the Ādi ! Only in adhy. 53, after having heard first the Bhārgava legends and then the story of the snake sacrifice (which had been previously related by the Bhārgava Pramati to his son Ruru), Śaunaka at last expresses the desire to hear the Mahābhārata of Kṛṣṇa Dvaipāyana, which was narrated to king Janamejaya by Vaiśaṁpāyana in the intervals of that snake sacrifice (1. 53. 32 f.) :

Mahābhāratam ākyhānaṁ Pāṇḍavānāṁ yaśaskaram |
Janamejayena yat pṛṣṭaḥ Kṛṣṇa-Dvaipāyanas tadā ||
śrāvayāmāsa vidhivat tadā karmāntareṣu saḥ |
tāṁ ahaṁ vidhīvat puṇyāṁ śrotum icchāmi vai kathām ||

This completes our survey of the Bhārgava material in the Mahābhārata.[1] But even this analysis does not give an adequate idea of the total number of Bhārgava references in the Great [63] Epic. The Bhārgavas regularly occur as static figures, along with other ancient sages, in the descriptions of martial combats, festive gatherings, state functions, council meetings and all important assemblies. Outstanding incidents of their history are frequently alluded to, briefly, even in the course of other narratives. The names of their heroes are habitually introduced in similes and metaphors : they are the standards of comparison (*upamāna*), to which everybody else is compared, especially the epic heroes. Thus a man is praised by saying that his intelligence is like that of Śukra. A warrior is eulogized by saying that in heroism he was the equal of the Bhārgava Rāma. Bhīṣma is once praised by saying that he could not be defeated even by Rāma. In other places the valour and effulgence of Cyavana and Aurva are utilized for the sake of a passing comparison. The devotion of Sukanyā to her husband

[1] The following sages should probably further be included among the Bhṛgus : (1) *Ārṣṭiṣeṇa*, a sage, mentioned several times in the Āraṇyaka ; a legend is told about him in the Baladeva-tīrthayātrā (Śalyaparvan) ; (2) *Gṛtsamada*, mentioned briefly in the Anuśāsana ; (3) *Veda*, who was the teacher of Uttaṅka and chaplain of Janamejaya and Pauṣya ; (4) *Paila*, one of the pupils of Vyāsa ; and (5) *Māṇḍavya*, who curses Dharma in the celebrated story (*upākhyāna*) of Aṇīmāṇḍavya in the Ādi. The part they play in our epic is small, and therefore they have been ignored in this paper. Moreover, none of them, except Gṛtsamada, is actually called a Bhārgava in our epic. Śrī-Kṛṣṇa himself was distantly connected with the Bhārgavas, being a descendant of Yadu, the son of Yayāti by the Bhārgava Devayānī.

Cyavana has been made proverbial by constant citation. These details could not be considered in the present paper for want of space.[1]

Retrospect

From the legends preserved in our epic it should seem that the Bhārgavas were a Brahmin clan, perhaps more intimately associated with the ancient Kṣatriyas than most of the other Brahmin clans, being largely connected with them by matrimonial ties. Thus Cyavana is said to have married Sukanyā, the daughter of king Śaryāti. Ṛcīka had married Satyavatī, the daughter of king Gādhi of Kānyakubja and sister of the famous Viśvāmitra. Jamadagni's wife Reṇukā is likewise said to have been a princess by birth, being a daughter of king Prasenajit of Ayodhyā. The Bhārgavī Devayānī was moreover married to king Yayāti : one of the very few *pratiloma* marriages on record in Brahmanical literature.[2] King Vītahavya had been adopted and made a Brahmin by a Bhṛgu, and his descendants became Bhārgavas.[3] On the other hand some of the ancient Bhārgavas seem to have come seriously into conflict with the Kṣatriyas. The relations of Rāma Jāmadagnya with the Kṣatriyas are so well known and have been repeated above so often that it is [64] unnecessary to dilate upon them here. But even in the case of Aurva and Jamadagni, the epic has to relate conflicts with the Kṣatriyas, which have been alluded to above.

In these conflicts the Bhārgavas are represented in our epic as irascible sages, domineering, arrogant, unbending and revengeful. To our epic bards they are at the same time omniscient and omnipotent. Supermen, who had become so chiefly by virtue of their rigid austerities and the magical or spiritual powers acquired by them. Owing to these occult powers, the Bhārgavas were like gods walking on earth, or rather greater than mere gods. Thus Bhṛgu pronounces a curse on Agni—a god fervently lauded and worshipped by the simple Aryans—for no faults of his. He also cursed (according to one version) Nahuṣa, who had been elected king of gods and who had become arrogant and irreligious owing to this sudden elevation to power. The wizard Cyavana paralyzed the arm of the recalcitrant Indra, a high god of the Vedic Aryans. Jamadagni would shoot down the Sun, another Aryan god. The Bhārgava Uttaṅka, when about to curse Śrī-Kṛṣṇa, the supreme god of the Bhāgavatas or Vaiṣṇavas, was gently pacified by the *avatāra*. The kings of the earth are of course like vermin before these Bhārgavas. The mighty Haihayas tremble before the infant Aurva, who blinds them by his effulgence, and they have to beg for mercy on their bended knees. King Kuśika grovels at the feet of Cyavana and meekly submits to all varieties of indignities for fear that the great sage might curse him.

---

1 Even these may be considered later, if a suitable opportunity presents itself.

2 Two others : Apnavāna's with Nahuṣa's daughter Ruci, and Prabhākara's mentioned by PARGITER, *Anc. Ind. Hist. Trad.*, 304 f.

3 Devāpi, brother of Śantanu, becomes Arṣṭiṣeṇa, a sub-class of the Bhṛgus.

Bhṛgu, the eponymous ancestor of the Bhārgavas, was one of the *prajāpatis*. While the other *prajāpatis* like Dakṣa are said to have issued from different limbs of Brahmā, Bhṛgu is represented as having sprung from Brahmā's heart, the noblest of the internal organs of man of god.[1] In another context in our epic, it is implied that Bhṛgu was the greatest of the *maharṣis*, though his name is not included even in the list of the famous Seven Sages.

But the Bhārgava most popular with our bards is surely Rāma Jāmadagnya. The bards love to dwell on his martial exploits, repeating them whenever the slightest opportunity for it presents itself. The shadow of this colossus overspreads the entire epic, excepting the short tale at the end of the poem. In our epic he is not yet a full-fledged *avatāra*, but on the high way to be ele-[65]-vated to that rank, surreptitious efforts being made to make the epic document his divinity. He conquers the whole world, alone and unaided; such is the prowess of his fierce austerities. He frees the earth of the burden of Kṣatriyas thrice seven times and makes the gift of the earth to Kaśyapa, his priest, who divides it among Brahmins. Rāma fights even the enemies of the gods, with the same assurance and success, enemies whom the gods themselves could not subdue. As the Bhārgava Rāma is the perfect warrior (*sarvaśastrabhṛtām varaḥ* a phrase the bards love to apply to him), three of the leading warriors of the Kaurava army—Bhīṣma, Droṇa and Karṇa—are said to have been initiated into the science of arms by Rāma Jāmadagnya, though the latter according to the epic itself, lived at the end of the Tretā Age and the Kuru Pāṇḍava war took place at the end of the Dvāpara.

The epic contains a number of episodes (*upākhyānas*) relating to the Bhārgavas, such as, the Aurvopākhyāna (Ādi), Kārtavīryopākhyāna (Āraṇyaka), Ambopākhyāna (Udyoga), Vipulopākhyāna (Śānti), and Uttaṅkopākhyāna (Aśvamedha), and so on. The entire Pauloma and a large section of the Pauṣya *two independent sub-parvans of the epic*, are also devoted to the legends of the Bhārgavas. Besides these there are important discussions and discourses attributed to some of the celebrated Bhārgavas, such as the Bhṛgu-Bhāradvāja-saṁvāda, the Cyavana-Kuśika-saṁvāda and the Mārkaṇḍeya-samāsyā.

Another striking feature of these Bhārgava legends in our Mahābhārata is the frequent repetition of these legends on different occasions in the course of the epic. Thus the legend of Uttaṅka, the myth of the altercation between Cyavana and Indra, the story of Droṇa's obtaining weapons from the Bhārgava Rāma, and the account of Karṇa's pupilship under him, is each told *twice*, in different contexts. The legend of the birth of Jamadagni and Rāma is related in all *four* times. That the Bhārgava Rāma exterminated the Kṣatriyas thrice seven times is mentioned *ten* times, in nearly

---

1 *Īśvaraḥ sarvabhūtānāṁ hṛd-deśe 'rjuna tiṣṭhati* | Bhag. Gītā.

identical form (*triḥsaptakṛtvaḥ pṛthivī kṛtā niḥkṣatriyā purā*, which appears to have been a slogan of the bards) ; but the humiliation of the pride of the Kṣatriyas by the Bhārgava Rāma is mentioned about a *score* of times.

It is to be noted that the Bhārgavas spring into this promi-[66]nence all of a sudden in the Mahābhārata. We look in vain for any reflection of their phenomenal power and glory in the Vedic literature.[1] There the Bhārgavas are frequently alluded to as devoted to the fire-cult and they appear in the rôle of a group of ancient fire priests. They are said to have procured fire for mankind. In the Battle of Ten Kings, the Bhārgavas are mentioned with the Druhyus. In many passages they are associated with the Aṅgirases. The Atharvaveda is also known as Bhṛgvaṅgiras, and it seems certain that both the Bhṛgus and the Aṅgirases dabbled a great deal in the black art and were feared on that account. That they probably came into conflict with other clans and especially perhaps the Kṣatriyas is indicated by the fact that in the last-named Veda the name of Bhṛgu is chosen to exemplify the dangers incurred by those who oppress Brahmins. The Sṛñjaya Vaitahavyas succumb as the result of an attack on Bhṛgu. The Aitareya Brāhmaṇa shows Bhṛgu in a similar light.

Thus we see that the Vedic references give no ground for explaining the eminence of the ancient Bhārgavas implied by the epic account. These references supply nevertheless rudimentary clues of ideas and sentiments which were probably magnified in the imagination of the remote decendants of a powerful ancient clan, influenced strongly by the cult of ancestor worship. Thus, for example, the close connection of the Bhṛgus with the fire cult may perhaps serve to explain the part that Agni plays in many of the Bhārgava legends in the Mahābhārata. The Cyavana-Aśvins legend of the epic finds some support in the statement of the Ṛgveda to the effect that the Aśvins rejuvenated Cyavana, making him "acceptable to his wife and a husband of maidens." The Brāhmaṇas amplify this account. The connection of the Bhṛgus with the Atharvaveda explains the element of witchcraft in the Bhārgava legends of our epic, such as, for example, the revival of the dead by the Bhārgava Śukra, or the paralyzing of the arm of Indra by Cyavana and of the creation of the monster called Mada, mentioned above. That the Bhṛgus had in some way championed the cause of Brahmins against other clans is, as [67] already mentioned, supported by a reference in the Atharvaveda. Their intimate association with the Aṅgirases implied in the Vedic literature is reflected faithfully in many of the stories and genealogies of our epic.

Taking a collective view of these Bhārgava references in the Great Epic, we cannot avoid the conclusion that the Bhārgava heroes occupy a surprisingly large portion of the canvas—which is said to depict the Bhārata War—filling up as they do much of the available space of the background.

[1] MACDONELL and KEITH, *Vedic Index*, vol. 2, p. 109.

And it is more than probable that if the epic is examined yet more minutely, still further evidence of Bhārgava material, hitherto undiscovered, will be brought to light. Their myths and legends are uniformly distributed over the entire extent of the Great Epic with the exception of some short and unimportant *parvans* (10 and 15-18) at the end (comprising in all not more than 2500 stanzas, a negligible fraction of the epic), books on which the average reader of the poem bestows but scant attention. The figures of the Bhārgavas have also been magnified to colossal proportions, painted with a thick brush and in vivid colours. In short, the Bhārgavas are represented in our epic—the Mahābhārata, the epic of the Bharata's or the epic of the Bhārata War—throughout as *the* people. How does that come about?—"*Cui bono?*", as the Roman lawyer would have asked.

To imagine that all this fulsome eulogy liberally showered upon the heroes of the Bhārgavas, and the interminable repetition of their stories and legends are entirely unconscious—at least unintentional—and without any ulterior motive, being just ordinary features of epic treatment, would be indeed naïve.[1] In the first place, we have very clear and definite evidence of the fact that our epic has been consciously and deliberately expanded at least in *one* instance: the surreptitious addition of a bunch of Bhārgava legends to the Kuru-Pāṇḍava epic in the shape of the so called Paulomparpan in the Ādi which is entirely made up of Bhārgava legends and has not even the remotest intrinsic connection with the story of the epic. Then we have equally clear and definite evidence of the tendentious "Bhṛguization" of older legends, which occur in the epic itself in *two* forms, one with and the other without some important Bhārgava element, to wit, the Stories of Sixteen Kings (Ṣoḍaśarājikiya) and the Nahuṣa-[68] Agastya legend. We have also noticed that our Mahābhārata contains two variant openings, one of which is clearly inspired by a Bhārgava,[2] both for-

[1] There is only one explanation of the childish exaggeration and this repeated mention on the annihilation of the Kṣatriyas by the Bhārgava Rāma. A deep analysis of the motives underlying this (phenomenon) would suggest that these fabrications are only a form of 'over-compensation', and endeavour to make the Bhṛgus feel important and 'worth while', after the disastrous blow to their ego-ideals. It is the psychological revenge of the Bhṛgus who were all but exterminated by the Kṣatriyas. The slaughter of the Bhṛgus admitted by the Bhṛgus themselves in the Aurva legend deserves all the credence which unfavourable evidence by a witness against one's own self ordinarily does; what the Bhṛgus in turn did to the Kṣatriyas—namely, the annihilating the Kṣatriyas by Bhārgava Rāma 3×7 is known to us only from the account of the event from Brahmin sources. This myth—the dream of the Bhṛgus—is the sublimation of that intolerable inferiority feeling which had been repressed, but which was clamouring for expression.

[2] This was noticed by HOLTZMANN, *Das Mahābhārata*, vol. 2 (1893), p. 12. "Es liegt hier die Einleitung des *Mahābhārata* der *Bhārgava* vor, gerade wie im Gesetzbuche des *Manu* die Fassung der *Bhārgava* sich eingedrangt hat". He did not follow, however, this fruitful idea any further, being misled by the immediate

There is only one explanation of the childish exaggeration and this repeated insistence on the annihilation of the Kshatriyas by the Bhargava Rama. A deep analysis of the motives underlying this phenomenon would suggest that these fabrications are only a form of "over-compensation", an endeavour to make the Bhrigus feel important and worth while, after the disastrous blow to their ego-ideals. It is the psychological revenge of the Bhrigus who were all but exterminated by the Kshatriyas. The slaughter of the Bhrigus is admitted by the Bh. themselves, the Rama legend also shows all the indecision which unfavourable criticism by writing against ones own self ordinarily does, what the Bhrigus in turn dealt to the Kshatriyas — namely, the annihilation of the Ks. by Bhargava Rama xx7 is known to us only from the account of the event from Brahmanic sources. This myth — the dream of the Bhrigus is the sublimation of that intolerable inferiority feeling which had been repressed, but which was clamouring for expression.

Not only is the clan ancient, its legends also are highly interesting. So suggestive in fact are the early myths of this clan that they had in former years engrossed the attention of many a student of Indian mythology, and called forth a variety of interpretations. Thus Bergaigne looked upon the Bhṛgu myth of the Ṛgveda as merely a more developed form of the early tradition about the descent of fire and identified Bhṛgu with Agni. A. Kuhn and A. Barth agreed in regarding the Bhṛgus as personifications of the lightning flash, and Kuhn tried to harmonize the Greek myth regarding the descent of fire with the Vedic. A. Weber, as already remarked, saw in a legend preserved in the Śatapatha Brāhmaṇa a relic of primitive Indo-germanic mythology. But even the later legends of these people are not without a certain amount of grandiosity. Just consider the figure of Paraśurāma: a matricide, annihilator of the Kṣatriyas and finally an *avatāra* of Viṣṇu, all in one.

The popularity of the Paraśurāma legend in India is attested by the number of places, scattered all over India, which are associated with his name and his exploits and held sacred to his memory.[1] Near the Kangra District of the Panjab there is a very ancient temple dedicated to Paraśurāma (a name not yet applied to him in our epic). In the State of Udaipur there is a sacred pool where Rāma is said to have bathed and atoned for his sins. In the Bijapur District of the Bombay Presidency, an axe-shaped rock marks the spot where Rāma is represented as having washed his famous axe (*paraśu*), which has given him his nick-name Paraśurāma, Rāma-with-the-Axe. Even this irresistible axe of his has been deified, and there is in Mysore State a temple dedicated to it. Gokarṇa shows an old tank dedicated to Mahādeva, which is said to have been built by the son of Jamadagni. Even the Lakhimpur District of distant Assam has a pool to show to which, according to popular belief, Paraśurāma had surrendered his dreaded axe, and which attracts pilgrims from every part of India.

Notwithstanding the absorbing interest of the Bhārgava myths, it is primarily not their interpretation that is attempted here.

1 Cf. Anujan Achan, ~~citing the Imperial Gazetteer~~, *The Paraśurāma Legend and its Significance*, p. 8 f. The paper was read at the Eighth Session of the All-India Oriental Conference (Mysore 1935) and has since been published separately with the special sanction of the Government of Cochin.

* Religion Védique (1878-83), 1. 52-56.

† Herabkunft des Feuers und des Göttertranks (1859), 8 ff. [2 Mythologische Studien, vol. 1 (1886), 10 ff.]

‡ Les Religions de l'Inde (Paris, 1885), 8

§ op. cit. 13 ff. [2 14 f.]

‖ ZDMG 9 (1855). 242.

tunately preserved by the conservative instinct of the redactors, helped by a process of conflation peculiar to the Mahābhārata, which tolerates a close juxtaposition of discrepant versions. We have further indirect testimony of the effort made to connect some Bhārgava or other with the propagation of the epic. We are thus told that it was the Bhārgava Uttaṅka who instigated Janamejaya to undertake the snake sacrifice at which the Mahābhārata was first publicly recited. Our Āstīka is that tale which was narrated to the Bhārgava Ruru by his father Pramati. And last but not least, we must take account of the very important fact that the Kulapati Śaunaka himself, before whom the Mahābhārata is said to have been recited by the Sūta Ugraśravas, was also a Bhārgava ! So when Śaunaka says that he wants to hear the history of the Bhārgavas before anything else (1. 5. 3) :

tatra vaṁśam ahaṁ pūrvaṁ śrotum icchāmi Bhārgavam |,

the reason for this peculiar predilection of the host of the Sūta is very evident.

But it might be contended that we are unnecessarily emphasizing the Bhārgava element ; that the Mahābhārata was or has come to be an encyclopaedia of Brahmanic tradition and it therefore contains also all the Bhārgava legends—in a slightly exaggerated form perhaps. The epic itself says (1. 56. 33) :

yad ihāsti tad anyatra yan nehāsti na tat kvacit |

That is undoubtedly true, to a certain extent. One can, however, easily convince oneself that the diaskeuasts who boldly conceived the colossal idea of converting the popular Epic of the Bhāratas into the *Encyclopaedia Brahmanica*, though generally catholic in their selection of Brahmanic legends and doctrines, and eclectic as regards their religious and philosophical outlook, yet they [69] were probably not entirely without their preferences and prejudices, and that they do not apportion anything like the same amount of space and breadth of treatment to the myths and legends of other Brahmanic families such as the Āgastyas, Ātreyas, Kāṇvas, Kāśyapas, Gautamas, Vāsiṣṭhas, and so on. The legends of these other families or clans are by no means entirely ignored in our Mahābhārata, but they are comparatively few in number and hardly ever repeated. They appear like negligible details on the vast canvas of the epic and are easily lost sight of in this colossal accumulation of apparently most heterogeneous elements, which are all the same carefully balanced so as to produce a more or less homogeneous impression. Very differently treated are the Bhārgava legends in our Mahābhārata. To make any impression by the side of the titanic figures of the old epic like Bhīṣma and Karṇa, Kṛṣṇa and Arjuna, the Bhārgavas had to be magnified a great deal and their legends, which were probably not so well known then

---

sequel. "Unser *Mahābhārata*," he remarks, "kehrt aber sofort wieder zur anderen Fassung zurück. In Folgenden erzählt nicht *Pramati den Ruru*, sondern, wie früher, *Ugraśravas dem Śaunaka*"

as now had to be repeated. And we accordingly find that the legends have been repeated, so often that the redactors themselves must have in time come to believe in them ; and the figures have been magnified, so liberally that they appear almost to eclipse the heroes of the Great Epic itself.

Just for the sake of contrast, we might compare the other great epic of India, the Rāmāyaṇa, for Bhārgava references. That epic also is a Brahmanic epic, containing a host of Brahmanic legends and stories. The result of his quest for Bhārgava references will astonish the reader. The references are remarkably few and extremely meagre. About our Bhṛgu, a *vibhūti* of Śrī-Kṛṣṇa, the only thing recorded in the Rāmāyaṇa is that his wife was decapitated by Viṣṇu ! Cyavana has been introduced in Vālmīki's epic only to narrate some stories. The solitary reference to our Rāma Jāmadagnya (*sarvaśastrabhṛtāṁ varaḥ*) has been noticed above ; it is the one in which he challenges Rāma Dāśarathi and is worsted in the encounter ! We learn nothing more about Jamadagni from the Rāmāyaṇa than the bald fact that he was slain by Arjuna Kārtavīrya. Aurva, who as an infant had blinded the Haihayas by his effulgence, is not mentioned at all, so far as I know. Comment is superfluous.

[70] Now there can be no question that all this Bhārgava material in our present Mahābhārata is entirely foreign to the plan of the original saga of the Bhāratas, occurring as it does almost wholly in the episodic portion of the epic. There should be, therefore, in my opinion no hesitation in concluding that *in our version of the Mahābhārata there is a conscious—nay deliberate—weaving together or rather stitching together of the Bhārala legends with the Bhārgava myths.*

The question how precisely this Bhārgava element, which we find concentrated mostly in the *upākhyānas*, came into the cycle of the Bhārata legends is intriguing, but unfortunately the answer is largely a matter of speculation. Even according to the traditional view, it was *not* the work of Vyāsa, the reputed author of the Mahābhārata, because the diaskeuasts have been fortunately frank enough to admit that *his* work, the Bhārata, which originally consisted merely of 24,000 stanzas, had no episode to speak of (1. 1. 61) :

caturviṁśatisāhasrīṁ cakre Bhāratasaṁhitām |
upākhyānair vinā tāvad Bhārataṁ procyate budhaiḥ ||

It could again hardly have been the work of Vaiśaṁpāyana, the direct pupil of Vyāsa, according to tradition, who is said to have recited the Bhārata of Vyāsa, in the presence of Vyāsa himself, as he had been taught by his *guru*, during the intervals of the short snake sacrifice celebrated by king Janamejaya.

The case was different with the next recorded recitation of the Mahābhārata : it was by the Sūta Ugraśravas in the presence of the Bhārgava Śaunaka during the twelve-year sacrifice instituted by the latter (1. 1. 1 ff ; 4. 1 ff). Even before the recitation commences, Śaunaka explicitly asks the

Sūta who had come there to recite his Mahābhārata, to narrate first of all the history of the Bhārgavas and, as directed by his host, the Sūta obediently does so. There is a very clear shifting of the centre of gravity. Here we have a different milieu and a different interest. The scene changes from the bustling and scintillating pageantry of the Kaurava Court to the reflective calm and leisure of the sylvan retreat of the Bhṛgus.

Few scholars, I imagine, would now be inclined to deny that our epic text has undergone momentous alterations in the course [71] of its long and eventful history. It is now generally recognized that the Bhārata, like the popular lays, ballads and early epics of all countries and all people, has always been a *fluid* text, adjusted to the varying needs of the occasion and the differing tastes of the audience. No disparagement or condemnation of the text is thereby implied. The process is quite normal, inevitable and in a wider sense wholly right. To continue to be a vital force in the life of a progressive people, the epic must be a slow-changing book. The fact of expurgation and elaboration is only an outward indication of its being a book of inspiration and guidance in life, and not merely a book lying unused and forgotten on a dusty book-shelf. And this is no drawback in the case of our text. Therein lies on the contrary its capital interest and importance for us. It is a rapid motion picture reel of many ages of Indian culture—not necessarily factitive history—arranged in a naïve fashion : something like the sculptured panels on the gateways and the railings of the Buddhist Stūpa at Sanchi or the mural frescoes of Ajanta, with scenes telescoped all in one plane, without much regard to perspective or perhaps with its own peculiar technique of perspective.

As already remarked, it seems probable that in the formative period of the epic a powerful Bhārgava influence—direct or indirect—has been at work, so to say behind the scenes, in shaping our epic for us. This element had obviously obtruded itself upon the original nucleus, certainly after the time of the original author Vyāsa and probably after that of Vaiśampāyana. The next traditional link, however, in the transmission of the epic is the Sūta. Is the Sūta then responsible for the conversion of the Bhārata into the Mahābhārata? Now I do not doubt that some of the Sūtas probably were gifted versifiers, able to compose *ex tempore* short bardic poems and to improvise lays to suit them to the varying tastes and requirements of the audience. But if we consider these Sūtas capable of composing on the spur of the moment such masses of narrative episodes and didactic discourses as we find in our Mahābhārata, we shall be crediting these minstrels with an accomplishment far beyond their natural capacity. Nobody is, however, so credulous nowadays as to imagine the Sūta as the author of those extensive innovation that must [72] have been necessary in order to convert a heroic poem of about 24,000 stanzas (taking the traditional figure as a rough guide for our speculations) into an encyclopaedia, of the present dimensions.

We are not in any case, as far as I can see, constrained to accept every single statement of the epic in its *exact* literal sense. And when I say that, I mean no disparagement either of the text ; far from it. Our epic does not pretend to be a dry, prosaic, matter-of-fact chronicle, nor a statistical history in the modern sense, based upon a laboriously compiled critical apparatus. If it were that, it would surely not have lived for 2500 years. We have on the shelves of our libraries hundreds of ponderous tomes and compendiums of national and world history, prepared along approved lines by laborious professors of history. But hardly anybody reads these works twice, and they are mostly forgotten, in a generation or two, by an understanding and ungrateful posterity. The Mahābhārata never was a scientific chronicle of that type and it would be egregious folly to regard it as such. It is above all an inspired poem. It was actually regarded by later generations as a *kāvya :*

kṛtam mayedaṁ bhagavan kāvyaṁ paramapūjitam |,

the highest type of Indian *poetry,* like its sister epic, the Rāmāyaṇa. It was before everything else a work of art, creative art, idealistic in conception, informed with deep religious feeling, permeated by a conscious didactic purpose, focussed more on ideas and ideals than on facts and figures, in which people were not interested then so much as now ; a work in which a moral was conveyed by a parable, an elusive truth by a tangible facile myth. And to the inspired creators of a traditional book of that type we must at least allow poetic licence and common imagination.

The entire story that the Sūta had heard the epic at its first recitation by Vaiśaṁpāyana and reproduced it *verbatim* at Śaunaka's bidding, having committed it to memory after a single hearing, is so obviously unnatural and improbable that it seems clearly more appropriate to regard it merely as a poetic fiction, a "frame-story," the most popular of Indian devices of literary composition. But there is no symbolism without a basis, however difficult it may [73] be for us to reach the elusive subconscious or unconscious. To my mind, the frame-story of our Mahābhārata is directly an unconscious admission of the fact that the Bhārata had at a critical stage of its evolution passed into the sphere of influence of the Bhṛgus, through the medium of the wandering minstrel. The Bhārgava influence is implied in the person of the Kulapati Śaunaka. The Sūta, who used to recite the poem in the Heroic Age, is kept on, with due regard to traditional usage, to give the new recension a setting appropriate to it and indicating the source at the same time.

The influence of the Bhārgavas in the narrative portion of the Great Epic is very evident and can hardly be disputed. But their influence in an entirely different sphere, though less tangible and therefore more difficult to demonstrate, is to my mind nevertheless probable : I mean the incorporation into the epic of large masses of didactic material, concentrated chiefly in the Śānti and Anuśāsana, especially so far as it concerns the Dharma and Nīti elements. Though the philosophy of the Mahābhārata is often times rather shaky, being in places abstruse and confused, and though the religious beliefs which find expression there are perplexingly eclectic, oscillating between Vaiṣṇavism and Śaivism, between Henotheism and Pantheism, there can be no two opinions about the fact that the Mahābhārata offers a very sound and complete exposition of Dharma and Nīti according to Indian theorists, a feature which has given this venerable old monument of Indian antiquity its rank as Smṛti and its abiding value and interest to the Hindus, nay to all true children of Mother India.

Now it happens that Dharma and Nīti are just the two topics in which the Bhṛgus had *specialized* and with which their names are prominently associated. The connection of the Bhārgava Śukra with Nīti, which is proverbial in the Mahābhārata, is so patent that it does not need to be especially pointed out. The connection of the Bhṛgus with the Dharmaśāstra is perhaps not so well known, but is nevertheless equally certain. One has only to recall that, according to a tradition preserved in the work itself, our Manusmṛti, the most famous and popular of ancient Indian works bearing on the Dharmaśāstra, is the ancient Code [74] of Manu in the form in which it was communicated to mankind by Bhṛgu and is therefore even commonly known as the Bhṛgusaṁhitā, an explanation which I see not the slightest reason to question or doubt. It is also recognized that there is intimate connection between the Mahābhārata and the Manusmṛti. The Manusmṛti, it may be pointed out, has an introduction not unlike in conception to the first chapter of our epic : a few stanzas agree to some extent even in their wording. The opinions of Manu have been frequently cited in our Mahābhārata (*ity evaṁ Manur abravīt*). According to BÜHLER'S computation, there are about 260 stanzas of the Manusmṛti, that is nearly 10 per cent. of the total, which are again found *verbatim* (or with only slight variations) in *parvans* 3, 12 and 13 alone of the Great Epic.[1] Then on the side of the Mahābhārata, Dharma is the foundation on which the whole stately edifice of the Great Epic has been reared, and to a great extent also the material of which it is composed. Our Mahābhārata is itself a *dharma-grantha*. The putative hero of the epic, Yudhiṣṭhira is called Dharmarāja, himself a son of Dharma ; he is Dharma incarnate. The Bhārata was a *dharma-yuddha* : *yato dharmas tato jayaḥ*. The field of battle was a *dharma-kṣetra*. Nārāyaṇa incarnated himself as Śrī-Kṛṣṇa to restore the fallen Dharma. The essence of the book (*Bhārata-sāvitrī*), embodying the moral of the story, is given as (B. 18. 5. 62 f.) :

ūrdhvabāhur vīraumy eṣa na ca kaścic chṛṇoti me |
dharmād arthaś ca kāmaś ca sa kimarthaṁ na sevyate ||
na jātu kāmān na bhayān na lobhād
dharmaṁ tyajej jīvitasyāpi hetoḥ |
nityo dharmaḥ sukhaduḥkhe tv anitye
jīvo nityo hetur asya tv anityaḥ ||

---

1 BÜHLER, *The Laws of Manu* (S. B. E. 25), p. LXXX.

The infiltration of masses of Bhārgava material in the shape of Bhārgava myths and legends, the manner of its treatment, and even that strange admixture of the Epic with the Dharma and Nīti elements, which latter especially has so long puzzled many inquirers into the genesis of the Mahābhārata, thus appear to find a simple and straightforward explanation in the assumption of an *important unitary diaskeuasis of the epic under very strong and direct Bhārgava influence.* But this does not at all [75] imply that the text has remained untouched after this first diaskeuasis; far from it. Like all traditional works, it was a slow-changing book; and additions and alterations, as already remarked, must have been made in it continuously throughout its long history of about 2500 years.[1]

These further additions were in the main probably made in the first instance by the Bhārgavas themselves in the centuries that immediately followed the first important diaskeuasis under Bhārgava supervision, since it is most likely that just as the different collections of Vedic hymns, the various Brāhmaṇas and the ritualistic manuals were all, for some time, the closely guarded property of diverse Vedic schools and families of sages, which had respectively cultivated and developed them, so also our remodelled Bhārata, now elevated to the rank of the Fifth Veda, must have remained for some time in the exclusive possession of the Bhārgavas as their close literary preserve. That would, in my opinion, account for the apparent homogeneous character of this heterogeneous mass: it all came from different hands, but out of the same mould.

If the above considerations have any validity, they might help us to lift up a corner of the thick veil enveloping our Great Epic and allow us to have a covert peep into its history. Such a peep would show that there existed in India, in very ancient times an epic poem of about 24,000 stanzas, attributed to Vyāsa (the "Expander"), which described in great detail the Bhārata War and sang the glory of the Pāṇḍavas. This heroic poem, the Bhārata, which used to be recited by the Sūtas mostly at royal courts and had in course of time become very popular, was at a critical stage of its history appropriated by the Bhṛgus (who had certainly specialized in the Dharma and Nītiśāstra and probably also developed leanings towards Viṣṇuism), with the idea of developing the epic into a vehicle of popular instruction and edification combined with entertainment. These anchorites, full of age-old wisdom

[1] The most conspicuous instances of such latter additions (not found in all mss. even):
Ādi: 1. The Brahmā-Gaṇeśa episode; 2. Kaṇikaniti; 3. Śvetakī-upākhyāna.
Āraṇyaka: 1. Sūrya-stotra (B. 3. 3. 36-69); 2. Additions to Mārkaṇḍeya's discourse (B. add. 193-198, 200).
Virāṭa: Durgāstotra.
Bhīṣma: Durgāstotra.

and wonderful masters of the art of myth-weaving, took from the Sūtas the Bhārata and gave back to the world the Mahābhārata, the same book yet different. In the process of the redaction by the Bhṛgus, the work, naturally and to an extent unconsciously, received that characteristic and indelible stamp [76] which was predetermined by the eventful history, the natural proclivities, the special endowments, and the peculiar "Weltanschauung" of the Bhṛgus. It was this little episode in its history that necessarily gave our poem the anomalous character of an Epos and "Rechtsbuch" combined. It may be surmised that this remodelled Bhārata remained for some considerable time in the hands of the Bhārgavas, who had developed it and so to say re-created it, as their exclusive literary property, and they exploited it thereafter and propagated it in their own way. The colossal success of the Bhārgava recension of the ancient Epic of the Bhāratas, a success which in one sense was richly deserved, was the indirect cause of the neglect and subsequent disappearance of the original heroic poem, which probably still existed at the time of the composition of the Āśvalāyana Gṛhya Sūtra (3. 4. 4).[1] Like other branches of the hieratic literature, when the epic at last passed out of the hands of the Bhṛgus and became the common property of the literati of India, it still remained a fluid text, not entirely closed to minor alteration and expansion, but retained its character as a traditional work, revered and cherished by the people as the work of Maharṣi Vyāsa and serving still as a vehicle of popular education, inspiration and edification as intended by the Bhṛgus. The further we pursue the study of the traces of Bhārgava influence on the Epic of the Bhāratas, the clearer, it seems to me, will become the history of our Mahābhārata, the Great Epic of Bhāratavarṣa.

VII. The Oldest Extant MS. of the Adiparvan.*

Introductory.

A discovery of capital importance for Mahābhārata studies is the accidental but singularly lucky find by Mānyavara Gurujiu HEMRAJ Panditjiu, C.I.E., D.P.I., the well-known savant of Nepal, of a new Nepālī MS. of the Ādiparvan, which according to the Panditjiu is between seven hundred and eight hundred years old, and therefore easily the oldest extant MS. of the Mahābhārata. It was only a few years ago that I had remarked in the "Prolegomena" to the Ādiparvan : "Only those who know the difficulties in the way of obtaining any MS. from Nepal will be in a position to appreciate fully the debt which the editor and the other members of the Mahābhārata Editorial Board, and beyond that the whole world of Indologists, owe to the Rajaguru. [202]

---

1 N. B. UTGIKAR, *Proc. & Trans. 1st. Or Conf.* (1922), pp. 46-61 : "The mention of the Mahābhārata in the Āśvalāyana Gṛhyasūtra."

* [*ABORI* 19.201-262].

Sankritists have much to hope for from the dispassionate efforts of this truly patriotic and cultured Rajaguru, who loses no opportunity of placing his immense learning and unbounded resources freely at the disposal of all serious workers in the field of Sanskrit research ". How prophetic those words have proved and how the Rajaguru has more than justified our expectations, is manifested in the recovery of this singular old Nepālī MS.

The MS., of which complete collations and specimen photos (reproduced here in facsimile[1]) were kindly sent to me for my use by Rajaguru HEMARAJ Panditjiu, was recently acquired by him and is in his possession. The material is palm-leaf and the writing, which is throughout uniform, is in old faded ink. It contains only the first parvan of the Mahābhārata, but is complete in itself, there being no folios missing. The average folio measures 21" × 2¼" and each folio contains uniformly 7 lines of writing, except the last folio, which has only 4½ lines. The MS. is not dated but the high antiquity claimed for it is authenticated, apart from its antique look,[2] by convincing internal evidence. The best proof is that it is almost entirely free from those modern accretions which are given in Appendix I of the Ādiparvan Volume, as also in great part from those other smaller insertions which are listed in the foot-notes. More astonishing still is the fact that out of the textual *emendations* hazarded by the editor, fifty per cent. are actually documented by this MS. It is therefore no exaggeration to say that this remarkable MS. opportunely affords welcome support to the Critical Edition in most crucial matters. Moreover many of the variant readings of the new MS. are difficult and obscure, marking out its text as distinctly archaic. And, finally, in many of its readings it agrees fairly closely with a certain other MS. from Nepal, which is symbolized as $\tilde{N}_3$ in the critical apparatus of the Ādi, and which is again the oldest *dated* MS. of the the Ādiparvan. The tradition is therefore fairly complete and well attested.

[203] The greatest value of this MS. lies, as hinted already, in its corroboration of the constituted text of the Critical Edition. Indirectly it attests and justifies, as an independent witness, the principles according to which the reconstruction of the epic text is achieved, thus placing the constituted text on still surer foundations.

Long Insertions of the Vulgate.

Hitherto, it may be observed, the data of the Śāradā and the " K " versions had mainly to vouchsafe for the purification of the epic text attempted

---

[1] The photographs are of the written surface of the first and last folios and two intermediate folios (one of which latter is the penultimate folio of the MS.).

[2] I have compared the script with the specimens reproduced in BÜHLER'S *Paleographische Tafeln*. It comes closest to the script of Tafel VI, No. XI (Cambridge MS. No. 1691, 2 of A.D. 1179).

in the Critical Edition. Now, the omissions of the constituted text are supported from a *new* source and from an entirely *different* version, the Nepālī. Our MS. is in fact surprisingly free from most of the matter pronounced to be spurious on the evidence of the then available MSS. of different versions. The *longer* insertions given in Appendix I are conspicuous by their absence in this MS. Here is a list of the long passages which are missing in the new MS.

No. 1 : The Brahmā-Gaṇeśa complex ; inserted at different points in K_{4-6} Dn Dr $D_{2-12.14}$ S, i.e., om. in its totality only in K_{0-3} D_1.

No. 13 : A passage of six lines ins. in K (except K_1) V_1 (marg.) Da Dn D_{1-7} $G_{1.2,4.5}$.

No. 14 : The Purāṇic story of Aruṇa, who is made to act as the charioteer of the Sun ; ins. in K_4 (marg.) Ñ V_1 B D (except D_5, D_2 on suppl. fol.) T_1 $G_{1.2.4.5}$.

No. 41 : Names of the hundred sons of Dhṛtarāṣṭra ; ins. in $K_{3.4}$. $Ñ_{2,3}$ V_1 B D (except D_5).

No. 42 : Story of the birth of Abhimanyu ; ins. in $K_{3.4}$ Ñ V_1 B D (except D_5).

No. 43 : Story of the birth of Karṇa ; Ins. in K_4 Ñ V_1 B D (except D_5).

No. 61 : Details of the marriage of Pāṇḍu and Mādrī, subst. for 1. 105. 4-7, in K_4 Ñ B D.

No. 62 : Story of the birth of Duḥśalā ; ins. in *all* MSS. except $Ś_1$ K_{0-3}.

No. 71-72 : Details of the picnic (jalakrīḍā); ins. in K_4 Ñ B D.

No. 75 : Story of *piṣṭodaka* given to Droṇa's son ; ins. in *all* MSS. except $Ś_1$ K_{0-3}.

[204] No. 76 : Arjuna's pre-eminence among the pupils of Droṇa ; ins. in K_4 Ñ B D T_2 $G_{1.2.4.5}$.

No. 78 : Description of the conquest and annexation of Drupada's kingdom by the Pāṇḍavas exacted by Ācārya Droṇa as *gurudakṣiṇā* ; ins. in K_4 Da_1 Dn D_2 (supp. fol. *sec m.*)$_{4,5}$ S.

No. 80 : Installation of Yudhiṣṭhira as heir-apparent ; ins. in *all* MSS. except $Ś_1$ K_{0-3}.

No. 81 : Kaṇikanīti : ins. in *all* MSS. except $Ś_1$ K_{0-3}.

No. 85 : Story of the boat sent by Vidura for the use of the Pāṇḍavas ; ins. in *all* MSS. except $Ś_1$ K_{0-3},

No. 118 : Śvetakī-episode ; ins. in *all* N MSS. Cf. also passage No. 120 ins. in T_2 $G_{3.4}$, and No. 121 ins. in $Ś_1$ $K_{0,1-4}$.

Short Insertions of the Vulgate.

Like these long insertions our MS. omits most of the *short* insertions given in the foot-notes to the constituted text. There are more than two thousand of such passages, the majority naturally from the Southern Recension. The following instances, selected at random, of "short" passages omitted by our MS. may be mentioned for the sake of illustration : 128*, 220*, 250*, 301*, 313*, 402*, 429*, 463*, 528*, 558*, 560*, 564*, 573*, 693*, 756*, 892* , 1001*, 1036*, 1038*, 1129*, 1131*, 1188*, 1242*, 1308*, 1312*, 1330*, 1331*, 1341*, 1365*, 1368*, 1377*, 1379*, 1444*, 1477*, 1492*, 1494 *, 1503 *, 1515 *, 1516 *, 1517 *, 1686 *, 1729 *, 1742 *, 1793 *, 1824 *, 1847*, 2132*.

These, it may be noted, are some of the many passages (extending from three to twenty lines) which are found in all N MSS. (except $Ś_1$ K)—with or without some S MSS.—but which are omitted by our MS. The following omissions from among these deserve special notice :

128* : This is a passage of 72 lines, consisting of the longer version of the contents of the Āraṇyaka-parvan, found in certain MSS. of the Northern Recension. It may be noted in passing that in its Parvasaṁgraha chapter, the new MS. gives *throughout* the shorter version, which has been adopted in the Critical Edition and which agrees with the version of this adhyāya in P. P. S. SASTRI's edition of the Southern Recension.

560* : By omitting this, our MS. omits the reference to Pāṇḍu, found in *all* N MSS, except those of the Kaśmīrī Version.

[205] 693* : This is a passage of sixteen lines and contains the famous couplet *na jātu kāmāḥ kāmānām* etc., recurring in many places.

892* : This passage, occurring after 1. 89. 51, is found in *all* N MSS. In the place where it is inserted there appears to have been a lacuna in the original, filled up by the two recensions in different ways. In the constituted text the place is marked by asterisks.

1036* : Details of Bṛhaspati's cohabitation with Mamatā, wife of Utathya and the *godharma* mentioned in that context, inserted in *all* N MSS. except $Ś_1$ K_{0-2} $Ñ_{1,3}$.

1341* : A passage of ten lines found in *all* MSS. except $Ś_1$ K. It describes the approch of Droṇa to Rāma Jāmadagnya for the astravidyā.

1793* : A passage of seven lines found in *all* MSS. except T_2 $G_{1,5,6}$ M.

These significant omissions, major and minor, prove that the text of our MS. is *shorter than that of all other MSS. hitherto known*. Accordingly we find that in the Parvasaṁgraha chapter of this MS. the figure of the stanzas for the Ādi is given as 7784, which brings down the figure of the Vulgate by eleven hundred and the figure even of the Śāradā MS. by two hundred stanzas ! It is however, curious that it apparently has the same number of adhyāyas as the Critical Edition viz. 225, while the Parvasaṁgraha figure for the same is 218 both in this MS. and the Critical Edition. In other words in differing from its own Parvasaṁgraha figure, our MS. exactly agrees with the critical text ! The number of adhyāyas in the Vulgate, it may be noted, is 234, while that of the Southern Recension can be computed to extend to about 250 adhyāyas. On the other hand, the number of adhyāyas in the Kumbakonam edition reaches the astonishing figure 260 !

Small Infiltrations.

Even though our MS. is appreciably shorter than any other MS. of the Ādi so far known, we cannot indeed suppose it to have been absolutely free from inflation and contamination. This MS. has in fact just a few insertions not countenanced by the Critical Edition. For instance :

[206] App. I, No. 12 : The *first three* lines of this passage (of sixteen lines) are *substituted* in our MS. in place of 1. 19. 1-2. This substitution is common to $\tilde{N}_3$ also ! The passage is characteristic of all N MSS. except those of the Kaśmīrī Version.

App. I, No. 33 : This passage is found in all N MSS., the Kaśmīrī Version showing variation only in sequence. The passage is inserted after 1. 56. 31, and is a continuation of the eulogy of the Mahābhārata, serving as an introduction to that redaction of the epic which begins with the episode of Uparicara. Here our MS. agrees with $\tilde{N}_1$ in omitting lines 3-11.

App. I, No. 58 : This passage also is a common heritage of all N MSS. It describes how Sūrya, when invoked by Kuntī, presses her to have sexual intercourse with him.

Besides these major additions, some insertions from the footnotes to the constituted text have filtered their way into our MS. The number of such passages is not very large, being about ninety, and they consist mainly of *single lines.* These are the passages in question : 90*, 220*, 288*, 291*, 476*, 478*, 479*, 485*, 494*, 495*, 549*, 601*, 678*, 708*, 709*, 710*, 750*, 868*, 873*, 875*, 879*, 903*, 906*, 909*, 962*, 999*, 1004*, 1013*, 1017*, 1018*, 1022*, 1068*, 1087*, 1096*, 1104*, 1110*, 1120*, 1124*, 1141*, 1142*, 1144*, 1146*, 1148*, 1155*, 1162*, 1166*, 1173*, 1178*, 1186*, 1196*, 1212*, 1219*, 1224*, 1230*, 1240*, 1305*; 1309*, 1357*, 1430*, 1436*, 1463*, 1470*, 1623*, 1644*, 1665*, 1698*, 1786*, 1789*, 1796*, 1812*, 1815*, 1818*, 1855*, 1882*, 1883*, 1919*, 1920*, 1921*, 1922*, 1951*, 1953*, 1960*, 1975*, 2016*, 2087*, 2097*.

All these insertions are uniformly met with in all N MSS., or at least in the majority of N MSS., and not a single one of them is sporadic.

An insertion of a single stanza from the *yadāśrauṣam* section (adhy. 1) is the only *unique insertion* in this MS.

Conflation of Mahābhārata texts.

Here we may note, in passing, the light this MS. sheds in an indirect way on how the text gradually gets inflated. At several places we find additions made *marginally* by another and a later hand. For instance, after 1. 5. 26, we find a marginal insertion of two lines सेयमित्यवगच्छामि etc., which is taken from a passage [207] of eight lines found in all N MSS. (except $K_{0.2}$ D_5). Again, after 1. 19. 15 we have a marginal addition of two lines

महानदीभिर्वह्वीभिः etc., of which the first line is merely a *variant* of a line included in our text, but the second is an "additional" line found chiefly in late Northern MSS. of the Central Group. It is clear that the copyist of such a MS. as this, without further investigation—which of course is not his business !—cannot determine whether the lines added in the margin belonged to its origial exemplar, or whether they were taken from some other source. It is not the custom of the copyist to be very squeamish about such things. He copies whatever he finds before him, provided it makes sense and has something to do with the epic. It is thus that the corpus has got gradually inflated to its maximum capacity. Cf. the example of K_1 cited in the Ādiparvan Volume (Prolegomena, p. XII).

Minor Readings.

Let us now consider the individual readings of our MS. Here also the agreement of this MS. with the constituted text is quite remarkable. That it cannot and must not be expected to have complete agreement with the constituted text is only obvious ; like all other Mahābhārata MSS., it also represents a particular version of the epic, and nothing more.

Our MS. shows in point of readings the *greatest* agreement with MSS. of the Nepālī group : quite naturally, as it is written in the same script and belongs to the same provincial version. In particular, its agreements with $\tilde{N}_3$, the best and the oldest MS. of the Nepālī version belonging to our apparatus, are unique and striking. The total number of variant readings in our MS. amounts approximately to a little more than 2500. Out of these, its unique agreements with $\tilde{N}_3$ (or in a few places along with one or two other MSS.) against all other MSS. count over 500. This shows that our MS. definitely belonged to the Nepālī version, and is not a copy of a MS. of the Śāradā or "K" version—a very important point though it has marked affinities in many a place with the latter groups. Here are appended about sixty instances, chosen at random, as specimens of the *unique* agreements of our MS. with $\tilde{N}_3$.

[208] 14.17^b लोभाभिभूतया (for लोभपरीतया)
16.26^b सर्वेषां तपसा (for रसानां पयसा)
16.31^c श्रान्तैः (for सर्वैः)
17.6^c देवेन (for चक्रेण)
17.24^d गिरिमभितः प्रतन्य (for गगनमभिप्रपद्य)
19.4^a संयुतं (for सत्त्वैश्च)
21.3^d उवाच ह (for अभाषत)
27.23^a सगुणं (for सफलं)
30.15^d सत्तमाः (for पन्नगाः)
32.8^b प्रायशो (for भ्रातरो)
33.21^d समन्ततः (for सविद्युतः)
38.22^d ब्रह्मन्महामनाः (for राजा महातपाः)
44.14^d जगृहे तदा (for प्रत्यगृह्णत)
45.2^a राज्ञा (for ब्रह्मन्)
48.1^d पुरुषर्षभाः (for परमर्षयः)
48.10^d यज्ञे (for सत्रे)
52.4^d महाबलान् (for विषोल्बणान्)
53.34^d कथ्यते (for सूतज)
55.23^f अभिरोचितः (for अनुचिन्तितः)
56.19^c महीं चापि जयेत्कृत्स्नां
57.55^a गन्धवती (for सत्यवती)
60.5^d धृष्णश्चेति (for संवर्तश्च)
61.2^a चरितं (for तत्त्वेन)
64.34^b क्रमानपि (for अपैरर्द्विजैः)

71.26[f] शकलीकृतम् (for तिलशः कृतम्)
76.26[a] भजस्व तस्मान्मा (for वहस्व पित्रा मां)
79.16[c] दत्वा स्वं प्रतिपत्स्यामि
84.3[c] यश्च (for *सन्स्म)
89.33[f] संवरणं रणे (for स एनं समरे)
90.32[b] महौजसम् (for यमक्षयात्)
90.42 अभग्ना (for अरुग्वान्)
92.15[c] सूक्ष्मैः (for पुत्रैः)
93.14[c] द्यौश्चापि (for दिवे वै)
93.33[cd] अष्टौ वसूंस्तान्मुनिसत्तमः (for राजन्वसूनष्टौ तपोधनः)
94.55[b] वशस्थाः (for विधेयाः)
94.84[a] न तदन्यो (for नान्यथा तत्)
96.17[ab] प्राक्संचार्यद्भिः (for ते द्रागभ्राजद्भिः)
99.6[b] आशीर्वरो (for आसीत्तरी)
100.1[b] सा पुनः (for शनकैः)
103.17[a] तोषयामास (for वृत्तेनाराध्य)
111.12[b] तत्र मानवाः (for मनुजा भुवि)
111.26[a] जातं ते (for नष्टं मे)
111.28[d] भगिन्यां (for स्वैरिण्यां)
113.7[d] पुराभवत् (for सनातनः)
115.6[a] नार्हो (for स्तम्भो)
116.7[a] एकां गतां (for आत्मसमां)
122.26[d] सम्यक् (for श्राम्यन्)
123.71[b] दशभिः (for निशितैः)
134.10[cd] पुरतः पौरैः (for पुरुषैरूपुः)
134.24[d] स्पर्शैर्ना (for प्रयोगैः)
136.12[d] वह्निभिः (for मन्त्रिणा)
141.2[d] राक्षसानां यशोहर
143.22[d] मणिहमचितेषु (for पद्मोत्पलयुतेषु)
149.7[a] फलं प्राप्य (for परं-पापं)
149.7[d] कुतस्त्वात्मवतो (for श्रेयो आत्मवधो)
149.11[b] न च कर्ता (for न नृशंसं)
154.16[d] सकांश (for नगरं)
157 4[b] सत्येन (for शाठ्येण)

Here it is necessary to emphasise the curious circumstance that while the new MS. is almost on a par with Ñ$_3$ in respect of *individual* readings, it is far superior to Ñ$_3$ in so far that it lacks about ninety per cent. of the *insertions* which Ñ$_3$ has in common with the Vulgate, that is to say, the Bengali-Devanāgarī group. It thus gives its welcome support to the Śāradā-K group and our Critical Edition as regards that large mass of passages in which [209] these texts are lacking. It may be incidentally remarked that Ñ$_3$ is relatively purer than the other two Nepālī MSS. and occasionally has definite leanings towards the Śāradā or Kaśmīrī version. These additional passages in MSS. like Ñ$_3$, we may reasonably infer, were gradually added by the epic artists, who worked out the details and filled in the lacunæ of this colossal composition. There must have been a free give-and-take of these passages in the extensive comparisons of different manuscripts of the epic text at holy places and centres of pilgrimage and seats of ancient learning. Beginning in the lowly way of marginalia and *śodhapatras*, these additions must have got embedded in the text, through their transmission from copyist to copyist, undergoing in this process a strange variation of details.

In a small percentage of cases, our MS. shows, it must be admitted, readings documented mostly by Southern MSS.—with or without support of a few other N MSS. It is naturally the most difficult thing in the world to decide in these cases whether this *sporadic* agreement is due to late contamination or to primitive connection through the lost archetype. In the light of such variants, some readings of the Critical Edition will have to be reconsidered, and it may, in sporadic cases, be found necessary even to alter slightly the readings of the Ādiparvan in the Critical Edition. That work must however be left over now for further research by a future generation of scholars.

Unique Readings.

Like all MSS. modern or ancient, our MS. has quite a large number of *unique* readings, that is to say, readings which have not been found in any MS. so far collated for the Critical Edition. They consist of variants of proper names, consciously or unconsciously manipulated ; synonyms or paraphrases ; and sometimes of mere transpositions of words and phrases ; or even insignificant variants of expletives and verse-filling particles. In a few instances the variants are obscure and archaic, but generally weak and inconsequential as compared to the readings of the Critical Edition. The Mahābhārata problem is made a problem of problems and a problem *sui generis* by the amazing diversity of MSS. in all imaginable details ; and our MS. is not [210] behindhand in liberally contributing to this diversity. Here I specify a few samples of *unique* readings of the new MS. :

1.181^{b} विनयः (for विक्रमः)
1.194^{b} परायणम् (for सनातनम्)
2.77^{b} गरुडस्य (for गन्धर्वाणां)
2.26^{b} सप्त श्लोकशतानि (for तथा नव श०)
2.104^{a} श्लोका ग्रन्थसहस्रे तु
2.136^{d} महात्मसु (for जिगीषया)
2.139^{c} समरे (for सचित्रं)
2.214^{cd} प्रीतः पश्यन्पुरवरे यथा (for वीरान्पश्यत्पुनरागतान्)
7.11^{d} जुह्वते (भुञ्जते)
13.15^{a} एकमनुव्रतः (for एव समास्थितः)
13.44^{c} प्रसन्नात्मा (for सुमहता)
20.12^{a} त्राता ततः (त्वमुत्तमः)
43.25^{b} भार्या (for भर्त्रा)
57.12^{d} स (for यन्नवेत्)
59.41^{d} तथाष्टमः (for च सप्तमः)
67.30^{d} हेतुज्ञो (for क्षेत्रज्ञो)
68.66^{c} बाला (for राजन्)
71.58^{b} पञ्च (for दश)
79.21^{d} तज्जरायां न कामये
84.17^{d} पुण्यान् (for पश्यन्)
88.25^{d} लभेदस्मत्सलोकताम्
102.16^{b} वेदाध्ययनसंगताः
108.1^{d} वैशंपायन (for आनुपूर्व्येण)
112.27^{b} कुशास्तरणशायिनी
114.38^{d} सुमहान् (for तुमुलः)
118.19^{b} श्लक्ष्णेन (for शुक्लेन)
132.8^{d} कार्यं साधु (for कारयेश्वा)
134.22^{a} अग्निना दाहदग्धेषु
147.18^{d} सुदुःखिता (for सुखान्विता)
158.18^{a} विष्णुपदी (for चैकवप्रा)
158.50 क्षत्रं वज्रस्य भाजनं
178.5^{b} नयनैः (for हृदयैः)
179.19^{d} सैनिकाः (for सुस्वनाः)
180.9^{b} सुखानि (for वसूनि)
186.7^{c} चित्राणि (for चाग्र्याणि)
190.8^{a} अभ्यजनोपपन्नं (for अर्थिजनोपशोभितं)
191.6^{a} ऋद्धिः (for भद्रा)
194.2^{d} नैवेह शकिताः प्रभो
195.5^{a} निजं (for यथा)
199.32^{c} शङ्खैः (तल्पैः)
201.18^{a} महादेवं (for प्रभुं देवं)
207.18^{b} प्रपद्य शरणं प्रभुं
207.23^{d} त्रीणि वत्सरान् (for त्रिहिमाः समाः)
211.24^{c} दिव्यान् (for राजन्)
214.30^{b} प्रार्थयन्कनकप्रभः
218.18^{a} संप्रतीकार०
218.22^{c} दिग्भ्यश्चैवा° (for विवशाश्चा°)
223.9^{d} अस्मात्परिविध्यै° (for हि नः परिरक्षै°)

Our Emendations.

Now we may turn to what is perhaps the most surprising feature of our MS. That is the support our MS. affords to the constituted text of the Critical Edition, with regard to the *emendations* attempted therein. It is remarkable to find that this single MS., which is certainly older than any of the MSS. we had before, supports and confirms, as already remarked, fifty per cent of these emendations. Out of the total of thirty-six emendations [211] made in the Critical Edition the following eighteen are corroborated by our MS :

30.7 प्रतिगृह्यतामिदानीं* मे (hypermetric !)
37.10 दिवं स्तब्ध्वेव* विष्ठितः
51.8 अथो* इन्द्रः स्वयमेवाजगाम (hiatus)
57.20 क्रियते *उच्छ्रयो नृपैः (hiatus)
84.13 ततो लोकान्महतो *अजयं वै (hiatus)
92.50 अष्टेमे* वसवो देवा (double sandhi)
98.8 अन्तर्वत्नी *अहं भ्रात्रा (hiatus)
103.5 श्रूयते यादवी कन्या *अनुरूपा (hiatus)
110.20 नाहं श्वाचरिते मार्गे *अवीर्य° (hiatus)
110.28 यदि *आवां महाप्राज्ञ (hiatus)
147.2 रोरवीथो *अनाथवत् (hiatus)
149.6 श्रेयो *आत्मवधो मम (hiatus)
157.13 पञ्चकृत्वस्त्वया *उक्तः (hiatus)
207.17 कुले *अस्मिन्बभूव ह (hiatus)
214.9 धर्मराजे *अतिप्रीत्या (hiatus)
219.3 *संत्रासित इवाभवन्* (shortening *metri causa*)
224.5 संतप्यमाना *अभितो (hiatus)
224.9 तथाग्नौ ते *परीत्ताश्च[1]

Now, even though these emendations were put forward more as a hypothesis than as a dogma (Prolegomena p. XCIV), they have evoked severe criticism from certain scholars. It will therefore be advisable to consider here some of these criticisms in the light of the readings of our new MS.

Professor A. B. KEITH, in his review[2] of the Ādiparvan, admits that, " the editor has quite justly relied often on the maxim that the more difficult reading is to be preferred to the simpler, since it is easy to explain the latter as correction of what was poorly understood by careless scribes ", but continues, " we need not, therefore, accept as a necessarily correct theory the view that we are to restore hiatuses, whenever we find variants in the MSS., which might be explained by assuming that they are the different efforts made by scribes, who were not accustomed to hiatus to remedy the irregularity ". Whether the said view represents a correct theory of Mbh. text-reconstruction or not may be best judged from the circumstance that out of the eighteen emendations which are actually documented and attested by this new MS., not less than thirteen were made just on the ground of [212] *hiatus* ! A glance at the above list will convince the reader of the truth of this contention.

---

[1] One stanza 1. 71. 36 in which there is an emendation is unfortunately omitted in the new MS.

[2] *Indian Culture*, Vol. 3, pp. 766-771.

In all these thirteen instances there are violent fluctuations in the MS. readings. These uncommon fluctuations pointed towards the possibility, which this MS, has turned into a certainty, that they represent more or less independent attempts at correcting some solecism to which the scribes, editors or commentators would naturally take violent objection. It is natural to infer that this solecism is the hiatus to which a steadily increasing antipathy is noticeable as we pass from the earlier to the later Sanskrit literature. It is well-known that Vedic texts frequently contain hiatus which does not cause any serious offence to the susceptibilities of the modern reader, but the same hiatus in the work of a poet of the classical period would be rated as a capital blunder. The view of HOPKINS (which Prof. KEITH endorses) to the effect that there is nothing peculiarly epic in hiatus, and that it is found in precedent and subsequent poetry, is quite non-committal, and, if anything, favours our position. The point at issue is the legitimacy of the hiatus in the subsequent literature and not merely its occurrence. It is quite legitimate in the earlier literature, but comes to be progressively regarded as a solecism and therefore is an anthema to scribes bred and brought up in the classical tradition. It is no doubt carelessness only, as Prof. KEITH observes, in the later stages of the growth of Sanskrit literature, but not necessarily so throughout its history. Prof. KEITH himself has not much faith in his own scepticism and consequently much of his criticism loses point, as he concedes, though reluctantly, the validity of certain restorations of hiatuses.

Prof. KEITH has altogether missed the significance of the variation of MSS. between particles like, *hi*, *ca*, *tu*, *vā*, in these instances of emendations. It is true that these particles show great variation from MS. to MS., as is only natural in the corpus of a fluid text. But the scribes did not go out of their way to vary the text and to replace deliberately one particle by another. Often enough these small particles are very instructive in determining the complex relationship of MSS. Our present MS., for instance, agrees with Ñ_3 scores of times in the choice of just [213] these particles against all other MSS. But we need not press the point too far. It is sufficient to note that the variation is not as arbitrary as it might at first sight appear. Moreover, it is easy to understand that these small particles do come in very handy whenever the question of avoiding a hiatus arises and can be sandwiched between the vowels without disturbing the metre.[1] This is clearly the simplest and most natural mode of avoiding the hiatus and explains the violent fluctuations of the text. That it is not the only mode of avoiding the seeming blunder may be seen from 1. 57. 20 *kriyate *ucchrayo nṛpaiḥ*, where T G have entirely recast the pāda, changing it to : *kurvanty ete dhvajocchrayam.*

---

[1] Cf. HOPKINS, *The Great Epic*, p. 199 f. : " In both metres, to avoid hiatus, irrational particles are often inserted. A good example is : purā kṛtayuge tāta hy āsīd rājā *hy* Akampanaḥ, vii, 2,029, where B., 52, 26, omits the first hi ".

So the proof of an original hiatus does not always rest upon a mere variation of particles, as Prof. KEITH thinks.

Prof. KEITH starts from the conviction (which is quite *a priori*), that if at all a hiatus occurs, it must occur either between the *pādas* where the absence of *sandhi* is natural ; or else before a vocative, where it is easy to feel a natural pause. He does not grudge the restoration of hiatus in 1. 99. 15 ; 103. 5 ; 110. 20 ; 119. 11 etc. on these grounds. In 1. 57. 20 *kriyate *ucchrayo nṛpaiḥ* and 1. 100. 2 *niśīthe āgamiṣyati,* he haltingly admits the validity of the restoration of hiatus and tries desperately to defend it on grounds of metrical facility. He is adamant, however, when it comes to—what he styles—" unmotived " hiatus. He has exemplified his scepticism in the following instances.

In 1. 147. 2 he considers *roravīthas tv anāthavat* as more legitimate.

Proceeding further, Prof. KEITH says that it is very difficult to believe in 1. 207. 17 *kule asmin babhūva ha* : since such a hiatus as this is " unmotived ". He can, however, easily persuade himself to believe that " the *saṁbabhūva* of a large body of MSS. was erroneously curtailed to *babhūva* with the result that *kule 'smin* had to be extended " !

In 1. 119. 11 *tathty ukte Ambikayā,* the position according to Prof. KEITH is " uncertain " ; *tv* may be right before *Ambikayā.*

[214] In 1. 98. 8, *antarvatnī aham Bhrātrā* may be explained, in the opinion of Prof. KEITH, " by emphasis " ; but it is quite probable, he adds, that " *tv* is original, *ty* would be a blunder for it and *hy* a correction ".

1. 224. 5, *saṁtapyamānā abhito* is quite " needless ", according to Prof. KEITH. The MSS. suggest, according to him, *saṁtapyamānān* as " clearly correct ". " Misunderstanding of the accusative ", we are told, " as following on the previous line has led to the mere corrections *saṁtapyamānā bahudhā* or *purato* ".

In 1. 157. 13, *pañcakṛtvas tvayā uktaḥ* " seems unmotived and the variants of the MSS. hardly justify it ".

Prof. KEITH calls 1. 110. 28, *yadi āvāṁ mahāprājña,* " very dubious ", and in 1. 51. 8, *atho Indraḥ svayam evājagāma* according to him is " not at all certain ".

1. 214. 9. is an interesting case. The pāda in dispute reads *Dharmarāje *atiprītyā,* which is an emendation. It was first criticized by the late Prof. WINTERNITZ as being " really unnecessary ". A reply was given to his criticisms in these *Annals* by me and I have devoted three pages of the journal (vol. 16. pp. 108-110) to explain the circumstances which, in my opinion, necessitated the emendation. Prof. KEITH was left unconvinced by these arguments. Rejecting this explanation, he dogmatically lays down : " in 1. 214. 9, *Dharmarāje hy atiprītyā* should be read ; the variant *tv* is normal, and the hiatus is unmotived ".

Now that most of these unmotived, needless, dubious, illegitimate, unnecessary hiatuses are actually documented and are no longer merely my conjectures, I am intrigued to know what hidden motives Prof. KEITH will discover in them in order to explain their occurrence in an authentic MS. in the possession of the Rajaguru of Nepal.

It is sad that Professor WINTERNITZ should not have lived to see some of his doubts about the readings of the constituted text finally dispelled by the evidence of this MS. The discovery of this valuable MS., so consequential for the text-criticism of the Ādiparvan, would certainly have delighted the heart of this veteran scholar, who took a passionate and life-long interest in epic studies. The text of the Critical Edition objected to in the [215] following places by the late lamented Professor WINTERNITZ is supported by our MS.

57.20^b क्रियते *उच्छ्रयो नृपैः
57.21^b हास्यरूपेण शंकरः
57.58^c दृश्यतोद्
91.8^{cd} मनसाध्यायम्
92.45^c न च तां किंचनोवाच
92.50^a अष्टमे*
93.11 देवदेवर्षिसेवितम्
214.9 धर्मराजे *अतिप्रीत्या
215.2,5 प्रयच्छताम् and संप्रयच्छतम्
216.10^a यत्
218.14^a जलधारामुचोऽऽकुलान्
218.27 ब्यातिष्ठन्त

I append below the collations of the new Nepālī MS. exactly as they were received from Panditjiu HEMARAJ, omitting only a few corrupt readings which are obvious mislections by copyists.

COLLATIONS OF THE NEPĀLĪ MS. OF THE ĀDIPARVAN OF THE MAHĀBHĀRATA BELONGING TO GURUJIU HEMARAJ PUNDITJIU C.I.E. OF NEPAL

☞ Corrupt readings have been mostly ignored in this list. The readings in parenthesis ( ) are those of the Critical Edition. [U] after a reading shows that it is unique to this MS., and not found in any other MS. collated for the Critical Edition. The MS. symbols after a reading show that the reading is elsewhere found in those MSS. *only*.

Adhy. 1

9 ^{d}) तु (for वै) [U]
18 ^{c}) यथावत्सर्षिभिस्तुष्टया
27 ^{d}) अक्षरम् (for अक्षयम्)
29 ^{a}) अक्षतं (for अचिन्त्यं) [U]
34 ^{c}) तथा (for आपो)
^{d}) समाः (for तथा) [U]
35 ^{b}) क्षणाः (for क्रमात्) [U]
40 ^{a}) दिवःपुत्रो (for दिवस्पुत्रो)
^{c}) स (for च)
41 ^{a}) पूर्वं) for सर्वे [U]
^{b}) पुत्रास्तेषां तथापरः
48 ^{a}) इतिहासस्य वैयाख्या [U]
48 ^{c}) इति (for इह) [U]
49 ^{a}) महाज्ञानं (for महज्ज्ञानं)
^{d}) समासग्रन्थधारणम्
50 ^{a}) पर्व्वादि (for मन्वादि) [U]
51 ^{b}) विशेषतः (for मनीषिणः) [V_1]
54 ^{b}) तदा (for पुरा) [U]
57 ^{a}) यत्पृष्टो (for पृष्टः सन्) [U]
60 ^{c}) वृत्तञ्च (for दुर्वृत्तं)
63 ^{c}) अतिरूपेभ्यः (for अनुरू°)
67 ^{cd}) अरण्य एव सजनो न्यवसन्मृगयारतः [U]
70 ^{c}) सर्व्वेषु (for पुण्येषु) [U]

[216] 71 ^{a}) यत् (for च)
73 ^{a}) श्रुत्वा (for दृष्ट्वा)
77 ^{c}) पुरप्रवेशे (for आसन्न^{o}) [V_1]
79 ^{a}) तेधीत्य वेदानखिलान्
95 ^{c}) कृत्वा (for ज्ञात्वा) [U]
97 ^{b}) कुलक्षयम् (for कुलक्षये)
98 ^{f}) अचेतसम् (for अचेतनम्)
99 ^{b}) पाण्डवस्यामितौजसः [M]
100 ^{d}) श्रियन्तां क्षत्रियो (for श्रियमक्ष^{o})
101 दृष्ट्वा (read ^{o}ष्ट्वा)नि (for युक्तानि)
102 Om.
104 ^{b}) Om. च
109 ^{c}) यत् (for तत्) [U]
112 ^{b}) मोक्षितं (for मोक्षणं)
118 Om.
122 Om.
125 ^{c}) न चैषां (for नैषां)
122 ^{a}) यदा वायुः शक्र^{o} (for यदाश्रौषं शुक्र^{o})
133 ^{c}) अन्यं (for पार्थं) [U]
834 ^{c}) तस्य चैवार्जुनेन (for सैन्धवे चार्जु^{o}) [U]
138 ^{a}) नागपुरं (for ^{o}बलैर्) [U]
140–141 Om.
142 After 142, ins. :

यदाश्रौषं महाधनुर्वेदकल्पं
क्षिप्रं सेतुं समरे वाहिनीनाम् ।
भारद्वाजं संयुगे सीदमानं
तदा नाशंसे विजयाय सञ्जय ॥ [U]

143 ^{a}) रण आचार्यं (for द्रोणमाचार्यं) [Corrupt]
150 ^{c}) भग्नपक्षं (for ^{o}दर्पं)
154 ^{c}) तेन (for येन)
155 ^{c}) मुक्तं (for दत्तं)
156 ^{c}) द्वैपायनं केशवं (for ^{o}नः ^{o}वो)
^{d}) शपानाम् (for शशाप)
166 ^{d}) काक्षीवन्तं तमोविसम्
167 ^{b}) महाभिमजितं धमम् [M_1]
169 ^{c}) चित्य^{o} (for चैत्य^{o})
173 ^{d}) द्रुदः (for द्रुमः) [K_4]
174 ^{a}) वेणुः (for वेनः)
175 ^{d}) निषधो नटः (for नैषधो नलः)

178 ^{b}) वृद्धायुधः (for वृद्धेषुधिः)
181 ^{b}) विनयः (for विक्रमः) [U]
184 ^{c}) शाखा (read ^{o}खा) कृता (for शाखानुगा)
186 ^{d}) [S] तिवर्तितुं (for निवर्तितुं)
187 ^{a}) विधिना विहितं (for विधातृवि^{o}) [U]
188 ^{b}) संक्षिपति (for संहरति) [U]
^{c}) निर्दहेत्तु प्रजाः कालः [U]
194 ^{b}) परायणम् (for सनातनम्) [U]
195 ^{a}) असच्च (for असत्सत्)
196 ^{a}) तत् (for यत्) [U]
197 ^{a}) यतं यतिवरा गुप्ता
198 ^{d}) विमुच्यते (for प्रमु^{o})
199 ^{c}) श्रुत्वा (for शृण्वन्) [M_1]
200 ^{d}) चिन्तितम् (for संचितम्) [K_6]
202 Om.
204 ^{d}) मयायं प्रचरिष्यति
205 ^{c}) चैव (for चापि) [U]
^{d}) असंशयः (for न सं^{o})
208 Om.
209 ^{a}) भारतत्वात् (for भारवत्त्वात्)

Adhy. 2

2 ^{a}) मम वै (for यदि वो)
3 ^{b}) प्रहरतां (for शस्त्रभृतां)
7 ^{d}) परिकीर्त्यते (for ^{o}कीर्तितम्)
8 ^{b}) लिङ्गितः ख्यायते भुवि [U]
^{c}) तथैव (for तेनैव) [U]
12 ^{b}) द्विजसत्तमाः (for मुनि^{o})
^{d}) सुमताः (for विश्रुतः)
16 ^{d}) अभिसंज्ञितः (for अभिधीयते) (B_4 V_1 G_1)
20 ^{b}) रथा (for तथा) [U]
21 ^{b}) नवैव च (for तथा नव) [K_4]
23 ^{c}) यस्ते (for यां वः) [U]
29 ^{d}) आस्तीकं चादितः स्मृतम्
[217] 31 ^{a}) Transp. आत्मेव and वेद्नि-तव्येषु [U]
32 ^{b}) निर्मिता (for अर्पिता) [U]
37 ^{d}) राज्यलाभः (for राज्यलम्भः)
38 ^{d}) श्रेया हरणहारिका
42–43 Transp. 42^{cd} and 43^{ab}
46 ^{b}) मृगस्वप्नभवं (for ^{o}भयं) [U]
50 ^{c}) Transp. प्रजागरं and ततः [U]

52 ^{a}) निर्वेदपर्व (for विवाद°) [U]
^{c}) नियार्त्रा पर्व विज्ञेयं
54 Reads 54^{cd} after 55 [M_1]
^{d}) ततश्चाद्भुतमुच्यते
57 ^{b}) चोत्तमम् (for चोच्यते)
60 ^{b}) तीर्थवंशमनुत्तमम् [U]
^{c}) सुबीभत्सं (for तु बी°)
71 ^{d}) पर्वसंग्रहे (for ° ग्रहः)
After 71, ins. 93* (om. line 4)
74 ^{b}) ह (for च)
77 ^{b}) गरुडस्य (for गन्धर्वाणां) [U]
78 ^{d}) दिवः (for दिवि) [U]
89 ^{d}) राज्यार्धसर्जनम् (for °शासनम्)
90 ^{cd}) तवदुपाख्यानं (for तत्र उपा°)
[Corrupt]
95 ^{f}) उत्तममेधसा (for °तेजसा) [U]
96 ^{b}) सह श्लोकशतानि (for तथा नव श°)
[U]
101 ^{a}) मन्युरभवत् (for मन्युरुद्भूतो)
^{b}) अकल्पयत् (for अकारयत्)
103 ^{b}) तवाख्यातं मया मुने [K_{0-6}]
104 ^{a}) श्लोका ग्रन्थसहस्रे तु [U]
105 Om. 105^{cd} [K_{0-1}]
106 ^{f}) पाण्डवस्यामितौजसः [U]
108 ^{d}) परिदेवितम् (for °देवनम्)
111 After 111^{ab}, reads 127^{ab} [G_{1-6}]
Om. 111^{cd} [T_1 G_4]
113 ^{c}) महाभागैः (for °वीर्यैः) [U]
122 Om. 122^{cd}
123 Reads 123^{ab} after 126
124 ^{b}) वातवेगसमो (for वायु°) [G_1]
128 ^{c}) आख्यानशते (for अध्याय°)
[U]
^{e}) एकान्नसप्ततिः (for एकोनस°)
[U]
136 ^{d}) महात्मसु (for जिगीषया) [U]
137 ^{b}) नः (for नौ)
^{d}) महात्मनोः (for °मतिः) [U]
139 ^{c}) समरे (for सचिवं) [U]
145 ^{c}) स्वयं गतः (for स्वयमागात्) [U]
151 ^{d}) संधिविग्रहसंज्ञितम्
152 ^{d}) नव श्लोकशतानि च
159 ^{a}) यत्र (for पत्र) [U]
164 ^{b}) जरासंधश्च पार्थिवः [U]
170 ^{b}) विवादः (for संवादः) [M_1]
^{d}) आख्येयसंज्ञितम् (for आक्षेपसंहितम्)
[Corrupt]
172 ^{c}) एकान्नसप्ततिः (for एकोनस°)
[U]
176 ^{b}) उच्यते (for अर्थवत्) [U]
^{c}) एकान्नषष्टिः (for एकोनषष्टिः) [U]
183 ^{a}) यत्र शोकार्ता (for पुत्रशो°)
186 ^{a}) नैवम् (for मैवम्) [U]
192 ^{a}) यत्र ताः क्षत्रियाः शूरा
^{b}) निष्ठान्तान् (for दिष्टान्तान्)
194 ^{d}) प्रकीर्तिताः (for उदाहृताः)
195 ^{f}) °वैक्लव्याश्रुप्रवर्तनम्
196 ^{c}) आपेदे (for आपन्नो)
^{d}) कुरुराजो (for धर्मराजो) [U]
^{f}) संबन्धिमातुलान् (for °बान्धवान्)
200 ^{b}) द्वादशैतत्प्रकीर्तितम् [U]
202 ^{b}) नु (for नि-) [U]
204 ^{b}) यत्र शासनम् (for चानुशा°) [U]
205 ^{d}) षष्टिश्चान्यन्यदर्शितम् [Corrupt]
206 ^{b}) पर्वोक्तं तदनन्तरम् [U]
212 ^{c}) समुत्सृज्य (परित्यज्य)
[218] 214 ^{cd}) प्रीतः पश्यन्पुरवरे यथा (for वीरानपश्यत्पुनरागतान्) [U]
215 ^{b}) तद्दृष्ट्वा स्वयमुत्तमम् (for दृष्टाश्चर्यमनुत्तमम्) [U]
218 ^{c}) द्वाचत्वारिंशत् (for द्विच°)
[K_4]
219 ^{a}) एव (for एकं) [U]
229 ^{cd}) अष्टाध्यायाः प्रसङ्ख्याताः श्लोकान्यञ्च शतञ्च यत्
231 ^{b}) Transp. शतं and तथा
234 ^{a}) निखिलं (for अखिलं)
[K_4 D_2]
243 ^{b}) विज्ञेयं (for विन्यस्तं)

Adhy. 3

1 After तस्य ins. आसन् [$\tilde{N}_1$ M_1]
Transp. उग्रसेनः and भीमसेनः
[B_{1-3}]
2 चाभ्यगच्छत् (for अभ्यागच्छत्)

3 रौषि (for रोदिषि)
4 Om. तत्र
6 After स तां ins. मातरं [$\dot{N}_1$ D_5]
7 पुत्रदुःखार्ता (for °शोकार्ता)
अभ्यगच्छत् (for उपागच्छत्)
8 नापराधी (for अनपकारी)
11 गतः (for यातः)
After गतः, ins. सन्
12 अभिहतः (for अभिमतः)
15 Om. तस्याः (after मच्छुक्रं पीतवत्याः)
Om. सर्वाः (before पापकृत्याः)
20 प्रवेशयामास (for प्रेषयामास) [U]
22 Om. उपायम्
24 अयोदो (for आ°)
25 भवता (for भगवता)
Om. गच्छ
27 आह्वानशब्दं (for आह्वानाय शब्दं)
28 रोद्धुं (for संरोद्धुं)
भवन्तं (for भगवन्तम्)
29 नाम्नास्त्विति (for नाम्ना भविष्यतीति)
30 Om. इति (after अवाप्स्यसि)
38 Before रक्षित्वा, ins. स
39 पीवानमपश्यत् (for पीवानमेव)
दृष्ट्वा चैनमुवाच (for दृष्ट्वोवाच)
42 उपाध्यायस्याग्रतः (for उपाध्यायगृहमागम्योपाध्यायस्या°)
43 Om. अपि (after तथा)
Om. च (before अन्यत्)
पीवानेव चासि (for पीवानासि)
45 नाभ्यनुज्ञातम् (for अननु°)
47 Before असि, ins. एव च
48 स्तनात् (for स्तनं)
52 Om. स (before तैः)
54 Om. भो (before उपमन्यो)
60 a) पूर्वौ (for पूर्वगौ)
b) Om. वा
c) सुवर्णावरजौ (for सुपर्णौ विरजौ)
62 d) सासात्रा (for सत्तमा)
64 b) प्रतिष्ठान्या (for प्रधिष्वन्या)
65 a) द्वादश (for द्वादशारं)
b) एकम् (for एकाक्षम्)
d) विषीभयः (for °दतम्)

67 a) Om. दश
69 cd) नासत्यावमृतावृधासते (for °मृतावृतावृधावृते)
76 अभ्यवादयत्तदाचचक्षे (for अभिवाद्याच°)
80 किंचित्कालं (for कंचि°)
शुश्रुषणा च (for शुश्रूषमाणेन)
81 गुरुधूर्षुं (for गुरुषु धूर्षु)
86 परिहीयेत् (for °हीयते)
[219] 87 आदिश्य (for प्रतिसमादिश्य)
88 उत्तङ्कः स शुश्रुषुः (for °ङ्को गुरुषु°)
89 Om. स (before वसन्)
92 भवतः (for भवन्तम्)
95 ते वयमनुज्ञाता (for सोऽहमनुज्ञातो)
गच्छाम (for इच्छामीष्टं)
97 After आज्ञापयतु, ins. मा
98 तां (for एनां)
99 Om. गृहं (before गन्तुं)
After आज्ञापयतु, ins मा
After भवति, ins. इति
100 तमुपाध्यायिनी (for सैव-मुक्तोपा°)
कुण्डले भिक्षितुं तस्य क्षत्रियया पिनद्धे (for भिक्षस्व°)
101 प्रातिष्ठत् (for °ष्ठत)
104 After तमाह, ins. स
106 Transp. उत्तङ्कः and आसीनम्
111 Om. स
113 Om. शीघ्रं
115 Om. त्रिः पीत्वा
118 Transp. तेन तस्य and सद्भावेन
121 पौष्यसकाश अगच्छत् (for °काशमाग°)
123 प्रकरिष्ये (for तत्करिष्ये)
124 उपाहृतं (for उपहृतं)
125 संयोजयामास (for भोज°)
126 Om. सकेशं
128 अन्नस्याशुद्धिभावम् (for अशुचिभावमन्नस्य)
132 b) निशितः (for निहितः)
d) नावनीता (for °नीती) [$K_{1\cdot3}$]
134 After शापो, ins. न
137 After अभिसृत्य, ins. अथ
139 a) यदैरावतराजानः (for य ऐरा°)
140 a) सुरूपा बहुरूपाश्च
b) अप्यथो (for तथा)

143 a) ये चेदमुपशृण्वन्ति
145 c) ह्यवसतां (for निव°) [Ñ$_1$ M$_{1\cdot3\cdot5}$]
146 c) हि सद्युक्ति (for महद्युक्ति) [U]
147 Transp. एवं and स्तुवन्
अधिरुह्य (for अधिरोप्य)
154 Transp. स and एनं
155 उपेयुः (for ईयुः)
156 आधमस्व (for धमस्व)
157 आधमत् (for अध°)
158 उपधूपितः (for धूपितः)
159 इमे ते (for एते)
160 जग्राह (for प्रतिजग्राह)
161 तम् (for एनम्)
एतत्क्षणम् (for क्षणादेव)
162 मातिं (for मनो)
166 After तक्षकेण, ins. मे
167 तन्त्रं (for तन्त्रे)
Om. अधिरोप्य पटं
177 Om. स
181 c) अद्य देव (for अन्यदेव) [U]
d) किमिदं कुरुषे नृप
183 b) परिवर्द्धयामि (for परिपालयामि) [U]
c) नस्तत्क्रियां तां (for वा किं क्रियतां) [U]
186 a) कामं कालं (for कार्यकालं) [U]
193 c) उत्तङ्कवाक्यमाविष्टो [U]

Adhy. 4

1 Om. पौराणिको
Om. द्वादशवार्षिके
2 कृतातिश्रमः (for कृतश्रमः) [U]
Om. ताम्
करवाणि (for ब्रुवाणि) [U]
3 प्रवक्ष्यामः (for प्रक्ष्यामः)
भवान् (for तद्भगवान्)
4 b) वेद चासुरसंकथाः [K$_2$ G$_{2\cdot3}$]
5 b) गृहपतिः (for कुलपतिः)
10 c) सूतपुत्रपुरः कृताः
[220] 11 b) द्विजः (for ततः)

Adhy. 5

2 d) श्रुतपूर्वं (for श्रुताः पूर्वं)
5 f) भार्गवो द्विजसत्तम [U]
8 d) पूर्वपितामहः (for °महात्)
9 d) नियतव्रतः (for नियतेन्द्रियः) [B$_5$]
12 d) यतव्रतः (for यशस्विनः) [U]
13 d) पुलमो (for पुलोम) here and in the sequel [U]
16 a) तत् (for तां) [U]
b) हृच्छयातिनिपीडितः [U]
18 b) पृष्टमनेन ते (for पृष्ट ऋतेन वै) [U]
c) वै (for मे)
26 After 26, ins. (marg. *sec. m.*)
सेयमित्यवगच्छामि नानृतं वक्तुमुत्सहे ।
अनृतं हि सतां लोके हृदि नैवावतिष्ठति ।

Adhy. 6

5 Om. (? hapl.) 5^{cdef}
6 c) सूतं (for सूतिं)
8 a) Transp. स and एवम् [K$_{0\cdot1}$]
12 c) तु (for च)
13 c) अतिक्रुद्धः (for अभिक्रुद्धः)

Adhy. 7

9 d) सर्वशः (for पर्वसु) [D$_{6\cdot7}$]
11 d) जुहुते (for भुञ्जते) [U]
16 c) देवमुखं (for °मुखो)
21 d) Transp. सर्वं and शुचि [U]
23 a) स्वाग्निः (for वाह्निः) [U]
b) प्रत्युक्तवाथ (for प्रत्युवाच)
24 d) तत्र (for सर्वाः) [U]

Adhy. 8

2 d) शुनकस्त्व यतोभवत् [U]
7 a) Transp. तं and गर्भं [U]
10 b) सर्वैं रूपगुणोन्विता [Corrupt]
c) प्रमद्वरेति वै तस्या [U]
13 d) वह्निदैवते (for भगदै°) [U]
16 d) स दष्टाङ्गे (for भृशमङ्गे)

Adhy. 9

3 a) शेतेसौ (for शेते सा)
5 b) यतव्रतः (for धृत°)
c) तथाद्यासौ (for तथाद्यैव)
d) उत्तिष्ठतु यशस्विनी [K$_1$]
6 b) दुःखार्त (for दुःखेन)
8 d) लप्स्यसेथ (for प्राप्स्यसीमां) [U]

9 c) करिष्येऽहं (for °ष्ये तं)
11 d) Before उत्तिष्ठतु, ins. च
12 a) तथा (for ततो) [U]
c) एवं (for इदं)
16 a) एतत्तु चरितं सर्वं [U]
c) तपसोथ प्रवृद्धस्य
18 b) °वर्षसाम्

Adhy. 10

2 a) भुजगं सदैव हन्यां [U]
5 b) डुण्डुभस्य (for भुजगस्य)
c) अहनत् (for अवधीत्)
6 b) गिरा (for इव)

Adhy. 11

1 c) भ्राता (for तात) [U]
2 b) इव (for अथ)
3 a) Transp. लब्ध्वा च and स [U]
6 c) हसतेतत् ते (for °तेदं ते)
[Corrupt]
8 a) च निःश्वस्य (for विनिः°)
9 a) तथ्यं (for वाक्यं) [B_5]
b) मे संशितव्रत (for तन्मे धृत°)
c) हृदये (for हृदि ते) [U]
d) सदा तव (for तपोधन) [U]
12 b) वर (for स्मृतः)
{221} 12 d) हिंसेत् (for हिंस्यात्)
[G_6 M_1]
17 b) इति (for अपि) [U]

Adhy. 12

3 a) वत्स (for सर्वम्)
4 a) त्वथ (for चापि)

Adhy. 13

1 a) पुरा (for राजा)
3 d) ब्रवीहि तम् ((for वदस्व मे)
5 d) तपस्विनः (for यशस्विनः)
6 d) °वासिषु
8 c) Transp. आस्तीकं and आख्यानं
11 d) अवाङ्मुखान् (for अधोमु°)
12 d) वै ह्यधोमुखाः (for वा अधो°)
15 a) संततावेको (for संततिस्त्वेको)
b) श्रुतिः (for श्रुतः)
d) एकमनुव्रतः (for एव समास्थितः)
[U]
17 d) पुत्रक (for सत्तम) [G_1]
18 d) अनुशोचितुम् (for अनुकम्पितुम्)
23 a) करिष्येति (for करिष्यामि)
25 d) उपायास्ये (for उपयंस्ये) [U]
28 d) मोदन्तु (for मोदन्तां)
36 b) तां ददौ (for प्रददौ) [U]
43 d) सहस्वैः (for सहिताः स्वैः) [U]
44 c) प्रसन्नात्मा (for सुमहता) [U]

Adhy. 14

3 a) आयुष्मज्जयम् (for आयुष्य मिदम्)
[$\tilde{N}_3$]
5 b) पितामहसुते (for प्रजापति°)
6 c) परया मुदयान्वितः [K_2 $\tilde{N}_3$]
9 b) ईदृशम् (for ईप्सितम्) [$\tilde{N}_3$ T_2]
13 b) परिचारकाः (for °चारिकाः)
d) तु (for च)
15 d) अपश्यत (for अदृक्षत*)
16 c) रोषसंतप्तः (for °संपन्नः)
17 b) लोभाभिभूतया (for लोभपरीतया
[$\tilde{N}_3$]
21 d) तदा (for सदा)
23 d) बुभुक्षितः (for °क्षतः)

Adhy. 15

8 d) सुमनोहरम् (for °हरैः)
9 b) बहुरत्नमयं शिवम् [$\tilde{N}_3$]
c) उद्विग्नाः (for उद्विद्धं)
10 d) तदा नियमसंभृताः
11 cd) अचिन्तयत्सुरेष्वेतन्मन्त्रयित्वाथ
सर्वथा [$\tilde{N}_3$]

Adhy. 16

3 c) अभूत् (for अभो) [U]
8 c) अमृतार्थ (read °र्थं)न्तु (for
अमृतार्थाय)
d) निर्मथिष्याम ते (for °महे)
10 a) तमूचुः (for ऊचुश्च) [U]
11 c) स शैलस्तस्य (for तस्य शैलस्य)
12 b) ततो (for तथा)
f) देवदानवाः (for दैत्यदा°)
14 d) अथाक्षिपत् (for अवाक्षि°)
19 b) विनिर्धूता (for विनिष्पिष्टा)

24 ^{d}) सर्वशः (for सर्वतः)
25 ^{a}) नानारसाः (for नानाविधाः)
26 ^{b}) सर्वेषां तपसा (for रसानां पयसा) [$\tilde{N}_3$]
31 ^{a}) ददानि (for ^{o}मि) [U]
^{c}) श्रान्तैः (for सर्वैः) [$\tilde{N}_3$]
34 ^{b}) [अ] मृतात् (for घृतात्) [U]
35 ^{c}) मरीचिकवचः (for ^{o}विकचः) [U]
^{d}) नारायणशिरोग्रगः [U]

Adhy. 17

1 ^{b}) महाप्रहरणानि (for नानाप्र^{o})
[222] 4 ^{d}) पीतवान् (for प्रापिबत्) [$\tilde{N}_3$]
6 ^{c}) देवेन (for चक्रेण) [$\tilde{N}_3$]
8 ^{d}) जग्राह (for ग्रसति) [$\tilde{N}_{1\cdot3}$]
13 ^{c}) ^{o}मालीनि [$\tilde{N}_3$ D_n]
^{d}) प्रपेतुः (for निपेतुः) [$\tilde{N}_3$]
14 ^{b}) निपेतुः (for निहताः) [K_4 $\tilde{N}_3$]
15 ^{a}) हाहारवाः संबभूवुः [$\tilde{N}_3$]
^{b}) समन्ततः (for सहस्रशः)
16 ^{b}) संनिकर्षेण (for ^{o}र्षे च) [$\tilde{N}_3$]
18 ^{b}) महाभये (for भयावहे)
20 ^{d}) अजय्यविक्रमं (for ^{o}य्यमुत्तमम्) [$\tilde{N}_3$]
22 ^{c}) दितिजवरान् (for दितिदनुजान्) [$\tilde{N}_3$]
23 ^{a}) अतिलेलिहत् (for अवले^{o}) [U]
24 ^{a}) तथासुरा गिरिभिरदीनमानसो
^{d}) गिरिमभितः प्रतन्य (for गगनमभिप्रपद्य) [$\tilde{N}_3$]
25 ^{c}) प्रतिगलिताग्रसानवः (for प्रविग^{o}) [$\tilde{N}_3$]
27 ^{b}) पवनपथं (for गगन^{o})
28 ^{d}) ह (for च) [$\tilde{N}_3$]
29 ^{c}) सर्वतः (for सर्वशः) [U]
30 ^{c}) ददुः (for ददौ)
^{d}) बलिभिरिह (for बलभिदथ)

Adhy. 18

1 ^{c}) तत्र (for यत्र)
4 ^{b}) and (5 ^{b}) दासभावाय (for दासीभा^{o})
9 ^{a}) स (for तु)
10 ^{b}) शापस्तत्राम्वमोदत
11 ^{f}) कश्यपाय (for काश्य^{o})

Adhy. 19

1–3 For 1^{a}–3^{b} subst.:
ततस्ते पणितं कृत्वा भगिन्यौ द्विजसत्तम ।
जग्मतुः परमप्रीते परं पारं महोदधेः ॥
कद्रू च विनता चैव दाक्षायण्यौ विहायसा ।
महान्तमुदकागारं क्षोभ्यमाणं महास्वनम् ॥
[$\tilde{N}_3$]
3 ^{c}) तिमिंगलगणाकीर्णं [D_5]
^{d}) तदा (for तथा)
4 ^{a}) संयुतं (for सत्त्वैश्च) [$\tilde{N}_3$]
^{cd}) Om.
5 ^{ab}) Om. [$\tilde{N}_3$]
6 ^{cd}) Om. [$\tilde{N}_3$ M_5]
After 6^{ab}, ins. (marg. *sec. m.*)
महानदीभिर्बह्वीभिस्तत्र [तत्र] सहस्रशः ।
(cf. v. l. 15^{ab})
आपूर्यमाणमत्यन्तमुद्धूतमिव चोर्मिभिः
(cf. v. l. 291*)
9 ^{b}) क्षोभद्वैधसमन्वितम् [U]
^{d}) सर्वतः (for सर्वशः)
10 ^{d}) रत्नागारं (for रत्नाकरं) [$\tilde{N}_3$]
11 ^{b}) अमितौजसम् (for ^{o}जसा) [U]
15 ^{b}) स्पर्धमानं (for स्पर्धयेव) [$\tilde{N}_3$ $G_{2\cdot3}$]
^{d}) तत्र तत्र समन्ततः
17 Om.

Adhy. 20

3 Om. [K_1 D_5 M_1]
4 ^{a}) चापि (for चैव)
7 ^{c}) स महान् (for सुम^{o})
8 ^{b}) असुरोत्तमाः (for असुरार्दनाः) [$\tilde{N}_3$]
9 ^{c}) अदूरम् (for अदूरात्) [$\tilde{N}_3$]
10 ^{d}) अनुत्तमः (for ^{o}त्तमम्) [U]
12 ^{a}) त्राता ततः (for त्वमुत्तमः) [U]
13 ^{b}) हरसि (for दहसि). [$\tilde{N}_3$]

Adhy. 21

1 ^{b}) कामवीर्यौ (for महावीर्यौ)
2 ^{d}) दासभावम् (for दासीभावम्)
3 ^{d}) उवाच ह (for अभाषत) [$\tilde{N}_3$]
7 ^{a}) सर्वदेवेश (for देवदे^{o})
[223] 13 ^{c}) स्थितिः (for तिथिः)
14 ^{a}) शुक्लश्च (for शुक्लस्त्वं) [U]

^{b}) By transp. तथा त्रुटिः

17 ^{d}) त्वं वेदान्यधिगमयन्ति (for वेदाज्ञान्यभिग°) [U]

Adhy. 22

3 ^{d}) असक्तं (for अजस्रं) [G_3]

4 ^{a}) संप्रवृत्तम् (for संप्रनृत्तम्)

Adhy. 23

1 ^{b}) द्वीपम् (for देशम्)

^{d}) पक्षिसंघविनादितम्

4 ^{a}) उपघ्नन्निरिव (for उपजिघ्रन्निः)

5 ^{e}) पुण्यं (for रम्यं) [M_1]

11 ^{d}) तथ्यं (for सत्यं)

Adhy. 24

8 ^{a}) मरुतः (for मारुतः)

^{b}) च (for तु)

^{c}) Transp. ते and वह्निः

10 ^{a}) निशाम्य (for निशम्य)

12 ^{c}) त्वरितं (for त्वरिताः)

Adhy. 25

2 ^{a}) विनि [ः] सर्प (for विनिर्गच्छ) [$\tilde{N}_3$ M_1]

4 ^{b}) निष्क्रम (for निष्पत) [$\tilde{N}_3$]

7 ^{b}) प्रभुः (for पितुः)

^{d}) उत्तमः (for उद्यतः)

9 ^{a}) अत्तव्यम् (for भोक्तव्यम्) [$K_1 \tilde{N}_3$]

10 ^{c}) चास्य (for तस्य) [U]

12 ^{a}) तु (for च) [K_1]

^{d}) कृतम् (for कर्तुम्) [U]

15 ^{c}) गुरुशास्त्रेण बद्धानाम्

17 ^{a}) एतं (for एवं)

21 ^{a}) यस्य (for तस्य)

^{c}) हि (for असौ) [$\tilde{N}_3$]

22 ^{a}) यं (for तं)

31 ^{b}) रोहणिपादपः (for रोहिणपा°)

^{c}) अथ वृक्षं महाकायम्

32 ^{a}) इयं (for एषा)

33 ^{c}) अभिहत्य (for अभिपत्य) [G_3 M_1]

^{d}) पतन्स (for बभञ्ज)

Adhy. 26

2 ^{a}) तां भङ्क्त्वा सुमहाशाखां

3 ^{b}) उपतत्य (for अनुपत्य)

^{d}) चैव (for एव) [$\tilde{N}_3$]

^{f}) पर्वतांश्च विचालयन् [$\tilde{N}_3$]

7 ^{c}) अनभिध्येयं (for °भिज्ञेयं)

20 ^{a}) Transp. ततः and स

23 ^{b}) महात्मनः (for समन्ततः) [$\tilde{N}_3$]

24 ^{b}) तदा (for तथा)

25 ^{b}) युताः (for युक्ताः)

27 ^{c}) प्रावर्तन् (for प्रावर्तन्त) [U]

^{d}) भयदर्शिनः (for °वेदिनः) [$\tilde{N}_3$ B_{3m}]

28 ^{b}) व्यथन्निव (for व्यथान्वितम्) [$\tilde{N}_3$ G_1 M_3]

29 ^{e}) येषां (for तेषां)

30 ^{b}) देवासुरेष्वपि (for °रेऽपि च)

31 ^{a}) इव (for अपि) [K_3 $\tilde{N}_3$]

32 ^{b}) ह (for हि)

^{d}) ववृषुः (for ववर्षुः)

^{e}) मुकुटांश्चैषां (for मुकुटान्येषां)

^{f}) व्युत्थितानि (for उत्थितानि)

39 ^{b}) Transp. स and न

Adhy. 27

1 ^{ab}) Transp. अपराधः and प्रमादः

3 ^{a}) कामरूपी (for कामचारी)

8 ^{d}) बृंहितान् (for सहि°) [U]

9 ^{b}) तपोनितान् (for तपोधनान्) [Corrupt]

[224] 13 ^{b}) देवराजभयङ्करः

^{c}) भूतानां (for ° देवानां)

14 ^{c}) स्यात् (for अद्य) [$\tilde{N}_3$]

21 ^{d}) देवश्रेष्ठं (for मुनिश्रेष्ठं) [U]

23 ^{a}) सगुणं (for सफलं) [$\tilde{N}_3$]

27 ^{d}) त्रैलोक्यपूजितौ (for ते लोकपू°)

29 ^{a}) एतौ (for एकः)

^{b}) कारयिष्यतः (for °ति)

^{c}) लोकसंभावितौ वीरौ

^{d}) कामवीर्यौ विहंगमौ

Adhy. 28

2 ^{a}) चापि (for चैव)

8 ^{c}) निक्षिपेमां (for विक्षिपे°)

9 ^{d}) अर्दयन् (for आर्द°)

17 ^{d}) युध्यमानमनेकशः

18 Transp. 18^{cd} and 19^{ab}

^{d}) पतगेन (for तपनेन)

20 ^{b}) विनतात्मजः (for °तासुतः)
21 ^{a}) महाबला महावीर्याः

Adhy. 29

1 ^{b}) मरीचिकनकोज्ज्वलः [Ñ$_{3}$ T$_{2}$]
2 ^{d}) क्षुरधारम् (for तीक्ष्णधारम्) [Ñ$_{3}$]
3 ^{a}) ज्वलितार्कप्रभं (for ज्वलनार्क°) [Ñ$_{3}$ B$_{4}$]
^{c}) घोररूपिणमत्यर्थं [Ñ$_{3}$]
4 ^{b}) पर्यावर्तत (for पर्यव°) [U]
^{c}) अनन्तरेण (for अरान्तरेण) [Ñ$_{3}$]
5 ^{c}) महारौद्रौ (for °घोरौ) [U]
6 ^{d}) ददशे (for ददर्श)
11 ^{b}) वीर्यतः (for वीर्यवान्) [D$_{5}$ T$_{2}$]
20 ^{d}) कथंचन (for कदा°)

Adhy. 30

1 सुपर्ण उवाच (for गरुड उ°)
2 ^{b}) सन्तोत्मबलसंस्तवम् [Ñ$_{3}$]
^{c}) यदि (for तव)
15 ^{d}) सत्तमाः (for पन्नगाः) [Ñ$_{3}$]
20 ^{a}) द्विधाकृता (for द्वैधीकृता)

Adhy. 31

4 ^{d}) एव (for तु) [U]
7 ^{a}) नीलानलौ (for नीलानीलौ) [Ñ$_{3}$]
9 ^{a}) निष्ठूरिको (for निष्ठूनको)
^{d}) मुद्गलपिण्डकः (for मुद्गरपि°) [Ñ$_{3}$]
18 ^{b}) अयुतानि (for अर्बुदानि) [Ñ$_{3}$ G$_{4.5}$]

Adhy. 32

1 ^{c}) त्वभिविज्ञाय (for त्वथ वि°)
2 ^{c}) आस्थाय (for आतस्थे) [Ñ$_{3}$ G$_{1}$]
3 ^{b}) तपोधनः (for तपोरतः)
4 ^{d}) नियतेन्द्रियः (for विजिते°) [K$_{2}$ Ñ$_{3}$]
5 ^{c}) प्रशुष्कमांसत्वक्स्नायुं [Ñ$_{3}$ G$_{3}$]
^{d}) जटामुकुटधारिणम् [Ñ$_{3}$]
8 ^{a}) [ऽ]पि (for हि) [Ñ$_{3}$ M$_{1.5}$]
^{b}) प्रायशो (for भ्रातरो) [Ñ$_{3}$]
^{d}) भवता अनुमन्यताम् (for तद्भवाननु°) [Corrupt]

9 ^{c}) आतिष्ठं (for आतिष्ठे)
12 ^{b}) त्यक्ष्यामि (for मोक्ष्यामि) [K$_{1}$ Ñ$_{3}$]
18 पितामह उवाच (for ब्रह्मोवाच)
20 ^{b}) भुजगपतिः (for भूतपतिः) [Ñ$_{3}$]
23 ^{c}) सर्वं (for सर्वा)
24 ^{a}) अन्तर्भूमौ (for अधो भूमेः)

Adhy. 33

3 ^{a}) यथासृष्टो (for यथोद्दिष्टो)
12 ^{a}) Transp. नागाः and तत्र [Ñ$_{3}$]
16 Transp. 16^{cd} and 19^{ab} [U]
19 ^{d}) ब्रह्मवध्यं भविष्यति
21 ^{d}) समन्ततः (for सविद्युतः) [Ñ$_{3}$]
[225] 21 ^{d}) समन्ततः (for सविद्युतः) [Ñ$_{3}$]
27 ^{d}) कृतं कार्यं (for कृतमेवं)

Adhy. 34

9 ^{b}) विषोज्ज्वलाः (for विषोल्बणाः) Here and in 10^{b} [U]
^{d}) वारयितवान् (for निवारितवान्)
12 ^{b}) जनिष्यति (for भविष्यति) [U]

Adhy. 35

4 ^{c}) संस्थाप्य चैव (for समाप्यैव च)
^{d}) उदागमन् (for उपागमन्) [U]
7 ^{c}) अस्य त्वं (for देवेश) [Ñ$_{3}$]
^{d}) इह (for अस्य) [U]

Adhy. 36

7 ^{b}) शीलगुणोपपन्नः (for वीतभयक्लमः सन्) [Ñ$_{1\text{-}3}$]
8 ^{c}) अवरेणासीत् (for इति विख्यातो) [S$_{1}$ K$_{1}$ Ñ$_{3}$]
9 ^{b}) धनुर्धरवरायुधः [U]
13 ^{c}) परिक्षितो नरेन्द्रस्य
16 ^{b}) संशितव्रतः (for °व्रतम्)
22 ^{c}) गृहमेधिना (for गृहमीथिवान्) [Ñ$_{3}$]

Adhy. 37

1 ^{b}) क्षेपसमन्वितः (for कोप°)
4 ^{a}) तात (for तस्य)
5 ^{a}) मृगयायां वै (for मृगयां यातः) [Corrupt]
8 ^{d}) मृतं सर्पं (for सर्पं स्कन्धे) [Ñ$_{3}$ G$_{6}$]

9 ^{a}) तेसौ (for अथासौ)
[Corrupt]
10 ^{a}) एतत् (for एवम्)
25 ^{d}) विभो (for तथा)
26 ^{a}) एत्य (for अद्य)

Adhy. 38

3 ^{b}) तात (for पुत्र)
5 ^{d}) मनीषिणाम् (for महात्मनाम्)
7 ^{b}) आचरन् (for आहरन्)
9 ^{d}) परश्चापि तपस्विनाम्
11 ^{c}) तत्करिष्याम्यहं तात
13 ^{d}) महामनाः (for महातपाः)
[K_1 $G_{1.4.5}$]
22 ^{d}) ब्रह्मन्महामनाः (for राजा महातपाः)
[$\tilde{N}_3$]
27 ^{a}) स (for वै) [$\tilde{N}_3$]
37 ^{e}) त्वरितः (for त्वरितं)

Adhy. 39

1 ^{c}) दग्धम् (for दष्टम्) [$Ko._2$ $\tilde{N}_3$]
3 ^{b}) एवम् (for एनम्) [$\tilde{N}_3$]
12 ^{a}) तद्विषं हत्वा (for यद्विषं हन्या)
[$\tilde{N}_3$]
14 ^{c}) यतमानस्य (for घटमानस्य)
[$\tilde{N}_3$ G_2]
15 ^{d}) इह (for इतो)
16 ^{d}) गृहीत्वा (for गृहाय)
17 ^{d}) निवर्त द्विजसत्तम [$\tilde{N}_3$]
25 ^{c}) तदा (for तथा)
32 ^{d}) तं निवेश्य (for संनि°) [U]
33 ^{b}) अन्ववेष्टितः (for अभिवे°) [D_4]

Adhy. 40

6 ^{b}) समन्त्रिणस्ततः (for समेत्य सर्वे)
7 ^{a}) अग्रमतिः (for आर्यमातेः)
[Corrupt]
10 ^{a}) नगेषु (for वनेषु)
11 ^{c}) Om. वै [U]

Adhy. 41

5 ^{b}) गर्तेषु त्राणम् (for गर्तेऽ*तांस्त्राणम्)
8 ^{d}) ब्रह्मन् (for अस्मिन्)
9 ^{a}) तस्य (for ततो)
13 ^{a}) Transp. तात and तपसः
^{c}) त्वस्मिन् (for ब्रह्मन्)
17 ^{b}) अद्य (for अस्ति) [U]
[226] 23 ^{a}) चैव त्वं (for वै ब्रह्मन्)
25 ^{c}) तपोरतिं (for ° रतं)
27 ^{b}) सहान्वयैः (for पितामहैः)
29 ^{a}) तं (for स)
^{c}) यथावृत्तम् (for °दृष्टम्) [$\tilde{N}_3$]

Adhy. 42

6 ^{c}) सनामां (for सनाम्नीं)
11 ^{b}) अ[illegible]मानि स्थिराणि च
15 ^{a}) सनामा (for सनाम्नी)
18 ^{d}) च स (for स तां)
20 ^{c}) वासुकिं (for वासुके)

Adhy. 43

2 ^{a}) कन्यां (for भार्यां) [$\tilde{N}_{1.3}$]
20 ^{d}) पश्चिमस्यां (for पश्चिमायां)
25 ^{b}) भार्या (for भर्त्रा) [U]
30 ^{d}) चिन्ताशोकसमन्विता
32 ^{c}) Transp. स्थितां and स्थितो [$\tilde{N}_3$]

Adhy. 44

2 ^{cd}) दीनाशयां (for दीनां तदा) [$\tilde{N}_3$]
11 ^{a}) तथा (for कुतो) [$\tilde{N}_3$]
12 ^{c}) मे (for ते)
13 ^{b}) तपोधनः (for तपोवनम्)
14 ^{d}) जगृहे तदा (for प्रत्यगृह्णत) [$\tilde{N}_3$]
19 ^{a}) चीर्णव्रतः (for चरितव्रतः)
21 ^{d}) समन्तात् (for प्रयत्नात्)

Adhy. 45

1 ^{a}) ततो (for तदा)
2 ^{a}) राजा (for ब्रह्मन्) [$\tilde{N}_3$]
^{b}) भूपतेः (for नृपतेः) [$\tilde{N}_3$]
3 ^{a}) जानन्ति हि भतुवन्तः [Corrupt]
11 ^{b}) दृढसक्तः (for दृढविक्रमः)
13 ^{b}) अजीजनत् (for अजायत)
15 ^{f}) सर्पेणाप्यनिवर्तितम् [U]
16 ^{a}) पुरुषव्याघ्र (for °श्रेष्ठ)
^{f}) सर्वभूतानुपालनम् (for °पालकः)
17 ^{b}) प्रियकृत् (for हितकृत्)
18 ^{c}) आचक्ष्व वै (for आचक्षध्वं)
[$\tilde{N}_3$]
22 ^{b}) ततायुधकलापधृक् [K_1 $\tilde{N}_{1.3}$]
^{d}) Transp. मृगं and पिता [U]

Adhy. 46

2 b) महातपाः (for °यशाः)
3 c) स यज्ञाय (for अनुज्ञातो)
f) तदा (for तथा)
7 c) सर्वभूतेषु (for °भूतानां)
11 d) स्वं (for तं) [$\tilde{N}_3$]
14 d) Here and in the sequel कश्यपः (for काश्यपः)
d) उद्यत (for एच्छते [U]
17 c) तथा विपन्नं (for मयाभिपन्नं) [U]
18 c) कं ते (for तेऽथ)
25 a) एनं (for एतं)
26–32 Om.
34 d) नेत्रयोः प्राप तं (for नेत्राभ्यां प्रततं) [$\tilde{N}_3$]
36 b) महात्मने (for दुरात्मने) [S_1 $\tilde{N}_3$ $D_{6\cdot7}$]
38 c) प्रयोगेण (for प्रसादेन)

Adhy. 47

1 c) वै (for स) [$\tilde{N}_{1\cdot3}$ G_6]
3 a) नो (for मे) [S_1 K_1 $\tilde{N}_3$]
4 d) प्राप्स्येयं वै सबान्धवम् [$\tilde{N}_3$]
6 d) परिपठ्यते (for कथ्यते नृप)
7 b) जनाधिप (for नरा°)
8 d) इव (for इति)
10 c) Transp देशं and तं
11 b) द्विजजनायुतम् (for द्विजगणायुतम्)
c) प्रभूतधनधान्यैश्च
[227] 15 f) संस्थाप्यते (for संस्थास्यते)
22 c) रावान् (for नादान्)
24 a) तुरगाः (for इन्दुराः)

Adhy. 48

1 d) पुरुषर्षभाः (for परमर्षयः) [$\tilde{N}_3$]
2 b) तत्र सत्रे (for सर्पसत्रे)
d) भयावहे (for महाभये)
4 a) वर्तयिष्यामि (for कथ°) [$\tilde{N}_3$]
6 b) कौत्स्येयजैमिनिः (for कौत्सार्य°) [$\tilde{N}_3$]
d) बोधिपिङ्गलः (for बोध°)
7 c) कमठकः (for शम°)
8 d) कुणिघटः (for कुटि°)
9 b) वयःस्वाध्यायशीलवान्
c) काहलो (for कहोडो)

d) शमसौरभः (for °सौभरः)
10 d) यज्ञे (for सत्रे) [$\tilde{N}_3$]
12 a) तेषां मेदोवहाः (for वसामे°) [$\tilde{N}_{1\cdot3}$]
18 c) तस्य (for तत्र)
26 b) वृत्तसंमतमं (for वृद्ध°) [Corrupt]

Adhy. 49

4 a) Transp. सा and तस्मै [$\tilde{N}_3$]
5 b) श्रुता (for श्रुतिः)
6 a) उच्चैःश्रवस्याश्वराज्ञो [$\tilde{N}_3$ G_1]
b) कुरुतेह मा (for न कृतो मम)
9 d) एधिवान् (for ईयि°)
12 d) तथा (for इति)
13 पितामह उवाच (for ब्रह्मोवाच)
16 a) न मोघं (for अमोघं)
17 c) दुःखसंप्राप्तं (for °संतप्तं) [U]
18 b) पन्नगेश्वर (for पन्नगोत्तम) [$\tilde{N}_{1\cdot3}$ T_2]
20 d) ज्ञापयिष्ये (for तोषयिष्ये)

Adhy. 50

1 c) भारताय (for °ताग्र्य) Here *et. seq.* in this adhy.
2 b) तथापरं (for °परः)
8 a) सूर्यसमानवर्चसः (for सूर्यहुताश°)
c) अन्यत् (for अद्य)
d) कदाचित् (for कथंचित्)
9 c) महीं (for क्षितिं)
d) सैव (for स्वेषु)
10 b) त्रिश्वकृत् (for °भुक्) [$\tilde{N}_3$]
c) प्रतीतो (for प्रदीप्तो)
12 b) तथा वै (for तथेह) [$\tilde{N}_{1\cdot3}$]
13 a) कद्वाङ्ग°
15 d) व्रतानाम् (for क्रतूनाम्) [$\tilde{N}_3$ M_4]

Adhy. 51

2 सभ्या ऊचुः (for सदस्या ऊचुः)
3 c) वाचं (for वाक्यं) [K_3 $M_{2\cdot4}$]
7 d) प्रसहिष्यति (for प्रदहि°) [U]
8 c) प्रमत्तः प्रजुहाव (for प्र यत्तः स जु°) [$\tilde{N}_3$]
9 b) परितः स्तूयमानः (for परिसंस्तू°)
c) अवगीयमानो (for अनुगम्य°)
d) After विद्याधरैः, ins. च [B_1]

12–15 Transp. 12–13 and 14–15
12 d) नद्गतो (for स्वतो)
15 राजोवाच (for जनमेजय उवाच)
a) बलाभिपन्नाय (for °भिरूपस्य) [Ñ$_3$]
b) तवानुरूपम (for यथानु°)
c) हृदिस्थं (for हृदि स्थितं)
16 b) जातवेदसम् (for °दसि) [K$_2$ Ñ$_3$]
18 d) विप्रं (for इदम्) [Ñ$_{1.3}$]
20 d) च (for नः)
22 a) अन्यत् (for अन्यं) [Ñ$_1$ G$_{1.2}$]

Adhy. 52

4 d) महाबलान् (for विशोल्बणान्) [Ñ$_3$]
[228] 5 b) सदः पालो (for सहः पैलो)
7 d) पिण्डसेक्ता (for °भेत्ता)
8 a) उच्छ्रिरः सूतपो (for उच्छ्रिखः सुरसो) [Ñ$_3$]
c) शिलीशलकणो (for °करो)
10 c) मेदः (for मोदः)
d) प्रमोहः संहताङ्ककः [Ñ$_3$]
11 b) पतिता (for प्रविष्टा)
12 a) एभिलः (for ऐण्डिलः) [Ñ$_{1.3}$]
b) वेणुस्कन्धः (for वेणि°)
c) शृङ्गवेरः (for °वेगः)
15 a) आमाकुठः (for आमाहठः)
b) हवनो (for मानवो) [Ñ$_3$]
c) मण्डवेदाङ्गः (for मुण्ड°)
16 a) नागः (for नाम)
17 b) सुचित्रः (for सुमित्रः)
c) पराशकः (for °शरः) [G$_6$]
d) कोणिस्कन्धः (for मणि°) [Ñ$_3$]
21 c) योजनायुतविस्तारा [Ñ$_{1.3}$]
22 a) कामवला (for कामगमा)

Adhy. 53

1 c) छन्द्यमानो (for °माने)
4 b) महात्मनाम् (for मनीषिणाम्)
cd) न वै संप्रतिभाति स्म येनाग्नौ न पपात सः [Ñ$_3$]
5 d) अभ्युदीरयत् (for अभ्युदैरयत्)
6 a) वितस्थौ (for वितस्थे) [Ko.$_2$]
d) गाञ्चकक्षान्तरा (for गोचकस्यान्तरा) [K$_3$ Ñ$_{1.3}$]

7 b) अभिचोदितः (for चोदितो भृशम्) [U]
18 c) च (for वै)
22 Om. [U]
24 a) तु (for स)
27 b) कीर्तितं (for कथितं)
d) अनेन (for तेन) [U]
28 a) प्रवक्ष्यामि च (for प्रक्ष्यामि चैव)
d) विचक्ष्व (for प्रचक्ष्व)
29 d) तथा कवे (for महाकवे)
30 d) तत्ते विचक्ष्व नः (for त्वं वै विचक्षणः)
34 d) कथ्यते (for सूतज) [Ñ$_3$]
35 a) तेहं प्रवक्ष्यामि (for ते कथयिष्यामि)

Adhy. 54

1 c) अभ्यगच्छत् (for अभ्यागच्छत्)
5 c) धर्मज्ञः (for ब्रह्मर्षिः) [Ñ$_{1.3}$]
d) सत्यः शुचिः प्रभुः (for सत्यव्रतः शुचिः)
13 b) राज्यं (for अर्घ्यं) [K$_{0.2}$ M]
15 b) प्रयत्नात् (for यत्नेन) [Ñ$_3$]
20 d) यथावृत्तं द्विजोत्तम
24 a) Trasp. तस्मै and राज्ञे

Adhy. 55

3 a) श्रोतृपात्रं (for श्रोतुं पात्रं)
b) प्राप्येयं भारतीं शुभाम् [K$_4$ Ñ$_3$]
17–21 For 17—21 (both incl.), subst. 476.* (for v. l. see below)
476* [(L.$_3$) Transp. सहिता and नगरात्
(L.$_4$) मित्रै (for मन्त्री)
(L.$_{11}$) तत्र (for चैव)
(L.$_{12}$) न्यवसन्तु महात्मानो (for प्राद्रवन्भयसंविग्ना)
L.$_{15}$) मात्रा सह परंतपाः (for धार्तराष्ट्रभयार्दिताः)
(L.$_{24}$) पाञ्चालेषु (for पञ्चा°)]
23 f) अभिरोचितः (for अनुचिन्तितः) [Ñ$_3$]
26 a) Transp. तत्र and ते [Ñ$_3$]
30 c) बभौ (for आबभौ) [Ñ$_3$]

31 After 31^{c}, ins. 478*, reading in 31^{d}, सव्यसाचिनं (for वै धनंजयम्).
After 31, ins. 479*.

[229] Adhy. 56

6 ^{a}) नागशतप्राणो (for नागायुत°) [U]
8 Om. [K$_{1\cdot3}$ Ñ$_{1}$]
10 ^{d}) परलोकं (for पितॄ°) [U]
12 In place of 12, ins. 485* [Ñ$_{1}$]
19 ^{c}) महीं चापि जयेत्कृत्स्नां [Ñ$_{3}$]
24 Om. [Ñ$_{1}$]
26 After 26, ins. 494* & 495*
27 Om.
28 ^{a}) इमां (for इदं) [U]
^{d}) ब्रह्म गच्छेत्स शाश्वतम्
29 ^{a}) श्रावयेद्ब्राह्मणान् श्राद्धे
^{b}) यश्चेदं (for ब्राह्मणान्)
^{d}) उपावर्तेत्पितॄनिह
31 ^{d}) समुच्यते (for प्रमुच्यते) [U]
31 After 31, ins. (with v. l.) App. I, No. 33. (om. lines 3–11)

Adhy. 57

1 सदा किल (for स कदाचित्)
3 ^{b}) तपोधनम् (for °रविम्)
^{cd}) देवाः शक्रपुरोगास्ते राजानमुपतस्थिरे
5 देवा ऊचुः (for इन्द्र उवाच)
^{d}) पालयते (for धारयते)
8 ^{c}) धन्यश्च (for सौम्यश्च)
9 ^{d}) भूमिह [?] (for चेदिप) [Corrupt]
12 ^{a}) स्वकर्मस्थाः (for स्वधर्म°)
^{d}) सत्तम (for यद्भवेत्) [U]
14 ^{a}) सर्ववर्णेषु (for °मर्त्येषु) [Ñ$_{3}$]
16 ^{a}) लोकानाञ्च तद् (for लक्षणं चैतद्)
17 ^{c}) इष्टप्रमागम् (for °प्रदानम्)
18 ^{b}) भूयः (for भूमौ) [U]
20 ^{a}) तस्याः (for चास्याः)
24 ^{c}) तस्य (for तथा)
26 ^{b}) जनाः (for नराः)
^{e}) नरा दानमहायज्ञैः (for वरदान°) [Ñ$_{3}$ B$_{6}$ m]

27 ^{f}) च सः (for वसुः)
29 ^{e}) माचेल्लः (for मच्छिल्लः) [K$_{2\cdot3}$ B$_{1\cdot6}$ D$_{5}$]
31 ^{f}) परिश्रुतम् (for [अ] थ विश्रुतम्) [Ñ$_{3}$]
34 ^{b}) पर्वतद्वयम् (for पर्वतः स्वयम्) [T$_{1}$ G$_{1\cdot3}$]
41 ^{d}) तेजसः (for रेतसः)
42 ^{b}) च (for सः)
^{c}) आशु (for अथ)
45 ^{d}) आमिषकाङ्क्षया (for °शङ्कया) [Ñ$_{3}$]
49 ^{f}) स्त्रीपुमांसौ स्म मानुषौ [Ñ$_{3}$]
52 ^{ef}) जनयिष्यत्यपत्यन्तु स्त्रीपुमांसौ तु भामिनी [Ñ$_{3}$]
53 ^{a}) अतः (for ततः) [D$_{5}$]
^{d}) वै (for च) [U]
54 ^{e}) सत्त्वरूपसमायुक्ता [K$_{3}$ Ñ$_{3}$ M$_{5}$]
55 ^{a}) गन्धवती (for सत्यवती) [Ñ$_{3}$]
58 ^{b}) पारावारम् (for पारावारे)
59 ^{a}) तदा स (for तयोक्तः) [Ñ$_{3}$]
60 ^{c}) विस्मितार्थाभवत् (for °ता चाब्रवीत्) [Corrupt]
62 ^{c}) गृहं गन्तुं मुदा (for गन्तुं गृहं गृहे)
68 ^{a}) अतः (for ततः)
^{b}) प्रतिष्ठितम् (for परिश्रुतम्) [U]
73 ^{b}) अनुग्रहकाङ्क्षया (for °काम्यया)
77 ^{c}) आणीमण्डव्यः (for अणी°)
81 ^{d}) अकिल्बिषः (for °ल्बिषी) [U]
84 ^{b}) कर्ता हर्ता जगत्प्रभुः [Ñ$_{3}$]
86 ^{c}) दिव्यं (for नित्यं)
87 ^{b}) सर्वलोकपितामहः [Ñ$_{3}$ G$_{1\cdot3}$]
^{c}) धर्मसंस्थापनार्थाय
88 ^{f}) अर्थविदावुभौ (for अस्त्रविशारदौ)
[230] 89 ^{ab}) Transp. स्कन्नं and द्रोण्यां) [Ñ$_{3}$]
91 ^{d}) पञ्चाल्पात् (for पावकात्) [Corrupt]
93 ^{d}) देवप्रकोपनी (for °पनात्) [U]
101 ^{d}) सर्वशास्त्रविशारदाः
103 ^{d}) ततो (for वने) [U]
106 ^{b}) सर्वतः (for सर्वशः)
^{f}) कृतम् (for ततम्) [Ñ$_{3}$ G$_{1\cdot2}$]

Adhy. 58

1 c) ज्ञातुम् (for श्रोतुम्)
2 b) महौजसः (for महारथाः) [Ñ₃]
10 f) शतशो (for सर्वशो)
11 d) सशैलवनपत्तनाम्
13 a) कामक्रोधभवान् (for °क्रोदोद्भवान्) [Ñ₃]
b) जनाधिपाः (for नरा°)
21 c) अनुवर्तन्तः (for °पश्यन्तः) [U]
22 a) स्वधर्मनिरताः (for स्वकर्म°)
27 b) पुनः पुनः (for मनस्विनः) [Ñ₃]
28 b) खरोष्ट्रमानुषेषु (for °ष्ट्रमहिषेषु)
29 c) तदा (for आत्मना) [Ñ₃ D₄ G₃]
30 b) बलमदान्विताः (for बलसमन्विताः) [Ñ₃ B₃ Da]
d) देवलोकात् (for तस्माल्लोकात्)
32 b) प्रपीडयन् (for अप्यपीडयन्)
33 c) सर्वशः (for सर्वतः)
34 d) बलमदेन (for मदबलेन)
41 a) तस्याः प्रसादार्थं तदा [Ñ₃]
42 c) सर्वेषाम् (for लोकानाम्) [Ñ₃ G₆]
45 c) ततो देवान् (for तदा सर्वान्) [U]
46 d) सर्वशः (for चाब्रवीत्) [Ñ₃]

Adhy. 59

7 a) देवानां दानवानां च
d) [अ] हं (for वै)
11 b) Transp. इमाः and प्रजाः
12 b) दनायुः (for अनायुः)
c) प्रधा (for प्रावा)
16 c) जघन्य (read °न्यो) यः (for जघन्यजः)
25 a) इश्वपा (for इसृपा)
b) विरूपाक्षहरावुभौ [Ñ₃]
d) कुपटा कपदास्तथा [Ñ₃]
27 a) Transp. वंशे and प्रथिताः
c) दनुपुत्रास्तदा राजन् [Ñ₃]
29 a) गवेष्ठः (for गविष्ठः) [Ñ₃]
30 a) सिंही तु (for सिंहिका) [Ñ₃]
31 b) पुत्रपौत्रादि (for °पौत्रम्) [Ñ₃]
36 b) म (?भ) द्रकर्मिणौ (for मन्मक°) [Corrupt]
37 b) कल्पितस्ते तपस्विनाम्
c) Transp. असुराणां and सुराणां

38 d) गुणाद्भूतम् (for गुणभूतम्)
40 c) कुलकः (for कुलिकः) [G₁₋₂]
41 d) तथाष्टमः (for च सप्तमः) [U]
43 c) तेषां (for चैव)
44 a) अतः प्रभूतानि (for अतस्तु भू°) [Ñ₃ B₁]
d) असुरां मार्गणां (for अमूनामरुणां) [B₁ Da]
e) अन्येषां सुभगा वासाम्
f) प्रावी (for प्रावा)
47 c) प्रसूताहि (for प्रावासूत) [Ñ₃]
48 b) विद्युत्कर्णां (for विद्युत्पर्णा) [Ñ₃]
52 ab) Om. [U]
54 b) ब्राह्मणवैद्यसंनिधौ (for °देवसं°)
c) Transp. लभते and स
d) मतिं (for यशः)

Adhy. 60

1 d) परमतेजसः (for °मानसाः) [U]
3 a) वाह्नोऽपुष्कलः (for दहनोऽथेश्वरः)
[231] 4 a) मरीचिराङ्गराथीत्रिः
5 d) धृष्णश्चेति (for संवर्तश्च) [Ñ₃]
6 a) अत्रेः पुत्रास्तु बहवः
12 a) Transp. ददौ and स [Ñ₃]
13 b) निबोधत (for °ध मे) [U]
d) Transp. क्रिया and तथा
15 d) धर्मपत्न्यः (for सोम°)
f) स्मृताः (for स्थिताः) [Ñ₃ D₅]
17 b) Transp. अनिलः and अनलः
d) नामभिः (for अष्टाविति) [Ñ₃]
31 d) लोकधारणाः (for °धारिणः) [Da D₃]
40 c) कवि ऋषि [:] (for कविर्विद्वान्)
d) त्वृषिसुतो (for कवि°) [Ñ₃]
42 c) चैव (for चापि) [Ñ₃]
43 d) अनिन्दितः (for °न्दितम्)
51 d) सुताश्चासुरनन्दिनीम्
53 After 53, ins. 549* (transp. भार्या and पुत्रो)
54 b) धृतराष्ट्रीमथो (for °ष्ट्री तथा)
55 d) नराधिप (for जनाधिप) [K₁ Ñ₃ B₃₋₅]
56 d) [अ] पि (for तु)
57 b) शुकानेवमनुव्रता [Ñ₃]

c) कल्याणगुणसंपूर्णा [U]
58 b) अथ (for अपि) [Ñ$_3$]
d) हरिभद्रां मनामपि) [Ñ$_3$]
60 d) सुमराश्च परंतप
61 a) नाम (for नागं)
c) ऐरावणः (for °वतः) [S$_1$ K$_1$ Ñ$_3$]
64 c) दिशां गजांस्तु श्वेता च
d) श्वेतां जनयदाशुगाम्
65 b) सुरसा (for सुरभिः)
66 ab) Reads 66^{ab} after 67
b) कद्रुः पन्नगसत्तमान् [Ñ$_3$]
f) तथा (for सुता) [Ñ$_3$ V$_1$ Da]

Adhy. 61

2 a) चारितं (for तत्त्वेन) [Ñ$_3$]
4 b) पुरुषर्षभः (for दानवर्षभः)
7 d) बभूव नरेश्वरः (for आसीन्मनुजेश्वरः)
7 d) मनुजेष्विह (for मनुजेश्वरः) [Ñ$_3$]
12 d) स जज्ञे पुरुषर्षभः
13 b) जघन्यस्तु (for श्रीमान्यस्तु) [Ñ$_3$]
16 d) Om. सः
18 d) Om. सः
19 a) राजा (for राजन्)
21 d) संख्यातविक्रमः (for विख्या°)
24 c) सुवस्तुः (for सुवास्तुः) [Ñ$_3$]
25 a) सुरेहः (for अहरः) [Ñ$_3$]
30 d) बभूवर्षिकसत्तमः [U]
32 c) द्रुम इत्यभिविख्यातः [U]
34 a) सुवर्णः (for सुपर्णः) [U]
c) क्रोडीकीर्तिः (for कालकीर्तिः) [U]
36 b) [ऽ]सुरो मया (for महासुरः) [K$_{0\cdot1\cdot3}$]
39 a) दनायुषः (for अना°)
41 a) वीर इत्यभिविख्यातः
c) पौण्ड्रभक्षकः (for °मत्स्यकः) [U]
45 a) कालेयानां (for कालकायाः)
48 c) निषधाधिपतिः (for निषादाधि°)
53 b) नराधिपः (for परंतपः)
c) राजा (for राजन्)
54 b) राजेन्द्र कीर्तितः (for राजन्प्रकी°) [U]
55 b) कीचकः (for कीटकः) [Ñ$_3$]
56 d) नाम यः (for नामतः) [U]
57 b) पार्थिवः (for नामतः) [U]
58 d) वादधारो (for वाधटानो)
59 a) करूषकाः (for कारू°)
c) उद्धृतः (for उद्धवः)
61 a) एष (for एव)
64 d) स जज्ञे (for संजज्ञे)
[232] 69 d) °भयंकरः
78 e) दोषेण वै (for दोषाद्वेषः) [Ñ$_3$]
79 Reads 79 after 81
a) सुमहान्पुत्रात् (for °हाभागं) [Corrupt]
b) वरात् (for वरम्) [U]
80 b) स वै (for भुवि) [Ñ$_3$]
81 e) महद्दीप्तं (for समुद्दीप्तं) [U]
86 c) स संजज्ञे (for बृहत्कीर्तिः) [K$_3$ Ñ$_3$ V$_1$ D$_5$]
d) फाल्गुनस्यात्मजो वशी
87 a) अंशात् (for अंशं)
96 a) नातिदीर्घा न च ह्रस्वा [Ñ$_3$]

Adhy. 62

10 b) रसवन्ति (for फल°)
11 d) सवनकिन्नरम् (for °काननम्) [U]

Adhy. 63

2 a) खड्गचापधारैः (for खड्गशक्ति°) [Ñ$_3$ M$_{3\text{-}5}$]
d) नागशतैः (for योधशतैः) [Ñ$_3$]
6 d) वज्रपाणि (for शक्र°)
18 b) गदामुसलकंपनैः
19 d) स्म (for च)
23 b) समेभ्यन्तु (for समिध्य च) [U]

Adhy. 64

2 d) महादीरिणम् (for महदी°) [U]
3 c) मतिप्रह्लादजननं [Ñ$_3$]
5 c) षट्पदाघूर्णिततलं
7 a) हृष्टैः (for पुष्पैः)
8 a) मारुताघट्टिताः (for °तागलिताः) [Ñ$_3$]
b) कुसुमशालिनः (for °शालिनः)
c) तु (for स्म)
19 b) प्रत्यपूजयन् (for प्रत्यपद्यत)
20–22 Stanzas 20–22 are ins. on the margin.

21 b) फेनपुष्पप्रवाहिनीम्
23 a) After नदीम्, ins. च [U]
b) तत्र (for दृष्ट्वा) [T_1 G_6]
25 a) स तं (for तस्य) [$\tilde{N}_3$]
26 b) पदातिजनसंकुलाम्
29 d) आश्रममण्डलम् (for °ममुत्तमम्)
30 d) नानाद्विजगणैर्युतम् [U]
34 b) क्रमानपि (for अपरैर्द्विजैः) [$\tilde{N}_3$]
35 cd) Transp.(-तत्त्वार्थ-and-विज्ञान) [U]
36 d) मोक्षशास्त्रविशारदैः [$\tilde{N}_3$]

Adhy. 65

1 c) After नापश्यत्, ins च
4 d) प्रतिपूजयन् (for °पूज्य च)
[K_4 $\tilde{N}_3$]
5 b) ह (for हि)
c) अनन्तरं (for अनामयं) [$\tilde{N}_3$]
6 b) तथा (for तदा)
9 d) द्रष्टासि (for द्रक्ष्यसे)
12 a) का त्वं कस्य च (for कासि कस्यसि)
13 c) तेहं विज्ञातुं (for त्वामहं ज्ञातुं)
[$\tilde{N}_3$]
21 b) मा (for मां)
36 d) आवर्तयेत मा (for °येत्तथा) [U]
37 d) जितेन्द्रियमतिं स्पृशेत् [K_1 $\tilde{N}_3$]
41 b) राजन् (for देव) [$\tilde{N}_3$]
d) भो (for देव) [$\tilde{N}_3$]

Adhy. 66

1 c) ततः (for तदा)
4 b) आभिलक्ष्यघनी (for °लिङ्गती)
[$\tilde{N}_3$]
After 4, ins. 601*
[233] 5 a) लुब्धां वाससि संसक्तां
6 a) रूपगुणान् (for °गुणं)
10 c) शकुन्ताः (for शकुनाः)
12 c) शून्ये (for [ऽ]रण्ये) [$\tilde{N}_3$]
13 d) धर्मसाधने (for °निश्चये)
14 a) [?इ]यं (for च) [K_4]
16 d) मनुजेश्वर (for मनुजाधिप) [$\tilde{N}_3$]

Adhy. 67

2 a) सुवर्णमालां (for °माला)
4 a) मे (for मां) [$\tilde{N}_3$]
b) एष (for एहि)
c) वामोरु (for रम्भोरु) [U]
12 a) First च om. [$\tilde{N}V_1$]
13 b) Transp. धर्म्यौ and तौ [$\tilde{N}_3$]
15 d) नृप (for प्रभो) [$\tilde{N}_3$]
16 a) सर्वं (for सत्यं) [U]
b) याचामि (for वक्ष्यामि)
17 b) ब्रवीमि ते (for ब्रवीहि मे)
d) संगतं (for संगमः) [T_2 $G_{4,5}$]
18 c) विनेष्यामि (for नयिष्यामि) [$\tilde{N}_3$]
20 f) Transp. निवासं and स्वं
[$K\tilde{N}_3$ D_5]
24 a) Transp. च and तां
27 b) पुरुषेश्वरः (for पुरुषोत्तमः)
c) अध्यगच्छः (for अभ्यगच्छः)
[$K_{1\cdot2}$]
28 c) स (for यः)
29 b) Transp. चक्रे and तस्य [U]
30 a) तं (for सा) [U]
c) निधाय काये कान्तन्तु [U]
33 d) दुःषन्तप्रियकाम्यया [$\tilde{N}_3$]

Adhy. 68

5 c) Transp. व्याघ्रान् and सिंहान्
6 b) समीपतः (for समन्ततः)
9 b) अपि (for अस्य) [K_2]
10 f) सर्वलक्षणसंयुताम् [$\tilde{N}_3$ D_6]
11 d) गच्छत (for नयत) [$\tilde{N}_3$]
12 d) सहपुत्रां गजाह्वयम् [$\tilde{N}_3$]
16 b) परन्तपः (for सुरोपमः)
20 d) स्थाण्विवनिच [?श्च] ला (for
स्थाणुरिवाचला)
23 d) राजानम् (for वचनम्)
24 a) नाम (for अपि) [$\tilde{N}_3$]
b) किन्तु देवं (for कस्मादेव) [$\tilde{N}_3$]
25 a) तत्र (for अत्र)
c) कल्याणं बत साक्षीणा (?) (for
कल्याण* बत साक्षी त्वं)
27 b) वेत्थ (for वेत्सि) [U]
30 d) हेतुज्ञो (for क्षेत्रज्ञो) [U]
31 d) वियातयति (for नियति°)
32 a) अन्यथा (for आत्मना) [$\tilde{N}_3$]
37 b) सदपत्यं (for तद°)
38 d) पूर्वमेव (for स्वय°)
40 d) मूलन्तारिष्यतः (for मित्रं मरि°)
43 b) जनस्याध्वनि वर्तते

c) विश्वस्यः (for विश्वास्यः)
50 a) स्वां रामां (for रामाणां) [$\tilde{N}_3$]
d) हि (for च)
51 d) रामा ऋते (for रामामृते) [S_1K_1]
53 a) इमं प्रासं (for अनुप्रासं) [U]
54 a) विश्रतः (for विश्रति) [$\acute{S}_1$ K_1 $B_{1m \cdot 4-5}$]
55 b) तथाविधः (for तथा सुखः)
57 d) भुवि (for लोके) [$\tilde{N}_3$]
60 a) वाहुना स्वाङ्कम् (for ननु नामाङ्कम्) [$\tilde{N}_3$]
61 c) जातकर्मसु (for °र्मणि) [S_1 K $\tilde{N}_3$ D_5]
62 d) शरदां (for शरदः)
66 c) वाला (for राजन्) [U]
67 a) विप्रचित्तिः (for पूर्वचित्तिः)
68 a) एतासां (for तासां मां) [$\tilde{N}_3$]
75 b) Transp. च ते and पिता
d) प्रभावसि (for [अ] भिधास्यसि)
77 a) स चैव (for सदैव)
{234} 78 b) बालोऽतिबलवान् (for बालोऽपि ब°)
79 d) त्वं मेनका (for मेनकया) [U]

Adhy. 69

2 a) त्रिदशांश्चापि (for त्रिदशेष्वेव) [$\tilde{N}_3$]
b) अपि (for अनु) [$\tilde{N}_3$]
6 d) रूपवत्तमम् (for °त्तरम्)
14 a) ततः (for अतः)
c) दुर्जनम् (for दुर्जनः)
18 b) विसर्जितान् (for विवर्धितान्) [U]
19 b) कीर्तिवर्धनाः (for प्रीतिव°) [U]
20 f) त्वमावोढुम् (for वोढुं त्वमिह) [U]
28 a) एवमुक्त्वा तु (for एतावदुक्त्वा) [$\tilde{N}_3$]
29 a) भर्ता माता पिता (for भस्त्रा माता पितुः)
30 a) रेतोधः (for रेतोधाः)
cd) आहितोयं त्वया गर्भो मावमंस्थाः शकुन्तलाम् [$\tilde{N}_3$]
35 a) अपि (for अस्य)
c) चाप्येवमेवैतत् (for अप्येवमेवैनं)
d) आत्मना (for आत्मजम्) [$\acute{S}_1$ K_1 D_5]

37 After 37, ins. 678*
38 c) विप्रेन्द्रैः (for विप्रैश्च) [U]
40 b) मे (for वै) [D_5]
41 a) मन्यतैव हि (for मन्यते चैव) [$K_{0\cdot1}$ D_5]
42 d) Transp. क्षान्तं and ते [D_5]
45 c) अजरं (for अजितं) [$\tilde{N}_3$]
46 d) प्राप्य (for प्राप)
48 c) गोविमतं (for गोविततं) [$K_{0\cdot2}$ D_{a1}]
49 c) तु (for च) [U]
d) भरता (for भारता)
51 c) यथामुख्यान् (for °मुख्यं)
d) भारतान् (for भारत) [$\tilde{N}_3$]

Adhy. 70

2 b) कौरवाणां (for पौर°)
3 c) प्राचेतसः (for प्रचे°)
5 d) संश्रितः सुतान् (for संशितव्रतान्) [U]
7 b) पुत्रिकात्वे (for पुत्रिका) [S_1 $K_{0\cdot1}$]
8 d) सप्तविंशतिम् (for सप्तविं°)
9 c) मरीचं (for मारीचः) [U]
d) अदित्यां (for आदित्यान्)
11 d) यतः (for ततः) [$\tilde{N}_3$]
e) ब्रह्मक्षत्रादयो यस्मात् [U]
12 b) संहितम् (for संगतम्)
14 c) नाभागादिष्टदशमान् [K_2]
20 a) सर्विभिः संक्रुद्धैः (for महर्षिभिः क्रुद्धैः)
c) बलमदात् (for मदबलात्)
22 c) शतायुश्च (for वनायुश्च) [$\tilde{N}_3$ $G_{4\cdot6}$]
23 b) रजरं यमनेनसं [$\tilde{N}_3$]
28 b) पाञ्चिम् (for पाञ्चम्)
36 c) स [?सा] ह्यं (for कार्यं)
40 a) त तस्य न (for न ते तस्य) [$\tilde{N}_3$]
41 c) तवादाय (for समास्थाय) [K$\tilde{N}_{1\cdot3}$ D_5]
46 b) ह (for च) [K_0 D_a]

Adhy. 71

2 b) त्वया द्विज (for द्विजोत्तम) [$\tilde{N}_3$]
d) राज्ञो वंशकरान् (for पूरोर्वंश°)
6 c) पौरोहित्याय (for °हित्येन)

8 c) Transp. न and तान्
10 a) ते[ऽ]थ (for ते तु)
12 a) तु (for स)
d) Transp. न and स [D_3 G_3]
13 b) मुनिम् (for कविम्) [$\tilde{N}_3$ D_5 G_1]
[235] 16 d) वचनमब्रवीत् (for वाक्यमुवाच ह) [$\tilde{N}_{1\text{-}3}$]
17 c) कथम् (for कचः)
d) मे (for मां) [U]
18 b) परवान् (for परमं)
c) अनुजानीस्व (for °मन्यस्व) [U]
20 d) काव्येन (for शुक्रेण) [$\tilde{N}_3$]
21 b) वै गृहीतवान् (for प्रत्यगृह्णत) [$\tilde{N}_{1\text{-}3}$]
24 b) नियतव्रतचारिणम्
26 f) शकलीकृतम (for तिलशः कृतम) [$\tilde{N}_3$]
28 d) चैव (for तात) [$\tilde{N}_3$]
30 a) शक्ष्याप्य (for शक्येन)
b) तम् (for अहम्)
31 b) प्रयुक्का [? read क्त्वा] (for प्रयुज्य)
32 c) कचो (for ततो)
34 b) Transp. वाक्यं and पितरम्
36 a) एनं (for एवं) [D_5]
After 36^{ab}, ins. 708* (with v. l.)
c) सुरद्विषश्चैव (for सुराश्च विश्वे च)
d) उपस्थाने सन्नमति प्रभावात्
After 36, ins. 709* (with v. l.)
37 b) तपोनिधिः पिता (for पिता तपोधनः) [$\tilde{N}_3$]
38 After 38, ins. 710*
39 b) शिष्या नागताम्सूषयन्ति (for शिष्यं नागतं सूचयन्ति) [$\tilde{N}_3$]
40 Om.
43 c) आसुरीं स्वश्च मायां (for आसुरी चैव माया)
48 c) अवेक्ष्यैषा (for समीक्षेथा) [U]
52 b) चैवमवाप्य घोरं (for चैव तथाविधोरं) [$\tilde{N}_3$]
56 c) दैवविमूढभावात् (for °बुद्धीन्) [$\tilde{N}_3$]
58 b) पक्ष (for दक्ष) [U]
d) त्रिदिवालयम् (for त्रिदशालयम्) [K_2 $\tilde{N}_3$]

Adhy. 72

1 b) निसृष्टं गुरुणा तथा [U]
3 d) Transp. भूयो and मम
5 b) त्वं ज्ञातुमर्हसि (for भजितु°) [$\tilde{N}_3$]
8 c) निबोध (for तथैव) [$\tilde{N}_3$]
9 a) मे पुत्रो (for पुत्रो वै) [$\tilde{N}_3$]
10 a) हन्यमानेन (for °ने च) [U]
b) त्वया कच (for कच त्वयि) [U]
11 a) सौहार्देनानुरागेण (for ° र्दे चानुरागे च) [U]
12 b) शुभव्रतम् (for °व्रते) [U]
c) Transp. त्वं and मह्यं [$\acute{S}_1$ $K_{0\text{-}2}$ D_5]
20 a) च (for न)
b) नेति यथात्थ (for यत्त्वं मामात्थ)
21 c) क्षिप्रं (for शीघ्रं) [$\tilde{N}_3$]
d) द्विजपुङ्गव (for °सत्तमः)
22 d) मुदा युताः (for मुदान्विताः) [U]
23 d) भागभाक्च (for °भाङ्नौ)

Adhy. 73

8 a) वक्षं त्वं (for मे वक्षं)
18 a) हि (for [अ] सि)
d) सत्यं (for सर्वं)
19 d) Transp. स and न [$\tilde{N}_3$]
21 a) संभ्रान्तं (for संशान्तं)
25 a) प्रत्वरितं (for वै त्व°) [M]
26 c) महाभ्रमन् (for °भाग) [$\tilde{N}_3$]
30 a) वास्तु वा मा वा (for मेऽस्तु वा मास्तु)
36 d) ईश्वरं (for ऐश्वरं) [Cd]

[236] Adhy. 74

3 b) नियच्छति (for निरस्यति) [$K_{0.2\text{-}4}$ $\tilde{N}_3$]
8 d) चातिबलाबलम् (for चापि ब°)
11 a) अभिनन्दति (for अभिभाषन्ति)
After 11, ins. 750* (with v. l. as in K)

Adhy. 75

6 [c]) Transp. धर्मश्च and सत्यं च [$\tilde{N}_3$ B_5 G_3]
7 [a]) अवहाय (for अपहाय)
[d]) After अन्यद्, ins नः [KD_5]
10 [c]) च (for वा)
11 [a]) यदस्ति किंचिद्द्रविणं [$\tilde{N}_3$]
[c]) चेत् (for ते)
14 [b]) शर्मिष्ठाम्प्रतिकामये [U]
[d]) दद्यास्त्व (for दास्यति)
18 [a]) Transp. सा and यं
20 [c]) त्वामनुयास्यामि (for त्वां तत्र या°) [$\tilde{N}_3$]

Adhy. 76

12 [c]) को नाम (for किंनामा)
13 [ab]) Transp. कृत्स्नः and मे वेदः [$\tilde{N}_3$ D_5]
15 [d]) माम् (for तन्मा) [$\tilde{N}_3$]
18 [c]) After ऋषिश्च, ins. अपि
19 [a]) एकभावोऽभवा (for एकदेहोऽभवा) [$\tilde{N}_3$]
25 [d]) विषहामि (for विवहामि) [$K_{1\cdot2}$ M_5 Cd Arj. (comm.)]
26 [a]) भजस्व तस्मान्मा (for वहस्व पित्रा मां) [$\tilde{N}_3$]
[b]) पित्रा (for त्वं हि)
29 [d]) Transp. नान्यं and लोके
32 [b]) वरये वरम (for वरयस्व यथा)
[c]) तस्मिन् (for अस्मिन्)
33 [d]) समवाप्नुहि (for °वाप्स्यसि)

Adhy. 77

16 [a]) अनृतं (for वचनं)
[c]) सर्वधनातिपाते (for °नापहारे) [M]
18 [d]) वक्तुम् (for कर्तुम्)
25 [a]) स (for च)

Adhy. 78

1 [a]) सा (for तु) [$\tilde{N}_3$]
3 [a]) अभ्यागमत् (for °गतः)
[b]) वेदवेदाङ्गपारगः (for धर्मात्मा वेदपा°) [$\tilde{N}_3$]
5 [d]) श्रोतुम् (for वेत्तुम्) [$\tilde{N}_3$ D_5]
6 [b]) Transp. रविं and यथा
[d]) Transp. शक्तिः and नासीत् [$\tilde{N}_3$]
8 [b]) संप्रधाय (for °हस्य)
11 [d]) जगाम हरितं वनम्
14 [a]) प्रसूत (for वि°)
15 [d]) ताम् (for तस्य) [U]
18 [d]) मे (for किम्)
20 [a]) भर्ता (for राजा)
23 [c]) त्वरितां (for °तं)
25 [a]) च (for तु)
28 [c]) मयि (for मम) [K_4 $\tilde{N}_3$]
30 [b]) स्वयम् (for प्रियम्)
32 [a]) यो (for वै) [$K_{0\cdot3}$ $\tilde{N}_3$ D_5]
35 [b]) मत्त्य° (for मद°)
[c]) मिथ्यावृत्तस्य (for ° चारस्य) [U]
36 [b]) नहुषात्मजः (for नाहुषस्तदा) [$\tilde{N}_3$ D_5 G_3]
37 [d]) न (for मा)

Adhy. 79

4 [a]) सहस्रवर्षाणां (for वर्षसहस्रे तु)
6 [b]) स्वयौवनैः (for स यौ°) [D_4 G_3]
[237] [c]) तात (for चैव) [$\tilde{N}_3$]
[d]) तज्जराहं न कामये [$\tilde{N}_3$]
7 [d]) Transp. ते and वै
9 [a]) ते (for तु) [K_1 $\tilde{N}_3$]
[b]) प्रतिदास्यामि (for पुनर्दास्यामि)
[c]) प्रतिपद्येहं (for प्रतिपत्स्यामि) [U]
10 [a]) Transp. कामये and जरां
16 [a]) ते (for तु) [$\acute{S}_1$ $\tilde{N}_3$]
[c]) दत्त्वा त्वं प्रतिपत्स्यामि [$\tilde{N}_3$]
17 [d]) जरायां न कामये (for जरां नाभिका°)
19 [a]) नोडुपप्लवसंतारो [$\acute{S}_1$ $K_{0\cdot1}$]
[d]) प्राप्स्यसि (for [अ] वाप्स्यसि) [$K_{2\cdot4}$ $\tilde{N}_3$ Dn]
21 [d]) तज्जरायां न कामये [U]
22 [d]) तत् (for त्वं) [U]
24 [a]) वरः (for प्रियः) [$\tilde{N}_3$]
25 [c]) किञ्चित्कालं (for कंचित्कालं)
30 [a]) पुत्र (for वत्स)
[b]) ददानि (for ददामि)

Adhy. 80

1 [a]) रूपेण (for वयसा) [$\tilde{N}_3$]

^{b}) वयसा (for ययातिः) [$\tilde{N}_3$]
2 ^{d}) इ (for हि) [$\tilde{N}_3$ B_4 D_5]
10 ^{c}) च मे (for चैव)
11 ^{a}) राजन् (for राजा) [D_5]
12 ^{a}) तु नृपं (for नृपतिं) [$\acute{S}_1$ K_1 D_5]
20 ^{a}) तु (for मे)

Adhy. 81

2 ^{d}) यदा (for यथा) [$\tilde{N}_3$]
3 ^{a}) स्वर्गवासं (for सुरवासं [$\tilde{N}_3$]
8 ^{b}) पुण्य° (for सत्य°) [U]
9 ^{d}) सर्वपापप्रमोचनीम्
13 ^{a}) पूजयश्चित्यं (for पूजयामास)
15 ^{d}) पुनः (for नृपः)

Adhy. 82

4 ^{d}) कथयस्व राजन् (for कथयेह सत्यम्) [$\tilde{N}_3$]
5 ^{c}) ते राजन् (for त्वं राजा) [U]
11 ^{c}) नाममर्मसु ते (for वा मर्मसु ये)
12 ^{a}) नास्तीदृशं संवदनं

Adhy. 83

2 ^{b}) गन्धर्वेषु पतत्रिषु (for गन्धर्वमहर्षिषु)
3 ^{a}) यदभ्यमंस्थाः (for यदावमंस्थाः)
^{d}) पतितोसि (for पातितासि)
11 ^{a}) च (for तु)
^{b}) चैवेन्द्रसमानरूप (for देवे°)
13 ^{d}) साधुः सदा गतिः (for चाभ्यागतः प्रभुः) [$\tilde{N}_3$ B_3 D_a]

Adhy. 84

2 ^{b}) युञ्जे (for प्रयुञ्जे) [$\tilde{N}_3$ $B_{3.4}$]
3 ^{b}) नाभ्यवादः कथंचन (for नाभ्यवदः कथंचित्) [$\tilde{N}_3$]
^{c}) यश्च (for *सन्त्स) [$\tilde{N}_3$]
4 ^{b}) पारलोक्यम् (for पापलोक्यम्)
^{c}) सन्तः सतां (for सन्तोऽसतां)
5 ^{a}) गतन्तत् (for महद्वै)
14 ^{b}) शतयोजनान्ताम् (for °नायताम्) [$K_{0.3}$ $\tilde{N}_3$ G_{4-6}]
15 ^{a}) अमरं (for अजरं) [$\tilde{N}_3$]
^{b}) दुरासदम् (for दुरापम्) [$\tilde{N}_3$]
17 ^{a}) अथ (for तथा) [D_5 G_1]
^{d}) पुण्यान् (for पश्यन्) [U]
19 ^{b}) गगनात् (for नन्दनात्) [$\tilde{N}_3$]
^{d}) अनुक्रोशतां (for अनुक्रोशात्) [U]

Adhy. 85

1 ^{a}) यदा वसन् (for °वसो)
[238] 3 ^{a}) तत्र (for तस्मिन्)
5 ^{a}) नरेन्द्र (for नरेण)
6 ^{a}) तुदत् (for तु तान्)
^{d}) भौमं ह्यनन्तं (for न भौममन्यं) [$\tilde{N}_3$]
7 ^{a}) ब्राह्मणो (for कर्मणो)
8 ^{c}) प्रपतन्तः (for °ततः)
^{d}) दीप्तदंष्ट्राः (for तीक्ष्णदंष्ट्राः) [U]
9 ^{b}) रौद्रा (for भौमा) [U]
10 ^{b}) तद्वत् (for तद्वै) [M]
14 ^{d}) क्षणेन (fos क्रमेण) [U]
16 ^{c}) उपहितं (for उपचितिं)
17 ^{b}) निकृष्यते (for निघृष्यते)
^{d}) नात्मानं वेदयते (for केनात्मानं चेतयते) [$\tilde{N}_3$]
19 ^{b}) भजन्ते (for व्रजन्ति) [$\acute{S}_1$ K_1 $\tilde{N}_3$ G_3]
27 ^{c}) तस्मः श्रेयः (for तास्मिःश्रेयः)
^{d}) प्राप्नुते (for प्राप्नुयुः)

Adhy. 86

5 ^{a}) त्यगृहश्च राजन् (for *नगृहश्च नित्यं)
11 ^{a}) ग्राम्यान् (for ग्राम्यम्)
12 ^{ab}) After अनिकेतश्च ins. अपि
13 ^{c}) हि (for [अ]स्य) [U]
15 ^{b}) तथा (for सदा) [$\tilde{N}_3$]

Adhy. 87

2 ^{a}) अनिकेतं (for °केतो)
^{b}) संयतम् (for संयतः)
^{d}) एकतरं (for पूर्वतरं) [$\tilde{N}_3$]
3 ^{d}) अन्यं (for सोऽन्यत्) [$\tilde{N}_3$]
4 ^{a}) असत्यम् (for अपश्यम्)
6 ^{b}) विप्रहीणः (for विप्रकीर्णः)
^{c}) अनन्तं (for अनन्तरं)
^{d}) स्वरयन्ति (for स्वरन्ति)
9 ^{d}) ततो (for तथा) [$\tilde{N}_3$]
12 ^{b}) वापि (for चापि)
14 ^{b}) सप्तान्यहानि (for सप्ताप्यहानि)

^{c}) भूतपृष्टा (for °पृच्छा) [K$_{2-4}$ D$_5$]
15 ^{a}) ददानि पत मा (for ददामि मा प्रपत)
16 ^{c}) After दैवावेशात्, ins. च [U]
17 ^{e}) कुर्यांच पूर्व (for कुर्यामपूर्वं) [K$_3$ Ñ$_3$ B$_1$ D$_4$]
18 ^{b}) वसुमान् (for वसुमना)

Adhy. 88

1 ^{a}) पृच्छेहं (for पृच्छामि)
3 ^{a}) ददानि (for ददामि)
6 ^{b}) Om. इह [K Ñ$_3$ D$_5$]
7 ^{a}) हृदयेन चापि (for °येनापि विद्वन्)
^{b}) अवमन्ये (for अवमंस्था:)
8 ^{d}) अवहाय (for उपास्से ह)
11 ^{a}) यदर्होहं तद्ददध्वं
^{c}) °नन्दामि (for °भ्रूणोमि) [K$_1$ Ñ$_{1\cdot3}$ D$_5$]
12 ^{a}) संप्रवक्ष्यन्ते (for प्रतिह°) [Ñ$_3$]
^{cd}) यानारूढा नरा वाहानभिवाञ्छन्ति शाश्वतान्
13 ^{a}) विवक्ष्यन्ति (for हि व°) [K$_2$]
^{c}) प्रकाशन्तो (for °शन्ते)
^{d}) ज्वलिता (for ज्वलन्तो) [Ñ$_3$]
14 ^{b}) विहायसम् (for °यसा)
^{c}) अत्र यास्यामो (for अनुया°)
^{d}) यथा (for यदा)
15 ^{c}) विरजः (for विरजा:)
^{d}) देवसद्मगः (for °द्मनः)
16 ^{b}) नृपते नृपाः (for नृपसत्तमाः)
17 ^{a}) अहम् (for पूर्वम्) [U]
20 ^{c}) नरपते (for नृपते) [Ñ$_3$ G$_{4-6}$]
24 ^{b}) मानवेषु (for मानुषेषु) [Ñ$_3$ G$_1$]
After 24^{cd}, ins. 868* (with v. l. as in K$_1$)
^{c}) सर्वेथ लोका मुनयश्च देवाः
25 ^{c}) द्विजातिभ्यः (for द्विजाग्र्येभ्यः) [Ñ$_3$]
{239} ^{d}) कथेदस्मत्सलोकताम् [U]

Adhy. 89

1 ^{b}) वंशाधरान् (for वंशकरान्)
2 ^{a}) वीर्यहीनो (for शीलहीनो) [Ñ$_3$]
5 ^{d}) वंशभृत् (for वंशकृत्) [Ñ$_{1\cdot3}$]
7 After 7, ins. 873*
8 ^{a}) महोत्साहा (for महेष्वासा) [Ñ$_3$]
9–10 The ten names ending with यु are spelt with युं. After 10^{cd}, ins. 875*
10 ^{e}) त्वासीत् (for तात)
^{f}) राजसूयाश्वमेधभाक्
11 ^{ab}) मतिनार इति ख्यातो राजा परमधार्मिकः
14 ^{a}) ततः (for सुतान्) [Ñ$_3$]
^{b}) पञ्चभूतोपमा नृपाः [Ñ$_3$]
^{d}) सुतान् (for नृप)
15 ^{a}) अथ सुषन्तं (for शूर भीमौ च)
^{b}) प्रभूतवसुमेव (for प्रपूर्वं व°)
17 After 17, ins. 879*
11 Transp. 18^{ab} and 20^{ab}
20 ^{a}) नरेन्द्रस्य (for महीन्द्रस्य)
^{c}) ततो दिविरथो (for ततः स वि तथो)
23 ^{a}) कृत्स्नां (for सर्वां)
25 ^{a}) तथा (for तदा)
29 ^{d}) अपि महात्मनः (for अमिततेजसः)
30 ^{a}) जनरूपिणं यं (for °पिणयोः) [U]
^{b}) नराधिपम् (for जनाधिपम्)
32 ^{b}) कृतैर्नानाविधैस्तदा [U]
^{e}) भरतान् (for भारतान्)
33 ^{a}) चेमां (for चैव)
^{f}) संवरणं रणे (for स पनं समरे) [Ñ$_3$]
35 ^{c}) नदीविषमपर्यन्ते
^{f}) भरता (for भारता)
37 ^{d}) भरताः (for भारताः)
^{f}) सुवर्चसः (for °र्चसे) [Ñ$_3$ D$_a$ D$_1$]
38 ^{a}) समाविष्टमुषितं (for समामष्टमी मुष्टं) [Ñ$_3$]
42 ^{b}) सुषाव (for सुषुवे) [K$_2$ Ñ$_3$]
43 ^{b}) कुरुजङ्गलम् (for कुरुजाङ्गलम्)
44 ^{b}) चैत्ररथं (for चित्र°)
^{d}) तस्य (for चास्य) [Ś$_1$ Ñ$_3$]
^{f}) अजायत (for व्यजा°) [Ñ$_3$ T$_2$G$_3$]
45 ^{a}) अनिष्वतः (for अभिष्वतः)
45 45^{ab} is repeated (with v. l.)
^{d}) शिल्पसः (for शल्मलः) [U]
47 ^{d}) सस (for सर्वे)
51 ^{b}) सौण्डिकः (for कुण्डिकः) [Ñ$_3$]
^{c}) हस्तो विकर्कः (for हस्ती वितर्कः)

[e]) वहिःश्रवाः (for हविःश्रवाः) [$\tilde{N}_{2\cdot3}$ $B_{1\cdot3m}$]
53 [b]) धर्मोहितेप्सया (for धर्मपरीप्सया)
54 [b]) नराधिपाः (for महारथाः)

Adhy. 90

1 [d]) ये (for मे)
2 [b]) मामिति (for मामति)
3 [a]) पुण्याम् (for दिव्याम्) [$\tilde{N}_3$]
5 [b]) सताम् (for अहम्) [$\tilde{N}_3$]
6 [a]) यथा (for पुरा) [K_3 $\tilde{N}_3$]
[b]) पुरा (for मया)
11 After पूरोः, ins. तु
12 परीतस्वं प्राचीन्वान् (for प्राचिन्वन्तम्) [U]
14 अहंयातिः (for अहंपातिः)
15 कृतकार्यस्य दुहितरम् (for खलु कृतवीर्यदु°) [U]
17–18 सुरार्चनः (for भरा°) [$\tilde{N}_{1\cdot3}$]
19 अयुतानायुः (for अयुतनायी)
आजहार (for आनयत्)
23 अजीजनत् (for अजनयत्)
25 After सरस्वत्यां, (ins. गुणसमुदितं)
[240] आहरत् (for आजहार)
26 समासे (for निवृत्ते) Before तस्यां, ins. स
31 [a]) Transp. माता and भक्ता
32 [b]) महौजसम् (for यमक्षयात्) [$\tilde{N}_3$]
35 विजयां (for जयां) तस्य (for तस्यामस्य) [U]
40–41 From तस्यामस्य up to संप्रिया नाम Om.
42 अभमा (for अरत्वान्) here & below [$\tilde{N}_3$]
45 अजनयत्पर्यश्रवसं (for अस्य जज्ञे पर्यश्रवाः यमाहुः) [K_2]
46 Om. पुत्रान् [$\tilde{N}_3$ $B_{5\cdot6}$]
48 [a]) कुमारः (for कराभ्यां)
[d]) Here and in the sequel शांतनु (for शंतनु)
50 Om. गङ्गां [$\tilde{N}_3$]
51 मातरम् उदावहत् (for उदवहन्मातरम्)
गन्धकालीम् (for °काली)
52 Before द्वौ, ins. अन्यौ

56 अविचिन्तयत् कार्यं न (for चिन्तयामास) [$\tilde{N}_3$]
उच्छेदं व्रजेत् (for उच्छिद्यते)
61 Om. तत्र
63 After कुन्ती, ins पृथा
66 After विवर्णरूपः, ins. तथा
68 Om. त्वं
70 Om. तां
71 Om. स
इति चाप्युक्तम् (for इत्युक्तः) [$\tilde{N}_{1\cdot3}$]
77 After 77 ins. 903* (with v. l.)
78 शंकिता विदुरसुमन्त्रितेन (for शकिता विदुरमन्त्रितेन)
81 अविन्दन्त (for °न्दन्)
83 यौधिं (for यौधेयं)
84 बलधारां (for बलधरां)
85 भद्रभाषिणीं (for the first नाम)
After उदवहत्, ins. स्वविषयग्राम्या- जगाम कुशली; अतीव गुणवन्तं वासुदेवस्य दयितं अजनयत् (for जनयामास)
87 After उपयेमे, ins. मद्रराज्ञो द्युतिमतो दुहितरम्
88 नाम राक्षसं घटोत्कचं (for राक्षस्यां घटोत्कचं नाम)
उत्पादयामास (for जनयामास)
89 After 89, ins. तेषां वंशकरोऽभिमन्यु
90 Om. अभिमन्युः
91 After 91, ins. 906*
93 After उपयेमे, ins. त्वन्मातरं भवान् (for अस्य)
94 भवतोपि (for जनमेजयात्तु)
After पुत्रौ, ins. जज्ञाते
95 शतानीकस्यापि वैदेह्यां पुत्र उत्पन्नोऽश्वमेधदत्तः
96 [a]) Om. तु.
[cd]) Om.
After 96[ab], ins. the following passage followed by 909*
ते धन्यः पुण्यः पवित्रः सततं श्रोतव्यो ब्राह्मणैर्नियमवद्भिरनन्तरं क्षत्रियैः स्वधर्मनिरतैः प्रजापालनतत्परैर्वैश्यैरपि श्रोतव्योऽभिगम्यश्च तथा शूद्रैरपि

त्रिवर्णगुणभिः श्रद्धानैरिति ॥ ९६ ॥
909* Om. विमत्सरा मैत्रा देवपराः,

Adhy. 91

1 ^{d}) संशितव्रतः (for सत्यविक्रमः)
2 ^{b}) राजसूयशतेन (for वाजपेय^{o})
3 ^{c}) ह्यासन् (for *आसन्)
6 ^{a}) सोपख्यातो (for अप^{o})
9 ^{b}) कश्मलाभिहतो नृपः [Corrupt]
[241] 13 ^{c}) न तच्छक्यं न कर्तुंञ्च [Ñ$_3$]
17 ^{c}) चिकीर्षामि (for करिष्यामि)

Adhy. 92

2 ^{b}) स्त्रीरूपधारिणी (for श्रीरिव रूपिणी)
4 ^{b}) यशस्विनीम् (for मन^{o})
^{c}) करोमि (for करवाणि)
7 ^{c}) भजतीं राजन् (for भजमानां त्वं) [Ñ$_3$]
^{d}) दिव्यां काम्यां (for राजन्कन्यां)
15 ^{c}) सूक्ष्मैः (for पुत्रैः) [Ñ$_3$]
21 ^{f}) वाङ्गना (for वाङ्गने)
22 ^{b}) संप्रष्टव्या (for प्रष्टव्या सा)
30 ^{c}) देवता (for देवी वा)
^{d}) गान्धर्वी (for गन्धर्वी) [Ñ$_1$]
32 ^{d}) [अ] थाभ्यनि (? न) न्वद् (for अभ्यगच्छद्)
39 ^{d}) वै (for सा)
44 ^{a}) क्षिप्रं (for पुत्रं) [S$_1$ Ñ$_3$]
46 ^{b}) प्रहसतीम् (for प्रहसिताम्)
^{d}) सुतम् (for पुत्रम्) [U]
47 ^{b}) मम (for इति) [Ñ$_3$]
49 ^{d}) वै (for अहं)
50 ^{a}) जाता (for देवा) [Ñ$_{1\text{-}3}$]
53 ^{d}) जन्मनो (for जन्मतो) [Ñ$_{1\text{-}3}$]
55 ^{a}) एवं (for एष) [Ñ$_3$ D$_5$]
^{c}) तत्प्रसूतं (for मत्प्र^{o}) [Ś$_1$ Ñ$_3$]

Adhy. 93

1 ^{d}) योनिम् (for तनुम्)
3 ^{c}) प्रपद्यन्त (for उदपद्यन्त) [Ñ$_3$ D$_{8\text{-}1}$]
6 ^{d}) सर्वर्तुकवनावृतम्
8 ^{b}) अभिशब्दिता (for अतिगर्विता)
13 ^{a}) अथ भार्यातु (for तु भार्या वै)
14 ^{c}) चौश्चापि (for दिवे वै) [Ñ$_3$]
15 ^{a}) स्वाधीनां वसुदोग्ध्रीं च
27 ^{b}) [अ] नघ (for नृप) [Ñ$_3$ D$_2$]
^{e}) ततः (for तदा) [Ñ$_{1\text{-}3}$]
30 ^{a}) गां (for तां)
33 ^{cd}) अष्टौ (for राजन्), and तान् मुनिसत्तमः (for अष्टौ तपोधनः) [Ñ$_3$]
35 ^{c}) Transp. न and लेभिरे
37 ^{c}) तात (for तदा) [U]

Adhy. 94

1 ^{a}) एष (for एवं) [Ñ$_3$ M$_3$]
4 After 4^{ab}, ins. 962*
5 ^{a}) अपि (for आसन्) [Ñ$_3$]
^{b}) पुरुषर्षभे (for भरतर्षभ)
8 ^{b}) नृपतिसत्तमैः (for ^{o}तिभिस्तदा)
11 ^{c}) ^{o}तपोख्यातः [Ñ$_3$]
12 ^{c}) सूर्यकल्पो [ऽ] भूत् (for सूर्यसंकाशो)
^{f}) क्षमित्वे (for क्षमया)
18 ^{b}) अथ (for अष्टौ) [Ñ$_3$]
20 ^{a}) च (for स)
29 ^{d}) Transp. तं and कुमारं [Ñ$_3$]
30 ^{b}) अरजोम्बरसंवृताम् [Ś$_1$ K]
^{c}) स तां (for सतीं)
31 ^{b}) अविन्दथाः (for अजायिथाः)
38 ^{a}) पौरवस्तु पुरं (for पौरवाः स्वपुरं)
42 ^{b}) वनं ततः (for समन्ततः) [Ñ$_{1\text{-}3}$]
46 ^{cd}) Om.
48 ^{d}) मतः (for ततः) [Ñ$_3$]
55 ^{b}) वशस्थाः (for विधेयाः) [Ñ$_3$]
^{c}) इव (for इह)
56 ^{d}) यत्त्वमात्थ (for यथा मात्थ) [Ñ$_3$]
58 ^{d}) शतैरपि (for शतादपि)
59 ^{c}) अविनाशात्तु (for ^{o}शाय) [Ñ$_3$]
60 ^{a}) त्रयी विद्या (for त्रयो वेदा)
^{b}) सन्तानमपि चाक्षयम्
60^{c}–61^{d} Om. [Ñ$_{1\text{-}3}$ V$_1$ B$_6$]
61 ^{f}) देवतानां (for उत्तमानां)
64 ^{a}) राज्ञो (for ज्ञात्वा)
^{b}) ज्ञात्वा सर्वम् (for कृत्स्नं चैवम्)
[242] 74 ^{b}) पुरुषर्षभ (for भरतर्षभ) [Ñ$_3$]
84 ^{a}) न तदन्यो (for नान्यथा तत्) [Ñ$_3$]
88 ^{d}) इति (for दिवि) [Ñ$_3$]

92 ^{d}) प्रत्यवेदयत् (for संन्यवे°)
[K$_2$ Ñ$_3$]

Adhy. 95

4 ^{b}) पुरुषर्षभे (for भरतर्षभ)
9 ^{a}) विपुले (for तुमुले) [Ñ$_3$]
14 ^{a}) °कुशलं (for °कुशलो)
^{d}) पर्यपालयत् (for प्रत्य°)

Adhy. 96

1 ^{a}) चैव (for भीष्मो) [Ñ$_3$]
6 ^{b}) नामानि (for नामसु) [Ñ$_3$]
10 For 10^{cd}, subst. 999*
17 ^{ab}) प्राक्संचार्यन्भिः (for ते द्राग्भ्राजभ्भिः)
[Ñ$_3$]
18 ^{b}) सदश्चोद्यतधूर्वरान्
21 ^{b}) परिवार्य तम् (for °वारयन्)
24 ^{b}) सर्वशस्त्रभृतां वरः
28 ^{b}) पररथार्दनः (for °बला°)
^{c}) तद्वाक्यकालितः (for तद्वाक्या-
कुलितः) [U]
After 28, ins. 1004*
30 ^{a}) विनिवर्तितं (for निवर्तमानं) [Ñ$_3$]
^{b}) राजानं सर्वपार्थिवाः
37 ^{c}) हत्वा (for अमृन्दात्) [Ñ$_3$ B$_8$]
38 ^{e}) चास्य शैलेन (for चाप्यथैकेन)
[K Ñ$_{1\cdot3}$ D$_5$]
39 After 39, ins. 1013*
41 After 41, ins. 1017*
43 ^{a}) तान् (for [अ]रीन्) [Ñ$_{1\cdot3}$ D$_2$]
44 ^{a}) सुता (for स्नुषा) [Ñ]
^{cd}) For 44^{cd}, subst. 1018* [Ñ$_{1\cdot3}$]
46 ^{a}) स तत् (for सतां) [Ñ B$_1$]
50 ^{a}) तदा (for तया)
51 ^{b}) धार्मिकैर्धर्मकोविदैः
54 ^{a}) चैव (for चापि)
55 ^{a}) प्रतिरूपेण (for °रूपोऽसौ) [U]
59 ^{f}) कुरुजाङ्गलैः (for °पुंगवैः)

Adhy. 97

1 After 1, ins. 1022* (with v. l.)
2 ^{b}) भानि (read °मि) नी (for मा-
निनी)
5 ^{b}) वा (for च) [Ñ$_{1\cdot3}$]
^{cd}) वेद (for वेत्थ; in both places)
[Ñ$_3$ D$_6$]
10 ^{c}) महाबाहो (for महाभाग)
12 ^{a}) तु (for च)

Adhy. 98

1 ^{c}) राजा परशुना पूर्वं
^{ef}) Om. [Ñ$_{1\cdot3}$]
3 ^{c}) वसुधा (for पृथिवी) [U]
4 ^{b}) ततस्ततः (for समन्ततः)
5 ^{ef}) Om. [Ñ$_{1\cdot3}$]
6 ^{a}) तथो° (for अथो°)
7 ^{d}) सोभ्यपद्यत (for सोऽन्व°) [Ñ$_{1\cdot3}$]
12 ^{c}) तत्तेजः (for तं रेतः)
13 ^{a}) ब्रूहि (for वदे) [Ñ$_{1\cdot3}$]
^{b}) एक- (for अत्र) [Ñ$_3$]
15 ^{b}) सर्वभूतहितेप्सिते
17 ^{c}) महान् (for तदा)
20 ^{b}) तदा (for ततः)
28 ^{b}) ममेवैमे (read °वेमे) (for °वैत)
29 ^{a}) हृष्ट्वा (for मत्वा)
33 ^{d}) Transp. मातः and कुरु [Ñ$_3$]

Adhy. 99

5 ^{a}) After त्वम्, ins. हि
[243] ^{b}) तपो महत् (for परा गतिः)
6 ^{b}) आशीर्विरो (for आसीत्तरी) [Ñ$_3$]
12 ^{b}) उत्सृज्यतामयम् (for °ज्य मामकम्)
[K$_2$ Ñ$_3$ G$_2$]
15 ^{d}) After च, ins. अपि [Ś$_1$ KÑ$_3$]
29 ^{a}) विधानविहितः (for विधातृ°)
36 ^{c}) तथा तव महाप्रज्ञे
41 ^{a}) After कथं, ins. च
^{b}) पालयितुं (for धारयितुं)
^{d}) संवर्धयिष्यति (for तं व°)
43 ^{d}) प्रतिपद्यते (for °द्यताम्) [Ñ$_3$]
44 After वैशंपायन उवाच, ins. 1068*
45 ^{c}) भारतानां (for भर°)
46 ^{d}) [अ]थ (for च)
47 ^{a}) त्वयाधीना (for तवाधीना) [Ñ$_3$]
^{b}) पुत्रं प्रापय मां तदा
^{d}) एतं (for एव) [Ś$_1$ K$_1$]

Adhy. 100

1 ^{d}) सा पुनः (for शनकैः) [Ñ$_3$]
2 ^{d}) After निशीथे, ins. हि
3 ^{a}) तु (for तत्)

^{b}) शुभा (for शुभे)
^{d}) कुरुसत्तमान् (for °पुंगवान्)
4 ^{d}) शरणं प्रविवेश तत्
15 ^{f}) विवर्णा समपद्यत [Ñ$_3$]
17 ^{b}) [अ] सि (for [अ] पि)
28 ^{b}) [अ] मितौजसः (for महात्मनः) [K$_0$ Ñ$_3$]
^{c}) [अ] धर्मज्ञः (for °तत्त्वज्ञः) [Ñ$_3$]
After 28, ins. 1087*
29 ^{c}) समासाद्य (for °वेद्य) [Ñ$_3$]
30 ^{a}) एते (for एवं)
^{b}) वै विदुरादयः (for द्वैपायनादपि) [Ñ$_3$]

Adhy. 101

4 ^{b}) वर्ततः (for तिष्ठतः)
10 ^{d}) सर्वान् (for चैव)
14 ^{d}) ऋषयोथ (for मुनयो°)
15 ^{b}) भारत (for सर्वतः)
^{f}) [इ] ति (for [अ] सि) [Ñ$_3$]
After 15, ins. an additional colophon
16 After 16, ins. 1096*
17 ^{a}) श्रुत्वा च वचनं तेषां [Ñ$_3$ D$_n$]
^{b}) निश्चिन्त्य (for निष्क्रम्य)
23 ^{d}) ईदृग् (for ईदृशी) [U]
25 ^{b}) धृतः (for कृतः)
27 ^{b}) महौजसः (for महात्मनः) [K$_{0-2}$]

Adhy. 102

6 ^{a}) धर्मक्रियायज्ञशीलाः
^{b}) सत्यधर्मपरायणाः [Ñ$_3$]
^{d}) ततः प्रजाः (for प्रजास्तदा) [Ñ$_3$]
7 ^{c}) [अ] भ्यनन्दन्त (for °वर्धन्त)
8 ^{a}) च (for वै) [S$_1$ K$_1$ Ñ$_3$]
11 ^{c}) °सभावप्र–
After 11^{cd}, ins. 1104* (with v. l.)
12 ^{d}) प्रभूताभिप्रवर्षितः [K$_0$ Ñ$_3$]
16 ^{b}) वेदाध्ययनसंगताः [U]
18 ^{b}) चाविभो (for चाभिभो) [Ñ$_3$]
19 ^{b}) नरेषु (for नरेभ्यः)

Adhy. 103

1 ^{a}) सर्वम् (for सम्यक्)

10 ^{d}) कौरव (for भारत) [Corrupt]
13 ^{b}) तदा (for शुभा)
14 After 14, ins. 1110*
17 ^{a}) तोषयामास (for कुलेनाराध्य) [Ñ$_3$]

Adhy. 104

3 ^{a}) अग्रजामथ (for °जातेति)
4 ^{c}) तत्र (for घोरं)
7 ^{d}) Transp. पुत्रः and तव [Ñ$_{1-3}$ D$_n$ D$_1$]
[244] 8 ^{b}) तस्य (for तेन)
9 After 9, ins. App. I, No. 58 (with v. l., omitting lines 8, 10, 11)
10 ^{b}) संबभूव तया सह
^{c}) तत्र वीरः समभवत्
^{d}) वरः (for वरम्)
12 ^{c}) ववतां (for वदतां) [Ñ$_{1-3}$ D$_5$]
^{d}) पुनः (for ततः)
After 12, ins. 1120*
13 ^{cd}) उत्ससर्ज कुमारं तं जले कुन्ती महाबलम्
16 ^{c}) उपस्पृश्य सदा (for आ पृष्ठतापात्) [Ñ$_{1-3}$]
^{d}) च (for स) [S$_1$ K$_{1-3}$ Ñ$_3$]
17 ^{a}) तस्मिन्काले च जपतः
^{b}) तस्य वीरस्य धीमतः
^{d}) वसु किंचिन्महीपते [Ñ$_3$]
18 ^{a}) शक्रो (for इन्द्रो)
^{b}) समुपागमत् (for भूतभावनः)
^{c}) कवचं (for कुण्डले)
^{d}) फाल्गुनस्य हिते रतः
19 ^{a}) स शरीरात्समुत्कृत्य
^{b}) तं निसर्गजम् (for रुधिरस्रवम्)
^{c}) विप्ररूपाय शक्राय After 19, ins. 1124* (with v. l.)
20 ^{a}) ददौ शक्तिं सुरपतिः
^{b}) वाक्यश्चेदमुवाच ह
^{e}) यं जेतुमिच्छसे सङ्ख्ये [Ñ$_{1-3}$]
21 ^{a}) प्राङ्नाम तस्य प्रथितं
^{b}) क्षितौ (for श्रुतम्)
^{c}) कर्णो वैकर्तनश्चैव

Adhy. 105

1 ^{a}) सर्वरूपगुणोपेता

2 ^{a}) महास्कन्धम् (for गज°)

^{b}) वृषभाक्षं (for ऋष°)

5 ^{c}) परिक्रीय (for °क्रीता) [S_1 $K_{1\cdot3}$]

^{d}) ततः (for तदा)

6 ^{a}) महास्कन्धं (for गज°) [G_1]

^{b}) वृषभाक्षं (for ऋष°)

^{c}) Transp. पाण्डुं and दृष्ट्वा

10 ^{a}) बहूनामागसां कर्ता

^{a}) वैरी सर्वकुलक्षितान् [$\tilde{N}_3$ T_1 G_5]

^{c}) मगधराजस्य (for °राष्ट्रस्य) [$\tilde{N}_3$]

12 ^{b}) पौण्ड्रेषु च नरर्षभ

14 ^{d}) कुरुकर्मसु (for कर°)

18 ^{ab}) कम्बलाजिनरत्नानि राङ्कवास्तरणानि च

20 ^{d}) आहृतः (for उद्धृतः) [U]

23 ^{ef}) Transp. लोकं and दृष्टा

24 ^{a}) नानादेश° [$\tilde{N}_3$]

^{b}) यानैरुच्चावचैरपि [$\tilde{N}_3$]

^{d}) तथाविधैः (for [अ] थाविकैः)

26 ^{c}) च (for तु) [U]

27 ^{c}) सर्वभूतानि (for सर्वशः पौरान्)

Adhy. 106

7 ^{b}) [आ) भरणानि (for शयनानि)
[$\tilde{N}_{1\cdot3}$ B_5 D_4]

Adhy. 107

5 ^{b}) स्य (? read त) स्य महात्मनः (for तेन महात्मना)

8 ^{d}) अलभीत् (for अग्रहीत्)
[Corrupt]

12 ^{c}) द्विवर्षसंहितां (for °संभृतां)

17 ^{d}) कुतोऽपरे (for कुतोऽन्यथा)
[Ś$_1$ $K_{2\cdot3}$ Ñ]

19 ^{a}) त्वष्ठीला (for *अष्ठीला)

^{b}) बभूव शतधा (for *अभवच्छतधा)

21 ^{d}) पुनः (for ततः)

24 After 24, ins. 1141*,
followed by line 1 of 1142*

25 After 25, ins. 1144*

27 ^{c}) तथ्यं (for सत्यं)

[245] 29 After 29, ins. 1146* (with v. l.)

31 ^{b}) विशां पते (for महीपते)
After 31^{ab}, ins. 1148* (with v. l.)

32 ^{a}) कुलार्थे पुरुषं (for एकं कुलस्यार्थे)

33 ^{b}) द्विजैस्तदा (for द्विजोत्तमैः) [U]

^{c}) तदा (for तथा)

34 ^{d}) चैव (for चैका) [K_3 Ñ D_4]

36 ^{c}) सुतस्तस्य (for ततस्तस्यां)
[Ś$_1$ D_5]

37 ^{d}) चैव शताधिका (for चैकाथ दुःशला)

Adhy. 108

1 ^{a}) एषां (for तेषां) [K_{2-4}]

^{d}) वैशंपायन (for आनुपूर्व्येण) [U]

2 ^{d}) Transp. समः and सहः

3 ^{c}) दुर्मनश्च (for दुर्मुखश्च) [$\tilde{N}_3$]

5 ^{b}) विकटासनः (for विकटः समः)
[$\tilde{N}_3$]

6 ^{ab}) Om.

9 ^{c}) अश्वकेतुः (for अश्वसेनः)

10 ^{a}) कुण्डशायी (for पण्डितको)

11 ^{b}) नागदन्तोग्रयाय्यपि

^{c}) खण्डकुण्डश्च (for निषङ्गी पाशी च)

^{d}) कुण्डधारो धनुर्धरः

12 ^{d}) दृढरथाः (for °रथः)

13 After 13^{ab}, ins. 1155*

14 ^{b}) सर्वे सर्वास्त्रकोविदाः [$\tilde{N}_3$]

^{c}) इति पुत्रशतश्चैकं

^{d}) शताधिका (for प्रकीर्तिता)

16 ^{b}) सर्वे सर्वार्थकोविदाः [$\tilde{N}_3$]

^{cd}) Om.

18 ^{a}) चापि समये (for समये राजा)

^{b}) धृतराष्ट्रो महीपतिः

^{d}) विधिना भरतर्षभ

Adhy. 109

1 ^{d}) ब्रह्मवादिना (for °विस्तम)

9 ^{b}) बुद्ध्या विरहितास्तथा [$\tilde{N}_3$]

13 ^{a}) वा (for च)

^{b}) इत्यपि (for इष्यते) [$\tilde{N}_3$]

15 ^{b}) शस्तः कस्मात् (for कथमस्मान्)
[K_0 $\tilde{N}_3$ B_1]

^{d}) हि (for वै) [Ñ $B_{5\cdot6}$]

16 ^{b}) प्रमुञ्चति (for वि°) [U]

17 c) बहुभिः (for इषुभिः) [K_3 $\tilde{N}_3$]
19 After 19^{cd} ins. 1162*
e) कर्तुं (for कान्तं)
f) तत्त्वया विफलं (for यत्त्वया वितथं)
22 b) सर्वधर्मार्थतत्त्ववित् [$\tilde{N}_3$]
23 b) ये नराः (for मानवाः)
c) विग्राह्याः (for निग्राह्याः)
25 b) [अ] नागसम् (for [अ] संशयम्)
31 c) दुःखार्तः (for शोकार्तः)

Adhy. 110

2 b) स्वेन (for बत) [$\tilde{N}_3$]
12 b) दश पञ्च वा (for द्वे च पञ्च च)
16 d) निमेषादिष्व्यवस्थिताः
17 d) सुनिर्णिक्तात्मकिल्बिषः
21 b) [ऽ]न्यं (for [ऽ]न्यां)
24 b) लोकपाः (for सोमपाः)
26 After 26^{cd}, ins. 1166* (with v. l.) [$\tilde{N}_3$]
30 a) °समाचारः
36 f) आवरणानि (for आभर°)
38 b) परमान्विताम् (for °मात्मिकाम्) [Corrupt]
43 b) नागसेनम् (for वारिषेणम्) [$\tilde{N}_3$]

Adhy. 111

6 After 6^{ab}, ins. 1173*
9 a) अतिक्रमेन्न यान्पक्षी
[246] 12 b) तत्र मानवाः (for मनुजा भुवि) [$\tilde{N}_3$]
d) शश्वद्धि धर्मतः (for शतसहस्रशः) [K_3 $\tilde{N}_3$]
13 d) धर्मवित्सु (for °विद्भिः)
14 a) तु (for च)
15 After 15^{ab}, ins. 1178*
15–16 Reads 15^{c}–16^{b} after 12 (?)
17 b) महर्षिणा (for महात्मना)
18 a) अस्मिन् (for अस्ति) [U]
19 a) देवश्रेष्ठं (for दैवदिष्टं)
20 d) प्रीतिकरं ह्यसि (for प्रीतिमवाप्स्यसि)
23 d) धर्मवादिनः (for °मादितः)
26 a) जातन्ते (for नष्टं मे) [$\tilde{N}_3$]
b) मे (for हि)
d) पुरा (for तथा)
27 b) Transp. षट् and पुत्राः
28 c) पौनर्भवेयः (for °भवश्च)
d) भगिन्यां (for स्वैरिण्यां) [$\tilde{N}_3$]
29 a) दत्तः क्रीतोपविक्रीतः [$\tilde{N}_3$]
30 a) पूर्वं पूर्वमसंभावे
d) [ऽ]पत्यम् (for पुत्रम्)
32 a) [अ]हं (for [अ]घ)
33 d) पुत्रजन्मनि (for [अ]पत्यज°)

Adhy. 112

7 c) परमदुर्धर्षः (for °धर्मिष्ठः) [$Ś_1$ K $\tilde{N}_3$ D_5]
8 c) तत्र (for ततो)
d) देवर्षिभिः सह (for सह महर्षिभिः)
13 After 13^{ab}, ins. 1186* (with v. l.)
14 b) Transp. ददौ and धनम्
c) अनन्तरञ्चान्नदानान् [S_1 K_0 $\tilde{N}_3$]
d) क्रतूत्तमान् (for महा°) [$\tilde{N}_3$]
16 a) च (for तु)
d) यक्ष्मणा समगृह्यत
19 b) भर्तृविनाकृता (for पुत्र°)
27 b) कुशास्तरणशायिनी [U]
28 c) कृपणामनाथां करुणां
29 a) तस्या (for तस्यां)
b) विपलन्त्याः (for °पन्त्यां)
30 b) हि (for [इ]ह)
31 a) आत्मनीये (for आत्मीये च)
32 d) भर्त्रा (for भद्रा) [K] (except K_1) [$\tilde{N}_3$]
33 b) भरतर्षभ (for मनुजाधिप)
34 b) [अ]पि नरर्षभ (for भरतर्षभ)

Adhy. 113

2 c) यथोक्तं (for त्वयोक्तं)
4 d) चारुहासिनि (for °लोचने)
6 e) प्रमाणदृष्टो (for पुराण°)
7 d) पुराभवत् (for सनातनः) [$\tilde{N}_3$]
8 d) विस्तरशः (for °तः)
20 e) विभाण्डकस्य (for उद्दालकस्य)
21 a) वामोरु (for रम्भोरु)
b) [अ]पत्यकर्मणि (for °जन्मनि)
24 a) धर्म्याणि (for सर्वाणि) [$\tilde{N}_3$]
26 a) वर्णेषु (for कालेषु) [$\tilde{N}_3$]
32 e) पूर्वं (for तत्र)
33 c) संश्रितात्मानं (for संशिता°) [$\tilde{N}_3$]

35 For 35^{cd}, subst. 1196*
37 ^{d}) यथा नौ स्यात्प्रजा प्रभो
38 ^{b}) मन्त्रवतां (for तत्त्वविदां) [U]
40 ^{a}) च (for न) [K$_3$ Ñ$_3$ D$_5$]

Adhy. 114

1 ^{a}) संवत्सराधिके (for °राहिते) [Ñ$_3$]
3 ^{a}) संयुक्ता (for संगम्य)
^{d}) हितम् (for वरम्)
6 ^{b}) भवितेति विचिन्तयन्
7 ^{a}) राजन् (for राजा)
21 ^{b}) तथा (for तम्) [Ñ$_3$]
23 ^{a}) मित्राणां (for देवानां) [Ñ$_3$]
247] After 23^{ab}, ins. 1212* (with v. l.)
28 ^{b}) तस्मिन्वाग् (for वागुवाच)
After 28, ins. 1219* (om. line 1)
29 ^{a}) कौन्ति (for कुन्ति) (here and elsewhere)
31 ^{b}) सोमकैः (for केकयैः)
34 ^{b}) शिवि° [Ñ$_{1.3}$]
38 ^{a}) देवस्थानां (for देवऋषीणां)
^{d}) सुमहान् (for तुमुलः) [U]
41 ^{c}) वै (for [ऽ] भूत्) [Ñ$_3$]
43 ^{b}) दिव्यालंकार°
After 43^{cd}, ins. 1224*
44 ^{c}) गोपश्च (for गोपतिः) [K$_{0.1}$]
48 ^{b}) प्रख्यातौ (for विख्यातौ) [K$_3$Ñ$_3$]
50 ^{c}) काची (for साची) [Ñ$_3$]
51 ^{d}) मनोहरा (for मनोरमा) [U]
52 ^{d}) [अ]थ (for च)
53 ^{d}) मुञ्जकस्थला [Ñ$_3$]
61 ^{a}) तपसा (for तेजसा)
^{b}) महावेगा (for °क्रोधा) [K$_3$ Ñ$_3$ D$_5$]
62 After 62, ins. 1230*
65 ^{c}) स्वैरिणी (for चारिणी)
^{d}) Transp. पञ्चमे and बन्धकी
66 ^{a}) सर्वं (for सत्त्वं)

Adhy. 115

2 ^{b}) विगुणोऽपि (for विगुणेऽपि)
6 ^{a}) नार्हो (for स्तम्भो) [Ñ$_3$]
8 ^{a}) मत्वा (for ज्ञात्वा)
9 ^{d}) Transp. कुरु and प्रियम् [Ñ$_3$]
11 ^{c}) आधिराज्यं हि (for आधिपत्यम्) [Ñ$_3$]
14 ^{a}) प्लवेनैव (for प्लवेनेव)
15 ^{a}) कुन्ती (for माद्रीं) [Ñ$_3$]
16 ^{a}) एका (for एव)
18 ^{d}) रूपद्रविणवित्तमौ [Ñ$_3$]
19 ^{a}) चैषां (for तेषां) [Ś$_1$ K$_1$]
21 After 21, ins. 1240* (with v. l. as in Ñ$_3$)
22 ^{c}) तदा (for पृथा) [Ñ$_3$]
23 ^{d}) यातॄणां (for नारीणां)
26 ^{ef}) Om. [U]

Adh. 116

7 ^{a}) एकां गतां (for आत्मसमां) [Ñ$_3$]
9 ^{b}) नान्वपद्यत (for °बुध्यत) [B$_6$]
12 ^{b}) कुरुसत्तम (for °नन्दन)
15 ^{b}) तदा (for वचः)
21 ^{b}) सभाग्या च भृशं मया [Ñ$_3$]
23 ^{b}) श्रेष्ठं (for ज्येष्ठं)
24 ^{a}) स्वभर्तारं (for इह भ°) [U]
25 ^{d}) After ज्येष्ठा, ins. मे
29 ^{d}) Transp. प्रियं and कुरु

Adhy. 117

1 ^{a}) दृष्ट्वा (for कृत्वा)
^{d}) समेत्य मुनयस्तदा [K$_0$ Ñ$_3$]
7 ^{a}) पुरीं गत्वा (for पुरा भूत्वा) [U]
16 ^{a}) दिव्यान् (for सर्वान्) [Ñ$_3$]
^{b}) अभिवन्द्य ते (for अभिवाद्य च) [Ñ$_3$]
21 ^{d}) तत्र (for तस्य)
26 ^{c}) पश्यन्तः (for पश्यतः)
^{d}) परां प्रीतिमवाप्स्यथ

Adhy. 118

18 ^{c}) जना आशु (for जलेनाशु) [U]
19 ^{b}) श्लक्ष्णेन (for शुक्लेन) [U]
22 ^{d}) वस्त्रैश्च (for अनल्पैः)
27 ^{b}) पाण्डवैः (for बन्धुभिः)
29 ^{b}) शिश्यिरे (for सुषुपुः)

[248]

Adhy. 119

1 ^{ab}) Transp. राजा च and भीष्मश्च [K$_3$ M$_3$]

d) स्वधामृतसमं (for °मयं)
4 b) पुरुषर्षभम् (for भरत°)
5 a) तथा (for तदा) [$K_{2\text{-}4}$ Ñ$_3$]
7 After 7, ins. 1305*
10 b) पुत्रशोकनिपीडिताम् [Ñ$_3$]
11 a) त्वम्बिकया (for *अम्बि°)
14 d) तेजसाभवन् (for पाण्डवा°)
15 a) लक्ष्यप्रहरणे (for लक्ष्याभिहरणे) [U]
18 a) गलेषु (for पादेषु)
d) °शिरोरुहान् [Ñ$_3$]
21 d) द्रुमात् (for द्रुतं)
23 a) धार्तराष्ट्रैस्तु (for °राष्ट्राणां) [Ñ$_3$]
26 d) विनिहन्यताम् (for संनि°)
28 a) विनिश्चयं पापं (for स निश्चयं पापः)
29 After 29, ins. 1309*
33 a) वातं (for वासं)
41 d) तस्मात् (for तदपि) [M]

Adhy. 120

2 b) गौतमः (for नामतः)
8 d) उत्फुल्लहृदयो (for °नयनो) [Ñ]
19 a) सोपि तौ निहितौ

Adhy. 121

6 d) ब्रह्मविदां (for धर्मभृतां) [U]
7 c) भरद्वाजः (for भारद्वाजं)
d) प्रत्यपद्यत (for प्रत्य०) [U]
19 d) सागरमालिनी (for नग°) [Ñ$_3$]
21 b) सर्वशः (for भार्गव)

Adhy. 122

1 a) आगम्य (for आसाद्य)
5 d) प्रवर्धति (for प्रवृश्चति) [Ñ$_{1\text{-}3}$ T_1]
6 b) नैवमुपाकृधि (for नवमुपाकुरु) [K_2 Ñ$_3$]
8 b) श्रुतम् (for कुलम्)
c) विवादं सख्यं च (for सख्यं विवाहश्च)
11 After 11, ins. 1357* (omitting l. 2 and with v. l.)
12 a) ते (for तु) [$K_{0\text{-}3}$ Ñ$_3$]
19 d) करवाम ते (for °महे)
22 d) एषाम् (for एवम्) [M]
23 b) सुसंस्कृतम् (for सुसत्कृतम्) [U]
25 d) °जिघृक्षया [Ñ$_3$]
26 d) सम्यक् (for भ्राम्यन्) [Ñ$_3$]
28 a) मे सखा सदा (for समासाद्य मां)
32 b) समुपागमम् (for पुनराव्रजम्)
35 c) मां ब्रवीषि (for आत्थ मां त्वं)

Adhy. 123

2 a) समाहूय (for तदा°)
7 b) हयेषु (for रथेषु)
c) रथेषु (for अश्वेषु)
8 d) कौरवान् (for पाण्डवम्)
14 a) Transp. परया and श्रद्धया [K_0 Ñ$_3$ D_5]
18 a) तं (for स) [K_3 Ñ$_3$]
23 a) अन्वजानन् (for अभ्य°)
25 c) वने (for च ते)
26 c) समासाद्य (for समागम्य)
33 d) दीयतामिति (for संप्रदीयताम्)
35 c) तव (for त्वया) [U]
d) इति (for मम)
36 d) तदा (for सदा)
40 b) गदायोग्यौ (for °योग्यां)
41 d) दारुकौ (for त्सारुकौ) [Ñ$_3$]
43 d) सौष्ठवे चापि (for °वेन च)
44 d) परन्तप (for नराधिप)
[249] 47 b) सर्वशः (for सत्वरः)
50 b) महाधनुः (for °रथम्) [Ñ$_3$]
54 d) वृक्षं (for भासं) [K_3]
58 d) निपात्यताम् (for निशम्यताम्)
60 c) भासं (for लक्ष्यं)
62 a) एकं (for एनं)
66 b) क्षुरप्रेण शितेन सः [Ñ$_3$]
67 b) फाल्गुन (for फल्गुन) here and in the sequel
71 b) दशभिः (for निशितैः) [Ñ$_3$]
74 e) वीर (for नाम)
78 f) पुनर् (for पुमान्) [U]

Adhy. 124

6 c) समायुक्तान् (for पराक्रान्तान्)
16 ab) Om. [S_1 K (except K_4)]
29 d) प्रयोगं (for °गे)
32 d) कुञ्जरौ (for गौवृषौ)

Adhy. 125

2 ab) ही (in both places for हा)

13 ^{a}) तुमुला (for [अ]तुला)
^{c}) प्रस्रवसंयुक्तैः (for °संमिश्रैः)
15 ^{c}) रक्तान् (for रक्ते) [U]
18 ^{a}) प्रमुदिते (for समु°)
20 ^{b}) [अ]भवद्गिरिः (for [अ]सृज द्गिरीन्)
21 ^{a}) Transp. प्रांशुः and ह्रस्वः [$\tilde{N}_3$]
25 ^{b}) [अ]नघ (for [अ]भवत्)
28 ^{a}) Transp. किं नु and गिरयः [$\tilde{N}_3$]
32 ^{d}) गदाग्रपाणि[:] समवस्थितैः स्थितः

Adhy. 126

2 ^{b}) कुण्डलोज्ज्वलभूषणः [$\tilde{N}_{1\cdot3}$]
6 ^{b}) सर्वं तत् (for सर्वतो) [$\tilde{N}_3$]
^{d}) अथ (for इव) [$K_{0\cdot3}$ D_5]
15 ^{b}) Transp. त्वया and वृणे [S_1 K_{1-4} $\tilde{N}_3$]
20 ^{c}) सकाशे (for समक्षं)
28 ^{d}) वाग्भिः सुव्यञ्जिताक्षरैः [$\tilde{N}_3$]
32 ^{d}) कुलभूषणः (for °वर्धनः)
39 ^{b}) प्रत्यजानत (for °भाषत)

Adhy. 127

1 ^{d}) ज्वलन्निव (for ह्रयन्निव) [$\tilde{N}_3$]
2 ^{d}) तमवन्दत (for सम°)
4 ^{b}) अतिविक्लवः (for स्नेह°)
8 ^{b}) प्रस्फुरिताननः (for °ताधरः) [U]
14 After 14^{c}, ins. 1430* (with v. l)
15 ^{c}) आदित्यसदृशं (for °संकाशं)
^{d}) प्रजास्यति (for जनिष्यति) [cf. $\tilde{N}_3$]
19 ^{b}) अग्रकरे (for अथ करे)

Adhy. 128

2 ^{d}) शिष्यात् (for सा स्यात्) [U]
10 ^{b}) नराधिप (for नरर्षभ) [K_0 N_3 V_1]

Adhy. 129

2 ^{a}) तथा (for ततो) [$\acute{S}_1$ $K_{0\cdot2\cdot3}$]
3 ^{b}) प्रतिचक्रुर्यथागमम्
4 After 4^{ab}, ins. 1436*
11 ^{b}) परिपूज्य (for प्रति°) [$\tilde{N}_3$ $D_{n\cdot1}$]
^{c}) पृष्ट्वा पाण्डोः पुरावृत्तं
18 ^{a}) यदि हि त्वं पुरा राज्ये [$\tilde{N}_3$ $G_{4\cdot5}$ M]

^{b}) भवमानः स्थितो नृप [$\tilde{N}_{1\cdot3}$]
^{d}) अवशेष्वपि (for °शे जने) [Corrupt]

Adhy. 130

5 ^{b}) बलादिभिः (for °वितः) [U]
^{c}) पितृपर्यागताद् (for पितृपैतामहाद्) [U]
[250] 7 ^{b}) कौरवा (for पौरवा)
8 ^{a}) महाराज (for मया तात)
^{b}) भाविनं (for भावितं)
11 ^{c}) ततः (for तदा) [$\tilde{N}_3$]
13 ^{b}) नाश्वत्थामा न (for न क्षत्ता न च) [$\tilde{N}_1$ M]
14 ^{d}) विशेषतः (for मनस्विनः) [$\acute{S}_1$ $K_{0\cdot2\cdot4}$ $\tilde{N}_3$ D_5]
18 ^{b}) प्रच्छन्नः प्रयतः (for प्रच्छन्नं तु यतः)

Adhy. 131

15 ^{c}) वन्दितान् (for वर्धितान्) [$\tilde{N}_{1\cdot3}$]
16 ^{d}) अभ्यनन्दन्त (for °वर्तन्त)
18 ^{b}) राज्यलंभाय (for राज्यलाभाय)

Adhy. 132

8 ^{d}) कार्यं साधु (for कारयेथा) [U]

Adhy. 133

4 ^{a}) समापृष्ट्वा (for तथा पृष्ट्वा) [$\tilde{N}_3$]
13 ^{a}) तथावदतः (for तथावादिनः)
17 ^{c}) चाभिवन्द्य (for अभिनन्द्य)
18 ^{c}) पांडवं ज्येष्ठं (for पाण्डवश्रेष्ठं)
^{e}) प्राज्ञः (for प्राज्ञं)
^{f}) सर्वधर्मार्थदर्शिवान् [D_5]
28 ^{d}) पाण्डवैः (for चाब्रवीत्) [$\tilde{N}_3$]
29 ^{d}) प्रत्युक्तो (for इत्युक्तो)

Adhy. 134

8 ^{b}) भरतर्षभ (for °र्षभाः)
10 ^{cd}) पुरतः पौरैः (for पुरुषैरुरुषुः) [$\tilde{N}_3$]
13 ^{e}) सौम्य (for सोम्य)
14^{e}–15^{b} Om.
After 15, ins. 1463*
21 ^{d}) सुयोधनवशे (for °मते)
22 ^{a}) अग्निना दाहदग्धेषु [U]
After 22^{cd}, ins. 1470* (with v. l.)

24 ^{b}) पक्षसंश्रितः (for °संश्रितः)
^{d}) स्पर्शैर्नां (for प्रयोगैः) [$\tilde{N}_3$]
26 ^{b}) चरन्तौ (for चराम) [$\tilde{N}_3$]

Adhy. 135

6 ^{d}) आश्वासकारणम् (for विश्वास°)

Adhy. 136

1 ^{c}) संप्रेक्ष्य (for संलक्ष्य)
4 ^{c}) वधार्येह (for निधा°) [$K_{0.2.4}$ $\tilde{N}_{1.3}$]
10 ^{c}) ततः (for तदा) [K $\tilde{N}_1$ D_5]
11 ^{d}) तत् (for यत्)
12 ^{a}) हा हा (for अहो) [$\tilde{N}_3$]
^{d}) वह्निभिः (for मन्त्रिणा) [$\tilde{N}_3$]

Adhy. 137

5 ^{a}) धीमान् (for भीष्मो) [$\tilde{N}_{1.3}$ $M_{3.5}$]
16 ^{a}) कुरवः (for कौरवाः)
^{b}) शोकसमन्विताः (for °परायणाः) [U]
18 ^{a}) निदावैद् (for विज्ञाय)
21 ^{d}) वयम् (for भयात्) [$\tilde{N}_{1.3}$]

Adhy. 138

2 ^{c}) यातिगुल्मांश्च (for दारु°) [$K_{0.3.4}$]
6 ^{a}) अगामक्षय चोद्देशम् [$\tilde{N}_{1.3}$ M]
13 ^{d}) नरोत्तम (for तदा नृप)
14 ^{a}) गव्यूतिमात्रमागम्य [K_0 $\tilde{N}_3$]
18 ^{b}) अनागसमनर्हतीम् [S_1 K $\tilde{N}_1$.]
^{c}) इमां (for इह) [K_{1-4} $\tilde{N}_{1.3}$]

Adhy. 139

1 ^{a}) Transp. तत्र and तेषु [$\tilde{N}_3$]
[251] 2 ^{f}) अपश्यस्त्स (for °श्यत) [K_3 $\tilde{N}_{1.3}$ D_5]
5 ^{c}) स्नेहस्रवः (for °स्रवान्) [$\tilde{N}_3$]
11 ^{d}) भरतर्षभाः (for °र्षभ) [$Ś_1$ $K_{2.3}$ $\tilde{N}_{1.3}$]
12 ^{d}) जाग्रन्तम् (for जाग्रतं तु) [$K_{0.2.3}$ D_{m1} G_2]
15 ^{b}) क्रूरोपबृंहितम् (for °संहितम्) [$\tilde{N}_3$]
^{c}) हि बलवान् (for [ऽ] तिबलवान्)
^{d}) भ्रातृसङ्गतम् (for °सौहृदम्) [K_3 $\tilde{N}_3$ G_5]
16 ^{a}) मुहूर्तमपि (for °र्तमिव) [K_2 $\tilde{N}_{1.3}$]
17 ^{c}) महात्मानं (for महाबाहुं)
23 ^{c}) अन्विच्छे (for इच्छामि) [K_3 $\tilde{N}_3$]
27 ^{b}) कनीयांसः (for कनिष्ठान्) [$\tilde{N}_3$]
^{d}) अपि (for इव) [U]
28 ^{a}) वने (for इमान्) [K $\tilde{N}_{1.3}$]
^{d}) कामार्थमिह (for कामार्त इव) [$\tilde{N}_3$]

Adhy. 140

5 ^{a}) भीम (for वीर) [K_0 $\tilde{N}_3$]
^{c}) इमं मम पृष्ठं (for इमां मम श्रोणीं) [$\tilde{N}_3$]
6 ^{c}) नयिष्यामि (for गामि°) [K_4 $\tilde{N}_3$]
7 ^{a}) पृथुलश्रोणि (for विपुल°) [$Ś_1$ $K_{1.2.4}$ $\tilde{N}_3$]
9 ^{b}) उभौ (for इमौ) [K_0 $\tilde{N}_{1.3}$]
^{d}) संघातं चाप्युरो महत् [$\tilde{N}_3$]
12 ^{a}) तया संजल्पमानस्य [$\tilde{N}_3$]
^{c}) क्षुद्रो (for क्रुद्धो) [Ś $K_{0\ 2.3}$ $\tilde{N}_1$]
14 ^{d}) सुसूक्ष्मं तनुवाससम् [$\tilde{N}_3$]

Adhy. 141

2 ^{d}) राक्षसानां यशोहर (= 4^{f}) [$\tilde{N}_3$]
4 ^{b}) [ए] व (for [अ] थ) [$\tilde{N}_3$]
9 ^{a}) वक्राङ्गाः (for क्रव्यादाः) [cf. $\tilde{N}_3$]
^{c}) संप्रहृष्टा वै (for भुवि संहृष्टा) [$\tilde{N}_3$]

Adhy. 142

15 ^{a}) समालिङ्गय (for °श्लिष्य) [Ko $\tilde{N}_{1.3}$ $M_{6.8}$]
^{b}) पुनः पुनः (for परस्परम्)
16 ^{c}) विभ्राजतु (for विभ्राजेतां)
24 ^{d}) गुणशतावपि (for °ताधिकम्) [$Ś_1$ Ñ]
25 ^{d}) [ए] वं (for [अ] थ) [$\tilde{N}_3$]
26 ^{d}) निपात्यताम् (for निहन्यताम्)
29 ^{b}) स्वरम् (for स्वनम्) [U]
34 ^{b}) महारथाः (for परंतपाः)

Adhy. 143

6 ^{b}) कालपरीतया (for °प्रतीक्षया) [$\tilde{N}_3$]
8 ^{a}) वीरेणानेन चैवाहं [$\tilde{N}_3$]

11 ^{b}) पतिः (for सदा) [Corrupt]
^{d}) नरर्षभाः (for °र्षभान्)
12 ^{a}) प्रवक्ष्यामि (for वाक्ष्यामि)
^{b}) अभीप्सताम् (for °प्सतः) [Ś$_1$ K$_{1\cdot3}$ B$_5$ D$_5$]
20 ^{a}) पुण्येषु (for रम्येषु) [Ś$_1$ K$_{0\cdot1}$ Ñ$_{1\cdot3}$]
22 ^{d}) मणिहेमचितेषु (for पद्मोत्पलयुतेषु) [Ñ$_3$]
23 ^{b}) वैडूर्यसिकतेषु (for °तासु)
25 ^{a}) रम्येषु (for पुण्येषु) [Ñ$_3$ G$_3$ M]
^{d}) देवतायतनेषु च [Ñ$_3$]
27 ^{d}) महाबलान् (for °बलम्)
[252] 28 ^{d}) महारथम् (for °बलम्) [Ñ$_3$ T$_2$ G]
36 ^{b}) तां (for तं) [K (except K$_1$)] [Ñ$_{1\cdot3}$]

Adhy. 144

13 ^{b}) धर्मनित्यो (for °पुत्रो)
14 ^{d}) [अ]संशयम् (for °शयः)
15 ^{b}) महाबलाः (for °रथाः)
^{d}) सदा (for तदा)
16^{c}–18^{b} inserted marg. *sec. m.*

Adhy. 145

3 ^{b}) [उ]त (for च)
5 ^{b}) कौन्त्या भैक्षं (for भैक्षं कुन्त्याः)
7 ^{b}) राष्ट्रे (for राजन्) [Ñ$_3$]
8 ^{b}) पुरुषर्षभाः (for भरत°)
13 ^{d}) यः कुर्यादुषितं (for यत्कुर्युरुषिताः)
15 ^{d}) सदृशं (for सुकृतं) [Ś$_1$ K Ñ$_3$]
19 ^{d}) विगताननम् (for विकृता°) [Ñ$_{1\cdot3}$ B$_5$]
22 ^{d}) परमसंमतम् (for °मकं मतम्) [Ñ$_{1\cdot3}$]
29 ^{d}) शोककरो (for दुःख°) [K$_1$ Ñ$_3$]
31 ^{d}) रतिम् (for गतिम्)
34 ^{b}) सुतं (for सुतां)
^{c}) बालम् (for बालाम्)
36 ^{c}) नेति (for नैव)
40 ^{a}) कृछ्रम् (for कृछ्राम्)

Adhy. 146

9 ^{b}) सर्वकामधनेश्वरः [Ś$_1$ K$_{0\cdot1\cdot3}$]
16 ^{d}) वेदस्मृतीमिव (for वेदश्रुतिं यथा) [Ñ$_3$]
18 ^{c}) अनर्थवशम् (for अनर्ह°) [U]
20 ^{b}) तव (for मम) [K$_1$]
22 ^{c}) गन्तुं ब्रह्मन् (for न तु ब्राह्मण)
31 ^{b}) महान् (for मया)
^{d}) जीवितम् (for [अ]जीवितम्) [Ś$_1$ K$_1$ Ñ]

Adhy. 147

1 ^{b}) निशाम्य तु (for निशाम्य तत्) [Ñ$_{1\cdot3}$]
5 ^{c}) तारणात् (for तारयेत्) [Ñ$_3$]
6 ^{b}) मयि (for [अ]पि
9 ^{d}) भवेयम् (for म्रियेयम्) [Ñ$_3$ D$_2$]
16 Reads 16^{cd}, after 1623* (cf. 18)
18 ^{d}) सुदुःखिता (for सुखान्विता) [U]
After 18, ins. 1623* (cf. 16)
21 ^{a}) पिता रुद (for रोदीस्तात)
^{c}) Transp. सर्वान् and तान्
^{d}) सोपतिष्ठति (for °सर्पति) [K$_1$]

Adhy. 148

1 ^{c}) ह्यपकर्वेयं (for *अप°) [K0 Ñ$_3$ D$_5$ M$_3$]
10 ^{b}) ते (for ये) [Ñ$_3$]
12 ^{c}) संचयेनास्य (for °ये चास्य)
13 ^{a}) कथं (for मया) [Ñ$_3$]
^{b}) अस्माभिः समुपार्जितम् [Ñ$_3$]
16 ^{a}) शोकार्णवे (for दुःखा°) [Ñ$_3$]
^{e}) अतो (for ततो) [U]
^{f}) उपयोक्ष्यति (for °भोक्ष्यति)

Adhy. 149

7 ^{a}) फलं प्राप्य (for परं पापं) [Ñ$_3$]
^{d}) कुतस्त्वात्मवतो (for श्रेयो *आत्मवधो) [Ñ$_3$]
8 ^{a}) नन्वहं (for न त्वहं)
[253] 11 ^{a}) तत्कुर्यात् (for कुर्याश्च)
^{b}) न च कर्ता (for न नृशंसं) [Ñ$_3$]
12 ^{d}) कदाचन (for कथं°)
20 ^{c}) तत् (for तम्) [M]
^{d}) ताम् (for तौ) [U]

Adhy. 150

15 ^{b}) मतम् (for महत्) [Ñ$_{3}$]
16 ^{a}) वृकोदरबले (for °बलो) [K (except K$_{1}$) Ñ$_{3}$ D$_{5}$]
^{b}) न जातो न जनिष्यति
20 ^{d}) [आ]चरितो (for चरितो) [K$_{4}$ Ñ B$_{5}$]
21 ^{d}) मतम् (for श्रुतम्) [U]
25 ^{a}) मां (for स)
26 After 26, ins. 1644*

Adhy. 151

9 ^{b}) प्रेक्षमाणो (for नेक्ष°)
11 ^{d}) च (for सः) [U]
14 ^{a}) प्रासं (for क्षिसं) [Ś$_{1}$ K$_{0\cdot1\cdot3}$ D$_{5}$]
19 ^{d}) क्रमेन (for श्रमेण)

Adhy. 152

6 After 6, ins. 1665*
7 ^{a}) तत् (for तं) [Ñ$_{3}$]
8 ^{b}) कल्य एव तम् (for काल्यमेव तु)
15 ^{a}) परिपृष्ट्वा (for °पृच्छ्य)
^{d}) विश्वास्य (for आश्वास्य)

Adhy. 153

4 ^{b}) विप्रं (for विद्वान्)
6 ^{b}) सरितस्तथा (for विविधानि च)
9 ^{d}) मनुजर्षभाः (for पुरुष°) [Ñ$_{3}$]

Adhy. 154

9 ^{d}) द्विजोत्तम (for द्विजर्षभ)
13 ^{a}) द्रोणो (for चापि)
^{c}) महाक्षं (for ब्रह्माक्षं) [Ñ$_{3}$]
16 ^{d}) सकाशं (for नगरं) [Ñ$_{3}$]

Adhy. 155

1 ^{a}) द्रुपदस्त्वमर्षी नृपतिः [S$_{1}$ Ñ$_{3}$]
2 ^{a}) स (for वै) [Ś$_{1}$ K Ñ$_{1\cdot3}$ D$_{5}$ M$_{5}$]
8 ^{c}) उपामन्त्रयामास (for तावाम°)
10 ^{c}) यथाकामम् (for °न्यायम्) [Ñ$_{3}$]
18 ^{d}) भुञ्जते स्म (for भुङ्क्ते चापि) [cf. Ñ$_{3}$]
20 ^{b}) नु (for [इ]दं)
21 ^{d}) मा (for त्वं)
22 ^{c}) यस्मात् (for तस्मात्) [U]
24 ^{b}) प्रसह्यंत नं वै भुवि [Ñ$_{3}$]
35 ^{a}) Om. अव [Corrupt]
36 ^{b}) [उ]पयाजाभिमन्त्रितम्
39 ^{b}) संप्रययौ (for च प्र°)
43 ^{b}) प्रवाति वै (for प्रवायाति) [Ñ$_{3}$ B$_{1\cdot5}$ M$_{3\cdot5}$]
After 43, ins. 1698*
48 ^{a}) उक्त्वा तु (for उवाच) [D$_{5}$]

Adhy. 156

5 ^{a}) द्रष्टुं हि (for दृष्टानि)

Adhy. 157

4 ^{b}) सत्येन (for शास्त्रेण) [Ñ$_{3}$]
13 ^{b}) मुहुः (for पुनः) [K Ñ$_{1\cdot3}$]
14 ^{a}) जज्ञे (for जाता)

Adhy. 158

2 ^{b}) सोमश्रवाह्वयम् (for °वायणम्)
3 ^{d}) महारथः (for °यशाः)
7 ^{a}) प्राची (for घोरा) [Ñ$_{3}$ M$_{6\cdot8}$]
8 ^{d}) कर्मचारेषु (for कामचारमिह)
[254] 10 ^{c}) गर्हन्ति पुरुषान्सर्वान् [Ñ$_{1\cdot3}$]
^{d}) गृहस्थान् (for बलस्थान्) [Ñ$_{3}$]
13 ^{c}) वासं (for वाकां) [Ñ$_{1\cdot3}$ B$_{5}$ m D$_{1}$]
14 ^{a}) कौणपाः (for कुणपाः)
15 ^{c}) वा (for च)
16 ^{c}) रणे क्रूरान् (for क्षणे क्रूरे)
18 ^{a}) विष्णुपदी (for चैकवप्रा) [U]
^{b}) वाशुचाकाशगा (for शुचिराका°) [Corrupt]
^{d}) [अ]लकशब्दताम् (for °नन्दताम्) [K$_{0\cdot2-4}$ Ñ$_{1\cdot3}$ B$_{1}$]
22 ^{b}) आयस्य (for आनम्य)
^{c}) अमोचत् (for मुमोच) [Corrupt]
24 ^{a}) बिभीषिकां वै (for °षिकैषा)
^{b}) प्रयोजयेत् (for प्रयुज्यते) [Ñ$_{3}$]
25 ^{b}) कामये (for लक्षये) [Ñ$_{3}$]
31 ^{d}) परित्राणम् (for पति°)
32 ^{a}) महाभाग (for °राज) [U]
34 ^{b}) गन्धर्वि (for गन्धर्व) [U]
37 ^{a}) शस्त्राग्निना (for अस्त्रा°) [U]
40 ^{d}) मम (for मह्यं)

41 ^{c}) यथा (for मया) [Ś$_1$ K$_{1.2}$]
^{d}) त्वयि निबोध (for प्रतिनि°) [K (except K$_1$) Ñ$_3$]
50 ^{a}) क्षत्रं वप्रस्य भाजनं [U]

Adhy. 159

4 ^{cd}) Om. [Ś$_1$ K Ñ$_{1\text{-}3}$]
10 ^{d}) आत्मनः (for आश्रितः) [Ś$_1$ K (except K$_4$) B$_5$ G$_1$]
14 ^{b}) कथञ्चन (for परंतप) [Ñ$_{1\text{-}3}$ B (except B$_6$) D$_2$]
15–16 Transp. 15^{ab} and 16^{ab} [U]
19 ^{a}) लब्धम् (for लब्धुम्)
21 ^{b}) वा (for च)

Adhy. 160

3 ^{a}) तु (for स) [Ñ$_{1\text{-}3}$ T$_1$ G$_2$]
12 ^{d}) तदा (for सदा) [U]
13 ^{a}) °माल्योपहाराभ्यां [K$_{0\text{-}4}$ Ñ$_3$]
21 ^{b}) उरुयशोभुजः (for °यशा भुवि)
30 ^{a}) तस्या (for अस्या)
32 ^{d}) °ताडितः [K$_{0\text{-}3\text{-}4}$ Ñ$_{1\text{-}3}$]

Adhy. 161

8 ^{c}) कमलपत्राभे (for °गर्भाभे)
17 ^{a}) भूतेषु (for लोकेषु) [U]
19 ^{c}) हे (for ते) [U]

Adhy. 162

4 ^{ab}) Om. [Ñ$_{1\text{-}3}$]
7 ^{a}) क्षुत्पिपासाश्रमार्तं स [Ñ$_3$]
^{d}) महीपते (for °तले) [Ñ$_{1\text{-}3}$ G$_1$]
18 ^{d}) यथेच्छकम् (for °च्छसि) [B$_{1\ 3\text{-}5}$ D$_4$]

Adhy. 163

17 ^{d}) मुनिसत्तमः (for राजसत्तमम्)

Adhy. 165

10 ^{c}) अमृतनिभं (for °रसं)
13 ^{b}) पृथुपक्षसमावृताम्
19 ^{b}) यथेप्सिताम् (for ममेप्सिताम्)
20 ^{a}) चापि (for चासि)
22 ^{a}) °प्रचुदिता
^{c}) रम्भायमाणा (for हम्भा°)
35 ^{b}) प्रभवात् (for शकृतः)
36 ^{c}) वर्बुरान्मूछान् (for बर्बरान्म्लेच्छान्)

25A

38 ^{a}) शस्त्रवर्षेण (for अस्त्र°) [U]
^{b}) वध्यमानं (for काल्य°) [U]
39 ^{b}) किञ्चित्ते सैनिकस्तवा [Ñ$_3$]

{255} Adhy. 166

20 ^{b}) वनम् (for पुनः)
34 ^{b}) रक्षसोपहतेन्द्रियः

Adhy. 167

10 After 10, ins. 1786*
11 ^{a}) अनुगम्य (for अनुगतः) [Ñ$_{1\text{-}3}$]
^{b}) नाश्रमाभिमुखोगमत्
21 ^{c}) रक्ष आददितुं (for रक्षो अत्तुमिह) [Ñ$_3$ M$_{6\text{-}8}$]

Adhy. 168

4 ^{c}) तस्मात् (for घोरात्) [Ñ$_3$]
^{d}) रक्षसो (for राक्षसात्)
6 ^{a}) विप्रयुक्तो (for °मुक्तो) [Ś$_1$ Ñ$_3$ G$_3$]
8 ^{a}) महाप्रज्ञ (for °भाग) [Ñ$_3$]
10 ^{a}) अवमन्यामि (for °मंस्यामि) [U]
14 ^{b}) सह तेन वै (for सहितोऽनघ)
^{c}) ख्यातां पुरवरां (for ख्यातं पुरवरं)
19 ^{b}) पताकाध्वजभूषितम्
25 ^{c}) नृपतिः (for राजर्षिः) [Ñ$_3$]
^{d}) पोदनं (for पोतनं) [U]

Adhy. 169

7 ^{a}) इति न ते (for तातेति) [K$_1$ Ñ$_{1\text{-}3}$ M$_3$]
^{b}) तात एष महानृषिः
8 ^{c}) तात (for तस्य) [Ñ$_3$]
9 ^{d}) महातपाः (for °मनाः)
15 ^{b}) ददतो (for भृगवो) [cf. Ñ$_3$]
18 ^{c}) महीपालाः (for महेष्वासाः) [Ñ$_{1\text{-}3}$]
19 ^{a}) उत्साद्यमानेषु (for उच्छिद्य°)
20 ^{a}) [अ]न्यतरा (for °तमा) [Ś$_1$ K$_1$ Ñ$_3$]
^{b}) दध्रेथ (for दाधार) [K$_1$ Ñ$_3$]
22 ^{b}) क्षत्रियाः पुनः (for क्षत्रियर्षभाः)
23 ^{d}) गतार्चिश्च (for शान्ता°) [Ñ$_3$]

Adhy. 170

12 ^{b}) °पन्नगान् [Ñ$_3$]
17 After 17, ins. 1789* (with v. l.)

19 ^{a}) लोके (for तात) [$\tilde{N}_3$]
^{c}) एतत् (for एवं)
^{d}) चात्मनात्मा निपातितः
21 ^{c}) न नः (for तपः) [U]

Adhy. 171

2 ^{b}) भवितुम् (for जीवितुम्)
6 ^{d}) ततो (for तदा) [U]
7 ^{a}) संपूर्णकामा इव मे
8 ^{c}) धारयेयम् (for दधारयेम्) [Corrupt]
17 ^{a}) तेजो (for तेऽग्निः) [$\tilde{N}_3$]
23 ^{c}) लोकान् (for धर्मान्)

Adhy. 172

2 ^{b}) सर्वधर्मभृतां (for °वेदविदां) [$\tilde{N}_3$]
6 ^{b}) शक्तितः (for युक्तितः)
8 ^{d}) पुनरागमत् (for समुपां°) [U]
9 ^{a}) ततः (for तथा)
^{c}) तत्राजग्मुरमित्रघ्नं

Adhy. 173

2 ^{b}) पुरा तेन महर्षिणा [?]
After 2^{cd}, ins. 1796*
^{e}) एतन्मे संशयं (for कृतं तेन पुरा)
14 ^{b}) सुनृशंसवान् (for °कृत)
^{d}) पशुम् (for मृगम्) [$\acute{S}_1$ K $\tilde{N}_{1\cdot3}$ D_5]
16 ^{b}) °कर्शिता
[256] 23 ^{b}) काममोहितः (for शाप°) [U]
^{d}) संभ्रान्तो (for स तस्या)

Adhy. 175

2 ^{d}) सङ्गतान् (for सगणान्)
3 ^{a}) ते (for तान्)
^{b}) धर्मचारिणः (for ब्रह्म°)
8 ^{b}) यशस्विनी (for मन°)
12 ^{d}) महाव्रताः (for यत°)
14 ^{a}) देयान् (for दायान्) [$\tilde{N}_3$]
17 ^{b}) प्रतिपूज्य (for °गृह्य) [U]
18 ^{d}) पतिम् (for वरम्)
19 ^{d}) भवेत् (for बहु) [$\tilde{N}_{1\cdot3}$]

Adhy. 176

6 ^{d}) निवासं (for निवेशं)
9 ^{c}) [अ] नानम्यं (for °यम्यं)
10 ^{c}) लक्ष्येण समितं (for यन्त्रेण सहितं) [U]
14 ^{c}) ततोर्चिता (for तेऽभ्य°)
After 14, ins. 1812*
15 ^{c}) शिशुमारशिरं (for °पुरं)
16 ^{b}) भूमिदेशे (for °भागे) [$\tilde{N}_3$ M_5]
18 ^{b}) परार्ध्यागरभूषितः
21 ^{b}) °धूपितैः
24 ^{b}) महाबलपराक्रमान्
^{d}) मृष्टागुरु° [Corrupt]
27 ^{c}) Here and in some places in the sequel पञ्चाल° (for पाञ्चाल°)

Adhy. 177

5 ^{a}) [अ] बलश्रैव (for बलश्रैव)
9 ^{c}) सुचित्रः (for सुमित्रः)
11 ^{b}) चित्रसेनः (for चन्द्र°)
^{d}) अदण्डो (for सुदण्डो)
12 ^{d}) महान् (for तथा)
15 ^{b}) पौरवः (for कौरवः)
After 15, ins. 1815*
16^{cd}) Om.
17 ^{b}) महामतिः (for °बलः)
18 After 18^{a}, ins. 1818* (with v. l.)
^{b}) सारिमेजयः (for सार°)
^{d}) जल्ली (for झिल्ली)

Adhy. 178

3 ^{b}) [अ] थ (for [अ] पि) [U]
5 ^{b}) नयनैः (for हृदयैः) [U]
6 ^{a}) तथा° (for अथा°) [U]
7 ^{a}) सुधर्माश्च (for सुपर्णाश्च) [U]
9 ^{d}) कृष्णः (for पार्थान्)
12 ^{d}) कन्दर्पबाणानुगता (for °बाणाभिहता)
16 ^{b}) निष्पिष्यमाणा (for निष्कूज्य°) [$K_{0\cdot2-4}$ M_{5-3}]
^{d}) दृष्यंति ह स्म प्रविभग्नचित्ताः [$\tilde{N}_1$]
18 ^{d}) च (for स)

Adhy. 179

11 ^{b}) त्रिषु (for कर्म)
19 ^{a}) सैनिकाः (for सुस्वनाः) [U]
20 ^{b}) [अ] मित्रकर्षणः (for [अ] रिनिषूदनः) [U]

22 ^{c}) वरदाममाल्य (for वरमाल्यदाम) [cf K_1]

23 ^{c}) [अ] चिन्त्य राज्ञः (for [अ] चिन्त्यकर्मा) [K]

Adhy. 180

2 After 2, ins. 1855* (with कन्यका for कालिका) [$Ś_1$ K $\tilde{N}_1$]

3 ^{a}) ते हन्मैनं (for निह^{o}) [$Ś_1$ K G_6]

4 ^{b}) दुरात्मानं (for ^{o}चारं) [$\tilde{N}_1$ $B_{3\text{-}5}$ D_5]

[257]* 5 ^{d}) नानुदृष्टवान् (for नैव द^{o}) [U]

9 ^{b}) सुखानि (for वसूनि) [U]

10 ^{a}) चैव (for एतत्)

13 ^{c}) महात्मानौ (for ^{o}वीर्यौ) [U]

16 ^{d}) भीमः (for पार्थः) [U]

18 ^{a}) सिंहर्षभमत्तगामी (for मत्तर्षभतुल्यगामी) [$\tilde{N}_1$]

Adhy. 181

4 ^{a}) आयम्य (for आदाय) [$\tilde{N}_2$ B_3]

^{b}) महाबलः (for ^{o}रथः)

9 ^{b}) शितैः (for त्रिभिः)

31 After 31^{ab}, ins. 1882* (with स्वपराद्वापि सर्वथा as posterior pāda)

^{d}) योत्स्याम हृष्टवत् (for ^{o}महे वयम्) After 31, ins. 1883*

Adhy. 182

2 ^{c}) कृष्णां (for कन्यां)

4 ^{a}) च (for हि)

7 ^{b}) शोभिष्यति (for तोषि^{o})

8 ^{a}) अधर्ममेवं (for ^{o}र्मभाजं) [U]

14 ^{d}) सस्मार भरतर्षभ

Adhy. 183

1 Om. [U]

5 ^{c}) मधुप्रवीरौ (for यदु^{o})

8 ^{a}) दिष्ट्या सर्वे पावकाद्वास्थ मुक्ता

Adhy. 184

3 ^{d}) निवेदयामासुः (for निवेदयांचक्रुः) [D_4 M_5]

5 ^{d}) चतुर्थी (for चतुर्णां)

6 ^{a}) ददस्व (for ददाहि) [S_1 K D_6]

^{b}) सिंहर्षभतुल्यरूपः (for मत्तर्षभ^{o})

7 ^{d}) [ऽ] प्युपजह्नुः (for [ऽ] भ्यव^{o}) [$\tilde{N}_1$ V_1]

9 ^{d}) सा तु (for पत्तः)

18 ^{b}) पौत्राः (for पुत्राः) [K_2 G_1]

Adhy. 185

8 ^{c}) स्थितां (for स्थितौ)

11 ^{d}) द्वितीयं (for द्विजातेः) [U]

12 ^{d}) [ऽ] भिसङ्गात् (for ^{o}दाहात्) [U]

16 ^{b}) वरदो वरार्थी (for द्रुपदो वरार्हः)

20 ^{b}) प्रसमीक्ष्य (for समुदीक्ष्य) [V_1 $M_{3\text{-}5}$]

21 ^{d}) तथैव (for तां चैव) [U]

23 ^{c}) या (for न) [U]

25 ^{a}) एवंगते (for नैवं^{o})

Adhy. 186

5 ^{d}) यानानि (for द्रव्याणि) [$\tilde{N}_1$]

7 ^{a}) वर्माणि चर्माणि (for रथाश्ववर्माणि) [$\tilde{N}$ D_n D_1]

^{c}) चित्राणि (for चाग्र्याणि) [U]

9 ^{d}) [अ] दीनसत्त्वाम् (for ^{o}सत्त्वाः)

Adhy. 187

13 ^{c}) वाचा (for राजा)

26 ^{d}) कथंचन (for कदा^{o}) [U]

Adhy. 188

1 ^{d}) [अ] भवादयन् (for ^{o}पूजयन्)

2 ^{a}) प्रतिलभ्य (for ^{o}नभ्य) [U]

3 ^{b}) [अ] क्लिष्टकर्मणा (for [अ] मिततेजसा) [D_5]

4 ^{d}) स्वयंवरे (for विशां पतिः) [$\tilde{N}_3$ B D_4]

Adhy. 189

4 ^{d}) ह्ययाम (for प्र^{o}) [S_1 $K_{1\text{-}2}$]

10 ^{d}) यत्र देवी गङ्गा सततं प्रभाता

18 ^{c}) उग्रधन्वा (for ^{o}तेजा) [U]

19 ^{a}) निवर्तयैतं (for विवर्तयैनं)

22 ^{b}) प्रावेपतातों मनशोभिषङ्गात्

[258] 24 ^{d}) क्षेप्व (for क्षेप्ध्वम्)

27 ^{c}) [अ] स्मात् (for [अ] स्मान्

29 ^{b}) इवं (for इहं) [U]
31 After 31^{a}, ins. 1919*
After 31, ins. 1920*
38 After 38^{a}, ins. 1921*
39 ^{a}) [अ]वेक्ष्य (for [अ]वाप्य)
^{b}) [अ]तिरूपत्रुह्याम् (for इव रूपिणीं च)
After 39^{ab}, ins. 1922*
48 ^{a}) उपागता (for तदा°) [K_3]

Adhy. 190

1 ^{b}) वर्जनाय (for कार्यमेतत्)
^{d}) उपयाता (for उपपन्नं) [U]
8 ^{a}) [अ]न्यजनोपपन्नं (for [अ]र्थिजनोपशोभितं) [U]
^{b}) विकीर्णपुष्पोत्पल°
^{c}) प्रभूतरत्नौघ° [U]
12 ^{b}) परीणयामास (for समानयामास)

Adhy. 191

6 ^{a}) ऋद्धिः (for भद्रा) [U]
7 ^{b}) °गुणान्विता
12 ^{b}) क्षौमवाससम् (for °संवृताम्)
13 ^{d}) शतशो भाजनानि च (= 15^{d})
14–16 Transp. 14^{ab} and 16^{ab}, and om. 15
17 Transp. 17^{ab} and 19^{ab}.
18 ^{b}) तदा (for तथा) [$Ś_1$ $K_{3\cdot4}$ $Ñ_1$ V_1]

Adhy. 192

1 ^{b}) समुपद्दीयते (for समुपनीयत)
3 ^{b}) न्यवधीद् (for [अ]भ्रामयद्) [U]
^{c}) भ्रामयामास (for त्रासयंश्चापि) [U]
^{d}) नृवरान् (for पुरुषान्) [U]
5 ^{a}) दृष्ट्वा (for श्रुत्वा) [$Ñ_{1\cdot3}$]
^{b}) राजन्पाण्डुसुतान्स तान् [U]
6 ^{c}) पुनर्जातानिव स्वैतान्
20 ^{d}) तथा (for तदा)
21 After 21, ins. 1951*
22 After 22, ins. 1953*
26 ^{b}) शक्नुमः (for शक्नुवः)
^{c}) वक्ष्यामः (for वक्ष्यावः)
29 ^{d}) सपुत्रपशुबान्धवान्

Adhy. 193

3 ^{a}) [अ]पि (for तूर्णं) [$Ñ_1$]
4 ^{b}) सुभृतैः (for सुकृतैः) [$K_{0\cdot3}$]
10 After 10 ins. 1960* (with v. l.)
13 ^{b}) महीम् (for महत्) [$K_{2\cdot3}$ $Ñ_1$]
14 ^{d}) यथाशास्त्रं (for °अर्थं)
16 ^{c}) लोप्त्रघातैः (for °हारैः) [$Ś_1$ $K_{1\cdot3\cdot4}$]
^{d}) पात्यन्तामासकारिणः
19 ^{c}) साध्वी वा यदि वासाध्वी

Adhy. 194

2 ^{c}) तदा (for यदा)
^{d}) नैवेह शकिताः प्रभो [U]
6 ^{b}) विद्यते (for शक्यते) [V_1 D_5]
8 ^{c}) पंच (for तं च) [U]
9 ^{b}) धनव्रतः (for °प्रियः) [$Ś_1$ $K_{0\cdot1\cdot4}$]
12 ^{d}) विचारणा (for °रय) [U]
13 ^{ab}) मित्राणि च प्रभूतानि बलवन्ति दृढानि च [U]
15 ^{d}) पञ्चाल्यसदनं प्रति
19 ^{c}) प्रसह्य (for प्रमथ्य) [U]
20 ^{a}) सम्मानदानेन (for साम्ना न°) [U]
^{b}) [अ]द्य (for च) [$Ś_1$ K (except K_2) $Ñ_1$]
23 ^{a}) महावीर्यै (for °प्राज्ञै) [U]

{259} Adhy. 195

5 ^{a}) निजं (for यथा) [U]
8 ^{d}) नः (for)
9 ^{c}) त्वाम् (for तव) [$K_{0\cdot3}$ V_1 G_1]
^{d}) भजिष्यति (for भविष्यति) [U]
13 ^{a}) पार्थां (for वीरा)
19 ^{d}) राज्यं तेषां (for तेषामर्धं) [$M_{3\cdot6-8}$]

Adhy. 196

1 ^{b}) तव (for नृप)
25 ^{d}) भाषताम् (for भाषितम्) [U]
28 ^{b}) ब्रवीषि (for °मि)

Adhy. 197

13 ^{b}) स्वेषु (for तेषु)
16 ^{d}) स्वयम् (for अपि) [U]
19 ^{c}) पाण्डवे ज्येष्ठे (for पाण्डवश्रेष्ठे)
23 ^{a}) तु विग्रहम् (for निर्विग्रहम्) [U]
After 23, ins. 1975*

29 ^{d}) न भविष्यति (for विनशिष्यति) [U]

Adhy. 198

24 ^{d}) एतदेव मतं मम

Adhy. 199

6 ^{a}) सदा (for ततो) [U]
9 ^{b}) पाण्डुपुत्रो (for धर्म^{o})
24 ^{b}) गदतो (for इदं वचो)
^{d}) कौरवैः पाण्डवर्षभ [U]
25^{abcd}) Om.
32 ^{a}) शय्यैः (for तल्पैः) [U]
37 ^{d}) सर्वभाष्यविदः (for ^{o}भाषाविदः)

Adhy. 200

3 ^{c}) नरव्याघ्रा (for महाभागा) [U]
5 ^{d}) व्याघ्रा इव (for प्राप्तराज्याः) [U]
8 ^{d}) ते (for च) [B_3 G_2]
9^{ab}) Om.
22 ^{c}) क्रमेण (for कामेन) [U]

Adhy. 201

4 ^{d}) द्विधैवैको भवत्कृतौ
14 ^{b}) पाहीति (for त्राहीति) [U]
15 ^{a}) नोपयाताम् (for ^{o}याति) [U]
18 ^{a}) महादेवं (for प्रभुं देवं) [U]
24^{c}–26^{d} Om.
29 ^{c}) नित्यः प्रमुदितः सर्वः

Adhy. 203

5^{c}-6^{b} Om.
12 ^{d}) स विश्वकृत् (for ततस्ततः)

Adhy. 204

5 ^{a}) महोद्याने (for वनो^{o}) [$\dot{N}_{1\cdot3}$ D_6]

Adhy. 205

8 ^{d}) [अ] भिमन्यते (for ^{o}मर्शति) [U]
17 After 17^{ab}, ins. 2016*
30 Om. with colophon

Adhy. 206

2 ^{c}) मौक्षाश्च (for चौक्षाश्च) [T_3 G_4]
7 ^{d}) प्रथमो (for प्रवरो) [$\acute{S}_1$ K (except K_2)]
18 ^{c}) राजन् (for पार्थ)
19 ^{d}) [अ] भिमूर्छिता (for [अ] स्मि^{o})
25 ^{f}) ते (for वः) [U]
28 ^{c}) न च मे (for स च ते) [U]

Adhy. 207

3 ^{b}) यज्ञानुद्दिश्य सत्रिणाम्
[260] 5 ^{d}) पुरुषर्षभः (for भरत^{o})
6^{ab}) Om.
13 ^{d}) मणपुरं (for मणलूरं) here and in the sequel
18 ^{b}) प्रपद्य शरणं प्रभुम् [U]
19 ^{b}) एकं प्रसवजं (for एकैकं प्रसवं)
20 ^{c}) एका तु मम कन्येयं
^{d}) हेत्वादनी (for उत्पादनी) [$\acute{S}_1$]
23 ^{d}) त्रीणि वत्सरान् (for त्रिहिमाः समाः) [U]

Adhy. 208

6 ^{d}) कुरुसत्तम (for ^{o}नन्दन)
8 ^{c}) सहसा (for तरसा)
14 ^{d}) वन्द्या (for वर्गा)
16 ^{c}) तपस्विनम् (for रूपवन्तम्)
18 ^{b}) [अ] द्भुतमुत्तमम् (for ^{o}तदर्शनम्)

Adhy. 209

20 ^{d}) एताश्चाप्याशु मोक्षय
24 ^{c}) यं (for तं) [U]

Adhy. 210

5 ^{d}) उभौ (for ऋषी) [K_4 $\dot{N}_1$ V_1]
11 ^{d}) सदाच्युतः (for महाद्युतिः)
12 ^{d}) दर्शनम (for भारत)
19 ^{a}) पार्थो (for सर्वैर्) [U]

Adhy. 211

10 ^{b}) बभ्रुर् (for भानुर्)
13 ^{b}) महाद्भुते (for ^{o}शुभे)
24 ^{c}) दिव्यान् (for राजन्) [U]

Adhy. 212

8 ^{c}) काञ्चनाङ्गेन (for आकाशगेनैव)
12 ^{d}) समंततः (for सभां ततः)
19 ^{d}) तुमुलं (for संकुलं)
31 ^{d}) अर्जुनेन पराजयः

Adhy. 213

6 ^{d}) इतः (for इति)
12 ^{d}) प्रभुः (for ततः)

13 ^{f}) आगतः (for आविशत्)
14^{ab}) Om.
15^{ef}) Om. [Ś$_1$ K$_1$]
17 ^{b}) रक्तकौशेयवासिनीम्
19 ^{a}) अभिवाद्य (for अभिगम्य) [U]
26 ^{d}) महामनाः (for °यशाः)
28 ^{b}) जल्ली (for झिल्ली)
32–33 Om.
38 ^{b}) कुन्तीपुत्रो (for धर्मराजो)
42 ^{a}) उपावृत्तविदेश्यानां [Corrupt]
^{d}) चन्द्रार्कसमतेजसाम् [U]
45 ^{b}) स्वलङ्कृताम् (for सुवाससाम्)
After 45, ins. 2087*
49 ^{a}) पाणिग्रहणिकं (for पादग्राह°)
^{d}) संबन्धं प्रति मानयन्
51 ^{b}) महाधनः (for °नदः)
57 ^{f}) मृगयां स महायशाः
After 57, ins. 2097*
68 ^{d}) व्याताननमहाभुजम् [B$_{1\cdot5}$]

Adhy. 214

3 ^{a}) सर्वकामार्थान् (for धर्म°) [U]
8 ^{a}) पार्थाः (for विप्राः) [U]
20 ^{b}) तथा (for शुभैः) [D$_{1\cdot2}$]
30 ^{b}) प्रार्थयन्कनकप्रभः [U]
31 ^{b}) चीरवासाः (for कृष्ण°)
32 ^{b}) ज्व वै (for भ्राजमानं) [U]

Adhy. 215

3 ^{d}) [अ]र्थस्य (for [अ]स्रस्य) [U]
9 ^{b}) मेघेनाभिः [? भि] प्रवर्षति
[K$_{3\cdot4}$ Ñ$_1$ D$_{1\cdot2}$]
12 ^{a}) उक्तोब्रवीच्छूरो (for उक्ते प्रत्युवाच)
[G$_{5\cdot6}$]
15 ^{a}) शरैः समर्थो (for शरेश्च मेऽर्थो) [U]

[261]

Adhy. 216

5 ^{d}) सर्वशस्त्रप्रवाधि (for °प्रमाथि)
[Ś$_1$ Ñ$_1$ D$_2$]
12 ^{b}) शक्रायुधसमावुभौ [Ñ B$_3$ D$_n$ D$_4$]
13 ^{b}) सिंहलाङ्गूललक्षणः
16 ^{c}) तदा (for रथं)
17 ^{d}) जयः (for [ऽ]र्जुनः)
28 ^{d}) कुर्यात् (for जीयात्)

Adhy. 217

6 ^{b}) भ्रातॄन् (for मातॄन्)
9 ^{a}) तद्देषु (for सर्वेषु)

Adhy. 218

6 ^{a}) स निर्गन्तु (for विनि°)
10 ^{d}) खगतान्भरतर्षभः
14 ^{c}) वितस्थे (for वियत्स्थो) [K$_{0\cdot3\cdot4}$]
15 ^{b}) [अ]मृतम् (for [उ]त्तमम्)
18 ^{a}) संप्रतीकार° [U]
22 ^{b}) स्वरोषाग्निदशो चिरात् [K$_{0\cdot4}$]
^{c}) दिग्भ्यश्चैवा° (for विवशाश्चा°) [U]
23 ^{d}) वधार्थिनः (for रणा°) [U]
27 ^{d}) हतौजसः (for महौजसः)
[Ś$_1$ K$_1$ V$_1$]
31 ^{d}) विचक्रो (for विचक्रं) [U]
38 ^{b}) महावने (for °हवे)
^{d}) भूतोत्पाताय (for °त्सादाय)

Adhy. 219

4 ^{b}) [अ]तिवेगवत् (for जनार्दनः)
17 ^{cd}) °नृप° (for °नर°)

Adhy. 220

4 ^{b}) विषां पते (for तथागते) [V$_1$]
22 ^{a}) सर्वलोकानां (for °देवानां)
31 ^{d}) विवर्जय (for विसर्जय)

Adhy. 221

3 ^{c}) संसीदयन् (for संदीपयन्) [U]
14 ^{d}) सर्वेषां (for पूर्वेषां) [U]
19 ^{d}) धरेत (for ध्रियेत)

Adhy. 223

9 ^{d}) [अ]स्मात्परिविध्यै° (for हि नः
परिरक्षै°) [U]
10 ^{d}) शरणैषिभिः (for °षिणः) [Ś$_1$ K$_1$]
11 ^{b}) त्वत्तो (for तथा) [K$_2$]
14 ^{b}) समृद्धः (for समिद्धः) [U]

Adhy. 224

1 ^{c}) दीप्तांशुं (for [अ]शीतांशुं) [Ñ$_1$]
10 ^{b}) च (for तु)
^{c}) समर्थस्त्वञ्च वक्ता वै
^{d}) न स्वास्ति (for तेष्वस्ति)
13 ^{b}) यस्थार्थे (for यदर्थं)

[d]) सपुत्त्वे (for का°) [U]
15 [b]) यो लम्बेत सुमन्तधीः [U]
[c]) अवमान्य ततो लोको [U]
16 [ab]) °मानोमी रेरिहाणी [U]
17 [b]) पुनः (for ततः)
19 [cd]) एकैकस्य न पुत्रांस्ताम्क्रोशमानावपश्यत [U]
20 [d]) Om. न [U]
21 [a]) °मान एकैकं
[c]) नोच्यते (for नोचुस्ते) [U]
[d]) सम्मतैः (for तमृषिं) [U]
22 [b]) कतमस्तस्य चानुजः
23 [c]) [अ] पि (for [अ] स्मि)
[262] 24 [b]) °जे तव (for °जेन वा) [S_1 $K_{0\cdot1}$]
25 [a]) यत्र (for यस्त्वं)
29 [a]) अवध्यानेन (for अप°) [G_{2-4}]
32 [b]) उपासदन् (for उपासिरे) [$K_{0\cdot4}$]

Adhy. 225

4 [c]) देश (for देशात्) [S_1 K (except K_2) $D_{1\cdot2}$]
[d]) क्षेममन्यं (for अन्यं देशं) [$Ś_1$ K (except K_2)]
7 [b]) शतक्रतुः (for सुरेश्वरः)
9 [cd]) गृहीतुं तं च शक्रो वै ददौ कालं चकर्ष च [Corrupt ?]
15 [b]) स पशुपक्षिणम् (for समृग°) [$K_{0\cdot3\cdot4}$ D_5]
16 [a]) दग्ध्वा (for जग्ध्वा)
17 [d]) चरतां यत्र वान्छत [Corrupt]
19 [a]) तदा (for ततः) [U]

VIII. The Rāma Episode (Rāmopākhyāna) and the Rāmāyaṇa *

SLUSZKIEWICZ's elaborate dissertation[1] on the recensions of the Rāmāyaṇa has revived the interest in the question of the relationship between the Rāmāyaṇa and the Rāma Episode of the Mahābhārata, a question which appears to have been first mooted by WEBER.[2] WEBER had contented himself with formulating the four logical alternatives : (1) the Rāmopākhyāna is the source of the Rāmāyaṇa ; (2) the Rāmopākhyāna constitutes an epitome of the Rāmāyaṇa, but of a Rāmāyaṇa more primitive than the epic in its present form ; (3) the Rāmopākhyāna represents an epitome of the Rāmāyaṇa, but an epitome modified somewhat by the compiler of the Episode himself ; and lastly ; (4) the two poems are derived independently from a lost common source. The alternatives worked out by WEBER may be admitted ; but then logical possibilities, unfortunately, do not carry us very far in historical investigations.

JACOBI, who has dealt with the question at great length in *Das Râmâyaṇa, Geschichte und Inhalt* (Bonn 1893), held firmly to the opinion that the Rāmopākhyāna was based on the Rāmāyaṇa, on *our* Rāmāyaṇa, on the Rāma Epic as we have it,—the episode forming a rather careless abridgment

* [*A Volume of Studies in Indology* presented to Prof. P. V. KANE, 472-87].

1 Eugeniusz SLUSZKIEWICZ, *Przyczynki do badań nad dziejami Redakcyi Rāmāyaṇy* (*Contributions à l'histoire des recensions du Rāmāyaṇa*) = Polska Akademia Umiejetności Prace Komisji Orientalistycznej Nr. 30 (Kraków 1938), pp. 1-86.

2 "Ueber das Rāmāyaṇa", *Abhandlungen der Berliner Akad. der Wiss.*, Phil-hist. Klasse, 1870, 1-88 (see especially, p. 36 f). Referred to by JACOBI, *Das Râmâyaṇa, Geschichte und Inhalt*, p. 71 f.—Cf. also E. W. HOPKINS, *The Great Epic of India* (New Haven, Yale University Press, 1920[2]), pp. 58 ff.

of Vālmīki's epic (*op. cit.* p. 70). In discussing the question he has drawn attention to certain passages in the Rāmopākhyāna which presuppose a knowledge of the Rāmāyaṇa, and which would be indeed unintelligible if the reader did not know certain facts and circumstances which were detailed in the Epic but omitted in the Episode. This argument [473] seems to be not quite as sound as it appears at first sight; because, for the allusions in question, the compiler of the Episode might have been indebted to any other source or sources which likewise contained those explanatory allusions which happen to be omitted in the Episode. The allusions do not point unequivocally to any one single definite source.

But JACOBI did not of course base his case on this fact alone. He strengthened it from another side. He pointed out (*op. cit.* pp. 72 ff.) about a dozen passages which the Episode had in common with the Epic. These parallelisms carry naturally far greater weight than the allusions mentioned above. Exact verbal agreement between the works of two poets, even though they may be working on the same theme, are always suspicious. The human mind is not easily duplicated. Similar *ideas* may arise independently: but the *words* in which they become clothed are still something personal and characteristic, varying with each individual.

JACOBI attached special importance to one particular stanza in the Episode,—a veritable doggerel which, (according to JACOBI) was evidently a copy of the perfect Rāmāyaṇa stanza—once heard never forgotten:[1]

सागरं चाम्बरप्रख्यमम्बरं सागरोपमम् ।
रामरावणयोर्युद्धं रामरावणयोरिव ॥

The Mbh. caricature of this stanza, according to JACOBI, was:

दशकन्धरराजसून्वोस्तथा युद्धमभून्महत् ।
अलब्धोपममन्यत्र तयोरेव तथाभवत् ॥

JACOBI was of opinion that this stanza of inferior form proves borrowing because it is inferior. This unquestionably proved also, JACOBI argued, that the Episode is merely an epitome of our Rāmāyaṇa. The argument is again not quite conclusive, and the point has been contested by HOPKINS. "A great poet," says HOPKINS, "is more apt to take a weak verse and make it strong than is a copyist to ruin a verse already excellent" (*Great Epic*, p. 63). Whatever the merits of this latter contention, JACOBI's *conclusion* appears to be correct in the main, though his argument is certainly fallacious. JACOBI should have stopped short with the stanza. The Mahā-

---

[1] *Op. cit.* p. 74: "Sollte aber noch Jemand davon Zweifeln, so verweisen wir auf den schon oben p. 14 citierten Vers: sâgaram câ'mbaraprakhyam . . . Dieser wirklich grossartige Vers, der einmal gehört nicht wieder vergessen wird, wird in Mbh folgendermassen wiedergegeben: Daśakandhara-rājasūnvos . . ' Nach Inhalt und Form eine klägliche Umschreibung, die sich auf den ersten Blick als Nachahmung verrät."

bhārata stanza appears to be—and very probably is—a weak [474] imitation of the Rāmāyaṇa stanza. The fallacy lies in the extension that the Rāmopākhyāna is therefore a weak imitation of the Rāmāyaṇa. The relation between the two stanzas does not necessarily prove anything about the relationship between the Rāmāyaṇa and the Rāmopākhyāna *as wholes*.

WINTERNITZ[1] has already warned us that each stanza of the Mbh. must be judged on its own merits,—it may be added, ***when we want to use the stanza for historical and comparative purposes.*** We could not find a better example of this dictum than the stanza on which JACOBI has relied for establishing the posteriority of the Rāmopākhyāna. The stanza has an intricate history. Though found in all our old printed editions, the MS. support for it is surprisingly meagre. Of the two lines comprising the stanza, the second was found only in Bengali MSS. in addition to some stray Nāgarī MSS. ; but the first line is itself known in two variant versions ! The form known to and cited by JACOBI, namely,

दशकन्धरराजसून्वोस्तथा युद्धमभून्महत् ।

alternates with another :

ततः प्रववृते युद्धं रामरावणयोर्महत् ।

which appears to be an attempt at remedying the awkwardness of the former, which was the subject of JACOBI'S strictures.[2] *Both lines are however completely missing in Kaśmīrī and Southern MSS. (besides many old Nāgarī MSS.*[3]*)*! This fact leaves no room now for doubting that the stanza in question is but a very late addition to the Great Epic. It can therefore naturally prove nothing whatsoever about the age or the character of the original Episode to which it has been secondarily appended by a recent interpolator. All disquisitions based on this stanza from the Rāmopākhyāna have consequently become futile. We must look for other criteria.

This only shows how very precarious are the conclusions that are based on the Vulgate text of the Mbh. And it is very remarkable that many of those very passages that have been used in the past for literary-historical purposes have turned out to be unhappily but also unquestionably spurious.[4]

---

1 *History of Indian Literature* (Calcutta 1927), p. 469 : "the date of each section, nay sometimes of each single verse, must be determined separately, . . ."

2 *Op. cit.* p. 74. Cf. footnote on p. 473 above [= 388].

3 For instance, in the fragmentary Devanāgarī MS. of the Āraṇyakaparvan belonging to the Bombay Branch of the Royal Asiatic Society, Bhau Daji Collection, No. 245.

4 I cannot give a better instance than that of a passage which was cited by H. OLDENBERG to illustrate his Ākhyāna theory. It is well known that OLDENBERG always maintained that the oldest form of epic poetry in India was a mixture of prose and verse, the speeches being in verses, while the events were narrated in prose. In this connection he drew attention to the story of Śibi in the Vanaparvan (adhy. 199 of the Bombay ed.). This adhyāya which OLDENBERG (*Das Maha-*

[475] However the fact that one particular stanza cited by JACOBI has turned out to be unauthentic does not affect his general conclusion about the relationship between the Rāmopākhyāna and the Rāmāyaṇa which, in my opinion, is quite well-founded and can be supported on other grounds.

As far as I can judge, the minute *differences* in the details of the story, which have been pointed out and exaggerated by some critics of JACOBI'S theory, tell us nothing whatsoever about the matter which is the subject of discussion. The verbal *agreements* have, on the other hand, an unusually great probative force. To strengthen the case of JACOBI, we need therefore a large number of *agreements*. I had this fact in mind when I was studying the Rāmopākhyāna for my edition of Vanaparvan or—to give it its correct name—Āraṇyakaparvan.

JACOBI had found just twelve concordances. They are obviously too few. But their actual number should be very much greater, even if we exclude the epic *iterata* and standing phrases, which are the common heritage of the epic bards and which have been listed separately by HOPKINS in an Appendix to his *Great Epic*. It would be premature, it seems to me, to discuss the question which of the existing versions of the Rāmāyaṇa our Episode stands closest to. That question can be taken up only when we have a really critical edition of the Rāmāyaṇa, which is promised by my friend and colleague Professor RAGHU VIRA of Lahore from his International Academy of Indian Culture. In the meantime, I shall just register the concordances which I have been able to find, irrespective of the versions of the Rāmāyaṇa to which they may belong.[1] A scholar who knows his Rāmāyaṇa better than I do would naturally be able to handle the question with more com-[476]petence and find more concordances. But in the absence of such an exhaustive study by a *savant* who has mastered both the poems, the following table which I have prepared may be found useful. I have consulted only the Bombay edition (published in 1888 by the Nirnaya Sagar Press) and GORRESIO'S edition (1843-1867). Of the latter edition, moreover, the last volume (Uttarakāṇḍa) was not available to me and therefore could not be utilized.

---

bharata, p. 23) regarded as a survival from the oldest form of our great epic can now on manuscript authority be proved to be one of the latest interpolations in the epic. We are not concerned with the date of this passage. The passage may be of hoary antiquity—though I doubt it personally—, but it certainly never formed a part of the oldest strata of the Mahābhārata : that much we can now say with confidence. One sees how even a scholar like OLDENBERG can make abysmal blunders in the estimation of the age and character of passages of the Mahābhārata.

[1] I must acknowledge here the help I have received from Mr. M. V. VAIDYA, M.A., and Pandit KRISHNAMURTI SASTRI, two of my assistants in the Bhandarkar Oriental Research Institute, in tracing out and identifying the parallel passages listed below.

Concordance of Parallel Passages in the Mbh. (Ramopakhyana) and the Ramayana.[1]

Mbh. Āraṇyakaparvan (Rāmopākhyāna), Crit. Ed. (B. = Bombay Ed.)	Ramayaṇa, Bombay Ed. (=B.) (G. = GORRESIO's Ed.)
(1) 258. 2^d (B. 274. 2^d) हत्वा गृध्रं जटायुषम्	B. 1. 1. 53^b (G. 1. 1. 58^d) गृध्रं हत्वा जटायुषम् (G, like Mbh., हत्वां गृध्रं ज°.)
(2) 258. 4^b (B. 274. 4^b) किंवीर्यः किंपराक्रमः	B. 3. 34. 2^b (G. 3. 38. 2^b) किंरूपः किंपराक्रमः (G, like Mbh., किंवीर्यः किं°.)
(3) 258. 5^d (B. 274. 5^d) रामस्याक्लिष्टकर्मणः	B. 5. 42. 34^b : 43. 9^b ; 6. 41. 77^b ; etc. (G. 5. 38. 31^b ; 6. 16. 79^b ; etc., etc.) रामस्याक्लिष्टकर्मणः
(4) 258. 9^d (B. 274. 9^d) रामस्य महिषीं प्रियाम्	B. 3. 50. 26^d (G. 4. 49. 24^d) रामस्य महिषीं प्रियाम्
(5) 259. 13^{ab} (B. 275. 13^{ab}) सर्वे वेदविदः शूराः सर्वे सुचरितव्रताः ।	B. 1. 18. 25^{cd} सर्वे वेदविदः शूराः सर्वे लोकहिते रताः ।
[477] (6) 259. 30 (B. 275. 30) परमापद्गतस्यापि नाधर्मे मे मतिर्भवेत् । अशिक्षितं च भगवन् ब्रह्मास्त्रं प्रतिभातु मे ॥ [J]	B. 7. 10. 30^{cd}-31^{ab} (G. 7. 10. 30) परमापद्गतस्यापि धर्मे मम मतिर्भवेत् । अशिक्षितं च ब्रह्मास्त्रं भगवन्प्रतिभातु मे ॥ (G, like Mbh., transp. ब्रह्मास्त्रं and भगवन्)

[1] Stanzas identified by JACOBI have been marked in the list with " J " : thus [J]. A few of the other passages have been noted by SLUSZKIEWICZ also, and have been marked with " S " in the list. SLUSZKIEWICZ'S arrangement seemed to me rather complicated and confusing. From his various lists it is difficult to estimate the actual range and extent of the similarities.

(7) 259. 31 (B. 275. 31) यस्माद्राक्षसयोनौ ते जातस्यामित्रकर्शन । नाधर्मे रमते बुद्धि- रमरत्वं ददामि ते ॥ [JS] (B धीयते for रमते and ददानि for ददामि.)	B. 7. 10. 34^{cd}-35^{ab} (G. 7. 10. 34) यस्माद्राक्षसयोनौ ते जातस्यामित्रनाशन । नाधर्मे जायते बुद्धि- रमरत्वं ददामि ते ॥ (G, like Mbh., °कर्शन for °नाशन, and वर्तते for जायते.)
(8) (259. 36^{ab}) (B. 275. 36^{ab}) विभीषणस्तु धर्मात्मा सतां धर्ममनुस्मरन् । (B मार्गमनु° for धर्ममनु°.)	B. 7. 10. 6^{ab} विभीषणस्तु धर्मात्मा नित्यं धर्मपरः शुचिः ।
(9) 260. 7^{d} (B. 276. 7^{d}) कामरूपबलान्वितान्	G. 1. 20. 14^{b} कामरूपा बलान्विताः G. 1. 19. 28^{b}
(10) 261. 6^{b} (B. 277. 6^{b}) रमयामास हि प्रजाः [S]	रञ्जयामास हि प्रजाः
(11) (261. 9^{b}) (B. 277. 9^{b}) मत्तमातङ्गगामिनम्	B. 2. 3. 28^{b} (G. 2. 2. 13^{d}) मत्तमातङ्गगामिनम्
(12) (261. 15^{c}) (B. 277. 15^{c}) संभाराः संभ्रियन्तां मे	B. 1. 8. 14^{c} [cf. 1. 8. 11^{c} ; 12. 3^{c}] (G. 1. 11. 15^{a}) संभाराः संभ्रियन्तां मे (G च for मे.)
(13) 261. 17^{cd} (B. 277. 17^{cd}) आशीविषस्त्वां संक्रुद्ध- श्चण्डो दशति दुर्भगे । [S] (B दशतु for दशति.)	G. 2. 7. 3^{ab} आशीविषस्त्वां दशतु मढे मन्दितमानिनि ।
[478] (14) 261. 18^{ab} (B. 277. 18^{ab}) सुभगा खलु कौसल्या यस्याः पुत्रोऽभिषेक्ष्यते ।	B. 2. 8. 9^{ab} (G. 2. 7. 4^{ab}) सुभगा किल कौसल्या यस्याः पुत्रोऽभिषेक्ष्यते । (G कौशल्यां सुभगां मन्ये and °षिच्यते for °षेक्ष्यते.)

(15) 261. 22^{cd} (B. 277. 22^{cd}) अवध्यो वध्यतां कोऽद्य वध्यः कोऽद्य विमुच्यताम् । [JS]	B. 2. 10. 33^{ab} (G. 2. 9. 11^{cd}) अवध्यो वध्यतां को वा वध्यः को वा विमुच्यताम् । (G अवध्यो बध्यतां कोऽद्य and बध्यः for वध्यः)
(16) 1245* (line 1) (B. 277. 24^{a}) पृथिव्यां राजराजोऽस्मि [S]	G. 2. 9. 13^{c} पृथिव्यां राजराजोऽस्मि
(17) 261. 25^{ab} (B. 277. 26^{ab}) आभिषेचनिकं यत्ते रामार्थमुपकल्पितम् । [S]	G. 2. 12. 3^{cd} आभिषेचनिकं द्रव्यं रामार्थमुपकल्पितं ।
(18) 261. 25^{d} (B. 277. 27^{d}) वनं गच्छतु राघवः	B. 5. 33. 21^{d} (G. 5. 31. 15^{d}) वनं गच्छतु राघवः
(19) 261. 33^{ab} (B. 277. 34^{ab}) अयशः पातयित्वा मे मूर्ध्नि त्वं कुलपांसने । [S]	G. 2. 76. 7^{cd} मम चाप्ययशो मूर्ध्नि पातितं लुब्धया त्वया ।
(20) 261. 39^{d} (B. 277. 40^{d}) शरभङ्गाश्रमं प्रति	B. 3. 5. 20^{d} (G. 3. 9. 15^{d}) शरभङ्गाश्रमं प्रति
(21) 261. 40^{c} (B. 277. 41^{c}) नदीं गोदावरीं रम्याम्	B. 3. 64. 3^{a} (G. 3. 68. 30^{c}) नदीं गोदावरीं रम्यां
(22) 261. 42^{cd} (B. 277. 43^{cd}) चतुर्दश सहस्राणि जघान भुवि रक्षसाम् । (B राक्षसान् for रक्ष°.)	B. 5. 37. 16^{ab} (G. 5. 35. 17^{ab}) चतुर्दश सहस्राणि राक्षसानां जघान यः ।
{479} (23) 262. 3^{b} (B. 278. 3^{b}) कच्चित्क्षेमं पुरे तव [JS]	B. 3. 35. 41^{ab} कच्चित्ते कुशलं राजल्लँङ्कायां राक्षसेश्वर
(24) 262. 12^{c}. (B. 278. 13^{a}) अपक्रान्ते च काकुत्स्थे	B. 3. 40. 20^{a}, 22^{a} (G. 3. 44. 18^{a}) अपक्रान्ते च काकुत्स्थे

(25) 262. 22^{cd} (B. 278. 23^{ab}) हा सीते लक्ष्मणेत्येवं चुक्रोशार्तस्वरेण ह । [JS]	B. 3. 44. 24^{ab} (G. 3. 50. 22^{cd}) हा सीते लक्ष्मणेत्येव माक्रुश्य तु महास्वनम् । (G हा लक्ष्मणेति चुक्रोश त्रायस्वेति महावने ।)
(26) 262. 27^{d} (B. 278. 28^{b}) विशेयं वा हुताशनम्	G. 3. 51. 41^{b} प्रविशेयं हुताशनं
(27) 262. 30^{c} (B. 278. 32^{a}) अभव्यो भव्यरूपेण [JS]	B. 3. 46. 9^{a} (G. 3. 52. 14^{c}) अभव्यो भव्यरूपेण (G °रूपां तां for °रूपेण.)
(28) 262. 33^{cd} (B. 278. 35^{cd}) मम लङ्का पुरी नाम्ना रम्या पारे महोदधेः । [J]	B. 3. 47. 29^{ab} ; 48. 10^{ab} (G. 3. 53. 35^{ab} ; 54. 14^{ab}) लङ्का नाम समुद्रस्य (B and G both second time मम पारे समुद्रस्य.) मध्ये मम महापुरी । (B second time लङ्का नाम पुरी शुभा; G second time लङ्का नाम महापुरी.)
(29) 263. 8^{ab} (B. 279. 9^{ab}) सा ददर्श गिरिप्रस्थे पञ्च वानरपुंगवान् ।	B. 3. 54. 1^{cd} (G. 3. 60. 5^{cd}) ददर्श गिरिशृङ्गस्थान् पञ्च वानरपुंगवान् ।
(30) 263. 11^{b} (B. 279. 14^{b}) वने राक्षससेविते	B. 3. 57. 16^{b} (G. 3. 64. 18^{d} ; 66. 2^{d}) वने राक्षससेविते
(31) 263. 22^{b}. (B. 279. 25^{b}) व्यपविद्धबृसीघटम् (B ° मठम्.)	B. 3. 60. 7^{b} विप्रविद्धबृसीकटम्
[480] (32) 263. 39^{a} (B. 279. 43^{a}) रावणेन हृता सीता	B. 3. 71. 21^{c} (G. 3. 75. 37^{a}) रावणेन हृता भार्या (G, like Mbh., सीता for भार्या.)
(33) 263. 40^{b} (B. 279. 44^{b}) हंसकारण्डवायुता	G. 3. 79. 40^{d} हंसकारण्डवायुतां

(34) 263. 41^{ab}
(B. 279. 45^{ab})

संवसत्यत्र सुग्रीव-
श्चतुर्भिः सचिवैः सह । [J]
(B वसते तत्र for संवसत्यत्र.)

B. 3. 72. 12^{cd}
(G. 3. 76. 36^{cd})

निवसत्यात्मवान्वीर-
श्चतुर्भिः सह वानरैः ।
(G तस्मिन्वसति सुग्रीवश्चतुर्भिः सचिवैः सह ।)

(35) 264. 2^{d}
(B. 280. 2^{d})

जगाम मनसा प्रियाम्

B. 4. 30. 6^{d}
(G. 4. 29. 5^{d})

जगाम मनसा प्रियाम्

(36) 264. 23^{ab}
(B. 280. 23^{ab})

मैन्दश्च द्विविदश्चैव
हनूमांश्चानिलात्मजः ।
(B द्विविदश्चापि.)

B. 4. 50. 6^{ab}
(G. 4. 50. 6^{ab})

मैन्दश्च द्विविदश्चैव
हनूमाञ्जाम्बवानपि ।
(G द्विविधश्चैव, and जाम्बवाननलः)

(37) 264. 27^{d}
(B. 280. 27^{d})

का त्वरा मरणे पुनः [S]

G. 4. 15. 21^{b}

का त्वरा मरणे पुनः

(38) 264. 32^{d}
(B. 280. 32^{d})

पुष्पिताविव किंशुकौ

B. 6. 90. 37^{d}
(G. 6. 70. 11^{d})

पुष्पिताविव किंशुकौ

(39) 264. 34^{ab}
(B. 280. 34^{ab})

स मालया तदा वीरः
शुशुभे कण्ठसक्तया ।

B. 4. 12. 41^{ab}
(G. 4. 12. 47^{ab})

स तया शुशुभे श्रीमान्
लतया कण्ठसक्तया ।
(G, like Mbh., वीरः for श्रीमान्, and मालया for लतया.)

(40) 264. 37^{b}
(B. 280. 37^{b})

वक्त्राच्छोणितमुद्वमन्

B. 4. 48. 20^{d}
(G. 4. 48. 22^{d})

वक्त्राच्छोणितमुद्वमन्
(G °मुद्गिरन्.)

[481] (41) 264. 42^{b}
(B. 280. 42^{d})

तापसीवेषधारिणी

G. 5. 18. 21^{b}

तापसीवेषधारिणीं

(42) 264. 55^{ab}
(B. 280. 56^{ab})

अविन्ध्यो नाम मेधावी
वृद्धो राक्षसपुंगवः । [S]

B. 5. 37. 12^{ab}
(G. 5. 35. 13^{ab})

अविन्ध्यो नाम मेधावी
विद्वान्राक्षसपुंगवः ।
(G तेजस्वी for मेधावी

Mbh.	Rām.
(43) 264. 64^{c}-65^{a}, 65^{d} (B. 280. 65^{c}-66^{a}, 66^{d}) असकृत्खरयुक्ते तु रथे नृत्यन्निव स्थितः । कुम्भकर्णादयश्चेमे रक्तमाल्यानुलेपनाः [S]	B. 5. 27. 21^{cd}, 33^{a} (G. 5. 27. 16^{ab}, 22^{a}) रथेन खरयुक्तेन रक्तमाल्यानुलेपनः । कुम्भकर्णादयश्चेमे
(44) 264, 66^{cd} (B. 280. 67^{cd}) श्वेतपर्वतमारूढ एक एव विभीषणः । [S]	G. 5. 27. 23^{ab} श्वेतपर्वतमारूढ एक एव विभीषणः ।
(45) 265. 4^{d}-5^{d} (B. 281. 4^{d}-5^{d}) वसन्त इव मूर्तिमान् स कल्पवृक्षसदृशो यत्नादपि विभूषितः । श्मशानचैत्यद्रुमव– द्भूषितोऽपि भयंकरः ॥ [S]	B. 5. 22. 29 (G. 5. 20. 24^{cd}) स कल्पवृक्षप्रतिमो वसन्त इव मूर्तिमान् । श्मशानचैत्यप्रतिमो भूषितोऽपि भयंकरः ॥ (G which has only the latter half °द्रुमवद् for °प्रतिमो, like Mbh.)
(46) 265. 8^{ab} (B. 281. 8^{ab}) सीते पर्याप्तमेतावत्- कृतो भर्तुरनुग्रहः ।	B. 5. 24. 21^{ab} (G. 5. 25. 20^{cd}) सीते पर्याप्तमेतावद्- भर्तुः स्नेहः प्रदर्शितः । (G भर्तुस्नेहनिदर्शनं for the posterior half.)
[482] (47) 265. 17^{cd} (B. 281. 17^{cd}) तृणमन्तरतः कृत्वा तमुवाच निशाचरम् । [JS]	B. 3. 56. 1^{cd} : 5. 21. 3^{ab} (G. 3. 62. 1^{cd}) तृणमन्तरतः कृत्वा रावणं प्रत्यभाषत । (B second time शुचिस्मिता. G वाक्यमब्रवीत् for °प्रत्य.)
(48) 265. 21^{a} (B. 281. 21^{c}) न चैवोपयिकी भार्या	B. 5. 21. 6^{c} (G. 5. 23. 4^{a}) नाहमौपयिकी भार्या
(49) 266. 1^{c} (B. 282. 1^{c}) वसन्माल्यवतः पृष्ठे	B. 4. 28. 1^{c} (G. 4. 27. 1^{c}) वसन्माल्यवतः पृष्ठे

(50) 266. 49^{c}
(B. 282. 51^{a})

निर्दग्धपक्ष : पतितो

B. 4. 58. 7^{a}
(G. 4. 58. 8^{a})

निर्दग्धपत्र : पतितो
(G, like Mbh., °पक्ष : for पत्रः)

(51) 266. 58^{ab}
(B. 282. 60^{ab})

तत्र सीता मया दृष्टा
रावणान्त : पुरे सती ।

B. 5. 65. 11^{cd}
(G. 5. 66. 10^{ab})

तत्र सीता मया दृष्टा
रावणान्तःपुरे सती

(52) 266. 67^{c}
(B. 282. 70^{a})

क्षिप्तामिषीकां काकस्य [S]
(B काकाय for काकस्य)

B. 5. 40. 4^{c}
(G. 5. 37. 4^{c})

क्षिप्तामिषीकां काकस्य

(53) 266. 67^{d}
(B. 282. 70^{b})

चित्रकूटे महागिरौ

G. 1. 4. 35^{b}

चित्रकूटे महागिरौ

(54) 267. 2^{ab}
(B. 283. 2^{ac})

वृत : कोटिसहस्रेण
वानराणां तरस्विनाम् ।

B. 4. 39. 19^{cd} ; 40. 18^{cd}
(G. 4. 39. 27^{cd} ; 40. 17^{cd})

वृत : कोटिसहस्रेण
वानराणामदृश्यत ।

(B second time शतसहस्रेण for कोटि°, and तरस्विनाम् for अदृश्यत. G, first time कोटी°, and गोलाङ्गूलैर् for वानराणाम्; G second time कोटी° and like Mbh. तरस्विनाम् for अदृश्यत.)

[483] (55) 267. 4^{cd}
(B. 283. 4^{cd})

गोलाङ्गूलो महाराज
गवाक्षो भीमदर्शन : ।

B. 4. 39. 19^{ab} : 6. 42. 28^{ab}
(G. 4. 39. 27^{ab} : 6. 17. 20^{ab})

गोलाङ्गूलमहाराजो
गवाक्षो भीमविक्रम : ।

(B second time गोलाङ्गूलो महाकायो गवाक्षो भीमदर्शन: G first time गोलङ्गूल°, and नाम नामत : for भीम°; G second time गोलाङ्गूलो महाराजो गवाक्षो भीमदर्शन :)

(56) 267. 44^{cd} (B. 283. 44^{cd}) दशयोजनविस्तार- मायतं शतयोजनम् ।	B. 6. 22. 72^{ab} (G. 5. 95. 12^{ab}) दशयोजनविस्तीर्णं शतयोजनमायतम् (G, like Mbh., आयतं शतयोजनं for शत°.)
(57) 267. 46^{d} (B. 283. 46^{d}) चतुर्भिः सचिवैः सह	B. 6. 16. 17^{d} ; 17. 7^{b} (G. 5. 88. 14^{d} ; 89. 3^{c}) चतुर्भिः सह राक्षसैः (G first time सचिवैः सह [like Mbh.], and second time सचिवैः सार्द्धं for सह रा°.)
(58) 267. 49^{b} (B. 283. 49^{b}) [अ] भ्यषिञ्चद्विभीषणम्	B. 6. 19. 26^{b} (G. 5. 92. 3^{d}) अभ्यषिञ्चद्विभीषणम्
(59) 267. 52^{b} (B. 283. 52^{b}) राक्षसौ शुकसारणौ (B मन्त्रिणौ for राक्षसौ.)	B. 6. 25. 9^{b}, 26^{b} (G. 6. 1. 12^{d}, 36^{d}) राक्षसौ शुकसारणौ
(60) 268. 10^{a} (B. 284. 10^{a}) आह त्वां राघवो राजन्	B. 6. 41. 78^{a} (G. 6. 16. 80^{a}) आह त्वां राघवो रामः
(61) 268. 11. (B. 284. 11.) अकृतात्मानमासाद्य राजानमनये रतम् । विनश्यन्त्यनयाविष्टा देशाश्च नगराणि च ॥	B. 5. 21. 11 (G. 5. 23. 9) अकृतात्मानमासाद्य राजानमनये रतम् । समृद्धानि विनश्यन्ति राष्ट्राणि नगराणि च ॥ (G भर्तारम् for राजानम्; and सुसमृद्धा विनङ्क्ष्यन्ति देशाश्च नग°.)
[484] (62) 268. 15^{a} (B. 284. 15^{a}) हन्तास्मि त्वां सहामात्यं (B सहामात्यैर्)	B. 6. 41. 79^{a} (G. 6. 16. 81^{a}) हन्तास्मि त्वां सहामात्यं (G अहं हन्ता सहा°.)

(63) 268. 16^{cd} (B. 284. 16^{cd}) अराक्षसमिमं लोकं कर्तास्मि निशितैः शरैः । [JS]	B. 6. 41. 67^{ab} (G. 6. 16. 68^{ab}) अक्षरासमिमं लोकं कर्तास्मि निशितैः शरैः । (G करोमि for कर्तास्मि.)
(64) 268. 17^{d} (B. 284. 17^{d}) रावणः क्रोधमूर्छितः	B. 6. 26. 6^{b} (G. 5. 47. 36^{d}) रावणः क्रोधमूर्च्छितः
(65) 268. 18^{b} (B. 284. 18^{b}) चत्वारो रजनीचराः	B. 6. 41. 84^{d} (G. 6. 16. 86^{d}) चत्वारो रजनीचराः
(66) 268. 36^{c} (B. 284. 37^{c}) नखैर्दन्तैश्च वीराणां	G. 6. 65. 22^{c} नखैर्दन्तैश्च वीराणां
(67) 270. 13^{d} (B. 286. 13^{d}) सस्कन्धविटपैर्द्रुमैः	B. 6. 52. 30^{d} (G. 6. 28. 32^{d}) सस्कन्धविटपैर्द्रुमैः
(68) 270. 14^{d} (B. 286. 14^{d}) हनूमान्मारुतात्मजः	B. 6. 52. 30^{b}, 32^{b} (G. 6. 28. 32^{b}, 34^{b}) हनूमान्मारुतात्मजः
(69) 270. 17^{b} (B. 286. 17^{b}) हतशेषा निशाचराः	B. 6. 52. 37^{d} (G. 6. 28. 40^{b}) हतशेषा निशाचराः
(70) 271. 4^{b} (B. 287. 5^{d}) भक्षयामास वानरान्	B. 6. 67. 96^{d} (G. 6. 46. 79^{d}) भक्षयामास वानरान्
(71) 271. 21^{ab} (B. 287. 23^{ab}) ततः सुतुमुलं युद्ध- मभवल्लोमहर्षणम् ।	B. 3. 25. 34^{cd} (G. 3. 31. 44^{cd} ; 6. 18. 23^{ab}) तत्रभूवाद्भुतं युद्धं तुमुलं रोमहर्षणम् । (G first time लोम° G second time तत्रासीत्सुमहद्युद्धं तुमुलं लोमं°)
[485] (72) 272. 1^{ab} (B. 288. 1^{ab}) ततः श्रुत्वा हतं संख्ये कुम्भकर्णं सहानुगम् ।	B. 6. 68. 6^{ab} (G. 6. 47. 2^{ab}) श्रुत्वा विनिहतं संख्ये कुम्भकर्णं महाबलम् । (स श्रुत्वा नि° for श्रुत्वा विनि°)

(73) 272. 26^b (B. 288. 26^d) भ्रातरौ रामलक्ष्मणौ	B. 6. 44. 36^d ; 45. 13^b ; 46. 1^d etc. (G. 6. 19. 54^b ; 20. 13^b ; 20. 1^d, 29^b etc.) भ्रातरौ रामलक्ष्मणौ
(74) 273. 5^b (B. 289. 5^b) कृतकर्मा विभीषणः	G. 6. 24. 42^d कृतकर्मा विभीषणः
(75) 273. 20^b (B. 289. 20^b) रावणिः क्रोधमूर्छितः	G. 6. 70. 19^b रावणिः क्रोधमूर्च्छितः
(76) 273. 20^d (B. 289. 20^d) शरानाशीविषोपमान्	B. 6. 88. 41^b (G. 6. 68. 5^b) शरानाशीविषोपमान्
(77) 274. 5^d (B. 290. 5^d) रावणो राक्षसेश्वरः (B राक्षसाधिपः)	B. 6. 95. 32^d ; 97. 2^d ; 100. 10^b ; 102. 2^d, 27^b ; etc. (G. 6. 80. 10^b) रावणो राक्षसेश्वरः (B राक्षसाधिपः in 97. 2^d and ff.)
(78) 274. 12^d (B. 290. 12^d) मातलिः शक्रसारथिः	B. 6. 112. 5^d (G. 6. 97. 6^b) मातलिः शक्रसारथिः
(79) 1298*, 1299* (B. 290. 19^c-20^b) दशकन्धरराजसून्वो- स्तथा युद्धमभून्महत् । अलब्धोपममन्यत्र तयोरेव तथाभवत् ॥ (MSS. v. l. for the first line ततः प्रववृते युद्धं रामरावणयोर्महत् ।)	B. 6. 107. 51^c-52^b सागरं चाम्बरप्रख्य- मम्बरं सागरोपमम् । रामरावणयोर्युद्धं रामरावणयोरिव
(80) 274. 21^d (B. 290. 23^b) शस्त्राणि विविधानि च	B. 6. 103. 29^b (G. 6. 88. 35^b) शस्त्राणि विविधानि च
[486] (81) 275. 25^d (B. 291. 26^d) वानराणां महात्मनाम्	G. 1. 4. 72^b वानराणां महात्मनां

(82) 275. 33 (B. 291. 34) यदि ह्यकामामासेवे- स्त्रियमन्यामपि ध्रुवम् । शतधास्य फलद्देह इत्युक्तः सोऽभवत्पुरा ॥ [S] (B मूर्धा for देह.)	B. 7. 26. 55^{c}-56^{b} यदा ह्यकामां कामार्तो धर्षयिष्यति योषितम् । मूर्धा तु सप्तधा तस्य शकलीभविता तदा ॥
(83) 275. 48^{d} (B. 291. 50^{b}) यावद् भूमिर्धरिष्यति	B. 6. 100. 56^{d} (G. 6. 81. 22^{d} ; 112. 102^{d}) यावद् भूमिर्धरिष्यति
(84) 275. 52^{ab} (B. 291. 53^{cd}) पुष्पकेण विमानेन खेचरेण विराजता । [S]	B. 6. 122. 26^{ab} (G. 6. 107. 25^{ab}) खगतेन विमानेन हंसयुक्तेन भास्वता । (G खेचरेण विमानेन कामगेन विराजता.)
(85) 275. 65^{c} (B. 291. 66^{c}) वसिष्ठो वामदेवश्च	B. 1. 7. 4^{c} (G. 1. 7. 1^{c} : 2. 69. 2^{a}) वसिष्ठो वामदेवश्च (G वशिष्ठो)
(86) 275. 69^{cd} (B. 291. 70^{cd}) दशाश्वमेधानाजह्रे जारूथ्यान्स निरर्गलान् ।	B. 6. 128. 95^{cd} (G. 6. 113. 10^{ab}) दशाश्वमेधानाजह्रे सदश्वान्भूरिदक्षिणान् । (G [like Mbh.] जारुथ्यान् for सदश्वान्.)

This cannot be considered as an exhaustive list.[1] In fact I must frankly confess that my study of the Rāmāyaṇa has been rather [487] perfunctory, and moreover it is difficult to identify passages in a work like the Rāmāyaṇa in the absence of a verse-index. A closer study of the Epic and Episode, I am confident, would result in the tracing of many more parallelisms in diction and phraseology. I must here add that I have intentionally ex-

---

[1] In the above list Nos. 5, 8, 23, 31, 79 and 82 were traceable to the Bombay ed. only ; Nos. 9, 10, 13, 16, 17, 19, 26, 33, 37, 41, 44, 53, 66, 74, 75 and 81 were traceable to GORRESIO's edition only ; while the remaining 64 are common to the two editions of the Rāmāyaṇa.—*En passant* I may add that even from these figures one can see that text of GORRESIO's edition is nearer to the Critical Edition of the Rāmopākhyāna than that of the Bombay Edition of the Rāmāyaṇa, a conclusion which is confirmed by the numerous agreements in individual readings between GORRESIO and our text as against the tradition represented by the Bombay text.

cluded such passages as show merely parallelisms in *ideas*, and I have strictly confined myself to exact *verbal* similarities. The greater the number of such verbal similarities the weaker becomes the case for HOPKINS. He, relying on the many minor differences in detail, argues that the fact that the subject-matter of the Epic and the Episode is treated differently in several particulars "points to different workings-over of older matter rather than to copying or condensing" (HOPKINS, op. cit. p. 63). HOPKINS loses sight of the fact that differences like those pointed out by him do not prove anything in such cases. Differences are natural and may be expected; nay, they could scarcely be avoided—as far as I can judge—when one is condensing a work of about 25,000 stanzas. But agreements in the bulk can never be casual or accidental; they show invariably identity of source. And the source, as already pointed out by JACOBI,[1] was not a manuscript of the Rāmāyaṇa, but a memorized version of it, current in the time of the adapter and in his locality. Then, I expect, the compilers of such works could hardly avoid the influence from oral tradition which existed then. In this restricted sense we must understand the statement that the Rāmopākhyāna is an epitome of our Rāmāyaṇa, a fact which we may regard as established on account of the numerous *verbal* agreements which have been shown to exist between the two poems.[2]

---

[1] *Op. cit.* p. 72.

[2] For my views on the relationship between the Mahābhārata and the Rāmāyaṇa, see my paper entitled "The Nala Episode and the Rāmāyaṇa" in *A Volume of Eastern and Indian Studies in honour of F. W. Thomas*, pp. 300 ff.

ARJUNAMIŚRA *

A commentator of the Mahābhārata who has suffered undeserved neglect at the hands of scholars and publishers alike is Arjunamiśra. Not only is Arjuna's commentary better than that of Nīlakaṇṭha, his text also is superior, in many respects, to that used or fixed by the Western commentator. And yet Arjuna's *Dīpikā* has never been published in its entirety[1] and, being difficult of access, is seldom consulted by scholars. HOLTZMANN has devoted a paragraph to him in his compendious work *Das Mahābhārata*, Vol. 3, pp. 67 ff., but WINTERNITZ does not mention him even once in the 130 pages he devotes to the Mahābhārata in his *Geschichte*. He is referred to *en passant* by BROCKHAUS, *ZDMG*, 6. 528 ; by TELANG, *Bhagavadgītā* Translation ; by Rajendralal MITRA, *Notices*, Vols. 5 and 6 ; and in some other manuscripts catalogues.

The version of Arjunamiśra, as I pointed out in the Foreword (p. v) to the first fascicule of the critical edition of the Mahābhārata (1927), is closely allied to the Bengali version. The simple reason for this affinity, not known to me then, is apparently that Arjunamiśra was a native of Bengal, to judge from the extracts from the colophons of his commentary recently published by Mahamahopadhyaya Haraprasada SHASTRI in the *Descriptive Catalogue of Sanskrit Manuscripts of the Asiatic Society of Bengal*, Vol. 5 (1928).

The few facts about Arjunamiśra and his commentary that I have been able to glean from the various available sources may be briefly summarized thus. The name of his commentary is variously given as (*Mahā-*)*bhāratārtha-* [566] (*pra*)*dīpikā* and *Bhāratasaṃgrahadīpikā*. The commentaries on the different Parvans have been handed down singly or in groups of a few Parvans at a time. Complete manuscripts of the commentary exist in Bengal, but even there they are not common. The manuscripts, which are written in Bengali and Devanāgari characters, bear various dates in the seventeenth or later centuries : the earliest hitherto reported date is Saṁvat 1676 (*ca.* A.D. 1620).

Arjunamiśra, who styles himself Bhāratācārya in the colophons of the manuscripts of his commentary, was the son of Īśāna, who was a "reciter" (*pāṭhaka* or *pāṭhakarāja*) of the Mahābhārata and who appears to have, like his son, borne the title Bhāratācārya. Arjuna is cited by name, by

---

* [*Dr. Modi Memorial Volume*, pp. 565-568.]

[1] The commentary on the Virāṭaparvan and the Udyogaparvan has been published by the Gujarati Printing Press, Bombay.

Nīlakaṇṭha once in his commentary on the Mahābhārata (*ad* 3. 291. 70) and is, therefore, certainly anterior to Nīlakaṇṭha, who belongs to the third quarter of the seventeenth century.[1] He in turn mentions among his predecessors the commentators Devabodha, Vimalabodha, Śāṇḍilya, Sarvajña-Nārāyaṇa, and he appears to have based his scholium closely on that of Devabodha. He wrote also a commentary on the well-known Vedic hymn Puruṣasūkta, to which he himself refers in the *Dīpikā* on Mbh. 14. 25. 26. TELANG (*op. cit.* p. 204) surmises that he is posterior to Śaṃkara, and HOLTZMANN assigns him to the thirteenth or fourteenth century : both without adducing any cogent reasons for their assumptions. Arjuna regarded and has treated the Harivaṃśa as an integral part of the Great Epic, elaborately defending this position : his commentary, therefore, embraces the supplement Harivaṃśa also.

Arjunamiśra lived in North India, in a town or village on the banks of the Ganges and, according to his own statement, compiled the great commentary on the Mahābhārata under the patronage of one Satyakhāna. [567] Relying on one Bengal Asiatic Society's manuscript examined by him, Haraprasada SHASTRI asserts that Arjuna was a Vārendra Brahman of North Bengal. The Mahamahopadhyaya may indeed be right in this, but I am not wholly convinced. I find it a suspicious circumstance that this word Vārendra occurs only in one place in one manuscript (No. 3422), while it is conspicuous by its absence in the others which contain a similar colophon. There is, however, another word which is often repeated in these colophons but not discussed by the Mahamahopadhyaya and which I think also contains a place-name. The word is spelt in the colophons variously as Campāheṭ(ṭ)iya, Campāheṭhi, Campiheṭika. It is used there as an attribute of *Kula*. I take the reference to mean that Arjunamiśra's family (*kula*) belonged to a town or village, called Campaheṭ(ṭ)i. Could this place be identified with certainty, we should have a very definite clue as to Arjunamiśra's provenance I am tempted to identify it with Campaháti mentioned in the *Imperial Gazetteer of India* (1885) as a "small village. . . . 15 miles south-west of Calcutta, in the district of the Twenty-four Parganās, Bengal" ; but owing partly to the erratic manner in which proper names are spelt in the *Imperial Gazetteer* and partly to the lack of sufficient data as to the situation of the place in question, the identification proposed above is necessarily uncertain.

Following the example of my predecessors, I have utilized Devanāgari manuscripts of the commentary of Arjunamiśra and treated his version as a sub-division of the Devanāgarī version. The two Devanāgari manuscripts I am using for my edition of the Ādiparvan are extremely corrupt. In fact all the manuscripts I have consulted—and they are all Nāgarī manuscripts —have been surprisingly corrupt. Not only that, the text they contain is

---

[1] PRINTZ, *KZ*, 44, 70 ff.

obviously contaminated from the vulgate text, as evidenced [568] by the glaring discrepancies that exist between the readings of the text and the *lemmata* in the commentary. This corruption of the Devanāgarī manuscripts I could not understand at first, but is, I cannot but think now, due to their being copies of Bengali originals. It would, therefore, be expedient to secure and use, whenever possible, good old Bengali manuscripts of Arjunamiśra's commentary, treating his version as an offshoot of the Bengali version. Arjunamiśra certainly seems to belong to the Eastern school of Mahābhārata commentators.

THE NALA EPISODE AND THE RAMAYANA *

There must be indeed very few Sanskritists who have read the justly popular Nala-Damayantī episode of the Mahābhārata and not felt disposed to echo the sentiments of A. W. V. SCHLEGEL that the poem "can hardly be surpassed in pathos and ethos, in the enthralling force and tenderness of the sentiments." [1] It is without doubt one of the most beautiful love stories of the world, striking on account of the simplicity of its style and the beauty of its imagery. Owing to its innate attractiveness and transparent lucidity, it has been the custom, since a long time, at almost all Western Universities, to begin the study of Sanskrit with the reading of this romantic little poem, for which purpose it is no doubt excellently suited. Its popularity may be judged from the fact that it has been translated not only into English, French and German, but also into Italian, Swedish, Czech, Polish, Russian, Greek and Hungarian among the European languages.[2] Every province of India can of course boast of its own version of this superb little epopee.

Regarded as an integral part of the Mahābhārata,[3] the episode is a palpable "interpolation", impending annoyingly the march of the epic story, and is forced upon the reader of the Epic in the most barefaced manner. During the exile of the Pāṇḍavas they receive a casual visit from a peripatetic sage called Bṛhadaśva. Yudhiṣṭhira—as is usual with him—complains to him of the misfortune which has overtaken him and his family, and asks the sage whether there has ever been a more unfortunate king than himself. Thereupon Bṛhadaśva forthwith relates the Nala story, in 27 adhyāyas, comprising something like 1100 stanzas or 2200 lines. There could be no clearer instance of deliberate interpolation, introduced with a coolness difficult to match. Yet we are really intensely grateful at heart in this case, as in the case of the Sāvitrī episode,—the two immortal stories that are known and loved throughout the length and breadth of India—that some meddlesome interpolator had the courage to interrupt deliberately the smooth flow of the epic narrative with these beautiful digressions and thus saved them [295] from falling a prey to the ravages of Time. And so with a number of other

* [*A Volume of Eastern and Indian Studies* in honour of F. W. THOMAS, C.I.E., 294-303.]

1 Cited by WINTERNITZ, *A History of Indian Literature*, Vol. I (Calcutta, 1927), p. 382, referring to *Indische Bibliothek*, I, 98 f.

2 WINTERNITZ, *op. cit.*, p. 238 n.

3 Āraṇyakaparvan, adhy. 53-79 (Bombay edition). In the Critical Edition these adhyāyas have been tentatively numbered 50-78. The abbreviation "B." in the references means the Bombay ed. of the Mahābhārata.

interpolations in the Great Epic. Many of them richly deserved to be "interpolated" in this Golden Treasury of the Myths and Legends of India.

Not only has the Nala-Damayantī poem what may be called a lively story-interest, but it is also clothed in a most attractive garb. The charmingly simple diction of this exquisite little poem is marked by a rigorous economy of words and "ornaments"; the construction of the story is also on the whole remarkably faultless: qualities which have endeared it to connoisseurs all the world over. The narrative, like a sylvan brook, runs its meandering course naturally and smoothly to its destined conclusion. And in spite of a few inevitable scenes of divine intervention and a little exaggeration necessary for artistic effect, we carry away the impression that the story rests on a foundation of fact, and we feel that it may all have happened, in those wonderful bygone times, exactly as it is narrated here.

In the whole length of this carefully and artistically constructed poem there is just one passage which is apt slightly to perplex a careful reader. It is the soliloquy of the Brahmin Sudeva in chapter 16 of the poem (B. 3. 68. 8 ff.). On reading this passage a discerning reader would notice for one thing a sudden change to a rather florid style, marked by a plethora of epithets and a rich embroidery of similes.

The situation is this. King Nala, having deserted Damayantī where she lay asleep, strode through the forest aimlessly until he met the snake-king Karkoṭaka, who, in return for a good turn done to him, transformed the handsome Nala into an ugly hunchback and advised him to go to Ayodhyā and seek service as a charioteer with king Ṛtuparṇa. Nala does so and remains at the court of Ṛtuparṇa in the service of the king. His whereabouts and identity are not known to any living soul besides himself: which is a *very important* point in the narrative. Damayantī, in the meanwhile, after a number of perilous adventures, reaches, by a fortunate coincidence, the palace of the queen of the Cedis, who is no other than Damayantī's own aunt (as is revealed later), who takes compassion on her and gives her shelter. In course of time the evil tidings of the fateful game of dice and the subsequent exile of Nala and Damayantī reached king Bhīma, Damayantī's father. Thereupon he called to him some Brahmins and enjoined them, with promise of rich gifts, that they should search for Nala and Damayantī and bring them back to him. One of these Brahmins, the fortunate Sudeva, comes to the country of the Cedis and there, in the palace hall, he sees Damayantī and recognizes her forthwith. On seeing the wan, unkempt and forlorn appearance of the beautiful princess of Vidarbha, he indulges in a soliloquy before addressing her directly. This passage, as already remarked, seems marked out from the rest of the poem by attempts at higher flights of imagination, approaching the requirements of what is known as the Kāvya style. Damayantī is here successively compared by Sudeva to Śrī (or Lakṣmī), to the full moon, to Rati (Cupid's consort), to the splendour of the full moon, to a lotus stalk, to a full-moon night, to a river, to [296] a lotus pool, again to a lotus stalk, and finally to the crescent of the moon (B. 3. 68. 10-17). That, however, is a minor matter.

The really perplexing part of the soliloquy is the way in which Sudeva refers to Nala in the following stanza (B. 3. 68. 20) :

duṣkaraṁ kurute 'tyarthaṁ hīno yad anayā Nalaḥ |
dhārayaty ātmano dehaṁ na śokenāvasīdati ||

"Extremely difficult is the trial of Nala who, deprived of her (scil. Damayantī), supports his body and does not pine away in sorrow !"

This can be properly said by a person who knows that Nala is heroically bearing the cruel blow of fate which had temporarily separated him from his beloved, and above all that Nala is alive. But for all Sudeva knew, Nala might have been dead. Here is a slight incongruity to start with. It might be argued that as it was not definitely known that Nala was dead, Sudeva was to a certain extent justified in assuming that Nala was alive, and so this outburst was after all not so very incongruous. But, even if he were alive, how was Sudeva to know whether Nala wanted to recover Damayantī ; in fact, to know at all what feelings Nala entertained then about Damayantī : they might conceivably have been even hostile, for all Sudeva could say. Such minute analysis of hidden motives and distant possibilities might, however, be regarded as captious criticism, when considering such an old-world love poem as this.

The disturbing thought however recurs when a few lines later we read (B. 3. 68. 23 ab) :

asyā nūnaṁ punarlābhān Naiṣadhaḥ prītim eṣyati |

"Through her recovery Nala will become happy indeed",

words which again definitely presuppose that Nala is alive and anxious to rediscover his lost Damayantī, neither of which facts could have been known to Sudeva, and whose assumption by him is quite gratuitous and most puzzling to the reader. Inappropriate to a certain extent are in the same context the adjectives *aprameyasya* and *vīryasattvavataḥ* (stanza 25) applied to Nala. Was it not through Nala's own insane infatuation for dice that Damayantī was reduced to this condition, and all that great disaster was brought upon the two families ? A discordant note is likewise struck by the words *Naiṣadho 'rhati Vaidarbhīm* (stanza 24), which under these circumstances seem peculiarly inappropriate. One rather feels at this stage that poor Damayantī had definitely made the wrong choice at the svayaṁvara : she would have been much happier had she chosen, in preference to the profligate Nala, one of the four gods who were wooing her.

Another very curious thing we notice about this passage is that while Sudeva waxes eloquent about Nala and his sufferings, he has no thought at the moment for king Bhīma, who is Sudeva's patron and who has dispatched him on this errand. Sudeva has not a word to say in this long soliloquy as to how glad the fond parents would be on seeing their beloved Damayantī and how happy Damayantī would be on being reunited to her kinsfolk. From [297] his present words we could never guess that he had been sent by king Bhīma or that he had any connection with the House of Vidarbha.

Our first thought is that the whole passage is one of those modern interpolations which have unintentionally disfigured many a fine old poem. The manuscripts do not however countenance such an idea. The passage is documented uniformly by all manuscripts alike. It is therefore not in any case a recent interpolation. Moreover the idea itself of the soliloquy is not by any means inherently inappropriate ; only the precise wording and some of the sentiments expressed seem a little incongruous.

We are therefore led to conclude that the poet's own knowledge of the real state of things, that Nala was not dead and that, repenting his hasty abandonment of Damayantī, he was then making reproaches to himself and was in fact longing to meet his lost Damayantī, had betrayed the poet into putting those words in the mouth of Sudeva, anticipating what was actually going to happen : a mistake common in the works of careless and inexperienced writers.

That this also is not the correct explanation of the anomaly follows, however, from the fact that almost all the lines forming this soliloquy of Sudeva recur almost *verbatim* in the long soliloquy of Hanumat in the Sundarakāṇḍa (adhy. 18 ff., ed. GORRESIO) of the Rāmāyaṇa at the time when he first sees Sītā in the Aśoka grove of Rāvaṇa's Laṅkā,—a soliloquy which, as will be made clear, is the source of the passage under discussion from the Nala episode.

The two situations, it will be recalled, have a superficial similarity. The heroine is lost, and messengers have been sent, by persons interested in her recovery, to find out her whereabouts. One of these messengers, more fortunate than the rest, suddenly and unexpectedly lights upon her, whereupon he just stands gazing at her and giving vent to his mixed feelings of joy and sorrow in the form of a soliloquy.

The one important difference between the two situations—a difference obviously overlooked by the adapter—is that in one case—the Rāmāyaṇa—the messenger, Hanumat, has been sent by Rāma himself, and the messenger therefore knows exactly the state of the mind of the husband of the missing princess ; whereas in the other case, the Nala episode, the messenger, sent by king Bhīma, has not only no knowledge of Nala's feelings towards Damayantī, but he does not even know whether Nala, *who is missing*, is alive or dead. And that makes a deal of difference. The words of the Rāmāyaṇa soliloquy are wholly appropriate in the mouth of the Monkey Chieftain ;

but the same words, in spite of a few necessary verbal alterations made by the adapter, prove on close scrutiny, as shown above, just a trifle incongruous in the soliloquy of Sudeva.

The extent of the similarity between the two passages will be clear from the following table in which the related lines are given in parallel columns.

	[298] Mahābhārata (Bom. ed.) 3. 68. 8 ff. [Emended][1]		Rāmāyaṇa (ed. GORRESIO) Sundarakāṇḍa[2] (Adhy. 18, 19, 21, 29)
8	mandaprakhyāyamānena rūpeṇāpratimena tām | pinaddhāṁ dhūmajālena prabhām iva vibhāvasoḥ ||	18 4	mandaṁ prakhyāyamānena rūpeṇāpratimena tām | pinaddhāṁ dhūmajālena prabhām iva vibhāvasoḥ || (cf. 10 cd also)
9	tāṁ samīkṣya viśālākṣīm adhikaṁ malināṁ kṛśām | tarkayāmāsa Bhaimīti kāraṇair upapādayan ||	18 22	tāṁ samīkṣya viśālākṣīm adhikaṁ malināṁ kṛśām | tarkayāmāsa Sīteti | kāraṇair upapādayan ||
10	yatheyaṁ me purā dṛṣṭā tathārūpeyam aṅganā | kṛtārtho 'smy adya dṛṣṭvemāṁ lokakāntām iva Śriyam ||	18 23cd 18 27ab	yathā purā vai dṛṣṭā me tathārūpeyam aṅganā | tāṁ dṛṣṭvā taptahemābhāṁ lokakāntām iva Śriyam |
11	pūrṇacandrānanāṁ śyāmāṁ cāruvṛttapayodharām | kurvantīṁ prabhayā devīṁ sarvā vitimirā diśaḥ ||	18 24	pūrṇacandrānanā śyāmā cāruvṛttapayodharā | kurvantī prabhayā devī sarvā vitimirā diśaḥ ||
12	cārupadmapalāśākṣīṃ Manmathasya Ratīm iva | iṣṭāṁ sarvasya jagataḥ pūrṇacandraprabhām iva ||	18 26	padmapattraviśālākṣīṁ Manmathasya Ratīm iva | iṣṭāṁ sarvasya jagataḥ pūrṇacandranibhām iva ||

1 The readings adopted here are readings of the "Vulgate," emended in the light of collations prepared for the Critical Edition of the Mahābhārata and available at the Bhandarkar Oriental Research Institute.

2 The text given here is that of GORRESIO. The Bombay editions have a slightly discrepant version, but most of the stanzas cited here do occur in the Bombay editions also which were compared by me.

Nala	Rāmāyaṇa
13 Vidarbhasarasas tasmād - daivadoṣād ivoddhṛtām | malapaṅkānuliptāṅgīṁ mṛṇālīm iva tāṁ bhṛśam ||	19 15cd Ikṣvākusarasas tasmād Rāvaṇenodhṛtā balāt | 18 16cd malapaṅkadharāṁ dīnāṁ maṇḍanārhām amaṇḍitām |
14 paurṇamāsīm iva niśāṁ Rāhugrastaniśākarām | patiśokākulāṁ dīnāṁ śuṣkasrotāṁ nadīm iva ||	21 14ab paurṇamāsīm iva niśāṁ Rāhugrastaniśākarām | 21 15cd patiśokāturāṁ dīnāṁ śuṣkasrotonadīm iva |
[299] 15 vidhvastaparṇakamalāṁ vitrāsitavihaṁgamām | hastihastaparikliṣṭāṁ vyākulām iva padminīm ||	21 14cd vidhvastapattrakamalāṁ vitrāsitavihaṁgamām | 21 15ab hastihastaparikliṣṭām ākulāṁ padminīm iva ||
16 sukumārīṁ sujātāṅgīṁ ratnagarbhagṛhoṣitām | dahyamānām ivoṣṇena mṛṇālīm aciroddhṛtām ||	21 16cd sukumārīṁ sujātāṅgīṁ ratnagarbhagṛhocitām | 21 17ab tapyamānām ivoṣṇena mṛṇālīm aciroddhṛtām ||
18 kāmabhogaiḥ priyair hīnāṁ hīnāṁ bandhujanena ca | dehaṁ dhārayatīṁ dīnāṁ bhartṛdarśanakāṅkṣayā	19 23cd kāmabhogavihīneyaṁ hīnā bandhujanena ca | 19 24ab dhārayaty ātmano dehaṁ tatsamāgamakāṅkṣayā ||
19 bhartā nāma paraṁ nāryā bhūṣaṇaṁ bhūṣaṇair vinā | eṣā virahitā tena śobhanāpi na śobhate ||	19 25cd bhartā nāma paraṁ nāryā bhūṣaṇaṁ bhūṣaṇair vinā | 19 26ab eṣā tasyānurāgeṇa śobhate 'py analaṁkṛtā ||
20 duṣkaraṁ kurute 'tyarthaṁ hīno yad anayā Nalaḥ | dhārayaty ātmano dehaṁ na śokenāvasīdati ||	19 26cd duṣkaraṁ kurute Rāmo hīno yad anayā vibhuḥ | 19 27ab dhārayaty ātmano dehaṁ na śokenāvasīdati ||
21 imām asitakeśāntāṁ śatapattrāyatekṣaṇām | sukhārhāṁ duḥkhitāṁ dṛṣṭvā mamāpi vyathate manaḥ ||	19 27cd imām asitakeśāntāṁ śatapattranibhānanām | 19 28ab sukhārhāṁ duḥkhitāṁ dṛṣṭvā mamāpi vyathitam manaḥ ||
22 kadā nu khalu duḥkhasya pāraṁ yāsyati vai śubhā | bhartuḥ samāgamāt sādhvī Rohiṇī śaśino yathā ||	19 28cd kadā tu khalu duḥkhasya pāraṁ yāsyati Maithilī | 19 29ab Rāghavasyāprameyasya Lakṣmaṇasya ca jīvataḥ ||

23	asyā nūnaṁ punarlābhān Naiṣadhaḥ prītim eṣyati | rājā rājyaparibhraṣṭaḥ punar labdhveva medinīm ||	19 22cd 19 23ab	nūnam asyā punarlābhād Rāghavaḥ prītim eṣyati | rājā rājyaparibhraṣṭaḥ punar labdhveva medinīm ||
24	tulyaśīlavayoyuktāṁ tulyābhijanasaṁyutām | Naiṣadho 'rhati Vaidarbhīṁ taṁ ceyam asitekṣaṇā ||	19 32	tulyarūpavayoyuktāṁ tulyābhijanalakṣaṇām | Rāghavo 'rhati Vaidehīṁ | taṁ ceyam asitekṣaṇā ||
25	yuktaṁ tasyāprameyasya vīryasattvavato mayā | samāśvāsayituṁ bhāryāṁ | patidarśanalālasām ||	29 6	yuktaṁ tasyāprameyasya satyaṁ sattvavato mayā | samāśvāsayituṁ bhāryāṁ patidarśanalālasām ||
[300] 26	ayam āśvāsayāmy enāṁ pūrṇacandranibhānanām |[1] adṛṣṭapūrvāṁ duḥkhasya duḥkhārtāṁ dhyānatat- parām ||	 29 7ab	 adṛṣṭaduḥkhā duḥkhasya na hy antam adhigacchati |

The question which of the two passages is the original one, need not detain us long. It is *a priori* not very likely that Vālmīki who is credited with having composed an epic of the size and rank of the Rāmāyaṇa would need to borrow the idea or the phraseology of such a commonplace soliloquy from a poem like the Nalopākhyāna. The redactor of the Nala story is, therefore, clearly indicated as the poet who would be under obligation for his inspiration to the Ādi-kavi. This *a priori* conclusion is happily confirmed in the present instance by the fortuitous circumstance that the passage turns out to be somewhat of a misfit in our poem. The anomaly, as has been suggested above, can be explained only on the supposition that the Nalopākhyāna lines were borrowed *en bloc* from a slightly different context. The exact phrasing of the speech of the messenger was originally conceived for a somewhat different set of circumstances as pictured in the Rāmāyaṇa, in which the soliloquy fits perfectly. The borrowed plumes, as is very often the case, do not fit the new incumbent as well as the adapter had imagined or at least hoped. We have, therefore, here an indubitable proof of the direct borrowing of some Rāmāyaṇa material by one of the Mahābhārata poets.—

[1] The corresponding line has been omitted by GORRESIO, but is correctly given in the Bombay (Nirnaya Sagar Press) ed. (1888), 5, 30, 7ab (cf. p. 83), and in the Gujarati Printing Press ed. (1916), 5. 30. 7ab (cf. p. 1856), both editions reading *aham* for our *ayam*. Both Tilaka and Govindarājiya mention (the pratika) *āśvāsayāmi*, showing that they knew the stanza.

not necessarily of course Kṛṣṇa Dvaipāyana Vyāsa, but one of the "Epigoni", the Vyāsäids, who carried on the good work commenced by Vyāsa.

* * * *

The conclusion that the idea of this soliloquy of Sudeva in the Nalopākhyāna of the Mahābhārata must necessarily have been borrowed by one of the redactors of the Great Epic from the Rāmāyaṇa is perhaps not without some significance for an understanding of the general interrelation of the Rāmāyaṇa and the Mahābhārata to which we may here advert in passing.[1]

The soliloquy discussed above is, as is well known, not by any means the only passage in which the Mahābhārata, shows contact with its sister epic,[2] and the question arises each time in the mind of the textual critic whether [301] the Mahābhārata or the Rāmāyaṇa is the source of the passage common to the two epics, a question to which, owing to the peculiar character and development of the Indian epics, no general answer is possible, though a partial solution of the problem may be attempted.

As remarked already, the Nala passage is not the only passage for which a parallel exists in the Rāmāyaṇa. In the Ādiparvan, for instance, in a cosmogonic chapter, I had occasion to draw attention to the fact that a passage of some 30 lines (1. 60. 54-67 of the Critical Edition) recurs almost verbatim in the Rāmāyaṇa (3. 14. 17-32, ed. Nirnaya Sagar Press). No definite evidence was available in that particular instance to show whether the passage was original to the Mahābhārata and had been borrowed by the Rāmāyaṇa, or *vice versa*, or again whether it had been borrowed by both epics independently from a third source. There seemed to me, however, to be some slight abruptness in the manner in which the stanzas were introduced in the Mahābhārata, which would suggest borrowing from the Rāmāyaṇa where the context is smoother; but, as the contents of the passage were of a very general nature, the third possibility mentioned above, namely that both epics owed the idea to a common (Purāṇic) source, could not be entirely eliminated.

The Sabhāparvan again supplies the well known *kaccit* chapter (adhy. 5), which has its counterpart in the Rāmayaṇa.[3] Here also the contents are of a very general character, having no direct bearing on the context of either the Rāmāyaṇa or the Mahābhārata, and the whole passage could well have been adapted by both epics independently from an older Nīti tractate.

On the other hand, in the Āraṇyakaparvan, commonly known as the

---

[1] The question has been discussed at some length by HOPKINS, *The Great Epic of India*, chapter 2 ("Interrelation of the two Epics"); and by WINTERNITZ, *op. cit.*, pp. 501-517. See now also EUGENIUSZ SLUSZKIEWICZ, *Przyczynki do badan nad dziejami redakcyi Rāmāyaṇy*. (*Contributions à l'histoire des recensions du Rāmāyaṇa*). Polska Akademia Umiejetności. Prace Komisji Orientalistyczne Nr. 30. Krakóio 1938.

[2] Several such passages are mentioned by HOPKINS, *op. cit.*, p. 73 ff.

[3] Cf. HOPKINS, *Amer. Journ. Phil.*, vol. xix, p. 149.

Vanaparvan, the Rāmopākhyāna closely follows in general our Rāmāyaṇa, notwithstanding some isolated though striking discrepancies between the two accounts.[1] There are also not wanting in the Rāmopākhyāna a few of our genuine Rāmāyaṇa stanzas which have been reproduced either verbatim or with but slight verbal alteration. To suggest that the Rāmopākhyāna was the original source which had inspired the revered Ādi-kavi to compose his Rāmāyaṇa would be again a *reductio ad absurdum*. The inevitable conclusion is that the diaskeuasts of the Rāmopākhyāna knew and summarised an extensive older Rāma epic. The only doubt is whether the redactors of the Mahābhārata had utilized *our* version of the Rāmāyaṇa or some other older version unknown to us, to which the discrepant traits of our episode might be traced. After an intensive study and a close comparison of the two texts, the late Prof. JACOBI had definitely expressed himself in favour of the former alternative, namely, that the Rāmopākhyāna was a passably accurate summary of *our* Rāmāyaṇa, the discrepancies between the accounts being due either to casual misconception or else to natural and unavoidable failure of memory, of which instances are common in summaries and abstracts.[2] [302] JACOBI'S view, it seems to me, now finds further confirmation from the instance discussed above of direct borrowing from our Rāmāyaṇa text in a case where there is no intrinsic reason whatsoever for any reference to the Rāmāyaṇa at all. Evidence seems to be, therefore, gathering to show that our Rāmāyaṇa text—or the bulk of it, at any rate—was used as a "source" by the diaskeuasts of the Mahābhārata. We can even go further and admit with JACOBI that the Rāmāyaṇa must already have been "generally familiar as an *ancient* work before the Mahābhārata reached its final form."[3] On the other hand it will have to be admitted that the Mahābhārata makes in various ways a distinctly more archaic impression, a fact which has led some scholars to regard it as even a much older work than the other epic. We thus arrive at the apparent paradox that the Rāmāyaṇa is older than the Mahābhārata and the Mahābhārata is older than the Rāmāyaṇa. The only way we can resolve this paradox is by supposing—as has already been suggested by WINTERNITZ[4] and other writers on the subject—that the period of composition of the Rāmāyaṇa, which is a work with a distinctly more unitary character, falls within the much longer period of the evolution of the Mahābhārata, which latter compared to the other is a very complex and complicated work indeed.

---

1 JACOBI, *Das Rāmāyaṇa*, pp. 71 ff.

2 JACOBI, *loc. cit. Contra* HOPKINS, *op. cit.*, p. 63 : "the subject-matter of the Kāvya and episode is treated differently in several particulars (details, loc. cit.) which points to different workings-over of older matter rather than to copying or condensing".

3 JACOBI, *op. cit.*, p. 71.

4 *Op. cit.*, p. 505.

This statement of the relationship between the two epics will appear perfectly valid and even natural when we remember that the evolution of the Great Epic of India falls into two distinct and separate phases, namely, the Bhārata and the Mahābhārata, the *caturviṁśatisāhasrī* (1. 1. 61 Crit. Ed.) and the *śatasāhasrī*, a fact which is documented in very clear terms by the work itself—and there is no reason to disbelieve it—but which for some unintelligible reason is not taken very seriously by people. Assuming, however, this to be a fact—which it undoubtedly is—we may hazard what seems to me to be a perfectly legitimate conjecture that the Rāmāyaṇa was composed in the interval which separated the Bhārata from the Mahābhārata. Thus, though we may admit that the Rāmāyaṇa was, as JACOBI says, a well-known work before the Mahābhārata reached its *ultimate* form, we must reckon with the possibility that when the Rāmāyaṇa itself (minus perhaps Books 1 and 7) was composed by the poet Vālmīki, the heroic poem Bhārata—the nucleus of our Mahābhārata—was already long in existence, current perhaps in some distant part of the country and in a different *milieu*. The Bhārata and the Rāmāyaṇa may have been indeed more or less independent products, different in origin and treatment. But when the Bhārgava redactors[1] set to work and converted the [303] Bhārata into the Mahābhārata, conceived on a much larger scale and with a much more ambitious programme, they had already the archetype of our Rāmāyaṇa text before them and they made full use of it, absorbing in their own encyclopaedic work all that they possibly could, and they were perhaps also influenced by it in no small degree. In fact the very impetus to the conversion of the Bhārata and the compilation of the Mahābhārata may well have been given by the contact with the sister epic, which appears to have had a more elevated ethical standard, a more serious didactic purpose, a much higher idealistic view of life, and a wider popular appeal.

A priori, then, whenever our Mahābhārata shows close *verbal* agreement with the *older* books of the Rāmāyaṇa, the presumption would be that we have to look upon the Rāmāyaṇa as the source, assuming of course that the common element is not of such a character that it could have been borrowed by both epics independently from a third source. It is naturally not excluded that the Rāmāyaṇa in its turn might have been influenced to a certain extent, at a still later epoch, in its further development, by the Mahābhārata, the new encyclopaedic Dharma Saṁhitā. In fact there is every indication that the interrelation between the two epics will reduce itself to a very complicated system of mutual actions and reactions, and it would be interesting to investigate the question more fully by collation of all possible parallelisms in ideas and expression between the two great epics of India.

---

1 For the part played by the Bhṛgus in the development of the Mahābhārata, see my "Epic Studies (VI) : The Bhṛgus and the Bhārata ; A text-historical study." *Annals of the Bhandarkar Oriental Research Institute*, Vol. 18, pp. 1-76 (particularly pp. 63-76).

EPIC QUESTIONS

No. 1 : Does Indra assume the form of a swan ?*

Mbh. (Crit. Ed.) 1. 57.21 : *hāsyarūpeṇa śaṁkaraḥ.*

This is the second pāda of a stanza occurring in the Ādiparvan which reads :

bhagavān pūjyate cātra hāsyarūpeṇa śaṁkaraḥ |
svayam eva gṛhītena Vasoḥ prītyā mahātmanaḥ ||

The Vulgate (1. 63. 21cd—22ab) differs from this only in so far that it reads the second quarter of the stanza as *haṁsarūpeṇa céśvaraḥ.*

I have discussed the text-reading briefly in the *Annals of the Bhandarkar Oriental Research Institute* (vol. 16, p. 100 f.) and justified it, in my reply to the late Professor WINTERNITZ, who in the course of a lengthy review[1] of the Ādiparvan had drawn attention to it, observing that as the reading was a *lectio difficilior* and was "far from certain" it requires a "wavy line". While admitting that the reading adopted in the Critical Edition was a *lectio difficilior* I contended that since the documentary evidence in its favour was complete, therefore it need not be regarded as uncertain and there was no need of a "wavy line." There would have been no reason for me now to revert to it but for two facts. On the one hand, it has been again, incidentally, criticized[2] by the late lamented Professor J. J. MEYER in his last publication, *Trilogie altindischer Mächte u. Feste d. Vegetation*[3] (Zürich-Leipzig 1937),—a thick opus with extremely rich and varied contents, enlivened as usual by the author's spicy wit and trenchant style. On the other hand, the reading receives some confirmation from a new and unexpected source.

MEYER argues for the reading of the Vulgate, characterizing the *hāsyarūpeṇa* of the Critical Edition as an astonishing ("verwunderliche") reading, and dismissing *hāsya-* as the stupid mistake of some scribe ("ein dummer Schreibfehler").

The context in which the Mbh. stanza occurs is as follows. The righteous king Uparicara Vasu, having laid down his arms, retired to the forest and

---

* [*Bulletin of the Deccan College Research Institute* 1. 1-7.]

1 *ABORI*, vol. 15, pp. 159 ff ; cf. p. 166.

2 Apparently, in complete ignorance of the previous discussion on the point in the *Annals.*

3 In the last part of the *Trilogie*, dealing with Indra. The reading in question is discussed on p. 5 f. The references are to the pagination of this part of the *Trilogie.*

began practising penance. Indra and the {2} other gods, apprehending trouble, appeared before him, and, dissuading him from continuing his fierce austerities, induced him to return to his royal duties. He should rule the kingdom of Cedi as Indra's special friend. As a mark of his favour, Indra presented Vasu with various uncommon gifts, among them a crystalline aerial car (*sphāṭikaṁ vimānam*) and a garland of unfading lotuses (known as *Indramālā*) which would protect the king against the missiles of his enemies and bring him wealth and victory (*vaijayantīṁ*). But he gave him also a bamboo staff (*vaiṇavīm yaṣṭim*), which would protect the good (*śiṣṭānām pratipālinīm*) and of course chastise the wicked. King Vasu brought home these precious gifts, according the wonderful staff full divine worship. That was how, we are told, the custom began of bringing from the forest, at a certain specified season, the staff, pole or tree, which was then set up, decorated with flowers, wreaths, flags, and with *piṭakas*—whatever these latter are—and worshipped in due form. Here we find the stanza cited above, which says in effect that on this occasion Indra is worshipped, according to ancient rites, in a certain form assumed by the god of his own accord, out of love for Vasu Uparicara.

What was this form? Was it the form of a *swan*, as the Vulgate has it and as MEYER argues? That is the question.

Before we try to answer this question, it would be well to examine the MS. evidence a little more closely than MEYER appears to have done. The important MS. reading (ignoring that of D_3), as given in the Critical Edition, may be put in the following synoptical form :

N (except K_1)	*haṁsarūpeṇa*	} *śaṁkaraḥ* (B_5 Dn) *césvaraḥ*.
K_1 M (= Text)	*hāsyarūpeṇa*[1]	
T. G.	*Yaṣṭirūpeṇa*	*Vāsavaḥ*.

To this we may now add the important, newly discovered eight hundred years old Nepālī MS. of the Ādi (of which I have given full collations in *ABORI*, vol. 19, pp. 201 ff.), which agrees exactly with K_1 M and therefore supports the critical text in an unambiguous manner.

Now let us see what MEYER has to say about these readings. According to him (p. 5), the original *césvaraḥ* (found in the Vulgate) was misunderstood as referring to god Śiva ; and, with a view to clarifying its meaning, it was deliberately changed by some scribe into *śaṁkaraḥ*, which latter is a well-known epithet of Śiva. And further *hāsyarūpeṇa* of the Critical

[1] The actual reading of K_1 is *āmmyahāmyarūpeṇa*, which is clearly corrupt. The original *s* has been wrongly transcribed as *m* : a common mistake in Devanāgarī transcripts of Śāradā MSS. ; there is moreover dittography. The portion of the text under discussion is missing in the Śāradā codex.

Edition is, according to MEYER, as already [3] remarked, nothing more than the stupid blunder of some copyist for the original *haṁsarūpeṇa*.

It may be made perfectly clear once for all that at least as far as the Mahābhārata text is concerned, the time when one could juggle with readings of MSS and lay down the law *ex cathedra* as to what is the original, what is an emendation and what is a scribe's mistake, is long past. It has now become a very much more serious and complicated matter, since the publication of the Critical Edition. To entitle anyone to a hearing, he must first of all show that he understands the critical apparatus and that he has studied the *stemma codicum* published by me on p. xxx of the Prolegomena of my edition of the Ādiparvan.

Let us now go back to the MSS. There we find that *śaṁkaraḥ* (of the Critical Edition) is documented by the whole of the Northern Recension (including the new Nepālī MS.) and the Malayālam version, while *céśvaraḥ* (championed by MEYER) is merely the reading of B_5 Dn ! Now one would like to know why what MEYER considers the original reading (*céśvaraḥ*) is found only in the *most recent* version represented by Nīlakaṇṭha (end of the 17th century) with the sporadic support of one aberrant Bengali MS. (B_5), while what he considers a recent emendation (*śaṁkaraḥ* is found in still older versions represented by MSS. scattered all over India from Kashmir to Malabar and from Gujarat to Bengal, including the distant Nepal and excepting (in addition to the Vulgate) only the Tamil-Telugu zone, which latter has moreover a third and divergent reading (*Vāsavaḥ*). How is it that only the Nīlakaṇṭha version has preserved the correct reading, while all other—much older—versions of North India together with the entire Malayālam version from the South contain what MEYER regards as a corruption? If *śaṁkaraḥ* of all N and M MSS. be a corrupt reading, as MEYER maintains, then Nīlakaṇṭha could have got his *céśvaraḥ* only by *emendation*, because I do not think that Nīlakaṇṭha had access to any really old Mahābhārata MSS., containing very original readings. In thousands of cases his text shows what can be proved, with absolute certainty, to be secondary, inferior, or corrupt readings.

This inability on the part of MEYER to recognize in a patently simple case what is original and what is secondary shows that he had only very vague notions of the relationship between the different recensions, versions and manuscripts. And the ignorance of this relationship is absolutely fatal to any attempt to discriminate between original readings and emendations and scribes' mistakes. You can never find out an original reading by selecting one which suits your purpose, or satisfies your æsthetic sense, or appeals to you in some other way, and then looking about for reasons in support of your *a priori* choice; because almost always "good" reasons can be found for nearly every reading. It is not a question of dialectic, but [4] of documentation. And no amount of tendentious arguing will refute the objective evidence of MSS.

MSS. in this case clearly prove that the process of alteration has been the reverse of what is imagined by MEYER. Here, it is evident, *ceśvaraḥ* has not been changed into *śaṁkaraḥ* for the sake of clarity, as MEYER maintains; but, on the other hand, *śaṁkaraḥ* has been very clearly changed into *ceśvaraḥ*—already rendered suspect by the expletive *ca*—perhaps, to avoid confusion, *śaṁkara* being here not the *nomen proprium* of Śiva, but an epithet meaning "beneficent, promoting welfare".[1]

We can now turn to the other word of the pāda, the more difficult of the two: was it *hāsyarūpeṇa, haṁsarūpeṇa* or *yaṣṭirūpeṇa*? MEYER (p. 5) rightly rejects the last. It is correct as far as the sense goes; but it can hardly be the original reading. Were it so, no scribe would think of deliberately changing it into the obscure and almost unintelligible *hāsyarūpeṇa* or *haṁsarūpeṇa*, both of which are, moreover, graphically unrelated with the former. From what we know of scribes' emendations they tend generally to simplify the text, not to complicate it. If that be so, then either *hāsyarūpeṇa* or *haṁsarūpeṇa* is the correct reading. Moreover *yaṣṭirūpeṇa* is confined (like *Vāsavaḥ*), to T G, and does not receive any support even from M, which in innumerable cases has preserved—in contradiction to the T G version—the original reading, which has been emended or simplified in T G.[2]

There remains, therefore, only the two alternatives—*hāsyarūpeṇa* given by K_1 M with the new Nepali MS, and *haṁsarūpeṇa* supported by N (except K_1). By the test of the agreement between independent versions,[3] *hāsyarūpeṇa* is clearly indicated as the original reading, since we have here an agreement between the independent versions of the extreme North and the extreme South, it being preferable to *haṁsarūpeṇa*, supported only by the central sub-recension. It is, moreover, undoubtedly the *lectio difficilior* (as was rightly observed by WINTERNITZ in the course of the review mentioned above), which accounts for its being surreptitiously ousted by the other. Both documentary and intrinsic probability are thus unquestionably in favour of the reading *hāsyarūpeṇa* adopted in the Critical Edition.

What indeed are we to understand by the *haṁsarūpeṇa* of the Vulgate? The word *haṁsa* has a number of meanings. MONIER WILLIAMS gives the following:

[5] a goose, gander, swan, flamingo (or other aquatic bird); the soul or spirit (sometimes 'the Universal Soul or Supreme Spirit', identified with Virāj, Nārāyaṇa,

---

[1] This point has been discussed by me in the paper mentioned above, *ABORI*, vol. 16, p. 101.

[2] For this point also cf. *ABORI*, vol. 16, p. 101.

[3] Cf. Prolegomena to Ādi, p. XCI.

Viṣṇu, Śiva, Kāma, and the Sun); one of the vital airs (Lex); a kind of ascetic; a man of supernatural qualities born under a particular constellation; an ambitious monarch (Lex.); a horse (Naigh); an excellent draught-ox (according to some, 'a buffalo'); a mountain (Lex.); a temple of a particular form; a kind of Mantra or mystical text; silver (Lex.); envy, malice (Lex.); name of two metres; (Music) a kind of measure; a mystical name of the letter *h*; a spiritual preceptor; name of a Deva-gandharva; of a Dānava; of a son of Brahmā; of a son of Vasudeva; of a son of Ariṣṭā; of a son of Brahmadatta and general of Jarāsaṁdha; of various authors; of one of the Moon's horses; of a mountain.

MEYER (p. 6) has cited copious examples for the meanings of *haṁsa* as the sun, the sun-god, as Viṣṇu and as Kṛṣṇa (son of Dharma).

Unfortunately none of these fit in the case of Indra. MEYER (p. 6) found, however, a loophole in the meaning of *haṁsa* as "sungod", and he surmised that perhaps the idea of this *haṁsarūpa* of Indra was to be dated back to the period when Indra was still recognized as a sun-god!

Nīlakaṇṭha, who has commented on this stanza, had naturally some difficulty in explaining this *haṁsarūpa*. According to him Indra was: *haṁsarūpeṇa yukto haṁsarūpī | tasya buddhisthasya rūpasya viśeṣaṇaṁ svayam eva* etc. To Nīlakaṇṭha the *haṁsa*-form is present only in the mind (*buddhistha*) of the worshipper. To MEYER, on the other hand, who was a realist with a vengeance, this explanation naturally did not satisfy. According to him (p. 4 f.), Indra, who is ordinarily invisible to mortals, takes on the *concrete* form of a swan, so as to be visible to Vasu and his subjects. MEYER further found (p. 5) the aquatic bird admirably suited to the mirth and gaiety and the sportive games that accompany the ceremonial.

Now which is the original and which is the emendation of these two readings? The characteristic of a scribe's emendation, as has been well said, is that it has all the appearance of improvement without its reality. Ours is a case in point. *haṁsarūpeṇa* is a phrase under which you can think all sorts of things, all equally vague; but on closer inspection they prove to be uniformly inadequate.

For why should Indra appear before Vasu, or the kings who followed in his footsteps, in the form of a *swan* of all things in the world, whether in a concrete shape before the eyes of his worshippers or in an abstract form in their minds? He had assumed one form already: that of the *yaṣṭi*, the staff. MEYER (p. 101) has himself established—absolutely incontrovertibly—that the tree or the pole or the staff which figures so prominently in the Indramaha ceremony, was worshipped, if not by Vasu, at least by the people whom the writer of the Mahābhārata account had in mind, as a symbol, [6] an image, or an incarnation of Indra himself, and not merely as a remembrance of a present from Indra to Vasu. As MEYER has pointed out, the Purāṇic writers, when speaking of the pole, refer to it unhesitatingly as "Indra" (or its synonyms "Śakra", etc.) in such expressions as *Śakrasthāna* or *Indra-*

sthāna, Indra (or *Śakra*): *pāda, Indraprayāṇa, Śakrotthāpana, Śakrocchraya, Indraṁ utthāpayanti, Puraṁdaram utthāpya, uttiṣṭhate* (or *niṣīdati*) *vajrapāṇiḥ*, etc. Viṣṇu-dharmottara 2. 157. 3cd. and (agreeing with it) Agnipurāṇa 268, 6cd say in so many words that *here is the god Indra himself*, come to earth (*bhūmiṣṭha*).

And what a funny form to assume for the thousand-eyed god of gods, who had performed a hundred sacrifices, the wielder of the thunder-bolt, the destroyer of enemies' forts, the killer of Vala (or Bala) and Vṛtra, and the hero of a thousand other wonderful exploits : the form of a bamboo staff, with wreaths and bells, flags and buntings hanging from it and with those curiously shaped *piṭakas*, some of which at any rate, *according to Meyer* (p. 96), were shaped like penies ! It was indeed a laughable form (*hāsyarūpa*), calculated to provoke mirth and laughter. And this form, it must be borne in mind, was not given to Indra by any man ; such a thing would have been very likely resented by him. The great god, wishing to do good (*śaṁkara*) to Vasu, had assumed it himself (*svayam eva grahītena*) out of his great love for the high soul Uparicara Vasu (*Vasoḥ prītyā mahātmanaḥ*). The jocular form—*krīḍāvatārarūpa*, as Devabodha[1] puts it—assumed by the mighty god on this occasion caused great merriment ; and the feast was accordingly celebrated with much laughter and gaiety, as described in the Bṛhatsaṁhitā, the Viṣṇudharmottara and other texts (MEYER, p. 103 f.).

Thus both documentary probability and intrinsic considerations support the reading *hāsyarūpeṇa Śaṁkaraḥ*. This reading is therefore not so astonishing as MEYER seems to have thought ; but it is astonishing that MEYER who had with praiseworthy diligence extracted and translated very lengthy passages from about a dozen original sources describing the ceremony in great detail, and not found anywhere (except in the Vulgate) the remotest reference to Indra's assuming the form of a swan or to his being represented as a swan, should have been so enamoured of the Vulgate reading, a reading which I am fully persuaded is nothing more than a scribe's emendation in the archetype of the Central group. But perhaps even MEYER's mistake is not so very astonishing : it is only an example of wishful thinking. Does it not connect Indra with the sun (*haṁsa*) [7] or at least with the sun-god ? And MEYER'S whole thesis (pp. 134-144) is that Indra was originally just not a rain-god or a thunder-god, but a sun-god, the vernal sun, the " genius " of fertility and vegetation, in fact, a phallic deity !

The redactors of the T G version were, perhaps, after all wise, in dis-

---

1 Devobodha has the gloss : *hāsa* (sic) *rūpeṇa krīḍāvatārarūpeṇa*. Here *haṁsarūpeṇa* would certainly not fit, as it is not clear how *haṁsarūpa* would be *krīḍāvatārarūpa*.—Devobodha is the *oldest* known commentator of the Mahābhārata, and, in my opinion, the best.

carding a reading which has caused so much confusion and misunderstanding, and adopted the plain and simple *yaṣṭirūpeṇa Vāsavaḥ*, which is a correct paraphrase of the original and has the additional advantage of being absolutely fool-proof.

I am convinced that this *haṁsa*-incarnation of Indra is nothing more than a *canard*.

II. The Parvasaṁgraha Figures.*

The Parvasaṁgrahaparvan (Ādi, adhy. 2) is a document of considerable importance.[1] But its value has been unduly exaggerated by some scholars, a circumstance which has led to some highly misleading results and some curious conclusions It is thus supposed that Kṛṣṇa Dvaipāyana Vyāsa had himself counted and noted down the number of ślokas he had composed, and that our Parvasaṁgraha was composed by Vyāsa himself. No doubt it is sometimes stated in the Parvasaṁgraha chapter that that sage had stated the extent of each of the eighteen parvans. But this attribution to Vyāsa is naturally only pūjārthe (*honoris causa*). It is nowhere suggested in the work itself that the first two adhyāyas of our epic were composed by Vyāsa. They could not be, because they are obviously only a report of the conversation which took place between the Sūta (Ugraśravas, son of Lomaharṣaṇa) and the sages assembled at Śaunaka's twelve-year sacrifice in the Naimiṣa Forest. The erroneous supposition regarding the authorship of this adhyāya has led to the naïve attempt on the part of some scholars to produce a text—a so-called critical text—of the Mahābhārata containing the same number of adhyāyas and ślokas as that given in the Parvasaṁgraha. Such an attempt is already negatived by our manuscripts and testimonia, which contain many variants of the figures in the Parvasaṁgraha. Thus the figures for the Ādiparvan itself vary, according to different sources, between 7984 (Kaśmīrī Version and the Critical Edition) and 9984 (Āndhra-Bhāratamu). That is sufficient to discourage any attempt at too close a reliance on the data of this adhyāya of the Ādiparvan. It has been common experience that figures in ancient works, if at all complicated, seldom come out right, and the figures of the Parvasaṁgraha are probably no exception to this rule.

[550] The figures given in the Parvasaṁgraha could have been obtained

---

* [Silver Jubilee Number, *ABORI* 23. 549-58].

[1] Cf. my Prolegomena to the Ādiparvan, pp. xcvii ff ; "Epic studies (III)" *ABORI*, vol. 11, pp. 277 ff.

[2] Cf. P. P. S. Sastri in the Introduction to vol. 15 of his Mahābhārata (Southern Recension), p. xxii : "Vyāsa's description of his Mahābhārata that he composed it in 18 parvas of 2,000 chapters and 100,000 stanzas is not a fanciful account but an accurate statement. And I have tried to substantiate this in this edition of the Principal Text of the Southern Recension."

in one of many different ways. The most probable suggestion has been that they were arrived at, not by actual *counting* of the stanzas, as we should ordinarily do now, but by *computing* the extent in some other way. Even now we speak of a story of 5000 words or a broadcast talk of 1500 words, and so on. The individual words are never counted in such computations; the figures are only approximations. The figures given in our Parvasaṁgraha chapter must be approximations of that type. They are not "ślokas" or stanzas as we ordinarily understand them; but are, properly speaking, what are technically known as, "granthas," a grantha being a unit of measurement of written matter equal to 32 akṣaras.

Assuming this to be the case, the first difficulty is that the figures given in the lists appear not as round numbers, as we should expect them to be, but are apparently correct to the last digit; for instance, the extent is given not as 8000 ślokas, but as 7987. We actually come across such figures as these: 6698, 7998, 8909, 14525, where true approximations would be 6700, 8000, 8900, 14,500, and so on. The approximation seems to me to have been reached by some such process as this. First, an average was obtained by counting carefully all letters in a certain number of lines. This average was then multiplied by the number of lines in a page and the total number of complete pages. The number of "granthas" of the last page, which was rarely fully written out, seems to have been computed separately, and added to the previous total. The grand total of letters (*akṣaras*) was then divided by 32 to give the number of "ślokas" or "granthas," fractions being omitted. That is how figures like those mentioned above must have been obtained. They are careful approximations, but approximations all the same. Moreover, as has been pointed out by me elsewhere,[1] it would be impossible to count the exact number of *stanzas* in a composite text made up of ślokas, triṣṭubhs, "fancy metres" and prose passages, which we actually find in many of the parvans of the Mahābhārata, as for instance in the Ādi, Āraṇyaka and Anuśāsana.

The figures we find in the Parvasaṁgraha chapter are fairly old; we cannot say now exactly how old. They are certainly prior to 1000 A. D., when the Javanese *Bhārata* and the *Āndhra Bhāratamu* were composed; because both these works contain similar lists, which agree in many particulars with our list.

Here are the figures given in three different sources.

---

[1] Prolegomena, p. xcix.

[551] TABLE I

Adhyāyas			Parvan	Ślokas		
C	B	A		A	B	C
South. Rec.	Jav. Version	Crit. Ed.	—	Crit. Ed.	Jav. Version	South. Rec.
218	818	218	I. ĀDI	7984	8884	9884
72	72	72	II. SABHĀ	2511	2511	4511
269	272	269	III. ĀRAṆYAKA	11,664	11,224	11,664
67	—	67	IV. VIRĀṬA	2050	2015	3500
186	186	186	V. UDYOGA	6698	6928	7998
118	117	117	VI. BHIṢMA	5884	5884	5884
170	170	170	VII. DROṆA	8909	8984	8909
69	69	69	VIII. KARṆA	4900	4970	4900
59	121	59	IX. ŚALYA	3220	3220	3220
18	18	18	X. SAUPTIKA	870	870	870
27	70	27	XI. STRĪ	775	770	775
339	333	339	XII. ŚĀNTI	14,525	14,525	14,525
156	—	146	XIII. ANUŚĀSANA	6700	—	12,000
133	133	133	XIV. ĀŚVAMEDHIKA	3320	4420	4420
42	92	42	XV. ĀŚRAMAVĀSIKA	1506	1508	1906
8	8	8	XVI. MAUSALA	300	300	300
3	—	3	XVII. MAHĀPRASTHĀNIKA	120	123	120
5	—	5	XVIII. SVARGĀROHAṆA	200	200	200
1959		1948	Total	82,136		95,586

(The average number of "ślokas" per adhyāya is about 45.)

[552] The above is a conspectus of the figures for the adhyāyas and ślokas of the eighteen parvans of the Mahābhārata according to (1) the Critical Edition, (2) the Javanese Version,[1] and (3) the Southern Recension by Professor P. P. S. SASTRI.

OBSERVATIONS ON THE FIGURES OF THE ABOVE TABLE.

I. *Ādi* : The first figure (8) of the Javanese number for the *adhyāyas* of the Ādi (818) is obviously wrong ; the other digits agree in the three texts. So we may take as correct the figures 218,[2] which is given us by the Critical Edition and Southern Recension, the Vulgate reading (227) being certainly a mistake.—The number of *ślokas* is no doubt a problem. I have adopted the figures given by the Śāradā MS. and one " K " MS. (K_1),[3] which is confirmed by the Rajaguru MS. from Nepal,[4] and I am still inclined to suppose that that was the original figure. The Javanese and Southern figures 8884 and 9884 respectively differ by 1000 exactly, the Javanese figure being the same as that of the Mid-Indian group (Bengali-Devanāgari).

II. *Sabhā* : The numbers are here absolutely certain. As regards the *adhyāyas*, there is perfect agreement between the three sources, all of them giving 72, which is also the exact number of adhyāyas of our Critical Edition of the Sabhā now passing through the press. The Vulgate figure (78) for the *śloka* is therefore unquestionably wrong.—The *śloka* number is also certainly 2511, as the Southern Recension, in which the first figure has been increased to 4, is demonstrably inflated to make it conform with the interpolated text, and the additional stanzas of the Southern Recension do approximately amount to 2000. The correct figures for Sabhā are therefore 72 and 2511.

[553] III. *Āraṇyaka* (commonly known as *Vana*) : As regards the *adhyāyas*, the Javanese records 272 against the concordant figure 269 of *all* Indian versions. The latter may be taken to be the right figure, the discrepancy of the Javanese, which is negligible, remaining unexplained.—The same is true of the figure for the *ślokas*, the concordant figure (11,664) of all Indian versions being the original Parvasaṁgraha figure.

IV. *Virāṭa* : The Javanese figure for the *adhyāyas* is unfortunately missing. But as our Critical Edition of the Virāṭaparva has successfully

---

[1] The figures for the Javanese Version have been taken from JUYNBOLL's *Adiparwa, Oudjavaansch prozageschrift*, Gravenhage, 1906. pp. 5-6. The passage is reproduced in a note by H. KERN, " Inhoudsopgave van 't Mahābhārata in 'T Kawi " in *Bijdragen*, ser III, Vol. IV, pp. 92-95, KERN has given in this paper a comparative table of the Indian and the Javanese figures.

[2] KERN, *op. cit.*, p. 95 also remarks that the Javanese figure 818 is incorrect, and that it should be 218.

[3] See the Critical Edition of the Adiparvan, p. 878.

[4] See my " Epic studies (VII)," *ABORI*, vol. 19 (1938), pp. 215 ff.

identified the adhyāyas on the basis of the colophons given in MSS., there is no reason to doubt that the correct figure is 67, as given by the Sanskrit Parvasaṁgraha.—The three sources give three different figures for the *ślokas*. The Southern Recension is obviously inflated, and may therefore be ignored, its figure having been revised—as in Sabhā—to accord with its interpolated text. It is likely that the Javanese translator has confused the Sanskrit words for 50 and 15 (*pañcāśat* and *pañcadaśa*). The first two digits of the figures given in the Critical Edition and the Javanese Version do agree. We may therefore reasonably assume the original figure to be 2050, which is given by the Critical Edition of the Parvasaṁgraha, though the two last digits naturally remain somewhat uncertain.[1]

V. *Udyoga*: The three sources agreeing exactly as regards the number of *adhyāyas* of the Udyoga, the figure 186 may be taken as certain.—The figures for the *ślokas*, on the other hand, are in a chaotic condition, the three texts giving three different figures 6698, 6928, 7998; which agree only in respect of the last digit! The figures for the ślokas remain, therefore, doubtful.

VI. *Bhīṣma*: The number of *adhyāyas* in the Bhīṣma is given by the Critical Edition and the Javanese Version as 117, but the Southern Recension gives their number as 118. In any case, the difference is not very significant, and the number may be assumed to be 117 or 118—There is no such doubt regarding the number of *ślokas*, which is unanimously given as 5884.

VII. *Droṇa*: There is likewise considerable agreement as regards the *adhyāyas* and *ślokas* of the Droṇa. The *adhyāya* number [554] is 170.—As regards the number of *ślokas*, the first two digits (89) are certain. And since both the Critical Edition and the Southern Recension agree on the figure 8909, that is indicated as the correct figure. The probability in favour of this figure is strengthened owing to the circumstance that the last two figures of the Javanese Version (84) are in all probability due to contamination with the previous śloka-figure 5884, which ends in 84. We may therefore adopt with confidence the concordant figure of the Indian versions 8909, the difference between the Javanese and the Indian numbers being 75; the error is in any event not more than 1 per cent.

VIII. *Karṇa*: The figures for Karṇa are exactly of the same type. The three sources agree in giving 69 as the number of *adhyāyas*.—The Javanese MSS. give the number of *ślokas* as 970, which is obviously wrong, it being almost certain that the word for 4000 has been omitted by the scribe by oversight;[2] so we get the original Javanese figure as [4]970. We may

---

1 See Raghu VIRA, *Virāṭaparvan*, Introduction, p. xxiv; and SUKTHANKAR "Epic studies (III)," *ABORI* vol. 11, pp. 277 ff.

2 KERN, *loc. cit.*, also recognizes that the first figure has been omitted by mistake in the Javanese text.

tentatively adopt the figure 4900, on the concordant evidence of Indian versions. The difference between the Indian and Javanese figures being only 70, the discrepancy is only about 1·4 per cent.

IX. *Śalya* : In this parvan there is fortunately no doubt about the *śloka* number, which is unanimously given as 3220.—And again, fortunately, as regards the *adhyāya* number, the discrepancy between the Indian (59) and Javanese (121) figures is so great that the Javanese may be ruled out as hopelessly corrupt. There is another test we may apply, the Javanese figure[1] (121) for adhyāyas gives the average of about 27 ślokas to an adhyāya, while the Indian average is 54. Now the total number of adhyāyas in the Mahābhārata is supposed to be 2000, and the number of stanzas 100,000 (śatasahasrāṇi[2]), which gives the average of ślokas to an adhyāya as 50 and that is much nearer the average for the Indian figure for the adhyāya number of the Śalyaparvan than the Javanese figure.

X. *Sauptika* : The figures for the Sauptika call for no remarks. They are uniformaly given in all the three sources as 18 and 870 respectively.

[555] XI. *Strī* : The sources do not agree as regards the number of *adhyāyas*, but the Javanese figure (70) which is nearly two and half times as large as the Indian (27) is extremely improbable.[3] We may therefore tentatively take the concordant Indian figure (27) as correct.—The difference between the Javanese and Indian figures for the *ślokas* is only five. It would seem that the last digit was lost in the Javanese tradition ; if that be so, the correct number is 775, as given unanimously by the Indian MSS.

XII. *Śānti* : The *śloka* figure for Śānti (14,525) is given unanimously by all the three of our sources, which is a fortunate coincidence and also a remarkable proof of the reliability of our tradition. The Vulgate figure (14,725) for the ślokas is positively wrong.—There is a difference of only six between the Javanese and Indian figures for *adhyāyas*, the Indian tradition giving the figure as 339, the Javanese as 333. The agreement between the different Indian versions is a weighty point in favour of 339, which we may tentatively assume to be the correct figure.

XIII. *Anuśāsana* : The evidence of the Javanese Version is unfortunately missing, the version ignoring this parvan altogether, for some reason which it is hard to guess. It cannot be argued that it is included in the Śānti, since there is no appreciable increase in the number of adhyāyas or

---

[1] KERN, *loc. cit.*, likewise considers the Javanese figure (121) as very suspicious.

[2] See the Critical Edition of the Adiparvan, additional passage No. 486*, given on page 241.

[3] As in the case of the Śalyaparvan, KERN (*loc. cit.*) regards the Javanese figure is very doubtful.

ślokas of the Javanese Version of the Śānti, as there would surely have been, had the two parvans been amalgamated as is done sometimes.[1] There being also no agreement between the various Indian versions, the figures for both adhyāyas and ślokas of the Anuśāsana remain uncertain.

XIV. *Āśvamedhika* : The number of *adhyāyas* is unanimously given as 133, which may therefore be accepted as the correct figure.—There is a discrepancy as regards the number of *ślokas* : the Critical Edition gives the figure as 3320, while the Javanese and the [556] Southern Recension agree in giving the figure as 4420, this being one of the rare instances in which the Javanese and the Southern Recension agree against the Northern Recension. The Southern Recension contains here an additional sub-parvan, comprising 23 adhyāyas and about 1700 ślokas, known as the Vaiṣṇavadharma parvan. There is no mention of any such parvan in the list of 100 pavans, given in the Parvasaṁgraha, though some Southern MSS. do insert, in another place, a line which mentions the Vaiṣṇavadharma among the contents of the Āśvamedhika. In this Section, Yudhiṣṭhira is instructed by Śrī-Kṛṣṇa in the Dharma of the Vaiṣṇavas, which seems hardly necessary, after the instruction he had received from Bhīṣma in more than 21,000 stanzas on general Dharma (Śānti and Anuśāsana). The higher Southern number must therefore be regarded as due to this inflation, and can in any case not be accepted. Nevertheless the peculiar agreement between the Javanese and the Southern is a disturbing factor. The number therefore may be regarded as doubtful.

XV. *Āśramavāsika* : There is not much doubt about the *adhyāyas* of this parvan, though the Javanese Version has a high figure (92) against the unanimous Indian figure 42, which may be assumed to be the correct figure.[2] —As regards the number of *ślokas*, there is a slight discrepancy of 2 between the Critical Edition and the Javanese Version, the former being 1506, the latter 1508. But the last digit in this number is not in doubt ; it must be six. The Southern Recension gives the figure 1906, which must be regarded as extremely doubtful, since even Professor SASTRI, who has edited the Southern Recension, could not find more than 1108½ stanzas for this parvan.[3] There has been clearly a mistake in the counting of the stanzas of this par-

---

1 It is perhaps worth noticing that so late a commentator as Vādirāja (cf. P. K. GODE, *ABORI*, vol. 17, pp. 203-210, who assigns him to the seventeenth century), treats the Śānti and Anuśāsana as one parvan and has colophons like :

इति श्रीमहाभारते शतसाहस्रिकायां संहितायां वैयासिक्यां शान्तिपर्वणि आनुशासनिके भीष्मस्वर्गारोहणं नाम षट्षष्टिद्विशततमोऽध्याय: ॥ इति शान्तिपर्व समाप्तम् ॥

—which is quoted by Professor P. P. S. SASTRI in the Introduction to vol. 17, (Anuśāsana Parvan, part 2,) p. xxiv.

2 KERN (*loc. cit.*) likewise suggests reading 42 for 92 of the Javanese.

3 It is interesting to note, as pointed out by Professor SASTRI, Nannaya's *Āndhra-Bhāratamu* gives 1106 as the figure of ślokas in the Āśramavāsika parvan. That probably is due to a fresh count.

van, and the Southern figure being palpably incorrect, we may utilize the approximate agreement between the Critical Edition and the Javanese Version and adopt 1506 as the probable original Parvasaṁgraha figure for the Āśramavāsika.

XVI. *Mausala* : All sources agree in giving the number of *adhyāyas* as 8 and the number of *ślokas* as 300, which may accordingly be taken as the correct figures. The text also seems to con-[557]-tain actually 300 stanzas. Consequently the vulgate reading 320, in the Parvasaṁgraha chapter, is clearly faulty and has been properly rejected.

XVII. *Mahāprasthānika* : The Javanese figure for the number of *adhyāyas* is missing ; but the Indian sources, including the MSS., uniformly divide this short parvan into three adhyāyas ; and the unanimous Indian reading cannot be called into question.—The number of *ślokas* may also be regarded as correctly given in the Critical Edition, which is supported by the Southern Recension, though the Javanese Version adds, erroneously, three to the number, giving the figure as 123. I surmise that this addition of three to the śloka number is a wrong transposition from the adhyāya number, which is missing in the Javanese Version. The Vulgate figure (320) for the ślokas is absurd and unquestionably incorrect.

XVIII. *Svargārohaṇa* : As in the previous case the *adhyāya* number is lost in the Javanese Version ; but there cannot be any doubt that the correct figure is 5, which is given by all editions and MSS. of the Mahābhārata. —The *śloka* number is unanimously given, by our three sources, as 200, which is a sufficiently correct approximation of the actual extent of this last parvan of the Great Epic ; and the Vulgate figure (209) may be unhesitatingly rejected.

The table on the following page gives the figures for the adhyāyas and ślokas, book by book, arrived at by a collation of the various extant versions of the Parvasaṁgraha chapter of the Ādiparvan.

[558] TABLE II

Table giving the authentic figures for the Adhyāyas and Ślokas of the eighteen Parvans of the Mahābhārata, based upon a collation of the MSS. of the Sanskrit Parvasaṁgrahaparvan and of the Javanese Version (ca. 1000 A.D.).

	Parvan	Adhyāya	Śloka
I.	ĀDI	218	?
II.	SABHĀ	72	2511
III.	ĀRAṆYAKA	269	11,664
IV.	VIRĀṬA	67	2050
V.	UDYOGA	186	?
VI.	BHĪṢMA	117 (or 118)	5884
VII.	DROṆA	170	8909
VIII.	KARṆA	69	4900
IX.	ŚALYA	59	3220
X.	SAUPTIKA	18	870
XI.	STRĪ	27	775
XII.	ŚĀNTI	339	14,525
XIII.	ANUŚĀSANA	?	?
XIV.	ĀŚVAMEDHIKA	133	?
XV.	ĀŚRAMAVĀSIKA	42	1506
XVI.	MAUSALA	8	300
XVII.	MAHĀPRASTHĀNIKA	3	120
XVIII.	SVARGĀROHAṆA	5	200

A STATEMENT REGARDING THE PROGRESS OF THE CRITICAL EDITION OF THE MAHĀBHĀRATA

Read by the General Editor, DR. V. S. SUKTHANKAR, *on the occasion of the publication of the Udyogaparvan and the presentation of it to the* RAJASAHEB OF AUNDH, *on 6th July, 1940*

MR. CHAIRMAN, LADIES AND GENTLEMEN,

On this happy and auspicious day, which is the twenty-third anniversary of the foundation of this Institute, I am glad to announce the publication of the edition of the UDYOGAPARVAN by Professor Dr. S. K. DE of the Dacca University, which is volume six of our Critical Edition of the Mahābhārata. This is, as you are no doubt aware, the third parvan to be completed by us. The Ādiparvan, edited by myself, was completed in 1933. It was followed three years later by the Virāṭaparvan edited by Professor Dr. Raghu VIRA of the Sanatan Dharma College, Lahore. And now we have the Udyogaparvan, which, I hope, will testify to our industry and perseverance.

The amount of matter published during the last 21 years, since the commencement of the work in 1919, may appear to you small. And it is a fact that some editions of the Mahābhārata which were begun long after we had started have already been long completed. But you must not confuse those editions with ours. Those other editions implied only work for compositors and proof-readers. Their procedure, which is very simple, is this. Older editions of the Mahābhārata are put in the hands of compositors, who proceed to manufacture a new edition, faithfully copying, in every detail, all the old mistakes and adding some of their own making, in the bargain.

When this Institute undertook to bring out a Critical Edition of the Mahābhārata, it was not meant to bring out a new edition in this time-honoured way, which has made the term "Indian edition" a synonym of a "bad edition." In Indian editions of the past, the paper was bad, the type was bad, the ink was bad, and the text also was generally bad. I do not wish to say that we have produced an ideal edition of the Mahābhārata, but I do maintain that we have taken a distinct step forward in that direction, and that our work has marked an appreciable advance in the technique of the editing of Sanskrit texts. And when I say that I am giving you not my own opinion but the considered opinion of savants, published repeatedly in the course of lengthy and elaborate reviews of our edition, in high-class and authoritative Journals throughout the world. The edition has been before the world of scholars for nearly fifteen years, and there has been a steady chorus of enthusiastic approbation greeting the appearance of every successive fascicule, whose publication is eagerly awaited by Indologists in all parts of the world.

When we say we are bringing out an edition of the Mahābhārata, we are really considerably underrating our own work. It is not merely a text-edition that we are preparing. What we have undertaken is a research into the Mahābhārata manuscript tradition, which, you will realize, is a very different thing and which—let me emphasize—has now been undertaken for the first time in the long history of our Great Epic.

Let us glance for a moment at the history of the project. Since 1897 there has been a steady and persistent demand for a critical edition of the Mahābhārata, which was wanted, as the late Professor WINTERNITZ put it, "as the only sound basis for all Mahābhārata studies, nay, for all studies connected with the epic literature of India." In 1904, as a result of the agitation which was kept up in Europe by certain Indologists, the International Association of the Academies of Europe and America undertook the work. And for that purpose, even some money was collected by the Sanskritists in England, through the Secretary of State for India, from certain sources in India, and the amount was placed in the hands of Trustees in England, which is still lying there, in the name of the Trustees, in some English bank. The last great European War put an end to this project of a European edition of the Mahābhārata, which ended as a matter of fact without achieving anything beyond some preliminary work. After that war, this Institute undertook the work, making a fresh start. The difficulty was of course the money. What really made it possible for the Institute to launch, some twenty years ago, this gigantic and ambitious scheme was the promise made by Shrimant Balasaheb PANT Pratinidhi, Raja Saheb of Aundh,—our worthy guest of this evening—to contribute a lakh of rupees to the Mahābhārata Publication Fund. Sir Ramkrishna BHANDARKAR, the then seniormost Ācārya of Indology in Western India, was naturally consulted. He is reported to have said that the project was certainly worth undertaking, but it would cost ten lakhs of rupees; and it was no use undertaking the work unless there were prospects of raising that sum. When he was assured that that amount would be found, he agreed to sponsor the undertaking, and as a matter of fact himself inaugurated it here, in this hall, in April 1919, by writing down the *mantra* of the Great Epic, *nārāyaṇaṁ namskṛtya* etc. The Institute, it may be observed, undertook then to prepare an edition in which all the different versions of the epic have been turned to account and which will meet with the highest requirements of critical scholarship.

With that our work has been [illegible]ked out for us. It divides itself naturally into five stages : (1) search for old and reliable MSS. ; (2) collation of the MSS. ; (3) constitution of the text with the help of the collations ;

(4) preparation of the critical apparatus, to be printed along with the constituted text ; and, finally, (5) seeing the matter through the press.

From the published volumes you will see that on every page from a half to two-thirds of the space is taken up by the critical notes, which give a very detailed account of the MSS. examined and collated and which form the bulk of our evidence for the text. It is this which necessitates laborious work and demands endless patience ; and its completion for the parvans so far published is, I consider, the abiding achievement of our edition. Our edition thus gives you not only a text, a critical text, but also a digest of the MSS. tradition of the Mahābhārata extending over nearly 2000 years. I may observe that in the case of every text, when the manuscript tradition fluctuates to any extent, it is only a careful study of the collations of the MSS., and nothing else, that can give you an authentic text ; just as when there is a dispute between two or more litigants an impartial judge trying the case would decide it only after examining the depositions and hearing the evidence of all the parties and their witnesses.

I am glad to say that the method which has been worked out by the Institute for dealing with the Mahābhārata textual problem has commended itself to all scholars who are competent to pass an opinion on the merits of the question. Professor Walter RUBEN, of the University of Ankara, who has made a close study of Rāmāyaṇa MSS., has declared that the same method may be applied, *mutatis mutandis,* to the Rāmāyaṇa also. Appreciative reviews of our edition, as I remarked already, have been published during the last thirteen years not only in Indian, but also in English, French, German, Italian, Czecho-Slovakian, Polish and American Journals. The scheme has been commended by the International Oriental Congress, by the All-India Oriental Conference and by many of the learned bodies specializing in Oriental studies. There have been heard a few dissentient voices, but they are mostly of persons who do not know the ABC of textual criticism and who have never even seen a Mahābhārata MS. in their whole life. Such uninformed criticism of self-styled scholars we may safely ignore.

But we need not rest on the judgment of other scholars alone, for a justification of our method. The correctness of the method adopted by us has been vindicated now by independent and objective evidence. The now famous Rajaguru MS., discovered in Nepal by the Rajaguru Pandit HEMARAJ, which is nearly 800 years old and is therefore the oldest extant MS. of the Ādiparvan, confirms not only many of the disputed readings of the critical text but justifies even some of the emendations made by me, which is—it will be admitted—unimpeachable evidence of the correctness of the method we have been following.

We have completed now in this fashion, as I said, three whole books of the Mahābhārata : the Ādiparvan, the Virāṭaparvan and the Udyogaparvan.

As for the other parvans, you are no doubt aware that the Sabhāparvan has been assigned to Professor Frankling EDGERTON of Yale University, who came over to Poona in 1938 in order to examine for himself the MSS. of the Sabhā which had been collated by the Institute for him, and also to give the finishing touches to his edition in consultation with me. His work has been lying with him ready for publication and would have been sent to the press long ago, but for this war, which is hampering inter-communication and delaying the publication of the parvan.

The next parvan we took in hand is the Vanaparvan (or rather the Āraṇyakaparvan, to give it its correct name), which is being edited by myself. It is passing through the press as rapidly as we can take it through. It will comprise about 1100 pages of our edition, of which nearly 700 pages have already been printed off. I hope to finish it—if nothing untoward happens to hinder its progress—by the end of this year.

As regards the Bhīṣmaparvan, which has been assigned to Rao Bahadur Dr. BELVALKAR, I am glad to report that considerable advance has been made by the editor in the preparation of the press-copy. Not only has Dr. BELVALKAR completed his draft of the constituted text, but the compilation of the critical notes has been taken in hand and is proceeding apace.

When the Bhīṣmaparvan is completed, which we hope to do in a little over a year from now, we shall have completed nearly 45 per cent. of this gigantic work. You will realize the amount of work that will be accomplished when I tell you that we shall have critically dealt with a little under 40,000 ślokas and printed about 4500 pages of our edition.

The collation work has made considerable advance and is a long way ahead of the publication. We possess now nearly complete collations of all the parvans up to the Anuśāsana, which means that we have nearly finished that part of our task ; because there remains now only the short tail, consisting of some easy and unimportant parvans, which I am confident, will offer no great difficulties either to the collator or to the editor.

I have given you, gentlemen, a very brief outline of the main work done under the name of the Critical Edition of the Mahābhārata. Our work has, moreover, given rise to many other subsidiary undertakings, which are being carried out by different scholars, in different places, to some extent independently of our work here.

Noteworthy among these works are the following four. Our edition has given to a student of the Dacca University a subject for a Ph.D. thesis entitled "Studies in Epic Grammatical Forms," which is an essay towards the compilation of epic grammar and which is based entirely on our edition of the Ādiparvan. Our Mahābhārata researches have further inspired another student of the epic to submit to the Bombay University a Ph.D. thesis on the Bhṛgvaṅgirasa element in the Mahābhārata. There is a third Ph.D. dissertation for which a subject has been furnished by our edition. The subject is the phenomenon of case-variation in the epic dialect, which is being investigated by a student of Dr. S. M. KATRE at the Deccan College Research Institute. A Spanish professor, Dr. Jose CAÑEDO, I understand, has planned an elaborate grammatical work on Epic Syntax, which has made considerable advance and which would have been published by now but for this war, which, as you know, is paralyzing all literary and scholarly activity in Europe.

I shall pass on to some minor studies which have arisen out of our Mahābhārata work. Arising out of his study of the Sabhāparvan, Professor EDGERTON has recently published three important papers. One of them is about the mention of the city of Rome in the Digvijaya section of the Sabhāparvan, which is the first time that a clear reference has been found in Indian literature to the name of the capital of ancient Italy, Romā. Another paper by him deals with the question of "Epic Triṣṭubh and its Hypermetric Varieties." A third paper by him concerns the reading and interpretation of a Sabhāparvan stanza, an old crux, which has become famous as the parable of the "Goat and the Knife" ("*ajakṛpāṇīya*").

In connection with his study of the Bhīṣmaparvan, which is being edited by him, Dr. BELVALKAR has published several valuable papers, among them the "Miscarriage of the attempted stratification of the Bhagavadgītā," the "Kashmiri Version of the Bhagavadgītā," and the "Cosmographical Episode in the Mahābhārata and the Padmapurāṇa." He has other papers in preparation.

You will thus see, gentlemen, that the time and the money spent during the last twenty years of silent and arduous work of the Mahābhārata Department of the Institute have not been spent in vain. The Institute has not only brought out critical editions of three of the parvans of the Mahābhārata, but it has built up an independent school of textual criticism and perfected the technique of the editing of Sanskrit texts. It has opened out new vistas of work with immense possibilities, which will occupy Indologists, I imagine, for at least half a century, if not more. It has stimulated vivid interest in Mahābhārata studies, which were languishing for want of a critical edition of the text. They are carried out now on a sound basis and in a scientific spirit, differing conspicuously from the somewhat gassy ebullitions of previous writers on the subject of the Mahābhārata.

The Critical Edition of the Mahābhārata is thus a comprehensive and many-sided literary activity, with ramifications in many directions. It is this aspect of our Mahābhārata work, I imagine, which impressed the British Academy in London and which induced that august body to vote a grant to our Mahābhārata Publication Fund in order to show its appreciation of the work which is being done by the Institute and which is not merely of national but international interest and importance.

It is gratifying to note that we have all along been staunchly supported in our enterprise financially by the Governments, the Princes and the People of India,—and at least by one University, the University of Bombay. During the last twenty years they have contributed in the aggregate some Rs. 3,50,000. That is a considerable sum, you will admit. But much more will be needed to complete the work. As we progress and inspire confidence among the people, who will begin to realize the great literary and scientific importance of this project, more help will, I am confident, be coming forth. Indeed there are indications that these are no false hopes. As the Secretary of the Institute, Dr. DANDEKAR, has just told you, the Sir DORABJEE TATA Charities have only recently, despite the prevailing financial strigency, sanctioned a grant of Rs. 5,000 for the Mahābhārata work, which has been a welcome addition to our attenuated resources, and for which we are extremely grateful to the Trustees of that Fund. Some of our annual subsidies, which had been granted for a fixed period of years, have expired. We have been endeavouring to get them renewed, and the response has been very encouraging, notwithstanding the chaos into which the war has thrown our national economy. Of the patrons whom we have thus approached, the first one to respond was the Chief Saheb of ICHALKARANJI, who, as the Secretary has just announced, has kindly promised to continue his patronage. This is a great encouragement to us and we are most grateful to the Chief Saheb, who is a staunch patron of learning and a great friend of all earnest students. On behalf of the Mahābhārata Editorial Board I must also express our most grateful thanks to Shrimant Raja Saheb of PHALTAN, who in response to our urgent appeal has, as announced by the Secretary, been pleased to continue his annual grant of Rs. 500 for the Mahābhārata work for a further period of five years. If the work is not finished by then, we shall again have to approach the kind Raja Saheb, who, I am sure, will again be pleased to renew the grant. Small though these donations be which we have now secured, there is no need to lose courage. They are indicative of good-will and confidence, which are worth a great deal. When the war clouds have passed away, better days will surely dawn for us ; when the thoughts of men will again turn to the preservation and growth of cultural values. We shall then have again, I am confident, the same share of bounty from our patrons of learning which we have hitherto enjoyed and which will help us to carry to completion one of the most important of our national projects.

July 6, 1940.

A STATEMENT REGARDING THE PROGRESS OF THE CRITICAL EDITION OF THE MAHĀBHĀRATA

[Read by Dr. V. S. SUKTHANKAR, on the occasion of the presentation of the Āraṇyakaparvan to Shrimant RAJASAHEB of Aundh on 5th January 1943.]

MR. CHAIRMAN, LADIES AND GENTLEMEN,

It is now more than seventeen years since I took over charge of the Mahābhārata work and reorganized, on somewhat different lines, this Department of the Institute, having profited by the experiences and experiments of my predecessor, the late lamented Mr. UTGIKAR. During this interval the Institute has published Critical Editions of four complete Books of the Mahābhārata : Ādiparvan (1933), Virāṭaparvan (1936), the Udyogaparvan (1940), and now the Āraṇyakaparvan (1942). These four parvans comprise, according to the Parvasaṁgrahaparvan, about 28,400 ślokas. In addition to this a fascicule of the Sabhāparvan edited by Prof. Franklin EDGERTON of Yale University (U. S. A.), which has been ready for some time and which could be taken up for printing only owing to the very generous special grant of Rs. 10,000 recently made by the Government of Bombay, is being published today. Furthermore, the press-copy of the Bhīṣmaparvan, which is being edited by Rao Bahadur Dr. S. K. BELVALKAR, is almost ready and is now undergoing final revision at the hands of its editor. It will be ready for being sent to the press very shortly. In fact the work is advanced as far that it can be got ready for the press within three months. But can we send it to the press? Not unless we can find a generous donor prepared to pay for the cost of the printing of the new volume, in these days when the cost of printing has almost doubled. The present financial situation of the Department is such that we can just manage to get the press-copies ready; but the large world of scholars outside the walls of this Institute, eagerly awaiting the appearance of our now-famous yellow-covered fascicules, must unfortunately be kept waiting until more funds are available.

Any way, during the past 17 years the Institute has critically dealt with the first 6 parvans of the Great Epic : the Ādi, Sabhā, Āraṇyaka, Virāṭa, Udyoga and Bhīṣma. The six parvans make up a total of about 36,800 ślokas, out of an aggregate of 82,150 ślokas, a portion which is approximately 45% of the entire Mahābhārata, excluding, of course, the Harivaṁśa, which I have kept out of my calculation in order not to frighten you too much. Even this is no mean achievement, I think. The part of the epic critically dealt with so far is, I imagine, in bulk about four times as great as the Greek epics, Iliad and Odyssey put together and one and a half times as our Rāmāyaṇa.

That a work of this nature and these dimensions is not one man's job is very very evident. Many friends, collaborators, sympathisers and patrons have contributed to such measure of success as has been achieved so far, and they include among them princes and potentates, curators and librarians, printers and parvan-editors, not to speak of the General Editor and his modest staff of collators in the background. Surely, the most potent among these multifarious contributory factors have been our generous patrons, who, out of regard for this venerable monument of Indian antiquity, this great and lustrous heritage of Bhāratavarṣa, have in the past liberally supplied the Institute, through all these years, with funds to carry on this costly but vital work.

Ladies and Gentlemen, I must tell you frankly this is a costly work. All good work costs money now-a-days! Good manuscripts cost money. Good printing costs money. Good editors cost money.

The British nation once paid out one million pounds for one rare Ms. of the Bible. Would India pay a similar amount for any book? Why not? Are the British people greater lovers of books, greater lovers of literature, greater lovers of religion, greater lovers of knowledge than we Indians? Certainly not. Great Britain is a small nation, a young nation, compared to India. And our love of knowledge, love of literature, love of scriptures, is greater. We are the inheritors of the great book, this "book of books" composed at a time when Great Britain was not yet entered on the map of civilized nations. And the entire cost of making this Critical Edition of the Mahābhārata is only one million rupees—and not pounds—which is only 1/15th of the cost of the Bible. We have collected and spent already 5 lakhs of rupees. We want now only 5 lakhs more. And we are not pessimistic about it. We have no reason to be that. When the war clouds have passed away, better days will surely dawn for us; then the thoughts of men will again turn to the preservation and growth of cultural values. We shall then, I am confident, enjoy the same generous support from patrons of learning as we have hitherto enjoyed and that will help us to carry to completion one of the most important of our national projects.

If you want me to point out to you just one man who is responsible for originating and furthering the project, he is sitting in front of you, I mean, Shrimant Balasaheb Pant Pratinidhi, the RAJA OF AUNDH.

The question may occur to you. Is it worth all this expenditure? Whether we realize it or not, we still stand under the spell of the Mahābhārata. Amid the deepest strands that are woven in the thread of our civilization, there is more than one that is drawn originally from Bhāratavarṣa and from Sanskrit literature. And well in the centre of this vast mass of literature, there stands this deathless, traditional book of divine inspiration, unapproachable and far removed from possibilities of human competition.

There is a danger that in our pseudo-scientific mood, we may be tempted to discard this great book, thinking that we have outgrown it. That would be a capital blunder! That would in fact mean nothing but an indication of our will to commit suicide, national suicide, the signal of our national extinction. For never was truer word spoken than when the late German Indologist Hermann OLDENBERG said that "in the Mahābhārata breathe the united soul of India, and the individual souls of her people." And why is that ? Because the Mahābhārata is the national saga of India. It is, in other words, the content of our collective unconscious. And just for that reason it refuses to be discarded. We must therefore grasp this great book with both hands and face it squarely. Then we shall recognize that it is our past which has prolonged itself into the present. *We are it* : I mean the real WE! Shall we be guilty of strangling our own soul? NEVER!

TABULA GRATULATORIA

Sadhuram Agarwal
V. S. Agrawala
K. V. Rangaswami Aiyangar
S. Krishnaswami Aiyangar
S. L. Ajrekar
A. S. Altekar
Andhra University
B. T. Anklesaria
Annamalai University
V. M. Apte
Director General of Archæology, Simla
A. S. P. Ayyar
B. B. R. A. Society, Bombay
S. K. Belvalkar
V. S. Bendre
V. K. Bhagwat, Principal Ram Narayan Ruia College
G. H. Bhat
University of Bombay
Bhawanrao Pant Pratinidhi Raja Saheb of Aundh
M. V. Bhide
S. S. Bhave
M. A. Chaghatai
J. B. Chaudhuri
A. M. Coyne, Principal St. Xavier's College, Bombay
A. K. Coomaraswamy
R. N. Dandekar
S. K. De
Deccan College P. and R. Institute, Poona
K. N. Dikshit
V. R. R. Dikshitar
P. C. Divanji
H. R. Divekar
S. R. Dongerkery
F. Edgerton
M. B. Emeneau
A. A. A. Fyzee
V. A. Gadgil
N. B. Gadre
J. R. Gharpure
P. K. Gode
Mrs. Gulab B. Gokhale
V. V. Gokhale
N. A. Gore
Narayanrao Baba Saheb Ghorpade
Y. R. Gupte
R. G. Gyani
K. K. Handiqui
R. G. Harshe
H. Heras.
M. Hiriyanna
Jagan Nath
M. R. Jayakar
K. M. Jhaveri
V. K. Joag
C. V. Joshi
P. M. Joshi
V. M. Joshi
B. Kakati
P. V. Kane
M. F. Kanga
D. D. Kapadia
Iravati Karve
Dr. & Mrs. S. M. Katre
Khalsa College, Bombay
Dharmanand Kosambi
D. D. Kosambi
M. N. Kulkarni
R. D. Laddu
Mrs. Mangalabai P. Laud
B. C. Law
M. T. B. College, Surat
Sir G. D. Madgaonkar
D. N. Marshall
St. Mary's College, Kurseong
Sir R. P. Masani
Ali Mahomed Mecklai
P. M. Mehta
Sir Chunilal B. Mehta
Lady Tapibai C. Mehta
V. V. Mirashi
S. N. Moos
Mulla Firoz Library, Bombay
K. M. Munshi
G. Srinivasa Murti, Director, Adyar Library
S. C. Nandimath, Principal, Lingaraj College, Belgaum
A. N. Narasimhia
Oriental Book Agency, Poona City.
De Nobili College, Poona
Sir R. S. Pant Sachiv, Raja Saheb of Bhor
D. S. Phatak
Shrimant Pratap Shet
H. N. Purohit
A. D. Pusalkar
V. Raghavan
G. S. Rajadhyaksa
Raghu Vir
Hema Chandra Ray
Panchanan Ray
H. G. Rawlinson
H. C. Raychaudhari
Royal Asiatic Society of Bengal, Calcutta
R. V. Sabnis
Diwan Saheb of Sangli
H. D. Sankalia
C. R. Sankaran
Santokh Singh
R. N. Sardesai
Lakshman Sarup
A. Banerji Sastri
School of Oriental Studies London
C. H. Shaikh
T. S. Shejwalkar
N. J. Shende
C. S. Shrinivasachari
Ludwik Sternbach
Lalnath L. Sukthankar
Dr. Mrs. Malinibai Sukthankar
Shantaram B. Sukthankar
Sitaram B. Sukthankar
G. M. Tambe
I. J. S. Taraporevala
University of Travancore
A. N. Upadhye
R. D. Vadekar
P. L. Vaidya
M. S. Vats
Siddheshwar Varma
H. D. Velankar
E. V. Vira Raghavacharya
B. J. Wadia
Sophia Wadia
B. K. Wagle
Seth Walchand Hirachand
Willingdon College, Sangli
Ramananda Yati
G. Yazdani
Shri Yogendra